The *Writer's* Handbook

Edited by
SYLVIA K. BURACK
Editor, The Writer

Publishers   THE WRITER, INC.   Boston

CONTENTS

PART I—BACKGROUND FOR WRITERS

PART II—HOW TO WRITE: TECHNIQUES

GENERAL FICTION

iii

SPECIALIZED FICTION

NONFICTION: ARTICLES AND BOOKS

PART III—EDITORS, AGENTS, AND BUSINESS

PART IV—WHERE TO SELL

THE WRITER'S HANDBOOK

1

EVERYTHING YOU NEED TO KNOW ABOUT WRITING SUCCESSFULLY—IN TEN MINUTES

By Stephen King

I. *The First Introduction*

THAT'S RIGHT. I know it sounds like an ad for some sleazy writers' school, but I really am going to tell you everything you need to pursue a successful and financially rewarding career writing fiction, and I really am going to do it in ten minutes, which is exactly how long it took me to learn. It will actually take you twenty minutes or so to read this essay, however, because I have to tell you a story, and then I have to write a *second* introduction. But these, I argue, should not count in the ten minutes.

II. *The Story, or, How Stephen King Learned to Write*

When I was a sophomore in high school, I did a sophomoric thing which got me in a pot of fairly hot water, as sophomoric didoes often do. I wrote and published a small satiric newspaper called *The Village Vomit*. In this little paper I lampooned a number of teachers at Lisbon (Maine) High School, where I was under instruction. These were not very gentle lampoons; they ranged from the scatological to the downright cruel.

Eventually, a copy of this little newspaper found its way into the hands of a faculty member, and since I had been unwise enough to put my name on it (a fault, some critics would argue, of which I have still not been entirely cured), I was brought into the office. The sophisticated satirist had by that time reverted to what he really was: a fourteen-year-old kid who was shaking in his boots and wondering if he was going to get a suspension . . . what we called "a three-day vacation" in those dim days of 1964.

I wasn't suspended. I was forced to make a number of apologies—they were warranted, but they still tasted like dog-dirt in my mouth—

and spent a week in detention hall. And the guidance counselor arranged what he no doubt thought of as a more constructive channel for my talents. This was a job—contingent upon the editor's approval—writing sports for the Lisbon *Enterprise,* a twelve-page weekly of the sort with which any small-town resident will be familiar. This editor was the man who taught me everything I know about writing in ten minutes. His name was John Gould—not the famed New England humorist or the novelist who wrote *The Greenleaf Fires,* but a relative of both, I believe.

He told me he needed a sports writer and we could "try each other out," if I wanted.

I told him I knew more about advanced algebra than I did sports.

Gould nodded and said, "You'll learn."

I said I would at least try to learn. Gould gave me a huge roll of yellow paper and promised me a wage of ½¢ per word. The first two pieces I wrote had to do with a high school basketball game in which a member of my school team broke the Lisbon High scoring record. One of these pieces was straight reportage. The second was a feature article.

I brought them to Gould the day after the game, so he'd have them for the paper, which came out Fridays. He read the straight piece, made two minor corrections, and spiked it. Then he started in on the feature piece with a large black pen and taught me all I ever needed to know about my craft. I wish I still had the piece—it deserves to be framed, editorial corrections and all—but I can remember pretty well how it looked when he had finished with it. Here's an example:

> Last night, in the ~~well-loved~~
> gymnasium ~~of~~ Lisbon High School, partisans
> and Jay Hills fans alike were stunned by
> an athletic performance unequalled in school
> history: Bob Ransom, ~~known as "Bullet" Bob~~
> ~~for both his size and accuracy,~~ scored
> thirty-seven points. He did it with grace
> and speed...and he did it with an odd courtesy
> as well, committing only two personal fouls
> in his ~~knight-like~~ quest for a record which
> *is basketball team*
> has eluded Lisbon ~~thinclads~~ since 1953...

4

When Gould finished marking up my copy in the manner I have indicated above, he looked up and must have seen something on my face. I think *he* must have thought it was horror, but it was not: it was revelation.

"I only took out the bad parts, you know," he said. "Most of it's pretty good."

"I know," I said, meaning both things: yes, most of it was good, and yes, he had only taken out the bad parts. "I won't do it again."

"If that's true," he said, "you'll never have to work again. You can do *this* for a living." Then he threw back his head and laughed.

And he was right: I *am* doing this for a living, and as long as I can keep on, I don't expect ever to have to work again.

III. *The Second Introduction*

All of what follows has been said before. If you are interested enough in writing to be a purchaser of this magazine, you will have either heard or read all (or almost all) of it before. Thousands of writing courses are taught across the United States each year; seminars are convened; guest lecturers talk, then answer questions, then drink as many gin and tonics as their expense-fees will allow, and it all boils down to what follows.

I am going to tell you these things again because often people will only listen—really *listen*—to someone who makes a lot of money doing the thing he's talking about. This is sad but true. And I told you the story above not to make myself sound like a character out of a Horatio Alger novel but to make a point: I saw, I listened, and *I learned*. Until that day in John Gould's little office, I had been writing first drafts of stories which might run 2,500 words. The second drafts were apt to run 3,300 words. Following that day, my 2,500-word first drafts became 2,200-word second drafts. And two years after that, I sold the first one.

So here it is, with all the bark stripped off. It'll take ten minutes to read, and you can apply it right away . . . if you *listen*.

IV. *Everything You Need to Know About Writing Successfully*
1. *Be talented*

This, of course, is the killer. What is talent? I can hear someone shouting, and here we are, ready to get into a discussion right up there

5

with "What is the meaning of life?" for weighty pronouncements and total uselessness. For the purposes of the beginning writer, talent may as well be defined as eventual success—publication and money. If you wrote something for which someone sent you a check, if you cashed the check and it didn't bounce, and if you then paid the light bill with the money, I consider you talented.

Now some of you are really hollering. Some of you are calling me one crass money-fixated creep. And some of you are calling me *bad* names. *Are you calling Harold Robbins talented?* someone in one of the Great English Departments of America is screeching. *V. C. Andrews? Theodore Dreiser? Or what about you, you dyslexic moron?*

Nonsense. Worse than nonsense, off the subject. We're not talking about good or bad here. I'm interested in telling you how to get your stuff published, not in critical judgments of who's good or bad. As a rule the critical judgments come after the check's been spent, anyway. I have my own opinions, but most times I keep them to myself. People who are published steadily and are paid for what they are writing may be either saints or trollops, but they are clearly reaching a great many someones who want what they have. Ergo, they are communicating. Ergo, they are talented. The biggest part of writing successfully is being talented, and in the context of marketing, the only bad writer is one who doesn't get paid. If you're not talented, you won't succeed. And if you're not succeeding, you should know when to quit.

When is that? I don't know. It's different for each writer. Not after six rejection slips, certainly, nor after sixty. But after six hundred? Maybe. After six thousand? My friend, after six thousand pinks, it's time you tried painting or possibly computer programming.

Further, almost every aspiring writer knows when he is getting warmer—you start getting little jotted notes on your rejection slips, or personal letters . . . maybe a commiserating phone call. It's lonely out there in the cold, but there *are* encouraging voices . . . unless there is nothing in your words which warrants encouragement. I think you owe it to yourself to skip as much of the self-illusion as possible. If your eyes are open, you'll know which way to go . . . or when to turn back.

2. *Be neat.*

Type. Double-space. Use a nice heavy white paper, never that erasable onion-skin stuff. If you've marked up your manuscript a lot, do another draft.

3. *Be self-critical*

If you *haven't* marked up your manuscript a lot, you did a lazy job. Only God gets things right the first time. Don't be a slob.

4. *Remove every extraneous word*

You want to get up on a soapbox and preach? Fine. Get one and try your local park. You want to write for money? Get to the point. And if you remove all the excess garbage and discover you can't find the point, tear up what you wrote and start all over again . . . or try something new.

5. *Never look at a reference book while doing a first draft*

You want to write a story? Fine. Put away your dictionary, your encyclopedias, your World Almanac, and your thesaurus. Better yet, throw your thesaurus into the wastebasket. The only things creepier than a thesaurus are those little paperbacks college students too lazy to read the assigned novels buy around exam time. Any word you have to hunt for in a thesaurus is the wrong word. There are no exceptions to this rule. You think you might have misspelled a word? O.K., so here is your choice: either look it up in the dictionary, thereby making sure you have it right—and breaking your train of thought and the writer's trance in the bargain—or just spell it phonetically and correct it later. Why not? Did you think it was going to go somewhere? And if you need to know the largest city in Brazil and you find you don't have it in your head, why not write in Miami, or Cleveland? You can check it . . . but *later*. When you sit down to write, *write*. Don't do anything else except go to the bathroom, and only do that if it absolutely cannot be put off.

6. *Know the markets*

Only a dimwit would send a story about giant vampire bats surrounding a high school to *McCall's*. Only a dimwit would send a tender story about a mother and daughter making up their differences on Christmas Eve to *Playboy* . . . but people do it all the time. I'm not exaggerating; I have seen such stories in the slush piles of the actual magazines. If you write a good story, why send it out in an ignorant fashion? Would you send your kid out in a snowstorm dressed in Bermuda shorts and a tank top? If you like science fiction, read the magazines. If you want to write confessions stories, read the magazines. And so on. It isn't just a matter of knowing what's right for the present story; you can begin to catch on, after awhile, to overall rhythms, editorial likes and dislikes, a magazine's entire slant. Sometimes your reading can influence the *next story,* and create a sale.

7. *Write to entertain*

Does this mean you can't write "serious fiction"? It does not. Somewhere along the line pernicious critics have invested the American reading and writing public with the idea that entertaining fiction and serious ideas do not overlap. This would have surprised Charles Dickens, not to mention Jane Austen, John Steinbeck, William Faulkner, Bernard Malamud, and hundreds of others. But your serious ideas must always serve your story, not the other way around. I repeat: if you want to preach, get a soapbox.

8. *Ask yourself frequently, "Am I having fun?"*

The answer needn't always be yes. But if it's always no, it's time for a new project or a new career.

9. *How to evaluate criticism*

Show your piece to a number of people—ten, let us say. Listen carefully to what they tell you. Smile and nod a lot. Then review what was said very carefully. If your critics are all telling you the same thing about some facet of your story—a plot twist that doesn't work, a character who rings false, stilted narrative, or half a dozen other possibles—change that facet. It doesn't matter if you really liked that twist or that character; if a lot of people are telling you something is wrong with your piece, it *is.* If seven or eight of them are hitting on that same thing, I'd still suggest changing it. But if everyone—or even most everyone—is criticizing something different, you can safely disregard what all of them say.

10. *Observe all rules for proper submission*

Return postage, self-addressed envelope, all of that.

11. *An agent? Forget it. For now*

Agents get 10% of monies earned by their clients. 10% of nothing is nothing. Agents also have to pay the rent. Beginning writers do not contribute to that or any other necessity of life. Flog your stories around yourself. If you've done a novel, send around query letters to publishers, one by one, and follow up with sample chapters and/or the manuscript complete. And remember Stephen King's First Rule of Writers and Agents, learned by bitter personal experience: You don't need one until you're making enough for someone to steal . . . and if you're making that much, you'll be able to take your pick of good agents.

12. *If it's bad, kill it*

When it comes to people, mercy killing is against the law. When it comes to fiction, it *is* the law.

That's everything you need to know. And if you listened, you can write everything and anything you want. Now I believe I will wish you a pleasant day and sign off.

My ten minutes are up.

2

TO BE A WRITER: WHAT DOES IT TAKE?

By John Jakes

You can answer the question two ways.

If you're an aspiring fiction writer, you might say something like, "It takes the ability to sense, imagine, and tell a strong story. It also takes talent for writing efficient dialogue that gives the illusion of reality and carries a lot of plot or characterization freight at the same time. Besides that, it takes good powers of description. . . ." You could spin out your answer to cover all the basic tools and techniques of the fiction writer's craft, and you would be right.

If you're an aspiring poet, you might mention meter and form first. A dramatist would think of structure and exposition. Those answers, too, would be right.

There's a second answer, though, equally correct but more fundamental. An answer that actually precedes the learning of technique, no matter what sort of writing you prefer.

By way of illustration, think about golf. I think about it a lot, because I love it, and I play badly. Obviously, good golf calls for certain skills. Strong, straight drives based on a good swing. Dependable putting. A keen eye for reading greens. Expert chipping to rescue your ball from a trap. But you can achieve none of that without certain broader fundamentals. Excellent hand-eye coordination and muscle memory (I don't have either one). Ability to concentrate. A liking for the game itself. All these underlie technique.

So, too, do certain attitudes underlie all the skills a writer must have. I call those attitudes states of being. During a professional career that spans thirty-seven years, I've thought about these states of being a lot. Added some, subtracted others. Finally distilled and described seven. I believe a writer must "be" all seven, even before taking the first steps toward technical mastery. Indeed, so crucial are these seven states of being, I believe that if you lack them, you will never be a professional, only an eternal novice.

Each of the seven is simple to describe, but profound in its impact on your life. Here they are, then . . . the seven "states of being" that support a writing career.

1. BE SURE. Do you really want to pay the price? It isn't small. Are you willing to isolate yourself day after day, session after session, year after year, in order to learn your craft the only way you can—by writing?

There are much easier, more pleasant ways to pass the time, though few so rewarding intellectually and spiritually. But it's no sin to be honest and admit it if you'd rather garden, fish, or socialize with friends than go it alone as a writer, with no guarantee of success. If you aren't sure you're up to all that writing demands of a person, go no further.

2. BE DETERMINED. This is a re-statement of one of my "three P's" of a writing career—practice. You must have guessed by now that I believe many parts of the writing process (though not all) can be learned, just as golf can be learned. It's true. You may never be a Fuzzy Zoeller or a Nancy Lopez—there are few out-and-out champions in any field—but, with determination and practice, you can probably become at least a part-time professional. To do it, however, you must write and keep on writing, trying to improve all the time.

3. BE PATIENT. This equates with the second of my "three P's," persistence. The writing profession is not, thank God, the record business. Idols are neither born nor made on the strength of a single three-minute album cut. A more substantial body of work is required. Nor do many stars emerge in the writing field at eighteen (only to be forgotten six months later). Except for a very few, a solid writing career usually arrives later in life.

Also, you must remember that publishing, like any other art that is part industry, changes constantly. Editorial people change jobs. A house or publication that rejects you this year may, under a new editor, say yes the next. Failure to realize this can increase your impatience to the danger point . . . the point at which you say, "What's the use?"

We live in an age of instant gratification. You won't get it writing . . . except for the joy in the work itself.

11

4. BE OPEN. This is the last of my "three P's"—professionalism. By being open, I mean being willing and eager to have all the flaws in your work exposed, so that you can fix them. I mean being anxious to have a working partnership with an editor who admires your strengths but won't spare you criticism of your weaknesses.

Don't let the editor do all the work, though. You must want to find the weak places for yourself, before the editor sees them. It is this rather cold-blooded attitude that sets most money-earning writers apart from dabblers and those who would rather talk about being a writer than do what it takes to be one. "No pain, no gain," runners say. It's the same with writing. Unless you're open to tough criticism and willing to do something about it, you'll never go the distance.

5. BE CURIOUS. Read everything you can read. Read widely, not merely in your chosen field of writing. Spend as much time as you can with your mouth shut and your eyes and ears open. Don't strive for attention . . . strive to go unseen in a crowd, on the beach, at a party. Watch people. Watch the sky. Watch a baby's repertoire of expressions. Watch the way sun puts shadow on a wrinkled garment. Nothing should escape your notice. Everything eventually contributes to what you write, even though the way it contributes is totally unknown to anyone, including you.

6. BE SERIOUS. Give unstintingly of yourself when you write. The kind of effort NFL players casually refer to as "110 percent." There's something to it.

Once again, if you dabble . . . withhold part of your energy . . . refuse to commit your whole mind and heart to the work . . . that will be reflected in a lackluster creative product. Give your work the best you have to offer at the moment you do it. Give it a clear head, and a body that's fit and rested.

On the other hand, while you're taking the work seriously, don't take yourself seriously. I abhor the kind of writer who can't laugh at himself . . . who can't avoid pretentious pronouncements (probably to cover a raging insecurity) . . . who carries "the gift" like a royal scepter and never stops waving it about for others to see.

Too many writers unwittingly play what I call Immortality Roulette. They get involved in worrying about their own reputations. How will they be remembered in a hundred years? They grow desperate, sometimes almost maniacal about it. They write nasty letters to harsh critics—or at least talk about doing it. They are happy or sad depending on a few words from a total unknown (most reviewers). The result of all this is often compensation in the form of overweening self-importance.

The saddest cases are the most marginal . . . those very competent popular writers who probably will be largely forgotten, except by a few trivia scholars or aficionados, as time goes by. Since most of us can't answer questions about posterity—a Hemingway, acknowledged a genius in his own lifetime, is a rarity—just do the best you can. No one can ask more, and what more can you logically ask of yourself? Posterity will take care of itself, with or without you.

7. BE YOURSELF. Above all, let who you are, what you are, what you believe shine through every sentence you write, every piece you finish. I don't mean preach. Just be natural. The originality and power of Tolstoy's *War and Peace* do not lie in the fact that he was the first to write a mammoth novel about Imperial Russia facing Napoleon. I don't know whether he was first or not. I suspect so; it doesn't matter. What matters is that he was unique, a singular person, and his great novel emerged from what *he* had to say about his homeland and its people in wartime. One of my favorite statements about writing, encountered so long ago I can't even acknowledge the source, is this:

"True originality lies not in saying what has never been said, but in saying what you have to say."

So there you are. Seven "states of being" you must achieve before you start your work in order to master the specific tools of your craft. Again, if you honestly feel these requirements are too tough—simply not for you—no one will blame or criticize you. But if you say, "Yes, I will be a writer because I can be all of those things . . . I am all of those things . . . or I'm willing to try to become them," then I predict eventual success for you.

Not enormous wealth, mind you. Not a best seller every year. Not immortality—just the solid satisfaction of being a *writer*. It's a proud and ancient profession . . . and it's a great feeling to achieve even a little success in the business of entertaining and enlightening millions with your own words. It's a calling very much worth the price.

13

3

THE WRITER'S COMPASS

By William Stafford

We writers try to help each other, sometimes. But there is a catch in this generosity: if you begin to rely only on what others say about your work, you may become like a compass that listens to the hunches of the pilot. You may be good company, but you are useless as a compass.

So, when we meet, say at a conference or workshop, we look each other in the eye with an estimate hovering between us. We know that our kind of activity has some complexities not evident to others, and we wonder if those complexities will be recognized in any interchanges about our craft.

For instance, we know that our work is insufficiently judged if much time is given over to assessing the topics of our work. We know that a critic who discusses whether we talk enough about Nicaragua or not, or human rights or not, or the general topic of enlightenment or not, is missing the mark.

We know that there is something supremely important in the creating of a story or poem that all too often will escape the attention of an outsider trying to assess it. And for those outsiders, general readers, even critics, it may not be devastating if they talk at large: the main point is that such readers be affected, no matter what they ascribe our influence to. But for us writers it would be fatal to be misled by superficial assessments; and in fact one of the main hazards for a "successful" writer may be the insidious intrusion of those outer assessments on the inner process that allows us writers to find our way.

We must have an inner guide that allows us to rove forward through the most immediate impulses that come our way. For us, our whole lives are our research; and caught up by our best subjects we become not just an expert, but the only expert there is. We have to be the sole authority for what comes toward us, where we are, with our unique angle of seeing.

Though this inner guide is difficult to talk about, it is supremely important; and it is different from that urge for money, publication, recognition, that is glibly identified as the bait for a writer. You can get lost, following the whims of the public. And the public can give you recognition, or withhold it; but afterward you must set forth again, alone.

If the most significant writing comes from this inner guidance, who will help you find it? Would it be someone who interposes the considerations of the marketplace while the delicate time of discovery is going on? Would it be the person who puts primary emphasis on your imitation of forms and strategies?

Let me plead, not for ignoring advice from wherever it comes, but for allowing in your own life the freedom to pay attention to your feelings while finding your way through language. Besides that audience out there in the world, there is some kind of ideal audience that you have accumulated within your individual consciousness—within your conscience!; and abiding guidance is your compass, one that constitutes what you have to contribute to discourse with others.

Moving back and forth from the inner to the outer world might be the way to your best writing.

Into the unknown you must plunge, carrying your compass. It points at something more distant than any local guidance. You must make "mistakes"; that is, you must explore what has not been mapped out for you. Those mistakes come from somewhere; they are disguised reports from a country so real that no one has found it. When you study that country, shivers run down your back—what a wilderness out there! What splendid stories flicker among those shadows! You could wander forever.

Odd words keep occurring to you—pauses, side glances—mysterious signals. What hidden prejudice brought that next word into your mind? If you hastily retreat to an expected progression, what shadowy terrain might you be neglecting? What revelations might you miss by any "expert" weaving of another well-crafted poem or story?

Like Don Quixote on his unorthodox steed you must loosen the reins and go blundering into adventures that await any traveler in this multilevel world that we too often make familiar by our careful threading of its marked routes between accustomed places.

And like Don Quixote you must expect some disasters. You must

15

write your bad poems and stories; for to write carefully as you rove forward is to guarantee that you will not find the unknown, the risky, the surprising.

Art is an activity in which the actual feel of doing it must be your guide; hence the need for confidence, courage, independence. And hence the need for guardedness about learning too well the craft of doing it.

By following after money, publication, and recognition, you might risk what happened to the John Cheever character who in like manner "damaged, you might say, the ear's innermost chamber where we hear the heavy noise of the dragon's tail moving over the dead leaves."

4

CONFESSIONS OF A BIBLIOPHILE

By Jerry Griswold

I'M NOT A BOOK COLLECTOR, someone who treasures first editions, fine bindings, and the like. Instead, like squawking ducks surrounding someone with a bag of bread crumbs, books have collected around me.

I realized this when I took an inventory of possessions for my homeowner's insurance policy. An event like that makes one think of books as objects—their number and location. And they are everywhere and of all kinds. In the kitchen, for example, the drawers and cabinets are filled with cookbooks, coloring books, and phone books.

I chuckle when the teachers of my children ask, "Do you have books around the house?" The bookshelves in my son's room lean forward precariously because they are filled to overflowing. There are books stacked in front of books in my daughter's nightstand, and some underneath. Between those bedrooms is the linen closet: stuffed with sheets, towels, and encyclopedias.

Our house doesn't look like a model home—one of those places where a few books are put on shelves to give that "lived-in" look. Upstairs, a cabinet in the hall contains six shelves of books, from Dr. Spock to *How to Sail*. The master bedroom has two nightstands: the drawers are filled with travel books; on top are stacks of current reading. The guest bedroom has two bookshelves (where the books are now arranged horizontally so that more can be packed in), as well as a couch and two tables (each with their piles of books). So much for guests! These books are permanent residents.

There are things I could tell you about books. Since I'm a college teacher and a literary journalist, I read, write, and talk about books, so I have several overflowing, six-foot bookshelves in my university office. The cheapest way to move books is by mailing them at the post office's special fourth-class "book rate"; and that is why, in the garage, there are fourteen boxes of books (mailed from Massachusetts when we moved to California). And like the Empire State Building, which residents of New York never visit but like to know they can if the desire ever strikes them, I have kept books on the off chance that I may wish to return to them; so, the attic of my parents' home in Seattle contains seven plastic-wrapped parcels of the books from my undergraduate days should a bizarre whim ever strike me to read once again, say, Immanuel Kant's *The Critique of Pure Reason*.

Books about living with less make up a large part of my collection. My wife would laugh to know that. She says if I were asked what three books I would take to a deserted island, I would respond: "Can I take one more?"

The book to take to a deserted island is, of course, one on shipbuilding, but questions like that are really something like the apocalyptic daydreams of people who find themselves surrounded by books and wish to sort them out. In a similar vein, I sometimes think of Aldous Huxley, whose books were all destroyed when his California house went up in flames. Learning of his loss, a publisher sent him their catalogue and said he could choose as many as he liked and they would be sent, *gratis*. I wonder what I would have chosen under similar circumstances? Or I sometimes think of the proposal I once heard of: toward the end of one's life, an individual would send his favorite books to a young person he admires. What would I send?

There is a real pleasure in such imagined lists. What are your favorite books? (*One Hundred Years of Solitude, The Great Gatsby*) What was your first and last book? (Haders' *Little Appaloosa,* Kidder's *House*) What books do you believe deserve more attention? (van de Wetering's *The Empty Mirror,* Beattie's *Love Always*) The largest? (a book with a title that amounts to a joke—*The Compact Oxford English Dictionary*) The smallest? The most expensive? The oldest?

But books, I sometimes forget, *are* objects. There are those that have their own smell: the straw-like aroma of my copy of *Treasure Island,* which was printed on inexpensive, wartime paper. Books that look terrific with lavish illustrations: *The Art of Maurice Sendak.* And those with pages that have a marvelous cottony feel: Sendak's *The Nutcracker.*

And these objects serve purposes. Books are good company: the one under the seat in the car, in a purse or suitcase, that you can read while waiting or traveling. If placed against an outside wall in a home, they can also serve as a form of insulation. And they make great gifts! Browsing in a used bookstore in a tiny Colorado town this summer, I came across just the Christmas gift for my sister who spent five years in Italy: an out-of-print copy of Ludwig Bemelmans' *Italian Holiday*.

When the number of books entering my life seemed unmanageable, I tried to turn the tide. I resolved to sell two books for every one I bought. That lasted for two months.

So, I've happily resigned myself to a life into which books frequently enter and rarely leave. When my family travels to shopping malls, I veer off to bookstores; even the franchised outlets provide a kind of methadone for booklovers. But I prefer privately owned bookstores. And stores that sell used books. And yard sales. And libraries filled with volumes in which people have scrawled such strange marginalia. What I like in all these, I've begun to recognize, is the eccentricity of the owners or the readers.

I think it was Virginia Woolf who looked at someone's bookshelves and said they contained all the right books but it was clear that the person was not a reader, since the shelves would also have contained some eccentric choices had that been the case. It is surprising what you can discover looking at others' bookshelves. Some may think us eccentrics, but booklovers sympathetically understand each other.

But I hope you will excuse me now, so I can be off to the day's other activities: finishing the book I'm writing, getting the mail with its fresh collection of book catalogues, on to the university to teach and talk books, and then a stop by the bookstore to pick up a Dr. Seuss story for my son and two novels that the store tells me I ordered. These new additions will go on top of the nightstand, if they don't go under the bed or on the bureau or. . . .

5

DON'T THINK: WRITE!

By Madeleine L'Engle

WHEN we write, for whom do we write? Or, as we would be more likely to ask, whom do we write for?

It sounds like an easy question to answer, and in some ways it is. But when it is applied to the matter of fiction, the logical answer—that we write for a specific audience—does not work. At least not for me.

Each year I teach at one or more writers workshops. I enjoy them for many reasons, not the least of which is the opportunity to meet other workshop leaders, often writers whose work I have long admired. Writing is a solitary profession, and a writers conference gives us a chance to get together. Another reason I enjoy the workshops is that I am forced to articulate what I have learned about the techniques of the craft of fiction writing; it is easy to get forgetful and sloppy. Having to explain imagery, simile, metaphor, point of view, is a way to continue to teach myself as well as the people who have come to the workshop.

At one workshop, I talked, as usual, about all the hard work that precedes the writing of fiction. Often there is research to be done. For my Time Trilogy I had to immerse myself in the new physics: first, Einstein's theories of relativity and Planck's quantum theory for *A Wrinkle in Time;* then cellular biology and particle physics for *A Wind in the Door;* and astrophysics and non-linear theories of time for *A Swiftly Tilting Planet.* For *The Love Letters* I had to learn a great deal more about seventeenth-century Portuguese history than I needed or wanted to know, so that the small amount needed for the book would be accurate. Before, during, and after research, the writer needs to be thinking constantly about the characters, and the direction in which the novel seems to be moving.

Does the story have the Aristotelian beginning, middle, and end? How do the events of the novel relate to me, personally, in my own journey through life? What are my own particular concerns at the time of writing, and how should they affect—or not affect—the story? When I actually sit down to write, I stop thinking. While I am writing, I am listening to the story; I am not listening to myself.

"But," a young woman in the class said in a horrified tone of voice, "my creative writing teacher says that we must keep the audience in mind at all times."

That is undoubtedly true for the scientist writing an article that is expected to be understood by people who have little or no scientific background. The writer will have to keep simplifying scientific language, explaining technical terms. Keeping the audience in mind is probably valuable for reporting in newspapers and magazines. The reporter is writing for the average reader; language should be neither so bland as to be insulting, nor so technical as to demand special knowledge.

As for lawyers, I assume they have each other in mind at all times as they write. Certainly they don't have most of us in mind. Their grandiosity appalls me. In a movie contract, I was asked to grant the right to my book to the producers, in perpetuity, throughout the universe. When I wrote in, "With the exception of Sagittarius and the Andromeda galaxy," it was accepted. Evidently the lawyers, who are writing to avoid litigation in a litigious world, did not anticipate a lawsuit from Sagittarius.

Of course I am being grossly unfair to many lawyers; I come from a family of fine lawyers. But the language used in a will or a contract is indeed a special language, and it is not aimed at the reader who enjoys stories, the reader of fiction.

Whom, then, does the writer of fiction write for? It is only a partial truth to say that I write for myself, out of my own need, asking, whether I realize it or not, the questions I am asking in my own life.

A truer answer is that I write for the book.

"But why do you write for children?" I am often asked.

And I answer truthfully that I don't. I haven't been a child for a long time, and if what I write doesn't appeal to me, at my age, it isn't likely to appeal to a child. I hope I will never lose the child within me, who has not lost her sense of wonder, of awe, of laughter. But I am not a child; I am a grown woman, learning about maturity as I move on in chronology.

A teacher, in introducing me to a class of seventh graders, said,

"Miss L'Engle has made it in the children's field, and she is now trying to break into the adult market."

I felt that I had better not explain to this teacher that I had no desire to break into the adult market and see my fiction in "adult bookstores." I am not interested in writing pornography. I did explain that my first several books were regular trade novels, which means that they were marketed for a general audience, not for children. And I explained that when I have a book that I think will be too difficult for a general audience, then we will market it as a juvenile book. It is a great mistake to think that children are not capable of understanding difficult concepts in science or philosophy.

A book that has a young protagonist will likely be marketed as a children's book, regardless of content. Since adolescents are usually more willing than their elders to ask difficult questions, and to accept the fact that the questions don't have nice, tidy answers but lead on to more difficult questions, approximately half of my books have young protagonists. But while I am writing, I am not thinking of any audience at all. I am not even thinking about myself. I am thinking about the book.

This does not imply anything esoteric. I do not pick up the pen and expect it to guide my hand, or put my fingers on the keyboard of the typewriter and expect the work to be done automatically. It is work. But it is focused work, and the focus is on the story, not on anything else.

An example of the kind of focus I mean is a good doctor. The good doctor listens to the patient, truly listens, to what the patient says, does not say, is afraid to say, to body language, to everything that may give a clue as to what is wrong. The good doctor is so fully focused on the patient that personal self-consciousness has vanished. Such focused listening does not make the doctor—or any of the rest of us—less ourselves. In fact, such focused listening makes us more ourselves.

The same thing is true in listening to a story as we write it. It does not make us any less writers, this strange fact that we do not think about writing as we are writing; it makes us more writers.

Then, of course, there is all the revising to be done. We do not always listen well. We do not always have our full attention on the story. Some scenes will need to be written and rewritten a dozen or more times before they work. We do have to revise with attention to infelicities of rhythm, flaw of syntax; there is, indeed, a great deal of conscious work to be done. But still, the writer is paying attention to the work itself, not the potential audience. I have, it is true, toned down scenes when the decision has been made to market a book as a "young adult" novel, because I know that young adult novels are read as often by nine- and ten-year-olds as by young adults. But such revisions are done long after the story has been listened to as attentively as possible, and cannot mutilate or betray the intent or integrity of the story.

It would be very inhibiting for me to have to keep an audience in mind. It would take a large piece of my mind off the story as it is unfolding, and I want all of my mind to be where it belongs: on the writing.

Have I had an audience in mind while I have been writing this piece? Not particularly. I'm telling myself things I need to remember. Nobody but someone interested in the writing of fiction is going to want to read this, so I am also writing for people who share my own concerns.

So, gentle reader (the Victorians seems to assume that all readers are gentle), give yourself the pleasure of forgetting earnestly to remember your audience at all times, and give yourself the fun of plunging deeply into your story, and having your mind focused on that, and nothing else. If the story that comes from this way of writing is a better story than the forcedly audience-centered story (and I am convinced it will be), it will have a wider audience. And isn't that what we hope for?—to reach as many people as possible, because we believe that what the story has to say is worth saying.

6

HOW TO FIND TIME TO WRITE WHEN YOU DON'T HAVE TIME TO WRITE

By Sue Grafton

Early in my writing career, I managed to turn out three novels, one right after another, while I was married, raising two children, keeping house, and working full time as a medical secretary. Those novels were never published and netted me not one red cent, but the work was essential. Writing those three books prepared the way for the fourth book, which *was* published and got me launched as a professional writer. Ironically, now that I'm a "full-time" writer with the entire work day at my disposal, I'm often guilty of getting less work done. Even after twenty-five years at it, there are days when I find myself feeling overwhelmed . . . far less effective and efficient than I know I could be. Lately, I've been scrutinizing my own practices, trying to determine the techniques I use to help me produce more consistently. The underlying challenge, always, is finding the time to write and sticking to it.

Extracting writing time from the fabric of everyday life is a struggle for many of us. Even people who are technically free to write during an eight-hour day often can't "get around" to it. Each day seems to bring some crisis that requires our immediate attention. Always, there's the sense that tomorrow, for sure, we'll get down to work. We're uncomfortably aware that time is passing and the job isn't getting done, but it's hard to know where to start. How can you fit writing into a schedule that already *feels* as if it's filled to capacity? If you find yourself lamenting that you "never have time to write," here are some suggestions about how to view the problem and, better yet, how to go about solving it.

First of all, accept the fact that you may never have the "leisure" (real or imaginary) to sit down and complete your novel without interruption. Chances are you won't be able to quit your job, abandon your family, and retire to a writers' colony for six weeks of uninterrupted writing every year. And even if you could, that six weeks probably wouldn't get the job done. To be productive, we have to make writing part of our daily lives. The problem is that we view writing as a luxury, something special to allow ourselves as soon as we've taken care of the countless nagging duties that seem to come first. Well, I've got news for you. It really works the other way. Once you put writing first, the rest of your life will fall into place.

Successful writers disagree about how much time is needed per stint—ranging anywhere from one to ten hours. I feel that two hours is ideal and not impossible to find in your own busy day. One of the first tricks is to make sure you use precious writing time for *writing* and not for the myriad other chores associated with the work.

"Writing" is made up of a number of sub-categories, each of which needs tending to. A professional doesn't just sit down and magically begin to create prose. The process is more complex than that, and each phase requires our attention. Analyzing the process and breaking it down into its components will help you understand which jobs can be tucked into the corners and crevices of your day. In addition to actual composition, writing encompasses the following:

Planning—initiating projects and setting up a working strategy for each.

Research—which includes clipping and filing.

Outlining—once the material has been gathered.

Marketing—which includes query letters, manuscript typing, Xeroxing, trips to the post office.

And finally, *follow-up* for manuscripts in submission.

All of these things take time, but they won't take *all* of your time, and they shouldn't take your best time. These are clerical details that can be dispatched in odd moments during the day. Delegate as much as possible. Hire someone for these jobs if you can. Have a teen-ager come in one day a week to clip and file. Ask your spouse to drop off a manuscript at the post office on his or her way to work. Check research books out of the library while the kids are at story hour. Use time waiting for a dental appointment or dead time at the laundromat to jot down ideas and get them organized. Take index cards with you every place.

Now take a good look at your day. Feel as if you're already swamped from dawn to dark? Here are some options:

1. *Stay up an hour later each night.* At night, the phone doesn't ring and the family is asleep. You'll have fewer distractions and no excuses. You won't drop dead if you cut your sleep by an hour. The time spent creatively on projects important to you will *give* you energy. Eventually, you can think about stretching that one hour to two, but initially, stick to a manageable change and incorporate it thoroughly into your new schedule before tackling more. I used to write from ten at night until midnight or one a.m., and I still find those hours best for certain kinds of work.

2. *Get up an hour earlier,* before the family wakes. Again, shaving an hour from your sleep will do you no harm, and it will give you the necessary time to establish the habit of daily writing. Anthony Trollope, one of my favorite writers, worked for most of his adult life as a postal clerk, on the job from eight until five every day. His solution was to get up at five a.m. and write 250 words every fifteen minutes till eight— three hours. If he finished a book before the time to go to work, he started a new project at once. In his lifetime, he turned out forty-six full-length books, most of them while he earned a living in another capacity.

3. *If you're employed outside your home, try working en route.* British crime writer Michael Gilbert wrote 23 novels . . . all while riding the train to his work as a solicitor. He used the 50-minute transit time to produce 2 to 2½ pages a day, 12 to 15 pages a week. Buses, trains, commuter flights can all represent productive time for you. Use those periods for writing, while you're inaccessible to the rest of the world.

4. *What about your lunch hour?* Do you go out to lunch every day to "escape" the tensions and pressures of the job? Why not stay at your desk, creating a temporary haven in your own head? Pack a brown bag lunch. It's cheaper, among other things, and if you limit yourself to fruit and raw vegetables, you can get thin while you pile up the pages!

5. *Look at your week nights.* See if there's a way to snag one for yourself. You'd make the time if you decided to take an adult education class. Invent a course for yourself, called "Writing My Novel At Long Last" and spend three hours a week in the public library. I heard about a writer who finished a book just this way, working only on Tuesday nights.

6. *Weekends generally have free time tucked into them*. Try Saturday afternoons when the kids are off at the movies, or Sunday mornings when everyone else sleeps late.

7. *Revamp your current leisure time*. Your schedule probably contains hidden hours that you could easily convert to writing time. Television is the biggest time-waster, but I've also realized that reading the daily paper from front to back takes ninety minutes out of my day! For a while, I convinced myself that I needed to be informed on "current events," but the truth is that I was avoiding my desk, squandering an hour and a half that I desperately needed to complete a manuscript. I was feeling pressured, when all the while, the time was sitting right there in front of me . . . literally. Recently, too, I took a good look at my social calendar. I realized that a dinner party for six was requiring, in effect, two full days of activity . . . time I now devote to my work. I still have friends. I just cut my entertainment plans by a third.

Now.

Once you identify and set aside those newly found hours, it's a matter of tailoring the work to suit the time available. This can be done in four simple steps:

1. Make a list of everything you'd like to write . . . a novel, a short story, a film script, a book review for the local paper, that travel article you outlined during your last trip.

2. Choose three. If you only have one item on your agenda, how lucky you are! If you have more than three projects on your list, keep the remaining projects on a subsidiary list to draw on as you complete the items on your primary list and send them out into the marketplace. I generally like to have one book-length project (my long-term goal) and two smaller projects (an article, a short story . . . short-term goals) on my list.

3. Arrange items on the list in the order of their true priority. Be tough about this. For instance, you might have a short story possibility, an idea you've been toying with for years, but when you come right down to it, it might not seem important enough (or fully developed enough) to place among the top three on your list. My first priority is

always the detective novel I'm writing currently. I work on that when I'm at my freshest, saving the smaller projects for the period after my first energy peaks. Having several projects in the works simultaneously is good for you psychologically. If you get stuck on one, you can try the next. As you finish each project, the feeling of accomplishment will spur you to renewed effort on those that remain. In addition, by supplying yourself with a steady stream of new projects, you'll keep your interest level high.

4. Once you select the three projects you want to work on, break the writing down into small, manageable units. A novel isn't completed at one sitting. Mine are written two pages at a time over a period of six to eight months. Assign yourself a set number of pages . . . 1 or 2 . . . and then meet your own quota from day to day. Once you've completed two pages, you can let yourself off the hook, moving on to the next task. By doing a limited amount of work on a number of projects, you're more likely to keep all three moving forward. Don't burden yourself with more than you can really handle. Assigning yourself ten pages a day sounds good on the surface, but you'll soon feel so overwhelmed that you'll start avoiding the work and won't get *anything* done. Remember, it's persistence that counts, the steady hammering away at the writing from day to day, day *after* day, that produces the most consistent work and the greatest quantity of it.

Essentially, then, all you need to do is this:

> Analyze the task.
> Scrutinize your schedule.
> Tailor the work to fit.

I have one final suggestion, a practice that's boosted my productivity by 50%. Start each day with a brief meditation . . . five minutes of mental quiet in which you visualize yourself actually sitting at your desk, accomplishing the writing you've assigned yourself. Affirm to yourself that you'll have a good, productive day, that you'll have high energy, solid concentration, imagination, and enthusiasm for the work coming up. Use these positive messages to block out your anxieties, the self-doubt, the fear of failure that in fact comprise procrastination. Five minutes of quiet will reinforce your new determination and will help you make the dream of writing real.

7

THE WRITER'S EYE

By Randall Silvis

A PART of every successful writer is, and must be, amoral. Detached. Unfeeling. As nonjudgmental as a tape recorder or camera. It is this capacity to stare at pain or ugliness without flinching, at beauty without swooning, at flattery and truth without succumbing to the lure of either, which provides the mortar, the observable details, to strengthen a story and make it a cohesive unit. This capacity I call the writer's eye.

As a child, I was and still am fascinated by the peaks and valleys of people's lives. I was blessed—or cursed—with what was often referred to as "morbid curiosity." At the scene of a funeral, I would be the one trying to inch a bit closer to the coffin, one ear turned to the dry intonations droning from the minister; the other to the papery rustle of leaves overhead. I would take note of how the mourners were standing, where they held their hands, if there were any clouds in the sky, who wept and who did not even pretend to weep, which shoes were most brilliantly shined, the color of the casket, the scent of smoke from someone's backyard barbecue, a killdeer whistling in the distance.

This is how I would remember and record the day, the event. In the details themselves, unbiased, unvarnished and pure, was every nuance of emotion such a tragedy produced. The same held true for weddings and baptisms, for joyous moments as well as sad. Almost instinctively I seemed to know that every abstraction had an observable form: To remark that my neighbor, a tired and lonely man, was drunk again, said nothing; to say that he was standing by the side of the road, motionless but for his gentle, oblivious swaying even as the cars zipped by and blasted their horns at him, his head down, eyes half-closed, hands shoved deep in his pockets as he sang a mumbled "Meet Me Tonight in Dreamland," said it all.

The writer's eye discriminates. It does not and cannot record every detail in a particular scene, only the most telling ones. It is microscopic in focus, telescopic in intent. If, for example, you wish to depict a woman who is trying to look poised despite her nervousness, does it deepen the depiction to say that she wears a two-carat diamond ring on her left hand? Probably not. But if she is shown sitting very straight, knees and feet together, a pleasant smile on her lips as her right hand unconsciously and repeatedly pulls at and twists the diamond ring on her left? These details are in and of themselves emotionally pallid, but in sum, they add to a colorful, revealing whole. In such a description, the word *nervous* need never be uttered. Yet the conclusion is inescapable, and all the more acute because the reader has not been informed of the woman's uneasiness but has witnessed it for himself.

In my novel *Excelsior* (Henry Holt, October, 1987), one of the most important scenes is a moment of closeness between an inept father and his six-year-old son. The scene takes place in a YMCA locker room minutes after the father accidentally knocked the terrified boy, who cannot swim, into the pool. Bloomhardt, the father, despises himself for his own incompetence, and believes that his son does, too. But during a rare moment of openness, six-year-old Timmy admits *his* feelings of frustration and failure. At this point, it would have been quick and easy to state simply that Bloomhardt was relieved, grateful that his son did not despise him, and was filled with a fervent, though awkward, desire to reassure the boy. Instead, I chose to show his state of mind as evidenced in observable details:

Bloomhardt blinked, his eyes warm with tears. He leaned sideways and kissed his son's damp head. . . . He faced his open locker again, reached for a sock and pulled it on. He smiled to himself.

Bloomhardt's actions are elemental and, on their own, nearly empty of emotional value. But in the context of this passage and in relation to the man's and boy's characters as defined prior to this scene, these details are all that are needed to show the beginnings of a mutual tenderness, trust, and love.

The writer's eye is not merely one sense, but every power of observation the writer possesses. It not only sees, but also smells, tastes, feels, and hears. It also senses which details will paint the brightest picture, which will hint at an unseen quality, which will allow the reader to see beneath the surface of a character to the ice and fire of emotion within.

Think of each phrase of description, each detail, as a dot of color on a Seurat landscape. Individually, each dot is meaningless, it reveals nothing, neither laughter nor sorrow. But if you choose your dots carefully and arrange them on the canvas in their proper places, you might, with luck and practice, compose a scene to take the breath away.

8

THE BEST TRAINING FOR REAL LIFE—FICTION

By Michael Korda

LITERATURE—good, bad and indifferent—shapes our lives. When we are young, it is the stuff of our dreams, fantasies and ambitions, not only an escape from the far less interesting real world around us, but also a way of learning about things that all too often can't be learned at home. A child of divorced parents and far-flung relatives, I made a family of the Rostovs, in *War and Peace,* because they were everything my own family was not—close-knit, emotional, living for each other.

Psychologists suppose that *life* teaches us what we know, for better or worse, but it's most often from fiction that we form our attitudes about life. If we waited for life to teach us about romantic love, for example, we might never learn anything about it at all—we pick that up, early on, from romantic novels, whether they're by Emily Brontë, Jane Austen or Danielle Steel. It's to books, movies and TV that we turn, in childhood and adolescence, for information about love, feelings, relationships in the adult world, and when we ourselves inevitably *become* adults, what we have learned from those sources becomes part of us, part of the way we see life—more important, part of the way we see *ourselves.*

A generation of young Americans modeled themselves after—or at least saw themselves reflected in—Holden Caulfield, or Franny and Zooey, in much the same way that ten years later the attitude of young Americans toward war was radically altered by reading *Catch-22,* or toward drugs was changed by reading *On the Road.* Books provide not only role models, they also teach us lessons we never forget about courage, sacrifice, ambition and desire, right and wrong, love and hate, war and peace.

All the lessons of life are there, buried in great books and great drama, and the interesting thing is that we absorb them without a sense of being *taught,* without effort, for at the same time we are being entertained. Time spent reading is therefore never, under any circumstances, time wasted, provided that what we're reading is worthwhile.

I'm sometimes astonished to realize how much of my own perceptions of life are filtered through literature. If I hadn't been exposed to Hemingway, T. E. Lawrence and Orwell at an early age, I wouldn't have left college in 1956 to go fight in the Hungarian Revolution, and if I hadn't been sustained there by the notion that what I was doing was essentially a romantic, literary act, I don't think I would have survived. If I hadn't read about the grandeurs of the military life, I would certainly not have joined the British armed forces when I was 17, nor been able to look upon that experience as interesting and significant, rather than a painful and time-wasting episode of three years duration, as my family viewed it.

When you come right down to bedrock, Shakespeare tells us more about jealousy in *Othello* than we are ever likely to find out by reading a modern nonfiction bestseller on the subject, and Dickens tells us more about families than we are ever going to learn from the works of modern family counselors. Literature is not an *escape* from life, it is a way of *experiencing* life, on a larger scale—a way of understanding that what we feel and experience has been felt and experienced before, that our problems are not unique but have been faced by other people, and overcome.

That, in the end, is the most important lesson of literature: that we are *not alone* in suffering the problems of childhood, or adolescence, or love, or marriage, or pain, or even death; that others over the centuries have gone through the same things and survived. In real life, it is hard to find people who can talk to us about such things—or at any rate who can talk to us sensibly, frankly and openly, beyond the usual clichés—but literature is full of just such experiences, from which anybody who can read, can *learn*.

In the end, great literature teaches us about *ourselves*. It does *not* offer us pat, ready-made solutions, like self-help books; it offers examples and life experiences that help us, in good times or bad, to face our own problems.

It is one of the ironies of our present age that increasingly we trust only what is new, based on "research," whereas the real truths almost always lie elsewhere. The works of self-help gurus, in the end, are thin fodder compared to Tolstoy, Dickens and Balzac, or their more modern

33

equivalents, to the extent there are any. How many people do we know in this new age of materialism (which in so many ways resembles the Twenties) who remind us of Gatsby, desperately trying to compensate for his inner emptiness with glitzy material success? I can never reread *Gatsby* without thinking of the number of people I know who are having a lousy time in the middle of their own prosperity and success today, and who don't know *why,* despite the fact that F. Scott Fitzgerald understood it perfectly, and wrote about it better than anyone else.

Circumstances change, customs and habits die out and are replaced by others, but human nature doesn't change, and hence literature is never out of date. That is why *King Lear* still tells us all we need to know about the perils of old age and pride, and why *Oedipus* still reads as if it had been written yesterday.

When I was a child, I was often told not to spend so much time sitting by myself with a book. How would I learn anything about life, I was warned, if I spent it reading? As a child, I took these warnings seriously, though I managed to keep on doing just what I wanted to do much of the time. But now, decades later, I can see that the advice was wrong. I learned far more about life from reading books than I would have from playing in the park or tossing a ball around with other children.

What lessons I did learn in the park and on the playing fields I have long since forgotten, or have been disproved by experience. The lessons I learned from books have stayed with me—and have invariably proved to be true.

9

SHOULD YOU COLLABORATE?

By Marcia Muller and Bill Pronzini

When we mentioned to a fellow mystery writer that we had written a collaborative novel, he shook his head wonderingly. "And you're still *friends*?" he asked.

Indeed we are. In fact, we've since written a nonfiction book together, and are contemplating a second novel; and we've also done collaborative short stories, as well as co-edited several anthologies. It should be emphasized, however, that literary collaboration is *not* everyone's cup of tea. Most writers prefer to work alone. Of those who experiment with collaboration, many find it unsuccessful; a few have even suffered the loss of friendship because of it. It is not something to be entered into lightly.

But when a collaboration works, it can be highly rewarding for both partners, and in terms of their literary product. A successful collaboration is a work of fiction or nonfiction which is better than either party could have written alone. It is not the voice of one or the other, but a *third* voice created by the blending of two styles and visions.

There are other advantages to collaboration, as well. Writing, as we all know, is a lonely profession; working with a partner certainly alleviates some of that loneliness. (A warning, though: Any good collaboration is not half the work, as one might think, but usually *twice* the work.) Another advantage is the obvious one that two heads are better than one: Developing a fictional plot, for instance, can be a much easier chore for two people than for one.

There are various kinds of joint projects. One is ghostwriting. This is a partnership between a writer and a nonwriter who has special expertise, an unusual experience, or a specific story he wants to tell. The work may be fiction or nonfiction, and the nonwriter, rather than the writer, receives credit on the work. Closely akin to ghostwriting is celebrity collaboration in which the writer and the celebrity work together to produce an account of the celebrity's life or experiences. Both receive credit; one or both may do the writing. (Ghostwriting and celebrity collaboration are areas open only to professionals.)

The third type is the two-author collaboration—our area of expertise and the type we'll confine ourselves to here. This type may take various forms, and may of course be fiction or nonfiction. In most cases, both writers' names appear on the work, although some teams may prefer a single pseudonym. And depending on the individual writer's strong points and abilities, the workload is broken up in various ways. In collaborating on a novel, one popular method is for the person who plots best to create the basic storyline, while the other does most of the actual writing. Another—which we use—is joint plotting and joint writing.

Our recent mystery novel, *Double,* which features Muller's Sharon McCone and Pronzini's "Nameless Detective," was a joint project in every way. The plot, which had to be complex in order to accommodate the skills of both series sleuths, was developed during many hours of discussion and planning. At first we considered setting it in San Francisco, the city in which both our characters live and work; but then we realized the dramatic possibilities inherent in using a different locale, one with which Sharon was familiar but "Nameless" was not. We settled on San Diego, her hometown and the place where her family still lives. How to get both of them to San Diego at the same time? They attended a private investigators' convention at a posh beach hotel, where an old friend of Sharon's is head of security. Once we had this basic premise, the various intrigues and relationships that make up the plot began to suggest themselves. But that was still only the beginning of our work. We then had to structure the book so that each of us (and each of our detectives) would share more or less equal worktime.

Because there were two of us on the project, the first draft was written rather quickly and easily—but the fact must be stressed that we did no writing at all until our plot was established and each of our characters was sharply delineated. Starting a collaborative project prematurely, before the authors have a clear idea of the direction the book will take, can produce disastrous results.

Before *any* work is done on a collaborative project, two vital elements must be present in the partnership. The first of these is *trust*. By this we mean that each person must have faith in the other's commitment to the project, writing abilities, and professionalism in following the work through to completion. In a way it is an implied contract. You know your collaborator will put his best efforts into the project, will support you whenever you need reassurance or help, and vice versa. This doesn't mean that every collaboration is a complete 50-50 sharing of the workload; often circumstances such as other commitments or differences in ability prevent that. But each partner must trust that the other will contribute a fair share throughout.

How do you know if you can trust your collaborator? It's the same as in any other personal or business arrangement. You make certain assumptions about how your collaborator will work and live up to responsibilities. If you know the person well enough, these assumptions will usually prove correct. In our case, we had been reading each other's works-in-progress for years; each of us knew how the other approached the craft of writing. Because we have similar styles and outlooks, each was able to offer helpful suggestions to the other. If you do not know your proposed partner well, if you cannot proceed on a firm basis of faith and trust, *do not* enter into a collaboration. Mutual enthusiasm for an idea is not enough on which to base weeks or months of difficult physical and mental labor.

The second essential element is *willingness to compromise*. Disputes will inevitably arise: one partner's dazzling plot twist may seem hopelessly contrived to the other; one's stylistic flourishes may seem embarrassingly purplish to his collaborator. The only useful method of settling such disputes is to discuss them rationally and to effect some sort of compromise satisfactory to both parties.

In the writing of *Double,* for instance, a problem arose with the plot: The "Nameless Detective" simply did not have enough to do. Muller yielded to Pronzini's judgment on this matter, even though it meant more work for her (sections had to be restructured and rewritten in order to integrate "Nameless" more fully into the story), because "Nameless" is Pronzini's creation and because Pronzini has more experience in plotting than Muller. Another dispute concerned fictionalizing and shifting a bit of San Diego geography, which also necessitated restructuring and rewriting. Pronzini yielded to Muller because she once lived in San Diego and had strong feelings on how to fictionalize that setting in a realistically acceptable way.

As we move on to the various methods of collaboration and the additional problems that may arise, we think you'll see how strongly the presence—or lack—of trust and the willingness to compromise can affect the quality of the final product. Indeed, how they can determine whether or not there *is* a final product.

The question we're most often asked is: *"How* do you collaborate?" There is no easy answer, for we have written together and with others in a variety of ways. It depends on the nature of the project—novel, short story, nonfiction book, anthology, article such as this one; and it also depends on the partners themselves. Pronzini has collaborated with some ten different writers over the past fifteen years, and each method of working was at least somewhat different. (And yes, Pronzini is still friendly with all ten of those authors.)

One of the easiest methods—the one we used in *Double*—is for each person to write alternate chapters. We were fortunate in that we were using two series detectives who were well-established and who had distinct first-person voices; it wasn't necessary to blend our styles, only to maintain a consistency throughout in Sharon's and "Nameless's" dealings with each other and with the various other characters. This method also works well for nonfiction and for non-series, third-person novels in which multiple viewpoint is employed (such as in Pronzini's recent collaboration with John Lutz, *The Eye*).

A variation on the above method is for each person to write alternate sections, rather than single chapters or scenes. This method worked well in another meeting of San Francisco sleuths, *Twospot,* in which Collin Wilcox's Lieutenant Frank Hastings and Pronzini's "Nameless" joined forces. *Twospot* is divided into four sections of some seven chapters each, the first section narrated by "Nameless," the second by Hastings, and so on. This is an advantageous approach in a novel whose plot requires a number of scenes involving one character before another character can be introduced.

A third method is for both collaborators to write from the point of view of the same character, or about the same things, dividing the work as they see fit, and then in a subsequent draft to rewrite each other's material in order to create a smooth flow—the "third voice" we spoke of earlier. Again, Pronzini has had success with this method in his several collaborations with Barry N. Malzberg. Muller and Pronzini have also used it successfully on a short story and on nonfiction projects, one of them being this article.

A few words should be said here about work habits. In any collaboration in which both parties do the actual writing, it is important that both maintain a steady output; and for both to read and discuss regularly what each has written. It is much easier to mediate a dispute and effect a compromise early on in a project, while it is in its first-draft stage. Waiting until a book or story is finished and then arguing about it does neither the collaborators nor the work any good.

No matter how confident you feel when you set out on a collaborative project, problems of one kind or another will surely develop. Some will be easily solved, others not so easily. But you should be aware of the pitfalls at the outset.

Ego. It is natural to have pride in your work; it is also natural to bristle when a collaborator says, "That scene doesn't work," or "That's a terrible metaphor; we'll have to cut it." But keep in mind that as often as not the collaborator is right. We are not always the best judge of our own work. Therefore your ego *must,* in many instances, yield to trust and compromise. If it doesn't, if it becomes a major stumbling block once a project has begun, the project should probably be abandoned. No decent collaborative work ever emerges from a battle of wills.

Snags. These usually concern work habits, and they come in all sizes and shapes. A common one is that elusive malady called "writer's block." One collaborator comes down with it and is unable to proceed, while the other remains as productive as ever. Another snag may occur when one person writes more quickly than the other and gets too far ahead. Still another is the interference of outside commitments, such as a bread-and-butter job or other, nonliterary projects. As soon as any kind of snag occurs, you should try to work out an immediate solution or compromise. Perhaps the partner not suffering writer's block can offer strong moral support, or take on some of his collaborator's workload. Perhaps the faster writer can regulate his pace to that of the other's. Perhaps the one without commitments can alter or adapt this schedule to accommodate his partner's.

Major snags. These concern such elements as the central premise of the work, important plot points, thematic statements. When they confront you, it can seem as if the entire project is doomed to failure. But they, too, can usually be remedied with enough discussion and compromise. We were not immune on *Double:* We had a draft finished, we liked it, we felt it worked well, and yet . . . there was a solution to one of several crimes that didn't seem to be well-motivated. The only alternative solution we could come up with required extensive rewriting, the addition of scenes and chapters. How did we deal with this? By going back to our typewriters, of course, and revising accordingly. When such snags develop, you'll find that your collaborator's willingness to undertake greater amounts of work is in direct proportion to his commitment to the project. And we were both 100% committed.

Collaboration is a unique opportunity for two writers to create something better than either could have accomplished alone. But this is only true if the partners remain in sync with each other on all fronts. Otherwise, each would be much advised to pursue individual literary careers.

Remember: No collaboration is worth the loss of a friend.

10

"COMMERCIAL" VS. "LITERARY"—THE ARTIFICIAL DEBATE

By Jean M. Auel

NOT LONG ago I received a letter from an English teacher. My books are on her Required Reading List, and she mentioned that it pleased her that today's college students could get stirred up enough to ask questions about them. But one question came up repeatedly in one form or another in both her lit and creative writing classes, and she wondered if I would take a few moments to respond.

"My students, who are aware of the difference between what we English teachers refer to as 'literary' and 'commercial' writing, would like to know if you yourself classify your writing as commercial, and how do you see it as differing from literary work. They think it lies solely in amounts of imagery and symbolism. I think it is in the nature of the storytelling. I see you as a master storyteller appealing to mass audiences (commercial), who makes generous use of techniques (literary). But my students, who are convinced for some reason that a writer cannot be both commercial and literary, see you solely as a commercial writer."

This is a question that deserves an answer. It is especially telling that those who are in the process of learning how to discern the quality of writing, and still able to ask such questions, are doing so.

In his introduction to Masterpiece Theater's latest adaptation of *Goodbye, Mr. Chips* by James Hilton, Alistair Cooke recalled that the year before *Goodbye, Mr. Chips* appeared in print, Mr. Hilton was being hailed as a distinguished literary newcomer with the publication of his *Lost Horizon*. Then, Mr. Cooke noted, "he wrote this thundering best seller and was instantly relegated by the critics to the lowly ranks of a successful popular author."

When my novel, *The Clan of the Cave Bear,* was first published, it was nominated for Best First Novel by the American Book Awards and was given two other awards for "Excellence in Writing." But then it started to sell, and my next novels even more, and the knee-jerk response from certain critics was, if everyone likes them, they can't be any good.

This is nothing new. Shakespeare was a very popular writer in his day, who was disparaged because he wrote for the "masses." I doubt that even he imagined that his work would still be popular—and acclaimed—four hundred years later. Who, today, can say what books will still be around four hundred years from now, or even forty? History will decide that, not contemporary critics.

Probably long before they entered their present English teacher's class, those bright, questioning students, who are aware of the difference between what "English teachers refer to as 'literary' and 'commercial' writing," learned the accepted rules of the writing game. But there must be some nagging doubt, something that doesn't quite fit, since they want to know if I "classify my writing as commercial," and how I see it as "differing from literary work."

Why are students given such a narrow, limiting viewpoint from which to base their judgments, as though nothing else exists except "commercial" or "literary"? Not only must everything written be forced to fit within these two narrow slots, but the slots might even be mutually exclusive. A book, or a writer, might be put into one slot, but as soon as some arbitrary number of copies are sold, it is jammed into the other slot.

There is so much more to be gained by trying to understand what the author's purposes were in writing the novel and judging how well the work succeeded in accomplishing those goals. Think of the possibilities. Is the story meant to entertain? To educate? To clarify? To experiment? To express beautiful words? To search for meaning? To demonstrate the importance of some concept? To show the value of humanity, or the lack of it? Is it meant to scare you? To please you? To excite you? To sadden you or make you happy? None of these requires exclusivity. Novels can include any combination of these and other purposes, and whether or not a book is popular has nothing to do with it. Commercial vs. literary is an artificial criterion for establishing the value of a book, based on economics, not merit.

But what about imagery, symbolism, and storytelling? How do they fit into good writing, and why do some books sell better than others?

Before we get too much farther into this, there is one subject that should be dealt with immediately. To some people, any book that includes detailed sexual descriptions was written to be "commercial." Most of the mail I get is positive, but I do get a few letters from people who object to the sexual content, and those range from mild to vociferous. The comment made most often is, "Your stories are good enough without it, you didn't have to put that sex in there to sell books."

That's entirely true. I did not have to put it in there to sell books—nor did I. It was a carefully considered decision based on research, story line, and personal philosophy. As a writer, I feel that any human activity is proper for a novelist to explore, in all its ramifications, if it is essential to the story. The sexuality was used partly to define character, but more importantly to define a culture that certainly had to be different from our own. Looking at both archeological and anthropological evidence, I believe my interpretation is close to the reality of the era. I don't think they viewed this life-creating act as evil or dirty, nor were they ignorant of their own natural responses. The sexual content is not gratuitous; it is there because it was necessary to keep control of the images, to make sure that a reader did not bring a misperception to the story.

Why should anything be important to the story? Is story important? The students think that the difference between literary and commercial "lies solely in the amounts of and types of imagery and symbolism." The teacher thinks it "is in the nature of the storytelling," and sees me as a "storyteller appealing to mass audiences (commercial), who makes generous use of techniques (literary)."

Does that mean, as it seems to imply, that story or "storytelling" cannot be "literary"? If the literary category excludes stories, what are literary writers supposed to write? Just imagery and symbolism? Is that what is taught in textbooks? Is that, perhaps, why students (and many critics) are convinced that a writer cannot be both commercial and literary? That if the story is strong, particularly if it communicates in some way with many people, the work must be "solely commercial"?

What is imagery? Is it only figurative language? A clever metaphor? A pretty simile? Is the purpose of imagery to make readers stop and admire some author's wonderful words? Or is it that when they read a scene or a description, they are stimulated by the words to create an image in their minds?

43

I'm a visual writer. I see the story unfolding, I have a mental image of the setting, the characters, the action, then I search for the words to show it. I don't care about the clever metaphor that is going to impress some critic; I don't write for critics. I want the perfect word; the one to make you see or smell or taste, to feel what the characters are feeling, and to suggest more. I want to draw you into the scene, but be in control of it. I want every word to count, to move the story forward, unless I want it to slow down to change the pacing, or to make an important point about the story or the world it is set in. I use the imagery that best serves my purposes.

And what about symbolism? I went to the dictionary for this one. Webster's *New Collegiate* defines it as, "The art or practice of using symbols, especially by investing things with a symbolic meaning or by expressing the invisible or intangible by means of visible or sensuous representations." Language itself is symbolic. But does the author or the reader decide the symbolic meanings of a writer's work?

If they are successful, readers will discover it, but serious writers don't usually make conscious efforts to put "symbolism" into their work. It comes about as a result of their trying to suggest an idea or to develop a theme.

What about storytelling? One point seems to be overlooked when that word is applied to authors. "Storytelling" is no less writing than any other kind of writing. Authors don't actually *tell* stories. They are story writers. You don't see a person speaking to you; you see little black marks on a page. But if it is done well, you won't see the words. Instead, you will believe, for a while, that imaginary characters, living in a make-believe time and place, actually exist.

Some people have the impression that a book that reads effortlessly was also effortless to write. It is not true. I strive for that goal, but it takes thinking, planning, technique, and writing and rewriting and re-writing. Others think that a book that reads easily cannot be good, because good books are supposed to be hard to read. Yet, more than once I've picked up a dense and obtuse book, only to realize that most of the so-called complexity was the result of laziness. The same thing could have been said so much more simply, but the author hadn't bothered to rewrite. I like the definition for a professional that a ballet dancer once gave me: It is someone who can make the difficult look easy.

The best judge of good stories and, by far, the toughest critic is that

44

tiny percentage of the total population that is the reading public. You can't con the collective reader into pretending a book is wonderful, and paying for it, because someone with literary prestige says it is. People understand stories, enjoy them, and probably have from the beginning of time. A particular work may have other worthwhile qualities, but if it's not a good story, readers won't tell other people about it, or buy additional copies to give to friends and relatives.

From that point of view, you can define a "commercial" book as one with a good story, but then does "literary" mean any book that does *not* have a good story? The techniques or qualities that are considered when determining the value of good writing are used, though perhaps in an altered form, when writing stories, too. Not all stories are written to be commercial.

I wanted to write good stories, partly because I enjoy story, but I had another purpose, which was equally important, that required good stories and strongly affected the way I wrote. The Earth's Children series started with an idea for a short story, I thought, of a young woman living in prehistoric times with people who were less advanced. I don't know where the idea came from. Though I quickly decided writing the story was fun, I was soon frustrated because I didn't know what I was writing about.

That led me to the library for research, and there I made a discovery. Our prehistoric ancestors were not brutish, half-ape savages, "cavemen" barely struggling for existence. The world of the Ice Age Cro-Magnon was fascinating, a stone-age technology and a hunting-gathering culture that was rich, complex, and surprisingly sophisticated. At first I was amazed, and then a little angry. Why didn't I know this? Why don't we all? Those first modern humans shared their cold ancient world with another kind of Homo sapiens, Neanderthal, whose brain was actually larger, though not quite the same. Two different kinds of advanced humans, living at the same time in the same place; what a perfect setting for fresh, new, and exciting fiction.

There was my story idea, but grown and expanded. It fired my imagination. I wanted to share this exciting new vision. It was time someone took the new, updated version of "caveman" out of the dry scientific books and made it accessible to people. I decided that someone was going to be me! It had to be accurate, but I knew the only way to do it right was through fiction.

I've been a wide and eclectic reader, and learned long ago that the real power of fiction is its ability to make you feel. Nothing else can capture you, absorb you, and literally make you live the life of the characters the way fiction can. Because of this, fiction can be a powerful teaching tool. Our education system tries to teach using primarily intellectual processes, but it is much easier to learn if your emotions are engaged. Heightened emotions aid memory; incidents remembered most vividly are invariably associated with strong feelings. Primitive peoples have known this for a long time. That's why so much knowledge and information that had to be memorized was passed on through ceremony and story.

I set as my goal to write an accurate and convincing story that showed the humanity of those ancient ancestors in such a compelling way that ingrained perceptions would be changed when people read it. I was too excited to realize what a big order that was—or too ignorant. I didn't even know how to write fiction, and I was forty when I began.

I have never taken a class in creative writing, but then I'm not sure anyone could have taught me how to write these stories that are part novel, part historical fiction, part science, part speculation. I gleaned and selected what I needed from books about writing and from fiction, including literature textbooks. To draw readers in and make them feel that world, I had to learn about character, scene, description, theme, story, pacing, texture, and more. I had to learn to cram in detail, to build it in along with the characters, and incorporate it into the story line, so that it would enhance the vision without stopping the story.

And I certainly didn't want to freight these stories with obscure techniques or obvious literary gimmicks; can you imagine using minimalist criteria, for example? They would have bogged down completely. It would have been entirely inappropriate and would not have served my purposes. With the weight of physical detail, they have enough to carry as it is. Even the philosophies and new concepts were tucked in with the story detail so they would be assimilated unobtrusively as they were read. My novels have much to consider on several levels, but I want it to sneak up on the readers, make them think, in spite of themselves, later.

Have I fulfilled my purposes, achieved my goals? I'm not sure; I don't think any author ever really is. I tried to create an accurate, if speculative, world that would capture the readers' interest. I wanted them to get caught up and carried along by the story, and not only suspend their sense of disbelief while reading, but to think about it afterwards. Are the images strong; do the words make them see, and even more, feel? Are the characters complex and memorable? Can readers find a common reference or a symbolic relationship to their own lives? Does the story stay with them after they've closed the book? Has it changed their perceptions of our stone-age ancestors?

I have had very positive responses from the academic community praising the accuracy of these novels, and since the books are popular, I think the stories must be reasonably good, so perhaps I have succeeded in some measure. But that doesn't answer the question I was asked: Do I classify my writing as "commercial," and how do I see it as differing from "literary" work?

Consider this: If I had planned to write a commercial best seller, would I have chosen Upper Paleolithic "caveman" as my subject? A spy thriller, perhaps, or a Hollywood glitzy, a type of story already proven to be enjoyed by many readers, but how many bestselling "caveman" books were there ten years ago? When I decided to write, whether it would be "commercial" or "literary" was not even a consideration. In fact, that artificial debate never entered my mind.

11

ANSWERS TO QUESTIONS ON FICTION WRITING

By Sidney Sheldon

Q. *Do you think beginning fiction writers should write short stories before they try their hand at a novel?*

A. I think the decision to start out writing short stories before tackling novels is a personal one. It is up to the writer to determine what makes him or her comfortable.

Q. *What do you think is the most important characteristic of a protagonist? Or an antagonist?*

A. The most important characteristic of any character—protagonist or antagonist—is reality, making them absolutely believable.

Q. *How can a writer best develop his skill for self-criticism?*

A. There are two phases to writing a novel: the creative phase, and the editorial phase. I feel that it is very important for them not to occur simultaneously. When you are putting words on paper, don't be a critic, because that is inhibiting. When you have finished the novel, then you must be ruthlessly critical of what you have done. That first wonderful flush of creativity is over and you are faced with the reality of what is on paper. I think the best way to become self-critical is to read major writers and try to measure up to their standards.

Q. *You have been enormously successful as a playwright, screenwriter, and novelist. Is there one type of writing you prefer? Why? Do the techniques of one, like playwriting, overlap with fiction? How? And can a writer improve his dialogue writing by learning to write plays?*

48

A. My first love is writing novels. No other medium offers me such a vast canvas on which to spin sweeping, panoramic tales. I cherish this freedom of expression. However, it was my experience as a screenwriter and playwright that prepared me for writing books. A playwright deals with dialogue. If the dialogue is not good, the play will not be good, so the playwright's bread and butter depends on sharp dialogue-writing skills.

Q. *Are there ever characters that you have trouble with—i.e., that you think are important to the story, but that just don't seem to come across as real people?*

A. I have never experienced any problems with making my characters seem real. To me, they are real, and I share all of their emotions. However, I do run into trouble sometimes when I allow minor characters to run away with the story and take up too many pages, and then I have to go back and throw out the majority of those pages. As I have stated before, the character of Old Samuel in *Bloodline* is an example of my failure to keep a minor player in check. It was necessary for me to throw out 150 pages on Old Samuel.

Q. *How do you determine the length of a story?*

A. The characters determine the length of a story.

Q. *Your plots are always very complicated. How do you make them believable and convincing?*

A. I think my books are believable because the characters are real to me. I feel my readership senses that, and therefore comes to share my compassion for the characters and their plights and to care about what happens to them.

Q. *How do you choose the locale for your stories?*

A. I start with a single character, and the story evolves out of that character. I do, however, try to write about glamorous places because I think readers like to live vicariously through the characters. In *Rage of Angels* I thought Manhattan would be an exciting place for Jennifer

Parker to live and work. In *Master of the Game,* Jamie MacGregor was involved in the diamond business, so South Africa, London, and New York were logical locales.

Q. *Do you consciously try to balance your characters in one story— good versus evil, for instance? How do you determine the number of characters you include?*

A. I do not consciously try to balance my characters with regard to good versus evil. I do not believe in black or white characterizations. I think there is some good in the most evil person, as well as a bit of evil in the best of people. I try to make my characters as real as possible so that the readers can identify with them. As for the number of characters in a novel, I have never been concerned with a set limit. The number of characters does not matter, as long as they are all interesting.

Q. *Does it help writers as they develop to read their work aloud to others?*

A. I know writers who like to read their works in progress aloud, and the reactions from their audience are helpful to them. Many writing workshops use this technique where the listeners critique the work of the authors. Personally, I would find this approach very disconcerting. I prefer to work in private. Once my publishers have approved an idea for a novel of mine, they don't see a word until about two and a half years later, when I have completed and polished the book.

Q. *Do men fiction writers generally write more convincingly about men, and women novelists about women?*

A. I think it is very difficult for a man to get into the psyche of a woman, or for a woman to get into the psyche of a man. I don't know how good I am at writing about women, but I enjoy making them my protagonists for a variety of reasons.

Q. *Do you put a lot of your own experiences into your work?*

A. A writer has to be a magpie. You file away bits of colorful dialogue, an unusual gesture that someone makes, a bizarre manner of dressing, a unique philosophy—all these experiences can help make a novel more colorful and more realistic.

Q. *What is the novelist's main responsibility to his audience? What do writers "owe" their readers?*

A. I don't think that an author has a responsibility to his readers. His responsibility is to himself. He must set out to fulfill his original goal, which can be to entertain, instruct, frighten, etc. His obligation is to do his absolute best. If he succeeds in that, his readers will be satisfied.

Q. *Is there any chance for a relatively new writer to break into script writing for the movies or television?*

A. This question seems to head the popularity poll. Of course there is a chance. Everyone working in television, motion pictures, and the theater had to break into those fields. It was just as difficult yesterday as it is today, and it will probably be just as difficult tomorrow. You have to use a little ingenuity. The dilemma is this: The motion picture studios and the networks are desperate for new ideas and new talent. At the same time, if you are not an established writer, they won't let you past the front door. It is a paradox, but there it is. I used the Trojan Horse approach. When I went out to Hollywood a good number of years ago, I wanted to be a writer, but I could not get by the policemen at the front gates of the studios. I wrote a synopsis of Steinbeck's *Of Mice and Men,* sent copies to all the story editors at the various studios, and within two weeks was working as a reader at Universal. [The job of the story analyst, as they were called in those days, was to present the clearest possible picture of a story or script and to relate it in as readable a form as his or her ability would allow. In a sense, this could be called creative writing, even though the analyst was synopsizing someone else's work.] I was up at 4:00 every morning, working on original screen treatments. I sold the fifth one, and then they all sold. I was established as a screen-writer.

You have to find your own Trojan Horse. The Writers Guild of America can give you a list of agents and production companies. Most of them will not want to deal with unknowns. Make them aware of you. Let them know that you are serious. The best approach is to send them something you have written. Be persistent. You may get slapped a lot, but if you keep at it, you are finally going to be kissed.

Q. *Creating and releasing tension seem to be important aspects of your novels. You often seem to let your readers relax, but not too much; when this happens, you pull them back with sometimes unrelieved tension. Are there specific ways of doing this?*

A. I love writing cliff-hangers, and yes, there are certain techniques that can be used. The most important thing is to create characters in whom the readers are interested. Because if they are not interested in your characters, they will be indifferent to whatever dangers those characters might be subjected to. If you are writing a suspense novel, a good trick is to create a dangerous situation for your characters and end the chapter on that note. Start your next chapter with another group of characters, if possible. But do not immediately get your protagonist out of trouble. Build the suspense, and keep building it.

Q. *Much has been said about writing about what you know, from your own experience. Some novelists, however, feel that this is too limiting and constricting, and that the good novelist uses his or her imagination and inventiveness and turns parts of what he knows into the story for his characters to act out. How do you feel?*

A. It is an axiom that writers should write only out of their own experience. Whether you do or not depends on how much you believe in axioms. By all means write about what you know. Use your experiences. However, very few writers experience murder, rape, or suicide, and few of us have traveled to Tibet or Fiji, or have pillaged ancient villages or taken over conglomerates. All of us, however, can experience these things in our imaginations, for that is the world where writers live. There are certain cautions that must be taken. If you are going to write about ancient Cathay, research it. In the libraries of the world are the answers to any possible questions you might have. If you want a locale or an event to be real to the reader, it must first be real to you. You must be able to see it, touch it, smell it, before you can expect the reader to believe in it. When that happens, it will have become an actual experience for you.

52

Q. *Do you have any strong feelings about the use of flashbacks, how they should be used, or when? What devices do you use for transitions from past to present?*

A. Flashbacks are very tricky and have to be handled carefully. When you jump backward or forward in time, it is easy to confuse the reader. There are mechanical devices like asterisks and leaving extra space between paragraphs, but it is a mistake to rely solely on those methods. You have to phrase your sentences so that it is clear to the reader that you are now taking him back in time or forward in time, or that you have returned to the present. These are important guideposts, so handle them carefully.

Q. *Should fiction ever teach a lesson, preach, or be didactic in any way, even indirectly trying to convey a message?*

A. There is an adage in the motion picture business that all messages should be sent by Western Union. I think it is dangerous to write a novel that is purely propaganda. On the other hand, I think that every writer has the right, if not the obligation, to put forth his or her views. I happen to believe that we treat our elderly shabbily by shutting them away in institutions of one kind or another when they are no longer able to be useful members of society. In *A Stranger in the Mirror,* I wrote a scene in which my protagonist goes to visit his father, who is in such a place. I was able to convey my feelings to the reader, but it was all part of the novel, not a detour for preaching. I am appalled by the way our court system works, and in *Rage of Angels* I tried to convey some of my feelings. I think it is very healthy for characters to express your point of view, but your message will be much stronger if you do it entertainingly.

Q. *How important are the names of characters? Do they reveal anything about the characters, or do you mean for them to do so?*

A. I choose the names of my characters very carefully. I think names do conjure up an image of a person and I try to match the name with the image. There is one habit that even seasoned writers have that drives me crazy: They give several of their characters names starting with the same letter and having the same number of syllables, which makes it very difficult to tell them apart. In one novel I read recently by an author who has published more than twenty books, on one page there were four characters whose names began with the same letter. Make sure that all the names have a different ring to them so that the reader does not have to concentrate on who is who.

Q. *Is there an alternative to travel and "on-site" observation for an aspiring novelist who would like to write about foreign (to him or her) places and people?*

A. I travel all over the world to research my books. I am aware, however, that many novelists are not in a position to do that. There are several alternatives: There are public libraries which can be wonderfully helpful. There are people and organizations that specialize in doing research for writers. When I needed information about Philadelphia for my book, *If Tomorrow Comes,* I wrote to the Chamber of Commerce, told them what I needed, and they sent me some invaluable material. When I needed to know what the weather was like in New Orleans, I telephoned the weather bureau there. When I needed to know the name of the train station in Milan, I telephoned the Italian Consulate in Los Angeles. By using a little imagination, you will find that you can do an amazing amount of research without leaving your own town.

12

THE USES OF AUTOBIOGRAPHY

By Gail Godwin

THE FIRST story I ever wrote was about a henpecked husband named Ollie McGonnigle. Leaving the house one morning, Ollie is so happy to be "escaping" that he forgets to look where he is walking and falls into an open manhole. As he is climbing out, a man comes along and says: "Why didn't you watch where you were going!" Ollie hits the man over the head with his umbrella. That night, Ollie comes home to find that his wife has invited company for dinner. The dinner guest turns out to be the man Ollie hit over the head with his umbrella. And, moreover, this man is also . . . THE MAYOR OF THE TOWN.

Now, when I wrote this story (I was eight or nine at the time), there was no man living at our house. I was being brought up by my mother and grandmother. I doubt that I had even met a henpecked husband, except for Dagwood Bumstead, or Jiggs, in the comic strips. But the reason I wanted to write that story, and the reason Ollie was my sympathetic character, was because Ollie McGonnigle was myself.

That slapstick little man, full of eagerness to be out on his own in the morning, so eager that he ignores that voice of authority whose favorite expression is, "Watch where you are going," was I. Ollie McGonnigle, who wanted to make his own mistakes, without anyone saying, "I told you so!" was I. And how gleefully I let him wield his umbrella against complacent authority, even though I knew it was his denouement to knuckle under by suppertime. And how did I know that? Because that was my fate, each evening, when I washed off what little dirt I had been allowed to pick up outdoors and sat down at the table with the authorities. And, on those few occasions when I didn't knuckle under, my grandmother always won by threatening to call her cousin Bill—who really *was* the mayor of our town.

It is revealing to me, to leaf through that file of childhood stories. Ollie the henpecked husband; the one about the rich and lonely little boy who lived behind a high ornate fence and waited each day for the perfect friend to come to play with him; the one about the dog on holiday—from the dog's point of view. What did I know about husbands, about being rich, about being a dog, about being a boy? Yet, behind each disguise, the protagonist was the young author, working out a problem in her life: how to coexist with the authorities; how to put up with solitude until you found the right friend who could get through that fence of perfectionism you'd built around yourself; how it would feel if you could take a vacation from civilization altogether, and get down on your four legs, and run off snarling and panting, to raise hell— even though you get smacked with a rolled newspaper at the end of your outing.

In adolescence, I came out from behind my male/animal disguise and began to write about women. There was a story called "A Sunday in Early New England," which began:

It was the year 1663 and the day was Sunday. All over the New World, people were getting ready to go to church. Prudence Purity was quite upset, however, as she prepared for the long walk with her father and mother and six brothers to the meeting house. The reason for her frustration was that she could not seem to tuck into her hat one bright curl which made her look like a Jezebel.

Looking back, I see clearly that the pressing theme behind all my teen-age stories with female protagonists was how to make peace with the social structure into which I was born—and yet salvage that one bright curl that refuses to tuck itself into the contemporary bonnet. I tried historical distance. In another story, I tried humor. I tried pathos in still another entitled, "I Broke the Code" (rejected by *True Confessions*). The bright curl led me on . . . and still does.

Another theme that surfaced, around high school time, was the theme of choices. The most unsubtle and badly executed of these stories was called "The Choice." It was about a girl who had to decide whether to spend her money to attend a gala where she would be able to shake hands with the world's most beautiful woman, or on a jar of a certain face cream that the beautiful woman used. My heroine chose the face cream.

My first published story, while I was in college, was about an old newspaper vendor who had gone without lunch for a week so he could pay the admission fee to a traveling Rembrandt show at the local art museum. But when he arrives at the museum, he discovers the fee has been raised for that particular show.

I try to recall the impetus for writing that story, over twenty years ago. I believe I wanted to write about how it feels to aspire to art and not know whether you'll have the price of admission when you get to the gates—a theme that has continued to haunt me, in life, as well as art. I was to confront this theme again, years later, in my novel about an artist called *Violet Clay*.

It is easy to look back through your juvenilia and say, "Oh, that's what I was doing. Those were my pet themes. Of course!" What is interesting is that, though the writing has improved, the old themes haven't changed very much. I'm still writing about the importance of salvaging and showing that bright curl, while coexisting with society at the same time; I'm still fascinated by the choices one has to make. And the aspiration theme continues to attract me, as does its dark counterpart: the thwarted aspiration theme! I combined the two of them in my novel, *The Finishing School*.

All of which is to say: I believe our lives shape our fiction just as much as our fiction gives shape to our lives. I'm most comfortable speaking for myself, but I'm convinced that I'm speaking for my favorite writers, as well. They wrote what they wrote, not "out of the blue," but because their lives made it necessary that they write just exactly what they wrote at that particular time. They wrote to discover, to work out, to test their ideas in the process of writing. As they worked on their novels, they worked on their lives: on their vision of life. They tested it, revised it, expanded it. They found—as Tolstoy found, as he worked on *Anna Karenina*—that they often began with one set of attitudes and gradually discovered, draft by draft; that there was quite another attitude beneath that one. They revised their judgments as they became more implicated with their characters, they stumbled on new connections, they watched new insights, and, as their characters grew and changed, they found themselves growing and changing, too.

"Let there be no question about it," writes Dickens's biographer, Edgar Johnson, "what a writer has not experienced in his heart, he can do no more than coldly image from without. Only what he has proved within emerges from those depths with irresistible power, and when new figures lighted in strong emotion force themselves into his imaginative world, they are a projection of that inward reality, no matter how thoroughly the mere surface details may have been changed and disguised."

I write what I write because I am attracted to a certain subject, a certain theme, a certain character I wish to send off on a mission for myself. I write because I need to re-examine some memory that just won't go away, because I need to re-imagine something until I can discover the real truth that lay behind the literal happening. I write because I want to know how it feels to be another kind of person who will do things I can't or won't do. I write to explore alternative choices, life patterns that may run parallel to mine for awhile, then deviate, on a track I cannot follow—except in my fiction.

I'm dubious when anyone tells me, "I never write autobiographical fiction," just as I'm dubious when someone says, "I've got to hurry and finish this story, because I'm afraid someone else will steal the idea." I want to respond, "How can anyone steal something that only you can write?" And if anybody else can write it, what's the point?

When I'm working best, I feel I'm writing something I have to write, something nobody else in the world can write. I feel everything in my life contributing to the destination of this work, determining even the shapes of the sentences. I am always afraid I'm going to die before I finish it.

When a story or novel dies on *me,* and, with a feeling of nausea and sadness, I put it away in a folder (I can't stand throwing out months of effort), I have come to know that the reason it died was that it didn't belong to me in the first place. People begin stories or novels for many reasons. "Wouldn't that make a good story?" someone says. Or someone hands you a clipping ("I cut this out of a newspaper just for you. It's *your* kind of story"), and when you read the clipping, you either catch fire or you don't. Or sometimes you catch fire and start to write and then realize that the anecdote *was* the story; you don't want to know any more. Sometimes I know as soon as I read a clipping that it just does not call out to me in any shape or form. It has no place in my mythology. If I were forced to write it, I suppose I could come up with a workmanlike story, but it would be, to quote Edgar Johnson, *"coldly imaged from without."* And that's not how I write.

I write because I'm looking for answers as well as the right questions.

Because I'm seeking consolation, but also revenge. Because it makes me feel better every time I come up with the precise sentence and the vivid image that expresses an aspect of life that attracts me or haunts me. Everything I have written since that long ago story about Ollie McGonnigle and the mayor of the town was written because I needed to find out what my characters knew, and because I was the only person in the world who could write their stories. All my protagonists—slapstick, allegorical, disguised by gender or species, occupation or social class, or hardly disguised at all—are parts of myself.

13

HOW DO YOU LEARN TO WRITE?

By Ruth Rendell

POPULAR FICTION no more needs a formula than does the highest art in the mainstream novel. Indeed, I have always maintained that genre fiction, so-called, is better written as if it were mainstream fiction and that fitting it into a category is best forgotten. And one should write to please oneself. When I consider the number of readers who have written to me to ask why I bother about style and characters when all they need is the mystery, others who have written asking for more murders or fewer murders, those who have demanded only detective stories, and those who have asked for anything but detective stories, I wonder where I should be now if I had aimed to please a public rather than suited my own taste.

One myth I used to believe in has been thoroughly debunked. This is the illusion that writing cannot be taught. The truth of it is that the desire to write cannot be taught, and that desire, that longing, must be there. Perhaps it is all that must be there, for with care and awareness, and yes a certain humility, the rest may be learned. Innumerable books exist on the writing of fiction. There are more and more courses available. But I believe that the aspiring writer—come to that, the working writer—cannot do better than learn by reading other works of fiction. I read and read, more now than ever, and if my attitude to what I read has changed over the years, it is in that gradually I have brought to bear on my reading an analytical eye, a developing critical faculty, a hunger to learn more of the craft. Perhaps I have lost something thereby. Escape in fiction is less easy for me; identification with characters comes less readily; I no longer lose myself in the story. But I am first a writer. And I think these things well lost for my gain in knowledge of how to write, though I see how far I still have to go.

So what kind of fiction do I as a writer of crime novels read? Not crime fiction, not mysteries. Not any longer. I used to, and then I

60

became afraid that I would come upon the plot I was currently writing or the twist in the tail I was so proud of. The best crime fiction anyway—always excepting the pure detective story—is simply fiction with crime in it. I read and reread the great Victorian classics that once afforded me sheer pleasure and now teach me how to evolve and develop a story and cliff-hang my protagonist at the end of a chapter. I read the best contemporary British and American masters of fiction, every novel that comes out and gets acclaimed by reviewers or wins a prize or gets itself talked about, everything we see adapted for television. My favorite novel used to be Samuel Butler's *The Way of All Flesh,* and I still love it and reread it, but its place in my top admiration stakes has for two or three years been occupied by *The Good Soldier,* by Ford Madox Ford. It has been called the finest novel in the English language, at least the best constructed. I read it once a year. Its structure, its author's skill in dealing with time, the smooth swift movements of its narrative through and in and out of the years, its curiously intimate, despairing, aghast creating of suspense—these are all marvels.

I recommend *The Good Soldier* to everyone who asks me how to write. I hope it has taught me something. It ought to have imparted some of its own subtlety, its wonderfully understated withholding from the reader—until nearly the end—of a chain of secrets, an interwoven carpet of mysteries. Victorian ghost stories also have a lot to teach us. M. R. James knew all about the power of reticence in building tension that is an essential element in my kind of fiction. And more than any modern master of horror, Perceval Landon teaches the writer all he needs to know about fear and how to create it in "Thurnley Abbey," the most frightening story I have ever read.

I am always a little dismayed by people who ask me where I get my ideas and go on to say that though they want to write, they don't know what to write about. Any aspiring writer of the sort of fiction that aims to entertain and be exciting should begin at any rate with more ideas than he or she knows what to do with. They want to tell a story, don't they? Isn't this what it's all about?

I never base my characters on real people. I mean this; I am being quite sincere. And yet, and yet . . . all we know of people is through the men and women we are close to or have met or those we have read of or seen on film. Heaven forbid that we should base our characters on those printed or celluloid personages others have created. So only

61

reality and living people remain. I suppose that we create amalgams, taking an appearance here, a quality there, and eccentricity from elsewhere. Increasingly, I look through books of pictures, the works of old or modern masters, for my characters' faces: to Rembrandt's "Juno," Greuze's "The Wool Winder," Picasso's "Acrobats," and Titian's dark sorrowful handsome man with the gloves. And for characters' names I go not to the telephone directory but to the street names in the back of a gazetteer.

It is interesting how a character begins to form itself as one gazes at some marvelously executed portrait. Slyness must lurk behind those eyes surely, cruelty in that thin-lipped mouth, subtlety and finesse revealed by those long thin fingers. I wish I had known of this method when I first began and struggled unwisely to make a character fit the plot instead of the plot growing naturally out of the behavior of the characters. I wish I had known then the abiding satisfaction of contemplating, say, Umberto Boccioni's self-portrait and seen there a young man's inner doubts, suspiciousness, intellect, hyper-nervousness, and begun to see my way to putting his counterpart into a book.

From the first, though, I listened to people talking. My friends tell me that my books are full of the things they have said. "We had that conversation in your house with such-and-such and so-and-so." It's true. I don't use my friends for my characters, but I use what they say for my dialogue. I listen in pubs to people talking and in restaurants and at airports, in trains, in shops. And when I write down what they say, I repeat it in my head, listening with that inner ear for the right cadence, the ring of authenticity. Is this how it really sounds? Is this the rhythm? Would my man with the thin body and sad face of Picasso's harlequin, the thin lips and the delicate upturned nose, would he use quite that word in quite that way? And if not, it won't do, must be changed and listened to all over again.

A publisher friend once said to me that the next time he received a manuscript that began with the protagonist waking up, feeling depressed, and going down to make himself a cup of tea, he wouldn't read on. All too many first books do begin like this. My experience of reading the manuscripts of unpublished writers is not that they are badly written or unreal or silly or badly constructed, but they are deadly boring. They are dull. The characters have no life and are undifferentiated; every piece of information is fed to the reader in the first chapter; no care has been taken over accuracy or authenticity. If they are not exactly plagiarisms of other more exciting works, they are deeply derivative. Originality is absent. There is no evidence of the writer's own experience being put to use.

Of course, few of us have first-hand knowledge of violence, even fewer of murder. How many of us have had a child kidnapped or know of anyone to whom this has happened? We should be thankful for our lack of experience. And the writer's imagination will supply what is needed here. We all know what it is like to walk alone along a dark road at night, be alone in a house and suspect the presence of a marauder outside, hear a footfall or a door close where there should be no footfall and no closing door, suffer the suspenseful anxiety of waiting for some loved person who is late home, long for the phone to ring yet dread it, miss a train and a date, fear flying, suffer jealousy, envy, love, and hate.

These are the raw materials the writer must use. Journalists ask me if I have known many murderers, visited courts and prisons. I have known none, and it is twenty-five years since I was in a court. But I can read the great psychiatrists, the newspapers, look at faces in pictures, and I can use my imagination. If a would-be writer doesn't have an imagination, he or she should find it out young and serve the world in perhaps a worthier way by making a career in a government office or a hospital. Newspapers as sources of stories and portraits of psychopathic perpetrators of violence have their value but to my mind have been overrated by teachers of mystery writing. Sociological case histories and transcripts of trials supply better models.

I have never been much interested in writing about heroes and villians, and I think the time for a blackness and whiteness of characters, a Dickensian perfect good and utter evil, has long gone by. We have all read novels in which our attention has flagged halfway through. Sometimes this is because the characters are all so unpleasant that we lost interest in their fate. For even the worst character in a novel should inspire in the reader some fellow-feeling. It is an intriguing fact that in order to make readers care about a character, however bad, however depraved, it is only necessary to make him love someone or even something. A dog will do, even a hamster will do. I once had a character called Finn in a novel, a psychopathic hit man, almost irredeemable, one would have said. My aunt read the book and told me that for all his vices and all his crimes, she couldn't help liking Finn because he loved his mother.

Structure and the movement of my characters I used to find hardest. Moving people about I still find hard. It was Graham Greene, I think, who in giving advice on how to write about violent or dramatic action, recommended the paring down of the prose into brief sentences without adjectives or adverbs. And nothing else must be allowed to intervene, no descriptions of the room or the terrain or the people or the weather. While X is killing Y, let him do it bare, in Anglo-Saxon nouns and verbs, in short brisk sentences. This way the action will come across swift and shocking.

I've never had problems moving my characters in time. The associative process takes care of this beautifully for the writer. We all understand it; it works for us in reality. The stray word, the seldom-heard name of person or place, the sight of something or the scent—all these can evoke the past, and in fiction at any rate carry the protagonist back in time days, months, or years to when that was last heard, smelt, mentioned. There are subtler ways, but these will be learnt along the way.

Writing begets writing. Successful writing—and I mean not only worldly success but that private satisfaction that comes from doing something well—inspires the writer to do better, to attempt the scaling of greater heights, hitherto daunting obstacles. So when a technique has been mastered, instead of sitting back to rest and preen himself or herself, the writer should investigate more subtle methods. Smoother transitions in the matter of flashbacks, for instance, subtler differentiations of character by means of dialogue alone, atmospheres created without violent words or hyperbole but on a lower, more fearful key. And how to make that which is very, very hard look easy.

14

LET FICTION CHANGE YOUR LIFE

By Lynne Sharon Schwartz

THE LURE OF USING our own experiences in fiction is almost irresistible—not only for beginners but for seasoned pros as well. What could be more natural, or more inevitable? To tell what has shaped us, to cast the incidents of our lives in the form of narrative, with ourselves as heroes and heroines, is instinctive: It shows itself as soon as children acquire language. And personal experience is a vital source of fiction, one might even say the only source: what else *can* we write of but what we have seen, felt, thought, done, and as a result, imagined? As readers, we're touched most deeply by stories that possess, in Henry James's phrase, the sense of "felt life," stories the author has cared about and lived with and presented in all their intensity; the others lie stone cold on the page. Indeed, a corollary to the old saw, "write what you know," could be, "write what you care about."

But if all of the above is true, then fiction might be no more than faintly disguised autobiography, an indulgent exercise in self-expression. Fiction would be a sorry, impoverished thing indeed, deprived of the rich and incomparable offerings of the imagination and the unconscious, with their enigmatic leaps and turns. Thankfully this isn't so.

How do we make use of the tremendous stores of material our lives provide, and at the same time avoid boring our readers by being that most tedious of companions—the kind we all know and dread—who talks only of himself, by himself, and for himself?

The lamest excuse beginning fiction writers give in response to criticism is, plaintively, "But that's what really happened." Who cares, I'm tempted to ask. To put it more tactfully: If you want to write fiction that others will love to read, you have to be willing to sacrifice parts of your life. Or if that sounds rather extreme, let's call it giving up "the way it really happened" in favor of a greater truth. For a story, in some unaccountable fashion, makes its own demands, like a child outgrowing the confines of the parental home. When you're willing to let the story's life take precedence over your own and go its way, you've taken the first step to becoming a successful writer.

Once you've embarked on that journey, the urge to tell what happened is slowly transformed into the desire to give events pattern and significance, to construct a *thing,* almost like a free-standing sculpture whose shape and contours are clear to all, with the power to delight, or amuse, or provoke, or disturb. Above all, to draw in an entrance. In its final form, while the construction may have been inspired by happenings in the writer's own life and may still contain their germ, it has taken on its own life. It has, sometimes in most surprising ways, gone beyond the writer's experience.

This doesn't mean you can't allow your deepest concerns into your fiction—quite the contrary. Look at the work of Jane Austen, who has left us the most witty, thorough, and painstaking account of nineteenth-century courtship and marriage rites in the middle classes; no sociological study could be more informative, not to mention enchanting. Little is known of Austen's personal life; we cannot say for certain who were her suitors or why she did not marry; we cannot point to episodes in her novels and trace their origins. What we do know is that she scrutinized the mating game in all its aspects, with a unique blend of irony, skepticism, and mellow acceptance. In other words, Austen managed to put her individual sensibility into her work in a far more profound way than by merely drawing on actual events.

As a humbler example, since it's what I know best, I'll use my own novel, *Rough Strife,* which also happens to be about a marriage. The story follows some twenty years in the life of a couple, Caroline and Ivan, who meet in Rome then return to the United States to live in Boston, Connecticut, and finally New York City—settings I chose because I knew them and felt on "safe" territory. During the time I was writing *Rough Strife,* a spate of novels appeared in which married women, weary and disgusted with the inequities of family life, were cutting loose to find independence and adventure. Something about the ease and abruptness of their flights from home bothered me; much as I sympathized with the problem of constraint, the solution seemed oversimplified. I was determined to write about a heroine who stayed to see it through, to learn where that route could lead. At the same time I, too, was determined not, fashionably, to abandon my marriage, a fact that surely influenced the book.

I suppose I planned, in some imprecise way, to have Caroline and Ivan face many of the issues my husband and I faced. But in the end the couple bypassed me to lead their own lives. Caroline, for example, surprised me by having a difficult time conceiving their first child. A mathematics professor, she has an affair with a graduate student, which leads to an abortion; later on, her second child with Ivan turns out to be hyperactive. Why, I wondered as I wrote, did I invent all that? Why did it invent itself, might be more accurate. Well, I wanted to illustrate the enormous effects that bearing and raising children have on a marriage, and those events heighten the illustration. They apply pressure and create tension. They arose from the imagination, wisely, I think, to serve the story.

At still another point the characters escaped me, quite against my will. I was writing a scene of a marital quarrel, with some rather acidic repartee. No one could have been more alarmed than I when Ivan suddenly turned violent, pushing Caroline to the floor. It was not at all what I had intended—not with these characters, anyway, civilized people, incapable of such behavior. In shock and horror, I watched a rape scene unfold. How much more shocking that it was coming from my own pen! And Caroline's reaction was equally horrifying. Instead of being indignant and repelled, she thinks she invited it in some way. She even feels sorry for Ivan in his guilt and remorse! The whole incident contradicted my beliefs as well as my experience—in real life I would have shaken them both to their senses. But this was not real life. This was the utter mystery and excitement of fiction, where characters rebel and demand their own errors and their own destiny, and we had best not stand in their way.

In the end, I had a novel about a couple whose story barely resembled my own. The only autobiographical elements left were a certain analytical turn of mind and a sense of the complex, ambiguous accommodations involved in living with another person. Whatever my original aims, I had written about the gradual process of accepting the results of one's uneducated choices. With the benefit of several years' hindsight, I can see that this notion of process, not the details of the plot, is what makes the book personal as well as, I hope, universal.

The same shifts occur in writing stories, only on a smaller scale. How well I remember lying awake one entire night with a gray spot jiggling before my eyes—something the doctors call a "floater," I later learned. It didn't let me sleep, and as the hours passed, I slipped into a miserable, unreasonable state of mind, berating myself for all the mistakes of my past, wondering what it all meant, if anything. . . . Anyone who's spent a sleepless night recently will know what I mean. The experience was so powerful and disturbing that naturally I wanted to write about it. The result was a story, "Acquainted With the Night," whose main character turned out to be a male architect ten years older than I. Why, I can't say. He too lies awake, victim of a floater, examining and agonizing over his past, which, needless to say, has nothing in common with my own. (I took the opportunity to give him a life full of moral crisis, without the straints I might have felt about detailing mine.) Again, the common and personal element, as well as the universal one, is simply the insomniac's painful and—in the light of day—distorted trip, a trip almost every reader has taken at one time or another.

The path leading to a newer story was more circuitous. Several years ago, a fire forced my husband and me out of the apartment building where we had lived for twenty years and raised our two daughters. Besides the shock and pain of losing our home, we and our fellow-tenants were outraged at the behavior of the landlord, Columbia University, in the aftermath of the fire. A lengthy court case ensued, with the tenants ranged against the power and willfulness of a large institution. Two years later I completed a book about the fire, the legal proceedings, and the social implications of institutions as landlords. Since I had written mainly fiction till then, I was prepared when friends asked why I hadn't turned my experience into a novel—what an ideal story it seemed, full of drama and conflict. My answer was, first, that the truth was topically urgent and needed to be told precisely as it happened; and second, that the story (plus the research it would entail) really didn't interest me as a novelist. I had been writing long enough to know that real estate practices, demographics, and the nature of bureaucracy were not my subjects.

Some time later, though, probably under the influence of many newspaper and magazine articles about homelessness in New York City, an imaginary family moved into my mind. Little by little their features became clear: they were newcomers from the Virgin Islands, the father was an electrician but temporarily working at a lunch counter, they were black, they were very proper and conventional, there were three young children. . . . They too had been forced out of their apartment by a fire, but unlike my family, they had had to accept the city's offer of a welfare hotel, a dismal and dangerous environment. The father, a proud man, found that intolerable, but with so little money what could he do? I became obsessed with the family until their story virtually wrote itself—"The Last Frontier," in which George and Louise Madison and their children move onto the stage set of a situation comedy, contrasting the whitewashed TV image of family life with their own reality.

None of the details about the Madisons corresponded to my own life—none, that is, except their condition of homelessness, and the resulting anger, frustration, and bewilderment. In those feelings that give the story its life, we were identical. One might say it is auto-biographical in the deepest sense.

The ability I've been discussing—giving up the facts for the broader reaches of the imagination—may sound daunting, but it comes with experience, and with the confidence and willingness to let the story take control. For almost always, at some point in the arduous process, the inner voice will whisper, "What if . . . instead of . . . ?" The secret is to listen, and to yield.

But that's not the only way. Some fiction gets written backwards, so to speak. In the case of *Balancing Acts* (my first novel, though it was published second), I was on the third draft and puzzled over why it wouldn't come right, when I finally grasped what the book was about and what its connection was to me.

I had begun it after a friend told me about her ten-year-old daughter's strong attachment to an elderly man, a volunteer teacher in her school. The man had just died, and the child was suffering the sort of grief—for the loss of a close friend—that most of us don't know till later in life. The story stayed with me—I didn't know why; one often doesn't—and I constructed a novel around it, with background and details far different from those of my own life. I couldn't help but notice, though, that the man in my novel had much in common with my father, and the thirteen-year-old heroine, with me. Not circumstantial matters in common, but affinities of temperament and attitude. Only on that third draft, when I realized that book was a particular emotional struggle on my part, connected with my aging father, could I rewrite it with coherence and conscious design. Plot, setting, and characters all remained the same, but I had found the autobiographical impulse at the core and could work outwards, using its energy.

Giving the imagination free reign, or conversely, locating the fertile source of a story, is exhilarating as well as productive. But it has its negative side (doesn't everything?). The upshot of letting fiction change the events of your life is losing parts of your past. It's not an overstatement to confess that looking over my work, I occasionally note bits that sound familiar, yet I can't quite remember whether they happened or whether I made them up. Did the neighbors down the street when I was nine years old really shout those awful things out the window, or did I imagine it? Or exaggerate it? Did that man in the boat really look at me in that seductive way? Was the path behind the country houses really as dark and lush with greenery as I wrote? And were my grandmother's glasses of tea with lumps of sugar as wonderful as I've made out? The line between memory and invention blurs; I can't say for sure what happened, and I have the sinking feeling that I've erased parts of my life in order to write stories over them. I may have given up more than I expected, becoming a writer. The only relief for such doubts is to go back and write some more. Because in the end, as the Roman poet said, life is short, but art is long.

15

SO YOU WANT TO WRITE A BESTSELLER?

By Barbara Taylor Bradford

When I'm on tour to promote a new novel, I meet many people in bookstores, TV audiences, and lecture halls, who tell me they want to be a bestselling novelist. They seek my advice. Generally, I tell them to sit down and do it, because that is the only way a book is ever written. However, I usually make a point of asking each one the same question: Why do you want to be a novelist?

Invariably they tell me that they want to make a lot of money and become a famous celebrity.

These are the wrong reasons.

There is only one reason to write a novel and that is because writing fiction is absolutely essential to one's well-being. It is to mine and it always has been. In other words, it is the work that really counts, the sense of creation that is the important thing to me.

Don't misunderstand me. Of course I want readers, every author does. But I have never sat down at a typewriter and told myself that I'm about to write a great bestseller. I have no idea if a book of mine is going to sell in the millions when I actually start it. How could I know, since I don't have a secret recipe? All I have is a story to tell about a number of characters who are very real people to me. I knew I wanted to be a novelist when I was a child in Yorkshire. I had no brothers or sisters so I invented playmates and told them stories. When I was ten, my father bought me a second-hand typewriter and I typed out these little tales and stitched them in a folder with a hand-painted title.

When I was 12 I submitted one—about a little horse, I think—to something called *The Children's Magazine* and it was actually published. I got ten and six for it. I have never stopped writing since.

The first novel I attempted was about a ballet dancer named Vivienne Ramage who lived in a garret in Paris! By this time I had managed to get a job on the *Yorkshire Evening Post* and had been to the Paris fashion shows with the women's page editor.

Paris totally overwhelmed me. I came back, and began this story. My ballet dancer was desperately poor and it was all terribly dramatic and suspiciously reminiscent of Dumas' *La Dame aux Camélias*! Anyway, I got to about page ten and suddenly thought: I've a feeling I've read this somewhere before.

I kept experimenting like that all though my girlhood. Being on a newspaper, doing the police beat, covering the coroners' courts, exposed me to life in the raw and taught me that you can't just write about the landscape or a room setting—a story is only interesting if it's about people. Their tragedies, their dramas, their joys.

That's what I'm dealing in now, human emotions. The hope is that I can get them down on paper in such a way as to touch a nerve in the reader so that he or she identifies and is moved. At 17 I was very much in love with being a newspaperwoman—a newspaper*man* I should say—even down to wanting a dirty trench coat. My mother accused me of having dragged it round in the street to make it grubby.

But my newspaper career didn't begin as a reporter. The only job I could get at the start was in the typist pool. First day I was still typing away long after everybody had gone home. As I was leaving I saw the wastepaper basket overflowing with the company's crumpled, vellum-like notepaper and I thought, I'm going to get fired for wasting their stationery. So I took a handful into the ladies' room, lit a match to it and threw it down the toilet.

Well, the blaze was so enormous I then thought: this way I'll be fired for being an arsonist! So I collected up the rest, smoothed it out and hid it in the bottom drawer of my desk.

For a week after that I took one of my mother's shopping bags to work with me and brought the telltale paper home in batches. I think I eventually got a job as a cub reporter because I was such an awful typist.

But I worked at getting moved, too—I did little stories and handed them in to my editor, who finally put me in the newsroom.

At 18, I became women's editor. When I was 20 I left Upper Armley, Yorkshire, for London and a job on *Woman's Own* as a fashion editor, followed by a stint as a reporter and feature writer on the *Evening News*.

Naturally, that was a job in which I met actors, film stars, novelists, screenwriters, politicians—people who were "achievers"—but I never expected to find success or be rich and famous myself. However, when I look back, I realize my mother always instilled in me a desire to do my best. I wanted to please her. She loved the theatre, movies, music and art and she got me my first two library tickets when I was still very small. When she died in 1981—only 5 weeks after I lost my father—I found those tickets in her purse.

I continued writing after I moved to the United States, where I have lived since my marriage in 1963 to a Hollywood film producer, Robert Bradford. I wrote non-fiction books between 1963 and 1974, mostly on interior design, and two books for children.

Between 1968 and 1974, when I was writing a syndicated column for American newspapers, I started four novels but discarded them all after a few hundred pages. One was set in Paris and North Africa. It was called *Florabelle*. I liked strong heroines from the start. That one was an actress.

Yet another novel was set in North Africa—I was smitten with Morocco at that time—and that tale was about a woman photo-journalist. My next was sited in the South of France. But the one I was writing when I thought of *A Woman of Substance* was called *The Jasper Cypher*. It was a Helen MacInnes-type suspense novel starting in New York and moving to Spain.

But obviously I was wrong, wasn't I? I should have been writing about Yorkshire, not Morocco. I got to chapter four and I thought, this is boring. I asked myself a lot of questions that day. It was like a dialogue with myself. I said: Well, what *do* you want to write about? What *sort* of book do you want to write? Where do you want to set it? And of course I knew, suddenly, that I really wanted to set it in England, specifically Yorkshire. Then I said: And I want to write about a strong woman.

So, having decided to write about a Yorkshire girl who emancipates herself and creates a big business empire, I could see it would be more effective if she were born poor and in an age when women were not doing these things, and to have her working for a rich family who falls as she rises.

After a couple of hours of thinking along these lines I had the nucleus of my plot and started to jot down a few notes and I thought, yes, she becomes a woman of substance. And I looked at that on my pad and thought, that's a marvelous title.

At a point like this I put paper in typewriter and tap out a few details. I might take two days experimenting with a name for the character. It has to have just the right ring. Then I create the other protagonists, maybe draw a family tree, listing names and ages, their relationships.

All the time I'm asking myself questions and answering them on paper. When is it going to start, how old is she, what is her background, what motivates her, why did this woman do what she did, become what she became? All my characters are totally analyzed, as if I were a psychiatrist.

I then transpose these notes onto index cards, and I maintain these character cards as if I'm dealing with real people—and they become very real to me. As I develop them, somehow the plot falls into place almost automatically.

Once I have title, characters and story line in note form, I divide the book into parts. It's a way to organize the material. In *A Woman of Substance* I got titles for the sections from the land—the valley, the abyss, the plateau, the pinnacle, the slope. It was a method of tracing the rise and fall of a life. In *Voice of the Heart,* I used the stage— overture, wings, Act 1, downstage right and so on. In *Hold the Dream,* the phases are entitled "Matriarch"—that's Emma Harte in old age— and "Heiress and Tycoon," which is the ascent of her granddaughter, Paula.

At this stage I write a piece like the copy on a novel's dust jacket, the bare bones of the story. Then I finish the outline, which is ten to 20 pages. That takes me about a week to ten days.

Once I get going on a novel, a good day is when I've written five finished pages. I usually start in longhand, using a fine nibbed pen (Sanford's Expresso, if you like to know that sort of thing) and then move to the typewriter.

Someone once asked me what a novel is and I said: It's a monumental lie that has to have the absolute ring of truth if it is to succeed.

It's easy to know when something is good and, in a way, it's easy to know when something is bad. But to know *why* it's bad, that's the thing. And how do you change it?

I've gone back and looked at my first attempts at fiction, and there wasn't too much wrong with them, except that I wanted basically to write about Yorkshire and didn't know it. So I wouldn't say to the would-be novelist: press on with *anything* you start. You could be on the wrong subject matter, as I was.

However, I now realize that as I labored, I was in effect honing my craft, teaching myself how to write a novel. I truly believe that learning the craft of fiction writing is vital and that you can't do that at classes. You can perhaps learn techniques—I borrowed library books on journalism when I was trying to become a reporter—but no one can teach you to write a novel. You have to teach yourself.

Basic writing ability is still not enough. A would-be novelist must also observe what I call the five Ds:

D for desire—the desire to want to write that novel more than do anything else.

D for drive—the drive to get started.

D for determination—the will to continue whatever the stumbling blocks and difficulties encountered on the way.

D for discipline—the discipline to write every day, whatever your mood.

D for dedication to the project until the very last page is finished.

Finally, there is a sixth D—to avoid! This is for distractions—perhaps the most important D of all, the enemy of all writers, whether would-be or proven.

Writing novels is the hardest work I've ever done, the salt mines, really. I sit long hours at my desk, starting out at six in the morning and finishing around six or seven in the evening. And I do this six and a half days a week, till my neck and shoulders seize up. I make tremendous social and personal sacrifices for my writing, but after all, I chose to be a novelist. Nobody held a gun to my head.

But in all truth, it's not possible to be a full-time novelist and a social butterfly, living the so-called glamorous existence of the bestselling novelist.

There's nothing which faintly resembles glamour about the work I do. I spend all of my working hours alone, facing a blank sheet of paper, and myself. For I have to dredge through my soul and my memories every day of my life.

When a book is finished I have to go on promotion tours. This may sound exciting. But it isn't. Taking a different plane or train every day and heading for another city is hardly my idea of fun; neither are crowded airports, poor hotels or bad food eaten on the run.

Then there are the fairytales. When reporters come to interview me they sometimes have a preconception. It's nothing to do with what they've learned about me, it's what they've decided without knowing me. They want to make me into Emma Harte. They want a rags-to-riches story. Somebody asked me the other day about my enormous change of lifestyle since I wrote a bestseller. Well, I started off simply enough but, to be truthful, my lifestyle changed when I married 22 years ago and went to live in Manhattan and also had an apartment in Beverly Hills.

But whatever I say, they're determined to write the story they want to tell. So the only thing I can do when I read a misleading story is smile and say, well at least they spelled my name right! But I'm not Cinderella, and never was.

Still, I admit that a bit of fiction about oneself is not much to put up with. I've been accused of dressing my Bichon Frisé puppy, Gemmy, in a diamond-studded collar and of wearing a £25,000 dress. I was due to go and stay with an old friend in Ripon and she roared with laughter when she read that. "Do I have to get a burglar alarm installed?" she kidded me. She knew a Yorkshire girl would never spend £25,000 on a dress, that she'd be doing something extraordinary if she paid £250!

So why do I go on? The answer is easy. I can't *not* do it. Writing is a means of self-expression for me, and it gives me great gratification. Especially when I know that a novel I have striven over truly works, not only for me, but for readers all over the world . . . readers who have derived enjoyment from my work, who have seen life through my angle of vision . . . who have been touched, enlightened and entertained. That is the greatest satisfaction of all.

And if you are a would-be novelist, hellbent on pursuing this career, then what better inspiration is there?

Ten Questions for Would-Be Novelists

Let us assume that the would-be novelist has both ability and a talent for using words. What else is required in the writing of fiction? I think I would have to ask you these questions.

1. Are you imaginative?

If you create characters in your imagination that are interesting and different and yet with whom the reader can identify, then you have a good start. If you can picture scenes between characters you create and can also feel caught up in their emotions, that's what I call imagination.

2. Have you got insight?

A novelist must be able to understand what makes people tick. Insight is being able to weigh someone up, to understand why they do the things they do. You must have compassion, and be willing to understand all points of view.

3. Can you get under the skin of a character, express his or her nature?

You have to be able to put the feeling and thought processes of your characters on paper effectively. I think writing up character studies is helpful. It teaches you how to develop a *whole* person on paper, remembering that nobody is all good, nobody is all bad; we are all made up with many complexities in our nature.

4. Can you make readers care about your characters?

That depends on whether you can flesh them out so that the reader believes they truly exist. I've found reading biographies very useful since they are about real people.

5. Can you really tell a story?

If it's to be compelling, make the reader want to turn the page to find what happens next, a novel has to combine structure, plot and action in a way that produces narrative drive. I have what I call my "loving ears"—two girlfriends I can ring and say: May I read you these few pages? That's what I sometimes do if I'm trying to say something complex, and their reaction helps me know if I've refined it enough. Do they want to "hear on"? Some feedback is helpful if you're feeling unconfident.

Structure is very important. Studying favorite books is good homework here. The structure of *Tai Pan* by James Clavell, who also wrote *Shogun,* is marvelous. And Wilbur Smith did a trilogy, *Flight of the Falcon, Men of Men* and *The Angels Weep,* which are all well-constructed novels. And the classics of course. There's nothing better than studying Dickens. And Colette. Colette, by the way, said: Two things are important in life. Love and work. I like that. Yorkshire people have the work ethic. My mother was always polishing a chair or making a stew and I still feel I must work all day, every day, or God will strike me dead.

6. Have you a talent for plots?

Working out story lines and getting them down in, say, ten pages is the best way of finding out. For myself, an event will trigger a plot. For instance, a former friend who was dying and wanted to make peace with me and other friends she had once hurt led to my plot for *Voice of the Heart.* The story line may "unreel" in the bath or on a bus in anything from ten minutes to an hour.

I never use anything exactly as it has befallen me or my friends, but I've seen so much of what happens to people that I know my plots are not too far-fetched, not larger than life. Nothing is larger than life.

7. Can you create a sense of time and place, mood and atmosphere?

I rely on memory for scenes from nature but I have occasionally taken snapshots for interiors. For *Voice of the Heart,* I photographed a *schloss* in Germany, to help me keep the mood of the place in my mind. Note-taking is another helpful tool, and sensible for people who don't have photographic memories.

I can't explain how you create atmosphere. I mean, Stephen King, the "horror" writer who wrote *Carrie* and *The Shining,* among many others, is brilliant when he creates an atmosphere of horror, and I think he does it with his choice of words. Atmosphere is not something visual, it's a feeling, and it's conveyed by particular words, so I too feel I must find the *exact* word and I'll spend hours sometimes to arrive at it. But, having said that, it's hard for a writer to analyze how he or she writes: I always fear I might analyze it away!

8. Do you have the knack of writing dialogue?

Dialogue has to do several things. It has to move the plot along and provide information of some kind. It has to delineate the character of the person speaking—or somehow reflect his personality. It should add to the flavor of the book, convey emotion or feeling. So it has to be very structured, even though it must sound natural.

Ask yourself if the dialogue you have written does all of these things, and if in all honesty you have to answer "no" you will almost certainly find that you can throw it out without loss—indeed it will be an improvement—to your book.

Written dialogue is totally different from spoken dialogue—write down a taped conversation and you'll see it's unreadable.

9. Are you organized enough?

If you want your novel to have a feeling of authenticity, then you must write from strength, from knowledge—and that means research. But the important thing about research is to be able to throw it away! Put it all in and it slows down the narrative drive. I might do a day's research just for a few lines of dialogue but it has to be integrated so it's not apparent.

An efficient filing system is vital, as are good reference books and address books that record sources—or you will waste precious time and work in a muddle. I have a table next to my desk where I keep handy a large dictionary and the *Columbus Encyclopaedia,* along with a thesaurus, *Bartlett's Familiar Quotations,* a world atlas, and maps of England.

10. Do you have a sense of drama?

There's so much drama every day in the newspapers, surely everyone has. Reading plays, watching movies helps to sharpen a dramatic sense, teach you what makes a "story." A book I go back to time and again is *Wuthering Heights.* Every time I read it I find something I hadn't noticed before. It is extremely emotional to me, a very Yorkshire book—though structurally it's said *not* to be good.

16

MAGICIAN, ACTOR, RUNNER ➡ WRITER

By Peter Lovesey

IT'S A PARTY and my host has steered me across the room to meet some people he says he knows I'll like. After we exchange names one of them asks, "What line of work are you in?"

"Ah." A pause for thought. Shall I admit to being a writer, or take some diversionary action, such as spilling my drink, or shouting "Fire!" or singing a couple of verses from "Some Enchanted Evening"? If not, I must face the inevitable questions; inevitable and always the same:

"Where do you get your ideas?"

I don't know the answer to this, so I generally say, "Anywhere I can."

The next is usually phrased in the form of a statement: "It must take a lot of self-discipline."

Then the questioning takes a personal turn.

"What did you say your name is?"

I give it.

There is a moment of silence, followed by,

"Should we have heard of you?"

A tough one, that. I can escape embarrassment by side-stepping ("No, it's not obligatory. What's your line of work?") or lying ("Oh, I don't often write under my own name."), because it only gets worse:

"Did you always want to be a writer?"

Actually, I didn't. I wasn't born with inky fingers. I didn't have a toy typewriter, and I didn't publish a book until I was past thirty.

The honest answer to that question is no. But what did I want to be as a child? Life before thirty must have had some relevance to my present way of life. What ambitions did I have in those so-called formative years? My earliest was to be a magician. I wanted to amaze and baffle my family and friends by sawing ladies in half. And, I'd better add, restoring them.

I was persuaded to give up conjuring for acting. I started as Joseph in a Nativity play and was sacked for overacting. I was a pure-born Method actor; I pushed the Innkeeper through the scenery when he told us there was no room. It was meant to provoke a genuine response, and it did. After the fight we were both demoted to humiliating non-speaking roles as angels. But I'd caught the acting bug, I wanted to be up there with Gielgud and Olivier.

The urge to act was eventually supplanted by an ambition to be a great long-distance runner, Great Britain's main hope for the 1956 Olympic marathon. I suppose I was one of the first joggers, running through dark suburban streets speaking a radio commentary as I went. I had to endure some strange looks. And there was more humiliation: After months of training, I finished last in the school cross-country race.

As it turned out, running made me into a writer. Facing the fact that I was constitutionally ill equipped for the marathon or even the 100 meters, I channeled my enthusiasm into supporting people who *could* run brilliantly. I made idols of the track stars I watched. I shouted for them, drew pictures of them, put them into ranking lists, and kept press clippings about them. Soon I started to catch out journalists in their facts. I don't suppose it helped them at all, but it helped my confidence. It made me believe that I could do better than they, but nobody else believed it. I wasn't an expert. I hadn't won an Olympic medal. I hadn't even coached an Olympic medalist. I was *Mr. Nobody.*

How do you become an expert overnight? Why, by picking out an area of knowledge that nobody else has bothered to investigate. I went to a newspaper museum and looked up reports of running events a century ago, fascinating to a twentieth-century reader: full of character, color, and eccentricity. I turned my discoveries into off-beat articles for track and field magazines. In a short time I was being described as "the world's foremost authority on the history of athletics." At that time, I was the *only* authority, so it was true beyond dispute.

Unfortunately, the magazine who dubbed me the world's foremost didn't pay me a cent. They published my articles for five years, and I was happy just to get into print. However, at the end of that time I looked at my best work and decided to tailor it into a book on long-distance runners. I went to a lot of trouble to get good illustrations. To his eternal credit, and may his tribe increase, a publisher picked it out of the "slush pile" of unsolicited scripts and liked it enough to publish it as *The Kings of Distance.*

The next year I was encouraged to enter a competition for a first crime novel. I used a nineteenth-century running background; what else would you expect from the world's foremost authority? *Wobble to Death* was unlike anything else in the competition and won the prize. I was launched as a mystery writer. I'm still writing mysteries, seventeen years later.

So what happened to those dreams of my childhood, to be a magician, an actor, or a marathon runner?

Magician, actor, marathon runner: As a mystery writer, I'm all of these. In my own way I'm doing the things I first dreamed of doing.

A magician? A mystery writer repeatedly performs tricks, showing the reader something that turns out to be misleading. Call it trickery, sleight-of-hand, or illusion, it comes down to unexpected effects. The best trick I ever pulled was bringing someone back to life after he'd appeared to be dead. The result was dramatic, but I can't claim any originality. Many fine writers used the device long before I did: I'm not giving too much away if, as examples, I mention Thomas Hardy in *Far From the Madding Crowd*; Evelyn Waugh in *Decline and Fall*; and, of course, Sir Arthur Conan Doyle in "The Empty House," the first story in *The Return of Sherlock Holmes*. Such a marvelous effect has to be used sparingly, or the element of surprise is lost. But there are numerous smaller illusions most of us try. There's the character who turns out to be someone else; the ambiguous suicide note; the poison that is also a cosmetic; the spy who is a double or triple agent.

Every conjurer is asked, "How is it done?" and he's supposed not to reveal his secrets. However, by the end of a book, every writer's secrets are laid bare. It's possible to look back and see exactly how it was done. The magic is in the plotting. May I suggest a useful way to learn how to be a successful writer-magician? Take a plot that has succeeded in surprising you. Study it again, analyze it, and summarize the main course of the plot on one side of a sheet of paper. Then have another look at the trick that surprised you. See how the facts were first presented to you and how the writer achieved the illusion. I promise you won't be wasting your time.

The magic, as I said, is in the plotting. Some writers will tell you that plotting is itself a mysterious process that happens without much conscious effort on their part. The book develops as they write it, and they don't know where the next day's writing will lead them.

My approach couldn't be more different. I believe in working out the entire plot before I start writing page one. Otherwise, I'd feel like a conjurer going out on stage without preparing his program. It's slow, agonizing, frequently unproductive work. Sometimes I worry at an idea for weeks and then reject it because I've proved to myself that it won't come out convincingly. The plot must be an excellent one, or why spend months or years of your life shaping it into a book?

I'm happy to pass on a few tips about plotting. I find it helps me at an early stage to give the characters real names, rather than A, B, or C, or "old man" or "blonde." It also helps to think up real locations, preferably places you know. Sometimes a particular setting, its streets and buildings, suggests twists that you wouldn't otherwise have thought about. And when you've reached an impasse, as I frequently do, it helps if there's someone in your life who won't mind having you explain the problem. Often the process of talking about it will clarify the difficulty. Even as I'm explaining why I'm stuck, inspiration strikes, and I see the way ahead. But choose someone *very* sympathetic, or he or she will think you quite mad.

My second ambition, you'll recall, was to act. As a writer, I'm acting all the time, with the bonus that I can invent my own dialogue as I go along. If the characters in a novel are to come alive, you need to give them convincing things to say in a realistic form. So I speak the conversations aloud as I write them, playing the parts and seeing if they have tension and drama.

The whole question of voice is crucial. After you've worked out a satisfactory—no, let's say it—brilliant plot, you need to decide what voice the writing will have. My latest mysteries have been written in the first person, with the narrator telling a tale in which he plays a leading part. In this way, the reader learns a lot about the character, whether he's forceful or unassertive, cynical or naive. It all shows through in the telling. And to get it right, I speak the lines aloud.

Even if I write in the third person, I invariably tell the story from the point of view of one or more of the characters. Once I rewrote an entire novel because I thought it would work better from someone else's point of view, and it did. I wouldn't want to give myself that task again, so now I spend time at the beginning deliberately deciding how to get it right: whose voice will tell the story.

Most actors will admit that in preparing a role they draw on their

82

observation of people they know. The same, I am certain, is true of most writers. I wouldn't recommend telling your friends that you based this or that character on them, but I believe in doing it. Even if they bother to read my books, they don't recognize themselves in the obscure settings I put them in. Besides, I make them do things my friends probably wouldn't admit to, anyway.

Ambition number three was long-distance running, and that, too, has relevance to my life as a writer. It's about endurance and fitness and pacing yourself. The prospect at the start, faced with that first blank sheet, is daunting, but once I'm ready, I set off and take it in my stride, and after two or three weeks Chapter One is complete. I don't care to think too much at the start about the time I'm likely to take, but as I go on it sometimes helps to have a finishing date in mind. My mysteries take anything from eight months to a year to finish. I'm slow for a full-time writer working eight or ten hours a day, but I rarely rewrite, so it's all progress.

Of course, it's a very hard slog. Hemingway said it was sometimes like drilling rock and then blasting it out with charges. Peter De Vries wrote, "I love being a writer. What I can't stand is the paperwork." Ask any marathon runner why he does it when he suffers constantly from blisters and leg pains, and you're likely to be told that it's about achieving something and the joy of getting there. For me, writing is compulsive for similar reasons. However hard it appears, it's still a fun run.

And the moral of all this? If you ever meet me at a party, don't ask me if I always wanted to be a writer, because you'll have heard it all before.

May your writing be magical, dramatic, and long-lasting.

17

BUILDING TENSION IN
THE SHORT STORY

By Joyce Carol Oates

THE most important aspect of writing is characterization—does a character come alive, is he memorable in some way? But the means of disclosing character is also important, for if a story lacks a strong narrative line, an editor or reader might not be patient enough to discover even the most stunning of fictional characters.

Novels are complex matters; the density of interest has to go up and down. Short stories, however, are generally based on one gradual upward swing toward a climax or "epiphany"—moment of recognition. A good chapter in a novel should probably be based on the same rhythmic structure as a short story. The novel, of course, can be leisurely while the average short story must be economical. Certain modern stories are so economical that single words or phrases are used to reveal the story's meaning—for instance, John Collier's "The Chaser," which ends with the words "au revoir" and not "goodbye."

While I think the best kind of contemporary story is much more rich and complex and daring than the Chekhovian-type stories so fashionable a few decades ago, still the writer must be careful to limit the range of his "secondary" material—descriptions, background. If he succeeds in winning the reader's attention by dramatic means, then the more important aspects of his story will be appreciated. We have all written wonderful little stories that are "hidden" somewhere in overlong, awkward, unsatisfactory masses of words.

Here are two examples of short story beginnings, each leading into a different kind of story:

1) "Let me tell you something about the Busbys," the old gentleman said to me. "The Busbys don't wash themselves—not adequately. And especially not as they grow older."

2) Just around the turn, the road was alive. First to assault the eye was a profusion of heads, black-haired, bobbing, and a number of straw hats that looked oddly professional—

The stories following these beginnings are to be found in *Prize Stories 1965: The O. Henry Awards*, edited by Richard Poirier and William Abrahams. The first story, "There," by Peter Taylor, invites the reader to listen in on a confidential, gossipy conversation: the words "Let me tell you" are intriguing enough, but the surprise comes in the second line. And we are introduced to a strange little town, "There," where each family seems to have a peculiar trait all its own—not washing properly, eating too much, narrow-minded complacency—and dying. Peter Taylor, the author of many excellent short stories of a rich, complex type, builds tension in a highly refined manner. We listen in on this old man's monologue, amused by his portraits of people back "there," and gradually we become emotionally involved in the pathos of his love for a girl who belonged to a family with a secret common trait—and then we find out, along with the narrator, that this common trait is dying. The girl has died young; the lover, now an aged man, has married someone else; there is no tragedy here, everything is muted and understated. But the story is unforgettable because Taylor has built so very gradually and unobtrusively the tension that arises out of the girl's impending death. Everything is past tense, but vitally alive.

The second beginning is from a story of mine, "First Views of the Enemy." Beginning with a near-accident, this story relies on tension building up within the main character's mind. A bus carrying migrant fruit pickers has broken down at the roadside, and when a young mother with her child drives by, one of the Mexican children darts in front of the car to frighten her. The tension between the young, American, rather materialistic woman and the socially-marginal people is the theme of this story. The woman arrives home safely, but she carries the image of this "enemy" with her into her expensive home, which now seems to her vulnerable. Her realization that she could lose everything she owns drives her to an orgy of selfishness as she locks things up, closes her drapes, even picks her most beautiful flowers and forces food upon her child. The tension is psychological, not active; the "enemy" does not appear after the first encounter. We see that the true "enemy" is the woman's hysterical selfishness, which she is forcing upon her child also.

Franz Kafka's classic, "The Metamorphosis," begins like this:

As Gregor Samsa awoke one morning from uneasy dreams he found himself transformed in his bed into a gigantic insect.

Incredible, of course. Unbelievable. But Kafka's mild-mannered prose proceeds on as if an event of no great dimensions has taken place. You, the reader, find out about Gregor's metamorphosis at the same time he does. You are surprised, yes, but so is Gregor—a quite ordinary young man, devoted to his family and his work. This surrealistic story is much more "realistic" in its ability to convince and emotionally involve than most slick fiction with its easily-recognizable people. But Kafka thrives on tension. He builds it from his first sentence on. Kafka is always asking, "What happens next?" and then he asks, "After that, what happens?" Like Simenon, he drives his characters to extremes and tests them. "The Metamorphosis" is beautifully constructed in three sections, each dealing with the tense relationship between the stricken Gregor and his family, until Gregor dies in order to release his loved ones. Tension is achieved on the literal level—what is going to happen to the insect-man?—and on the symbolic level—what will be the outcome of the "love" between members of a family when one of them is mysteriously stricken and is no longer "human"?

These three stories, widely differing in technique, build up tension through an accumulation of detail. If violence erupts in fiction, it should be the outcome of tension; it should not come first, nor should it be accidental. Action stories are of interest to certain audiences, but quality stories usually refine action onto a psychological level. There is "action"—movement—but it takes place in a person's mind or in a conversation. If someone finally kills someone else, it is simply the climax of a rhythmic building of tension that lasts long enough to be convincing but is short enough to be interesting.

Remember that tension created for its own sake is cheap; no one will read your story more than once. The tension is part of your technique but technique is only a means to an end; it is never the end itself. That is why the French "new novel" is so boring—it has no capacity to move us—while older, stormy works like *Wuthering*

Heights (which could only be "camp" to today's *avant-garde*) will be interesting to all imaginable future generations. I think the stress placed today on technique is misleading. A writer should imagine his scenes dramatically, as if they were to take place on the stage. There, empty, wordy passages are found out at once. It isn't "words" or "style" that make a scene, but the content behind the words, and the increase of tension as characters come into conflict with one another. "Words" themselves are relatively unimportant, since there are countless ways of saying the same thing.

A final suggestion: be daring, take on anything. Don't labor over little cameo works in which every word is to be perfect. Technique holds a reader from sentence to sentence, but only content will stay in his mind.

18

ABOUT THAT NOVEL

By Evan Hunter

STARTING: If you haven't got an idea for one, forget it. If you haven't got an idea you want to express on paper, in words, forget it. If you prefer putting paint on canvas, or rolls on your pianola or in your oven, forget it. You're going to be with this novel for a long, long time, so you'd better have *thought* about it before you start writing it. When it's ready to be written, you'll know. You'll know because you can't get it out of your mind. It'll be with you literally day and night. You'll even *dream* about it, but don't get up and rush to your typewriter. Go back to sleep. Only in movies do writers get up in the middle of the night with an inspiration. The time to go to the typewriter is when you're fresh and ready to do battle. There *will* be a battle, no question, a siege that will seemingly go on forever. So sit down, make yourself comfortable, and begin.

No outline at first, except the loose one in your head, draped casually around the idea. The thing you are trying to find is the voice. This is the single most important thing in any novel. The voice. How it will *sound*. Who is telling the story? Why is he telling it? If you're sixty years old and writing in the first person singular about a sixteen-year-old high school student, beware of the voice. It may be your own, and that is wrong. If you're writing in the third person, you can change the *tone* of the voice each time you switch to another character, but the *voice* itself must remain consistent throughout. The voice is your style. Except in my mystery series, I try to change my style to suit the subject matter of any novel I'm writing. I've come a hundred pages into a novel using the wrong voice, and I've thrown those pages away and started a new search for the right voice. Don't worry about spending days or weeks trying to find a voice. It will be time well spent. You'll know when you hit upon it. Things will suddenly *feel* right.

Once you've found the voice, write your first chapter or your first scene. Test the water. Does it still feel right? Good. *Now* make your outline. First of all, determine how long the book will be. The average mystery novel runs about 200 pages in manuscript, but a straight novel can be something as slim as *Love Story* or as thick as *Gone With the Wind.* You are the only person who knows in advance what your story is about. You are the only one who can figure how many pages you will need to tell this story. Take out your calculator. Are you writing a 300-page novel? O.K., how many chapters will you need? The length of each chapter will be determined by how much you have to *say* in that chapter. If you're depicting the Battle of Waterloo, it might be a trifle difficult to compress it into ten pages. If you're writing about a man putting out the garbage, you probably have only a scene, and you'll need additional scenes to make a full chapter.

Outline the novel in your own way, never mind freshman high-school English courses. I've outlined a forty-page chapter with just the words "Father-son confrontation." The outline is you, talking to yourself on paper. Get friendly with yourself. Tell yourself what you, as the writer, want to accomplish in any given chapter. "O.K., now we want a big explosion in the garage, and we want to see all these goddamn flames, and smell the smoke, and we want neighbors running over with garden hoses. Bring the little girl in at the end of the scene, shocked by what she's done." Got it? *Talk* to yourself. You don't have to outline the whole book. Just take the outline as far as your invention will carry it. Later, when you've written all the chapters you've already outlined, you can make another outline of the *next* several chapters. If a chapter is needed between something that has happened before and something that will happen later, and you don't know what to put between those two slices of bread, just type in the words, SCENE MISSING. You'll come back to it later. You're going to be here awhile.

MOVING: Set yourself a definite goal each day. Tack it on the wall. Ten pages? Five pages? Two pages? Two paragraphs? It doesn't matter. *Set* the goal, make it realistic, and *meet* it. If you're writing a planned 400-page novel, it will seem impossible ever to get it finished.

400 pages may be a year away. But your daily goal is here and now, and it's important to set that goal and meet it so that you'll have a sense of immediate reward. At the end of each week, on your calendar, jot down the number of pages you've already written. Store your kernels. Watch the cache grow. Keep the thing moving. If it bogs down, if you're supposed to write a tender love scene and you've just had a fight with your accountant, put the anger to good use. Jump ahead and write the Battle of Waterloo chapter. *Don't stop writing!* It's easier to go fishing or skiing—but sit at that damn typewriter, and look at the four walls all day long if you have to. There is nothing more boring than looking at the walls. Eventually, if only to relieve the boredom, and because you've made a deal with yourself not to get out of that chair, you'll start writing again. At the end of the day, read over what you've written. If you think it's lousy, don't throw it away. Read it again in the morning. If it still looks lousy, do it over again. Or if it's still bothering you, and you don't know why, move on. Keep it *moving*. The nice thing about writing, unlike public speaking, is that you can correct all your mistakes later.

CHANGING: The only true creative aspect of writing is the first draft. That's when it's coming straight from your head and your heart, a direct tapping of the unconscious. The rest is donkey work. It is, however, donkey work that must be done. Whether you rewrite as you go along—taking that bad chapter from the night before and putting it through the machine again from the top—or whether you rewrite everything only after you've completed the book, you *must* rewrite. But be careful. You can hone and polish something until it glows like a diamond, but you may end up with something hard and glittering and totally without the interior spark that was the result of your first commitment to paper. You're only a virgin once, but try to bring to each rereading of your own material the same innocence you brought to it the first time around. You will be rereading it *twenty* times before you're finished. Each time, ask yourself what you intended. Do you want me to cry when I read this scene? Well, are *you* crying? If you're not, why aren't you? Find out why you aren't. Did someone say something that broke the mood of the scene? Is that field of daffodils too cheerful for the tone of the scene? Has your heroine stamped her foot when she should be tearing out her hair? Work it, rework it. When you yourself begin crying, you've got it.

ENDING: How do you know when you're finished? You're finished when you're satisfied. If a scene is right the first time around, leave it alone. Tell yourself, "Terrific, pal," and leave it alone. You'll know you're getting to the end because you'll suddenly slow down. When that happens, set smaller goals for yourself. Instead of those five pages today, make it three. Your pace is slower because you don't want to let go of this thing. You've been living together for a long, long time, you've let this smelly beast into your tent, and you've grown to love it, and now you're reluctant to have it gallop out over the sands and out of your life forever. The temptation is to keep it with you forever, constantly bathe it and scent it, groom it and curry it, tweeze its lashes and tie a bow on its tail. *Recognize* the temptation and recognize too that everything eventually grows up and leaves home. When you've done the best you can possibly do at this time (there *will* be other books, you know) put it in a box, give it a farewell kiss, and send it out into that great big hostile world.

SENDING: Where do you send it? Be exceedingly careful in choosing your agent or your publisher. Don't send the book to anyone who charges a fee for reading it or publishing it. In the real world of publishing, people pay *you* for your work. The Society of Authors' Representatives (if you decide to go the agent route) will send you on request a list of reputable agents in the United States. The address is P.O. Box 650, Old Chelsea Station, New York, NY 10113. Just write and ask, enclosing a self-addressed, stamped envelope. If you decide to submit your manuscript directly to a publisher instead, a long list of publishers looking for various kinds of novels appears in *The Writer* Magazine, or in the market list in Part IV of this volume. Although some book publishers today have given up reading unsolicited manuscripts, many others still maintain reading staffs, and their sole purpose is to search for publishing possibilities. Send the novel manuscript out. One publisher at a time. Multiple submissions are frowned upon except when an agent is conducting a huge auction, and then the publishers are made aware beforehand that the book is being submitted simultaneously all over the field. Choose a publisher who has previously published your sort of book. Don't shotgun it around blindly. If your novel espouses atheism, don't send it to a religious publisher.

WAITING: So now your monster is out roaming the countryside, trying to earn a living. No, there it is in the mailbox. Damn thing. Wish you hadn't given it life at all. Tear open the package. Nice little noncommittal note. Thanks a lot, but no thanks. Despair. Chin up, kiddo, send it out again. But here it is *back* again. And *again*. And *yet* again. Plenty of publishers in the world, just keep trying. Pack it, send it, wait again. Why? Why wait? Why set up a vigil at the mailbox? Why hang around the post office looking like someone on the Wanted posters? You should be *thinking* instead. You should be mulling a new idea. *Don't* wait. What you *should* be doing is—

STARTING: If you haven't got an idea for one, forget it. If you haven't got an idea you want to express on paper, in words, forget it. If you prefer putting paint on canvas, or rolls on your pianola or in your oven, forget it. You're going to be with this novel for a long, long time, so you'd better have *thought* about it before you start writing it. When it's ready to be written, you'll know.

Write it.

19

USING IMAGINATION IN PLOTTING

By Joan Aiken

IT'S PERFECTLY possible, of course, to construct a plot *without* the use of imagination. A plot is a mechanical thing, like a coat hanger—the structure upon which the garment of fiction will be hung. You can look up a made-to-measure plot in Georges Polti's *The Thirty-Six Dramatic Situations,* and in that useful and amazing work of reference, almost any book or play that has ever been written will be found in embryo: "The Loved One Hated by Kindred of the Lover," for instance. Let's see . . . *Romeo and Juliet,* of course, *Pride and Prejudice, Beauty and the Beast.* "Recovery of a Lost One" covers *The Winter's Tale, Huckleberry Finn,* and *The Three Little Pigs.*

The point I am trying to make is that the plot itself need not be of great importance; the plot is the least of the writer's problems. When I was a child, an editor called Fothergill had the notion of passing out the same plot to a dozen different authors and persuading them to write a short story based on it. Then he published them in an anthology called *The Fothergill Omnibus.* All the stories were completely different, as each writer had handled the theme in his own way. The only drawback was that most of them were rather dull. Whatever its potential, a plot has no value unless it appeals to you personally. In which case, the simplest and most basic themes—Remorse, Mistaken Judgment, Unreasonable Jealousy—are sufficient for your coat hanger.

Where the use of imagination comes in is at the next stage: how you arrange your viewpoint, your time scheme, your characters; which feature will stand out and remain in the reader's mind. We all have our favorite books into which we dip from time to time. What do we choose? Not always an essential part of the plot. Often it is a side scene, or just a bit of description.

I'm going to discuss here a few aspects of plotting where imagination can be brought into play (naturally there are uncountable others). The elements I have chosen are time, character, deliberately setting yourself a problem, and some odds and ends, such as story order, incident, and how to give your imagination a prod.

Time, first. You have an idea for a plot, but it drags.

How about changing its pace and momentum by interweaving a causally connected story from an earlier period?

I'll illustrate with an example.

My novel *Midnight is a Place* is a riches-to-rags story of two children in an English Stately Home setting, who suddenly find themselves destitute and not only that, but ostracized and hated by everyone about them. An adequate plot, but nothing out of the common. Feeling this, I made use of the causal strands that had brought about this situation: a wild wager between two young rakes in which one of them had cheated, and the exile and death in poverty of one of them. This story is not told flat out in one piece but is revealed to the reader in fragments, interspersed between the present-day account of how the two children struggle to keep alive in highly adverse circumstances. The account of the past, coming through in this way, has the effect of enriching the contemporary thread of plot by giving it more dimension as well as verisimilitude. In real life, after all, we receive our information from newspapers, television, and from friends in just this way—not in one consecutive saga, but in fragments we must piece together to make a coherent account.

So if a plot seems to lack the richness that imagination can provide, *start further back*. What are the causes that brought your characters to the predicament they are in at the outset of your story? You must know a great deal about them before you begin—their history, their parents, even their grandparents. Having created this material, make use of it. Don't go back to the earlier point in time and start from there, but find a means of weaving those earlier strands into your present-day fabric.

Another use of imagination can be for problem-solving. How to set this up? Construct for yourself an apparently insoluble problem and then wait to see how your imagination will deal with the challenge.

Dorothy Canfield did this masterfully in the novel *Her Son's Wife*. The plot is extremely simple. A widowed schoolteacher, left with a young son and anguished memories of her revered husband, rears the son with such rigid, obsessional authority that he turns into a weak, obedient mother's boy, who then, in one feeble spurt of resistance while halfway through college, marries a selfish, illiterate slut whose only asset is vulgar prettiness. What *can* the mother do? The young pair have no money, they must live in her cherished, carefully tended house, which they reduce to a shambles. The setup is portrayed with excruciating fidelity. The mother decides that she can't endure it and accepts a better job in another town, leaving her beloved home to the feckless pair. But a few years later a chance glimpse of her adored little granddaughter, age three, left in the charge of good-time girls and street louts, obviously destined to grow up into just such another floozie as her mother, draws the grandmother home again. With an immense effort of will, she subdues her own feelings and refrains from adverse criticism or interference. But the situation is still just as bad: the son weakly unhappy, aware of his wife's defects but still infatuated by her; the daughter-in-law unfaithful, selfish, slovenly, self-pitying, hypochondriacal; and the child, bright, sweet-natured, but growing up wan and unhealthy from poor feeding, with terrible habits picked up from her mother.

What can the grandmother do? The reader honestly cannot imagine. The situation appears insoluble. The grandmother has already submerged her own nature to an almost incredible degree. Anything she does will be disruptive, almost bound to hurt the child or her son. Yet she is a strong-minded, capable woman. How can she liberate herself from this impasse?

It seems almost unfair to reveal her solution, for it is so startling, and yet, in essence, so simple, completely inevitable, built precisely upon existing foundations. The mother-in-law proceeds to exploit the wife's self-pitying disposition, and persuades her to take to her bed with an imagined ailment of the spine. There she is pampered and coddled with every possible attention, while order and routine return once more to the household, the son is able to find a better job, and the grandchild can grow up healthy and unaffected by her mother's slatternly influence. Soon the mother, fat and debilitated, could not get up even if she wished to. Thus, evil is done that good may come: The grandmother, aware that she has committed what amounts to a moral murder, condemns and despises herself, yet still feels it was the only thing to do. Her penance is on the way in any case: When son and granddaughter have left home, for another job and college respectively, and the protagonist (the grandmother) is making plans to take off to lead the independent, professional life that she has craved for so long, she finds that she is trapped. Her daughter-in-law can't do without her; she has, indeed, learned to love. "Don't leave me, Momma!" is her final cry.

Imagination can also be used to strengthen character. You have your plot—a good, workable story about an elderly man who holds a well-paid public position with practically no duties. Political events quite unrelated to him suddenly focus on him and his comfortable sinecure, and a disapproving newspaper article is written about it. Conscience-stricken, he decides to resign, and finally does so.

This, in essence, is the plot of *The Warden,* Trollope's first Barsetshire book: an exceedingly plain, straightforward plot. What turns it to magic, so that it will be read forever, and again and again by addicted readers, are the characters of the hero and his son-in-law. The hero, Mr. Harding, is a delightful old man, unworldly, musical, given to playing the cello for slightly longer than his auditors would wish, but humble, and, when he comes to think about them, absolutely certain about issues of right and wrong. We should recognize him if we met him in China. Mr. Grantly, the archdeacon, his son-in-law, is another absolutely three-dimensional character—acerbic, worldly, with hardly a grain of humor in his make-up, not at all a person with whom one would wish to live. And yet we absolutely love him. How did such characters leap into Trollope's mind, when some of his others—particularly his callow heroes—are so flat that they are no more than clothes-pegs?

An animal or an object may also be used as the imaginatively transforming agent. Peter Dickinson, a highly original writer, makes use of both. Quentin, a rat gifted with ESP, who can be used like a laser beam to kill people who believe in his power, is a notable feature of the thriller *Walking Dead,* about corruption and dictatorship in an imaginary Caribbean state. In *The Gift,* by the same author, telepathy also plays a part. The boy hero inherits this "gift" from his father's family, and so unwillingly tunes in on arrangements for a heist planned by the feckless father and some dangerous accomplices. One of these is hardly sane; it is the wild disruptiveness of his thought patterns, much more powerfully beamed out than those of normal people, that first alerts the boy to what is going to happen. But among these frantic transmissions, there is one that is beautiful and serene, the image of a stone, smoothly shaped and streaked with color, and it is the use the hero makes of this image and its reappearance at the close that make the story moving and memorable.

Can a writer deliberately harness imagination? It is certainly a faculty that all writers possess (otherwise they would never have taken to the profession in the first place). So how can it be invoked? What can be done if a piece of work seems flat and uninspired and clomps along rather heavy-footed?

First, critical processes must be brought into play. We are all our own best critics; if we take the pains, we can decide which are our better works. Any writer knows that feeling of awestruck astonishment on reading an earlier work thinking, "What a perfectly marvelous invention! How in the wide world did I ever think of that?" Sometimes it really does seem as if inspiration from some other source had temporarily taken over the typewriter.

Having refreshed your memory by a glance back at one of those really inspired pieces of writing, review your present work in a critical and comparative spirit. What element that was present *then* is lacking *now*? Are the characters ready-made and uninteresting, taken out of stock rather than created expressly for this story or novel? Is the style flat, uninspired? Are the events mechanical, or the outcome too predictable, too improbable? Often the fault can be traced to one particular ingredient, one episode, one character that is not pulling its weight (like the sister Mary Bennet in *Pride and Prejudice,* a minor flaw in an otherwise nearly perfect work). Can the character be replaced by some other person, perhaps even by an animal, or taken out altogether? Can the weak incident be replaced by some other happening or narrated from a different viewpoint, or—this is often the solution—simply deleted? Leave a line-space, take a deep breath, and write "twenty years passed." Then see what happens.

A leisurely pace is often the most important factor in this kind of revision. The imagination is a balky faculty; it will not be hurried. Sometimes it is simply waiting for new material. Then you witness a scene in a bus: a repulsive little girl, unpleasantly cute, is kicking up a fiendish fuss because she has to give up her seat to an elderly lady and sit on her father's lap. "I *wanted* to sit on that seat, *very much*!" she is yelling, and the fat, placating father is beseeching her: "Don't *be* like this, sweetheart. You are hurting Daddy's feelings very much!" Or you see an elderly man and woman on a railroad platform, at odds with one another. The husband keeps making some snarling remark, then walking out of earshot toward the platform edge and angrily shouting, "What? I can't hear you?" when his wife comes back with a riposte. At once, after some such experience, you can see how the relations between a pair of characters in your story can be handled. They may not be old and young, husband and wife, father and daughter: The creatures who finally appear in your work may appear to have no connection at all to the scene in the bus, on the station. Yet the flash was there, and it came just when you needed it.

Very, very often I find that the message is transmitted in a dream, or comes in one of those brief, acute waking flashes in the middle of the night. The unconscious has known, all along what the solution was to be but has not been able to make itself heard above the clatter of your typewriter.

Why should I have dreamed about a kitchen with black corrugated walls and ten copper stoves in it, with beer-making equipment in the room next door and a strong smell of brewing, perceptible even in the dream? I write my dreams down in my notebook, and then forget about them. Sometimes, weeks later, it suddenly becomes clear what part one of them has to play. Why should I dream about K.N.'s sitting room full of water? Why of a man with a coat hanger through the shoulder of his pullover and a hat on the coat.

In writing my novel, *If I Were You*, I discovered, just before it was too late, the lack of solidity in one character. The story is about substitution: The heroine, who wants time and peaceful surroundings in which to write a novel, is persuaded to take the place of another, richer girl, whom she closely resembles and who wishes to go off to become a missionary. (Period, 1815; the other girl's parents will not permit their daughter missionary aspirations.) I knew from the start how the story was going to end: The other girl's ambitions were going to be deflected the very first time a young man proposed to her. But I thought the young man who proposed was of no importance; I had planned him as a minor character, perhaps remaining offstage altogether, or, at most, appearing only once. But, then, why did I wake up in the middle of the night, announcing to myself, "His name is Lieutenant Dunnifage"? Surely, with an emphatic name like that, he must be destined to play rather more of a part in the plot? It was not until my editor had read the story and suggested that the ending, as it then stood, was both too abrupt and too implausible, that I saw how Lieutenant Dunnifage could be worked properly into the story and turned into a highly instrumental part of the climax.

Sometimes imagination can be constructively applied to the *order* of your story. Told chronologically, it is adequate, but unremarkable; how would it be if turned back-to-front, or posed in the form of a question?

I came across a delightful example of this recently in a picture book for very small children, *The Sneeze,* by David Lloyd and Fritz Wegner. "Once upon a time," it begins, "there were a hat, a ball, a bench, a girl, a man, a dog, a newspaper, and a suitcase." Then it proceeds to ask questions. "Who wore what? Did the girl wear the newspaper? Who threw what? Did the man throw the bench? Who jumped over what? Did the man jump over the dog?" In the end, it is all sorted out with great precision and charm, so that a simple sequence of events is transformed into a shapely, rounded narrative. But what was the genesis of such a method of storytelling? Why, the imagination, of course.

Imagination is such a tremendously strong part of us that it seems a pity we harness it so little to our daily needs. Like electricity during the Middle Ages, it is there, all around us. Like medieval man, we rub a bit of amber on a coat sleeve and observe with mild wonder that it will attract particles of paper to itself. We see the lightning strike the church steeple, but we have only the most rudimentary conception of how this force can be employed to run railways or warm whole populations or transmit messages across continents. Our imagination is dying to help us, if only we would listen to its urgent cries to be heeded.

20

THE READER AS PARTNER

By Tony Hillerman

SOMETIME VERY EARLY in my efforts to make a living as a writer, I noticed an odd little fact, trivial but useful: People just back from seeing the Rocky Mountains didn't describe the Front Range. They told me about the clump of mountain iris they'd seen blooming through the edge of a dwindling snowbank. Witnesses of a train wreck I interviewed when I was a reporter would describe the women's clothing scattered along the right-of-way and ignore the big picture. The fellow drinking beer after watching the rodeo would talk about the sounds the bulls made coming out the gate—not the derring-do of the champion rider.

I noticed my own brain worked that way, too: It would store a scattering of details in full color and with every stitch showing, but the general scene would be vague and ill-defined. I presumed that this was the way run-of-the-mill men and women remembered things, and thus, it would be useful for writers in the process of converting a scene that exists in our minds into words that would recreate it in the imagination of those who read what we write.

I doubt if there is anything new or original about this thinking or this tactic. Selecting significant details to cause the reader to focus attention exactly where it's wanted was being done with quill pen on papyrus and probably before. Except for those dilettantes of the "art for art's sake" school, every writer is engaged in a joint venture every time he writes. He looks at what's behind his own forehead and translates it into words. At the other end of the crosscut saw, the reader drinks in those words and tries to transmute them back into images.

It's a partnership. We work at it. So does the reader.

But we're getting paid for it, in money, fame (if we're lucky), and in the fun of controlling the process. The reader expects a different reward for the cash and time he or she invests. Even so, that reader is a working member of the team.

I always write with some clear notions about those for whom I write. They are, for example, a little more intelligent than I am and have a bit better education. They have good imaginations. They enjoy suspense. They are impatient. They are middle-aged. They are busy. They know very little about the specific subject I'm writing about. They are interested in it only if I can provoke that interest.

Given that, how should I go about my business? For example, how should I describe in physical terms this benign character I am about to introduce in chapter three? Not much, probably, if that character is to be important to the plot, and the reader is to come to know him from repeated meetings. But quite a bit if said character takes the stage only briefly.

Why this odd inversion? Because my intelligent, well-educated, middle-aged, imaginative reader knows from personal experience what various sorts of people look like. Therefore, if you use a character a lot, the reader paints his own portrait. For example, as far as I can remember, I have never given more than the vaguest descriptions of either Joe Leaphorn or Jim Chee, the two Navajo tribal policemen who are often the protagonists in my mystery novels. Yet scores of readers have described them to me. Tall and short, big and little, plump and lean, handsome and homely. The reader's imagination creates the character from his or her own experience, making the policeman look exactly the way he should look. Why should the writer argue with that? Why should the person who is investing money and time in reading my story be denied his role in the creative process?

Minor characters, I think, need more description. The reader is likely to see them only briefly through the eyes of the protagonist. He should be as curious about minor characters as is the viewpoint character— looking for the spot of gravy on the necktie, the nervous twitch at the corner of the eye, the dark roots of the bleached blonde hair, the scar tissue on the left cheek. Our reader won't see this minor actor enough to fit him into any personal mold.

Sometimes, of course, the writer must exercise more control over the image the reader would create. The story line may demand that the reader know the character is burly, has an artificial hand, and that his eyes tend to water if he stands too long reading the sympathy cards in the Hallmark shop. Otherwise, I count on the reader to perform his half of the task with no interference from me. I think he enjoys it more.

This notion of the reader as partner in a game of imagination affects how I write in many other ways. For example, there's that hard-to-define something that I think of as "mood." It exists in my mind as I write a scene. Sometimes it is merely the mental state of the viewpoint character through whose eyes whatever is happening is seen. But it can be more than that, or even different from that. For example, I may need to send signals to the reader that it is time for nervous anxiety, while the protagonist is still happily remembering that there's nothing left to worry about.

I tend to take on the mood of the scene—writing with lower lip gripped between my teeth when doom is impending, writing with a grin when all is well in chapter nine. I want the reader to join me in this mood. And here I'm on shaky ground. I simply have no way of knowing if my tactics work.

They involve engaging the reader's senses. I interrupt the dialogue or the action to show the reader through the eyes of the protagonist the dust on the windowsill, the grime on the windowpane, the tumbleweeds blowing across the yard, the broken gate creaking in the wind, the spider scurrying toward the center of its web, the stuffed weasel in its frozen leap toward the cowering quail in the taxidermy display. I have the reader notice the odors of old age, of decay, and of air breathed too often in a closed and claustrophobic room. I have him hear the sort of vague sounds that intrude into tired, tense silences. These are the sorts of signals my senses are open to when I am in this certain mood. If they don't contribute to causing it, at least they reflect it. Perhaps the same will be true for the reader.

Another mood. Another set of sensory signals. Take satisfaction-contentment-happiness (what my Navajo characters might call "hozro"). There's the smell of rain in the air (remember, I write mostly about a landscape where rain is all rare and a joyful blessing), the aroma of brewing coffee, the promising voice of distant thunder, the sound of birds, the long view through slanting sunlight of sage and buffalo grass, and the mountains on the horizon, a sense of beauty with room enough and time enough to enjoy it, and the good feeling of fresh-baked bread under the fingertips.

Unless some psychologist can come up with a universal catalogue of which objects/smells/sounds are connected in the mind of Average

Human with which mood, neither you nor I will ever know how effective this technique is. My conversations with those who have read my work suggest that sometimes I can make it work, and sometimes I fail. But I am working at it, using my only laboratory animal—myself—as guinea pig.

Someone I meet pleases me. I think I would like them. Why? Well, you know . . . there was just something about him. But specifically, exactly what was it? Go back, you sluggard, and remember. What was it, specifically and exactly, that first caused you to start looking at and listening to this stranger? It was the body language, the expression, that told you he was really and intently listening when you talked to him. Interested in you and in what you were saying. So how can that be described most effectively? And what else was there? The way he said things? The turn of phrase. To defer. Not to interrupt. The tendency not to overdescribe, to presume his listener was intelligent and informed. Whatever it was, isolate it. Remember it. Have it handy the next time you want to introduce this sort of person to the reader.

A scene depresses me, leaves me out of sorts and angry. Why? The coldness of the room, the dim, yellow light, the tarnish on the gold tassel on the rope, the arrogant stare of the hostess, the slick, clammy coolness of the surface of this table. . . . What else?

I awake at night from a bad dream, tense and anxious. Quick. Dissect the mood before it evaporates. Nightmares are rare these days for me. For a man who deals in suspense, fear, and tension, they are too valuable to waste. What was in it and in the darkness around the bed that provokes this uneasiness and anxiety? Specifically, what do you hear, or smell, or feel or see that causes this painful tension?

I have been doing this for years: stripping down people and places, dissecting their looks and their mannerisms, filling the storage bins of imagination with useful parts; doing the same with street scenes, with landscapes, with the weather. When I wrote only nonfiction, such stuff was jotted in my notebook—the telltale details I trained my mind to isolate and collect. The anthropologist squatted on a grassy slope beside an anthill, his callused fingers sifting through those tiny grains ants bring to the surface, frowning in his fierce hope of finding a chip from a Stone Age artifact. The same fingers sorting through the residue left on the sifter-frame over his wheelbarrow, eliminating the gravel, roots, and rabbit droppings, saving the tiny chips flaked from a flint lance point; finding a twig to fish out the angry scorpion and return him to the grass. And that final detail, I hope my reader will agree, does more than put him on the scene with me. It gives him insight into the character of the man who owns the callused fingers.

21

THE HIDDEN CENSOR

By Diane Lefer

TEN YEARS ago, I had file cabinets full of fiction I'd written, and not a single page of it had ever seen print. Today, I make my living as a writer and, looking back, I'm convinced that the major turning points in my creative life had less to do with discovering tricks of the trade than with recognizing the personal attitudes and emotions that were standing in my way.

The first important lesson, which didn't come easily, was:

Don't worry about what people are going to think of you.

One day, about ten years ago, I read a novel by Chaim Potok called *My Name Is Asher Lev,* about a Jewish artist, from a deeply religious Hasidic family, whose breakthrough as a painter comes when he incorporates crucifixion symbolism into his work—not that he wishes to convert, but the Christian imagery helps him express his perceptions of life. The result: Asher Lev gains renown in the art world, but his family cannot understand or forgive what he has done. The moral: The artist must express his own truth, no matter how painful the consequences may be.

Most of us don't face as clear-cut and difficult a choice as Asher Lev. Our families may not always approve of our work, but they aren't going to turn away from us in shock, either. But Chaim Potok's novel shook me up anyway. For the first time, I recognized the hidden censor who'd been at work in my head, interfering with the words I put down on paper without my even knowing it.

I had heard, of course, about other writers' inhibitions. Marcel Proust, for example, couldn't write *Remembrance of Things Past* until after his mother's death; he was too concerned that what he said might hurt her. But I'd never thought I suffered from that kind of block. After all, I had been writing stories for years. And anyway, I didn't think I had anything to hide.

105

In fact, every time I sat down to write, somewhere in the back of my mind, I was worried about what my family, friends, neighbors, and people I barely knew would think of my morals, my attitudes, my mental health. I had not been writing the heart and guts into my stories; I'd been avoiding certain styles and subjects, as though I was afraid people might confuse me with my characters, or that a story rooted in deep emotion might be too personally revealing. Yes, I wanted people to read and like my work. But I also wanted them to like *me*.

And I finally became convinced that you cannot do good work until you stop worrying about being liked. If you really want to be a writer, you finally have to make up your mind to ignore the possible consequences and pull out all the stops.

Anyway, after reading *My Name Is Asher Lev*, I sat down and wrote what turned out to be my first published story ("Huevos," published in *Redbook*). The plot hinged in part on a sexual double entendre, and I awaited publication nervously, steeling myself in advance for what my parents might say. (Remember, no matter how old you may be, your parents can still make you jump through hoops!) To my relief, they liked the story very much.

My second published story was about a widow from Maine who moves down to New York City. No problem, I thought. But this time around, my father was very unhappy with what he read. He thought the story was weird and that people would think it was the product of a "twisted mind"—which was not the kind of mind he wanted his daughter to have.

My father's reaction had been impossible to predict. So even though it upset me, it also liberated me. Trying to avoid offending people not only hurt my work—it was futile, as well.

I'm not suggesting that you be utterly ruthless and trample on other people's feelings without a second thought. If your work is largely autobiographical, your accounts of real events may hurt real people. And writers do get sued for libel—though I've noticed that while people do recognize events they've been involved in, they are less likely to recognize characters based on themselves, especially when the portraits are not complimentary. So think carefully and make up your own mind about your view of ethics, loyalty, and privacy.

For my part, when I deal with material drawn from life, I try to be semi-ruthless. That is, I get it all down on paper, no holding back. I don't consider anyone's feelings till the piece is done. Then there's time enough to decide whether to send it out and face the possible consequences, or to revise it and change all the identifying details, or to withhold it from publication, at least for the time being.

But no matter how careful and considerate you may be, no matter how entirely you rely on your imagination instead of your experience, get ready to face the fact that you're bound to ruffle some feathers.

When my first Regency romance *Twice Bought Bride* came out (published under a pseudonym by Dell), my elderly aunt accused me of lifting characters and incidents from our family history. I cannot imagine anything more removed from our family experience than Regency romance, and so I denied the charge and asked Aunt Anna which sections and characters she had in mind. She refused to discuss it further and only gave me a very knowing smile.

Be a good parent to your characters.

After talking about my father, it's only fair that I confess my own wrongdoing.

After giving my characters life, I tend to forget that they then have minds of their own. Again and again, like a mother who insists her kid get all A's and become a doctor, I've tried to make my characters conform to my preconceived expectations and ideas, i.e., my plot.

In trying to move a story along, I've tried to force characters to phone people they had no desire to talk to, to avoid old friends without any reason, to go places they didn't want to visit, and even to commit suicide. I've been terrible. I recently tried to break up a marriage, but every time I headed this poor couple toward divorce, the dialogue became artificial, and the prose fell flat. I was manipulating my characters, moving them like puppets, putting them through their paces just to set them up for the next turn of the plot. No wonder it all rang false. The couple, as I had developed them up to that point, didn't want to be divorced. I was forcing this momentous event on them for my own purposes . . . and it didn't work. At last, I acknowledged their right to stay together, and I modified my story line to take their desires into account.

If you want your characters to ring true to the reader, they have to seem real. And you get that effect by treating them as if they are. When you invent a story, you may feel it's one place in your life where you have total control. Forget it! Like a good parent, provide your characters with an environment and stimulation, then try to stay open-minded. Let their words and actions flow from their personalities and don't arbitrarily interfere. Develop them—but with respect.

Get to know your enemies.

For me, the purpose of literature is to expand the limits of each person's particular world and experience, and by the use of imagination, to transcend the mental habits and assumptions of daily life. The writer, like the reader, needs to explore other worlds. But at the same time, we're constantly told to "Write about what you know." And so, many writers rely heavily on autobiographical material. This can be a real problem.

People often ask me to look at fiction they've written, drawn from real-life experience and based on their recent heartaches and problems—the inexplicable cruelty of a lover, the tyrannical attitude of a parent, the irresponsible or self-destructive behavior of a child. With a few shining exceptions, these stories tend to be long on self-pity and self-justification, and short on real understanding. This is no coincidence—if we really had any wisdom about our own situations, we wouldn't get into such terrible conflicts to begin with. When it comes to our own lives, we are often blind to true insight.

As time goes by, it becomes easier to look back on, say, the folly of youth. But if you are trying to write about pain you've recently suffered—because you think it's a dramatic story, or because it seems therapeutic to do so—my advice is not to write from your own point of view. You've probably spent enough time as it is, trapped within your own feelings. Instead, stretch your imagination, and try to get inside the head of the person who hurt you.

An example: Back at the end of the '60s, I wrote a novel (unpublished) about an idealistic young student who falls under the spell of a charismatic writer who visits her college campus. The man turns out to be a fraud, and his followers—including my heroine—suffer tragic consequences.

Well, at the time, I was an idealistic young college student, and I very much understood and knew the desire to believe in something and someone. I identified with my heroine and naturally chose to write the story in her voice and from her point of view.

Editors who read the manuscript didn't see what was so engaging about the villain and why my heroine was so impressed. So I rewrote and expanded, amplifying her obsession and explaining *her* and what she wanted to see in this man. Each revision was progressively worse. The heroine became progressively more desperate and pathetic. The bad guy became progressively more of a symbol and less of a person. Like the heroine and like me, the book was very intense and earnest. It was also very bad.

Several years ago, I came upon the manuscript in the back of my file cabinet. I cringed a bit when I reread it, but I still liked certain passages in the scene in which my student and false hero first meet. Maybe, I thought, a short story could be salvaged from the novel's wreck.

I had always realized that the young woman never understood the motivations of the man she chose to admire. But as I reread the pages again, I saw for the first time that he was a mystery to me, too. I didn't know what would make someone act the way he did. Totally identified as I'd been with the character who was most like myself, I hadn't been aware that I was every bit as blind as she.

It suddenly occurred to me to let this nasty but charming villain tell the story in his own voice. To do that, I would humbly have to give up my own values, transcend my own ignorance, and enter foreign terrain: the enemy's seemingly inexplicable mind.

When the resulting story, "Peonies," was published, I was satisfied that my charismatic bad guy had come to life. He was not a sympathetic character, but he had at last emerged as a complicated human being and not just a symbol of evil.

As writers, we aim to explore and illuminate areas of life, experience, and the human heart, so even as we work at developing our craft, we can fall short if we fail to seek new levels of insight or if we neglect our own personal growth.

When we summon up the strength to stand by our art and accept the consequences, when we learn to relinquish total, arbitrary control, when we develop empathy and learn to put ourselves in the shoes of characters who perplex us or threaten us, we may conceivably become better people. We will certainly become better writers.

22

HOW WELL DO YOU KNOW YOUR CHARACTERS?

By Richard Martin Stern

A GREAT DEAL has been written about knowing what you are writing about—subject, locale, etc. But how well do you know your characters? Because they, not the setting and not the subject, are the story.

Characters are, or ought to be, people whom the all-important reader will get to know (and *know* is the operative word) in order to understand something about them and care about them in some way. You may want readers to like your characters—admire them, hate them, find them amusing or pitiful, honest or deceitful, heroic or craven, witty or dull (your choice, the list is almost endless)—but if you don't know them yourself, nobody else can be expected to find them anything more than unknown names on place cards at an empty table.

And by *knowing,* I do not mean simply being acquainted with in the sense that you can describe someone as having red hair or a facial tic and let it go at that. The someone—your character—must *do* something, which means acting *in,* or more likely reacting *to,* a given situation. Otherwise, even though you may have described him or her in detail, he or she remains merely a flat picture in black-and-white without shading, not even a statue, which is three-dimensional but is rarely something you can empathize with.

I am not implying that your character must come on like Gang Busters. He may do little and say less, he may say a great deal without lifting a finger, he may romp around like a madman without saying a word, or anything in between these extremes, but whatever he says or does must fit into the scene and give the reader a chance to understand something about your character as a person. In my view, it must also advance or even highlight the story.

All of that, I agree, sounds like a rather large order, and it is, but perhaps not as large as you may think for many, if not most, of the characters in your story. A few words or a single scene, carefully chosen, may suffice to set these "bit players" in the reader's mind *and* add to the story. Let me illustrate.

My most recent novel, *Wildfire,* concerns a massive forest fire in New Mexico mountains and the human as well as the technical problems involved in subduing it. At one point, with the fire totally out of control, there are reports of blasting on the forest's perimeter, prompting suspicions of arson. An Assistant Fire Boss is sent to investigate. He sees the crew chief who had reported the blasting:

> The crew chief on the perimeter was grimy and short-tempered. By the light of flames that leaped and cavorted through a patch of scrub oak and a sprinkling of juniper clinging to broken ground, Ben could make out streaks on the crew chief's face where sweat rivulets had dissolved channels through the accumulated dirt. His eyes seemed overlarge, as if carefully outlined in oriental kohl make-up. "Stupid goddam fool," the crew chief said. "I told the mother—"
> "Let me have it from the top," Ben said.
> "Goddam Highway Department idiot. Orders, he says. They're widening the highway, so come quitting time they set off charges and then clear away the broken rock the next day. You know what the son of a bitch told me? He said, 'So okay, you got a goddam fire. That's your worry. I got a job to do, and you can take your goddam fire and shove it. I'm through for the day and I'm going home.' They could just as easy as not set off another goddam fire, couldn't they?"

The crew chief is not named. Nor, beyond mention of his sweaty face, is he described. There is no need. He appears only in these few paragraphs, and his lines are short, but he is important in that he seems to illustrate the eternal conflict between unthinking people who go their own way doing their own little jobs regardless and those striving to accomplish a common good; in this manner he makes himself identifiable *and* adds to the story's drama.

For the major characters in your story—any story from a short-short to a 1000-page novel—the problems are, admittedly, larger, which means, of course, that you must know your leading characters more thoroughly and in greater depth.

These major characters should not be presented whole and entire on first meeting, because if they are, and continue to behave in exactly the same way throughout the story, they become stereotypes.

For example, when I watch Clint Eastwood ride into town and do away with the first batch of scoundrels, I have the feeling that I already know all that I am going to know about the character Eastwood is playing. The story line may be intricate and fascinating, there may be

111

moments of pathos or tragedy, the scenery will be breathtaking, and the action will roar on without let-up, but the hero who in the end rides off into the sunset leaves behind no more knowledge of himself than he revealed in the opening scene.

By contrast, consider Rhett Butler in *Gone With the Wind,* who, bit by bit, in scene after scene, emerges from the almost shallow riverboat gambler character he first appears to be into a real, sentient, loving and sentimental, although always dashing, person of depth, who lusts and suffers and bleeds—a whole man of stature.

Or take Scarlett herself, with her 17-inch waist and her adolescent thinking, who through trial and tragedy grows into full maturity, strong, even over-strong, but, like Rhett, a whole and complicated person with whom readers can identify and about whom they can care deeply.

Rhett Butler and Scarlett O'Hara are the kinds of characters you can, and will, remember precisely because they have grown and because they are not all of a piece, flawless, rounded, and whole as a glass paperweight. Each has weaknesses, flaws, "warts," if you will, and these imperfections, rather than detracting from character strength, instead enhance it by contrast.

How is all this accomplished? First and foremost, I will say again and again, by your *knowing* your characters, their strengths and their weaknesses, their likes and dislikes, the way they think and the way they tend to react in given situations, what they want from life and what they may be prepared to give or to sacrifice in order to get it, something—but probably not too much—of their background and perhaps something of how they managed to be where they are.

Secondly, the facets of your characters that you want to be seen and understood by the reader must have opportunity to emerge. And that means that you must provide the situations in which your characters can perform as you want them to. Again, not always easy, but always necessary. Stories are crafted, one step at a time. This is what makes the entire business both frustrating and enormously satisfying.

Some of what I have said, I grant, you may learn as you go along and get to know your character better, but from the character's first appearance in your story, you must know a great deal more about him than you allow your reader to see, on occasion so much more, in fact, that not all of your knowledge can possibly be fitted into the tale. Your problem then becomes choosing only those facets that fit the story. Lengthy case histories rarely have a place in a work of fiction.

Characters may change, of course, and frequently appear to do so during the course of a story. We are all affected by events that concern us, and your characters should be affected, too. But I would suggest that you beware of the sudden, whole, and complete transformation of a character regardless of the circumstances. Priests are not likely to abandon all at once a lifetime of peace and turn to dastardly crime.

Instead, and much better, what often *appears* to be character change is rather the emergence of, or new emphasis on, a facet of your character that has been there all along but is thoroughly understood only by you; you have craftily withheld this insight until the dramatic moment, so it can emerge with full force. It is this kind of sleight-of-hand, not deliberate falsification, that may prompt the reader to think, or even say aloud one of the warmest accolades a writer can hope for: "Of course! It couldn't have been any other way!"

I have said that characters are, or ought to be, real and understandable people. And not infrequently they have minds of their own, as you will discover as your tale unfolds. The clown frequently wants to play Hamlet; the hero may be too lazy or too interested in other matters to get on with being heroic; the female lead may be just too damned girlishly pure, or she may turn out to have distressingly firm tendencies in the other direction. You must know how to deal with all of them.

After all, they are—or ought to be—*your* characters, *your* creations, with perhaps a facet or two drawn from real life, but with most of their tendencies and characteristics assembled into a whole, and even invented in the workshop of *your* mind; and what you have brought into being, you'd better be able to control.

You'll play director, drill sergeant, father or mother confessor, teacher, judge, authoritarian and friend, and many more roles as well as that of writer before you are through. And you will emerge, or ought to, with a thorough, in-depth knowledge of each of these creatures of yours, and, I venture to say, with some kind of affection for them all. I would be willing to wager that Dickens had a sneaking liking even for Uriah Heep.

Most important, after all this soul-searching and turmoil on your part, your characters will finally emerge for the reader as what they must be: real people the reader can recognize and care about. *Then* you have succeeded.

23

LOVE FROM THE NECK UP

By Eva Ibbotson

I BEGAN my literary life in the fifties, as a writer of short stories for women's magazines.

To write those kinds of stories then was to accept the conventions that prevailed. If the hero and heroine kissed, they did so chastely, without physiological descriptions; they were presumed, at the end, to have come together in order to marry and, having done so, to live happily ever after. Love-from-the-neck-up-with-the-mouth-closed was the phrase I coined for their activities, mocking myself and making clear to my intellectual friends that I was well aware of the absurdity of what I was doing.

But secretly I very much enjoyed my work. I have always liked the discipline of working within limits and found total freedom hard to bear. (Consider the boredom one so often feels during "dream sequences" in musicals or films, where the rules of storytelling are suspended, and everything just goes on and on and on.)

And even more than limits, I liked love. I really loved love, from the word go. Romantic love with all its absurdities, its ludicrous determination of one man and one woman to commit themselves, each to the other, till the end of time. The forms this commitment has taken throughout history have been, for me, a never-ending source of fascination. Christian marriage, with its grandiloquent assumption that the partners can be all in all to each other till parted by death. . . . The orthodox Jewish tradition, in which a woman, shorn of virtually all legal rights, becomes—by the consent of those who love her—the kingpin, the lodestar (and frequently also the bane!) of her family. . . . The subtle, sensual delight that girls of the Orient took in serving their men. . . .

Of course, the feminists are right to be appalled by much of this, but I doubt if one can choose one's obsessions, and I—the child of parents

114

who separated when I was three years old—was stuck with an abiding interest in this kind of love. Altogether, I think I'm with the Jesuits when they say that a child is there, *entire,* by the time it's seven years old. I'll bet that Tolstoy, trotting beside his nursemaid through the Russian forests, was already shaking his fist at God. I wouldn't be surprised if Charles Dickens was still in ringlets and knickerbockers when he began to grind his (milk) teeth at the fate of the poor. And I can see the elders of Venice hurrying by with averted faces to avoid the questions of that brat, Marco Polo, about what happened when one left the city and went East.

The fifties turned into the sixties. I wrote my stories, and the mouths of my heroines stayed closed. My own marriage was a happy one, my four children were a delight. There was nothing in England at that time to make romantic love seem obsolete. The hippies, the flower children, might not be much concerned with marriage, and when they loved, it was clear that they proceeded from the neck down and with the mouth open—but I felt in no way alienated from their world.

My stories sold. I wrote my way gradually "upwards" into anthologies and "proper" books; I published two novels for children. Then, as my own children grew up, I decided to write a full-length romantic novel. But not *only* romantic: the book was to be funny, well-researched and intelligently written, and if a man picked it up by mistake, I intended that he should go on reading.

A Countess Below Stairs took me two years to write. It's about a young Russian countess, Anna Grazinsky, who comes to work as a housemaid in an English country house after the Revolution. In it, I treated my reader to a number of my minor obsessions: for music, for ballet, for the landscape of the English countryside. . . . But, yes, the heroine does marry the earl who owns the house, and, yes, her bodice remains unripped, her mouth closed.

Here is an exchange between Anna and the earl after she hears him cry out in a nightmare (he has been wounded in the war) and has gone to his room to offer comfort:

"Do you realize if this were two hundred years ago I could keep you here? Exercise my *droit de seigneur.* What would you do then?"

"I should scream," said Anna, disengaging her wrist. She got up and went lightly to the door; then she turned and said, grinning, "I 'ope!"—and was gone.

This novel was published on the understanding that I write two more. Tessa, the heroine of *Magic Flutes* (set in Vienna in the twenties), has the same half-humorous awareness of her potential for passion, but she too remains chaste until the end. In my latest novel, *A Company of Swans*, Harriet, traveling to the Amazon with a ballet company at the time of the rubber boom, does go to bed with the hero, but if her mouth is open, it is rather with wonder and awe, and marriage follows. And, since to describe the act of love is to risk describing some complicated aerobic workout, I show Harriet's feelings afterwards as she tries to memorize the room in which the miracle of her "ruin" occurred:

> . . . Because she had to remember this room. It was Rom's own room to which he had carried her from the Blue Suite, and she had to remember every single thing so that years later she could come back here in her mind. Even on her deathbed, she must be able to come back here and walk across the deep white carpet . . . particularly on her deathbed . . .

The years rolled by. My daughter married; I was a grandmother. And with my contract for three books fulfilled, I woke up in the mid-eighties and looked about me at the world of entertainment.

I watched plays and films in which love prided itself on bringing about intricate cruelties and pointless betrayals, ensuring for everyone a miserable end. I watched thrillers in which the "goodies" perished horribly and the "baddies," as often as not, went merrily on. I read children's books in which teen-age sex and the shoddiness of adults were the main theme. (Great authors must of course deal with serious themes—with incest and murder as much as with glory and endeavor— but I'm talking about *entertainment*.)

I tried to fit in . . . started a novel about child abuse, another about abortion . . . and abandoned them both. "I'm finished," I said to my husband and to anyone else who'd listen. "I'm out of touch."

Out of touch—that dread phrase! How often I've heard it . . . on the lips of young people who thought they were not mature enough to matter as writers, or old ones who thought life had passed them by . . . from women who lived in the provinces and believed that "real" life happened elsewhere, or men whose religious faith isolated them in a world of rationality. . . . Now it was my turn.

I became quite seriously depressed, paid attention to my physical ailments, and talked of giving up writing. I would keep chickens, run a bookshop, go to India and find a guru—anything except practice the craft I'd laboriously taught myself for thirty years.

What saved me was a girl called Shirlene.

On the train to York, on a visit to my mother, I sat opposite a homely woman of about my own age. Inevitably, we began to talk about our children. The woman had an only daughter, Shirlene, who was clearly the apple of her eye. Though a popular and friendly girl, "Our Shirlene" would never go out when they were showing old films on television. Shirlene loved these vintage movies; she liked the way there was a proper story and an end you could understand.

What sort of films, I asked, and Shirlene's mother said, "Oh, you know, Shirley Temple and Deanna Durbin and Fred Astaire. And those ones where James Stewart's putting things right. She likes things to be *nice*," said Shirlene's mother.

The train stopped at York and Shirlene was waiting on the platform. My image of her had been quite clear: one of those simple, homespun girls you still find in the north of England, wearing a tweed skirt and a cardigan. So the safety pin through her nose surprised me. Her hair surprised me too: puce on top and emerald green at the sides. Shirlene's ripped tousers were viciously studded, chains hung from her leather jacket.

And this was the girl who stayed home to watch Doris Day protect her maidenhood or watch Fred and Ginger waltz together in a cloud of tulle!

The scales dropped from my eyes. I remembered a number of things I'd heard and put out of my mind: A publisher telling me that those inordinately depressing and fashionable novels that win literary prizes are bought in quantity as Christmas presents but seldom actually read. . . . The experience of a friend who'd gone to see a much-hyped film about gang rape and found himself alone with an old bag lady who'd come to rest her feet. . . .

I remembered, too, a Jewish story of which I've always been very fond. An old rabbi is comforting a lost and bewildered member of his flock. "Remember, Moyshe," says the rabbi, "when you get up to heaven, God won't ask you if you've been Abraham or Moses; he'll ask you if you've been Moyshe Finkelstein. If you've been *you*."

I decided to be me: To have faith in the thousands of people all over

117

the world who still want to read about men and women pursuing, with humor and tenderness, a high ideal of love. To be grateful for the lifting of taboos, the broadening out of topics, to use the new techniques that films and television have brought to us as writers, but to be true to my own vision of what it is that entertains.

So I started a new book. This time my heroine's mouth will almost certainly be open, because that's the way mouths are these days, and it will be nice for her. But for all her faults and frailties, she'll be concerned with fidelity and goodness—and in the end she'll have her reward.

And those of you who have also felt discouraged—who are "out of touch"—too young, too old, too far away—won't you please join me?

After all, we owe it to Shirlene!

24

WHAT MAKES A FICTION WRITER?

BY B. J. CHUTE

THE other day, an interviewer asked me, "What makes a fiction writer?" and I could only answer, "I have no idea." It is a time-honored and shopworn question, and there are as many answers to it as there are writers, because all writers are different.

The interviewer, being neither time-honored nor shopworn but, on the contrary, young and lively, changed her question to "What makes *you* a fiction writer?" I felt I could answer that question reasonably well, and I did so by offering such (time-honored and shopworn) reasons as a natural bent for storytelling, a life-long habit of reading, a love of words, and all the etcetera of halfway answers which I hope were useful to her but which really did not satisfy me.

Thinking now about her question, I have been turning it over and over in my mind until I arrived, like Alice, at my looking-glass destination by walking away from it. I do not believe I know what makes me a fiction writer, but I do believe that there are four qualities without which one cannot write fiction at all.

The first, of course, is *imagination*. Imagination is as necessary to a novelist or short-story writer as the spinning of webs is to a spider and just as mysterious. It defies analysis (either one is a spider, or one isn't), and it has been quite properly called "the creative impulse." It has also been called the Muse, and, when the Muse vanishes, that yawning void she leaves behind her is known as "writer's block."

Imagination cannot be created, but it can be fostered, and this fostering is part of the writer's duty. It is not enough to congratulate oneself on having been gifted (lovely word!) with imagination, though it is certainly a major cause for rejoicing. The imagination, like the intellect, has to be used, and a creative writer ought to exercise it all the time. There is no idea, however insignificant or vague it may be, that the imagination cannot touch to new beginnings, turning it around and around in different lights, playing with it, *listening* to it. One of the most marvelous things about spiders (and writers) is the way they will launch themselves into space on a filament so infinitely slender as to be nearly invisible, and, lo, there is suddenly a bridge flung over the chasm, across which any fly (or any reader) can walk with perfect confidence.

The second quality I believe to be essential for writing fiction is *empathy,* which the dictionary properly defines as "mental entering into the feeling or spirit of a person or thing." As with imagination, one is to a degree born with empathy; but, like imagination, it can be fostered. Writers of fiction write from inside themselves, but they also write from inside other people, and, again, this is a kind of gift. It is what produces strong and believable characterization. *Madame Bovary* was written from the inside out. Flaubert seems to know not only the passion, the boredom, the despair and the terrible loneliness of that pitiful woman, but he also seems to know the most trivial light or shadow that falls across her mind. Imagination could create her, and her world, and the people around her, but it is Flaubert's empathy that makes his unhappy Emma not just credible but totally real. This is Melville's "subterranean miner that works in us all," and, although we cannot expect to be Melvilles or Flauberts, we can mine what we have. And if we do that, with honesty and intensity, who knows what lode of treasure we may strike?

The third quality is *style.* In its simplest form, style in writing can be defined as the way in which a thing is said. It is a much abused word, and it sometimes seems to me that it is woefully misunderstood by writers and readers alike. Style does not exist apart from the story, and, if five people tell an identical story, each one will tell it in a different style. The best style will produce the best story, and the listeners will turn to it even if they do not know why they turn. Style is a great preservative of writing, and no writer ought ever to think that a really good style is beyond his reach. But many writers do think so, and too many settle for second best when, in fact, they ought to be working all the time against any such preposterous limitation of their own capacities.

Once I ran across a description of style as applied to architecture, which is just as true of writing—"What is style? Clear thinking, really; the ability to use your head before you do anything with your hands." Sloppy thinking will produce sloppy style, and I am certain there is not a writer among us who has not stared hopelessly at the written page which reflects the muddy results. What to do? Go back, of course. Find out what you are trying to say, and, having found it, select the words that will make the reader see what you are seeing. Selection is vital to style. Because English is an incredibly rich language, there are many bad ways of saying something, and many good ways, but there is usually only one right way. This right way will be the writer's *own* way—in short, his style, or what Proust called "the underlying tune" which distinguishes one writer from another. This should represent the very best the writer has to offer. "Second best" will not do.

Take, as an example, a description from Nathaniel Hawthorne. He is introducing a minister, and all he wishes to say about him is that he is a serious person, wears a beard, and is dressed in the kind of dark clothes and tall hat that would have been affected by a clergyman of his time. There are perhaps a hundred ways of putting all these details together so that the reader can visualize the character sharply, and most such descriptions would probably take a paragraph, certainly several sentences. Hawthorne does it in seven words; his minister is "grave, bearded, sable-cloaked and steeple-crowned."

This is perfectly beautiful writing, and it is as exact as it is beautiful. The picture is instantaneous and vivid, and the tone is faultless. I do not know whether Hawthorne got those seven words right the first time, or whether he labored over them in rewrite after rewrite. Even successive drafts of his manuscript would tell us nothing, because the majority of a writer's work goes on in his mind. What matters is that every word in Hawthorne's description is the right one: *grave,* with its sonorous double meaning; *bearded,* just the simple piece of information to balance the poetic images that follow; *sable-cloaked,* concealing, mysterious, and darker than darkness itself; and, finally, the triumph of *steeple-crowned,* which makes us see not only the minister in his tall hat, but Church, Authority and Heaven as well.

It is true that the average writer is not a Nathaniel Hawthorne, but it is also true that none of these seven words is in the least obscure or recondite or self-conscious; each one would be available to any writer who was craftsman enough to persist in finding it. If a writer is willing to work all the time and in everything he writes to achieve the best style of which he is capable, the words will be there for him as they were for Hawthorne.

And this brings us, inevitably, to the fourth quality, which is *patience*.

Patience in a writer is many things, but most of all, I think, it is characterized by concern for the words on the page. The aim of this concern is "to see the thing and throw the loop of creation around it," as Joyce Cary said. (And notice how riveting the phrasing of that statement is; there's style for you!) What Cary calls "the thing" is the idea, the initial impulse, the product of imagination and empathy. The "loop of creation" is the finding of the right words that will make it possible for the reader to share the writer's special vision, and such words can be very evasive, very slow to come.

At rare and wonderful intervals, the stars in their courses do seem to join together, and the writer finds himself writing so effortlessly and with such precision that it almost seems as if he were taking dictation. These are the best of times, but they are certainly not ordinary. In ordinary times, the words on the page are merely adequate: they move the story along; the second draft will be easier; experience lends hopefulness. The worst of times are when the words will not come at all, and the writer feels as if he were floundering in a swamp or gasping for air in a desert. This can be really frightening, and it is here—in swamp or desert—that the quality of patience will spell the difference between disaster and survival.

In the dictionary, the second definition for the word *patience* is "calmness in waiting." I like this definition very much indeed, because there is a steadiness about it and a good deal of faith, and any writer needs both.

When the final draft of a manuscript is on paper, the words are all that really matter. Money, status, and fame are by-products; nice to have, but nothing permanent. If that statement seems idealistic, of course it is. It is meant to be. To call upon the dictionary once more, idealism is "the cherishing or pursuing of ideals, as for attainment." For the writer of fiction, the pursuit is through imagination and empathy, the cherishing is through style, and the attainment is through patience.

122

Excellence is simply idealism in action, and so high an aim is bound to fall short of the mark many times. I call to your attention the words of John Adams, written in February of 1776—"We cannot ensure success, but we can deserve it."

25

FIRST PERSON SINGULAR

By Donald Hamilton

LET US now consider the case of Ethelbert Hackworthy, one of the country's foremost producers of unpublished novels. With unquenchable optimism, Ethelbert is commencing a new book. In the opening scene, carefully planned to seize the reader's attention in a grip of iron, he brings his proud but impecunious young hero, John Pennywhistle, into the music room of rich old Senator Silverbuck's mansion, where pretty Mary Silverbuck is seated at the piano.

Ethelbert is going strong now; he's right in the groove. He has John look at Mary and think she's quite a dish. He describes Mary, tenderly, down to the last ruffle on her fashionable gown and the last freckle on her piquantly upturned nose. So far, so good. But now Bert realizes that something is missing. Great Heavens, he hasn't described John yet! Well, that's easy to fix; and he has Mary look up from her music. She sees John in the doorway, and thinks him a fine tall figure of a man, which leads naturally to a detailed description of John. . . .

Do you like this? Do you feel free to jump from character to character and from viewpoint to viewpoint whenever the fancy takes you? Well, I suppose that's your privilege. Certainly you have lots of company. Many very good, or at least very successful, writers operate in just this way; and after all, it's the way most movie and television scripts are constructed, isn't it, with the cameras cutting freely from one character to another? So what, if anything, is wrong with it?

As far as I'm concerned, everything is wrong with it. The typewriter—or word processor, if you're modernized to that extent—is not a camera, capable of recording only the surface of things, and people. Why throw away your ability to penetrate character and personality by using it as a mere photographic instrument? As a matter of fact, I hate this floating-viewpoint technique; in treating the reader to brief glimpses of all the people in a novel, it really presents a good look at none of them.

As a writer, I disapprove of it, which is O.K., since nobody's forcing me to use it. But more important, as an omnivorous reader, I detest it, because it cheats me out of a great deal of literary entertainment. Why? Just as I'm getting interested in a certain character, male or female, the fickle author switches his attention—and tries to switch mine—to a different character, female or male. As far as I'm concerned, this kind of jumpy writing (we might call it kangaroo writing, considering the way the viewpoint leaps around) is strictly expendable.

The corny scene with which I opened this article is one I actually wrote years ago to illustrate a literary piece I never managed to sell. At that time, I was naive enough to think that everybody shared my prejudice against writers who flitted from viewpoint to viewpoint. I took for granted that every sensible reader much preferred writers who stuck to one character through thick and thin. But the years have brought resignation, if not humility. I'm now hardened to the fact that a lot of readers and editors actually *like* the wandering viewpoint, and that a lot of fairly skillful writers employ it profitably. I will even admit that a truly good writer can get away with it, even with a cantankerous reader like me. But then, a truly good writer can get away with anything.

Even if you think it's perfectly fine to switch protagonists as the fancy moves you, you should be aware of the fact that there is another school of writing that's been around for quite a while. I seem to recall that Fielding stuck pretty tightly to Tom Jones; and Daniel Defoe concentrated on Mr. Crusoe, and didn't bother us much with Mr. Friday's intimate hopes and aspirations. So let's consider the alternative to the omniscient spy-in-the-sky kind of viewpoint treatment that's so popular today.

Some years ago I was very flattered when, reviewing several mysteries for a rather highbrow publication, Jacques Barzun referred to one of my early suspense novels as a first-person story. It wasn't, but the fact that he'd come away from the book thinking that it was showed that I'd achieved my goal. I'd put the reader into the mind of my character—one character—so firmly that the reviewer had laid the book down at the end with the impression that it had been narrated by that character, not by me. Which was exactly the effect I'd been striving for. Now I understand that many writers consider other techniques of viewpoint perfectly proper. I understand; but I don't necessarily agree.

But enough of my literary preferences. Let's just consider the problems of a single-viewpoint novel, as opposed to one written from multiple viewpoints. The basic problem is discipline. As you write about your single character, treating the rest of the cast as peripheral to him, or her, you'll be subjected to continual temptations. The plotting can be tough, if everything has to be filtered through the consciousness of one individual.

You'll hear seductive little voices whispering that the creative life would be much less laborious if, instead of sticking grimly to the thoughts and experiences of "he," for example, you just slipped next door for a minute and let the reader know what "she" or "they" were thinking and doing. Resist! Stay with it, work it out from the hero's viewpoint, if that's what you started with, and figure out how to tell him, and the reader, what the heroine or the villains were up to, while he was struggling desperately to free himself from the cruel bonds securing him to the rusty ringbolts in the wall of the secret cavern soon to be flooded by the rising tide. You know nothing that the hero doesn't know, you see nothing he doesn't see, you feel nothing that he doesn't feel.

The reward for such authorial self-discipline can be great: a kind of hypnotic intensity that leads the reader to identify himself completely with your character; an identification that can never be achieved if you spend two pages on this gent in Moscow followed by a couple of paragraphs about this lady in Washington followed by a whole chapter about this married couple—viewpoint shifting constantly between him and her, of course—in London.

There is a simple substitute for this difficult discipline: Just write your novel in the first person, and you won't be tempted to let the viewpoint wander. If your hero or heroine is "I" instead of "he" or "she," you'll never find yourself slipping into any other viewpoint accidentally, just because it makes the plot work out more easily. You're locked into one character for good or ill.

Many years ago when I asked an editor about the salability problem, I got the following answer: "I'd say there is no prejudice against first-person stories, but in general, first-person viewpoint is difficult to use successfully." The notion that first-person writing is tough in some mysterious way is held by many writers and editors, and that puzzles me tremendously. To me, it seems a very simple technique. It's self-policing. With only one viewpoint available to you, how can you goof? Of course, I've used it for well over twenty novels, so I should have mastered it by now; but I can't recall having any trouble with it even at the first.

There are just two hurdles to be surmounted when using first-person narrative. The first is the plotting, which, as I've already said, can be demanding whenever you stick to a single protagonist—whether you write in the first person or the third. Since your lone hero or heroine can't be everywhere, many things have to happen off stage, so to speak, and you have to avoid getting your book cluttered up with too many messages or messengers of doom, as your protagonist learns of dramatic disasters occurring elsewhere. But I've never found this a great handicap, and I don't see why you should.

More difficult to overcome for some writers is a second obstacle: If the story is to be narrated by the chief character in the novel, he or she has to be a fairly compelling character. An interesting author can write an interesting third-person novel about a dull character, enlivening the text with his own comments and observations; but a boring character is almost bound to tell a boring first-person story about himself. So consider your protagonist very carefully before you commit yourself to writing a whole book as told by or through him or her: Is he, or she, good enough, strong enough, intriguing enough, exciting enough, to carry it off?

Please understand, I'm quite aware that the multiple-viewpoint technique has a place in the literary scheme of things: Tolstoy would have played hell trying to write *War and Peace* through the eyes of a single character. For a truly big book, a panorama novel, it's obviously the way to go. But my feeling is that a lot of lazy writers use it, not because their books are so tremendous in scope, but simply because they can't be bothered to work out how to tell the story from a single point of view. For these writers, and for the beginner learning how to master the tools of the trade, planning and writing a whole novel about *one* character should be a valuable exercise, teaching the student many new things about the profession of writing.

I have a hunch that a novel so written might well turn out to be the best thing that author ever wrote. Of course I'm prejudiced.

26

THE WILLING SUSPENSION OF DISBELIEF

By Elizabeth Peters

ALTHOUGH Coleridge coined the useful phrase, "the willing suspension of disbelief," it has been the goal of storytellers since the pre-literate dawn of time and of writers since fiction began. Writers of suspense fiction particularly depend upon this gesture of good will on the part of the reader, but successful achievement of that goal depends upon the writer as well as the reader. Presumably, the reader of thrillers or novels of suspense starts each book in the proper mood of suspended disbelief, but he cannot sustain this mood if the author taxes his intelligence too much. How, then, does the writer of suspense fiction create an aura of plausibility which will allow readers to accept his creation, "for the moment," as Coleridge adds?

The so-called Gothic novel is a sub-category of the novel of suspense. In most cases, the term "Gothic" is a misnomer, for the romantic, "damsel-in-distress" thrillers which publishers label "modern Gothics" are not Gothics at all. Their ancestors are not Mrs. Ann Radcliffe's *The Mysteries of Udolpho* or Horace Walpole's *The Castle of Otranto,* but Wilkie Collins' *The Moonstone* and Charlotte Brontë's *Jane Eyre.* The true Gothic novel requires an atmosphere of brooding supernatural horror and a setting that includes ruined castles and desolate moors. I don't consider my books to be true Gothics, but it would be pedantic of me to object to the term, which is certainly more succinct than more accurate designations. I may then be forgiven if I refer henceforth to this form of fiction as "Gothic."

The most important thing for a writer of Gothics to recognize is that the genre is inherently incredible, almost as unlikely as a fantasy novel. Personally, I find it as easy to believe in the green Martians of Barsoom as I do in the adventures of Gothic heroines. Some writers of Gothics seem to feel that because their plots are fantastic, they need not be logical. The converse is true. The more fantastic the plot, the more important are those factors that invite belief, or, at least, the suspension of disbelief.

What are these factors? Some may be seen in the three elements of plot, character and setting.

The plot of a Gothic novel must be tight, consistent, and logical —within the given framework. Like the fantasy novel, which starts with a single fantastic premise, the Gothic begins with what I like to call an "initiating coincidence." The heroine happens to overhear a conversation between two people who are planning a murder; or she happens to accept a job as governess in an isolated household whose inhabitants all suffer from severe neuroses. None of these situations is very likely, but we can admit one such fortuitous occurrence in order to get our plot moving. From that point on, however—no coincidences, no lucky accidents. If the hero is walking down Main Street at the moment when the heroine, cornered by the villain, screams for help, the hero must have a reason for being on Main Street at that vital moment. It will not suffice to explain that he keeps in shape by jogging down Main Street every fine afternoon. If the heroine is to be rescued—and Gothic heroines always are—the rescuer must be brought to the spot by hard work and/or logical deductions.

Plausibility of character is as important as consistency of plot. The two are related, of course. A stupid heroine's foolish behavior can lead to plot complications. Indeed, the plots of the poorer Gothics seem to depend wholly on the heroine's incredible naïveté, as she falls into one pitfall after another. But it is difficult for the reader to identify, or even sympathize, with heroines of such consummate imbecility. Admittedly, Gothic heroines have a propensity for getting into trouble. It is one of the important elements of the Gothic plot, but it can also be one of the great weaknesses of the genre. Critics justifiably jeer at the dim-witted girls who take nocturnal strolls around grim old mansions. If you must get your heroine out of her nice, safe, locked room in the middle of the night, after two murders have already been committed, do give her a good reason for leaving that security. (I cannot think of anything that

129

would induce me to leave my room under those circumstances, except perhaps the voices of my children screaming for help.) Your heroine must have an equally pressing motive. Better yet, have her stay in her room and get into trouble in some less conventional manner. And no mysterious notes asking for a midnight rendezvous in the castle crypt, please. Critics sneer at that one, too. A heroine ought to have sufficient intelligence to check with the hero to make sure he actually sent the note before she ventures into a crypt.

The characters of Gothic novels are not profound or complex; in two-hundred-odd pages we do not have space for such luxuries, since we must spend a good deal of verbiage on plot and atmosphere. But if our characters are cardboard, they need not be absurd. They must not exhibit flagrant personality aberrations, or behave so idiotically that the reader begins to hope they will be murdered in the crypt, as they deserve to be.

Of course, the more fully developed and realistic your characters, the more plausible their actions will seem. One of the classics in the field, Daphne du Maurier's *Rebecca*, has a heroine who has always exasperated me by her timidity and docility; but she is believable, because she behaves in a way that is consistent with her background and her personality.

Atmosphere and setting are particularly important to thrillers of this type, and the same rule applies: the more unusual or exotic the setting, the harder you must work to give it an appearance of authenticity. In these days of jets and travel books, Samarkand is no more exotic than Paris or Rome. But you must make sure that your descriptions of these cities are accurate, and that you include enough details to convince the reader of the reality of the setting in which your heroine's wild adventures are to take place. I do not subscribe to the theory that a writer can write only about things he or she has personally experienced. I have personally visited all the cities and countries I have used in my books; but I could not have written about them without the aid of maps, photographs, and detailed notes taken on the spot. Perhaps a conscientious writer can do this with a city he or she has never seen—but it will require a great deal of work.

The rule holds even when you are inventing a setting. In one of my books, the action takes place in Rothenburg, a small German town I know fairly well, but for various reasons I decided to add an imaginary castle to that city instead of using an existing structure. I did almost as much research on the castle as I did on the city, reading about medieval castles and Franconian architecture, so that the description of my imaginary castle would agree with details of real structures of that period. If your characters do a lot of running around, draw floor plans. Readers love to spot discrepancies, and will write irritated letters if you have your heroine descend a staircase where no staircase can conceivably exist.

One useful trick to make sure that the reader will accept your devices of plot or of setting is to prepare him for them well in advance. A strategically located doorway, through which the hero gains entrance to the conference room—a secret passage whereby your characters can escape when danger threatens—these, and other devices, will seem more plausible if they are mentioned before you actually need them. Again, the more unusual the prop, the more carefully you must explain its presence. A secret passage in a medieval castle needs only a sentence or two of description, since the reader knows that medieval castles abound in such conveniences. A secret passage in a modern split-level house requires considerable explanation—and perhaps a brief character sketch of the eccentric individual who had it built.

Plot props require the same advance preparation. If the heroine's knowledge of Urdu is going to save her from a fate worse than death, or expose the master criminal, you must tell the reader early in the book that she is an expert in this abstruse language. If you do not, she will resemble Superwoman when she comes up with the information. And for pity's sake, if she or the hero is to be an expert in ichthyology or Egyptology, learn something about those subjects before you talk about them. I was once put off an otherwise readable Gothic because it involved a reincarnated Egyptian princess named Cha-cha-boom, or something equally absurd. No reincarnated Egyptian, fake or genuine, would have such a name, and the repetition of the inane syllables grated on me so strongly that I never finished the book. The author could easily have found an authentic ancient Egyptian name in the encyclopedia. I remember another book I never finished reading because the villain, a German sea captain, kept shouting "Grüss Gott!" in frenzied moments. If you do not know that "Grüss Gott" is a friendly greeting in southern Germany, have your villain stick to English.

You may think that few readers have much knowledge of Egyptology or other abstruse subjects. This would be a dangerous assumption. Archaeology is a popular field, and for some odd reason, which I mean to investigate one day, archaeology buffs seem to be especially addicted to thrillers. But that is not the important thing. The important thing is that plausibility depends upon the accumulation of consistent, accurate details. They really do add verisimilitude to an otherwise bald and unconvincing narrative. The reader may not consciously note all your errors; but a series of careless inconsistencies will tax the reader's willingness to accept your imaginary world, and a single glaring error may be enough to snap that fragile thread on which the suspension of disbelief depends.

Of course, you are bound to slip up occasionally, no matter how conscientiously you research your book. As I work through revision after revision, I come across howlers I can't believe I missed the first and second times. To my chagrin, a few of them escape me even in the third and fourth revisions and get into print, despite the additional efforts of my intelligent editors. In one of my books, written under another name, an integral plot prop was an old family Bible. Long after the book was published, a reader wrote to me inquiring how the Bible happened to survive the conflagration that had destroyed the equally ancient family mansion and most of its contents. "I can imagine several possible solutions," she added charitably, "but I do think you ought to have *told* us."

She was absolutely correct. I should have told her. And I would have done so, if I had noticed the discrepancy. However, errors of this sort are not in the same category as careless mistakes or poorly developed characters. An occasional gap in the plot or an error of fact will not be serious if the rest of the plot is as tight as you can make it, and if the other facts have been checked and rechecked.

I could go on, giving examples of the basic rule, but if you read many Gothics, you will spot plenty of other cases, of success and of failure. Of course there are some writers who seem to be able to break all the rules and get away with it. Don't bother writing to tell me about them. I know about them. I only wish I knew how they do it.

132

27

HANDLING TIME IN FICTION

By Jonathan Penner

"BEGIN at the beginning," the King of Hearts commanded the White Rabbit in *Alice in Wonderland*. "Go on till you come to the end. Then stop."

In fiction, the arrangement of time is rarely so simple. Odd as it seems, not all stories stop at the chronological end. Some have circular patterns, concluding in the middle of the events they narrate. One or two even run backwards, starting with the final event and ending with the first.

But it's the beginnings of stories that present the most nettlesome problems. The very notion of a "beginning" is not philosophically secure. Everything comes *from* something, which in turn comes from something else. The selection of any starting point is a more or less violent imposition of order upon the flux of events.

A more practical problem is that once you've selected what feels like a beginning—someone waking up in the morning, or someone getting sick with the flu, or someone's first day on the job—you may find that it's dull stuff. And the start of a story is where you *must* be interesting. Though wonderful scenes may follow, the reader won't get to them if the opening is a bore.

Fortunately, what occurs first *chronologically* needn't come first *narratively*. You can begin your story partway through its chain of events, choosing material that's vivid, suggestive, amusing, tense. You can introduce your central character, and provide at least a thread-end of plot.

The opening is a huckster, a harlot. Engage the reader, charm him, seduce him, until he surrenders to your cause—until the critic in him concedes that he is going to finish this story. Then you can go back in time for relatively dull but indispensable background information.

In a few stories, of course, the handling of time presents no problem. These stories usually comprise a single scene, with little need for background. They may deal with a span of time no greater than that required to read them: perhaps ten minutes in a character's life.

But usually the author must choose where to launch into the river of events. And though his journey is with the current, at some point he must portage upstream to inspect the watersheds from which his story springs.

How far should you carry your story's first forward rush before providing a flashback? How long should the flashback continue before you return to the main story?

Each story will dictate its own rhythms. But a fair principle, albeit one easier to state than to apply, is to continue forward from your opening point until the reader's curiosity about the past outweighs his curiosity about the future.

You won't, in general, insert a flashback right in the middle of fascinating action. That merely frustrates the reader, who is trying to find out what happens next—not what happened a long time ago.

But at a certain moment he will *want* a flashback. He'll want to know how things got like this, what makes these people the way they are. He may require orientation: time, place, relationships. This is the moment—when the story has completed its first advance—to direct the reader's attention to such anterior matters.

Now: how do you move back and forth between the two time periods—the one that's *narratively* first (which we're calling, for convenience, the "main" time period) and the one that's *chronologically* first (the flashback material)?

The technique chiefly involves the use of appropriate verb tenses—complemented by indicators such as "now" and "back then"—to let readers know where they are in time.

A detailed example follows. At the start of our story, fifteen-year-old Cameron Pearl is going to have his hair cut. But we also want to include a flashback, dealing with Cameron's barbershop experiences when he was a little boy.

We begin in the *simple past* tense. (Yes, some stories are told in the present tense, and require slightly different mechanics.) Verbs in the simple past tense are *italicized*.

(1) One morning soon after his fifteenth birthday, Cameron Pearl *entered* Willy's Barber Shop, sliding around the half-open door as though he *hoped* nobody would notice his arrival. But the place *was* empty except for Willy himself, slowly pushing a broom. He *welcomed* Cameron with a toothy grin. "Into the chair, young fella." In no time at all, the familiar laundry-smelling sheet *was* around Cameron's neck, and he *heard* the rapid snip-snip-snip of the approaching scissors.

Suppose we insert our flashback right here. To let the reader know what's happening, we switch from the simple past tense to the PAST PERFECT tense (the "had" tense). Verbs in the past perfect tense are CAPITALIZED.

(2A) Cameron HAD BEEN coming to Willy for haircuts ever since first grade. In the early years he HAD ENJOYED it.

If that's enough flashback, and we want to return to the main story, we let the reader know it by returning to the simple past tense:

But now, staring at the eternally half-filled bottles aligned on the shelf below Willy's mirror, all he *felt* was boredom and irritation. "Leave it long in back," he *sighed*.

Smooth enough. But suppose we want a longer flashback? Won't page after page of the past perfect tense—"had done," "had said," "had thought," and so on—become a nuisance? It will indeed. A more graceful technique is to ease into the simple past as soon as we've gone far enough with the past perfect to establish that this is indeed a flashback.

Here's an example. In all that follows, verbs in the simple past are *italicized* and verbs in the past perfect are CAPITALIZED. Please reread paragraph (1) above. Then continue on with the following, and watch for the switch.

(2B) Cameron HAD BEEN coming to Willy for haircuts ever since first grade. In the early years he HAD ENJOYED it—paging through magazines while he *waited*, climbing into the throne-like chair, the tickle of the shears, the hot lather, and finally the cool air on his awakened neck when he *left* the shop. Because there *were* busy streets to cross, he always *came* with his father, who in those days *had* a full head of silver-blond hair. Cameron *thought* it so handsome that he *hated* to see the first locks of it fall to the floor.

His father always *entered* the chair first, and Cameron would pretend

(Note this "would" tense, which is often useful in flashbacks. It indicates habitual activity in the past.)

to read *Esquire* or the *Police Gazette* while he *listened* to the conversation of the men. Regulars, most of them: men like Mr. Hastings, from the candy store, and Dr. Albrecht, and Mr. Kutzko, who *owned* the shoe store. When they *talked* politics, Cameron *felt* proud—his father *knew* more than anyone, and they all *listened* with respect. But when the discussion *turned* to sports, Cameron *sat* in dread. His father's unconcerned ignorance about baseball *was* shocking— Cameron himself *knew* more—and he *prayed* silently that his father would say nothing at all.

See? We've finessed our way out of that awkward "had" tense and are now narrating the flashback in the simple past tense. We can stay in the simple past for the rest of the flashback—though if it were extremely long we'd look for ways to remind the reader, every so often, that it *is* a flashback, not the main story. That would prevent a jolt when the flashback ends.

Now, let's prepare to end our flashback, to get on with the story of fifteen-year-old Cameron and toothily grinning Willy. Can we go straight back to the simple past tense with which we began the story?

No—because we've just been giving the flashback, too, in the simple past tense. The reader wouldn't know where one ended and the other began. So we unobtrusively return to the past perfect tense to finish the flashback. Again, watch for the switch.

Fortunately, his father never *did*—he only *nodded* gravely at the recitations of statistics, the predictions and postmortems. And gradually Cameron HAD COME to understand that this *was* all that wisdom *was*—knowing what you *knew* and what you *didn't*. It *was* a discouraging insight, and once he HAD HAD it, he *lost* a degree of respect for his father. And it *was* then that he HAD STARTED enjoying his visits to the barber less.

By returning to the past perfect tense, we've reminded the reader that this is a flashback. Next we'll signal, with a shift from the past perfect tense to the simple past (and with the extremely useful word "now"), our return to the main story.

Now, staring at the eternally half-filled bottles aligned on the shelf below

136

Willy's mirror, all he *felt* was boredom and irritation. "Leave it long in back," he *sighed*.

From this point, the story will continue forward in the simple past tense to its conclusion—or until the next flashback.

I should like to make one more point about flashbacks, a point also illustrated by our tale of Cameron Pearl. Many writers are under the impression that, in order to go back in time, you have to have your central character *remember* past events.

This is emphatically not so. In fact, few devices of fiction are cornier or phonier than forcing bouts of nostalgia upon your central character.

Yes, people do sometimes remember things—but seldom with the coherence and completeness that flashbacks require. Yet many a character in fiction is made to relive the past regardless of psychological plausibility, regardless of what would more likely occupy his mind at the moment. Character is falsified for the sake of the reader's education. "Stanley stared out the window, letting his mind drift back—back—back to the time when . . ."

But if you keep that glassy stare out of Stanley's eyes, how will you enter the flashback?

The answer is that you simply *tell* us what happened in the past. No need for Stanley or anyone else to glaze over and remember. Just tell us. Telling is narration: as used here, the words are synonyms. This is one of the things narration, or narrative, is for.

I think there are two reasons many writers are uncomfortable with narrative—with telling. The first is that they were raised on movies and television, in which almost nothing *can* be told. In a visual medium, everything must be dramatized—shown.

The other reason is that some writing teacher, perhaps in high school, issued a commandment: "*Show,* don't tell." Misapplication of this excellent advice has caused incalculable mischief.

What the aphorism *does* mean is that you shouldn't (for example) tell us "Cameron's father was prudent" and expect us to believe it. Instead, you've got to present Cameron's father in such a way—for instance, by having him stay within his area of expertise when shooting the bull in the barbershop—that the reader himself comes to the conclusion that the man was prudent.

"Show, don't tell," does *not* mean that you can't narrate your story! Notice that we didn't make Cameron sit there in the barber chair remembering his childhood. Fidelity to point of view requires that the flashback be limited to what Cameron *could* remember—it can't deal with material unknown to him—but not that he actually do the remembering.

We simply *told* the reader, "Cameron had been coming to Willy for haircuts ever since first grade." And our flashback continued from there.

138

28

THE LONG AND SHORT OF IT

By John Lutz

Short story or novel? Which should I write and why? What are the differences? Not just in word length—what are the *real* differences? These are questions that cross the fertile minds of a great many writers, novices and veterans, but especially those at the beginning of their careers.

First of all, let's see the short story as it really is. Since the demise of a number of high-paying markets for this form of fiction, the short story seems to have suffered an accompanying diminution in status in the minds of many who read, and write, popular fiction. There's a common misconception that a writer begins with short stories and, after gaining enough proficiency, moves on to the more demanding task of writing novels. Ain't so. Not any more than it's true that an Olympic gold medalist in the hundred-yard dash is merely in the process of working his or her way up to running a mile, and then the 26-mile marathon. The old saw that the shorter the piece the more difficult it is to write applies here, as it does in most instances.

While the novel is a somewhat forgiving form, the short story is a high-wire act: One slip can be fatal, as far as creating an effective work of fiction is concerned. If the illusion is punctured, the writer has lost the reader. The writer's miscalculation isn't diluted by many paragraphs and pages done right, as in the novel; one drop of acid in the relatively small vessel of the short story, and you have potent poison.

It is true that many writers begin by writing short stories and then move on to careers as novelists, but the reasons have more to do with economics than with levels of skill. It's also true that there are more short story writers who go on to write novels than there are novelists who later write short stories. Again, economics. Primarily. No getting around it, there's a greater return of money for effort in novels than in short stories. That, regrettably, is the state of the market.

139

But there's something else involved here. It's more likely that a short story writer will also be able to write novels, than it is that a novelist will also be able to write short stories. The skills involved in short story writing are somewhat different, generally more intense, and not within every writer's capabilities.

An editor once said of a short story writer known for his tightly written stories that he could write *War and Peace* on the back of an envelope. A good short story writer is able to pack maximum meaning and emotion into the fewest possible words, and that's a skill that can be extremely useful in novel writing. As a novelist, the writer of short stories is able to draw character, create situation, and set scene and mood in a few sentences or paragraphs, an ability many novelists don't possess. This isn't to be confused with the ability to condense; the short story writer actually tells it differently. The ability to write incisively and directly to the nerve is a skill, acquired by writing short stories and more short stories—and a skill worth cultivating. The art of economy might not be essential to a career as a novelist, but it sure helps.

No novel maintains constant mood and pace and climbs in a straight line to crisis, climax, and anti-climax. If novels were reduced to lines on graphs, they would appear as a series of peaks and valleys. It's how the valleys are handled that often determines the readability and success of novels. At those inevitable points at which lengthy explanation is necessary, or scenes must be set in detail, or clues must be planted, the novelist who can also write short fiction is able to use the short story writer's unique abilities to keep the novel moving with technique rather than situation, and to hold reader interest. Again, it's not the art of condensing, but that of knowing, of sensing, the essence of what needs to be related, and then penetrating to the core of it with the least possible digression and the greatest possible deftness. A slightly different skill from that usually employed in novels, and one learned only through writing short stories. I don't think it's inaccurate to say that a novelist's education isn't complete without some experience in writing short fiction.

But what are the really practical reasons for writing short stories as opposed to novels, aside from honing separate skills and laying the groundwork for a wider range of techniques as a novelist? While there isn't as much potential monetary gain in the writing of short stories, there also isn't as much time invested as in writing novels. Not as much bulk work. And a short story is more likely than a novel not only to sell more than once—to foreign markets and anthologies—but to keep on selling years, often decades, after the initial sale and publication. My agent recently sold Italian radio rights to a story I'd written over ten years ago. And at the same time sold to the same market a short story he'd had published when he was writing professionally in 1946, over *forty* years ago. Checks tend to turn up unexpectedly in the mailboxes of short story writers, and of course they're always welcome. So over a period of years, even decades, the time and effort involved in writing a short story can sometimes be very profitable. In fact, one writer I know makes a good living writing short stories almost exclusively, though this is something of a rarity these days and is probably going the way of the snail darter. The author established himself as a top-flight writer of short fiction in the years when there was a larger number of magazines publishing short stories. And while the market for short fiction has changed (and not for the better), it does seem to be improving lately. Or at least it is trying to improve. New magazines that print short fiction are born and most of them die, but there are survivors, and they seem to be hardy enough to withstand the rigors of the marketplace. The public never left the short story; with the elimination of most of the general magazines that published short fiction, the short story left the public. There is still, among people who read for entertainment and enlightenment, an appetite for short fiction.

More important than the above reasons for writing short stories, there are some short stories that *should* be told, and that simply aren't suitable for novel form. Narrow but powerful themes present themselves, as do intriguing situations and fictional characters who are best suited for direct and vivid tales without subplot or elaboration. At its best, the short story can attain the power of parable, something almost impossible for the novel. And, as we know, writers are at the mercy of their muse; they have some control over what they write, but not over what they *want* to write. In every writer there are tales that demand to be written.

For the novice writer, one of the advantages in the creation of short stories is that it is, I think, still easier to break into professional writing with a short story than with a novel. A few years ago I was on an award committee choosing the best mystery short story by a beginning writer. Several of the mystery magazines revealed to committee members which stories were first-publication authors, and I was surprised by the large number and by the quality of the stories. There's a wealth of talent out there; and it's producing quality fiction.

Once the beginning writer has a short story or two published, whether they're award winners or not, he or she has established professionalism and a track record. This can make it easier to sell that first novel, if that's what the writer has in mind. And that seems to be what most writers *do* have in mind.

One successful and well-known short story writer often says that he prefers writing short stories because "when I'm finished I'm the same person I was when I started." I know what he means. A novel's a lengthy proposition. It nags. Sometimes writing it is like keeping a dozen plates spinning at the same time, rushing from one end of the table to the other. That can be invigorating, even exciting. Also wearing. And a novel *does* simply take a long time to write; the author would grow and become a different person even if those months were spent watching television or reading instead of writing. Well, maybe not watching television.

Another analogy might be that of a painter working in oils, standing a few feet from the canvas, deciding on a dab here, a swipe there, a color blend here, not quite sure *precisely* what's been created until he or she moves well back and gains perspective. Not so unlike a novelist. No matter how much control you exercise over your material, there's always that distorting passage of time and experience between the first word and the last. Only when the first draft is finished does the novelist gain clearer perspective and *really* know what he or she has wrought.

But a short story is something you as a writer, after enough experience, will see whole within a relatively brief time after the first glimmer of idea. It's something over which you have much influence because early in the writing process you can catch it in your mind in its entirety. You can almost hold it in your hand as if it were a gem of your creation and turn it this way and that and polish it to your idea of perfection.

There's a mode, a mind-set, for writing short stories, and one for writing novels, and the rewards of each should be sampled in order to be a complete writer.

It pays in a number of ways for the novelist to work also in short story form—not to develop novelists' skills before moving on to longer fiction, but to develop different, *additional* skills that can prove valuable in

142

writing novels and provide an advantage over writers who throughout their careers stick to working in one length.

Shifting back and forth between short fiction and long can be difficult at first. It requires developing a sort of dual professional personality, and many writers seem unable to do this. But it's wise to find out if you're one of the people who can make this mental shift and see, think, and write in short story as well as novel form.

Novels can be a joy to create, but if you think you'd like watchmaking, diamond cutting, or building ships in bottles, and if you're willing to apply yourself with the necessary intensity for any of those tasks, short stories can offer their own keen and unique satisfaction—and give you specialized writing skills that will widen your scope as a novelist.

29

GETTING YOUR NOVEL STARTED IN TEN DAYS

By Genni Gunn

You've always wanted to write a novel but can find neither the time nor the starting point. You have unique experiences to record, hundreds of characters struggling to come out of your pen on to paper. What you need to do is make time to write and, perhaps most important, have a clear idea of *what* you are going to write.

A book is not written in one sitting. Even assuming you have a busy schedule, you need not wait to begin until you can afford to take a year's vacation from work. If your ideas are well organized, you can begin your novel now, by setting aside one hour a day in which to write.

Think of your novel as a jigsaw puzzle. Every day, you will examine one piece and put it in its proper place. The events, characters, and actions that first appear as a jumbled mass too big to tackle can be organized to make sense. You will need discipline and persistence.

Here's how to begin:

1) Set aside one hour a day for writing, if possible, the same time every day, so that eventually writing will become a habit.

2) Set up a place to write (preferably a desk where you can leave notes, typewriter, and necessary files) and return there every day to write.

Now you're ready to explore your novel idea. Where do you start? It is important to set realistic, achievable goals for each day. Here is a sample schedule for the first ten days:

Day 1. DEFINE YOUR IDEA. A novel begins as an idea. This can take the form of a character, an isolated event, or a lifetime struggle worth recording. Begin by asking yourself, "What is my novel about?" Write a one-sentence summary. If you can't do this right away, write down all the things you think your book is about. Read these over and condense them until you have *one sentence only*. Try to be as specific as possible.

At the end of your hour, type your finished sentence and tape it over your desk so it will always be visible as you write.

Day 2: LIST YOUR CHARACTERS under two headings: *Major Characters* and *Minor Characters*. Describe their relationship to one another. New characters may emerge as you write. Add them to your list. Fill in their descriptions later.

Day 3: LIST LOCATIONS AND SETTING in your novel: cities and towns (real or imaginary), houses, fields, roads, schools, etc., in which major events will take place. Fill in the detailed descriptions later.

Day 4: DEFINE YOUR CHARACTERS' GOALS. Your main characters must want something that they are unable to get. In one sentence, define *what* each of your main characters wants—tangible or intangible. As an example, here are three characters from an unwritten novel, and their three goals. At the end of Day 4, you should have a completed page that resembles the following:

GOALS

Paul wants: 1) money to settle pressing debts.
2) a means to live; a job.
3) a way to defend himself against his sister's accusations.
Alice wants: 1) to prove Paul's a swindler. She believes that before their aunt's death, Paul took money from their aunt that rightfully belonged to Alice.
2) her share of the money.
3) to keep Paul away from her adopted daughter, Judy.
Judy wants: 1) Paul.
2) her mother (Alice) to like Paul.
3) Paul to make a new start.

Day 5: LIST OBSTACLES that will prevent the main characters from getting what they want. These should be difficult for your characters to overcome; they can be other characters or physical or emotional impediments. Here, for example, are obstacles the characters described may have to surmount:

OBSTACLES

Paul: 1) Aunt Sophia, who was to leave him an inheritance, died penniless.
2) He has no skills with which to make a living. He is in his late thirties and feels he is too old to begin a trade.
3) His sister Alice.
Alice: 1) Paul won't divulge any information regarding his relationship with their Aunt Sophia prior to her death.

145

2) Paul is secretive about his financial affairs—she can't prove he has the money.
3) Her adopted daughter, Judy, is in love with Paul.

Judy: 1) Paul is not in love with her—he considers her his little niece.
2) Her mother distrusts Paul and won't let Judy see him.
3) Paul doesn't believe in his own ability to make a fresh start.

Day 6: PLAN THE CONCLUSION. Make up an ending for your novel. Write it in paragraph or point form and tape it over your desk. Characters often take on a life of their own and do things that are not what you had originally intended. Don't be afraid to rewrite the ending if your original version doesn't ring true.

Day 7: MAKE AN OUTLINE. The outline will serve as your guide while you're writing. (Update your outline if your story plot changes along the way.) When you are stuck in a chapter, choose something from the outline that interests you and begin writing about that event. It is not necessary to write chronologically. You may prefer to write separate sections of your novel and fill in the transitions later.

List the major events that will occur in your novel, not necessarily in detail.

Day 8: MAKE CHAPTER HEADINGS. Examine the events you listed yesterday. Separate them into chapters—with each chapter covering one major event. Now, write a one- or two-sentence summary description of what happens in each chapter. Tape the revised outline over your desk.

Day 9: SET UP FILES. Today will be an organizational day. Take blank file folders (either letter or legal size) and make a label for each one, using the following headings:
1) Characters
2) Locations
3) Chapters (one for each chapter heading)
4) Mannerisms
5) Speech patterns
6) General observations

These files will give you easy access to your information as well as suggest what to write about on those days when you lack inspiration. When you begin writing your novel, fill these files with the following information:

a) *Characters:* Write detailed descriptions—physical characteristics, emotional needs, family background, etc.—*know* your characters.

b) *Locations:* Where do your characters live? Where does the action take place in your novel? Think of writing as a visual art—write pictures for the reader.

c) *Individual chapters:* For your chapters in progress, notes, and ideas.

d) *Mannerisms:* Be observant. Record the way people show their emotions by body movements. To say, "He was angry" is vague and weak, but "He stamped his foot" *shows* the anger.

e) *Speech patterns:* Listen to people speak—the sound of their voices, the way they shape sentences, etc. This will be invaluable when writing dialogue, but remember that conversation is not dialogue. Give each of your characters distinct characteristics, perhaps a favorite phrase to repeat, short clipped sentences—whatever seems appropriate.

f) *General observations:* Keep a record of any thoughts you have about your novel or about human nature. You can always use these, even if not in your current project.

Make up you own file headings for other things that are important to your novel.

Day 10: WRITE YOUR OPENING PARAGRAPH. Begin your novel at that point at which your main character is faced with his or her major problem. Try to make your opening paragraph intriguing. Here is a possible opening for the novel example given earlier:

Paul had waited twenty years for his inheritance. He had squandered his time and what little money he'd earned with odd jobs on gambling and physical pleasures. After Aunt Sophia's funeral—a dull, dreary affair in which he'd been unable to feign sorrow—the will was read. Aunt Sophia died penniless.

This opening includes:
1) The main character
2) His predicament—therefore his problem
3) The necessary background to show the reader the gravity of his problem

If you're dissatisfied with your opening paragraph, put it aside and as you get new ideas, revise it.

From now on, each day, when you sit at your desk, you'll have a choice of things to write about. Look through your files for something that interests you. Describe characters, locations, mannerisms, or speech patterns and fit these into your novel later. Don't worry about the order. Get your story down on paper. You can fine-tune when you begin rewriting.

Set yourself realistic goals: One page a day for a year will yield 360 pages—a book-length manuscript. Half a page each day is even more realistic. Some days you'll write several pages; other days you'll struggle just to fill one. Most important, *stick with it!* Do nothing but write in the hour you've set aside, even if you only repeat a word to fill the page.

There are no easy ways to write a novel, no secrets, no shortcuts. It takes hard work, perseverance, and the belief that you have a story to tell.

30

DIALOGUE IN SHORT FICTION

By Hans Ostrom

WRITING effective dialogue is one major obstacle beginning fiction writers must overcome before they can write publishable short stories. Some of the problems beginning writers encounter in writing dialogue are fairly typical: the speech of characters is wooden, sounding like "essay talk" rather than "people talk"; or some lines are overburdened with meaning, serving only to get abstract points across and thereby failing as believable utterance. Lately, however, I have come to regard such typical problems as symptoms of a more basic difficulty: the inability or unwillingness of writers to *let their characters talk,* as opposed to *making them say what needs to be said.* To illustrate the difference between these approaches to writing dialogue, let me quote some dialogue from Bobbie Ann Mason's short story, "Shiloh." Norma Jean, Leroy, and Norma Jean's mother (Mabel) are talking:

> . . . While Norma Jean runs the vacuum, Mabel drinks coffee. She sets her coffee cup on a blueprint.
> "I'm just waiting for time to pass," she says to Leroy, drumming her fingers on the table.
> As soon as Norma Jean switches off the vacuum, Mabel says in a loud voice, "Did you hear about the datsun dog that killed the baby?"
> Norma Jean says, "The word is 'dachsund.'"
> "They put the dog on trial. It chewed the baby's legs off. The mother was in the next room all the time." She raises her voice. "They thought it was neglect."
> Norma Jean is holding her ears. Leroy manages to open the refrigerator and get some Diet Pepsi to offer Mabel. Mabel still has some coffee and she waves away the Pepsi.
> "Datsuns are like that," Mabel says. "They're jealous dogs. They'll tear a place to pieces if you don't keep an eye on them."
> "You better watch out what you're saying, Mabel," says Leroy.
> "Well, facts is facts."

Notice how in one way these characters fail to communicate. Norma Jean, after all, is either running the vacuum cleaner or covering her ears—deliberately not listening to her mother. Meanwhile, Mabel ignores the correction of "datsun" and plunges ahead with her tale. Leroy is intent on getting a Diet Pepsi, and even when he does respond to Mabel, he responds to her oblique but cruel reference to the baby he and Norma Jean have lost. Mabel closes this section of dialogue by ignoring Leroy's warning and sticking to her discussion of dachsunds.

Like this brief excerpt from "Shiloh," much dialogue in contemporary fiction—including stories by Raymond Carver, Ann Beattie, Alice Adams, and Frederick Busch, to name but a few writers—*appears* aimless, even chaotic. Characters seem to be talking at one another, not to one another, and if communication occurs, it occurs beneath the words that are actually spoken. For that matter, one can find similar dialogue in earlier stories, including such classics as Faulkner's "That Evening Sun" or Eudora Welty's "Petrified Man."

In contrast, much dialogue by beginning writers is, ironically, *too clear.* When characters talk too precisely and respond exactly to what has just been said, they are slaves to the points the author wants to get across rather than characters talking believably.

An extreme but well-known example of such dialogue occurred in Jack Webb's radio and television program, "Dragnet," in which dialogue served almost exclusively to move the plot forward or telegraph the theme. We can all recognize the kind of exchange that took place at the end of a conversation between a witness and one of the detectives:

WITNESS: "There was just one more thing, though."

DETECTIVE: "What's that?"

WITNESS: "Now that I think of it, Smith *was* carrying a suitcase."

Such dialogue is more glass than wooden in that we are supposed to look through it to see the plot unfold. And at the end of the show, someone—usually the character Joe Friday—would utter a speech designed solely to hammer home a platitude about crime and justice. Although beginning writers rarely suffer from such extreme cases of "Dragnet dialogue," they often enslave their dialogue to theme or plot and severely inhibit the believability of their characters' speech.

Dialogue for short fiction is not much different from dialogue for the theatre; it must *appear* artless, even aimless, although the art and the aim are only disguised, not discarded.

One key to achieving this kind of dialogue, I believe, is to "trust" your characters so well that you let them talk—as themselves—and in the process, they will serve your plot and conflict. You must trust them to such an extent that dialogue may actually become the plot and the conflict. Alienation of one kind or another is central to contemporary fiction, and letting characters talk *at* one another is one way to dramatize alienation.

Of course, letting characters talk is easier said than done. It requires an immense amount of discipline and of risk-taking by the writer. The bigger the theme or idea with which we are working, the more tempted we are to preach, to explain thoughts and actions, to intrude on what dialogue we do include. While these techniques are useful and often preferable to dialogue, they are, however, just as often indirect ways of shutting characters up, taking over for them. The short story form itself contributes to the temptation to stifle characters, for when we are trying to *compress,* the last thing we feel like doing is letting characters banter. (Novelists are not so hard-pressed.)

But out of banter can come surprises. Characters say things you don't expect them to say in ways that are surprisingly effective, and if they surprise you, the author who supposedly knows them, think how successfully they may surprise a reader who is meeting them for the first time.

As you are writing a draft, it is essential to resist the temptation to stop an exchange of dialogue simply out of impatience. (If there is an obvious place for narration or description, so be it.) You must also take the risk of letting your characters alter the plot or redefine the conflict— or redefine themselves. That is, letting characters talk can be a way of allowing them to go off on their own and of allowing a less conscious part of your mind to shape the story.

If you are writing the kind of story that is centered on character rather than on plot, then let your characters talk in early drafts. First, have a good idea of who the characters are, at least enough to know *how* they talk. Then have some general idea of where the scene might be headed, but be willing to let it drift from that destination. Then just let them talk—banter, argue, question, mumble, interrupt, misinterpret.

If you get impatient about the direction they're taking, "bribe" yourself by enjoying the language itself, the rhythm of phrases, the "bounce" of conversation. (And remember that since writing is rewriting, you are under no obligation to keep all of the words, and you'll have plenty of opportunity to cut or trim or reshape the dialogue.) Also, don't let any *one* character talk too much. Think dialogue, not monologue. For monologues are often ways of shutting characters up, and they are usually the voice of the author, not of the character.

If you do let your characters talk, and if you read aloud what they say, at the very least you will overcome the problems of woodenness and preachiness with which all serious writers of fiction grapple. In the process, you will frequently sharpen characterization, because writers know their characters (as we all know real people) partly, if not primarily, by what they say.

Finally, if you grant your characters the right to talk to each other in what may seem a random way, they may reveal and communicate previously hidden possibilities of the conflict or "story idea." Beginning writers in particular often refuse to let a character talk because they believe they know from the outset what characters need to say. As I've said, however, if characters are given the freedom to talk in early drafts of a story, they often tell the author what should be said and thereby point the way to a richer, livelier final draft. In most cases, fiction writers have nothing to lose and everything to gain by letting their characters talk.

31

THE LISTENING EAR

By Anne Chamberlain

"DUMB!" The unseen woman in the next booth exclaimed, "about as dumb as a coon in a tree, that's my opinion, and who knows better'n me?"

"You're the one as knows," an eager girlish voice supplied.

"More brains than you can shake a stick at, and turns them all the wrong way, that's my opinion. Why, let me tell you now what she done last Wednesday afternoon, nobody home, and in she snaked and I think she got into my parlor table drawer, read my postcards—my bills too, electric and the gas, she read, and that weren't the worst of it. Let me tell you . . ." The narrative slipped into a tantalizing whisper, incoherent to the casual listener. I was that listener, a traveler, enjoying a quick stopover meal at the village restaurant. Not having previously noticed the two women, I now realized that I probably wouldn't catch a good look if I left before they did. Fascinated, I lingered for a few minutes, and was rewarded with the suddenly loud, dramatic final line: "And then she ate the *whole* watermelon!"

Over the mountainous miles of the homeward drive, over the years since, this delectable tidbit remains one of the small treasures in my memory. A "treasure" it can be justly termed, for, with the intimate village atmosphere, the rural idiom and emphasis of the narrator, the avid (perhaps fawning?) attendance of her companion, this fragment limns a scene, hints at characterization, suggests numerous stories. What a sneaky, spiteful, absurd act, eating somebody's watermelon! And why would the marauder, obviously well known to the victim, indulge in so barbaric a feast? Were they feuding neighbors, rivals in quilting club contests, jealous sisters-in-law, or simply harborers of a longtime natural animosity? A humorous situation, certainly, which— as always with comedy—would be seasoned with sound psychological

153

undertones. Over the countless possibilities, the listener/writer can muse, fantasize, and, in due time, select that which seems most suitable to his particular talents.

For me as an author, cultivating an astute ear for dialogue is a lifelong process. Having grappled with the task of presenting dramatic scenes on paper, of distilling ordinary speech for extraordinary effects, yet of preserving the tones and rhythm of natural talk, I have become a student, a collector, and a connoisseur. Mine is not a calculated eavesdropping. The phrases, fragments of discussion, and sometimes complete anecdotes that reach my ears by chance are tossed into the air wherever people gather and talk, free to any and all who pay attention. They are often delightfully unexpected, and in afterthought, may lend themselves to fascinating interpretations.

In restaurants, airports, stores, hotel lobbies, elevators, the listener finds rich fields to explore. Settings for arrivals and departures may be especially fruitful:

"Please," a woman clutches at the arm of her escort; they are standing in line at the airport, he with a gleaming briefcase, she—apparently—about to say goodbye: "I ask you once more, Arthur, please . . ." He does not answer, nor does he look at her. Her fingers tighten on his sleeve. "Arthur, I'm asking," she murmurs, her voice sinking into a whisper.

For what is she pleading? That he phone at the customary time tonight, forgetting this morning's argument? That he look up the wayward son, who in the city of the father's destination, has recently moved in with an objectionable girl friend? That he think more carefully before he accepts the promotion that will take them from the home and neighborhood she has learned to love? Is he usually "Arthur" to her or, in more relaxed moments, "Art"? Does he remain silent because he is angry, or merely bored?

The listener knows only that she is serious about something, that he is adamant. An alert ear learns the importance of inflection. How many dozens of ways there are of saying "please"! Politely, as a vocal punctuation, urgently, sardonically, savagely, humbly, sometimes a mixture of emotions pour into the single syllable. "It isn't what he said, it's the way he said it," is the frequent plaintive tagline of an anecdote, when the narrator remembers the direct quote but realizes that—in itself—this fails to capture the impact. It is the desperate, last-minute quality of the airport woman's utterance, the breathlessness, the sleeve-clutching, the fading into a whisper that dramatizes her words. Were the writer to develop a story line from this episode, he would use the verbs, adjectives, and action detail to present the dialogue within its emotional context.

Perhaps Arthur is indeed expecting to be offered a promotion, his acceptance of which will take them and their children to a much larger city, a strange and—to Millicent, his wife—a frightening environment. It means transplanting their two youngsters, in sensitive early teen years, to more urban schools and (she suspects) more hazardous temptations. Ashamed as she is to admit it, she hates leaving the house she has cherished for years, the garden she has lovingly tended, the church and the women's clubs; oh, she loves him far more than any *place,* he surely knows this, but isn't she human, doesn't her own life, don't the lives of the children count? The present action, which seems to have evolved easily from Millicent's point of view, could be unfolded within the airport setting, as they arrive, check in, wait, continue the discussion that may have previously waxed into an argument, softened into mutual understanding, flared again into anger. Brief flashbacks, dramatizing the tensions, could be woven into the immediate scene, which builds to the last few minutes, as they stand in line. At this point, even though the situation may have been artfully developed, it would be temptingly easy to overwrite:

"Please," she begged wistfully, clutching at his sleeve, pouring her heart into this last minute entreaty, "I ask you once more, Arthur, please . . ."
Stone-faced, stubbornly silent, he stood, refusing to look at her.
"Arthur," tears surged into her voice. Her fingers tightened on his sleeve, as though she would hold him, draw him to her, fold him into her arms, "I'm asking . . ." Her voice sank into a whisper, a strangled sob.
He stared coldly and mutely into space.

This has too much trimming. Overembellishment is a weakness common to the writing of dialogue. If the author astutely employs other techniques, descriptions of characters and of setting, perhaps subjective delineation of the unspoken feelings of one or more of those concerned, the actual spoken exchange should need little adornment. Knowing Millicent and Arthur, through their airport wait and through the thoughts and the flashback episodes that have illuminated their tensions, the reader understands much of what is not spoken at their

155

parting. Seeing him board the plane, Millicent knows that some day she and the children will be boarding with him. Or she realizes, only dimly yet, as she turns from waving goodbye, that this time he is truly leaving, she is going home. One story possibility; airports bustle with them.

The listening author discriminates. It would impossible to hear, much less to heed, the countless words that may be spoken around one in the course of a crowded day. As a fiction writer, I have a built-in tape recorder, which, for my purposes, is more convenient and dependable than its mechanical counterpart. It receives constantly; it erases the superfluous; it may splice; it will store what seems worth keeping.

"I went downtown this morning—oh the loveliest day, I just can't tell you! Sunshine and breeze and spring everywhere, I danced, danced on my toes all the way, and right at the corner by the mailbox, you can't imagine who I saw, I ran right into her, I hadn't seen her for—you can't imagine how long!—centuries! And you'll never guess what she told me, she came right out with it—" the young woman babbles merrily to her hairdresser, a captive but not uninterested audience, "on the street, on the corner by the mailbox, I'll have you know, she told me, might have been saying, 'it's a nice day,' she was that nonchalant, she came right out with it—"

An individual's speech is as unique as his handwriting, his manner of dress, his voice, walk, gestures, his smile and his eyes. This woman talks in hyperbole, loves to prattle, and contrives through suspenseful hints to keep her audience attentive:

"She was divorced, that's what she said, cool as a cucumber, and then before I got over *that,* I mean I'd barely begun to digest it, she goes right on to say she's married again. Can you imagine! And all within five minutes, well no more than ten, and here I am, my jaw just dropping and she says, 'I thought you knew, didn't you know,' and I said no I didn't know, how could I, hadn't seen, hadn't heard a word about her in centuries and—" to a murmured question from the beautician, "didn't I tell you *who* she is? Well-l-l . . ." Into a genealogical chart she spins, spilling names, father, grandfather, uncle, aunts, first husband and, "a Hardquist, of course, and you do, well maybe you don't know the Hardquists but he, number one husband I mean, he was a chip off the old block, his father Jedson, *the* Jedson, and what I couldn't tell you, my dear, about Jedson Hardquist—"

Seated two chairs away in the beauty salon, I reflect that shocking news, delivered bluntly by a mailbox, might—for a minute or two—silence the babbler's torrential monologue. And I ponder over that

156

woman, "as cool as a cucumber," with the mixed-up marital history. And what about Jedson? I will be hearing more, for I, too, am a captive audience.

In dramatizing the speech mannerisms of the babbler, who can rapidly become a loquacious bore, the writer must aim to convey her effect on others without producing a similar tedium in the reader. One quoted paragraph, like that above, can characterize her compulsive gushiness, and additional phrases will suggest all that is not on paper. While the incessant talker is particularly difficult to harness in dialogue, the need for pruning and culling applies to the speech of all characters.

"No, I didn't know about the Hardquists," the beautician interposes pointedly. She is tired of the monologue. Perhaps she dislikes scurrilous gossip; too much of it whirls around her shop. And is there, in the weary but gentle rebuke of her tone, a distaste for the whole carefree society, the smug, prosperous, much-married and divorced people about whom she hears so much? A story, a hundred or more stories could be written from the point of view of a skilled and patient beautician.

In contrast with the fluent monologuist, the terse speaker, who favors a form of verbal shorthand, poses a different challenge to the writer. Often his reticence can be dramatized through the speeches addressed to him. In the hotel lobby, I notice the young wife greeting her husband enthusiastically:

"How was your morning?"
"Same as ever." He kisses her amiably and takes her arm, steering her to the dining room.

She has come into town from suburbia. They will lunch together, and I reflect that she is hungry for excitement and news.

"Same?" She pouts, teasing him. "Oh, you, it's always the same, same, same," and pats his arm, "but what about Chalmers? Anything happen?"
He motions toward the hostess, they are conducted to a table, sit down, order cocktails.

From this overheard exchange, I spin an imaginative continuation, just enough to suggest more:

157

"You haven't told me about Chalmers. . . ."

"Fired," he lights a cigarette.

"Oh no! Oh how terrible, was he upset, how did he take it? Oh poor Lydia—"

He has opened the menu. "Think I'll have the steak."

"Did he come in? Did you see him? What did he *do?*"

"Yes," he smiles to the waitress, as she places the cocktails before them, "I think we'll order now."

With this taciturn man, who may have excellent reasons for not wanting to tell his wife about Chalmers, the problem is to convey what he does not choose to say; much can be achieved through action detail.

Fine stories have been written without a scrap of dialogue; others have consisted entirely of spoken words. Most authors use direct quotes at high dramatic points, emphasizing and advancing the narrative. Often, I become so absorbed with other aspects of the story that I do not give enough consideration to the question: Would this character say this in this way? By cultivating the listening ear, I am more aware of natural speech and more alert to those weaknesses that may be distilled into direct quotes.

I have learned to be wary of the overly structured sentence, the too complete and well-rounded paragraph. It is not inconceivable (in writing, nothing is!) for the anguished husband, leaving his wife, suitcase packed and hand on doorknob, to address her: "Much as I love you and always will, our marriage has become totally incompatible, is beyond the help of counselors, and is mutually erosive to our respective personalities." Not inconceivable, as this husband may be a person addicted to eloquence; one does imagine that, if he used such terms, his wife willingly opened the door for him. It is more likely that he would speak briefly, might shout, mumble, lunge out of the house. Under intense emotional pressure, a character's talk is usually jagged, sentences incomplete, feelings too deep for balanced, measured phrases.

A vehement discussion may go on for thousands of words, lasting a whole evening, and to report it literally would not only cover dozens of pages but would bury the story in the process. I am, therefore, aware that I must delete and, if I listen as an author may, I find myself deleting swiftly, editing what I hear, saving what is worthwhile.

"I told him in no uncertain terms," said the portly man at the bus stop, "that his attitude was depressing. demoralizing, and disappointing." He paused, groped for another alliterative adjective, exploded triumphantly, "destructive." He bit at his cigar. "Yes," I told him—"destructive!"

His companion nodded sagely and stroked his drooping moustache. "You told him off, Fred, you surely did. I wish I had your gift for language. But what'd he say? Fred, what *did* he say?"

The bus arrived, they climbed on together, still talking. . . .

The listening bystander will not know what he said. Or how he managed to be all of those adjectives, rolled into one, or were these faults pure imaginings of a pompous fellow worker? Was our denouncer guilty of the very accusations he so relished? A distinct possibility. A story? I muse.

Cultivating the listening ear is an educational process that helps me write dialogue I have never heard until I imagine the characters and what they are saying; it is also a rich source, an inexhaustible mine of material. Of perhaps a thousand tidbits that I overhear and speculate about, only one or two may combine within the ever mysterious creative self to produce a story. Constant entertainment is at my command. I can turn on that tape recorder which, in the depths of memory, is always waiting, brimming with ideas.

How did matters finally work out for Arthur and Millicent? Maybe he wasn't considering a promotion, after all. She might have been pleading because, in the city of his destination, there lived that former secretary, the golden-haired and lynx-eyed, the sly and determined, with whom Arthur was still in touch. He had said it would be stupid, plain unfriendly not to look her up, at least to telephone; why, she and Millicent had been on good terms, hadn't they? She had made the mistake of protesting and had lighted the match—or had the fire been simmering already? Another story.

The babbler in the beauty shop prates on. In the next chair may be Old Jedson Hardquist's third wife, young, sharp-eared, new to town, rapidly absorbing important information. Or the patient beautician, scissoring deftly, may have had, as her last client, the carefree "cool as a cucumber" woman who had met the babbler at the mailbox. Anything can happen; the listener can pick and choose.

How did poor Chalmers react to being fired? Will the eager wife ever learn details from her cautious husband? Was the portly man's unknown target actually "depressing, demoralizing, disappointing, and destructive"? Delectable, that phrasing, in its pompous smugness.

Come to think of it, how big was that watermelon?

32

LEAVE THEM WANTING MORE

By Jean McConnell

THERE is an old adage in the theatre—always leave them wanting more. This might with profit be borne in mind by the writer of short stories. Perhaps the essential difference between the novel and the short story is that in writing novels you can meander—take time off to explore the byways—while in short story writing you must keep to the main road. But this could make for a pretty dull journey unless the way is enhanced by the writer's art.

So, the aim of the short story writer is to find the most economical way to convey an important point—a colorful image, at the same time moving the narrative forward. Sometimes it's just the choice of a single word: "The house was afire" does not conjure up the same picture as "The house was ablaze."

It is in dialogue that a writer can make points most speedily. We may laugh at a line like "You Jane . . . Me Tarzan," but in its context it puts across Tarzan's potential to learn to speak, the strong man's vulnerability, and his awakening sexuality.

It is an excellent test of a writer's ability to compress a sometimes complicated story line into short revealing speeches. Whereas in films the pictures provide the background detail, in the short story everything must be filtered in with no noticeable holdup in the main thrust of the plot.

How to do it? Where are the main opportunities?

It is in the opening paragraph of a story that the writer can make the most mileage. Often it is a good plan to begin the story where the action is already on its way, to plunge straight into a conversation. Here the dialogue must convey an idea of the setting and what has happened before, as well as some characterization and sufficient hint of conflict to make the reader want to know what is going to happen next.

Take the following example. This is from a short story of mine entitled, "Remember Me?" The story had to reach quite a high peak of drama in a very little time; therefore, all relevant information had to be fed in speedily, yet without coming over as bald fact:

"Remember me?"
The voice was at my elbow. I turned. The blue eyes smiled up into mine, the pert nose wrinkled, the pale gold hair swung sideways, shimmering. Shorter. It had once been waistlength.
The other wedding guests surged around us. My awareness of them blurred. Only she, standing there before me, was in sharp focus.
"Remember me? Elizabeth?"
Yes. I remember you.
This was the girl who took from me my first love. Who can ever forget that girl? Who ever forgets that first love? Even now, so long after, in this crowded room—standing nearby a husband I had loved dearly for five years—even now the memory came back to me painfully.

We have the setup—a wedding—a sudden meeting of old friends. Note the description of Elizabeth: the detail in which our heroine assesses her is the first point of significance. Her immediate reaction is intensified by the use of italics. Then we get a basic fact—Elizabeth stole our heroine's first boyfriend. So when we learn that her husband is nearby, we are aware of the possible threat.

One could have described the heroine's looks, or what the bride and groom were like—whether they were friends or relations or whatever. But none of this is necessary. The whole of the story then happens in the few minutes it takes the two young women to exchange half a dozen sentences. It is a memory replayed in the heroine's head, only coming back to real life when she has to introduce her husband to the predatory Elizabeth and find he seems to know her. Again, the finale is brief but the heroine's relief is complete, and the outcome entirely satisfactory for her.

"Is that woman a friend of yours?" he asked.
"She was. Once," I replied carefully.
He opened the car door and I climbed in.
Why, John? Why? Why? Why?
At last it came out as a word.
"Why?"
"That's the woman who broke up Tom's marriage. Six weeks later she left him flat."
"Oh."
"She's—" He hesitated, seeking the word.

161

It was important he should find the right one. Important to me. Too weak a term could indicate saloon-bar gossip. Too strong might imply a former intimacy.

"She's—?" I prompted.

"Unkind," he said simply.

It was the right word.

"I'm sorry if she's an old friend, honey." He patted my hand.

"No," I assured him as we moved off. "I scarcely remember her."

Another important point is to make every word not only count in its own right and move the tale along, but reveal something useful about the situation or characters at the same time.

Take this opening of a story of mine called "Fresh Fields":

Beginning (a)

"Gilly, would you look after the farm for us while we're away?"

"But I've no experience with animals."

"Oh, there are only a few hens and ducks and pigs."

Beginning (b)

"I'd sooner you took over than anyone else, Gilly."

"But I've no experience with animals."

"Rover loves you."

"I mean the hens. And the ducks. And the pigs!"

In example (a) we have learned the heroine's name and the basic situation: a request for help on the farm.

In example (b) we have learned that our heroine is someone to trust. That she's warmhearted. That she's rather comically timid of farm creatures. Already the readers feel they know this nice girl and suspect the story is likely to be humorous. The number of words used is virtually the same, so it was much better to use example b, which immediately established the style in which I wanted to write the story and also implied a lot more than example a.

Setting the style of a story at the outset is important. Take this opening, for instance, which is from my story, "The Search":

There was hardly a depth of soil between the kitchen flagstones and bedrock to bury a few fingers, let alone the body of a full-grown man—even if he were of slender build. For that matter the tell-tale signs of recent disturbance were not present. The Inspector brushed back the small tuft of weak hairs which were all that remained of an unruly boyish forelock. Two weeks, he pondered, two weeks the man had been missing. Not long. But long enough for a man who had said, "See you tomorrow night, Jack," to the barman at the pub. Too long for the man whose pedigreed Jersey cow had been due to calf at any moment. Long indeed for the daughter of the grocer who suspected she was carrying his child and believed he'd be pleased.

We know at once it's a crime story, and the remark about the fingers signals that it might be a gruesome one. The reference to "slender build" is also a plant for later—when the man is found sewn into a mattress. The description of the Inspector's hair engages the readers' sympathy and puts them on his side.

This story was only 1,100 words and all essential information was very usefully packed into the last three sentences of that first paragraph.

In writing a short story, the writer doesn't have much room to move, so he should go for the table and chairs and forget the cocktail cabinet and plant stand, by which I mean, concentrate on what is absolutely necessary and eliminate the trimmings—unless they are trimmings that are highly significant. Consider the following section from a story about a fairground stunt. A man is fasting to the point of death. He speaks to his wife.

"I'm finished."
"What ya talking about? Lyin' there with nothin' to do. You got it easy this time."
Easy, yes. Easy compared with holding a lighted candle to your flesh till the blisters rose. Easier than biting out the throat of a live chicken. He'd done these things to please the crowds. And the others for her private pleasure to earn the oblivion of the pinch of white powder she supplied in reward.

In a novel you might go on: "There was a time when . . .etc." But here there is no need—or time—to spell it out further. This particular story was called "All the Fun at the Fair," and the title itself added irony since it was a tragedy involving both murder and suicide.

Any author who has written stage plays recognizes that he must get the exposition over speedily and cleverly. Praise be for the invention of the telephone, whereby essential facts can be so swiftly imparted. The short story writer must also think along these lines, endeavoring to lay out his background entertainingly yet wasting no time in getting to the heart of the matter.

In a first draft, when you are finding your way through the plot, it is

163

inevitable that you overwrite. It is in the paring down that the challenge lies. Any story can be reduced to its fundamentals. What you are aiming at is compressing the length, while retaining the color, the flavor, the style. Things are easier if the matter is racy, light or humorous. Then a single word can jump-cut you along with good effect.

"Come up for a nightcap," he said.
"All right," I said.
Madness.

Or take this passage from my story, "Spring Break":

"What a marvelous break for you," everyone said.
"Yes!" I responded, and smiled and smiled.
Paul drove us to the dockside and his farewell was loving. As he waved from the quay, I thought I saw him glance at his watch. But perhaps not. I had to believe not.

The significance of the clock-watching—the impatience to be away— might have been dwelt on, but instead, the repetition of the word "not" works faster and surely better.

"Spring Break" was my original title for the story, but as published it was called "The Scent of Mimosa." My title had a double meaning: (a) a holiday and (b) the end of a love affair.

The magazine's title was perfectly relevant to the story and more romantic. In the end, it was just a matter of emphasis. Since it *was* a very romantic story, the magazine's choice was probably the right one.

However seductive, the descriptive passage is a space-waster unless it fulfills a secondary function of, say, implying the mood or attitude of a character. Consider the opening of "Spring Break":

It's the wrong time to leave the city. The thought nagged me warningly. Despite the bleak wind whipping through the colorless buildings and the windowbox empty and dank, it was the wrong time. Because of her. She had come into my life only a month or two ago. The change in Paul had been gradual, but it signalled itself at last even to my resistant mind.

This can perfectly well be written:

There was no doubt about it. It was the wrong time to leave the city. Because of her. She had come into my life only a month before. I knew it instantly. The change in Paul was obvious. I didn't want to understand. But I did.

164

Both examples are quite economical. The first takes time to establish a chillier mood. But the second gets straight to the point and thrusts the reader into the situation. It is for the writer to balance what he needs against what he has time for.

Often this task falls to the editor. And let it be said that the best of them are still highly skilled in this field and can cut to the bone yet still preserve the writer's original intention.

Nevertheless, the professional writer designs his piece to the correct length for the prospective market. And if it's to be the short story, then he must be fast on his feet. Ponder the fact that reducing the sauce usually enriches it. Let this be the objective.

Never forget that by confining yourself to the intriguing hint—the evocative word—you will have given your reader the infinite pleasure of using his imagination.

33

USING IMAGES IN FICTION

By Merrill Joan Gerber

THE WORD "IMAGE" means "picture," and all of us have been advised just how many words a picture is worth. Yet we know it's true that a picture strikes us as "whole" and stays with us in ways that dialogue and narrative do not. Using images in fiction writing allows us to vivify and illuminate as well as highlight and frame the actions and intentions of our characters.

Evocative images in a story are graceful signposts to the reader, pointing out to him (but not telling), suggesting to him (but not insisting), what we as writers mean to convey. Like symbols, images are effective on more than one level: They move the story along in a functional way, working on a concrete, literal level, while they also serve as an indicator in a more subtle way, giving clues to deeper meaning without seeming to lecture or explain.

In the title story of my collection of stories, *Honeymoon,* I introduce the "newlyweds" Cheryl and Rand by presenting the reader with images that work in a purely literal and physical way, but also serve to suggest the nature of the characters' relationship:

On their way out of the Bun Boy coffee shop in Baker, Rand gave Cheryl a quarter to buy a Bio-Rhythm fortune card from a vending machine. She stood in the hot desert wind, her skirt lashing about her legs like a whip, strands of hair flying into her mouth, while she laughingly read him the news that the biograph rated her low on luck, low on sex, and low on leisure plans, while it rated her high on health, endurance and driving.

My intention was to use images to give the reader a sense of who these two characters are and to hint at what their relationship to one another is like. In the first line of the story, Rand, who is old enough to be Cheryl's father, gives her a quarter, just as a father might give a child money to buy some little bauble out of a vending machine. I definitely meant to convey that idea—and found I could present it quite economically with that image. Furthermore, two other words, used innocently enough to describe the effects of a hot desert wind ("lashing" and "whip"), suggest something of what is to be revealed in the nature of this new marriage—a certain corruption. After they get into the car, Cheryl asks . . .

"So can I drive the rest of the way to Vegas now? . . .It's so boring just to look out the window. There's no scenery."

"Get in the car, please," Rand said, his pants legs flapping like banners in a used-car lot, ". . . and don't put another ding in my door."

"I didn't put the first ding in," she said, getting into his red Corvette. She automatically took a sip of water from the insulated cup hanging in a holder on the dash and made a face. "Yuck—hot."

"You just had a milkshake," Rand said. "Why do you have to drink old water?"

"I don't know," she said, shrugging. "I just saw it there. Don't worry about it."

More images: the man's pants legs flapping like banners in a used-car lot, to suggest what? A used-car salesman, perhaps; maybe a certain lack of integrity. And by his accusation that his wife "put a ding in his door"—he is suggesting that she broke his toy, the red Corvette. Cheryl's taking a sip of the hot water (and her subsequent "yuck") is the kind of thing a child would do. So the reader understands certain things without being told: Both characters are immature. He is petty, impatient, easily angered; she is easily bored (which may be why she married him—to get out of some other boring situation).

Later, when she thinks about why she married Rand, in defense against her mother's opinion of him ("more than twice your age, after you because you're a gorgeous young girl, you ought to be dating his sons!"), she describes boys her own age:

What did they know? The guys her own age were nothing, invisible, scarecrows on hangers. They glugged beer and walked to some drumbeat in their heads; she was sick of faded jeans and running shoes and guys who couldn't wait to turn you on with grass or with their own throbbing bodies . . . half of the guys she knew thought they would be famous rock stars; they couldn't even carry a tune.

At least for that moment we can identify with Cheryl, seeing the young men as she sees them, "scarecrows on hangers, glugging beer . . ."

167

When the newlywed couple get to Las Vegas, Rand instructs her to:

"Call room service and order us each a big shrimp cocktail," Rand said, his body reflected a dozen times in the mirrored room as he hung up his clothes in the alcove.

"I don't know if I want that," Cheryl said. "Maybe I want a hamburger."

"Call! Call!" he said. "Hurry up. When I get out of the shower I want it to be here."

And when it came, big white shrimp with pink tails and pink veins arched in a goblet over a snowball of ice, heads swimming in luscious red cocktail sauce, she knew he was right. It was exactly what she wanted. She chewed in a luxury of wanting the shrimp, grateful to him. When he came out of the shower she had eaten half of his shrimp, too—and he looked at the bloody plate and laughed, and peeled off his damp towel and swatted her. "That's what I love about you," he said. "Your healthy appetites, all of them."

The images here are sensual, the words are sensual: "luscious," "red," "luxury"; and there's an undertone of sexual suggestion—the bloody plate, his peeling off his damp towel, his "swatting her," his referring to her "healthy appetites, all of them." Also, his "body reflected a dozen times in the mirrored room" suggests a certain power he has over her; to her he is bigger than life.

All of this is accomplished without ever "telling" the reader what Rand's inclinations are, or how exactly Cheryl is attracted to him—but it's all there, in the evocative images of what he does and how he appears to her.

In another story in the collection, "At the Fence," we have the situation—simply put—of Anna, a middle-aged woman who is disturbed by a barking dog who lives with a young couple in the house next door. Anna hates the dog; he is ruining her peace, ruining her life. (Or so she thinks. But here is her first view of the dog):

The young man looks behind him, and there comes the dog—a sleek black Doberman trotting right to the door, his long snout coming up against the screen, his stubby tail wagging.

Not so bad, really, thinks the reader. Can it be that this animal, described rather pleasantly, is really ruining her life? But a moment later the young man's wife . . .

swings into view, wiping her hands on her blue jeans. She is perhaps a year or two younger than her husband, about nineteen . . . yet she comes to the door as if she owns not only this rented house, but also the world with Anna in it. She puts her hand on her husband's bare shoulder; only then is Anna aware of the thick black hair on his chest, the private hole of his navel looking at her eye. The girl has cornsilk blonde hair, long and thick, and she twists it, rope-like, over one shoulder as she stands there looking out. Her breasts are heavy and loose inside a blue T-shirt.

It is not the dog so much that Anna resents, as it is the mocking presence of this vital young couple who take for granted what Anna is losing: her youth, her joy in life. She sees herself as the victim of a great injustice: she is getting old too soon:

Anna thinks that it was just yesterday she was newly married, and now she's old. She doesn't believe the problems she's been thinking about these days could really be her problems. She hasn't had enough of starting out, she's just getting used to being grownup, being married.

The reader begins to understand that Anna feels trapped in her life, just as the dog is trapped in his yard. Therefore, it seems logical that each time Anna hears the dog begin to bark, she identifies with him.

. . . he begins a thin wailing, less eerie than the coyotes' wailing she hears at night from the hills, but burdened enough, an outward spiraling tornado of loneliness and misery. Then it will pause briefly before turning into an explosion of staccato barks, getting shriller and more panicky, till finally the animal is running from one end of the yard to the other, rattling the fence, clawing at the spaces between the boards, yipping and yapping in a frenzy that can go on, easily, for several hours without pause.

Anna says to her husband . . .

"No one has a right to do this, to destroy a person's peace, just because he likes the idea of having a dog. A man and his dog!—what a dumb romantic notion." At the same moment she is thinking that she would like [her daughter] to marry a man like the one next door. A man who has a dog—a man, who, with his woman and his beer and his ballgame, seems like the sort of man a woman should have, a man who protects his rights, who doesn't back down, who stands firm. She thinks of his hairy chest, and to her surprise something clutches low down in her abdomen in the place where the estrogen is running low.

So we see, by the images presented, a certain contradiction here. Anna thinks she hates the dog, perhaps hates the young man who owns him—and yet, there is some great ambivalence in her. She thinks about the dog:

169

. . . hardly a watchdog, hardly a man's best friend, just a whimpering, crazed, abandoned creature, without a mate, without a friend.

This is not really a description of the dog, it is the way Anna thinks of *herself.* Late one night, thinking that she will get even with the dog . . .

. . . Anna gets her two biggest pot covers and takes them out into the backyard. She holds them, poised like a cymbal player waiting for her cue in the pit of a great orchestra . . . Anna waits, counting the beats, as breathless as if the stars are her vast audience and this is her debut. And when it comes, first the whine, then the howl, then the full-fledged bass and treble of the mad dog's great range, she runs in her nightgown, barefoot, across the damp grass of the yard, runs to the fence and crashes the pot covers together in a series of clashes, bangs and shrieks till the night sky shakes with the lightning and thunder of her fury.

What the images here really convey is her yearning to have an audience, to have her debut, to enter the world, to be the center of attention. To count as a person! And yet whatever she does comes to a lessening, to destruction and misery:

Then . . . silence. She has terrified him. She feels her lip curl. Hah, good. She imagines the dog to be like a native in the jungle who witnesses a meteorite fall . . . Back in the house . . . Anna replaces the pot covers in the cabinet under the stove, but not before a sliver of silver metal, shredded from the edge of one of the covers by her wild banging, pierces her finger, drawing bright blood . . . The next day she buys a pair of ear plugs, little cylinders of wax and foam, and at night jams them into her ears as if she is corking up her vital fluids.

Anna's grief is immense—she rails at the gods and what does she get? More loss, her life's blood leaking from her, and more than ever, her sense of all she is missing, and losing, in life. The presence of the barking dog only underlines this emotion. By now she identifies completely with him; even as she goes out to see where at the fence she can best poison him, he trots into view and

pushes his snout against the space between the boards in the side gate. . . . The dog is licking her hand, dancing with pleasure at her company, his rear end wiggling in rippling convulsions. No one has been that happy to see her in a long time. . . .

These images convey the many things he means to her. He is her enemy, but he is also her precious friend and, like her, is lonely, desperate for friendship, and helpless to do anything about his plight.

He is also warm, alive, beautiful . . . sexual—all the things Anna wishes to be. Finally, after her husband, goaded by her, confronts the dog's owner, she fears that . . .

a real man has a dog and a gun. He will blast her children in the yard. Or strangle her cats . . . she imagines the young man right now stroking the polished barrel of his shotgun, and she feels herself arc out of bed and land on her toes like a ballet dancer. She hurries into the backyard. The stars are as sharp as at the beginning of creation. A tall palm at the far end of the yard is fanned out against the moon. There is a rustling in the brush on the other side of the fence as she approaches it. She whispers, "Here boy, come here," and the beautiful black dog with his princely face comes to the fence and thrusts his warm nose through the crack till it is cupped in her fingers.

Once again we have the image of her as performer as she "arcs out of bed and lands on her toes like a ballet dancer." The "beginning of creation" suggests a new life; she is going to take some action. The images that describe the dog have evolved so that the dog has changed from a crazed animal whom Anna hates to a beautiful prince whom Anna loves. And what is the function of the handsome prince in any fairy tale?

By the light of the moon she pulls and pries at a board in the fence until she wrenches it from the bottom rail. Making a tiny kissing sound with her lips she holds it aside and the dog pours through like a waterfall, shimmering and coursing down the length of her leg. She kneels and puts both arms around him, long enough to feel his hot breath on her face.

The "kissing sound" suggests the moment in the fairy tale when the animal (the beast, the donkey, the frog) is changed into the handsome human prince. Now the image of the dog—almost as her lover—takes on greater strength as she pulls him into the house with her, "leading him by his red collar."

He follows her out the front door and into the wide street where they both stand in silence panting in the cool air. His ears are up, his hind legs spread slightly apart. She bends quickly and gives him a sharp rap on his rump.
"Go!" she commands. "Go!"
He starts forward like a thoroughbred, like a whippet, a black arrow flying into the dewy night. She watches him gallop till his image begins to fade against the slurry blacktop. She doesn't breathe as she sees him pause, tense, and then leap in a single bound over the horizon. At that moment she realizes she has forgotten to climb upon his back.

171

The story ends there, with that image. In her brave moment of intimacy with the dog, she loses him. The woman is left behind.

Show—don't tell is an old truism taught by writing teachers to their students. Old truths are often the best. Using images to tell your story is an effective technique, eliminating the need for tedious exposition while opening up the mind (yours and the reader's) to poetry and picture.

34

WRITING SHORT STORIES

By Peter Meinke

For me, the hardest part of writing short stories is the plot, probably because I'm least interested in it. When I think of short stories I admire, I tend to remember characters, like John Updike's Marples, or Flannery O'Connor's good country people, and forget exactly what they did. If I waited until I had a plot clearly in mind before I got started, I'd still be waiting for my first story.

A short story is closer to a poem than to a novel. Tone, density, and intensity carry more weight than structure or logical development. In my stories, I usually begin with a character who interests me and let him (or her) take me where he wants to go. In the first draft, I follow. In the rewriting, I try to shape the story so it seems natural, or inevitable, or at least not totally arbitrary.

I "collect" characters in my notebook and often give them imaginary conversations. Before writing my story "The Piano Tuner," I had several characters in mind to write about—I think all of us can readily conjure up a fair number of characters who for one reason or another fascinate us—but I settled on one, perhaps because we were traveling on the Cape Fear River. I began to describe in my notebook a huge, frightening, unshaven drunken man, and to give him a number of speeches—about women, about cigarette smoking, about patriotism— that he seemed to want to say. I imagined him entering my house, which at that moment I was missing very much, and taking over. But on what pretext? He was becoming a real person to me, but like a Pirandello character, he was looking for a plot. All around me, as I wrote descriptions of this man, musicians were tuning their instruments.

Robert Frost said the secret of writing poetry is the ability to take advantage of happy accidents, and this applies as well to short stories. I knew nothing about tuning pianos, or expensive harps such as the one that eventually found its way into the story, but I knew those were just details. I had found a way to get this brute into my house, the beginning of a plot:

The piano tuner was a huge man, crowding the doorway. I hadn't known he was coming, but I got up from my desk to let him in; my wife was still out shopping. His head was small for his body, and his belt was almost hidden by the belly folding over it. I suppose I came up to about his shoulders, and the reek of his sweat was stunning. His stained T-shirt announced THE PIANO EXCHANGE.

After that, I had to do a little research. I had heard musicians talk about "bringing it up a tone"; I checked on what a tuning hammer was and what hand you held it in. You will be surprised at how few details you need to know in order to sound convincing. But there must be *some* details. We had an upright piano in our house, so I described it as well as I could, exaggerating its age and value. I must have been reasonably convincing, because after the story first appeared in *The Atlantic Monthly,* the president of the Piano Technician's Guild wrote a letter protesting that *their* piano tuners didn't behave like that! I was glad to hear it.

In my story the piano tuner gradually takes over the whole house. To make this believable, I had to make the speaker, the "I" of the story, wimpier and wimpier, while still retaining enough sympathetic traits for the reader to identify with him. I'm sure there's something of me in every character I create, even brutish dolts like the piano tuner, but there is a real temptation when you are speaking in a voice that at least in some ways resembles your own, to smooth him out, to make him likable, sensitive—well, sort of nice, like *yourself!* It's important to give the speaker whatever flaws are natural and in character, even though some of your friends might say, "I didn't realize you were such a klutz." (In my experience, whenever you write in the first person, no matter how bizarre the speaker's behavior or how entirely you "made him up," a fair percentage of your friends will identify you directly with the "I" of the story. Don't worry about it. Friends think about us a lot less than we think they do.)

I didn't know what the piano tuner was going to do, but I wasn't halfway through the story before I realized that he symbolized everything the WASP middle-class man was traditionally afraid of: brute strength, coarseness, rampant sexuality, anarchy, drunkenness. This realization also furthered the plot: a clash was inevitable.

174

In Wilmington we had watched a hopped-up black man standing in the middle of the street and doing karate kicks at cars—he seemed basically friendly and no one stopped or protested. I recognized that *he* would upset my central character, too, so I backed up and put him into my story, making him more menacing, a sort of partner with the piano tuner (the radio music at the end of the story implies he is back in the house). I guess what I'm saying is that you should just begin your story any which way, to tell it, to describe someone—and after you've got a good start, to look for its shape and meaning, like a potter with a lump of clay.

In that way, the plot will take care of itself, and if you're lucky, it will reverberate with suggestion for other people. The plot of "The Piano Tuner" is simple: A man lets another man into his house and lives to regret it. But people have written to me saying they think it's a symbolic tale of exploitation in the modern world, or a parable of the fierce energy of the artist versus the timidity of the critic, or a vision of the American male losing his masculinity. I hope all of these "interpretations" are true, and others as well. But I think it would be a mistake to sit down to write a story that would fulfill these interpretations. The writer works best when he or she is least self-conscious, especially in the beginning, and is just seized, like Coleridge's Ancient Mariner, with the need to tell a story.

Sometimes a plot idea will come to you early on, and this is a help as you work into your story: You have a direction in which to go. But because characters are more important than plot, you have to be willing to let your plot go and follow the characters instead. Also, there is a good chance that if *you* have a plot with a certain ending in mind, your reader will soon think of the same thing: The pre-plotted story stands a good chance of being not very surprising.

Another of my stories, "Even Crazy Old Barmaids Need Love," is a love story about a somewhat shady character named Daryl Dana and a Polish barmaid named Agnes (Agnieska). The "impulse" behind this story was just to describe a good bar. It begins:

It takes about six months to make a decent bar. When Phil Masters bought The Grouper he threw out the new jukebox with its rock songs and put in the old one of his father's with its mixture of golden oldies and country. He put in more lights and took out some tables. He kept the stuffed fish above the bar— an immense fat grouper with an expression of open-mouthed wild-eyed sur-

175

prise—but got rid of all the little black-and-white photos of the previous owner and his cronies holding up various fish between them.

The bar had been a biker bar, and my "idea" for the plot was to build up to a big climactic battle at the end, where Daryl Dana would get severely beaten up by the banished bikers but would prove himself brave enough and worthy of Agnes. In fact, that's the way I wrote it at first, with a great and bloody fight and a touching scene in the ambulance as they rode together to the hospital. But it didn't feel right: it seemed "programmed" and predictable and, more importantly, not true of the characters as they had developed, or at least not *showing something important about them* (anyone can get in a fight if he is unlucky enough).

So I muted the ending. This was a mature couple with checkered pasts, who would avoid confrontation if possible, in order to stay together. Daryl ducks the fight and has to decide if he can swallow his pride and return to the acting group he had earlier huffed out on:

He had already decided, and was steering them back through the sad streets, sweetened a little by the rich smell of old flowering trees with the lovely names: jacaranda, bougainvillea, magnolia, mimosa. He knew he was right because she held his hand tighter as they neared The Grouper. The party was still going on, more or less, though the noise was subdued and sober. Robertson was sitting at the end of a long scarred table, apparently declaiming a speech from some play. They watched through the window for a minute.
"Some show," said Daryl.
"Yes," she agreed. "Some show."
"Well, let's get our tickets." He pushed the door open and they walked in.

The ending sacrifices drama and excitement for more valuable qualities in a short story: credibility and suitability.

I suppose you can write a short story any way you want: unplotted, pre-plotted, loosely plotted, tightly plotted. My main point is that you should focus your energy and attention mainly on character: In the short story, the character *is* the plot.

176

35

REAL AND INVENTED PLACES

By Geoffrey Wolff

At the beginning of my novel *Providence,* there is an "Author's Note" that claims that "while the geography, neighborhoods, streets, and ancient history of my *Providence* are generally those of the New England city of Providence, Rhode Island, it is a place of the imagination. I have, for example, re-routed a river to suit my purpose, and every contemporary character who dwells within these pages is an invention; they who live and die here are not intended, should not be misunderstood, to be 'real.' "

Uh-huh. Sure. Tell us another. Hey, if that's the way you want it . . . Everybody knows about author's notes, those "purely coincidentals" attested to by writers dodging a lawsuit, or the cold-shoulder of kin, or—God forbid!—a bullet. Now, I'd hate to stand convicted of a want of cynicism, but let's just for the sake of amicable argument imagine that we have here an author's note that means exactly what it says, that the Providence of this book's title is a notion and region of one writer's dreams and inventions, a particular Providence, for better or worse singular, as different from the stories you build on the word providence as yours are different from your neighbor's.

If two people say "providence" and one thinks of a benign watchman while the other thinks of bad luck, those two will have a short and confusing conversation. They will not connect; neither will have what every storyteller wants and needs, an audience. If a writer makes a place called "Providence" and sets it in the high mountain ranges of Indiana, that whole-cloth creation, that fantasy, will assert its autonomy absolutely. That "Providence," as a setting, must create rather than inherit (and manipulate) a history, a context. No need in such a sci-fi "Providence" for an author's note, and no room for the Biltmore's Apogee, the Cheater's Club, the Turk's Head Building; no sense in naming the widest bridge in the world the Crawford Street Bridge.

Because the Providence I have made mine shares much geography but only some experience with the real city of Providence, Rhode Island, my novel may mislead, may disturb, may provoke skepticism in its citizens as to my motives, veracity, good will, and power to invent. Most of the questions such readers may raise about my novel are neither trivial nor stupid. Many of them drive directly to the heart of what fiction is and what it is not.

A couple of weeks ago I got a request from the producer of a local radio call-in talk show. She said the host of that show wished to interview me for a few moments in the early afternoon. I asked if her colleague had read the book, and she said he had not. That was O.K.: People are busy, and there are many books. To get a sense of this radio show I tuned in and learned from the host much about my book. He told his audience that while I had "disguised" it as a novel, *Providence* was no such thing. It was, he declared—his opinion unclouded by a reading of the novel—a "real book."

Well, he and I never did have our chat, but since then I have turned over in my mind, perhaps too obsessively, what in the world the fellow might have meant by the modifier "real" in his thumbnail sobriquet. Let's try to imagine his thoughts:

By "real" might he have meant true? If so, did he take into account the consequence on any narrative, in any mode, of point of view? I have in recent years written books of fact—a biography and an autobiography—and they taught me that the word truth, as meant by a scientist, a philosopher, or even a historian, is unavailable to literary narrative. Facts—the date of this person's birth, the address of that person's third house—may seem to be *there,* immutably, but they aren't. To be trivially plain, let me note that for a biographer to give a reader an industrialist's 1968 income on the "factual" evidence of that industrialist's 1968 1040 return is not necessarily to have written something true. More important, the storyteller's vantage, his partiality, conditions which facts live and which are suppressed. Art is above all a process of repudiation, whereby the chaotic thisness and thatness of life are shaped into a semblance of order, and this is as true of a "real" book—biography, let's say—as of an unreal book, like Henry James's *Washington Square,* Charles Dickens's *Tale of Two Cities,* Thomas Mann's *Death in Venice.*

But perhaps by "real" our radio host meant merely that he had heard tell that my *Providence* uses place-names that appear on city maps:

Benevolent Street, Atwells Avenue, Meeting Street. I have been asked if I fear being sued by the Biltmore for having set scenes in the downtown landmark. I hadn't considered the problem, frankly, any more than Scott Fitzgerald must have fretted about a lawsuit from New York's Plaza when he set that wonderful summer showdown between Gatsby, Tom and Daisy there. No reader thinks twice about finding Park Avenue in a New York novel, but for some Providence readers it has been a puzzling, perhaps irritating experience, to find *their* proper nouns in my damned book.

Why this might be so is not, for me, without interest, but let me indulge here in an aside about a place-name I am ashamed of, a place-name that my carelessness got wrong, and for me importantly wrong. You will find in my *Providence,* as you drive its pages east on Wickenden Street toward India, a place called "Fox's Point." Not a few people have remarked, with quite proper contempt, my pathetic adumbration of a real place, disfigured by my apostrophe *s,* called Fox Point. I'm irritated by my carelessness not because I got a "real" place wrong, but because I got a "right" word wrong. "Fox" Point is at least one hundred percent better than "Fox's" Point because it *sounds* better. A piece of writing, for me, *is* its sound. If the city of Providence has been in this book a principal character, my hero is the sound of the city's voices, its language, the expression of its singularity.

But I'm running ahead of myself, a little. I believe the reason some good citizens of Providence have felt proprietary about their city's proper nouns bears upon my license. I don't mean the liberties I have taken with the place, but my standing, my authority, my right to write about it. I am, after all, a newcomer, a relentless transient, California-born and raised in Florida, Seattle, Tennessee, Connecticut, here and there. My family moved here from Vermont, a ski town in the Mad River Valley.

I've got a theory about sightseers, self-serving, of course. My theory uses locutions like *sharp-eyed* and describes tourists like me as *putting their ears on.* Thing is, I believe this theory, because I know when we made our way to Providence six years ago I was astonished by it. It is one hell of a place, take the word of an outsider. Where it is beautiful, it is more beautiful than other cities of my experience. Its ugliness is in some places breathtaking. It has pizzazz, brass, presence, an idiom. Tell me if the place bores you. It has never bored me. I think one of the things the citizens of Providence have in common is a capacity for

179

astonishment. And one of the sources of our astonishment is the imagination, energy and sublime stupidity spent by fellow citizens eager to have what they have not earned. I mean that we suffer preposterous crimes here, and that we also enjoy the most wonderful damned crime stories. I mean that as an outsider I was quickly robbed of many belongings, and just as quickly enriched, brought to life, by the extreme acts and speech of my near neighbors.

And here, again, comes the question of license. There is judgment in my words. I'd like to think of my impulse as discrimination in its best sense, a sorting of what matters from what does not, but some Providence readers have asked, with varying degrees of decorous restraint and plain anger, where I get off coming here from wherever the hell and holding their city up, holding my version of their city up, to the world's view? And don't they recognize some of those faces, a bit of that recent history? Of course, of course. Any novel—or any novel by me—is a synthetic composition fabricated of found art (who could improve on the nickname "Moron"?) and bits and pieces taken from a rag-bag of observation, memory, dreamy invention, willful creation. This character's jug-ears come from the guy a desk ahead in the 4th grade; that woman's "jeepers" was heard years ago at a Los Angeles drive-in restaurant, uttered by a waitress working on roller skates.

A corollary version of the question of license and civic responsibility, more forward-thinking, asks why I had to hang out all that dirty laundry—those crimes, rip-offs, pains, erotic fixations, sudden and lingering deaths—for public view? Why couldn't I have looked on the bright side, seen the Preservation Society's good works, lauded benefactors and savants? Why such a heavy cargo of low-lifes?

First off, let me say that I know enough about the world to realize that Providence has no monopoly on crime, corruption, bozos, prisoners of sex, the dead and dying. This is so obvious that to say it seems silly, but it's worth remembering that a novel, if it's good, is not written to deplore, or even to mend. It is written to expose, sure enough, but not in the way an investigative newspaper or television report exposes. It is written to expose our deepest apprehensions. (If there is solace in hoarding, miser-like, miserably and meanly, our most precious secrets, this solace is set inexorably against the writer's calling. I mean that ladies' and gentlemen's distrust of writers is well founded; writers are temperamental enemies of good-mannered decorous reticence, except as such verbal reserve might have formal properties useful to their work's purpose, the telling of secrets.) The fiction I admire is written to show through words—which *are* a novel's deeds—how seemingly small choices—whether or not to open that stranger's locked door—ramify out, touching the lives of the polity, the community, the neighborhood, the family asleep upstairs when that choice gets made.

Providence, city of two hills divided by a downtown river valley where we all meet in court or commerce or to send letters to the world, is substantial enough to resonate with the consequences of a long, long history of good and bad choices. It is small enough to hold us all, so the act of one truly touches the many. I have found the city to be like an apartment house with thin walls. Its voices, like those coming from John Cheever's "Enormous Radio," have been magically amplified. I hear the thuds and scuffles next door, the awkward motions of love. My novel is written from the premise that acts *matter,* that individual decisions *are* a city's history. The acts I have chosen to explore in my *Providence* may seem superficially to be extreme acts. Maybe they are extreme acts, but who here would gainsay their dailyness? My ambition was, in fact, to explore the limits my characters impose on one another, and more important, on themselves. Lisa will pass counterfeit tens, but not twenties. Skippy will rob the downstairs of a house, but will essay no upper invasion, until he does. Baby will kill the Moron but can't, despite himself, kill Skippy. Adam is a man of the law, until he breaks it. Tom, ditto. What does it take to push the limits?

It takes pressure. Fiction is *about* pressure. Nothing personal: my novel, like most, draws its heat not from the sun, but from friction, discord, opposition. In a novel of consequence, I believe, someone wants something from someone who does not want to give it. A bribe. A wallet. Love. Immortality. A kind word. And friction is made sensible, available to the heart through the senses, by language. Thus the idiom of my *Providence* attempts, by its simulation of lazy ease or frantic compression, whether trailing off fecklessly or sprung to the breaking point in its urgency, to enact will and friction. There is in my novel's language a kind of verbal aggression that *is* the battle waged by "little people" against their masters. It is by language that we even the odds against such bullies as bureaucrats, criminals, unloving beloveds, and death. And whatever its powers, excesses, and failures, this language— the coarse and fine music of a city in a time—I learned at *this* time, in *this* city. For which Providence, my thanks, "real" thanks.

181

36

POINT OF VIEW: EXPERIMENT IN LIVING

By Marjorie Franco

A FEW years ago I walked into a New York office, gave my name to the receptionist and sat down. The receptionist, a young girl, turned to me and inquired, "Are you an actress?" "No," I said, disappointing her, "I'm a fiction writer." I had the feeling she wanted me to be an actress—it's more glamorous, I suppose—and to make amends I said, "Inside many a writer lives an actor." Nodding agreeably, but clearly dissatisfied, the girl returned to her work. Had she been interested I could have explained that writing, like acting, is an experiment in living, and that the writer (and the actor), by lifting himself out of his own particular life, looks at life from another point of view.

What is point of view, and what does it have to do with writing, or acting, or the persons behind either of these creative arts? The dictionary says point of view is a "position from which something is considered or evaluated." All right; that seems clear. The writer takes up a position from which to tell a story. What position? A reader might say, "That's simple; he tells a story in either the first or third person." It might seem simple, but for the writer it is not.

There are at least six third-person viewpoints and five first-person viewpoints, some rarely used. To discuss all of these or to discuss technique without a story to hang it on can be confusing. Even though the writer has an intellectual mastery of viewpoint techniques, he may not create a good viewpoint character. Writers learn by doing. Did Chekhov sit down and ask himself, "Should I adopt the position of concealed narrator and third-person protagonist narrator restricted, or what?" Or did he simply write "The Kiss"?

This is not to say that it is unimportant to learn technique, for a writer needs to learn as much as he can about the tools of his craft. But tools are only a means to something more, and a preoccupation with them can lead to mechanical writing. Viewpoint, then, is not a matter of manipulation, of attaching oneself, willy-nilly, to a position, to a character, and then telling the story through that character's mind and feelings. Viewpoint is organic, and writers have in common with the actor the method to make it work.

An actor trained in the Stanislavski method knows the psychology of his character; he knows *how* he does things because first he knows *why*. The actor tries to put himself in his character's place, to enter his world, live his life, master his actions, his thoughts and feelings. His truth. It is not enough merely to think of an emotion. Abstract emotions don't come across, or they fall into clichés. It is better to imagine what a character might think or do in a *certain situation*. Then the emotion comes of itself.

A writer uses a similar method of organic viewpoint. He puts himself in his character's place, enters his world, indeed creates his world, suffers his pains and celebrates his joys. If a writer has never laughed or cried at his typewriter, then I doubt if he has ever been deeply inside a character.

Before a writer takes up a viewpoint position he might do well to consider his own temperament and personality and the limitations these impose on his choices. Fiction is personal, as personal as the writer's imagination and emotional experience. New writers are often told, "Write what you know." I would broaden that by saying, "Write what you know emotionally." Love, hate, anger, joy, fear—these are universal. They become unique when they are connected to experience. Our emotional experiences are stored within us. Filtered through memory and a well-developed imagination, they can be called up, made fresh and organized into the work at hand. Creative imagination is the writer's valuable gift, and even though it is somewhat limited by his experience, within that sphere of experience it is unlimited in variety and combination. Hopefully the writer is always enlarging his sphere, adding to his storehouse with outward experience in reality.

Out of the sphere of my emotional experience I wrote "The Poet of Evolution Avenue" (*Redbook*), the story of a young wife and mother who was, also, a bad poet. She believed her creative gift was being hampered by the intrusion of her family. She had neither the

183

time nor the privacy to write a real poem. Time and privacy are practically forced on her in the form of a vacation alone in her father's California apartment, but it isn't until she is ready to go home that she is able to write a real poem, and then only because she doesn't want to go home empty-handed.

This story is based on the old Ivory Tower idea: a poet is more productive when isolated from the world. My poet discovered that she had been making excuses for herself, that her world was her stimulus, and that she had trouble producing poetry without it.

The idea for that story came out of my own emotional experience. Some years earlier I had gone to California to be near my father while he was in the hospital undergoing surgery. For three weeks I lived alone in his apartment, a large, tight-security building in which I rarely saw the other residents. I had brought my typewriter, thinking I would turn out a volume or two between hospital visits. It didn't work. I was accustomed to working with people around. Interruptions. Interruptions can be marvelous. They take the place of pacing, a necessary activity of some writers. I learned that I am not an Ivory Tower writer, ideal as that may seem; I need the stimulus of family and friends.

Every writer has his own voice, and it is up to him to find it and use it with authority. That voice comes through as male or female, child or adult, humorous or serious, but behind it, within it, is the author's brooding presence, his vision of life. He describes the world from his point of view. He is on intimate terms with his viewpoint characters. Henry James could imagine what his focal character (he is never named) in *The Aspern Papers* might think and do when he is forced to admit to the woman who loves him that he has been using her for his personal gain. But I doubt if James could have lived inside Bigger, as Richard Wright did in *Native Son*, and chased and killed the huge rat in a Chicago tenement. Who is to say one view is better or worse than another? Each is different, unique.

Recognizing his limitations, an author adopts a viewpoint position he can understand emotionally as well as intellectually. My story, "Miss Dillon's Secret" (*Redbook*), is about a teacher. I have never been a teacher, but teaching is within the sphere of my emotional experience. I have been a student, of course, and my husband, now a principal, was once a teacher. His experiences have rubbed off on me. I believe that a natural teacher is born, not made, that the qualities in such a person work together to make learning exciting. The title character in my story, Miss Dillon, is drawn from a real person, an experienced teacher whose students come back to visit her with their husbands and wives and children and grandchildren.

I adopted the viewpoint position of a young teacher who had worked with Miss Dillon. There were more decisions for me to make. Will I place myself inside or outside the viewpoint character? And how far inside or outside? This can be a difficult choice, for each character has its own limitations, and the author, to keep his voice appropriate to the viewpoint, puts limits on his "knowledge" accordingly. He seems to know less than he does. Consider, for example, Hemingway's camera-eye view which limits his "knowledge" to what can be seen from the outside. Or, at the other extreme, Joyce's deep internalizing, which limits him in the other direction.

For my viewpoint character I adopted a position somewhere in between. With the story told in the third person, my character's problems are external, but her discovery of Miss Dillon's secret is internal, brought about by an emotional experience with one of her former students.

We might ask ourselves certain questions concerning viewpoint: 1) Who will be the narrator? author, in first or third person? character, in first person? or nobody (omniscient narrator)? 2) From what angle does the narrator tell the story? Above, center, front, periphery, shifting? 3) Where does the author place the reader? Near, far, shifting?

Sometimes an author adopts a viewpoint position instinctively, and all goes well. The voice flows from a stable position. At other times an author finds himself tangled in clumsy sentences and tedious explanations, surrendering his surprises too early, battling predictability, placing his best scenes offstage. When this happens, the problem could very well be the viewpoint he chose. He may be looking from the wrong angle. Usually I can tell by the way it "feels" if I'm in a good or poor viewpoint. But not always. Four years ago I wrote a short story called "The Boy Who Cooked." The

185

title character, Benny, was the antagonist, and the viewpoint character was a woman protagonist whose name changed with each of the many versions I wrote. I couldn't sell the story. But I continued writing it, on and off, for four years, always keeping the boy, but frequently changing the characters around him, including the viewpoint character. The total number of pages devoted to that story runs into several hundred, which is some indication of my devotion to a character. But finally I gave up and put the story away.

Meanwhile, I had written and sold a story called, "No Such Thing as a Happy Marriage" (*Redbook*), in which the viewpoint character was a wife and mother named Jenny. Six months after that story was published, my editor, in a letter to me, mentioned Benny, the boy who cooked. Even before I had finished reading the letter, Benny, like Lazarus, rose from the dead. Why couldn't I write a new story for Benny? And why couldn't I surround him with the same cast of characters I had used in "No Such Thing as a Happy Marriage," with Jenny as the viewpoint character? I could, and I did. This time the viewpoint felt right; the voice flowed clearly from a stable position, and I wrote the story in a matter of hours. After four years of roaming through my typewriter, Benny had found his place, and his story, "The Boy Who Cooked," was published in *Redbook*.

The author's attitude toward a character (and his desire to create a similar attitude in the reader) can help determine the angle from which he views him. If the character is obviously sympathetic, the reader will identify. With some characters, however, the reader may feel only a tentative sympathy, until he is shocked into understanding by some revelation which allows him to feel complete sympathy. Sometimes, reader and character start out with a great distance between them. Perhaps their worlds are totally different. The author gradually pulls the reader into the character's world, and the reader ends by feeling sympathy. (I have this experience, as a reader, when I read Jean Genêt, for example.) A difficult relationship for an author to achieve is one in which the reader is forced to identify, perhaps unconsciously, with a character he dislikes. He is left wondering what there was about the story that fascinated him. What he may not realize is that, being human, we all have our share of unattractive qualities, and seeing them in someone else stirs our recognition. Playwright Harold Pinter frequently achieves this kind of relationship.

In my story, "An Uncompromising Girl" (*Redbook*), my aim was for tentative sympathy and eventual complete sympathy. As the author (concealed narrator), I speak in the third person through the focal character. The channels of information between author and reader are a combination of the author's words, thoughts, and perceptions, and the character's words, actions, thoughts, perceptions and feelings. I used the angle of the character attempting to see herself from the outside, but erring in her vision—a position which placed limits on my "knowledge" of the character.

Earlier I spoke of the writer's voice, which I related to his vision of life and which includes his entire personality. Now, to that voice I would add two more voices: the story voice, which is the pace, the music, the tone of the story; and the voice of the viewpoint character, since it is through his eyes that we see everything that happens. Actually, it is impossible to separate all these voices, fused as they are into a creation that has passed through a maturing process in the author's mind and found its way to the page, either in harmony or dissonance. But for the sake of clarity, let us for a moment consider the voice of the viewpoint character.

If a story is told in the first person through a character (and not the author), then that character's voice is ever-present, and the writer, like the method actor, must know the character's every thought, act, feeling and desire. He must know his truth, his conscious and unconscious life, what he wants, or thinks he wants, and the difference between the two. My story "Don't Call Me Darling" (*Redbook*), was written from such a viewpoint. I had to know my character's attitude toward herself as a woman pursuing a career. I had to know how she felt about women's rights in general. And how she felt about friendship and human communication. I had to understand her intellect, her ambitions, her habits, and her insights. When she spoke, she revealed herself as a careful individual, and this voice had to remain consistent throughout the story, even though some of her attitudes were undergoing a change.

When an author knows the details of action and speech in a

character, he is in control of his material. He can become more familiar with his character by spending time with him, engaging him in conversation or argument, as if he were a living entity. He may even want to get up from his typewriter to act out a detail, a gesture, or an entire scene, in order to visualize it more clearly in his mind. Creating characters, seeing them come to life, is an exciting experience.

The entire experience of a story, from start to finish—and it may cover a period of several years—is an exciting one, in spite of the hard work, frustration and failures. Not a small portion of that excitement lies in the discoveries that are made, for in any work of creative imagination one looks for insights. What does the story have to say? Does it reinforce a shallow view of life? Or does it open up new insights for the viewpoint character? When I write a story about a character who seems very real to me, am I not at the same time making a discovery about myself? Writing, like acting, is an experiment in living. It is looking at life from another viewpoint. And life can be exciting wherever it is lived, or re-created— on the stage, or on the page.

37

HOW TO BE YOUR OWN CRITIC

By Margaret Chittenden

One of our most difficult tasks as writers is to be objective about our own work. It's not easy to convince ourselves once a novel is finished that this is not necessarily the greatest story ever told. But we have to be honest with ourselves. We have to learn to criticize our manuscripts *constructively,* one step at a time. What should we look for?

From time to time, as I've read novel manuscripts by unpublished authors, I've discovered three main flaws that occur over and over again: the *beginning* is too slow, the *middle* is padded with irrelevant action, and the *ending* is either too long, or too unbelievable, or both.

Beginnings

The beginning of a novel should introduce your main characters, show where the story is taking place, and hint at the conflict. But none of these things should be revealed under static conditions. The story should get under way with the first word on the first page. The reader does not want to wade through a whole river of information and description of the characters before the story gets moving.

Yet many novel manuscripts that I've read either start out with long, long passages of exposition, or else they start with a paragraph of action and *then* go into long passages of exposition. It is not necessary to tell the reader everything about the main characters in the first chapter; you should hold back some of that information. Often, you can leave some of it out altogether. As the writer, you need to know everything there is to know about the main characters before you start writing the book, but you don't need to tell the reader right off about their parents, grandparents, ex-lovers, degrees they've earned in college, every happening in their lives that took place before the start of the story.

Usually, it's best to begin a novel with some kind of action going on, but not necessarily with the protagonist in an airplane circling the airport just before landing—a very popular opening that gives the main character lots of time for soul-searching. Instead, show the main character doing something, going somewhere, talking to someone. Make the opening *intriguing* and then continue with your characters in action, introducing *short* pieces of information that are essential. Later, you can weave in other essential acts through dialogue and in short quotes from the main character's thoughts. Be sure your reader can tell *where* the story is taking place. Don't open with pages of dialogue without giving at least a hint of the setting and who these characters are. Don't give the impression that the story is set in a drawing room and have it turn out to be in a car or an airplane.

Middles

The middle is the place where the novel should *develop*. Here again, writers often put in too much introspection on the part of the main character. Let your reader know what your main character has on his or her mind, but keep it brief. Also, when you write your original synopsis, make sure that enough *action* takes place in the middle section. Frequently, novel synopses by beginning writers have long beginnings and long endings, but the reader would have to take a giant leap between the two. The story doesn't grab the reader at the start and take him or her *suspensefully* to the end.

In plotting the middle, apply the law of cause and effect. Instead of simply asking, what comes next, ask yourself, what would happen as a *result* of this? When the synopsis is finished, go through and check for the *cause-and-effect*.

Here is an example from the synopsis of my novel, *This Dark Enchantment*. Karin has come to Quebec City to assist Charles in writing an architectural history of the city. *Because* of this she meets Doctor Paul Dufresne, whom she first sees being solicited by a seedy young man who looks as though he's on drugs. *Because* of what she sees, Karin suspects that Paul might be involved in drug dealing. *Because* of this, she is not receptive to his advances, and *because* of this . . . and so on. I don't write the synopsis this straightforwardly, but I do check to make sure it could read that way. Cause and effect—two much neglected, often forgotten words in novel writing.

Endings

If you have your causes and effects in proper sequence, the ending will be logical, though not too predictable. I try to sustain suspense in the main plot while tying up any loose ends in the sub-plots, so that the reader will want to stay with me till THE END. But once I've reached the end, when resolutions or solutions are arrived at, I try to exit as rapidly as possible.

It's also necessary to strive for *believability* in the ending. For example, if you've had your hero being really nasty to the heroine in the beginning—which seems to be a popular thing to do—you can't suddenly have him be sweet and lovable at the end, unless you've shown cause and effect in the middle. Some of the manuscripts I've read in which the hero and heroine ended up at the altar would not convince the reader that any sane woman would want this man, or even want to speak to him again.

Now that you've checked the beginning, middle and end of your novel manuscript, it's time to look at it page by page, word by word.

Try going backwards through the manuscript, one page at a time, so you don't get caught up in the flow of the story. Look first for too many *wells, justs* and *verys,* and cross out most of them. Then check spelling and grammar, looking especially for mistakes in syntax. (In a recent novel manuscript, I read the following: "Her shoulders squared and left the room.")

Check to make sure the nouns are specific, that you have written, "the weeping willow" rather than "the tree," the "cocker spaniel" rather than "the dog."

Scrutinize verbs. Try to replace passive verbs with active verbs. "David hugged Joanna" is stronger than "Joanna was hugged by David."

Cut out as many adjectives and adverbs as you can, and check punctuation. (I have a tendency to forget commas.)

Once all this nit-picking is done, make yourself very comfortable, preferably in a recliner, then read the book from beginning to end, pretending it was written by a writer whose work you don't particularly enjoy. If you find yourself going to sleep, take a long, hard look at the passage that brought on your fatigue. Try to read straight through, as a reader would, making brief notes in the margins of anything obviously wrong—sections that seem slow or dull or unbelievable or trite. Mark scenes that don't seem *visual* enough, transitions that are too abrupt.

Once you've finished this initial reading, revise all the things you've marked. Then read the whole manuscript again. Check the movement of the characters, so that you haven't had a character go off on a week's trip and then be present in a scene that takes place the next day. Check characterization. Have these invented people come to life? Can you see them—not just at the beginning, but all the way through? Do you *care* about them?

I try to check diligently to make sure my heroine has *acted,* not just reacted. I don't care for timid heroines. I want to be sure my young woman has done something for herself and not waited for the hero to initiate all the action. Has *your* heroine come through as a real, caring, compassionate, intelligent woman? If this is a romance novel, is she *worth* loving?

Take a close look at your hero. Is he a real human being with admirable qualities, or is he just an ad for jockey shorts?

Next, check on viewpoint. If the entire novel is told from the heroine's point of view, all of the action must be filtered through her point of view. The reader should not see, hear, learn or observe anything that the heroine cannot see, hear, learn or observe. Some editors have told me they don't mind seeing the viewpoint character from the outside occasionally, but I'm a purist about viewpoint. I try never to write, "Tears rolled down her beautifully sculptured cheeks." One: This sort of thing makes the heroine sound conceited. Two: Such a description jars the reader into looking at the heroine from the outside, instead of looking at everything through her eyes. When in doubt, I change the sentence temporarily into first person. I wouldn't write, "Tears rolled down *my* beautifully sculptured cheeks." So when I'm writing in her viewpoint, my heroine can *feel* her tears, but she can't *see* them. She can *look* at people, but she doesn't look at them with her "sparkling amethyst eyes."

If the writer presents the story from the main character's viewpoint, it's difficult to describe her completely, without using the trite device of having her look in the mirror, but it can be done. In my book *Song of Desire,* for example, Vicki's aunt tells her it's O.K. for her to look like an ad for sunshine and vitamins. Vicki herself complains that when people look at her they say, "Ah, a California Girl," and expect her to run around with a surfboard under her arm and not a thought in her head. Maintaining one viewpoint assures greater reader identification. It also gives unity to the emotions.

However, if your novel is written in multiple viewpoint, you still need

192

to check to be sure that you haven't bounced in and out of several characters' minds in a short space of time. Viewpoint-hopping can be very confusing to a reader.

Once you are sure the viewpoint is consistent, make certain all the characters' actions have been properly motivated, so no one does anything without having a reason. Then ask yourself if any of the dialogue sounds stilted. Do the young people talk as young people do, or do they sound like senior citizens? "That's exceedingly kind of you," for instance, is not something a young person would usually say today.

Next, try to unravel the various threads in your story to make sure you haven't dropped any halfway through the novel, and that they are all tied up at the end. In *Song of Desire,* for example, one thread dealt with the hero's acting career, another with the heroine's career as an interior designer. A third thread dealt with the hero's young sister and her adventures, and a fourth with thefts from a hotel. In a multi-layered novel, it's easy to lose track of one of the threads, so this aspect of the manuscript must be carefully checked.

After all these questions have been answered and all necessary revisions are completed, read the whole manuscript again. By now you should be thoroughly sick of it, so if it still holds *your* interest, it should hold an editor's and a reader's. After this final reading, put the manuscript aside and think the story through, making sure you haven't missed anything significant.

Your aim in all this self-criticism is to produce the best book you can possibly produce. Before you send a completed manuscript to an agent or an editor, it should be the best work you can do. This is the writer's responsibility, the writer's task, the writer's joy.

38

MIDDLE-OF-THE-BOOK BLUES
Ten Ways to Get Your Novel Back on the Track

BY PHYLLIS A. WHITNEY

MIDDLE-of-the-book blues! I get them every time, and sometimes more than once along the way. The enthusiasm with which I started out has evaporated. The excitement of discovering and developing a new set of characters, a new setting and situations, lies in the past, and freshness is gone. Boredom is a dreadful state for any writer, and it must be dealt with promptly.

Nevertheless, forcing oneself to write is not the answer. Boredom is usually a warning that all is not well, so that the creative part of the brain is balking. Fortunately, I've been adrift on these becalmed waters before, so it's not as frightening as it was the first few times it happened. Now I pay attention to the warning and take several specific steps to turn myself around and rekindle interest in my work. You may develop a different set of steps for yourself, or adapt some of these for your own use.

1. When I find myself stopped, it is often because I'm not clear about where I am going next, or because I'm taking a mistaken direction, and my unconscious is alerting me. The first thing I do is to talk to myself on paper—whether in pencil or on the typewriter. I discuss the problems with myself, looking for leads that will help me understand what is wrong, and how I can start my imagination working again.

I jot down every stray idea that occurs to me that might be used in future action. I find that the mere act of setting something on paper can stir up the creative juices. Since this isn't really writing-for-keeps, there's no strain. At this point I take care not to be critical of any notion that comes my way. The sorting out, the judging can come later. Being critical too early may stop the flow.

2. Next I re-examine each character in turn, testing for ways in which

unforeseen action can be produced. Is there some hidden relationship between this character and that one—something I haven't thought of before? In one novel it suddenly developed that one of my important characters had been married years before to a secondary character in the story. Like me, my main character knew nothing of this marriage. The moment I discovered this, all sorts of possibilities opened up. My imagination stopped balking and went into action—because I had fed it something intriguing to work on.

Conflict and interest can grow endlessly out of our characters. I always keep in mind Brian Garfield's advice to "jolt the reader." Our characters are full of surprises if we give them half a chance. So I try to open up those past lives and develop new and unexpected turns for my plot.

3. Settings, interior and exterior, are always good sources for new plot possibilities. Each background is different and individual, and the setting itself will provide endless story material.

When I went to Sedona, Arizona, for the background of *Vermilion,* one of my first impressions of that stunning Red Rock country was of a line of tall rocks that reminded me of Egyptian statues. Some seemed to have faces carved into them by nature. I saw such "statues" in the red rocks a number of times, and I took color pictures of them. Later, when I studied these snapshots at home, the mystical possibilities began to stir in my imagination until I had part of the main theme of my story.

Exploring your setting again when you reach a static period can furnish new material that will make you eager to get back to your writing. Out of just such feeding of the imagination does inspiration grow.

Whenever I travel to find a new background for a novel, I am on the lookout for anything mysterious, any setting in which something nefarious might happen. West Martello Tower is an old Civil War fortress in Key West that I roamed through and knew that I would want to use in a novel at some point. It is now the home of the Key West Garden Club, and a variety of tropical plants and trees have been planted within the fort's enclosure. The fort is built against a hill, so that it is partly underground, and there are vaulted brick passageways and ceilings—all perfect for scenes of mystery! The setting itself was a challenge to my imagination.

4. It is important for my characters to interact with my settings. In

Vermilion my heroine is haunted by the faces in the rock. The mystical elements provided by the imaginary character, "Vermilion," are brought out all the more by the setting itself. Until setting *integrates* with character, I have only a travelogue.

When I was writing *Domino,* set in the Colorado Rockies, I wanted to use a tiny ghost town that was blowing away to dust. In the plotting, I devised ways in which this little town could affect the heroine's life and become so forceful a part of the story that the book could carry the town's name in the title.

For me, one of the most stimulating preparations for writing is this deliberate examination of character and setting, to find the ties that chain them together.

5. Of course, in the process of collecting background material, the real people I meet who live in a particular place are endlessly fascinating. I talk to everyone who will talk to me, though I'm not looking for *their* stories: I like to make up my own. Encounters with strangers provide take-off points for story ideas, though these may not come to me until later. For example, I saw a woman on a pier in Key West flying a spectacular kite, and I was able to use her to pick up a scene that was lagging.

In Carmel, California, an elderly sculptor whom I met in the Monterey Library invited me to see his beautiful home. Of course I jumped at the chance, since I always need to discover how people live in the setting I'm visiting and will want to write about later on.

All these elements make a rich stew of material and later, just going through pictures and brochures and reading the notes I've taken can set me off on interesting story trails.

However, not being able to travel doesn't mean that I can't write. When I had knee surgery, I had to forgo a trip to Newport, but I wrote a book about it anyway, leaning heavily on photographs and research material and finding someone who would check my manuscript for mistakes.

Wherever one lives, there are interesting corners, villages, city streets. When I couldn't take a long trip, I wrote about the place where I live, Cold Spring Harbor on Long Island, which became the background for my novel *Rainsong.*

6. In the planning stages, I always look for ways in which to make my main character's situation intolerable. Putting on emotional pres-

sure leads to conflict, explosions, action. In the opening of *Rainsong,* my heroine's husband—a famous pop singer—has died under mysterious circumstances. To escape the furor of the media, she accepts an invitation to an old Gold Coast mansion on Long Island. In the quiet of this huge house, she hopes to recover her talent for song writing. I asked myself how I could jolt my heroine and make her situation even more unbearable and frightening. One night she hears music playing in the supposedly empty house. Her dead husband's voice drifts up to her, singing the "rainsong" she had written for him. There are chills aplenty here, and the pressure is on.

Since *Jane Eyre,* the character hidden away and kept secret from the heroine is always fascinating, and possible variations for developing plots from this situation are endless. I never mind if a story idea or character has been used before, as long as I can give it a new twist. In *Poinciana,* my heroine becomes aware of the old woman living in a cottage on the grounds of her husband's Palm Beach house. By doling out a little information at a time, I fed the heroine's curiosity (and the reader's), until the confrontation scene between the old woman and the young one could furnish real jolts, and bring about the realization that the situation was intolerable for both my heroine and the old woman.

7. Since none of our characters leaps into existence full blown but must grow out of the events that have shaped them, it pays to look into past happenings, which may have a tremendous effect on the present. Of course, I do some of this in the plotting stages for my novel, but I can do so even more effectively when I know my story people and have seen them in action.

Characters who are dead before the story starts can be almost as important in the action as the live characters. There are always secrets in the past that still influence and affect the present and make a splendid source of new action. (*Rebecca* is an outstanding example.)

In writing *Dream of Orchids,* I found that the second wife of the heroine's father—dead a year before the novel begins—was still very much alive in the memories of the other characters, because of events she had set in motion. Jolts and surprises again—and a rich source of story action to pull me back on the track.

Force your characters to make decisions, for this always results in action. If you find that your main character is drifting along without much drive, you may have found one source for your lagging interest.

Not only the main characters, but other characters as well, need to make choices. Such decisions force characters to plan and act—often against one another.

8. Research in books and libraries can be an endless source of exciting ideas. When I started work on my Key West novel, *Dream of Orchids,* I had no suspicion that I would become interested in the subject of orchids, or in action that involved diving to a sunken Spanish galleon. I am not an orchid fancier, nor have I ever done any scuba diving. But after bringing home ten books on raising orchids, I could write about them with some assurance, and the orchids themselves gave me all sorts of plot material, including attempted murder. My research included a visit to an orchid greenhouse in my own locality—with a list of questions in hand.

My agent had suggested wreck diving as a subject I might use for the Key West background. I resisted at first, feeling that it had all been done too many times before, and I didn't know anything about scuba diving and wasn't interested anyway. She paid no attention to such nonsense and mailed me four issues of *National Geographic* with accounts of treasure brought up in recent years from Caribbean wrecks. Eventually, I was able to write those diving scenes with confidence. I was under water in my imagination, while my typewriter stayed dry.

A rule learned long ago: *If you don't know, find out.* Once you have your facts right, your imagination can take you anywhere you want to go.

9. I like to be specific about the questions I must find answers for before I begin to write. Very early in my plotting phase, I jot down all those questions for which I have no answers.

When I feel becalmed, I take out the list, cross off those that have been answered, and add others to the list. Since I never throw away any of my plotting material, but keep it all in labeled envelopes, I can give you examples of some questions that I wrote down when I was in the middle of writing *Emerald*. They will mean nothing to anyone else, but may give you a glimpse of the method I have found worked for me.

What action does Linda take to protect Monica from suspicion in Saxon's death?

What does Carol learn from Henry Arlen, without realizing until later what he has told her?

What about Linda's quarrel with Saxon? When? Where?

These go on and on, and when nothing else works, I turn to my question list and pick one of them to *think* about *at that moment*. This is the time for thinking, not writing. When the answers begin to come, my interest grows and I can push ahead.

10. Somewhere during this time, I may search back into my own life and emotions. What have I felt deeply about? What has angered me? What has made me happy? Parallels between our own emotions and those of our characters are always important. We can pull those feelings out of memory and apply them to the people in our stories.

Discouragement need never be permanent. It only feels that way while you are going through it. Stir up your imagination. Put in new combinations, new energy—open all those closed doors! Once you see what's out there, you won't be able to resist stepping through to make the novel in your typewriter even better.

39

AGAINST NOSTALGIA

By Sumner Locke Elliott

HAVING BEEN born in Australia but having lived in the United States since 1948 and having written four-and-a-half novels with settings in Australia (the other half of one is set in California and New York), I am sometimes lauded, sometimes berated, for writing nostalgia. To both I object strenuously. *Webster's* defines nostalgia as "homesickness, a sentimental or morbid yearning for the past." In nearly forty years, I have never had a twinge of homesickness and most certainly no morbid yearning for the past, the past being generally the reason that I fled Australia. I am not prone to tears at "Waltzing Matilda" nor the smell of rain on eucalyptus leaves, and I am not bound to compare every harbor in the world to Sydney's. Possibly because I was born not unpatriotic, but un-nationalistic. I have never been easily aroused by the marching bands, the flags and confetti, or the insistence of mass enthusiasm. But I am moved more often by trivia, by hearing in my mind the raucous sound of thousands of green locusts (which is what they call cicadas there) in the quickening mornings of the marvelous Australian summers, which, unlike the summers of the east coast of America, are invigorating. I'm moved by the gift of a little mountain devil, which is a face of a small pointed elf with horns and which grows on a prickly bush in the Blue Mountains of New South Wales.

Of course there must be a trace of nostalgia in all memory. But even memory is fiction. The delineation of the past becomes the copyright of the individual and subject to his or her arrangement of the circumstances (as in Alan Jay Lerner's song, "Oh Yes, I Remember It Well"); what passes for the memory in my mind is not the same as in someone else's remembrance. Fiction, of course, frees us from the boundaries that confine us and undernourish the inherent drama in our work. It is the combination of memory and fiction that makes the work more readable in every way than the account even of some sensational event told with every facet of truth intact.

For me, at any rate, what memory does is impel the resolution of some action, and the memory is of no use without the resolution. Here, for instance, is the beginning of a short story that I have not yet written but the memory of the incident is vividly stored in my mind:

I am about seven years old. I am watching from a short distance two women in a lighted room. One is standing, the other seated in a chair. The one standing is my aunt. She is middle-aged and becoming stout; she has never been good-looking, and a heart condition has drawn little scarlet veins across her nose and cheeks. She wears her graying hair drawn back into a bun. She is dressed in a wool skirt and with a tweed cardigan covering a beige cashmere sweater or what Australians then called a "jumper." I have never liked her, and in some dim response out of starvation, she has poured gifts and protestations of love on me, which have only served to widen the gulf between us, because sometimes the responses of children are unmitigating. Her responses to my unrelenting disapproval have been expensive toy trains and riding boots of exquisite styling and leather, but she is wont not to risk exposure of herself in embraces or kisses. I watch her and the other woman deep in soft conversation. The other woman's back is turned to my aunt. Without warning, my aunt leans suddenly over the chair and kisses the top of the woman's head. I am appalled.

What could it mean? A simple demonstration of affection? Sublimated perversion? But the incident itself, the memory, is of no use unless it is projected into the scheme of a story, so that it becomes a link in the chain of emotional jousting that took place between aunt and nephew; it must be realized in the fuller context and resolved.

In my first novel, *Careful, He Might Hear You,* the same aunt is a major character, and in that book (the thought occurs to me more than occasionally that it was deliberate homicide), I contrived to have her die in a ferry accident. In real life (never as authentic to me as the fiction), she died as a result of the heart condition she had had for many years, and to my astonishment I wept inconsolably. She was in deadly fear of thunder and lightning, and when I visited her grave in 1974 on a trip back to Australia, as I alighted from the suburban train, a thunderstorm of such sudden ferocity broke that I thought, "Aha, she knows I am coming to her." But this is too pat for consideration in a book; it is the kind of trite metaphor that should be instantly rejected.

As I have said, memory is fiction. *Careful, He Might Hear You* was denounced by the only living person who could remember the event and who knew most of the participants. "Not the people *I* knew," she said. Naturally enough. I was disconcerted at first, foolishly believing she would have recognized every nuance of the time and of the characters that I had so carefully reproduced. It was through a different lens that she had looked at my world. This is part of the reason most people fail to recognize themselves as the original models of fictitious characters. How delightful it would be to know that the original Mr. and Miss Murdstone read *David Copperfield* in all innocence.

In a different sense the "I" character of the first-person novel is never really the author. Up to now I have avoided the use of the first person because I find it confining, and not being able to get into the minds of other characters is an irretrievable loss to me. This is especially so in the autobiographical novel, and in mine the principal character was myself as a child. I always felt completely disassociated from this child, never more so than when I first saw the film version of the book. It was not unlike looking at a photograph of one's self as a child.

I look at the photograph. It is in sepia. The upward-turned face with the carefully brushed clean hair is seraphic, trusting, virginal. I remember that at that age I was in love with a little girl named Beryl Garside. We were in Sunday school together. I recall the circle of baby chairs we sat in. In those days, little girls wore their best hats to Sunday school, and the hats were confections. Beryl had—to me—the most wonderful hats in the world, and many of them. Each Sunday she would be there resplendent in straw and ribbons that extended down her back. I loved to see Beryl's hats, I dreamed about them at night. Then one shocking rainy Sunday, Beryl appeared in a plain black felt hat, so unadorned and ugly that I could scarcely believe my eyes, and Beryl's pretty face mostly hidden under the wide brim seemed to have taken on an ugliness also. Without a second's thought, I leapt up, and snatching off the offending hat, slapped Beryl in the face, screaming, "I hate your hat, Beryl." Her consternation was more shock at my outrageous action than at the slap itself. Fancy dear little Putty Elliott doing such a thing, an angel like him! We are subject to the stranger in all of us.

Fifty years later, I was to write a scene in which a drunken bully

202

snatches the new hat off a frightened girl, yelling, "I hate that hat you're wearing," and throws it into a fountain. The bully's tipsy sycophants laugh loudly, and the wretched girl is forced into laughter also until the rich bully's fiancée says cuttingly to him, "Pay her. Pay her for the hat." The scene, which was in a book called *Signs of Life,* passed through my mind and onto the typewriter without the ghost of a memory of Beryl Garside until months later, when, reading the galleys, I almost tripped over the fact that I had resurrected my Sunday school disgrace.

It is easy to blame it all on the unconscious, which stores away everything that we would most like to forget. Often it is through our unconscious memory that we find the inspiration without knowing. But that fortunately is not nostalgia.

Occasionally, try as I may, I cannot fit the memory in. Or else it does not belong to the book. There is a little string of rather plaintive memories that I have considered for several books but which refused steadfastly to be included, or else were later wisely omitted. Again I see my plain aunt weeping to my good-looking male violin teacher, while I am told to wait outside in the corridor where somebody in the distance is practicing Kreisler's "Caprice Viennois."

The importance of balance can often be vital. For instance, I am usually opposed to scenes in which a major event or anything of a tragic or dramatic nature takes place during bad weather: In fiction writing, never have the storm outside when there is a storm within. At the picnic in ideal weather, the water rippling in sunlight, the drowsy hum of bees, the tablecloth laid out with the tempting food, the baby lamp chops grilling on the twig fire, wild flannel flowers and blue sky—then the child can be beckoned away behind a tree to be told of a terrible death in an accident.

Possibly this is a finnicky, old-maidish trickery. There are no rules to writing, and what is law to one writer can be anathema to another. I abhor descriptions of good-looking people, especially of beautiful women, often found in novels. Margaret Mitchell disposed of a leading character in American fiction in her opening sentence: "Scarlett O'Hara was not beautiful, but men seldom noticed it."

But the risk is that we do look back on the past with nostalgia. When I was growing up, I used to spend the long Christmas holidays with my cousins on a farm in another state. I had to travel overnight to Melbourne on the express. No more glamorous experience in memory could outdo the excitement of that train. I can still smell the musty odor of the compartments and see the sleeping cars with their softly lighted corridors over the dark red carpeting with the words "NSW Railways" woven into them, and the dark green leather seats, half of which let down out of the wall and became the upper berth, reached by a small ladder with velvet-covered steps, and I can feel the rhythm and sway of the train and the thick brown blanket that smelled faintly of smoke. In a moment, in a word or two, if I am not careful, I will be on a journey of such nostalgia as to make Dickens's Little Nell seem brittle. Nostalgia must be used only as background (and not go on for too long), the sounds of the rushing train must be there only to conceal partially the sounds of weeping in the next compartment, and then . . .

But I cannot write about the past and not mention the trams. Sydney used to be a tram city (Melbourne still is), and it was the most generally used public transport to and from the city to the suburbs. The trams were big, gray and dirty cream-colored, lumbering but capable of fairly high speed, attached by long poles to the overhead electric wires. They were not dinky and pretty like the San Francisco trolleys, and they were not trolleys; they were *trams*. Shirley Hazzard has described them as "toast racks," which is accurate—the open compartments at either end, the rows of seats, doors with windows that opened in the middle, and the narrow wooden running-boards on which the conductors with their heavy bags of change clung perilously to the sides of the rocking vehicle in all weather. Wedging his shoulder firmly into the door against the swaying of the tram, the conductor gave out the tickets and made change, walking along the little footboards not more than eight inches wide. I can still hear the snap of the leather strap he pulled and the tinkle of the bell in the driver's cabin when the last people had gotten off and others got on. I can see the names of the suburbs on the roller in front: BALMORAL, THE SPIT, TARONGA PARK ZOO, CROW'S NEST.

It is six in the evening. I am in a big two-storied white house overlooking the harbor, and I can hear the Dover Road tram climbing the upward curve of the hill outside with a grinding noise. I am in bed having bread and milk off a tray. I am four, and I am filled with delight.

That is nostalgia.

40

ONE CLUE AT A TIME

BY P.D. JAMES

FOR ME one of the keenest pleasures of rereading my favorite mysteries is their power to transport me instantly into a familiar world of people, places and objects, a world in which I feel at once comfortably at home.

With what mixture of excitement, anticipation and reassurance we enter that old brownstone in Manhattan, that gentle spinster's cottage in St. Mary Mead (never fully described by Agatha Christie but so well imagined), that bachelor flat in London's Piccadilly where Bunter deferentially pours the vintage port [for Lord Peter Wimsey], that cozy Victorian sitting room on Baker Street.

A sense of place, creating as it does that vivid illusion of reality, is a necessary tool of any successful novelist. But it is particularly important to the fabricator of the mystery: the setting of the crime and the use of commonplace objects help to heighten by contrast the intruding horror of murder. The bizarre and the terrifying are rooted in comforting reality, making murder more believable.

There is probably no room in crime fiction that we enter with a keener sense of instant recognition than the claustrophobic upstairs sitting room at 221B Baker Street. Baker Street is now one of the dullest of London's main thoroughfares, and it is difficult, walking these wide pavements, to picture those foggy Victorian evenings with the inevitable veiled lady alighting from her hansom cab outside the door of the celebrated Sherlock Holmes.

But we can see every detail of the room into which Mrs. Hudson will usher her: the sofa on which Holmes reclines during his periods of meditation; the violin case propped against the wall; the shelves of scrapbooks; the bullet marks in the wall; the two broad windows overlooking the street; the twin armchairs on each side of the fireplace; the bottle of 7-percent-cocaine solution on the mantel shelf; the desk with the locked drawer containing Holmes's confidential records; the central table with "its white cloth and glimmer of china and metal" waiting for Mrs. Hudson to clear away.

The mental scene has, of course, been reinforced countless times in films and on television, but what is remarkable is that so vivid a picture should be produced by so few actual facts. Paradoxically, I can find no passage in the books that describes the room at length and in detail. Instead, Sir Arthur Conan Doyle builds up the scene through a series of stories object by object, and the complete picture is one that the reader himself creates and furnishes in his own imagination from this accumulation of small details.

Few things reveal the essential self more surely than the rooms in which we live, the objects with which we choose to surround ourselves, the books we place on our shelves, all those small household goods that help reaffirm identity and provide comfort and a sense of security. But the description in crime fiction of domestic interiors, furnishings and possessions does more than denote character; it creates mood and atmosphere, enhances suspense and is often crucial to the plot.

In Agatha Christie, for example, we can be confident that almost any domestic article mentioned, however commonplace, will provide a clue, either true or false. A loose door number hanging on its nail; flowers that have died because no one watered them; an extra coffee spoon in a saucer; a picture postcard lying casually on the desk. In *Funerals Are Fatal,* we do well to note the bouquet of wax flowers on the malachite table. In *Murder at the Vicarage,* we can be sure that the tall stand with a plant pot standing in front of the window isn't there for nothing.

And in *The Murder of Roger Ackroyd,* we shouldn't be so intrigued by the corpse that we fail to notice how one chair has been strangely pulled out from its place by the wall.

All writers of mystery fiction use such devices, but few with such deceptive cunning. It is one of the paradoxes of the genre that it deals with that great absolute, death, yet deploys the trivia of ordinary life as the frail but powerful instruments of justice.

Because in a Christie mystery the puzzle is more important than either the characterization or the setting, she seldom describes a room in great detail. Hers is the art of the literary conjurer. How very different is the loving care and meticulous eye with which a novelist such as Margery Allingham creates for us her highly individual domestic interiors.

In *More Work for the Undertaker,* how brilliantly she describes every room of the eccentric Palinode family, so that the house itself is central to the plot, its atmosphere pervades the novel, and we feel that we know every secret and sinister corner.

But my favorite Allingham rooms are in *The Tiger in the Smoke,* with its opposing characters of the saintly Canon Avril and the psychopathic killer Jack Havoc. How simply described and how absolutely right is the Canon's sitting room. "It was the room he had brought his bride to 30 years before, and since then . . . nothing in it had ever been changed. It had become a little worn in the interim, but the good things in it, the walnut bookcase with the ivory chessmen displayed, the bureau with 13 panes in each glass door, the Queen Anne chair with the 7-foot back, the Persian rug which had been a wedding present from his younger sister, Mr. Campion's mother, had all mellowed just as he had with care and use and quiet living."

Right, too, in its very different style, is the sitting room of his dress-designer daughter, Meg, littered with its sketches of dresses and strewn with swaths of material and samples of braids and beads. "Between the demasked grey walls and the deep gold carpet there ranged every permissible tint and texture from bronze velvet to scarlet linen, pin-pointed and enlivened with draining touches of Bristol blue."

This is a highly individual room in the grand manner but without pretentiousness, and I'm not in the least surprised that after a dubious sidelong glance, Chief Inspector Luke decided that he liked it very much indeed.

A room I like very much indeed is Lord Peter Wimsey's sitting room in his flat at 110A Piccadilly. We see it most clearly through the eyes of Miss Murchison in Dorothy L. Sayers's *Strong Poison.* She is shown by Bunter into a glowing, book-lined room "with fine prints on the walls, an Aubusson carpet, a grand piano, a vast chesterfield and a number of deep, cozy armchairs upholstered in brown leather.

"The curtains were drawn, a wood fire blazed on the hearth, and before it stood a table with a silver tea service whose lovely lines were a delight to the eye." No wonder Miss Murchison was impressed.

After his marriage, of course, Lord Peter honeymooned with his

Harriet at Talboys, an Elizabethan farmhouse in Hertfordshire that Lord Peter bought as their country retreat, complete with inglenooked fireplace, ancient beams, tall Elizabethan chimneys, erratic plumbing and the inevitable corpse in the cellar. Meanwhile, the dowager Duchess of Denver was busying herself collecting the chandeliers and tapestries for the Wimseys' town house in Audley Square and congratulating herself that the bride "was ready to prefer 18th-century elegance to chromium tubes." I am myself partial to 18th-century elegance, but I still feel more at home in that bachelor flat at 110A Piccadilly.

Incidently, Talboys was modernized and completely refurnished, including the installation of electricity and the provision of additional bedrooms, before the murderer of its previous owner had been executed—in England a matter then of only a couple of months. That was remarkably speedy even for the 1930's. Today I am doubtful whether even the son of a Duke would be able to command such speedy service.

I myself work in the tradition of Margery Allingham and share her fascination with architecture and domestic interiors; indeed, it is often the setting rather than a particular character or a new method of murder that sparks my creative imagination and gives rise to a novel.

In my last book, *The Skull Beneath the Skin,* the setting is a restored Victorian castle on a lonely offshore island. Here the owner, obsessed with violent death, has created his own private chamber of horrors, a study decorated with old woodcuts of execution scenes, Staffordshire figures of Victorian murderers, mourning regalia and the artifacts of murder.

Here I have used the setting to fulfill all the functions of place in detective fiction; to illustrate character, create atmosphere, provide the physical clues to the crime and to enhance that sense of unease, of the familiar and ordinary made strange and terrible, which is at the heart of detective fiction.

And it is surely the power to create this sense of place and to make it as real to the reader as is his own living room—and then to people it with characters who are suffering men and women, not stereotypes to be knocked down like dummies in the final chapter—that gives any mystery writer the claim to be regarded as a serious novelist.

41

SUSPENSE WRITING

By Mary Higgins Clark

MY PUBLISHER recently forwarded a letter to me from a man who had just read my suspense novels. It was brief and to the point. The reader also wanted to be a writer and he had a question for me: "About how many words and pages are required to turn out a best seller like your own?"

My immediate response was a smile, but it was quickly followed by a feeling of sadness. I don't think that particular aspiring writer will ever make it. And while his question is almost unbelievably naive, it's not the first time it's been asked.

For some reason, I find it difficult to put down advice in an organized manner. Telling someone how to turn out a marketable suspense novel is rather like dancing with an octopus. Which hand (or tentacle) do you reach for first?

However, I think that by attempting to answer the kinds of questions that pop up in my mail and by explaining how a story evolves for me, I might be able to pass along some useful suggestions.

Therefore, with the understanding between us that this will not be a precise blueprint or an annotated "how to," shall we begin?

Question: "I'm eager to write a mystery, but can't think of a plot. Where do you get your ideas?"

Obviously the plot, like the foundation of a house, is the structure on which all else is built. No matter how glib the writing, how enchanting the characters, if the plot doesn't work, or if it works only because of flagrant coincidence or seven-page explanations at the climax, I believe the book is a failure. But where to get the *idea?* Easy. Pick up your local newspaper. The odds are that on the first page or two it contains news of at least one homicide, an aggravated assault, a bank robbery, a mugging, a jailbreak. There also may be a recap on a criminal trial that merits national attention, an update on a series of unsolved murders, and an item about the child who has been missing six months. In other words, material for a dozen short stories or novels.

Now for your own plot. Select a case, one that for whatever reason sticks in your mind. Begin a file on it. Cut out every newspaper item that refers to it. *Know* that case. If a defendant is indicted, try to attend some of the trial sessions. And then—and here's the key—use that case as a nucleus for your story. You're a fiction writer; invent, go further, say to yourself, "What if?"

Several years ago I decided I wanted to try my hand at a suspense novel. Like everyone else, I was faced with the decision: What shall I write? At that time there was a celebrated case in New York in which a young mother was accused of murdering her two children. She stoutly denied her guilt. Two juries rejected her defense. The case fascinated me. I had five children, and the thought of losing any of them gave me nightmares. The thought of not only losing them but being accused of *murdering* them was beyond comprehension. A voice in my subconscious whispered, "And then suppose it happened again?" *Where Are the Children?* was in gestation. Let me reemphasize my point: *Where Are the Children?* was not based on the actual case. I took two ingredients: the young mother accused of infanticide; the frantic denials of guilt. With these in mind I began to build the story.

In my opinion time and place are essential contributors to a successful suspense novel. I chose to set *Where Are the Children?* on Cape Cod for a number of reasons. The Cape offers privacy. New Englanders and particularly "Capeys" do not intrude. The stranger who rents the big house off-season will not be the subject of idle scrutiny. The Cape has mists and fogs, churning surf, nor'easter storms, weatherbeaten captains' houses perched high on embankments above the sea. All these enhance the atmosphere of terror and gloom.

A Stranger Is Watching has as a principal location the bowels of Grand Central Station. Why? There you find dark, damp tunnels throbbing with the echo of rushing trains and groaning machinery; stray cats; underground people silently flitting by; abandoned storerooms, eerie with accumulated cobwebs and grime. I explored the area and knew it was right. And I loved the possibility of the juxtaposition of kidnap victims bound and gagged near a ticking time bomb while overhead thousands of commuters rush through the terminal.

Like the Greeks, I believe in the containment of time. *Oedipus Rex* starts in the morning with the king observing the problems of his stricken domain. It ends a few hours later with his wife a suicide, himself blinded, his world vanished. The swiftness of the action adds to the shock value.

I believe that if you write a book in which people are kidnapped and the villain plans to execute them at a specific time, the suspense is considerably greater than if the reader is only generally concerned about the victims' welfare. In *Where Are the Children?* the reader knows that the kidnapper is planning to throw the children into the rock-filled surf at high tide, seven P.M. In *A Stranger Is Watching,* the time bomb is set to go off at 11:30 A.M. Hopefully as zero hour approaches the reader is sharing the anxiety of the protagonists.

Question: "When I start to write, all my characters sound alike. What am I doing wrong?" That's another good inquiry and a valid problem. Through trial and error, I evolved something of a system that has helped me. The key phrase is *know your people.* Do a biography of them before you begin to write your story. Where were they born? Where did they go to school? What do they look like? What kind of clothes do they wear? Are they sophisticated, easy-going, observant? Are they married? Do they have children?

Think of someone you know or knew as a child who reminds you of the character you're trying to create. Remember the way that person talked, the expressions he or she used. When I was inventing Lally, the bag lady in *A Stranger Is Watching,* I combined two people from my childhood. One was our cleaning woman, who used to come up the street invariably singing "lalala"; the other the proprietor of a hole-in-the-wall candy store near my grammar school. She was one of the homeliest women I've ever known. The boys in my class always used to make jokes about calling her up for a date. Together the candy store proprietor and "Lala," as we nicknamed our cleaning woman, merged into Lally. But then to get the feeling of authenticity, I haunted Grand Central Station and chatted with real bag ladies. One of them became the prototype for Rosie, the other bag lady in *Stranger.*

There are hundreds of examples of fine books which contradict what I'm about to say, but here it is anyhow. I like to write about *very nice people* who are confronted by the forces of evil and who through their own courage and intelligence work their way through to deliverance. Personally, I'm not comfortable with the non-hero or non-heroine who is basically so bad-tempered or self-serving that in real life I would avoid him or her like the plague. I myself don't get emotional satisfaction out of a book in which the villain is so desperately attractive that I find my-

211

self rooting for him to beat the system. My villains are, and probably will continue to be, as evil, as frightening, as quietly vicious as I can dream them up. I know I'm on the right track if I'm writing at night and no one else is home and when the house makes a settling noise, I uneasily start looking over my own shoulder.

Another key element in creating characters is to *orchestrate* them. Within the framework of the plot try to have a variety of people in whom your readers will not only believe but with whom they can identify. Never, never throw away a minor character. Let your reader understand him, know what makes him tick. And make it a cardinal rule that every minor character must move the story forward. Suspense by its very nature suggests an express train or a roller coaster. Once on board, you cannot get off until the ride ends. I am committed to the belief that this kind of speedy action is essential to good suspense writing.

Question: "Do you do much research before you start writing?" Yes. Yes. Yes. And as I am working on the book I continue to research. My book, *The Cradle Will Fall,* is about an obstetrician who experiments on and sometimes murders his pregnant patients. I read everything I could get my hands on about artificial insemination, *in vitro* pregnancies, and fetal transplant experiments. I interviewed and picked the brains of a doctor friend who is a researcher in a pre-natal hospital laboratory. I proposed "what if" questions to obstetrician buddies. Then when the book was completed I gave a Xerox to one obstetrician friend. I was in New York. He was in Minneapolis. I was on a tight deadline: He stayed on the phone with me four hours. I had a list of all medical references in the book, e.g. page 2 top line, page 8 fourth paragraph, etc. Jack reviewed every one of them with me. On some he said, "That's fine." On others, he'd suggest changes. For example, near the climax of the book, a desperate search is going on for the gravely ill heroine. Jack said, "It's an emergency. Two doctors are talking. Don't have Richard say, 'She'll need a transfusion when we find her.' Put it this way, 'We'll hang a bottle of O-negative.' "

The Cradle Will Fall is set in New Jersey. The protagonist, Katie DeMaio, is a young assistant prosecutor. My daughter is an assistant prosecutor in New Jersey. She was my expert in police procedure. She went over every line that referred to the working of the court, the prosecutor's office, trials, witness statements, etc. For example, after a murder scene I had the homicide detective post a sign, CRIME AREA. POSITIVELY NO ADMITTANCE. I remembered having seen a sign like that somewhere. My daughter said, "No, that's wrong. In a suspicious death, we'd leave a cop guarding the premises until the apartment has been thoroughly searched." In another chapter, I had the prosecutor televise the interrogation of a witness. She corrected me. "In New York that's being done sometimes, but it's still not legal in New Jersey." The point is that authenticity of detail gives the ring of truth to a book.

Question: "How much rewriting do you do when you're working on a book?"

Plenty. But rewriting is a two-edged sword. I know too many people who've spent months working over the first chapter of the projected novel. That's wrong. Get it down. Bumble through it. Tell the story. Then when you have fifty or one hundred pages typed you've got something to work with. It may be at that point you'll start again from the beginning because the book has a fundamental flaw that has become obvious. I wrote fifty pages of *The Cradle Will Fall*. In that first version Katie DeMaio is the twenty-eight-year-old wife of a prominent judge. She is in a minor automobile accident while he is away, stays overnight in the hospital, and while sedated witnesses a crime.

I soon realized something was wrong. I couldn't get worried about Katie. The reason became obvious. Here she is married to an interesting, handsome man, a Superior Court judge. I just knew that when John DeMaio got home the next day, he'd make very sure that no one would hurt his Katie.

How to solve the problem? John had to go. Instead of the *wife,* Katie became the young *widow* of Judge John DeMaio. Immediately, she is infinitely more sympathetic—vulnerable and alone in the large secluded house she inherited from him. A great additional plus is that we now have room for a love interest. Doctor Richard Carroll, the provocative medical examiner, is very keen on Katie, and she has been holding him off. The reader, we hope, becomes emotionally involved in the potential romance and worries that Katie is sealing her fate because she does not let Richard know she is scheduled for minor surgery. The doctor who will operate on her is planning to kill her.

So there we have it. As I warned in the beginning I suspect this advice has a disjointed quality. I tend to offer writing hints the way an old

County Sligo cousin shared her recipe for Irish soda bread: "Take a handful of this, a fistful of that, a pinch of whatever . . . . Now taste it, love. Does it need more caraway seeds and raisins?"

Nevertheless if any of this advice helps anyone, I'm glad. There is surely no sweeter satisfaction to the suspense writer than to hear a heavy-eyed friend say accusingly, "You kept me up half the night reading your darn book!"

42

SCIENCE FICTION TODAY

By Isaac Asimov

SCIENCE FICTION has changed enormously since I first began writing it, professionally, nearly fifty years ago.

When I submitted a story for the first time on June 21, 1938, there were three magazines in the field; only one of which, *Astounding Science Fiction,* was, in my opinion, quality. There was nothing else to speak of. An occasional amateur publisher put out a tiny printing of some poorly written science fiction novel. There were a few comic strips, notably *Buck Rogers* and *Flash Gordon,* and an occasional very primitive movie serial.

But now?

In the print media, science fiction novels are commonly found on the best-seller lists, both in hardcover and softcover. The book stores have shelves full of them. The movies and television find science fiction to be profitable blockbusters. Science fiction courses are taught in high schools and colleges. Short story anthologies exist by the hundreds. Science fiction is *big time*.

It might seem to you, then, that it must be a great deal easier to break into the science fiction field now than it was fifty years ago. After all, the target is so much larger now.

Unfortunately, I don't think that's so. Let us analyze the situation more closely. Fifty years ago, when sf consisted of three magazines and virtually nothing else, there were many other outlets for fiction. It was the heyday of the pulp-magazine craze. Every newsstand had dozens of them in every conceivable category: romance, mystery, western, jungle, war, horror, adventure. Some came out monthly, and some biweekly, and some even weekly. There were also "slick" magazines that published a great deal of fiction and paid much more than the pulps did.

Of them all, the science fiction magazines were the smallest in number, the least lucrative, the most specialized, and the least regarded segment. Almost none of the myriads of young people who had the itch to write considered science fiction as a possible outlet. The science fiction magazines drew their new prospects from among their own long-time fanatic readers, who had been reading science fiction since they had learned to read and had no interest in anything else. They didn't care for either fame or wealth, but wanted only to write that wonderful stuff they were reading and see their name in print in a science fiction magazine. There weren't many of those fanatics (usually abbreviated as "fans"), but I was one of them. I had been reading science fiction avidly from the age of nine, and I was eighteen when I made my first sale.

Under those circumstances, it was not necessary to be a great writer, you understand. There were few science fiction writers of any kind in those days, and still fewer good ones. If you were eager to write science fiction, knew grammar and spelling, and had read enough science fiction to know a new idea from an old one, that was about all that was needed.

Nowadays, all that has changed also. In the first place, the fiction market has contracted violently in the last fifty years (a result of the coming of the comic magazine, and then, even more important, television). The pulps are gone. What slicks exist publish very little fiction. In fact, the only branch of popular fiction that has expanded wildly in the last half century has been science fiction. (Mysteries and romances have done no more than hold their own over the long run.)

This means that of all the youngsters who grow up with the itch to be writers, a sizable percentage tend to flood into science fiction in large numbers. There are hundreds of excellent science fiction writers today, whereas, half a century ago, there were mere dozens of not-so-excellent ones. In addition, many of those who entered the field years ago are still there. The "big three"—Isaac Asimov, Arthur C. Clarke, and Robert A. Heinlein—whose books are sure-fire best sellers today, have been writing steadily for nearly fifty years. Clarke and Heinlein, despite their advanced years, show no signs of slowing down and I, of course, am still a youngster.

What's more, all these writers tend to write novels. That's where the money and fame are. And novels are precisely what a beginner would find difficult to do. A novel has a complex structure, with interlocking plots and subplots, with room for characterization to be developed and dialogue to show a certain depth and wit. If a beginner throws caution to the winds and determines to tackle a novel anyway, he finds it represents an enormous investment of time and effort, all of which (the chances are) will be thrown away except for what good the writing experience will do him.

The natural way in which science fiction writers broke into the field in my early days was to turn out short stories for the magazines. (There was, after all, nothing else to do since, at most, two or three novels were published each year as magazine serials.) Clarke, Heinlein, and I all got our start as writers of science fiction short stories for the magazines. We worked our way up to novels by stages.

Well, then, are there not science fiction magazines that publish short stories today, to say nothing of science fiction anthologies?

Yes, but skip the anthologies. The vast majority of them include reprints—stories that have already appeared in the magazines. That leaves only the magazines.

Unfortunately, the magazines have not expanded along with the rest of the field. There are four magazines today that specialize in science fiction. In order of age, they are *Amazing Stories* (previously *Amazing Science Fiction Stories*); *Analog Science Fiction/Science Fact* (which had once been *Astounding Science Fiction*); *The Magazine of Fantasy and Science Fiction;* and *Isaac Asimov's Science Fiction Magazine.* In addition, there are a couple of other magazines, which publish some science fiction. Most notable of these is *Omni,* which publishes two or three stories in each issue. It pays much higher rates than the others do, and consequently seeks its stories from among the established writers. (And there are a number of little magazines in the field, a good place for beginning sf writers to try, though payment rates are low.)

The magazine field, therefore, is not much larger than it was fifty years ago, and the competition is keener. The level of writing in the magazines is consequently substantially higher than it used to be, and my 18-year-old self, if transported into the present with no more talent than I possessed then, might not have been able to break in.

However, all is not lost. In the old days, when a writer established himself as a science fiction short story writer, he stayed there having nowhere else to go, and left that much less room for newcomers. Nowadays, as soon as a science fiction writer begins to make a name for himself in the magazines and has gained the necessary expertise, he shifts to writing novels. The result is that the magazines are forced to be on the continual lookout for new young writers. These new writers have to be good, to be sure—it is no longer enough that they feel warm to the touch—but the fact that they are unknown is not held against them.

But so what if the competition is keen? That makes the task the more challenging, and the triumph sweeter in the end. The rules are the same. You have to read a great deal of science fiction so that you gain some insight into what science fiction is and what makes it good. And you have to write a great deal of science fiction, because only by writing can you gradually learn the tricks of the trade. And you have to have an inhuman perseverance and develop a thick skin against disappointment and frustration. And don't think the world is picking on you. I suspect that Homer and Aeschylus had all the same experiences you had in getting started.

Perhaps something else occurs to you. It may seem to you that when I was just beginning (back in the Middle Ages) hardly anything was known about science and I could write freely about interplanetary travel and robots and all that stuff. Nowadays, however, we *have* interplanetary travel and robots, so what is there to write about? Hasn't science caught up to all the science fiction plots? Isn't science fiction dead?

Not at all! Nohow! The science fiction writer is tied to the front end of a locomotive that is speeding across the landscape. No matter how far and how fast the locomotive is going, the writer is looking ahead and sees an endless vista.

Scientific advance provides writers with fascinating new backgrounds. We used to think Mars had canals; now we know (not "think") it has extinct volcanoes. And we know Io has active volcanoes. And we know that Venus is as hot as hell—literally—and has no oceans. We can turn away from the tired old planets and make use of brand-new ones, and have the satisfaction of knowing that there's less guesswork and more knowledge now.

Again, we think of all the new concepts science has given us. We have neutron stars, and black holes, and quasars, and exploding galaxies, and big bangs. We have mesons, and hyperons, and quarks, and gluons. We have DNA and biogenetics. We have computers and microchips. We have jet planes and satellites of every kind and probes and shuttles. We have seen close-ups of Uranus and its satellites. We had *none* of that when I was starting out.

When I think of all these new scientific items there are to play around with now—and how little I had back in 1938—I am amazed that I was able to think up any stories at all in that medieval period.

Of course, we have to be careful of fashion. When I first started reading science fiction, it was all adventure and Sunday supplement science. It was written in primary colors and in jagged lightning streaks. It was ideal for a bright nine-year-old to get started on.

By the time I began to submit stories, however, it became fashionable to load them down with authentic science and to try to make the characters sound like real scientists and engineers. The 1940's and 1950's were the heyday of "hard science fiction" and that was my forte, and (to tell you the truth) I still write it even though it sounds old-fashioned today.

In the 1960's, there came a period of stylistic experimentation called "the new wave" which, it seems to me, made hard reading and wasn't very successful. However, it settled down into the literary style we have today.

So however much you may want to read the "old classics" (like Asimov) and however much you may enjoy them, you had better also read, and pay close attention to, the kind of material that is appearing in the magazines *now*. That is what you should be writing.

Of course, you may be asking yourself if you should be writing for the print media at all. Shouldn't you be breaking into movies and television, where the BIG money is?

Frankly, I don't know how that's done. I've never worked in the visual media myself except on two or three minor occasions when I was talked into it much against my will.

It is my experience that when you write for the print media, what you write is what gets published. If there is a need for revision, the editor asks *you* to revise, and the chances are even good that you will get to see a galley proof so that you can make sure that any last-minute editorial changes meet with your approval.

When you write for the visual media, however, you must apparently meet the requirements of the producer, the director, the various actors, the office boy, strangers who pass in the street, and the mother-in-law of any or all of these, each of whom changes your product at whim. If you are a real writer, money isn't going to compensate for never being free to write as you wish.

43

WRITING THE UN-HISTORICAL NOVEL

BY GARY JENNINGS

I AM REGARDED as an author mainly of "historical novels," though I have never in my life sat down to write any such thing. I staunchly maintain—and in these very pages I have said so before—that there really *is* no such thing as an "historical novel."

Unless a writer chooses to write about some imagined future, he or she *has* to write about the past, even if only yesterday's. Consider: It is not just a matter of tradition or convention that most novels are told in the past tense. The most up-to-date, hip and trendy "contemporary novel," about to be published tomorrow, is already a story about the past. I myself have toyed with the notion of doing a novel based on my adventures on Madison Avenue in the late 1950's—when all of us bright young admen considered ourselves the last word in up-to-date, hip and trendy—and, with some chagrin, I realize that the times, our society, our culture, all have changed so much in thirty years, that *that* would now be regarded as an "historical novel," if not a prehistoric artifact.

However, the novels that I have so far written have been set in more distant pasts—*Aztec,* 500 years ago; *The Journeyer,* 700 years; *Spangle,* 100 years—but only because, like any other novelist, I have chosen subjects, events, or characters that I knew would make a good story. It just so happened that those subjects were best represented, or those events occurred, or those characters lived in the past. I did not choose them because they were "historical."

And neither do the characters in my novels regard *themselves* as "historical," which brings me to the main point I want to make here. My fictional characters, as well as those drawn from real life—the Aztec named Mixtli and the journeyer Marco Polo and the circus troupers of *Spangle*—all think of themselves as up-to-date, hip and trendy, never once as "partakers in history." I may seem to be stressing the obvious, but I believe the point cannot be overstressed: that a

220

writer writing about the long-ago must constantly be aware that it was not *then* the long-ago. That deliberate and constant awareness may be the most important of all the factors that go into the writing of such a novel, and sometimes it can also be the most difficult factor to manage.

The author of a Napoleonic-era novel has remarked that the hardest thing she had to do, while writing it, was to bear in mind that on the night before the battle of Waterloo, nobody knew who would win it. No author is likely to have his Babylonian hero carrying a purse of coins dated "B.C.," or to have his Westphalian hero say to the heroine, "Well, goodbye, dear, I'm off to the Thirty Years' War." But the temptation is ever present to give our long-ago characters a foreknowledge they could not have possessed.

Even when an author copes adequately with that time-frame aspect, there is another horn to the dilemma. Write about Napoleon, and you expect nearly every reader to be familiar with the history. But write about even an obscure person or era, and you have to assume that *some* readers will be familiar with it. In other words, they already know, to some degree at least, "how the story comes out." That being so, how do you simultaneously stay true to history, keep your characters properly in their time frame, *and* still make the story grip a reader who has the advantage of 20/20 historical hindsight? Well, sometimes that can be done by playing the two horns of the dilemma against one another.

And that has never been better done than by Frederick Forsyth in his *The Day of the Jackal.* Every reader of that novel knew, from page one to the end, that that story never happened at all in real history; that Charles de Gaulle never got assassinated by a sniper; that he was, in fact, still alive and feisty when the novel was published. However, *none of the novel's characters knew that,* and that was what gave such a headlong urgency to the race to intercept the jackal sniper.

Still, that would not have been enough to rivet the interest of the reader already aware that de Gaulle never got shot. So Forsyth did more. He so persuasively took us through the sniper's preparations and made his modus operandi so likely to succeed, that the reader willingly suspended the disbelief of "this never happened," and came to believe that "by damn, this scheme *could* have worked," and voraciously read on to find out "how the hell did this *not* happen?"

Forsyth managed this so superbly because (1) he made his characters believable persons with believable motives and believable responses;

221

(2) he had done his homework, on everything from ballistics to the most minute details of the story's time and locale; and (3) by the accretion of those realistic details he achieved a verisimilitude that no reader could fault or resist, that convinced every reader to believe "this could have happened."

Now, on the art of delineating character, I will not expound; the subject is too vast to go into here. But the other two techniques—the accretion of details and the achievement of verisimilitude—are well within the capability of even the beginning writer, if he or she is willing to put in the labor they entail.

Reality cannot be flattened down onto a two-dimensional printed page, but verisimilitude can—the *illusion* of reality. It is done by (1) knowing every last detail of your story's time and place, from architecture to climate to customs, etc., (2) knowing every last thing about your characters, from birth to story-time: their upbringing and education, their trades and the tricks thereof, their look and dress, their individual traits and crotchets . . . and then (3) immersing yourself so thoroughly in them, their surroundings, and their story that you forget they are in any sense "historical" and you live their lives and adventures right along with them.

You do not, of course, shovel into your narrative every last detail you have unearthed in your research. It is fatal to let the reader see how hard you have worked—and it is unnecessary. If you know your characters, the period and the locale inside out, believe me, your own assurance will convey that to the reader—but *only* if you know all those things inside out. When you do throw in some detail of curiosa, try to do it offhandedly, not obtrusively, and please do make sure it's a detail that your reader would not also be likely to know. (For a simplistic example: everybody knows that Roman senators wore togas and Greek bacchantes wore chitons, but who knows what they wore *under* them?)

Here again, it is equally important to know what your characters could *not* have worn or used or mentioned in dialogue, lest they step out of their time frame and destroy the story's verisimilitude. A recent novel about England's William Rufus lamentably dispelled its 12th-century mood when the author (more than once) had this or that character remark of another that he was "as flighty as a hummingbird." (No Englishman ever saw a hummingbird until he got to the New World, four hundred years or so after King William's time.)

By the way—and not at all incidentally—be sure to double-check your sources of any information from times past. A reader of my *Aztec* wrote to castigate me because I had mentioned bees and honey in that novel, and, said she, the *Encyclopedia Britannica* avers that there *were* no bees in the New World. If any edition of the *Britannica* makes any such statement, it is dead wrong. (True, the Aztecs did not have domesticated honeybees, but it is likewise true that, if the New World had had no wild bees to do the job of pollinating, it would also have been a world almost nude of vegetation.)

If you can adroitly manage the accretion of enough realistic details, and thereby achieve verisimilitude—whether you are writing a novel or trying to placate an irate spouse by inventing an excuse for some misbehavior on your part—you stand a good chance of being believed, whatever lie you're embedding in the story. And, come right down to it, fiction is nothing but expert and believable lying.

In each of my novels set in the past, I have tried to employ that method—details = verisimilitude—but in the case of *Spangle,* it led me to use a system of organization that I had never used before, and some of you might also find it useful.

First, of course, as we all must do, I did my bookwork and legwork research. The bookwork was to bone up on the history, geography, dress, customs, etc., of a hundred years ago. The legwork meant visiting and traveling with actual circuses to learn from their experts the tricks of their trades—the details of everything from lion-taming to tightrope-walking. That took me to circuses all over the world, from Nashville to Leningrad, and I have to admit that it was fun. Or most of it was. Less glamorous aspects of the circus were also necessary to my story—things like the setup and teardown of the Big Top (sometimes in terrible weather); the logistics of supply, transport, scheduling; even details like the shoveling of menagerie manure.

On occasion, I found myself instructing the experts—and this illustrates what I have said about a novelist's having to know what his characters could *not* have known. An Italian trapeze artiste told me that he supposed his act would have been done no differently a hundred years ago. I had to correct him. At that time no trapezist had ever done any such feat as a triple or quadruple somersault; the trapezist Léotard had just then introduced the simple leap from one bar to the other. Also, not Léotard or any other circus performer of that time had glitzy

223

chrome-plated rigs, amplified music, strobe lights, etc. ("Per Bacco," muttered the artiste. "That's right, they didn't.")

Finally, home again and possessing far more information than I could ever cram into one novel, I conceived a curious system of organizing it all—the most outlandish-ever outline for a novel. It consisted of a sheet of brown wrapping paper, five feet wide and twenty feet long, scribbled and scrawled and diagrammed all over in different-colored inks. It might have been mistaken for the tracklines and timetables of every railroad in creation. The notes and diagrams began at one end of one side of the paper, with April 1865, ran all the way along that side of the paper, around the far edge and to the end of the other side—forty feet, in all—to June 1871.

To explain that, I must tell something about the story of *Spangle*. The circus that is the novel's collective "chief protagonist," finding itself impoverished and stranded in Virginia after the American Civil War, makes its way to Baltimore, sails to Europe, and there—traveling all over the continent—gradually recoups its fortunes, until it winds up in Paris just in time to be trapped in that city's siege during the Franco-Prussian War. The circus comprises a varying but always numerous cast of performers and crewmen and hangers-on, and they naturally have dealings with even greater numbers of "outsiders," including many real-life characters of the time. The circus travels through every kind of country, from the Shenandoah Valley to the Hungarian puszta and the Russian northland, and to cities as various as Baltimore, Florence, Vienna, Budapest, and St. Petersburg, before arriving in Paris.

Not only did I have to keep track of the whereabouts of each of my multitude of characters, their doings and interrelationships, the whole circus's triumphs and disasters and so on, during 1800 pages of type-script—I also had to keep track of significant dates and events, land-scapes and locales in the world that the circus travels through. And in those days it was a world of infinitely shifting political situations, alliances, even national boundaries. In brief, that Bayeux-tapestry thing plotted *Spangle* from the first page to the last and enabled me to have the circus always authentically situated in real time and place.

The outline truly was woven, like a tapestry, of warp and weft and intricate design. The long sheet of wrapping paper was divided by vertical lines, according to date and locale, and in those vertical spaces I scribbled the notes from my research as to what was going on then and thereabouts (just telegraphic code reminders to refer me to my more copious notebooks and file cards). Horizontally across those vertical warp lines, I wove the weft—long lines representing every one of my major characters, fictional or real, with notations along each line as to what each was doing at each time and place (for example, the developing complexity of an artiste's circus act), plus all of those characters' adventures and misadventures. Additional lines—diagonal, wiggly, criss-crossing—connected characters, to keep straight their interactions, romances, rivalries, enmities, etc. The tapestry, I am sure, would have been totally incomprehensible to anybody but its creator.

However, that peculiar outline did more than help me remember where everybody was—and when—and what he or she was doing at any specific point. It also enabled me to "live with" my characters, wherever and whenever they found themselves, and I could keep *them* from ever disrupting the time frame and mood of the story by having any pre-vision of what was to occur in the future. Also, in the occasional place where the circus itself did not provide enough action, incident, perilous situation or whatever, to keep the story lively, I could jump from the "horizontal-weft" to the "vertical-warp" notes, and bring in either true or based-on-true incidents from "outside" the circus. That was not often necessary—a circus is a perpetual adventure—but there *were* spots where real-life history was being even more dramatic than anything fictional that was going on under my Big Top.

Most of my writing colleagues and friends consider me woefully old-fashioned. I still prefer to compose (and even to do the grueling finished-typing of 1800 pages) on a manual typewriter, while they—ever so much more up-to-date, hip and trendy—have graduated to sophisticated computer word processors. Nevertheless, some of them have expressed awed admiration of the precision and flexibility with which I could work, using that "cumbersome, archaic, handwritten" roll of wrapping paper. It gave me an overview of *Spangle* that would be beyond the scope of any computer screen. As I say, I've never before resorted to any such system, and I may never do so again. (My next novel has a far less numerous cast of characters and covers a lot less territory.) But the Bayeux-tapestry layout worked splendidly for *Spangle,* and I hold no patent on it. If it appeals to you, and seems applicable to whatever novel you have in mind, feel free to imitate it. I wish you all success, and I won't even ask an acknowledgment.

44

WRITING REALISTIC WESTERN FICTION

By Elmer Kelton

IDEALLY, the only major difference between a Western and any other good, serious novel should be the subject matter, the setting. A good story is a good story, and a bad story a loser whether the setting is Paris or London, Cape Cod or Dodge City. The same general principles of characterization, plot and movement apply.

Being set in the West automatically bestows upon a story certain advantages and certain limitations. The main advantage is a loyal if sometimes-too-small readership receptive to the Western scene. The principal limitation is that it is unlikely to be taken seriously by most of the critical establishment, making it a stepchild in the literary family.

Because of this old prejudice—call it snobbery if you wish—much fine writing has been accorded the "averted gaze," ignored in favor of "relevant" material not half so well written.

The cliché view of the classic Western is a story built around a strong, unsmiling hero who stands seven feet tall and invincible against the worst of villainy, unselfishly sets all wrongs right, and then rides away into the sunset.

Certainly, such Westerns exist. They started in the days of Ned Buntline a century ago, and they continue to appear. There is an audience for the "utility Western," typical of the Saturday-matinee "B" Western film, in which the same frontier-town set and the same outdoor scenery are interchangeable, whether the story is set in Texas or Oregon.

But I am convinced there is a larger audience for a Western novel firmly and accurately grounded in history, the story growing out of conditions inherent in and peculiar to a specific time and place, its conflicts not falling neatly into black and white.

I made my first Western short story sale, to *Ranch Romances*, in 1947. Even so, after some fifty magazine stories and twenty-six published novels, I still consider myself a learner. I continually read and watch for a good story idea, for an interesting character I can interpolate into a novel.

Most of the rules that apply to other fiction apply to the Western. A writer who approaches the Western with a down-the-nose attitude is unlikely to get far in the field. Like any other form, the Western deserves the respect of its writer—respect for the rules of good storytelling and for the realities of history around which the story revolves.

Nothing turns me off faster than to get into a story and find anachronisms and inaccuracies about the time, the place and the people. Any serious writer of historical fiction studies the history that will be the foundation of his novel. The Western deserves no less. This study does not have to be drudgery. Doing the historical research is often the most pleasurable aspect of writing fiction. A writer who does not love history has no business writing about it.

A majority of my novels have been strongly grounded in history. Before I start to write, I study the setting of the story, the historical situations that will form the framework, and the people of the time and place, their problems, their beliefs. Old newspapers, diaries, and written reminiscences are invaluable.

Intricate plots have never been my long suit, though I admire writers who can bring them off. Rather, I rely upon characters and the historical situation to set the pattern. I like the story to grow out of the history to such an extent that the plot could not be transferred to some other time and place without radical surgery.

An example is an early novel of mine, *Massacre at Goliad,* still reprinted periodically in paperback. Two brothers emigrate to Texas from Tennessee some years before the Texas revolution against Mexico. They live through the situations and events that gradually build the atmosphere for revolution. In modern terms, one is a hawk, the other a dove. They become estranged because of their political differences. However, once the fighting begins, they are brought back together by their concern for one another.

My biggest historical novel has been *The Wolf and the Buffalo,* about the lives of a black cavalryman on the Texas plains in the 1870s and a Comanche warrior against whom he is pitted, the black man fighting the red man so the white man can have the land. This novel gave me an opportunity to dramatize the daily life of both the buffalo soldier and his enemy. Gideon Ledbetter, the former slave now in uniform, is on a gradual ascent, while Gray Horse, the Comanche, is witnessing the twilight of his people's way of life.

It struck me that the two characters had a great deal in common. It was a temptation to have them realize it and perhaps come together in some way, but in real life it did not happen. The fact that it should have but did not is one of the ironies of history. I *did* let one black trooper in the story see the parallel and try to act upon it, deserting the army and riding out into Indian country with the idea of proposing an alliance against the white man. What happens to him is what would have happened in real life, more likely than not. The first Indians he encounters shoot him out of the saddle. They see him as an enemy, simply a white man with a black face.

At the end of the story the two characters come together in the only way they would in real life: in combat to the death.

This brings me to what I consider the most important element in a Western, or in almost any other type of fiction: characters.

I wrote the final scene of *The Wolf and the Buffalo* with tears in my eyes. Working with those characters for two years, I had come to care about them as real people. I gloried in their triumphs and felt deeply their personal tragedies.

Well-developed characters have a way of taking charge of a story and leading the writer in directions not anticipated. Often they change details, and sometimes they cause major alterations to the intended plot line. Usually I let them go their own way, for my unconscious is quietly telling me this is the natural and spontaneous thing for them to do.

In a recent question-and-answer session, a reader said she did not understand why I should let characters take over. "They are your creation," she declared. "You can make them do what you want them to."

But to force them into my preconceived plan makes the story seem mechanical and contrived. When in doubt, I follow the character. He knows himself.

In *Stand Proud,* I started with a young Texan forced into frontier service for the Confederacy late in the Civil War, carried against his will into an ill-considered Indian fight (a real one, incidentally) that gave him a wound he would have the rest of his life. Wherever other men led him, he invariably suffered. As the years passed, he increasingly resisted

228

advice; he ignored any judgment not his own. His stubbornness caused him to make mistakes, a few with dreadful consequences. Not until almost too late in his life did he begin to acknowledge his dependence upon others.

Sound like a typical shoot-'em-up plot? I hope not.

These are not men seven feet tall and invincible. These are men five-feet-eight and nervous. They are vulnerable; they can lose, and the reader knows it.

What is more, their opponents, by and large, are not the dog-kicking villains of the old "B" Western. Often they can evoke a certain sympathy and understanding. Sometimes the reader is not sure how he wants the story to come out because he can feel empathy for both sides.

This brings up the question of conflict. The traditional image of the Western is a simple white-hat vs. black-hat yarn, a tall, strong, silent hero against a dyed-in-the-wool villain. It is an old war-horse plot, though one that a gifted writer can still make seem fresh and alive. I am not that gifted. When I have tried to use it, the old horse has shown all his ribs.

Somebody once suggested looking for plots at periods of traumatic change, when an old order is being pushed aside by something new. You can find these anywhere in history. We see them all around us today.

I like to use these periods of change as the basis for historical Westerns, for they set up a natural and understandable human conflict, often between honorable people, each side convinced that it stands for God and the right.

This type of conflict may be cataclysmic, like the clash of the Union and Confederate armies at Gettysburg. Or it may be small and intimate, like the conflict between a modern elderly couple who want to hang onto the family farm or ranch despite all of today's rural economic misery, and their grown children who want them to sell the homestead and retire to town.

At either extreme, the conflict is the same: change vs. resistance to change. It is the oldest plot in the world, and yet it is always fresh.

The conflict may be intensified when it is within the character himself as much as or more than between him and others.

There is a built-in hazard in doing a historical Western, or a historical novel of any kind: the possibility of losing the characters and the story amid all the spectacle. A few years ago we had a rash of 100th anniver-

229

sary celebrations of towns and counties in Texas. Many paid tribute to their past by staging historical pageants, parading costumed people, wagons, coaches, horses, mules, even Longhorn cattle and buffalo past the audience. The spectacle was grand, but with rare exceptions it was only that: a spectacle. The audience came away with little feeling for what it would have meant to be one of the historic personages represented. We saw them only from afar.

History provides the stage. The writer must provide the characters and make them walk and talk and breathe, feel joy and anger, exhilaration and despair. If he does not, he has simply a historical pageant, not a story.

A lot of myth surrounds the West, but the truth is there for the writer who wants to seek it out. The Western story does not deserve to be locked into any set pattern, any formula. It can be as varied as the land from which it springs.

It must be, if it is to survive in its second hundred years.

45

CREATING A SERIES CHARACTER

By Robert B. Parker

WHILE I have ventured outside the form upon occasion (*Three Weeks in Spring, Wilderness, Love and Glory*), it is the chronicle of a series character named Spenser that puts bread and Promise margarine on the table at my house.

Writing about a protagonist who has appeared before and will appear again presents some specialized problems. For instance, you have to find exposition tricks that will inform people who are reading you for the first time, without boring people who have read all your books in sequence. And, while both the writer and the reader are aware that the hero of a series is very unlikely to die, the hero doesn't know it. One has to be careful to render him as a man no less mortal than the rest of us.

But if there are problems in a series, there are also opportunities. If you create a character in one book that you like (Hawk, for instance, in *Promised Land*), you can use him again. And if you didn't get him right the first time, you have another chance, and another. Moreover, you have the chance to develop your hero over a sequence of books and during a span of real time. Thus Spenser, who first appeared when I was 41, can grow, as I have.

There are, then, a few things that are uncommon about writing a series of novels. But there is much more that is common to the craft. In each instance, series or not, I begin with what Henry James called a "treatment," a brief statement of story and locale and major characters. The treatment is normally about two pages in longhand. Don't be misled. This is the hard part. The treatment may take a month of sitting, several hours each day, thinking (my wife says thinking has always been especially trying for me, but one should pay her little mind. She once described me as looking like a Mississippi state cop). I didn't have to think up the protagonist when I set out on my first novel (*The Godwulf Manuscript*). Spenser sprang fully conceived from my imagination where he had been lurking since I wrote my age in single figures. Because I don't have to imagine the hero, I always start with the scene, i.e., the place, the circumstances, the people that I can write about, the academic scene, for instance, or the book-tour-talk-show scene.

From the treatment, I develop a chapter outline, still in longhand, that lays out the sequence. It's not very fancy (a chapter might be outlined in a sentence, "Spenser drives to Smithfield and talks with the police chief"), and it partakes of none of those insistent curlicues that you learned in school (if there's an A, there has to be a B, etc.). The whole novel gets outlined in five or six pages. It is primarily for my emotional well-being. It saves me from rolling a piece of white paper into the typewriter and then staring blankly not knowing what to write. The outline is there, Linus; I need only look. Sometimes I don't look at all. The outline to *The Judas Goat* was there beside me on the desk every writing day, and I never so much as glanced at it. Sometimes I follow it closely, sometimes I stop mid-book and re-outline something I haven't been able to get right. But I always know pretty much what the story is when I begin to write it.

Then, the outline completed, I have only to write the book. I'm not being cute. Once the story is conceived, the hard part is over. If you have the ability, then executing the book is merely a matter of sustained (though hardly exhausting) effort. Discipline (though hardly of monastic intensity) is required.

If you have the talent without discipline, you'll have thirty pages of a swell novel in your desk for the rest of your life and you'll publish a couple of good short poems somewhere. If you have the discipline without talent you'll have ten unpublished novels in your closet. There's a third possibility, I suppose. You could have discipline, no talent, and a knack, and be Harold Robbins. Ideally, perhaps, all three would be best. But of one thing I am certain. Writers write, and one is not a writer until one has written.

I set myself a minimum number of pages, as a way to get from beginning, through middle, to end. The number of pages varies with circumstance. I have never set the limit lower than two pages a day, or higher than five. Unless I'm on a roll, I stop when I've written my quota. If there is time left in my writing day, I'll turn to something else, but by writing my quota I have fulfilled my responsibility to the book that day.

Since my typescript tends to equate one-to-one to the printed page, five pages a day will give me a two-hundred-page book in forty days of writing. That sounds mechanical, and it is. It is a large task broken down into many small ones. When I can, I try to follow Hemingway's advice to stop while you're hot so it will be easy to start up next day. But sometimes I'm not hot for weeks on end and then I just do my quota. If you wait to be hot you'll accomplish that thirty-page novel mentioned above.

I am not compulsive about writing. I don't work weekends. I don't work nights. If one of my sons is performing, I go and watch. If my wife will take a trip with me, I'll travel. I don't bring a typewriter. If my novel comes out three days later, or two weeks later, it makes small difference. Writing is my livelihood, not my life. And while I can't conceive of not writing at all, I'm not compelled to do it every day.

On the other hand, I do have to do it regularly. I would assume most writers who succeed in publishing any quantity of work do it regularly.

I have always been more interested in the protagonist than in the plot, which is, I suppose, one reason I write largely in the first person. If you're in doubt, I'd urge you to try first-person narration. It's the natural storytelling mode ("You shoulda seen what happened to me at Hampton Beach last night"), and it helps prevent inflated narrative language. If you tell your story in the first person, it is very handy to invent some people who can help you interpret your hero by offering some objective comment. In *The Great Gatsby,* Fitzgerald took that technique to the extreme by having Gatsby's story told to us by Nick Carraway. It is, of course, part of Gatsby's tragedy that he doesn't understand what happened to him. He couldn't have explained it. Carraway had to.

Spenser talks of himself, but for the parts he can't or won't speak of, Susan Silverman serves. She helps us understand him. She helps him understand himself. Hawk too helps illuminate Spenser. The ways in which Hawk and Spenser are alike, and the ways in which they are not alike, are crucial in imagining Spenser.

An interesting story about dull people may be possible, but I can't think of one. For me, the plot is in large part a frame, a series of occasions in which Spenser is able to demonstrate what he is, to enact himself. But to speak of the two, plot and character, as if they were separable is misleading. "What is character," James said, "but the determination of incident? What is incident but the illustration of character?"

The best books are always about more than the plot anyway. They have echoes and implications. They are informed by a sense of how life is, or ought to be. George Higgins wrote about cops and robbers. But his books are also about the thinness of the line between them, and about the way a man should behave, and about the relationships among men in groups. In *True Confessions,* John Gregory Dunne wrote about a murder investigation. But he also wrote about brothers, and hierarchy and autonomy and Catholicism, and Irish-ness. "The only reason for the existence of the novel," James said, "is that it does attempt to represent life." Aspiring writers should give their days and nights to Henry James (and me).

Writing isn't as hard as writers lead you to think it is, but it does not lend itself to shortcuts. Clichés are shortcuts; avoid them like the plague. But there are other more subtle temptations to cut across the field. I remember a manuscript in which the author used one description for two people, something to the effect that they were both huge and bald and menacing. That's a shortcut. The novelist attempting in some way "to represent life" must recognize that rarely in life are two people identical, even if they are minor characters.

A writer does that not because he's lazy, but because he's impatient. He wants to get on with it. It takes some understanding and some self-control to come to terms with the fact that the careful representation of life *is* getting on with it.

I have sometimes made the remark that I don't think writing very teachable. But if you are going to pursue writing instruction despite that admonition (no one has ever lost money rejecting my advice), be certain that your teacher has done what he/she/it teaches. Many people understand reading, but only writers understand writing. An intelligent reader can often say what's good or bad about a piece of writing, and there are critics who have helped me understand my own work better. But only a writer can tell you how (if it can be told): a writer who publishes; for money. I believe that there are very few good novels that don't get published. In fact I believe there are none.

There are, however, good novels that don't get finished. There is no one right way. Each of us finds a way that works for him. But there is a wrong way. The wrong way is to finish your writing day with no more words on paper than when you began. Writers write.

46

HORROR OF HORRORS

By Graham Masterton

You have to make up your mind, of course, what terrible threat your characters are going to be obliged to face.

In my first horror novel, *The Manitou,* it was a three-hundred-year-old Indian medicine man, reborn in the modern age to wreak his revenge on the white man. In *Tengu,* it was a squad of Japanese zombies, invulnerable to almost everything including decapitation, who were trying to get their own back for Hiroshima.

Other terrors have included a sinister family who need other people's skin to keep themselves from growing old; a nasty religious cult who believe that the only way to get to heaven is to eat thy neighbor; and a demon who impregnates unsuspecting women in their dreams.

It isn't always necessary for your terrible threat to be totally original. Some of the finest horror novels have been fresh interpretations of well-worn themes. *'Salem's Lot,* Stephen King's breakthrough novel, was all about common-or-garden vampires; and *The Howling* by Whitley Strieber was a werewolf story.

You just have to make sure that no matter how wacky it is, your terrible threat is believable—at least for as long as it takes your reader to finish the novel. Unless it's believable, it won't be frightening, and if it isn't frightening, then you haven't delivered what your reader is looking for. And what your reader is looking for above everything else is fear.

Fear is the prime ingredient of all successful horror novels, although naturally you have to fulfil the terrible threat with which you have presented your characters. You can't write about vampires who never get around to sinking their fangs into anybody, or werewolves who don't tear anybody's lungs out, or zombies who stay in their coffins and don't shuffle around shopping malls dropping bits of themselves wherever they go.

But creating an atmosphere of fear is far more important (and far more difficult) than creating a moment of disgust. It is the atmosphere of brooding evil that will make your horror novel successful . . . the feeling that you implant inside your reader's reluctant mind that the terrible threat is hanging not only over your characters but over him, too.

If you succeed in making your readers sleep with their bedside lights on, then you've achieved something special.

Now, how do you go about creating this atmosphere of fear?

First of all, you mustn't ignore the principles of good storytelling. Your horror novel must have a beginning, a middle, and an end. Your characters should be believable and believably motivated—and that goes for your vampires and ghouls, as well as your heroes and heroines. No matter how outlandish the Threat From Beyond that you choose to visit on them, your characters should react the way that real people would react. If you're not sure how, go to a horror movie and watch the audience instead of the picture. You'll be fascinated by the responses you see in people's faces. And what you'll find particularly striking is how often people laugh with terror.

You should establish firm ground rules for yourself about what your Threat From Beyond can and can't do. Vampires can go out only at night; they're hypersensitive to crucifixes and garlic; they can be killed by a stake driven through their hearts. Werewolves can never remember what they were up to while they were werewolves and can be killed only with silver bullets.

Many of my Threats From Beyond have been based on ancient legends, and I have retained the characteristics that were described in the original folk stories. In *Tengu,* the evil mastermind of a horde of vengeful Japanese zombies was a diminutive dwarf called Kappa. I based him on cunning Japanese water-demons called Kappas, who drag men, women, children and livestock into lakes and suck their blood. The Kappas' one weakness is that they have concave, saucer-shaped heads which are filled with water, and this water gives them their strength. If you can persuade a Kappa to bow his head, the water will pour out, and he will lose his power. In *Tengu,* I adapted the legend to make Kappa a hydrocephalic who is eventually suffocated when his huge head drops forward, constricting his neck and suffocating him.

In *The Pariah,* a Mexican skeleton-demon called Micantecutli can be subdued by freezing; and the nasty family in *Picture of Evil* can be wiped out if their portrait is destroyed.

There must be a way in which your hero can eventually win out over the Threat From Beyond. How your hero finds out what it is, and how he attempts to carry it out, can be as desperate and as complicated as you like, and you can bluff and double-bluff to scare your reader even more: *Is that nice Mrs. Stephenson next door really a vampire or not? She's still wearing her crucifix, but . . .*

Similarly, your hero should be restricted by his morality and his conscience, and perhaps by other more mundane factors, too, like the fact that he simply can't afford to spend his time chasing demons, unlike the wealthy Duke de Richelieu in Dennis Wheatley's supernatural novels. Or maybe he's got a messy divorce to deal with, as well as the Thing That Eats Entrails.

Whatever kind of horror novel you're writing, never forget that you're still dealing with the fundamental struggle between Good and Evil, and for any struggle to be involving and meaningful, it has to be played out according to understandable rules. There is no tension in any confrontation if there aren't rules, whether that confrontation is chess, tennis, pro-football, or fighting malevolent demons from another dimension.

It isn't always necessary for your hero to overcome the Threat From Beyond completely. I often like to leave a tingling little element of doubt at the end of my horror novels. But it *is* necessary for the sake of the reader's satisfaction that Good should have proved itself during the course of the struggle to be superior to Evil. We all need to be reassured that honesty and purity and clean shining teeth will always win out over deceit and corruption and careless personal hygiene.

This needn't necessarily apply to short horror stories, some of the very best of which end up with the principal character facing the most hideous of extinctions. But a full-length novel requires very much more investment from your readers in terms of time and emotion and character identification, and they will feel frustrated and cheated if you feed your principal character to the Threat. Imagine the audience dissatisfaction if *Jaws* had finished off Roy Scheider instead of the other way around!

Having chosen your Threat and the general outline of your story, take a very close look at your characters. As a general rule, the more bizarre your Threat, the more ordinary your characters should be. In my award-winning novel *Charnel House,* the hero is a sanitary engineer working in San Francisco. He reacts and behaves like a sanitary engineer, all the way through the book, although his character is deepened and changed by his encounter with an age-old demon:

The old man came into my office and closed the door.
He said, almost apologetically, "It's my house. It's breathing."
I picked up my ballpen. "Could you tell me your name, please?"
"Seymour Wallis. I'm a retired engineer. Bridges, mainly."
"Okay, and your problem is noise?"
"Not noise," he said, softly. "Breathing."
"Maybe you have a downdraft in your chimney," I suggested. "Sometimes the air comes down an old stack and finds its way through cracks in the bricks."
He shook his head. "It sounds like some kind of animal breathing. I know it's hard to credit, but I've heard it for three months now, and it's quite unmistakable."
I turned back from the window. "Are there any odors? Any unpleasant deposits? I mean, you're not finding animal excrement in your larder or anything like that?"
"It *breathes,* that's all, like a German shepherd on a hot day. Pant, pant, pant. All night long, and sometimes during the day as well."

So, reactions are important. They have to be believable and consistent with your character's background and personality. I personally think that in horror fiction it's a mistake to make your principal character too brave. The gradual finding of courage within himself or herself, the discovery within his or her own personality of previously unrealized strengths, is an important part of making the character believable. And, if the character is believable, the horrors that he or she has to face are going to be all the more believable, too.

Your readers will also be able to identify with this growing sense of courage, and finish the novel feeling that they, too, have faced up to the Threat and come out on top.

Take a great deal of care with the location and general ambience of your horror novel. Some of the most frightening horror stories have been set in perfectly ordinary everyday locations, but there is something to be said for choosing a setting that is isolated or unusual. Various rural locations have worked well: Appalachian mountaintops where none of the telephones work and most of the locals have near-together eyes and carry axes around with them, or downtrodden communities in the middle of the Texas plain where corrugated-iron doors bang monotonously in the wind and unseen eyes keep boring into the back of your head.

The purpose of choosing locations like these is to isolate your characters from the usual aids and comforts of civilization while at the same time not trying to be too Gothic and bizarre. Perhaps the finest creator of alarming rural locations was H.P. Lovecraft, who could frighten his readers just by describing his own invented New England landscape—and that was before he got on to the story itself:

> When a traveler in north central Massachusetts takes the wrong fork at the junction of Aylesbury Pike just beyond Dean's Corners he comes upon a lonely and curious country. [Note the unsettling use of the word "wrong." You're only on the first sentence, and already you've been led astray.] The ground gets higher, and the briar-bordered stone walls press closer and closer against the ruts of the dusty, curving road. The trees of the frequent forest belts seem too large, and the wild weeds, brambles and grasses attain a luxuriance not often found in settled regions. When a rise in the road brings the mountains in view above the deep woods, the feeling of strange uneasiness is increased. The summits are too rounded and symmetrical to give a sense of comfort and naturalness, and sometimes the sky silhouettes with especial clearness the queer circles of tall stone pillars with which most of them are crowned.

Lovecraft did tend to overdo his forbidding settings sometimes. All his gorges are of "problematical depth," and all his houses have "rotting gambrel roofs." All his local characters have the "mental and physical stigmata of degeneracy and in-breeding." But his technique of leading his readers away into an unnerving country that is only just on the edge of the world we know is worth the appreciative study of anybody who wants to write horror.

John Farris uses the same technique to great effect in his novel *Wildwood,* in which "the town site had been laid out by a man with a talent for camouflage and misdirection" and in which the inhospitable and monotonous countryside is thick with "bog and bramble and bear wallow."

I used New England myself as a location for my novel *Picture of Evil,* but I tried to create the house in which the evil characters dwell out of glimpses and smells rather than straightforward graphic description:

240

They made their way cautiously along the darkened path. At length they reached a high red-brick wall, heavily overgrown with clematis, bare and brown now, and dripping with rain; and Maurice opened a rusted iron gate, which squeaked dolefully. Beyond the gate was a brick-laid yard and then the dark outline of a huge house. There were no lights at any of the windows, and as Laura followed Maurice toward the front porch, she could smell freshly turned earth, and drains, and damp.

At last we come to the horror itself: the moment when the Threat gets to chomp people, or mince them up, or drain their vital juices, or whatever your chosen Threat actually does. Just how much chomping or mincing or draining actually goes on (and how explicitly you describe it) will depend on what kind of readership you are aiming for. There is a dedicated category readership which will always buy books with plenty of vivid blood and guts—usually high school juniors, servicemen, blue-collar workers, and prison inmates. Then there is a more general but more demanding readership which will buy a horror story provided it is involving and well-written, rather than plain gory.

Choose your words very carefully when describing scenes of horror. The more matter-of-fact you are in your language and your treatment, the more goosebumps you can raise on your readers' skin without being tasteless. You don't need to gloat and lick your lips to make a blood-thirsty scene come alive. In fact, you may be in danger of losing your readers' sympathy if you do.

If you want to study moments of horror written in a hair-raising but completely acceptable way, you would do well to turn to the *Reader's Digest,* which regularly carries stories of the nasty things that have happened to real people. Here's a typical quotation from "Bear Attack," an article that appeared in a recent issue:

> Shooting pains jerked Rollins back to reality. As the bears tried to get a better grip on his neck, he bit deep into the cold, damp earth. Now one bear was clawing at his back, while another gnawed at his skull . . . . As he lifted a hand to his head, his fingers slid under his warm, soggy scalp as if it were a hat.

What you can learn from the *Reader's Digest* articles is how people really react to horrific situations, and your fictional moments of true horror will become even more telling by the use of authentic descriptions.

There are few more telling compliments to the horror novelist than to have readers complain that his books are "stomach-churning," when in fact he has used no gruesomely graphic language whatsoever. Here is a scene from *Picture of Evil*, which a great many readers told me was "excessively bloody":

Vincent killed the girls, somehow. Such an act of violence was completely out of character. But he knew there was nothing left for him to do. It was like clubbing seals. Ermintrude knelt in front of him, and he beat her twice, so that her skull broke. Netty, he dragged from her wheelchair, and threw face down on the floor, and hit her as hard as he could on the back of the head.

It was, of course, the imagery of clubbing seals that made so many readers imagine that they had read about blood. If you choose your images well, you need never use the words "gore" or "guts" or even "blood." I'm not saying that I *never* do, but what I'm preaching is the powerful effect of restraint.

The horror novel is one of the most difficult and interesting of media. To my mind, it is still in its infancy, but the comparatively recent acceptance of the importance of horror fiction both as entertainment and literature bodes very well for any talented writer who wants to try his or her hand at it.

Read as much current and classic horror fiction as you can, from Poe on. Discover what has been tried before, and how well, or how badly. Then all you need is a sheaf of blank paper and the will to frighten your fellow human beings to death.

47

ON WRITING SCIENCE FICTION

By Ursula K. Le Guin

I LOOK over my typewriter, out the study window, forty miles north to the mountain called "The Lady"—Mount St. Helens. Since the May 18, 1980 eruption and the May 25 ash-fall, people keep saying to me, "You're a science fiction writer—you should write a story about the volcano!" And I can only stare, and whimper, "But—But—"

I could attempt to describe what the eruption looked like from my study window. I could research and write up a history of the volcano. I could tell the true story of the old man who wouldn't leave his home at Spirit Lake (but that's been better done already in a country song). I could write poetry that has the volcano in it somewhere, some day. There's a great deal any writer could write about the eruption, and the ash-fall, and the people involved. But the one thing no writer could make of it, now, is a science fiction story. Science fiction is about what hasn't happened, but might; or what never will happen, but this is what it might be like if it did.

St. Helens happened. The Lady blew. Having seen that pillar of darkness towering seventy thousand feet above my city, I know that the most and best any artist could do with it is to try—and fail—to describe it.

Before May 18, a major eruption of St. Helens was an *idea*. Since then, it's an *event*. Science fiction works with ideas. It is basically an intellectual form of literature—with all the limitations, and all the potentialities, that go with the dominance of intellect.

I hear a polite mutter in my mind's ear: "The woman is nuts. Brainless heroes bashing brawny villains to rescue bronze-bra'd princesses while boring through Hyperspace towards Beta Bunthi, home of the Bug-Eyed Yrogs—this is intellectual?"

Well, no. But it isn't science fiction, either. It's space opera. Let me define my terms. As far as I can make out, "science fiction" and "speculative fiction" are the same thing—and so henceforth I'll call them SF, which nicely includes both. "Fantasy" covers all imaginative fiction, but may be used as a category including all imaginative fiction *except* SF and horror stories. It also includes "science fantasy." As for "space opera," in print or on the screen, it is to SF what "sword and sorcery" is to fantasy: the stuff produced for mass sales. Not steak, not hamburger, just baloney. Mindless, macho, and miserably imitative; but with a thirty-million-dollar budget it can be lots of fun and very pretty.

Space opera not only borrows hardware and gimmicks from SF, but also filches the great imaginative themes, such as space travel, time travel, alien beings, other worlds. But instead of using them as metaphors of the human condition, as SF does, space opera makes them into meaningless decorations. They are not part of the structure of the work, but serve instead to disguise it. You peel off the space suits and the tentacles, and guess what? Howdy, podner! Welcome to Hyperspace, Texas!—And, frankly, I miss the horses.

A real SF story, book, or film is fundamentally different. It starts with an act of the mind, a step from *is* to *if,* a reach of the imagination into the nonexistent. But it is not a leap into the impossible or the absurd. Indeed, SF dreads absurdity and loves logic almost as much as Mr. Spock does. In SF, the risky act of imagination is controlled by the thinking mind, the intellect. And therefore the discipline it accepts most naturally and gracefully is that of science. Real science: a respect for fact, and a sympathy with the patient way science arrives at fact.

Fantasy makes its connection to ordinary-daylight-outside-the-book-cover-reality through the emotions and through ordinary physical perception. (I could go on about that, but this chapter's about SF, not fantasy!)

SF makes its connection with ordinary-day-light-etc.-reality through ideas—principally the evidence of science and the speculations of the thinking mind. In SF, there is a reason for what happens, and it is a rational reason. The events of the story make sense in a cause-and-effect system. No matter how wildly imaginative they are, they don't happen just because the author likes it that way, or thinks it "feels right." Fantasy admits such reasons unknown to Reason. But SF doesn't. In SF, the questions "Why?" and "How?"—asked at any point in the story—should be answerable.

This doesn't mean that an SF story is an educational lecture with some fictional sugar-coating. Anything but! The ideas are the seed, not the tree—the blueprint, not the building. An SF story that hasn't *grown from* its ideas, but just flatly states them, is dull stuff.

A very few SF writers are practicing scientists, in such various fields as psychology, anthropology, biology, astronomy. Most are not. My impression is that the knowledge of science used by most SF writers comes from self-education—reading books and articles on subjects that interest them. (As for myself, the total of my formal training in science is one semester of anthropology and one of geology.) The point is, what's wanted is not a great mass of technical knowledge, but an attitude towards knowledge—an attitude of curiosity, above all. If learning facts and finding how events connect together bores you, then you probably don't read much SF, and certainly wouldn't enjoy writing it.

Let me try to illustrate this apparently paradoxical situation. Let's take a typical crazy SF invention: A five-hundred-foot-tall woman lands on Earth. Now, first of all, does she walk up Main Street, mashing a Honda at every step, and sit down for a rest on the First National Bank building?

In fantasy, she could. In the space opera movie, she does. In SF, she doesn't, because she can't. If she's really a woman just like us only a hundred times taller, she's too heavy to stand up, let alone walk. Crushed by her own weight—the gravitational pull of the Earth—the poor thing is lying there dying of internal injuries. We know that beings of our general type and mass cannot exceed a certain size, under our local conditions. Brontosaurus was at the limit for a land animal, and he wasn't any five hundred feet tall. Even Bill Walton has problems. And we are following Delany's Law. S.R. Delany, a most innovative writer of SF, put it this way: "Science fiction must not contradict *what is known to be known.*" And we know that it is known that solid 500-foot ladies are impractical.

But what if she's a projection of a five-foot Alien who is staying up in her space ship above the Earth until she finds if it's safe to arrive in person? She meant to beam down a five-foot projection, but the beamer got the size wrong. The technology involved—perhaps using holographic images—is not known to be impossible. Or, what if she really is five hundred feet tall, but, since she comes from a giant gas planet like Jupiter, she is made of airy, gauzy stuff, with almost negligible weight and mass? Realizing that she got the size wrong, she compresses herself into the shape of a five-foot woman weighing 3½ pounds, and walks briskly into the First National Bank building, holding her breath. . . . Well, this is

245

getting pretty hard to explain, but I'm not sure that we've contradicted anything that is known to be known. And so long as that rule is kept, SF is perfectly free to invent. It just has to make sure, as it goes along, that it doesn't contradict *itself*. The pieces must hang together.

Figuring out how it hangs together, all the where-why-what-and-whether, is half the fun of SF, for both the reader and the author. There's so much to know about our friend in the First National Bank Building—what life is like for someone as gauzy and compressible as a silk scarf, and what the weather is like on her home planet, and what kind of society her people might have, since they are all very fragile, very agile, and able to change size and shape at will. And what might have brought her here to Earth, and, as a matter of fact, what she's doing in the Bank. Madame, what are you up to in there?

"Prrswit frumbo rigpot thoom," she says into her Vox-Coder, which instantly prints out in English: * I * AM * GATHERING * MATERIAL * FOR * A* SEARINGLY * REALISTIC * STORY * ABOUT * BANK * TELLERS *

Fantasy and SF certainly overlap, but there is a real difference between them, and in general I believe they are best not muddled up together. A fantasy element—something rationally unexplainable—can be very annoying in an SF story, and often looks like what it is: a bit of laziness on the author's part, sloppy or wishful thinking. The reverse mix, SF intruding into fantasy, often occurs in books for young people by authors who are basically distrustful of the power of fantasy, and so try to explain away the whole thing—"But it was really all a dream!" That's a cheat, and the kids know it.

There is one more thing about SF that I feel I have to mention, but don't want to, because it is so undignified. In workshops I call it PSG. PSG stands for Pseudo-Scientific Garbage. It isn't meant as an insult, merely as a description. After all, the truth is that science fiction is not true. It isn't science. It's fiction. Although it starts from a known fact or an educated guess or at least a crazy but plausible hunch, and although it tries loyally not to contradict what is known to be known and not to stumble over its own internal logic—still, the whole thing is made up. And, especially if it's set in the future or on a different world, *all the details* have to be made up. Here's where the PSG comes in, and here's where the gift for SF may shine brightest.

For example: that Vox-Coder our Alien was using. I didn't explain that it's an instant translating machine, voice-activated. I didn't really have to. It's not a big step from the little hand-carried translator-computers we have right now. The Vox-Coder seems not only possible, but probable. Yet, the more you happen to know about language and translation, the less probable it may seem. Here evidence from one science (computer technology) contradicts evidence from another science (linguistic theory), and you have to take your choice. But your choice is warped by the fact that translators are so handy in SF. Without them, all the Aliens have to spend months learning English, or the Terrans have to painfully learn Voobish. So we gave our 3½-pound Alien a ¼-ounce Vox-Coder. And so I call it, with all due respect, a piece of PSG.

All interstellar space ships are PSG.

Much PSG is truly common property in SF. You learn it simply by reading SF. (Anybody who tries to write SF without having read it is wasting his time and ours.) There's a good deal of genuine sharing: the word "FTL," for example, meaning Faster Than Light. Anybody can fly an FTL ship. More often you don't borrow the name—Vox-Coder, phaser, pinlighter, etc.—but take the general idea and deck it out your own way. Of course you also are free to make up any gimmick or device you want or need, and this is fun. Much of the joyful inventiveness, the shock and beauty of SF is in its PSG. I think of Philip K. Dick's fully automated and highly verbose taxicabs, which tend to argue with their customers, sometimes becoming quite emotional. . . . Of Vonda McIntyre's gentle replacement of the hypodermic needle by the serpent's tooth. . . . Of H.G. Wells's lovely, shimmering Time Machine. . . . Of the pleasure I had trying to figure out what it would feel like to be a woman this month and a man next month and both/neither in between. . . . PSG, all of it. *Taxicabs don't talk!* Only if you're perfectly sure of that fact should you write a story about talking taxicabs.

In 1968 I wrote a book, *The Lathe of Heaven* (and in 1979 WNET/TV made a movie of it). At a climactic point of the book, Mount Hood erupts, and then the extinct volcano inside Portland city limits, Mount Tabor, erupts, and the whole Cascade Range goes off—except Mount St. Helens.

Why did I deliberately leave her out, knowing that she was in fact the likeliest to erupt? I can't explain. When I was writing the book I looked at her out the window, the "misty, blue-grey cone" which is in the story but not here in the real world any longer; and she must have whispered to me, "Sshh. Quiet. I have my own plans."

And I'm very glad I got it all wrong. My job's fiction. I'll leave the reality business to the Lady.

48

PLOTTING THE REALISTIC DETECTIVE NOVEL

BY MARCIA MULLER

RECENTLY I WAS having dinner with a fellow writer, and for once we were not talking shop. Instead, we were discussing a mutual friend who was having problems. After a while my friend looked thoughtful and said, "Maybe we shouldn't be talking like this. After all, remember what Sharon said about her last case: You can't understand what goes on in another person's life unless you exist inside it."

Sharon is my private detective, Sharon McCone, who to date has appeared in seven novels. And what my writer friend didn't realize at the time is that she had just paid me one of the greatest compliments of my career. Her casual quoting of Sharon told me that I had created a real character and a real situation—ones that could be remembered and applied to situations in everyday life!

In the course of our reading we've all run across characters and stories that have such reality that we remember them long after we've forgotten our best friend from high school or what happened to us in the summer of '62. In many detective novels, we encounter situations so strange that any investigator would insist they couldn't possibly happen; yet we believe in them implicitly, cheer for the hero the whole way, and heave a sigh of relief when everything is finally resolved. What makes these stories so believable? Why do we remember some novels long after we turn the last page, while we dismiss others as mere gimmickry—and often don't bother to read to the end?

The answers to these questions lie in the novels' characters. A realistic detective novel is *not* about cardboard characters sitting around a drawing room, puzzling over mechanical clues to a bloodless murder. It *is* about real people who exist in a world that is not all that dissimilar to the reader's world. What happens to these people in the course of the novel is extraordinary, and their response to the events may be unusually courageous or clever, but the realistic backdrop against which they act convinces the reader that the story actually could happen.

To make your reader believe—and become involved in—the plot of your detective novel, not just your hero but also your villain and your secondary characters must be believable. These are the people who will develop as you plan and write your book; who will interact with one another; and whose actions will suggest plot twists, red herrings, or even a better ending than the one you had first envisioned.

The development of the plot of my novel *There's Nothing To Be Afraid Of* is an example of how characters create a story. I wanted to write a book set in San Francisco's Vietnamese refugee community. I had researched the subject and knew that many of the refugees had been resettled in the Tenderloin district of the city—an area previously the sole turf of the poor and homeless, prostitutes and pimps, drug addicts and pushers. I knew that the refugees were changing the character of the neighborhood, and that the changes, while positive, had caused resentment and conflict with the long-time inhabitants. My research provided a factual basis from which I could begin to speculate: What if that resentment flared into violence—a campaign of terror directed against a group of Vietnamese living in one of the Tenderloin hotels? What if the campaign resulted in a murder? That, I decided, was the problem Sharon would be asked to investigate.

I now had a real setting for my novel and a situation that could very well occur in real life. I also had in mind several types of people who were likely to become involved in such a conflict, but I needed to create distinct characters. I made a list, named individuals, removed a few who didn't quite fit, added a few more. The final cast included a Vietnamese family, the Vangs; a street preacher, Brother Harry; a homeless man who quoted poetry, Jimmy Milligan; a flower seller, Sallie Hyde; and a porno theatre owner, Otis Knox. But at this point, these were merely names on paper. Next, I had to make them real.

To be truly believable, every fictional character must have a past, a present, and hopes for the future. Some of these details may be relevant to your plot, some may not. Some you may reveal to your reader, others you may choose to conceal until the unraveling of your mystery. But you should be aware of all of them. They are what flesh out your characters, give them a frame of reference, and allow them to act and react to the situation around them. And in turn, the acting and reacting of the characters help you to structure your plot.

In writing the detective novel, it is essential to remember that you are not merely creating a sleuth, or a victim, or a criminal; instead, you are writing about a real flesh-and-blood person who also *happens* to be a sleuth, victim, or criminal. This person does not exist in a vacuum; he has a life outside of the immediate story, consisting of a family, home, romantic entanglements, friends, political opinions, food preferences, hobbies—and much more. You may choose not to bring in all of these facts—they may not be relevant—but you should be aware of them, since they may come in handy at some point in your book. For instance, Sharon is an amateur photographer, able to read negatives, a skill that allows her to discover the motive for the murder in her fourth case, *Games To Keep the Dark Away.* I did not invent this hobby merely for the purpose of solving that case; it was something I had always known about her, but I had not mentioned it in the earlier books because it was not relevant.

Creating an existing context for your character is particularly important in the case of a series character. When I began writing about Sharon McCone (several years and many abortive attempts before she finally saw print), I created a biography for her. This contained details about her family and upbringing, her educational and work history, and such other things as political leanings, likes and dislikes in food, what she finds attractive and unattractive in men, even color preferences and the style of furniture she favors. As the series has progressed, many of these details have altered, because in fiction, as in real life, people change in response to the conditions around them. For example, Sharon originally preferred modern furniture, but after a case involving Victorian houses, she recognizes a fondness for older things. And, as each of her cases brings her into contact with violent death and evil, she becomes more worldly-wise and perhaps a shade more cynical.

The milieu in which your character exists should also include details of home life and friends. Sharon once lived in a rundown studio apartment in San Francisco's Mission district; she recently bought a house in the Glen Park area and has the usual first-time homeowner's problems. At All Souls Legal Cooperative, she is surrounded by friends and co-workers: her boss, Hank Zahn; her close friend, tax attorney Anne-Marie Altman; Ted, the efficient secretary and intrepid worker of cross-word puzzles. In addition, she meets people through her cases: former lover Lt. Greg Marcus, current love Don DelBoccio, and antique dealer Charlie Cornish—to name three who reappear from novel to novel. This supporting cast lends Sharon's world an air of authenticity, and often provides fodder for subplots or the main plot. These friends' actions and reactions affect Sharon, providing further impetus for character change, which is the stuff life—and a good story—are made of.

An example of character development from *There's Nothing To Be Afraid Of* may further clarify how this process works. Hoa Dinh never appears before the reader; he is a murder victim when we first see him. But it is essential that we know a great deal about him: first, because he has been murdered, and the motive for a murder is usually personal; and second, because the reader needs to care about Hoa in order to care about the search for his killer.

From my research about the Vietnamese refugees, I knew what Hoa's past and present typically would have been. On that factual basis, I built specific details. Hoa is only sixteen at the time of his death. He has fled Vietnam with his family, narrowly escaping drowning when their boat almost sank in the South China Sea; he has been shunted between refugee camps and temporary housing; he has finally achieved some stability in his permanent home in the Tenderloin, and is attending electronics classes. Hoa's hopes for the future should have been bright, but he is murdered before he can realize them. Hoa now has a past, present, and shattered hopes for the future. He is now a tragic human being, not just an anonymous victim. Other details, concerning Hoa's feelings toward his present situation and the activities these feelings prompted, were essential to the unraveling of the plot and had to be concealed until the proper moment came to reveal them.

I developed the other characters on my list in a similar manner, giving them unusual pasts, problematical presents, and, in some cases, fears rather than hopes for the future. And eventually the circumstances of one of them suggested a motive for the harassment of the Vietnamese and the murder of Hoa Dinh. From that, I was able to project a tentative solution to the case.

The first five or six chapters of my novels are usually devoted to developing the situation and the characters and setting up complications. During this stage—even though I have the motive and solution firmly in mind—I like to keep the plot fairly flexible and open to change. The characters begin to act and interact, sometimes in unusual and surprising ways that suggest red herrings and further complications. These complications always lead to a richer plot than I've originally envisioned; often they can lead to a totally new solution.

In *There's Nothing To Be Afraid Of,* the interaction between two characters in the subplot acted as a catalyst that enabled Sharon to put several pieces of information together, leading directly to the solution of the crime. I decided that the subplot would concern All Souls Legal Cooperative, Sharon's employer: A dissident group of attorneys is trying to wrest control of the co-op from the group that founded it.

My first character was Hank Zahn. I know Hank well: He is from an upper-middle-class background; he fought in Vietnam, returned home disillusioned, and joined the protest movement. After law school, he founded All Souls. That is Hank's past. His present is troubled: Some of the attorneys want to "bring all Souls into the eighties" and do away with the concept of low-cost legal services for the underprivileged upon which the co-op was founded. Hank's hopes for the future are to continue serving his clients along those lines.

The other faction is led by Gilbert Thayer, a new partner. Gilbert's background is similarly privileged, but he is younger than Hank, has recently graduated from law school, and hopes to make a great deal of money. At present, he sees All Souls as a vehicle for furthering that ambition and is trying to turn it into a big-time law firm—and do away with the sliding fee scale.

Given Gilbert's character, it is logical that he go about his plan in a bombastic, abusive manner—which he does. On the other hand, Hank has a low-key, contemplative personality. He withdraws to think things over and then emerges with a clever plan designed to force Gilbert's hand, resolving the situation at the co-op—and in doing so, providing Sharon with the nudge she needs to solve her case.

In the above example, both men act and react in ways that are logical and consistent with their particular frames of reference. Gilbert always blusters and alienates others; Hank always thinks things through and devises clever plans. It is this logic that makes the solution to the take-over attempt at All Souls believable.

Your plot should always be based on your characters acting in ways that are logical with the past, present, and future you have devised for them. The body-finding scene (one of the most difficult to write in crime fiction) provides a good example of this. When Sharon McCone discovers a body, she does not panic, scream, or run away (as I might do), because she has discovered bodies before and is aware of what to do—check to see if the person is really dead. On the other hand, Sharon is an emotional woman, so she does not conduct herself casually or coolly at a murder scene; she feels and reacts with the appropriate seriousness and sadness.

How can you ensure that your characters are acting in a logical and realistic manner? The best way is to put yourself in their shoes, keeping in mind the frame of reference you have created for them. In *There's Nothing To Be Afraid Of,* one of the minor characters also finds a body. She is not a professional investigator, nor is she experienced with this sort of violent death, so she would not check the person's pulse and call the police as Sharon would. To figure out what her logical reaction would be, I first reviewed what I knew of the young woman: She was easily frightened, had a family to whom she was close, and was not overly trusting of the police. Then I put myself into the situation: It's dark, there's a dead person on the floor, I'm scared. What would *I* do— given this young woman's background? Panic and run to get help from my family, of course. And that's exactly what my character did.

In all your characters' actions—whether as momentous as those on finding a body or as simple as deciding what to have for breakfast— place yourself in the situation, *keeping in mind the person's particular frame of reference*. This is sure to help you come up with a logical reaction that will also move your plot along to a realistic conclusion.

In assessing how plausible the plot of your detective novel is, you may want to ask yourself the following questions: Is my story based— however loosely—upon actual fact? Have I created a situation that— given those facts—could probably happen? Are my characters representative of types who would be likely to become involved in such a situation? Have I developed them fully, with an eye to the larger context in which they live? Are their actions—and thus the movement of my plot—logical and consistent with their particular frames of reference?

Once you have answered "yes" to these questions, you will feel confident about allowing your characters' interactions to create the clues, red herrings, and plot twists that will make your plot truly baffling. These, however, are merely mechanics, and only as good as the people who discover the clues, fall for the red herrings, and untangle the twists. In the detective novel, the crime is only as interesting as the person who commits it and the person who solves it.

49

SEEING AROUND CURVES

By Martha Grimes

SOMETIMES I wonder if painters and potters are asked, "How far along are you?" with that portrait or vase, or "How much have you done?" with that landscape or bowl. Such well-intentioned inquiries into the progress of a novel make me feel a little cross and, in a way, slightly stupid, as if I, naïve traveler on the Orient Express, were asked to describe the Venetian canals before my feet had left the platform in Victoria.

People seem to grasp the idea that a painter does not see an orange or an ear floating in his mind's eye, and a potter does not see a neck or a handle. But perhaps because we all "write" in some sense, there is a certain familiarity about pages, and they think progress can be charted by counting them. Perhaps paintings and pots are seen spatially, as a whole, but stories and novels are seen as linear. An eye doesn't "follow" an ear in a portrait, but it's a dead cert that page two will follow page one in a book. And because of this, when I say "a hundred and fifty pages," my interrogator might answer, "Ah. Halfway through, then." No, definitely not, I tell him, no more than I'd have painted half a face if I had got down the eye and the ear.

But if one sees writing in this way—as linear—it is understandable that one might be more likely to look at it as a trip, with marked distances to go between colorful chapter stop-offs. And the mystery writer especially may lean toward this idea of inventing a sort of TripTic or map or other means of charting the territory he intends to cover, then peopling it with characters, and drenching it with atmosphere. Since it is true that in a mystery there should be no loose ends and no clues unaccounted for, it is likely that one might think all story plot problems are resolved in good time.

This assumption that the emphasis in the mystery novel is on eventful happenings or crises—like the murder itself, for it is most often

254

murder—sometimes obscures the fact that the ax doesn't hang in the air, but must be dropped by someone's hands on someone's head. It also assumes that we who write it must know about Venice before we leave Victoria Station. Yet few people know exactly what their destination will look like before they get there or even if they will reach it. So we don't know where we are until we see what it looks like, and we don't know who we are until we see what we do. No one can see around curves no matter how far he sticks his neck out the window. Plot—the territory we want to chart—depends on the characters as much in a mystery as it does in any other novel; character directs the whole journey.

Many writers apparently do very well by mapping out the trip before they start, by sorting out what we might think of as the central elements of plot in a mystery—the perpetrator, the victim, the means, and the motive—and getting them into place by means of outlines, summaries, and synopses. On the other hand, there are writers who just go ahead and climb aboard the train, uncertain even of their destination, perhaps taking their chances that some unknown factor will keep the train from derailing.

I suppose I work this way because I find it so difficult to untangle plot from character, to invent crises for strangers. Nor do I think the device of the character sketch written ahead helpful, because what Tony had for tea when he was seven doesn't interest me unless at twenty-seven he's going to lace someone else's tea with cyanide. Plot, character, setting all seem one huge tangled skein when we set out to write. And because it's difficult to untangle the elements, you might think that the Grand Design should be set down before you have characters bumping into one another on the platform. Line them up and make them behave, for heaven's sakes! There goes the Colonel, making for the café. *Thwack!*

Now let's say that the sketches, the outlines, the synopsis, or the plot summaries are all approaches that you feel will at least get you aboard the Orient Express. You take your character-sketched people along and thus you and Sybil and Grimthorpe and the Colonel manage to get into the dining car (oddly lacking in ambiance since you would hardly have included that in your plot synopsis). The four of you are having a good gossip and being quite friendly, all of you with copies of the outline/sketch/synopsis before you.

255

You're all in a pretty good mood, except when the Colonel becomes rather churlish because he can't get the waiter's attention. Of course he can't because there is no waiter; he was not in the TripTic.

Now, Sybil, Grimthorpe and the Colonel read over the outline/sketch/synopsis. And there the trouble begins. Fortunately, the dining car is unpeopled—since the background passengers weren't in the synopsis—and the four of you can have a high old time:

Sybil is furious because you're having her marry Grimthorpe when the Orient Express hits Venice. Sybil claims she wants to marry Anthony.

Who's Anthony, you wonder? watching her dampen her finger and plaster a spit-curl to her cheek as she gazes out at the empty (truly empty) countryside.

"Sybil," you ask patiently, "*why* must you marry Anthony?"

"Well, *I* dunno, do I?" Then she rolls her eyes and adds, "I s'pose because he's ever so 'andsome. . . ." She swings her leg and twirls a cheap sequined bag. . . .

But Sybil's supposed to be a marchioness. Why is she coming on like a shopgirl?

Grimthorpe's mouth twitches as he looks down his knobby nose at Sybil and announces he wouldn't have her on a bet.

The Colonel's face is beet-red because he can't find a waiter, yell as he might.

You now realize something's wrong and wonder how the devil you're going to get out of this mess as the Orient Express chugs along to Paris. The only thing you're sure of is that they'll all detrain in Venice—

Until the train rolls into Paris, and Sybil just gets off. Anthony lives in Paris. . . .

The reader is certainly familiar with what is practically a cliché—that after a while the "characters simply take over." This is actually one of those wonderful remissions (or reprieves) for the writer, when everything seems to be on automatic pilot, and the people in your book "come alive," and appear to know what they're going to do and how they're going to do it. You would be willing to believe that the Muse indeed visiteth at such times. The Muse or Tinkerbell or Inspiration or something. But since you know that characters do not clear the mental compartments and take over themselves, it must be some other part of your mind doing it, and all of the scenario above is probably the

256

unconscious ditching the lovely plot complications of the conscious mind. In other words, Sybil (part of you) has a reason for tuning out all of that highbrow marchioness stuff; you simply don't know what it is, any more than you can see around curves. But you will eventually know why, and eventually round the curve. That you will either go mad at worst or type away in a state of controlled hysteria (at best) is something writers like me have to put up with if they want to get to Venice.

All of this revolves pretty obviously around another question that makes me cross: "Where do you get your ideas?" *Idea* is a word that seems frighteningly all-encompassing and makes me think of Carl Sagan neatening up the cosmos. *Idea* really does sound as if the interrogator is asking you where you got your *plot*. And the whole point is—how on earth do you know what people are going to do (correction, what you're going to *have* them do) until you see what they've done so far?

Perhaps I'd opt for the word (if there must be one) of "notion." That sounds far more frivolous, something rather small and capable of being grasped. It could be *anything*. The "notion" for *The Man with a Load of Mischief* came purely from the name of a pub. That a pub would have such a strange name led me on the further notion that a mystery set in England and having something to do with pub names might be interesting. My original detective was an effete, snobbish aristocrat, whose only saving grace was the wit of Oscar Wilde. Unfortunately, I had to toss that one out, since I don't have the wit of Oscar Wilde. Anyway, this character ultimately became Melrose Plant, and by that time, Scotland Yard had insinuated itself into the mystery in the person of Richard Jury. Perhaps the reason I am so fond of British pub names is that the germ of an idea can be found in so many of them. *The Anodyne Necklace* was irresistible for this reason. The notion of someone's killing for a necklace with curative powers was all I climbed aboard with.

The initial "notion" might be anything concrete—scene, sound, smell. I think if you confuse "notion" with "theme," you are definitely on the wrong platform, and you'll be sitting on your suitcases forever. *Theme* is an abstraction; it is not a cause but an effect.

The notion for my novel *The Old Fox Deceiv'd* was nothing more than a mental image of a youngish woman walking along a dark and cobbled

257

street. In this case, it was a setting that attracted me, and memories of the quintessential English fishing village called Robin Hood's Bay that I had visited ten years before. I was writing this plotless book when in one day I saw, in three different places, a woman dressed in black and white. It was Halloween, and one of them, in a black cape, was walking across a low-rising hillside. The three became a composite that begins the story:

> She came out of the fog, her face painted half-white, half-black, walking down Grape Lane. It was early January and the sea-roke drove in from the east, turning the cobbled street into a smoky tunnel that curved down to the water. . . . The wind billowed her black cape, which settled again round her ankles in an eddying wave. She wore a white satin shirt and white satin trousers stuffed into high-heeled black boots. The click of the heels on the wet stones was the only sound except for the dry *gah-gah* of the gulls.

Here, it was setting and atmosphere that intrigued me. I liked the idea of a young woman walking along the pavement of an English fishing village, and that someone be waiting in either a door- or alleyway, and that a knife come slashing down. I had no idea (1) who the girl was, (2) why she was being murdered, (3) who was murdering her. When I wrote the opening quoted above, the only additional thing I knew was that the young woman was either going to or returning from a costume party. That made me think of the various "disguises" and the endless possibilities arising therefrom for murder and mayhem.

I have probably used about every banal convention of the British novel of detection I can think of (hoping, of course, nothing appears to be banal in the end) simply because I like them. Bodies dumped in snow, letters dipped in vitriol, corpses stuffed in trunks. I have not actually used the near-holy device of the train schedule for some reason, but I imagine it will come up at some point.

When I sit down to write a book the only thing I'm sure of is that I'm there at the moment. Talent isn't guaranteed, but discipline is at least dependable, like any other habit. Fortunately, it's more productive than smoking and drinking. Flannery O'Connor said that although she might not come up with an idea for the allotted time she was there, at least she was there in case one happened along.

I have been asked (sometimes accusingly) why in the world I, an

American, would set her books in England. Like Sybil, "I dunno." Probably I was on my way to Venice and got off, by some quirk, in Little Grousdean, where I sit around in the local pub with Sybil and Grimthorpe and the Colonel, arguing over train schedules and drinking Old Peculier.

50

PROCESS AND PLOT IN THE HISTORICAL NOVEL

By Dee Brown

No writer is likely to undertake a historical novel unless he or she is keenly interested in certain periods of the past. My favorite time and place is the 19th century in America, especially the latter half. Most of my books, fiction and nonfiction, are set in that time, and almost every one of them originated from some simple incident of history, a true event that challenged my imagination. Quite often a provocative appetizer will pop up unexpectedly while I am doing research for another book.

Such happenings may be barely chronicled; often they are incomplete and slightly mysterious. They may remain as lines in my notebook or hang in my mind for months or years until out of a rising curiosity I begin to seek out the people and places involved, and perhaps begin the research that may or may not result in a historical novel. Like Shakespeare, who foraged through ancient tomes in search of ideas for plays, I spend a good lot of time with old publications.

Let us assume that I have chanced upon an account of a rather gruesome murder that occurred in Baltimore in the 1840s. I have found the report in an old volume about antebellum crimes, or in a contemporary newspaper. There is something familiar about this particular murder, but days pass before the connection is made. Then suddenly I realize that the murder was quite similar to the one committed in Edgar Allan Poe's story "The Tell-Tale Heart."

What a find! I think that Poe must have based his famous short story upon this actual murder. But no, a hasty examination of a biography of Poe reveals that although he was living at the time, the murder occurred four years after his story was published. At first I am disappointed, but then I begin to conjecture that perhaps the murderer read "The Tell-Tale Heart" and then acted upon it. I wonder what Poe must have thought, if he read about a murder that seemed modeled upon his invention.

A bit of rereading of the Poe biography reveals that the author was in and out of Baltimore, trying to raise money to start a new magazine, around the time of the murder. I ask myself: Is there a historical novel here? And I immediately begin to build a scaffolding to see if it will sustain a novel-length tale of the past.

Should Poe be the protagonist? Or should the unknown murderer be the lead character? Or an officer of the local police determined to solve the crime? Is the murderer a man or a woman? I know that Poe pursued and was pursued by two or three young women during the last years of his life.

I examine other biographies of Poe and decide to set the framework of the novel sometime after the death of his wife. Why not 1849, the last year of his life, when Poe was forty, and everything was unraveling for him, when even his friends suspected him of madness? In my imagination he comes to Baltimore after reading about the murder that is so similar to the one he invented four years earlier. He loves puzzles; he wants to solve the riddle of this crime, find the murderer. I know that Poe died in Baltimore after a five-day drinking bout with some men of "doubtful company." Had he found the killer who modeled his crime after that of "The Tell-Tale Heart"? Was Poe himself murdered because of what he had discovered?

Before constructing a plot, I must know the background, the physical setting of the story. Baltimore of the 1980s bears little resemblance to Baltimore of 1849, but if practicable, a visit there could be rewarding. I go to get the feel of the place, to view the surrounding countryside, to gaze upon the waterfront and inhale the odors of the river and the bay. Even more rewarding are visits with a notebook to Baltimore museums and restored houses, and most important of all, to libraries.

A map of the city around the year 1849 is essential. I find one and decide to have it enlarged to mount upon the wall above my workroom desk. I study histories of Baltimore and make photocopies of accounts of the city in the mid-19th century. I examine contemporary drawings and photographs. On a microfilm reader I peruse local newspapers of 1849, making special note of events that might enliven my story. Advertisements must not be overlooked, nor schedules of trains and sailing times of ships, nor prices of commonly used commodities.

I hope that out of all this collected jumble of the past will spring ideas for scenes, for characters, for action. I take my prizes home with me and immerse myself in them. At the same time I consult reference books from my own collection. (Every writer who works in the past requires standard works on historical costumes, uniforms, furniture, houses, railroads, boats, tools, foods, geography, and so on.)

First of all, I must know the clothing that my characters will wear. Baltimore was a premier railroad town in the 1840s, and I must know what the locomotives and passenger cars were like. My characters will see and may travel on boats that are in the harbor, and I must know the different kinds of vessels that would have been there in 1849. Photography had recently come into use and was instantly very popular, and I think I may use it in my story. I refresh my knowledge of early photography.

During this period of research, I try to imagine living in Baltimore in the year I have set my story. Time and movements are much slower, medicine is almost powerless against diseases that strike suddenly, attitudes toward life and death are different. Yet I must remember that human nature, the emotions, are much the same as now.

After some weeks of this saturation in the past, I am ready to create the characters who will play out my as yet vague plot. Some of them have already begun to step forward out of the shadows. Edgar Allan Poe is present, fully formed, his appearance frozen in photographs made in his later life. I remind myself that I must not violate history by placing him where he could not have been, and that what I make him say or do must conform with what is known of his personality, his patterns of behavior.

In contrast to Poe is a character I am inventing, a Baltimore police detective. He must be described and named, a biography of his past created. I think of him as being a native of the city, a former railroad laborer, then an army officer in the Mexican War, who on his return home finds employment as a police officer and is then sent to London to study the new police system at Scotland Yard. (This means I must do some research on early Scotland Yard methods of solving crimes.) At the time of the murder, my police detective has recently returned from London, eager to put to use what he has learned.

There are two women characters, opposites perhaps: one who lives in Baltimore and was a friend of Poe's late wife Virginia; the other, an amateur poet from New England who is slightly mad, like Poe, and who has been pursuing him for several months. How these characters are developed, the roles they will play, depend somewhat upon the plot. For the time being I let them grow in my imagination, as the plot begins to develop.

The murdered man I think of as an old sailor—miserly, misanthropic—who lived in a rooming house. The murderer is now known to me, but not the motivation as yet. I must decide at what point in the story this person will be revealed to the reader. Will it be better to reveal the identity of the murderer early so that the reader can watch the pursuit and see the dangers arising to the pursuers? Or should the identity be left to surprise the reader near the end?

Other questions arise in my mind. Should the detective at one point suspect Poe of being the murderer? Should Poe himself in one of his more acute depressions fear that he may be the murderer? The plot is developing.

Now it is time to decide from what viewpoint to tell the story. Through an omniscient narrative voice, the fly on the ceiling that sees all, or from one character's viewpoint? First person or third person? I draft an opening scene, in which the detective first arrives at the place of the murder, writing it in the third person, and then writing it again with the detective telling it as he sees and feels it. The latter seems more promising, but the final decision will be made later, after a few more trials.

Another chore that I undertake after writing the first draft is a reading in search of anachronisms in the narrative, and modern slang in the dialogue. Some readers may not notice or mind such discords, yet I'm certain that many react as irritably as I do when a 19th-century character pulls the zipper on his flight bag and greets his companions with a "Cool, man!" or "Hi, guys!"

Conflict. That is the essential ingredient, the basis of the plot. The source of suspense that keeps writer and reader on edge until the conflict is resolved. In this story, there will be major conflicts between the police detective and Poe, conflicts between the two women, and growing menace from the murderer as the differing skills of Poe and the detective come closer to revealing who the killer is. Not until the conflicts are resolved is the story told. And so the plot develops.

What has been outlined here is applicable, with varied modifications, to almost any historical novel in any setting. The story could be treated as a romance novel or a mystery, straight adventure, pure melodrama, a comic satire, or as a serious psychological novel. Through personal preferences, and through trial and error, writers of historical novels soon find the methods and the genres of fiction they are most comfortable with.

What we all seek is to create vivid characters in a compelling story, so believable that when a reader finishes the novel, he feels that he has truly lived through a past time. When I have finished the first draft, I always ask myself if the novel has added something to my knowledge of the past, and if it has not, then I know I must go back and find where I failed. Too much "furniture" of the past can burden the plot, of course, yet if I have failed to surround my characters and narrative with the contemporary political, social, and economic forces that determine attitudes, then I have probably added little to a knowledge of the era in which my novel has been set.

51

HORROR FICTION: EXPLORING THE DARK SIDE

By William F. Nolan

OVER THE PAST DECADE, I have chosen to concentrate on writing short horror fiction. I've often been asked why. Simple. Horror fiction offers the serious writer a wonderful opportunity to explore a wide variety of characters under stress, characters faced with bizarre situations, within the commercial framework of terror-suspense.

I am challenged as a writer as I explore the dark side of the human animal. We are all capable, under pressure, of aberrant behavior, and the more strain our minds are subjected to, the more we revert to that darker self. The thing that has always frightened me most is a human mind out of control—and I often write about people who have slipped over an emotional edge.

In my "Saturday's Shadow," I move inside the head of a cop who has gone over that edge; he kills his own sister to save her from what he believes to be a deadly shadow, which is, of course, only in his mind. In "One of Those Days," my protagonist hears mice singing in the walls, watches a cat with a baby in its paws cross a busy street, and finally realizes that his psychiatrist has turned into a shaggy dog. But these are all in his mind. . . .

My story "Ceremony" deals with *group* madness. It concerns a professional hit man, a killer for hire, who is lured to a small village in Rhode Island and who himself becomes a victim—trapped by sweet-talking "normal" folk who are actually as mentally twisted as the killer himself. Yet they *seem* so nice.

Which brings us to characterization. As writer, it is my job to make certain that the readers *accept* these people, not as monsters, but as individuals who have adjusted their moral values to fit their own desperate needs. This makes them all the more frightening.

Many beginning horror writers make the mistake of thinking that if the scare elements are horrific enough, then the story will succeed. Put in enough vampires and ghouls, they say, and you don't need to worry about creating real people. In truth, horror fiction cannot be separated from mainstream fiction in this regard. Solid characterization always serves as the core, or central pillar, of any really effective story. In order to frighten a reader, you must create people your readers can recognize and identify with. Once they are willing to accept your characters, once you have won their emotional rapport with characters they believe in, they'll go along with you as storyteller. They'll follow your characters from a sunny street into the darkest alley—from sanity to nightmare. You must, therefore, graft a muscled skin of reality over your skeleton of terror.

The more realistic the external elements of your story, the more effective it becomes when you let loose the horror. Stephen King's great success in the terror genre can be attributed, mainly, not to the horrors he creates, but to the *people* he creates. In his novel, *The Shining,* he did not take his characters into the nightmarish hotel until he had fully established them as three-dimensional human beings. It took him 100 printed pages to do this. Then, and *only* then, was he ready to engulf his characters in the real terrors of the book.

In my short story "Trust Not a Man," I spend 98% of the story in building my character—a lonely young girl searching for a man she can love and trust. The reader identifies with her troubled past, her sadness, her empty life. Then she discovers she has become involved with a man who is about to assault her—and she reacts by feeding him to a large, flesh-eating thing in her greenhouse. I devote only four paragraphs, at the end of the story, to the horror. The rest is all buildup to this moment. By then the reader is ready to accept the horror *emotionally*. My skeleton has been fleshed with reality.

Beyond character, mood is an all-important factor in effective horror fiction. Atmosphere. The stage must be set for the events that follow. Very early, most often on the first page, I try to establish a sense of disquiet, of something *wrong,* an aura of dread, however subtle. Let me cite some openings from my work to demonstrate this.

Here's how I begin "The Yard":

It was near the edge of town, just beyond the abandoned freight tracks. I used to pass it on the way to school in the mirror-bright Missouri mornings and again in the long-shadowed afternoons coming home with my books held tight against my chest, not wanting to look at it.

266

The key words here are: *abandoned . . . long-shadowed . . . not wanting to look at it . . .* These words convey an atmosphere of isolation, darkness, and fear. Or let's look at the opening of "Dead Call":

Len had been dead for a month when the phone rang. Midnight. Cold in the house and me dragged up from sleep to answer the call. Helen gone for the weekend. Me, alone in the house. And the phone ringing . . .

Again, the key words: *dead . . . midnight . . . cold . . . alone.* What I'm demonstrating here is that terror has to be constructed as carefully as an office skyscraper or a fine automobile. A terror tale must be layered, with one effect built over another; it must achieve a *cumulative* effect just as, with music, a good symphony builds in intensity. Terror, then, must be carefully orchestrated.

Consider what may well be one of the most terrifying scenes ever written—the "woman in the room" scene in King's *The Shining*. It's five pages long, and each paragraph builds toward the author's horrifying climax. King starts with the boy, Danny, standing outside the room he fears. He has a pass-key but doesn't want to use it. His body trembles. He hums to himself. A stream of thoughts and images races through his mind. He opens the door, and we get a description of the room. Dark. Turns on a dim light. The bathroom door is ajar. Danny is scared because he knows *something* awful is in there. Big white tub in there, with a shower curtain drawn around it. Danny goes in, draws back the curtain. A long-dead woman is in the tub. Bloated and purple. She *sits up*. Horrified, Danny bolts from the bathroom, runs to the outer door. But it's closed. He hammers on it, telling himself that this corpse can't really hurt him, that it isn't real. And just when he almost has himself convinced, a pair of fishy dead hands close on his neck. . . .

King has *layered* this scene to gain his impact. Each sentence takes us deeper into the boy's nightmarish encounter. By the time those dead hands touch him we have been emotionally prepared to react *with* him, to be frightened and shocked.

Another key element in effective horror fiction is what I call "the echo effect." A good horror tale must leave the reader with something to think about beyond what is obvious in the story on the surface. It must resonate within the reader's psyche. I often construct a subconscious "basement" beneath the main floor of my narrative, creating a double level.

Example: In "The Halloween Man," the *surface* narrative concerns the frantic efforts of a young girl to escape from what she believes to be a ghoulish creature who appears on Halloween night to collect children's souls. She ends up, at the story's climax, hiding in her room—and when her father attempts to calm her increasing fears, she is certain that *he* is the Halloween Man. The reader is left with the question of the ghoul's ultimate reality. Did he actually inhabit the father's body or did he exist *only* in the mind of this frightened girl? Thus, my echo effect.

In another of my terror tales, "Fair Trade," the narrator, under arrest for murder, describes a bizarre journey into town with an animated dead man who attacks and kills a citizen. The narrator *could* be telling the truth or he could be making up a lurid story to cover the fact that he is indeed the real killer. The reader is left to ponder both levels of reality. The tale leaves an echo behind in the reader's mind.

There are, of course, many ways to construct a plot, but a favorite method of mine is to begin with a very ordinary situation and allow it to become more and more offbeat. Take my story "The Partnership." I begin with a folksy fellow named Tad Miller, who's chatting idly with the waitress in a roadside café. Tad tells us all about himself, and we *like* the guy. He's a good ole boy. He tells us that Sally, who runs the place, likes him. ("Most folks do. And that's nice. Person wants to know he's liked, even if he keeps mostly to home.")

Tad also tells us about his partnership with Ed. All very homey and comfortable. Stranger comes in. He and Tad get to talking. Tad ends up taking the stranger out to show him through an abandoned funhouse near the lake, in an old, closed-down amusement park. That's where we meet Ed—who just happens to be a giant half-rat-half-water creature with a razor mouth and glowing red eyes. Ed gets the stranger for dinner, and Tad gets the guy's fancy wristwatch. A partnership. My plot has taken the reader from light into darkness, from the ordinary to the extraordinary. And our guide has been good ole Tad.

Try not to give the reader what the reader may expect. The more familiar the situation, the easier it will be to take your reader wherever you wish. In my "Dark Winner," a man takes his wife back to Kansas City to visit his old neighborhood. Ordinary, right? Not quite—because the man discovers that his evil childhood self is waiting inside the house of his youth, waiting to claim him, body and soul. Adult is absorbed by child, leaving the wife alone and powerless.

What about a party? We've been to countless parties in our lives. Why not start with a man invited to one late at night? I did just that in my tale "The Party," in which we meet David Ashland, a hard-drinking man with an unhappy past, who is attending what seems to be just another cocktail party but which quickly takes on a surreal aspect. The party builds to a feverish pitch, and Ashland flees but finds he cannot leave the building. To his horror, he finds that the *same* party, with the same people, is going on in every room of every floor—a party that will never end. And, final irony, all the booze is watered! David is trapped in his own special hell.

And, as author, I took the reader there by saying, hey, let's go to a party.

Stories such as these sneak up on the reader; they are, in a sense, almost playful. But they have hidden teeth. They bite.

Let me sum up with my feelings about art versus exploitation. I've been asked what I think about the "slice and dice" school of horror, the films and stories that drench the audience in blood and gore. I have strong feelings about them. They anger and nauseate me. They fail to examine the human condition; they simply exploit it. The true art of fear is achieved through a layered use of sensual effects as the writer (or filmmaker) manipulates mood, atmosphere, and character to his subtle purposes. And, for me, that's the operative word: subtle. I have found that with horror less is often more.

As writer, I prefer to allow my audience to fill in the graphic details of horror, since nothing on paper or on film can match the horrific images we can conjure up inside our own heads. And that's the prime target: the human mind.

Your audience is out there, waiting to be frightened. So go ahead, sneak up on 'em and scare their socks off.

They'll love you for it!

52

AUTHENTICITY IN CRIME FICTION

By Dorothy Uhnak

I HAVE ACQUIRED a reputation for authenticity and accuracy in presenting in my novels an investigation or examination of a crime. It would be obvious to suggest that since I spent fourteen years as a detective, it would be natural for my writing to reflect a certain expertise. But—

I never worked on a homicide investigation, yet I deal with murder in my novels.

I never worked a narcotics deal, yet I describe such events.

I have never been inside the office of the Police Commissioner or the office of the District Attorney, yet I have used both as settings.

I never, as a police officer, extended the boundaries of an assignment, yet my characters have done so on occasion.

I have not worked as a detective for a long time, and the law—and its enforcement procedures—have changed, been redefined, as have the police departments. As has society.

Despite my background and experience as a detective (which gives me a head start over other writers), I still must do considerable research to achieve the authenticity I require in my crime fiction writing. And this quality is essential not only for settings and procedures, but particularly in my characterization. For without that, I feel my novels would fail.

It is not my aim in my novels to tell a "cop story" per se. I deal with questions of morality and choices that confront businessmen, doctors, lawyers, bricklayers, students, shipping clerks, writers, dentists, teachers—people in all walks of life. My novels focus on the tightly defined world of the police officer, but also attempt to examine the larger world in which he lives, because that is a world in which I am comfortably knowledgeable. However, in aiming for the authenticity of my characters, it is essential for me to remember that no one is "born a cop."

By the time he becomes a police officer, an individual brings a

270

minimum of twenty-one years of individual history, philosophy, view-point, psychological orientation and self-image, which includes exposure not only to family and friends but to the influences of his immediate and extended society. In creating a character, I look back to my own association with fellow police officers. I've worked with a large assortment of personalities with a range of interests and abilities: a man who designed and tailored his own clothing; a talented jazz pianist who just "picked up" piano-playing; a cartoonist with strong political opinions; a magician who helped get us through long, boring stakeout hours. I've worked with deadly bores and with storytellers who could hold their own as professional stand-up comics; with men who were apolitical, far right, far left, dead center; with religious fanatics who loved preaching to prisoners (literally a "captive audience"); others who used religion for political advantage, and those who kept their beliefs to themselves. I've worked with men who did the job as honestly and as professionally as possible and with men who misused the authority inherent in law enforcement.

To achieve authenticity in my characters I research the time frame in which they live. My novel *Law and Order* was a generational novel covering about forty years in the lives of a family. The characters took on flesh and substance only when I was thoroughly familiar with the time, place, and "climate" in which they lived and which shaped them.

In writing about contemporary police officers, one must be aware of the differences in their life experiences, as compared with the environment that shaped their older colleagues and predecessors. Police officers in the past have been "true believers" and upholders of the status quo; have usually had some military service; believed in authority, right and wrong, law and order, a black-and-white moral code. The world has changed drastically since the fifties and sixties. Young law enforcement officers now bring with them *their* historical times, shaped in the revolutionary sixties and seventies and into the eighties. Old "truths" have been discarded. Sexual and social mores are relative and open to interpretation. Drugs are socially accepted by many of the younger generation, and many of the new cops have tried them. A writer cannot describe the working cop of today by reflecting the historical view of the older police officer. It does not apply, and everything that shapes the individual must be taken into consideration.

My background as police officer stands me in good stead. I make note

271

of *all* salient facts: physical locations, political climate, official procedures (which must be updated from time to time), the emotional state of the characters, and their actions. This provides the necessary authenticity that frees me to probe the *character* of the person, because I know that a lieutenant is functioning in his squad. He's doing what a lieutenant is supposed to do.

That's a given. I can then get on with creating the *man* behind the lieutenant's shield. At times, when my story seems to bog down, the actual process of an investigation that I learned as a detective will help me get things going again.

But even with all this, I would be lost without the backup of good research. There are excellent police science textbooks on criminal procedure, investigative procedures for specific crimes, court and lab routines. From consulting a relevant textbook, I know what I as the investigator would be doing next; whom I would logically speak to, question, examine. There are also any number of college-level courses in criminal justice and police science—more available now than at any other time. Most police departments in large cities maintain a public information officer who will cooperate with writers. Small police departments have usually been generous with their time and personnel. One important suggestion: When requesting information, always address a letter to the top person—the commissioner or chief. He will then refer it to someone who will assist you far more enthusiastically, knowing the request came from the "boss."

By following proper procedures, you can introduce new characters logically, and researching authentic cases, understanding inherent progression of events and the accepted line of reasoning will provide the authenticity essential to the reader as well as for the writer. As a reader, I have often lost interest in a story or novel if the author has made a glaring mistake in either law, procedure, jurisdiction, or assignment.

The act of gathering information also provides insight into official mentality. While I was working on *The Investigation,* I started with a simple telephone inquiry: How many assistant district attorneys work in the borough of Queens? I just wanted an off-the-top-of-the-head number for an offhand remark to be made by one of my characters. Unfortunately, I began my inquiry at the lowest official level. I was switched up the hierarchy *six* times, until I found myself at last speaking to the second-district-attorney-in-command (not a minor position).

He gave me the information I wanted, but only *after* I answered a dozen of *his* questions, e.g., Why do you want to know? Is this a political novel? How does this office enter into the story—specifically? Why did you choose this particular case? Whom did you say you worked for when you were a detective? Did you ever know a guy named. . .?

There are times when stretching the rules is allowable for the sake of the story, but this should be done only when you are doing it *deliberately*. Otherwise, more and more mistakes creep in, and the result is a flabby story. In instances in my book in which I allowed individuals to devote nearly all their working time—in some cases their non-working time—to the investigation at hand, I have knowingly violated authenticity. Detectives nearly always work on multiple cases and practically never when they're off a case. However, I always strive to make it seem not only plausible and natural but officially acceptable when they "go outside the lines" somewhat.

It is the writer's prerogative, of course, to create and develop a story in any way he or she chooses. However, if a writer sets out to write what will be offered as an accurate portrayal of an event in the police world, I feel that it is incumbent on that writer to set the framework within the authority of authenticity.

A Selected List of

REFERENCE BOOKS FOR MYSTERY WRITERS

BARZUN, JACQUES, and TAYLOR, WENDELL HERTIG. *A Catalogue of Crime*. New York: Harper & Row, 1971.

BRIDGES, B. C. *Practical Fingerprinting*. Revised by CHARLES E. O'HARA, with a foreword by AUGUST VOLLMER. New York: Funk & Wagnalls, 1963.

CHAPPELL, DUNCAN, and FOGARTY, FAITH. *Forcible Rape: A Literature Review and Annotated Bibliography*. (National Institute of Law Enforcement and Criminal Justice, Law Enforcement Assistance Administration, U.S. Dept. of Justice) Washington, D.C.: Government Printing Office, 1978.

Cunliffe, Frederick, and Piazza, Peter B. *Criminalistics and Scientific Investigation*. Englewood Cliffs, N.J.: Prentice-Hall, 1980.

De Forest, Peter R., Gaensslen, R. E., and Lee, Henry C. *Forensic Science: An Introduction to Criminalistics*. New York: McGraw-Hill, 1983.

Fox, Richard H. and Cunningham, Carl L. *Crime Scene Search and Physical Evidence Handbook*. (U.S. Dept. of Justice, Law Enforcement Assistance Administration, National Institute of Law Enforcement and Criminal Justice) Washington, D.C.: Government Printing Office, 1973.

Goddard, Kenneth William. *Crime Scene Investigation*. Reston, VA.: Reston Publishing Co., 1977.

Hagen, Ordean A. *Who Done It? A Guide to Detective, Mystery and Suspense Fiction*. New York: R. R. Bowker, 1969.

Hall, Angus (ed.). *The Crime Busters: The FBI, Scotland Yard, Interpol: The Story of Criminal Detection*. London: Verdict Press, 1976.

Keating, H. R. F. (ed.). *Whodunit? A Guide to Crime, Suspense & Spy Fiction*. New York: Van Nostrand Reinhold, 1982.

Kirk, Paul Leland. *Crime Investigation* (2nd ed.). Edited by John I. Thornton. New York: Wiley, 1974.

———. *Crime Investigation; Physical Evidence and the Police Laboratory*. New York: Interscience Publishers, 1953.

Laurie, Peter. *Scotland Yard. A Study of the Metropolitan Police*. New York: Holt, Rinehart and Winston, 1970.

O'Hara, Charles E. *Fundamentals of Criminal Investigation*. Springfield, IL: Charles C. Thomas, 1966.

Penzler, Otto (ed.). *Detectionary*. Woodstock, N.Y.: Overlook Press, 1977.

Schultz, Donald O. *Crime Scene Investigation*. Englewood Cliffs, N.J.: Prentice-Hall, 1977.

Smith, Myron J. *Cloak and Dagger Fiction: An Annotated Guide to Spy Thrillers* (2nd ed.). Santa Barbara: ABC-Clio, 1982.

SÖDERMAN, HARRY, and O'CONNELL, JOHN J. *Modern Criminal Investigation* (5th ed.). Revised by CHARLES E. O'HARA. New York: Funk & Wagnalls, 1962.

STEINBRUNNER, CHRIS, and PENZLER, OTTO (eds.). *Encyclopedia of Mystery and Detection*. New York: Harvest/HBJ, 1984.

53

ELEMENTS OF THE POLICE PROCEDURAL NOVEL

By Rex Burns

Given the development of the writer's sense of which words live and which don't — a development that for me comes as much through reading as through writing — I think the areas most pertinent to a successful police procedural are four: research, setting, plot, and character.

These divisions are, of course, artificial. As in any "recipe," the elements blend and influence each other; and in any art such as cooking or writing, the whole is greater than the sum of its parts. But though each writer must discover for himself this sense of life or wholeness, some of the basic elements contributing to it can be distinguished. Let's begin with research.

The kind of research I favor is quite basic: my main source for information is the daily newspaper. I figure that if a newspaper article about a crime interests me, it will interest other readers. Naturally, the newspaper story must undergo a metamorphosis before it comes out as fiction. For one thing, there are the questions of libel and plagiarism; and, for another, too great a reliance on the facts as reported can cause a story to become quickly dated.

More important is the question of a good yarn — an interesting newspaper article is only a germ, a bud. It provides a sequence of events and an indication of setting for the full-grown fiction. For example, the following paragraph from a UPI newswire release was the nucleus of a chapter of a novel I was working on: "The raids in Cordoba began when a small airplane, circling the city to apparently coordinate the attacks, threw a bomb that exploded without causing injuries near a provincial bank about 11 A.M." In short, a newspaper article can provide a rich source of actual whats, wheres, and whens. The whys and the whos are the novelist's responsibility.

A second good source of information for the police procedural writer is court records. Affidavits, depositions, and transcripts — in addition to

276

the writer's sitting in on court hearings — help provide not only events and incidental tidbits for a story, but also the language of narration. Increasingly, a cop, especially a senior officer such as a detective, must understand the technology of the law. Every technology has it jargon, and this can be found in legal records and in courtrooms.

Both newspaper stories and court records are as valuable for what they leave out as for what they offer. To get some of that which is left out, read the story with the questions "how?" and "why?" in mind. For instance, that favorite phrase of reporters, "police, acting on a tip from an informant . . ." gives rise to such questions as: Which policeman? Who was the informant? What incentive did he have for informing? What kind of communication — telephone, written, conversational? Who believed the informant? Who didn't? How much time passed between the tip and the raid? These and similar questions come up when the novelist begins creating the fictional world which will embody any actual events he chooses to use.

Though the writer's imagination furnishes the answers to such questions as those asked above, that imagination can be stimulated by a third kind of research which I've found to be most beneficial: interviewing. A policeman, like almost everyone else, enjoys talking about his work, and most municipalities have programs for bettering police-community relations. And a writer — despite what his neighbors may think — is a member of the community. In a larger town, check with the department's public information office. Departments in smaller towns tend to be less formal, and I think somewhat less accessible, perhaps because their manpower tends to be insufficient and the training less professional, generating a defensive attitude. The prosecutor's office and the sheriff's office are also worthwhile avenues of approach. For me, this interviewing tends to be quite casual and takes place during a duty watch; there's a lot of time for conversation during eight hours of riding in a patrol car.

Armed with some specific questions derived from reading newspapers and reports, the interviewer can start filling in those blanks found in the documents. The answers don't have to be related to the same cases read about — in fact, I like it better if they aren't. The novelist deals with probability, and patterns of common behavior offer more freedom for the invention of particulars than does the mere reporting of facts, which is where the journalist ends and the novelist begins. Unlike what takes

277

place on most television talk shows, an interviewer-novelist should be a good listener and, speaking for myself, a copious but surreptitious notetaker. It also helps to train your eye for such minutiae as manufacturer's labels, model numbers, organization charts — in short, anything that gives quick specific detail for your story's setting. Interviewing also provides the latest slang and technical jargon.

The manner of introducing those technical terms into the narrative varies. If a character honestly might not know what a particular device or procedure is called, he can simply ask someone in the story. The character and the reader become informed together. I use this device sparingly, since my characters in the Gabe Wager books are generally professional and well-trained. (Moreover, as a reader, I get damned irritated when a story's development is continually interrupted by some idiot who needs everything explained to him.) Another means of introducing technical terms is to use the phrase in normal dialogue and let the descriptive passage carry the explanation: " 'Let me have the Kell-Kit,' said Wager. Sergeant Johnston handed him the small body transmitter. . . ." Or, for variation, the equation may be reversed: " 'Let me have the body transmitter,' said Wager. Sergeant Johnston handed him the small Kell-Kit." I'm not sure if police departments have yet surpassed the federal government in the use of acronyms and arcane initials, but these are an essential part of bureaucratic jargon. It is a rule of thumb in writing first to use the full phrase, then, in the next sentence or two, the more common initials: "Wager turned to his little book of Confidential Informants. The first C. I. was. . . ." No explanatory passage is needed, and the action moves without interruption.

Research, then, is the foundation for the police procedural, and on that foundation are built in setting, plot, and character. Setting is, of course, easiest to create if it's well known to the writer. For the Gabriel Wager stories, that means Denver. Ironically, my editors more than once pointed out that a street which I invented wasn't on their map of Denver, or an odd-numbered address should be on the north rather than south side of a particular avenue. But the familiarity I mean is as much in flavor as in fact, and its manner of presentation is — for me — impressionistic. The single well-chosen detail that captures the flavor of the setting and gives focus and life to an otherwise sketchy scene is part of the economy I associate with the "grittiness" of a police procedural. A gothic, a novel that explores states of mind, or a sci-fi fantasy may call

278

for more sweeping and panoramic descriptions to create a mood or sustain a romance. But I find harmony between a spare style and the realistic police story. Since this descriptive technique tends to emphasize action rather than setting, and since a police procedural is akin to a report — and a report is usually about "what happened" — the emphasis on concrete and concise detail feels right to me.

The concern with what happened brings us to plot. Plot is not just *what* takes place but *why* it takes place. The police procedural may or may not use the mystery as the basis of suspense. If the police do not know who the perpetrator is, then unraveling the mystery becomes the plot — i.e., the gradual revelation of motive and opportunity. But often, in life as well as in fiction, the police do know who the villain is, and the plot centers on gathering enough evidence for a viable court case. The manner of getting this evidence is quite tedious and even dull — questioning fifty or a hundred witnesses, long hours of surveillance, studying accounting records. The problem for the storyteller in the police procedural field becomes one of remaining true to reality without boring the reader. One technique that fits the police procedural is focusing attention on new methods of surveillance or on the ever-changing avenues of legal presentation. Here, research is indispensable. Another device is to give your detective more cases than one. This is by no means unrealistic, but a good story requires that the cases somehow work together toward a single conclusion. That's the old demand of art for unity, a unity seldom apparent in real life.

Another very familiar technique for maintaining interest is the foil — someone who offers byplay for the protagonist. A foil should serve a variety of purposes, all contributing toward the unity of the novel. The character used as a foil — a rookie, for instance — may be a device not only for explaining police procedure, but also for revealing the protagonist's character through his reaction to the foil's activities.

I try to make character as interesting as case. The strongest novels are those with living characters to whom the action is vital, and this holds true for any tale, even a plotless one. But whether it's a who-done-it or a how-to-prove-it, the police story is fundamentally an action story, and in it the development of character should not impede the action. Ideally, character development and action should coincide; but where they do not, I tip the balance in favor of action, possibly because I envision the Gabe Wager series as one long novel of perhaps fifteen volumes, and this view gives me plenty of room to let the character grow.

279

There are several other concrete devices that aid the quick presentation of character without interrupting the action. One device especially useful for creating secondary characters is the "signature" — a distinctive act, speech pattern, or habit of thought that identifies and distinguishes one character from another. This signature may be simple: one secondary figure from *The Alvarez Journal* smokes cigars, another has an old man's rumbling cough, a third speaks administrative jargon. Or, if the character is of more importance to the story, a combination of signatures may be used to flesh him out. At its worst, this device generates cliché characters — the western bad man with his black hat and sneer. At best, the signature makes the character become alive and individualized — the girth, thirst, and cowardice of Falstaff. The problem, of course, is to characterize without caricaturing — unless your aim is satire. The novelist's ability to create real characters can be improved by reading other writers who are very good at it: Shakespeare, Flaubert, Faulkner. Another means is "reading" friends and neighbors: What exactly is it that distinguishes one of your acquaintances from another? Given universal human qualities, what makes one individual different from another?

Minor and secondary characters, while absolutely necessary, do not give life to the action. Rarely can any story, police procedural or other, do without a protagonist. Again, because of the importance of action in police procedurals, the writer is faced with the need for an economical development of his main character. The technique I have chosen for my Gabe Wager series is by no means new: It's the familiar "recording consciousness" of Henry James, the restricted third-person point of view, in which every event and concept in the story is presented from the perspective of a single protagonist. I've found several advantages to this device: The action proceeds and the protagonist's character is revealed at the same time. The reader is faced with the same limitations of knowledge as the protagonist, and thus the element of suspense is heightened. Using third person rather than first person puts distance between the reader and the protagonist and offers another dimension to the story, which helps the reader through those necessary and authentic but often slow stages of a case's development.

This narrative technique also has shortcomings. The author can't give the reader any information that the protagonist does not have, thus leaving little chance for irony or depth. For this point of view to work, the

280

author must also have a total understanding of the protagonist. While it may not be relevant to the story, it is nonetheless necessary if the character's actions are to be consistent.

First-person narration achieves many of the same results but brings an even closer identification between author and character. Think of the popular image of Mickey Spillane, for example. I prefer third person because it enforces objectivity and quite possibly because, unlike Gabe Wager, I'm not a good cop.

Focusing all the action through Wager's perspective, then, contributes to a unity of action and characterization in which action dominates but character development follows quite closely and, I hope, unobtrusively. I try to achieve this by placing a heavy emphasis on dialogue. By its very nature, dialogue is dramatic — the characters are onstage talking rather than being talked about by a narrator. Again, the signature is very important, and I play a little game of trying to see how many lines of dialogue I can put together without having to state who is speaking. The idea is that each character's voice should be distinct enough to indicate the speaker.

I place the police procedural in the category of literary realism. The contemporary, the probable, the routine, determine my choice of a realistic subject. Once I select my subject, the elements of research, setting, plot, and character are indispensable, and, in my Gabe Wager police procedurals, all of these elements must contribute to the action.

54

HOW DO YOU TELL A GOOD
SCIENCE FICTION STORY?

By Susan B. Weston

LISTENING to Isaac Bashevis Singer on a radio program recently, I heard advice useful to any writer, but especially important to those of us writing science fiction and fantasy stories. If you sit down to send a message, Singer warned, you'll probably ruin your story; but if you sit down to tell a story, you might just send a message.

The temptation to preach seems particularly hard to resist for writers extrapolating futuristic stories from present situations. "Change your ways!" many science fiction writers seem to be shouting. "Repair this"—acid rain, the greenhouse effect, midwestern drought, the exhaustion of fossil fuels . . . you know the list. It includes any massive environmental change that would wreak social havoc. But of course the message—"Don't let this happen, or else!"—is implicit in the material. The novelist's job is to tell a good *story*.

How do you tell a good science fiction story?

Remember that familiar chestnut, "write about what you know"? It seems such sensible and obvious advice. After all, literature is a feat of realization—making real with words. How can you possibly realize what you *don't* know? Is it possible to write fully realized science fiction? But you must become a "literalist of the imagination," to quote from Marianne Moore's famous poem, "Poetry." In that poem, she also suggests that a good poet must be able to create "imaginary gardens with real toads in them."

The first step in my writing begins with that imaginary garden. When I write, those toads won't come to life until they're perched on palpable rocks and shaded by chlorophyll-producing leaves. I have to create a richly detailed and plausible setting, because my characters emerge from it, interact with it, are defined by it. For me, setting leads to character leads to plot.

My science fiction novel, *Children of the Light,* is set in a small midwestern farming community three generations after a nuclear war. I had done one kind of research, studying government documents and various books on the consequences of a limited nuclear war; now I had to turn abstract knowledge into reality that could be felt. To transport myself to that faltering future community, I did focused "imagination exercises." Everywhere I went and everything I did was dissociated from its context here and passed through the filter of that imagined future. In front of my suburban house, for instance, I walked on a sidewalk buckled from winter freezing; grass grew up in the cracks. Suppose no one repaired this concrete ever again? What would it look like twenty winters from now?

There'd be no electricity, of course, no fuel delivery. Anyone surviving the disaster would need to gather fuel. Perhaps the wooden houses would be dismantled for firewood. I imagined my house dismantled, the basement exposed to the elements, all the useless machines rusting. And my neighbors' houses, all dismantled. As I washed dishes or tossed clean laundry into the drier or removed a convenience food from the freezer, I'd think: Oh, no running water. No washing machine. No refrigeration.

For weeks, I did these preliminary exercises, trying to set my feet firmly on that future ground by continually rehearsing what would be altered in the daily routines of my own comfortable middle-class life. Though the characters were still an indistinct communal band, I was beginning to know them because I knew the hard ridge of callouses raised along their palms, their knotted shoulder muscles. I knew what they did all day long, and how, and where.

To individualize this raggedy malnourished crew, I rather arbitrarily assigned each character some distinctive physical trait. There was a dwarf with a big booming voice. A mute with a tremor. A sallow young woman with a strident infectious laugh. And so on. Their somewhat grotesque physical traits were useful to the reader as "identifying tags" that also served to emphasize the genetic and environmental damage these people had to cope with. Each distinctive trait became my starting point for more fully developing the character. When does the dwarf's voice shrink to fit his real size? Why does the mute get so excited about pictures of windmills and generators? What makes the sallow young woman laugh?

283

I wrote the novel from the third-person point of view, using an omniscient narrator for descriptions and transitions, and moving into the limited third person—inside someone else's head—to gain emotional immediacy and closeness. No matter whose point of view controlled any given scene, I made sure that everyone else in the scene was either interacting or sleeping. But sometimes a character threatened to remain a lifeless comic book figure, flattening out a scene or dulling the edge of a conversation. Then I resorted to "monologue exercises," rewriting the entire scene from that person's point of view.

The first-person monologue is a basic tool in characterization. It helps you hear a character's distinctive voice, imagine what it's like inside someone else's head, and walk the proverbial mile inside someone's ill-fitting shoes. If a monologue exercise failed to bring a recalcitrant character to life, I knew I had to delete that character from the story. When it succeeded, the mystery characters emerged from the shadows so vigorously that they often surprised me with the things they said and did.

Letting the characters dictate the plot—and have priority over it—often yields some unexpected results. I used the oldest device in the writers' manual when I made my central character a stranger to the community, a time-traveler stunned by the grimness of the future he has stumbled into. The "stranger in town" device is usually coupled with an obligatory conversation in which someone *explains* all about this dreary world. Exposition presented in such a conversation is apt to be dull and awkward. I tried, instead, to imagine Jeremy's first scene in Idamore from the perspective of all the characters.

How would *you* react if someone began insistently asking about things you take entirely for granted? Suppose someone asked, "What do you call these little houses on wheels that are all over the place? Cars? Where'd they come from anyhow, all these cars?" When Jeremy poses similar questions to Helena, she thinks—not surprisingly—that he's slightly retarded. Only a dimwit could wonder what had happened to the birds, or why the trees were so small, or what time of year it was.

I might have had Helena explain to Jeremy that the birds were killed off by a radioactive dust cloud generated by a nuclear explosion in the year such and such, just after the twenty-six-minute war started by so and so over such and such an issue. More interesting—and ultimately more plausible—is a dramatic exchange between the bewildered representative of our world and the future citizen possessing only distorted information. Here's part of the exchange:

"The birds," said Jeremy. "Why did the birds go away?"
"Dim, dim," Helena said to herself, looking at the ground and shaking her head. "You remember, Jeremy," she said in her false-patient voice. "The birds left after the time of the light."
"What light?"
Helena rolled her eyes. Then she rubbed her nose—less a scratch than a gesture of impatience. "You know. The light."

By staying close to the way this scene would feel to each person in it, I found a surprising vein of light humor. This comic ingredient persisted, at first making me uneasy. Who's ever heard of comedy in a post-nuclear holocaust novel? There were several scenes I almost chucked into the wastebasket for their inappropriate tone. After prying tubers from the icy water of the pond, for example, Helena basks bare-breasted in the sun. Jeremy is unaccustomed to casual conversations with half-naked women, so we get this silly sequence:

Something soft fell on her, and she let out a shriek as she clawed it off. "Sorry I startled you," said Jeremy, once again walking away. "I brought you a dry shirt. Put it on. I need your advice."
"I thought you put on a thinking *hat*," she said.
"Huh?"
"Is this a *thinking* shirt?"
"I'm in no mood for jokes, Laney."
They were obviously having one of their misunderstandings, so Helena fell silent, buttoning the large shirt stiff with soap and fresh air. "I have on the shirt," she said, but Jeremy continued to pace around the edge of the pond with his hands in his pockets.

What I soon discovered through the prism of comedy was the tension inherent in these scenes: eroticism, anger, tenderness, sadness, and frustration were all lurking there. Comedy became my own key to unlocking the full human dimensions of this future world.

I wrote *Children of the Light* scene by scene, groping my way closer to the characters, letting the story emerge from their conflicting experiences and concerns. Obviously I'm not one of those efficient writers who start with a plot outline and proceed to time lines and flow charts.

285

For writers whose creative processes resemble mine, I'd recommend Constantin Stanislavski's *An Actor Prepares*. I've found that Stanislavski's exercises can help the fiction writer who has to be an inspired actor creating not just one authentic character, but an entire society.

55

WRITE TO SELL

A 3-Point Checklist That Works

By Samm Sinclair Baker

WHY do some writers make sales and collect sizable checks again and again . . . while others, perhaps you, are beaten back repeatedly by discouraging rejections? Is there some "magic" by which rejected writers can be transformed into published professionals? Is there immediate help for you if your work isn't selling?

Yes . . . the reasons for rejections are often surprisingly clear and simple—once you know how to identify and correct them for your own benefit. You'll gain some valuable eye-openers by applying these three basic checkpoints. They can open new pathways to selling what you write.

The primary reasons for failure to sell were affirmed vividly for me when I was the judge of a contest for beginning writers. Employing these practical insights has worked for me and for other selling writers. They're bound to work for you, if you'll follow through with them intelligently—*never giving up.*

Take advantage of these three checkpoints in analyzing any manuscript before you submit it for publication, and you'll uncover crucial, costly flaws. Making necessary corrections and revisions before you submit your article can mean the difference between sale and turndown.

First, study these recommendations; then apply them to the piece you've just finished—and to others that didn't sell. Concentrate on reading your article objectively, line by line, as though you were the editor. Now, as editor rather than writer, *you* must decide whether or not to buy the piece for publication. Be ruthlessly honest as you ask yourself, "Is the manuscript faulty, judged by any or all of the checkpoints?"

If yes, revise, rewrite—or start all over again. It often pays to discard the entire piece if it doesn't measure up. Finally, you'll be thrilled by the improvements you can readily make, once you realize exactly what is wrong. That's *self-help in action,* since you'll have a simple method to use profitably in planning and completing everything you write to sell from now on.

CHECKPOINT # 1

Will This Subject Interest Enough Readers?

The great editor of *Good Housekeeping,* John Mack Carter, enlightened me about editorial needs. He said that there are three subjects of outstanding interest to most women and many men today. Readers, he emphasized, are constantly seeking new, usable information about: *Diet . . . Sex . . . Money.*

If you write in the categories of these prime subjects—offering fresh, easily grasped approaches—you'll certainly have a better chance to sell than if your piece is about something as far-out as "The Prevalence of Fire Ants in Abyssinia." Obviously that's a wild exaggeration to make an essential point: *Write what interests most others, not just what pleases you.*

Of course, you don't have to confine yourself to those three basic themes. Yet, even within that seeming limitation, the possibilities for writing that sells are practically unlimited. For example, consider the many variations, such as:

DIET: "DROP POUNDS NOW WITH 12 DELICIOUS NEW RECIPES."

SEX: "ENCHANTING NEW HAIRSTYLES BOOST SEX APPEAL."

MONEY: "ADD INCOME WITH EASY NEW WORK-AT-HOME IDEAS."

It comes down to the old saw: Feed your pets what *they* want to eat, not what *you* like. Similarly, choose a subject that is of high interest to other people, realizing that editors are people, too. Analyze carefully in advance the interests of the specific reading audience you're trying to reach. Otherwise, you'll waste time and effort and invite discouragement and frustration. Smart subject selection is fundamental if you *write to sell.* Clearly, selling interests you. . . . or you wouldn't be reading this.

A common mistake of beginners is the I-I-I approach—writing about your personal experiences. That's relatively easy, but get it out of your head that anything that happens to you is of interest to others, unless it will appeal to a wide audience. Editors groan when a manuscript begins, "I remember Aunt Clara very well. I loved her deeply, and I'll always treasure sweet memories of her. . . ."

How many magazines readers care about your Aunt Clara or your Uncle Ted? How many of the same readers would be interested in an article that begins: "The weekend reducing spa business is booming, but what can a brief stay at a spa do for you realistically? Can it help you lose weight, keep on taking off pounds and inches, and stay slim from then on? For the answers, I interviewed five men and five women who had been to various weekend spas a month earlier. Here's what they reported. . . ."

Aren't your chances of selling the spa piece infinitely better? Checkpoint #1 is clear: Before you write on any theme, think of where you're going to aim for publication. Then consider the subject through the editor's eyes. Realize that, as editor, you must interest the largest possible number of your readers, so you'll buy only articles most likely to do that. To sell the articles you write, *you must fulfill the editor's needs.* For a men's magazine, for example, you would interview mainly men.

CHECKPOINT #2
Are Your Opening Lines "Reader-Grabbers"?

An editor of a mass circulation magazine (a neighbor) brought home for the weekend a huge briefcase loaded with articles submitted for publication. He said, "Before I take you sailing, help me weed out which of these pieces have possibilities for an issue coming up soon." I protested, "It will take me forever to get through these."

"You'll be finished in less than a hour," he assured me. "You can usually tell by reading just the first paragraph whether to discard it or go further. If the opening sentences don't hook you, reject it—the writing rarely gets any better."

Here are a couple of examples to show how much the opening sentences matter in the articles you write. Again, read them as though you're the editor examining the two following submissions on the same general subject. Based on the opening paragraphs alone, which manuscript would you have read with greatest attention?

(A) "Everyone in the neighborhood spoke well of Maryann Browne. She could usually be seen sitting in the old rocker on her front porch, swaying slightly as she knitted patiently hour after hour. We were all deeply shocked when we heard that her family doctor, whom we all knew, let it be known through the grapevine that she had cancer."

(B) "I'm a cancer patient, in the midst of that uneasy purgatory known as remission. After a year that would make the cast of *Dynasty* shake its collective head in disbelief, I am trying to get well. I *will* get well. That is, if people let me. The cancer may not kill me. But I'm not at all sure about the public."

The article that was bought, and appeared in a leading magazine, was "B." As a casual reader, I turned the pages rather idly, but the opening brief paragraph grabbed me. The writer telling flat out that she is afflicted with the dread disease led me on with the promise of hope in "remission." I was hooked further by the unexpected challenge in the surprising dramatic twist that "the public" might keep her from getting well. The public? That's *me!* Now *I* was involved. How could I stop reading?

It's obvious why I—or you—as editor, would, if offered a choice, probably reject "even without reading any further than that first paragraph. Why should I care or be particularly interested in someone I don't know—Maryann Browne—just because people "spoke well" of her? There's nothing very thrilling about a woman sitting in an old rocker on her front porch, knitting patiently hour after hour. Sure, I (and you) feel sympathy for anyone with cancer—but that's not enough to *compel* me to read more. Result: rejection. I'll bet that the discouraged writer never realized why her piece didn't sell—as you understand the reason now.

What's your next step? As an aspiring, determined writer, you'll gather all of your rejections for reexamination as soon as you can. You'll reread the opening paragraphs carefully, objectively, with fresh, clear-sighted analysis—as if through the editor's eyes. Do your opening lines reach out and grip readers, pulling them into the rest of the article? If not, rewrite until you have created a solid reader-grabber, even if it means rewriting a dozen times. You'll have a far better chance of having your writing read and bought.

Here's one more self-teaching example to help you avoid rejection slips in the future, or turn your past rejects into sales: A fine professional writer wanted to sell an article on beauty care to one of the best-paying, top-circulation women's magazines. But she knew there was tremendous competition in the beauty article field, not just from other free-lance writers, men and women, but from the magazine's staff writers.

She put her creativity to work and sought out one of the most popular photography models, who agreed to coauthorship. There was just one problem, as she knew too well: Most women might feel that they couldn't learn from a model who started with "perfect features." So the writer tackled the dilemma head-on with this opening paragraph:

You don't have to be born with perfect features to have a model's face. [Really? Tell me more. . . .] Many of the world's highly paid models are not necessarily natural beauties, but they do have the ability to put their best face forward. That means skin care and carefully applied make-up. I'd like to share with you some of the very special beauty secrets I've learned during my career as a model.

That's the hook—the grabber—the promise from a top model to share her beauty secrets with you. Possibly you're asking yourself, "Why didn't I think of a creative idea like that, and write an opening that would make the sale to an editor?" From now on, I hope you will.

I've reworked the opening paragraphs of my books up to twenty and more times, until I felt as sure as I could be that I'd fashioned an irresistible promise, the hook that would seize and hold the reader. One of the best examples I know is the start of the best-selling diet book of all time, *The Complete Scarsdale Medical Diet* (which I coauthored with Dr. Herman Tarnower). The opening proved a salesmaker.

The doctor is speaking:

"I, personally, explain *The Complete Scarsdale Medical Diet*'s phenomenal popularity in two words: 'It works.' A slim trim lady said to me recently, 'Your diet is beautifully simple, and the results are simply beautiful.' I just say, 'It works.'"

A reader-grabber like that can work for you. Check your opening lines repeatedly to make sure they convey convincing promise of worthwhile reading ahead.

CHECKPOINT #3

Have You Done Enough "Self-Editing"?

"A superb cook knows when to take a dish out of the oven so it's neither underdone nor overcooked," an editor commented. "But most of the manuscripts I reject are either underwritten—not enough thought and work put into them—or overwritten—too many words to say too little, not enough careful cutting."

When I've been involved on the editing end, I've found that many 20-page manuscripts would have been more acceptable if cut to 15 or even 10 pages. Yet, when I've suggested this to earnest individuals, the reaction usually has been, "You want me to cut out what I've worked so hard to put in? The writing is good, isn't it?"

Yes, the writing may be good—but, as the cliché affirms, it can be "too much of a good thing." Any word that isn't effective and essential should be eliminated. Stop and think what "edit" means. According to dictionaries, "to edit" means "to make written materials suitable for publication." Next time you're about to send out a manuscript you've written, ask yourself . . .

• *Have I worked this over specifically, so it's "suitable for publication," saying exactly what the reader needs and wants to know?*
• *Have I been too lazy to go back and cut again and again?*
• *Am I too much in love with my own words to edit sufficiently?*

A big part of successful professionalism grows from enough self-editing. It pays to review and rework every page repeatedly, asking each time, "Is this word necessary?" This chapter was more than three times as long before I cut-cut-cut, to make it most understandable and useful for you. Yes, it hurts to cross out words, paragraphs, pages you've sweated over, but it's essential to successful editing.

After over thirty years of writing and seiling, I still check every piece according to all three of the preceding checkpoints. That discipline keeps working for me. There are other factors that can make or break a sale. Some, such as timing and a magazine's overstock, are often out of your control. Regardless of such unforeseeable obstacles, these three basic checkpoints can and will work remarkably for you—when you *write to sell.*

56

WRITING ARTICLES FROM PERSONAL EXPERIENCE

By Rita Milios

WHEN I first began my professional writing career, I had the same goals as many other writers, amateur or pro. I wanted my work to be read by thousands of people in some of the nation's largest and most popular magazines. How could a novice writer achieve such dramatic results in a short period? I found that doors opened widest to me when I submitted one particular type of magazine article—the personal experience piece.

Many of my personal experience articles are what I call "emotional stories." Magazines are looking for more emotion, more real life. By filling this need, I have established a successful writing career. In just four years, my personal experience articles have been published in such magazines as *Reader's Digest, McCall's, Woman's World,* and many more.

The potential of a personal experience article lies not in the nature of the experience itself, but in the ability of the writer to turn an experience into an interesting, instructive, moving piece. "Slice-of-life" essays that reflect human nature are sought by many magazines, large and small; and the personal experience piece, because it requires no research, is one of the easiest articles to write.

Here are a few basic steps that I follow when writing personal experience articles, with good results:

STEP 1) *Begin your article at a dramatic point.*

A good way to hook your reader is with a dramatic lead that appeals to his or her emotions. However, I do not always begin with the *most* dramatic event. Instead, I start with the one that has true dramatic value and at the same time can provide a good lead into the rest of the article. Often this involves a flashback to fill in pertinent details. But once the flashback has been completed, usually by the end of the first or

293

second page, my piece flows on in a steady forward progression to the end.

For example, I began "Our Bond of Love," which sold to *Lady's Circle,* with my thoughts as I lay in a hospital bed receiving news of my desperately ill newborn son.

> The doctor entered the room quietly, cautiously. His eyes held a look of concern and dread that betrayed his calm.
> "I'm sorry, Mrs. Milios," he said gently. "I'm afraid I bring more bad news."
> *No! Stop!* my mind cried. *I don't want to hear it. I can't take any more. Please, why can't you keep it from me? I can't change anything, and it hurts too much to know the truth. Why can't you just lie to me?* But I couldn't say that. "What is it?" I asked in a wooden voice.

Clearly, there is a crisis here, and the reader is hooked with both empathy and curiosity. What is the bad news? How will it affect the narrator? What will happen next? Once I had captured my reader's attention, I used a flashback to tell how I got into this situation and what possibilities lay ahead.

STEP 2) *Convey your thoughts and emotions.*

Since personal experience articles involve emotion and are written in the first person, if you're afraid to show your feelings, this type of writing might not be for you. But strong emotions elicit strong reactions. You have to try to relive the emotion of the experience, to create a scene that rings true and seems real. By recreating the scene complete with thoughts and emotions you can make your reader experience it, vicariously sharing with you all the intensity, insight, and understanding that the experience brings. And by sharing some of your "bad" feelings, you can create a bond with your readers and give them an unexpected "gift," helping them face negative emotions they may have repressed.

On several occasions, friends who have read "Our Bond of Love" have told me, "I had those same feelings and I felt so guilty," or, "Reading your story made me understand that those feelings are normal, that they're O.K."

STEP 3) *Choose an experience that readers can relate to.*

Not every reader has experienced a flood or a fire or catastrophe similar to the one you are writing about. Yet, most readers relate to these kinds of articles because of the emotion and the insights and understanding the piece provides. Readers look to the problems of others to find solutions to their own problems. And every reader has at some time faced fear, love, anger, and some kind of "life's-not-fair" situation.

But what about the lucky writer who has lived a relatively normal life? What personal experiences or everyday events can he or she successfully turn into articles? These can be as effective as a dramatic piece in eliciting a response from your reader. Most readers appreciate a simple anecdote about everyday life that uplifts or inspires them. In "Blackberry Pickin' Time," I used vivid descriptions to create a feeling of nostalgia in an anecdotal article for *Yesteryear* magazine:

> I remember the day Mama dragged the old coal buckets down from the attic. They were black with soot and laced with cobwebs, for they hadn't been used since we moved into the new house with the modern oil burning furnace. But we scrubbed those buckets till they shined.
> "We're goin' blackberry pickin'," Mama said.

Religious magazines often buy inspirational first-person anecdotes. "The Day God Rode the Bus," which sold to *Aspire,* was the story of a simple kindness from a stranger that had far-reaching effects.

> "What can I ever do to repay you?" I asked the boy, certain that anything I could do would be inadequate.
> He said, "Simply help someone else when they need you."

Normal, everyday experiences often provide the best insight into human nature. And it is these insights that editors and readers are looking for.

STEP 4) *Share with the reader the insights and lessons you have learned.*

Every crisis, every experience teaches you something about life. What insights or lessons did your experience give you that you can share with your readers to help them face and resolve a similar problem or to understand themselves better? Don't be afraid to spell it out.

My article, "What Did I Teach My Child Today?" written for *Living with Preschoolers,* is about setting good examples. All parents know that they should set a good example for their children, but how many of us realize the full extent to which our actions are mimicked? ("My children, little sponges that they are, soaked up everything that I said or did.") And how many fully realize the responsibilities of parenthood until it is too late? (. . . "I suddenly realized that when I took on the job of parent, I also assumed the job of being a full-time adult, even though there are times when I don't feel big or strong or smart at all.") Sharing insights such as these bring reader and writer closer together, and add "significance" to your article.

STEP 5) *Marketing the personal experience article.*

You've finished your article, but can you sell it? Who will buy it? Almost any general interest, women's, or religious magazine, if you have written the article well. Is the emotion real? Can your reader relate to the feelings? Are they universal? Have you shared the lessons that you learned? If so, you are ready to choose the most suitable market for your story.

Go through the market listings and watch for such phrases as these: ". . . seeking meaningful stories of personal experience" (*McCall's*); ". . . looking for articles that give practical examples from real life" (*Christian Home & School*); ". . . want personal narratives that are true and have some universal relevance" *(Guideposts).*

A knowledge of individual magazine styles is important. For instance, I know that *Reader's Digest* likes narrow escapes. *Woman's Day* likes everyday situations with good insights and problem-solving techniques. *Redbook* likes "Young Mother's Stories," and *McCall's* often looks for medical miracles. Religious magazines like articles that inspire or uplift. The same experience might have to be written differently for each of these markets to fit in with the editorial style of the particular magazine. Gearing each personal experience article to the proper market requires careful study of each magazine, but it pays off. Good marketing skills mean fewer rejections.

Finally, when querying an editor about a particular personal experience article, make special note of its significance for the readers. Will your piece inspire them? Give them courage? Will it make them feel better to know that they are not alone in their feelings? Will it help them? If so, how?

When writing your personal experience article, make it *real.* Do your best to move your reader, inspire him, make him cry. Make your story *live*.

57

RESEARCH TIPS TO HELP YOU WRITE

By Alden Todd

IT HARDLY NEEDS stating that research is essential to good writing, because our words must convey authenticity, accuracy, and precision if we want readers to give us their confidence. This is true both in fiction and in non-fiction. Carelessness in research can lead to all kinds of embarrassments—misplaced dates, incorrect names, impossible meetings, and so on. We must, therefore, lay a solid groundwork of carefully researched facts for your writing, and sometimes this process requires considerably more time than the writing itself. The following tips can be helpful in improving and speeding the research that underpins good writing.

1. *Thinking through a research plan*. In doing research for writing, the beginner often makes the mistake of rushing to the first possible source of information that comes to mind, instead of considering several possibilities and then choosing the best order to follow. This order can be written down as a research plan and revised as work progresses.

In researching history, biography, and events of the recent past, particularly when looking for material in written form, a writer can get good results by playing detective and asking these questions:

Who would know? Who could care? Who would care enough to have it in print? The answers can often lead directly to the printed matter or to the people you'll need to interview.

Thinking through your plan of research may save you an hour or day, or even longer. Too much time is often spent in hunting for the written materials that might be spent more productively in actually doing the research. An important element in research skills lies in getting one's hands on the right material fast. Therefore, the writer whose work is based on solid research and who wants to be most productive should learn everything possible about the available reference books and periodicals, the local libraries, and what specialists to ask for the necessary information.

2. *Finding the right library.* It is natural to turn to the town or city public library as the first source of resource material. Because it must serve the entire community, the public library generally holds a much larger collection of reference books and other materials than the ordinary card holder realizes. So it is always a first good step to find out what standard reference works your public library has. In many places, counties have organized interlibrary loan systems; the local staff can tell you which cooperating public library can supply the books you need.

Bear in mind that the biggest library in your community is not always the best for your purposes. If your subject is art, you care only about the depth of its art reference collection. In fact, the small, specialized library often has a far better collection for your specific purpose than the large public library does. It is usually less crowded and staff members are more likely to know the collection thoroughly. The same is true of a departmental library of a large university system.

To find out about special libraries near you, ask the reference librarians whether they have a local or regional directory of the Special Libraries Association (SLA). Such directories are compiled for many metropolitan regions of the country for interlibrary loans and job placement. Librarians usually keep their SLA Directory behind the desk and show it only on request. The local directory of special libraries in law firms, medical centers, social work agencies, businesses, clubs, and many other places can be of great help to the writer. If the local SLA Directory is not available, ask for the national library directory and look in it for all the libraries in your area.

Writers often ask whether a person not connected with a company, professional school, or organization that maintains its own library can gain admission to it. In every case, I have found that if one asks permission to use such a library for a special purpose, such as writing an article, the librarians have been friendly and cooperative. Do not be timid: Special libraries can give you more help per hour spent in research than the large general library.

In localities where there is a college library, it is worth exploring the possibility of using that collection—either through a friend with a college connection or perhaps under a program that permits local residents to use the library for a fee. And within many universities, one often finds subsidiary libraries on special subjects (e.g. medicine, law, business, astronomy) in different parts of the campus, each with its own admission policies.

3. *Finding reference books.* The best way to find if there are standard reference books on your subject is to consult an experienced professional librarian acquainted with your field, if possible in a special library devoted to that field. Do not waste time browsing through reference book shelves in the hope of finding what you want. It's much more efficient to find people who know their collections, then state precisely what you want to find out, and ask for reference books that will help you.

Of course, you can start out by looking in the library catalogue under various subject headings to see which books the library carries on your subject. You may find a dozen books that are useful, or you may draw a blank. It's a matter of how broad or narrow your subject is, and how detailed the subject categorizing is.

The standard directory of reference book titles is the *Guide to Reference Books,* issued by the American Library Association and revised regularly. This is a comprehensive, 1,000-page, two-column work containing brief descriptions of books on all kinds of subjects. An experienced librarian can help you find the headings and pages relevant to your topic. It is worth the time of any serious researcher/writer to become generally familiar with the contents and organization of this valuable sourcebook.

A particularly useful and inexpensive guide to reference books that writers would do well to acquire for themselves is the paperbound *Reference Books: a Brief Guide,* by Bell and Swidan, published by the Enoch Pratt Free Library (400 Cathedral Street, Baltimore, MD 21201). This is the best low-price guide to reference works that I know, and it has been kept up to date by dedicated editors who are professional librarians.

One fast method of making at least a preliminary choice of books to consult on much-explored subjects is to look at the brief bibliographies that are appended to articles in major encyclopedias, such as *Encyclopedia Britannica.* You might not otherwise know where to begin among the many books that have been written on such subjects as George Washington or heart disease. Also, the sources suggested in the encyclopedia articles have passed the scrutiny of specialists and are authoritative.

Another useful reference work for your research is *Subject Guide to Books in Print,* an annual that lists more than 600,000 book titles currently in print and available from U.S. publishers. They are indexed with cross references under 63,500 subject headings. Here you can find all U.S. books in print on a particular subject. A companion guide is *Paperbound Books in Print,* which lists current books by title, author, and subject. Subject headings are not as numerous as in the subject guide to hardcover books, so within the more than 100 listed subject-areas, you must search for suitable titles.

Finally, the *Guide to American Directories* will tell you whether there is a directory in your field that would help you in your research.

4. *Finding periodical articles.* Most libraries subscribe to the *Readers' Guide to Periodical Literature,* which indexes by author and subject the articles published in about 200 periodicals. But for a comprehensive index of subjects published in other periodicals, academic publications, and learned society journals, the *Readers' Guide* is not sufficient, because it mainly indexes articles in general circulation magazines and covers relatively few others. To find such specialized articles, the researcher/writer should consult one or more other indexes that cover specialized magazines and journals. Examples are *Applied Science & Technology Index, Art Index, Business Periodicals Index, Education Index, Index to Legal Periodicals,* and the like. Ask a professional reference librarian what specialized periodical indexes are available, and you will discover how much depth they add to your research.

Note: You may have to visit a special library to locate some of these indexes as well as the back issues of periodicals to which they refer.

5. *Finding specialists and people who know.* There is, of course, more to research than turning to what others have written. Much that the writer wants to find out has not been put on paper, so he must frequently locate experts who can be interviewed, whether in a face-to-face meeting, by telephone, or by letter. It all depends on how accessible the expert is. As a writer you should, however, always remain a bit

skeptical, remembering that what you learn from someone else may only be that person's version or opinion of a past event and should be subject to the same critical scrutiny as that with which you approach a book or article.

One very handy way to find experts and specialists in all parts of the country is to use the *Encyclopedia of Associations,* which can be found in good reference—and sometimes business—libraries. The 1987 edition contains information on more than 23,000 national and international organizations operating in the U.S., including hobby clubs, professional societies, trade associations, labor unions—in fact, every sort of association in which members have a common purpose. Each entry in this multi-volume encyclopedia includes an association's address, purpose, activities, executive officers, and the titles and frequencies of publications. By writing or calling the association headquarters, you can locate a chapter or individual members in your city or region, and call on them for information in their special field.

Another way to find people with a special knowledge in a different part of the country is to consult *Editor & Publisher International Yearbook,* an annual directory of the daily and weekly newspapers of North America. For daily newspapers, it lists the editors and specialized reporters in various departments—music, sports, gardening, theater, and others. There is also the newspaper library, which contains clippings and memos about important happenings in the locality. I have called on newspaper editors and reporters several times in the course of my research and have always found them cordial and helpful.

6. *Using public relations sources.* Public relations professionals can be of great help to the researcher and writer. Their offices go under various names—public relations, PR, publicity, public information (the term used in government), press relations, and, in embassies, press attaché. Whatever the title, these are people whose job it is to supply information to the press and public on behalf of an organization, institution, or individual.

In recent years, the PR function has become so important in the U.S. that the person best equipped to supply information about an institution is often the PR director—not the president or chief executive officer. But no one seeking information from a PR source should park his critical faculties at the door. Researchers should be as careful in accepting what PR professionals tell them as they would about statements read in a journal article or a book. Similarly, one must be cautious and critical dealing with the public information officer of a university, government agency, manufacturing company, or airline. It is the researcher's job to separate the factual and valid from what may be exaggerated or even untrue.

Writers may sometimes become so fascinated and engrossed in their research that they lose their sense of time and purpose. The writer must recognize that the final purpose is writing, and that research is a subsidiary though necessary means to reaching the final goal.

58

HOW TO WRITE A WINNING QUERY

BY LINDAANN LOSCHIAVO

A WINNING query letter is the key to getting a go-ahead on an article. Whether you're a novice or an established free lancer, it's usually a waste of time to propose your article ideas to an editor over the telephone—or to submit your finished product over the transom. Most editors don't like to be interrupted by calls unless you're already known to them and also if your topic is timely and urgent. And to write the whole piece without a preliminary nod from an editor is unwise. What if the magazine has just bought a piece on a similar subject? Even if that isn't the case, the "slush pile" piece is never considered as carefully as an article that's been assigned or requested on speculation.

To get that assignment or the agreement to read your work "on spec," sharpen up your query-writing techniques.

Hammering out the "hook"

An intriguing opening is called a "hook" because it *must* catch a busy editor's eye. Start off with your best. A great deal of material is rejected because its presentation is second-rate. However, if your proposed idea and style grab the *editors* right away, they'll be more willing to believe your final draft will grab their *readers.*

Here are some examples of my finely honed hooks, queries that brought positive responses from editors the first time out.

About eight million Americans wear contact lenses. Several million more wear eyeglasses. Now orthokeratology is making corrective lenses obsolete. Haven't heard of this new procedure? It's about time you did. ("Orthokeratology Is Making Things Perfectly Clear," *Ambassador Magazine*)

As you read this, several phones are ringing in the Greater New York area. A pregnant teen-ager is thinking about running away from home. A 30-year-old veteran has just been released from the hospital after his fourth operation—and he's contemplating suicide. A housewife's alcoholic second husband is beating

303

up her preschoolers. A 72-year-old blind man is depressed and lonely. Who's at the other end of the telephone? A trained, para-professional counselor in a hot-line crisis intervention center in one of the five boroughs, calming, advising, reassuring, *listening*. ("My Name Is Joseph. I'm Going to Kill Myself," *The New York Times Magazine*)

Most women diet before their weddings in order to look slim in their gowns and (ever after) in their wedding albums. What a shame then to ruin it because of poor eating habits during the honeymoon. Here's how your brides can enjoy themselves and *still* return home with no excess baggage around their hips. ("Staying Slim and Fit on Your Honeymoon," *Mode for Brides* [an Australian publication])

Now that you've read some good hooks, here are a few poor ones:

There are crisis intervention centers all over New York City. Listeners hear all kinds of exciting stories. I know your readers would find this provocative. (*Poor:* See why this flat-footed version is devoid of drama? Merely *telling* it's fascinating material, not demonstrating it by some heart-stirring vignettes, is unconvincing, boring, flat.)

I've been reading *(name of magazine)* for years. I think it's the best women's magazine on the newsstand. (*Poor:* This is amateurish and sounds like a fan letter, not a query.)

I've noticed you've never printed an article on _____, so I'd like to do one for you. (*Poor:* Maybe this is a taboo topic at that particular magazine. Even so, always make your lead *dance*—not limp along.)

Why were my three queries successful? Partly because their leads blended essential ingredients: instant reader identification, promises of help, and dramatic presentation. For instance, most airline passengers either wear glasses or know someone who does. Who would pass up a chance to improve his or her vision? Similarly, many New Yorkers would either sympathize with the troubled callers or identify with them and also want to know how to dial for hot-line help. Last, all brides go to great lengths to look their best on their wedding day.

There's a silent message as well. The hooks demonstrated that both my style and my subject matter would captivate an audience. Yours should, too.

Constructing the body of a query

This "silent message" in·your hook or opening paragraphs should echo throughout the query. Your next few paragraphs must reveal that you (a) write well, (b) have a topic worth developing, and (c) can deliver what you're proposing. How? *Show*—don't just tell.

Highlight your preliminary research. *Poor approach:* "I'm planning to interview several therapists to learn about dealing with difficult people." *Good approach:* "Sometimes you can simply ignore difficult people. Sometimes you can't. Then what? 'It's not what you argue about with a difficult person—but *how*,' observes Vincent D. Foley, Ph.D., a New York psychologist." (A condensation of Dr. Foley's advice follows.) Promising to offer innovative tips or solutions is never as effective as serving up a tempting summary of lively direct quotes in a query.

Stress selling points. *Good phrases:* "Few people know about this unique procedure," "it saves consumers time and money," and so on. Are there news pegs? Is this timely? If possible, tie your article to the latest discovery, an anniversary, a holiday. If none of this is possible, emphasize why the audience of that publication would find your feature enjoyable or useful.

Describe your researching, interviewing, or writing methods. Setting these forth inspires confidence. *Poor approach:* "My article will cover the latest methods of whitening your smile." *Good approach:* "What's involved in the newest methods of whitening a smile through bleaching? Doctors Rudolph and Eisdorfer will explain—step-by-step—how it's done, how long it takes, how much it costs. They'll also discuss what's *not* involved: no pain, no drilling, no tooth reduction, no huge bills."

Emphasize your credentials

Conclude the query with your credentials. If you have published articles, list them with names and dates of magazines—tailored to this particular market or this topic, when possible. For example, if you're querying the editor of a men's fashion publication, stress that you've written for similar magazines. If you're proposing a self-help piece, note the other how-to features you've done and where they have appeared.

If you have no publication credits, emphasize some of your other qualifications. For example, if I were proposing an article "How to Run with Hand Weights"—and if I had no other exercise features ever printed—then I might say, "I've been jogging for three years, and I've taught a year-long seminar on using hand weights in aerobics. Also, I've been promised an exclusive interview by Leonard Schwartz, M.D., the Pittsburgh physician who invented Heavyhands." (Besides, if you master query writing, soon you *will* have plenty of credits to include.)

Whether or not you're a published author, if your query is well-crafted, competent, witty, appealing, the *product* itself gives you more authority than your *promises*.

Some General Guidelines for Your Query

• Type it single-spaced on good white bond or your letterhead.

• A clean keyboard and fresh typewriter ribbon make a good impression—on you.

• Keep your letter brisk, bright, and brief; a single sheet of stationery should suffice. (Exception: if the "Writer's Guidelines" indicate otherwise or if your idea requires a detailed, complex proposal.)

• Consider outlining your query first, a professional time-saver. Group the points that are most dramatic, salable, and pertinent. Then decide on the most effective arrangement. Model your letter on that skeleton.

• Avoid beginning with the pronoun "I" or starting too many paragraphs with it. Vary your syntax and sentence length until your text sounds rhythmic.

• Duplicate the magazine's *tone* in your query. Are their articles typically chatty, warm, urbane, arch? Demonstrate that your voice can chime right in with their regulars.

• Are you a novice? Conclude by offering to do the manuscript "on speculation," which means that an editor is agreeing *only* to read it— not necessarily to buy it.

• Write tightly and truthfully. Don't overstate, oversell, or overestimate an editor's patience.

59

ARTICLE OUTLINES BRING SALES

By William E. Miles

"Put it before them briefly so they will read it, clearly so they will appreciate it, picturesquely so they will remember it and, above all, accurately so they will be guided by its light."

Give Joseph Pulitzer a prize for this nearly century-old advice to reporters! Although the publisher of the New York *World* was referring to newspaper stories, his remarks are just as applicable today to magazine article outlines. Brevity, clarity, color, accuracy—that's the gift-wrapping of the package you are inviting an editor to open when you submit an outline of a subject you hope will spark his interest in your article.

An outline should be kept as short as possible, preferably one page single-spaced. Sometimes, of course, the subject demands more detailed explanation—but try not to let it exceed two pages. Within this framework, fill it with enough colorful facts and figures to catch the editor's eye and indicate the authenticity of the material.

Typed on a separate page or pages, the outline should be accompanied by a brief covering letter and sufficient return postage. A sample covering letter might read like this: "Would you be interested in taking a speculative look at a 2,000-word article on the order of the attached outline? My articles have been published in . . ." (naming some of the magazines you have sold to or listing whatever other qualifications you may have). Then, paper-clipped to the covering letter, the outline itself. For example:

Pranks for the Memory

Practical jokes are probably so-called because they are practically never a joke to the victim—who often winds up on something funny as a crutch. Even Mark Twain, an inveterate practical joker much of his life, confessed in his later years that he "held the practical joker in limitless contempt."

307

The late Bennett Cerf, another humorist who held practical jokers "in low esteem," once waxed particularly indignant over the dirty trick perpetrated on a Chicago bridegroom. After passing out at a bachelor party, he awakened to find his right arm in a cast. His fun-loving friends told him he had broken it in a brandy-inspired brawl—forcing him to spend his entire honeymoon with a perfectly good arm in a painfully tight cast.

Such practical jokers, according to Cerf, are "under no circumstances to be confused with humorists." But American history, dating back to pre-Revolutionary War days, is filled with hundreds of other examples of more harmless exercises in hilarity that don't deserve the harshness of his critical verdict.

One of the earliest of these was conceived by General Israel Putnam, a hero of the French and Indian War, after being challenged to a duel by a British army officer. Putnam selected as his choice of weapons two powder kegs into which he bored holes and inserted slow fuses. When the fuses burned down to an inch of the kegs, the British officer beat a hasty retreat—from barrels filled with onions!

But some practical jokes turn out to be really practical—as in the case of a "green" engineer at the General Electric plant who was assigned by old-timers as a prank the "impossible" job of frosting light bulbs on the inside. Marvin Pipkin not only found a way but, at the same time, devised a method of strengthening the bulbs so they would last much longer—cutting the cost to consumers in half!

An article of mine, based on this outline, appeared in *Elks Magazine*. If this makes the outline approach to article sales sound easy, it isn't. An outline is only the bare bones of an article and no skeleton key guaranteed to unlock all editorial doors. For every idea that clicks, you may receive a dozen or more rejections. And sometimes the article itself is rejected after the outline has received a speculative O.K. For one reason or another, the article may just not live up to its billing.

But whether it does or not, outlines are not only attention-getters, but time-savers. A complete article can take a month or so to research and write and another month or so languishing in editorial offices awaiting a decison. An outline, on the other hand, requires only cursory research—enough to establish an intriguing lead and some supporting information. Only after the "go-ahead" (if you get it) do you need to start researching the subject in depth.

Editors also answer queries far more rapidly than they return articles—so even a rejection has its bright side. If the query is turned down, you've saved yourself unnecessary work in more ways than one. When outlines are returned, as they usually are, there's no retyping involved (except for another covering letter), if you decide to try elsewhere.

Another important aspect of an outline is that an editor, who likes the general idea, may have some suggestions of his own as to how he'd like it

308

handled. An article I sold to *The Lion* is a good example of this. My original idea was to take a swipe at juries because of the way they were influenced by clever lawyers (and sometimes their own ignorance) into returning strange, far-out verdicts. I had no solutions to the problems in mind when I submitted the following outline to the editor:

THE TROUBLE WITH JURIES

FBI statistics show that 90 out of every 100 murderers are arrested, 50 receive some sort of punishment, and two are sentenced to death. This means that almost half of all accused killers are acquitted after their mandatory trials by jury in cases of first degree murder—presumably the guilty as well as the innocent.

This assumption was borne out by an investigation of the jury system in Pennsylvania which disclosed some juries had reached their verdicts by drawing straws or flipping coins. Other jurors were found to have rushed through their deliberations in order to get to a dance or a lodge meeting on time.

Although Thomas Jefferson described juries as "the best of all safeguards for the person, the property and the reputation of every individual," many legal experts regard them as outmoded relics in this modern age. Trial by jury stems from trial by oath in which the accused, swearing to his innocence, was supported by twelve "oath-helpers," or compurgators, who attested to their belief in his statements. This "jury of peers" was intimately acquainted with the defendant and the circumstances of the alleged crime. But in our day, as Dr. Joseph Catton points out, an attempt is made to select persons who know *nothing* about the offense. "There are those who believe," he adds wryly, "that today's jurors know nothing about anything."

Other criminologists contend that a modern jury is generally made up of persons unfamiliar with the law who often miss the significance of technical rulings by the judge. Even in cases where court rulings are simple and understandable, the jury sometimes ignores them. There is one actual case on record in which members of the jury, disregarding the evidence and the judge's charge, all knelt in prayer—and came up with a verdict!

The editor replied: "I'd be happy to consider your article 'The Trouble with Juries' with one important condition. I'd like to see the piece conclude with some constructive recommendations from authorities on how the jury system could be improved and/or replaced by better systems."

Further research incorporated his suggestions into the article whose whole thrust was changed, including the lead, when it appeared in *The Lion* under the new title, "Of Juries and Judgments."

The lead (aside from the idea) is probably the most important part of an outline, because it's the first thing to attract an editor's eye. One good means of accomplishing this is to tie it to a particular city or state even though the actual subject matter may range far afield. Here's an outline with just such a lead that resulted in a sale to the *Chicago Tribune Sunday* Magazine:

Chicago's long history of accomplishments includes the honor of being the first city to introduce what some engineering experts have called one of the ten most complex and ingenious inventions of the past hundred years. Back in 1893 it put the "zip" in the zipper when a sample of the original slide fastener was placed on display at Chicago's Columbian Exposition for use by the Fair's hootchie-kootchie dancer, Little Egypt, as a rapid skirt-release.

But it was the zipper, not the stripper, that caught the eye of a visitor to the Fair—Colonel Louis Walker of Meadville, Pa.—and he hired the inventor, Whitcomb L. Judson, to improve his original patent on a "locker or unlocker for automatically engaging or disengaging an entire series of clasps by a single continuous movement."

After years of experimentation, the device was finally perfected in 1913 and, four years later, a Brooklyn tailor made the fastener famous by attaching it to money belts which he sold to sailors at the Brooklyn Navy Yard. The Navy itself was soon using the fastener on flying suits. And during the depression, a dress company tried out the novelty as a sales booster—taking the industry by storm. Soon the zipper's long story of "ups and downs" was over. Its slide to success had begun!

Leads come in all shapes and sizes and there are dozens of other ways of writing that all-important first paragraph whose purpose is to sell a particular editor on a particular idea. For instance, the "striking statement" lead:

Lightning, the silent partner of thunder, has frightened more people—and killed fewer—than any other common danger. In fact, your chances of being killed by a lightning bolt are one in a million.

The editor liked this outline lead well enough to keep it intact when my article "Striking Down Lightning Myths" was published in *Wheels Afield*.

Another editorial eye-opener is the "news peg" approach—tying the article to a current happening or upcoming event—or the "anniversary angle" like this outline lead for my article "Meters By The Mile" that appeared in *The Rotarian* more years ago than I care to remember:

Ten years ago last October 1,500 parking meters went on trial in New York City. They were immediately found guilty by protesting motorists who charged that they interfered with their constitutional privileges of life, liberty and the pursuit of free parking space . . .

But why go on? The point is that, varied as they were, all of these leads had one thing in common—an ability to grab the editor's attention and keep him reading. From these examples, you can see that I like to write a lead (and sometimes an ending) that will be used more or less "as is" in the finished article if the outline receives an editorial O.K.

This gives the editor a good idea of what to expect—not only of the subject but of the style in which it will be written. For an outline must persuade the editor that you not only have a good idea, but possess the ability to handle it well.

60

REFLECTIONS OF A BIOGRAPHER

By Elizabeth Longford

INSPIRATION COMES to biographers as much as to novelists but cannot be commanded by any cerebral tricks. Nevertheless one can do something to help it breathe.

In the last 20 years, I have worked out a "writing day" for myself. I write best in the morning, though not immediately after breakfast. I use that first hour to write letters or shopping lists; even the laundry list loosens me up and gets me going with a pen. Writing out-of-doors suits me best, either in the Sussex garden or on the Chelsea balcony. Outdoor sounds seem to absorb the distractive parts of my brain and leave the rest free to concentrate. It may be that I have got used over the years to writing in some degree of noise indoors: children in the same room or myself on a train journey. The only place I can't perform is at a desk on a straight-backed chair. Writing late at night seems more inspirational than it is. I seldom find the results come up to scratch when I reread them next morning. Indeed, problems that appear insoluble at midnight have a way of smoothly solving themselves at midday.

Structure and chronology are among the perennial problems. How to deal with the subject's personal and public life? They happen simultaneously, whereas in the biography there may have to be some measure of separation. Should it be separate chapters? Or separate sections within the same chapter? I have used both methods, though the former more with public male characters who tend, conveniently for the biographer, to compartmentalize their lives. Women, even public women, are more "open plan."

I reread endlessly what I have written and make continual corrections: sometimes substantial ones involving rearrangements of material, more often verbal changes. Really obstinate problems have to be solved with the help of manual labor—preferably gardening. Clearing the ground for a rosebush clears away the mental rubbish as well.

All these techniques to be developed for what? Biography. Not for the (superior) arts of fiction or history. I think biography chose me, as it chooses most of its operators. And chose me because I wanted to write in the ways it had to offer. Michael Holroyd, author of *Lytton Strachey,* has said that biography is the nearest art to the novel. It is about people, and it thrives on imagination, to decipher them if not to create. I prefer to work on people who were or are *there,* as a doctor or teacher does, not so much on might-have-beens. I like to see them in my mind's eye as a novelist does but also to see the actual letters they wrote, the clothes they wore. There is a special excitement in handling their possessions that seems to generate extra perceptiveness.

I like my subject to be encapsulated in a life, as history is not. All the same, my biographies must always to some extent be a "Life and Times of . . ." The balance between "Life" and "Times," however, is one of the most difficult to achieve. A reviewer said there was not enough historical background in my first biography (*Queen Victoria*); when I tried to repair that omission in my second (*Wellington*), another reviewer said there was too much. Can one win? Help has come, notwithstanding, from two guidelines, the first offered by Cecil Woodham-Smith, biographer of Florence Nightingale: "Always keep your narrative moving." That means, among other things, avoidance of too much argument with other historians, a pastime in which academics delight. My second rule is never to lose sight of my subject for more than a page or so. I aim at the maximum of background detail with the minimum of digression.

Another elusive question of balance concerns sympathy with one's subject. I could never write a biography of, say, Hitler, though I recognize the need for such works; perhaps the author's righteous indignation supplies the adrenaline usually produced by enthusiasm. Every self-respecting biographer tries to avoid hagiography like a plague of treacle.

Perhaps the thing I am really striving for is empathy. While sympathy merely means fellow feeling, empathy means "the power of projecting one's personality into, and fully understanding, the object of contemplation." I can do this only with someone I like. Incidentally, the one thing that makes biography unreadable is to lecture or rebuke one's subject.

Detection is another aspect of biography that I like: both the probing into character and the weighing up of fact versus legend. A Catch-22

313

situation is often involved at the beginning of these researches. If one reads secondary sources first—other authors' books—one may be prejudiced by them before one has had time to form one's own opinion; but if one goes straight into the original sources—letters and diaries—one may not be sufficiently well equipped to detect the hidden evidence on some controversy or problem. My own solution has been to read (or reread) *one* general account first and then dive into the primary sources.

Questions of fact or legend require exhaustive research but are sometimes solved by accident, occasionally too late, alas, for one's current book. I could not decide, for example, whether Queen Elizabeth II kept a real diary or merely a brief engagement record. After the publication of *The Queen*, I happened to mention this doubt during a lecture to a conference of American university women in London. One of them came up to me and said: "I *know*. When our group was introduced to Her Majesty, I asked: 'Ma'am, do you keep a diary? If so, how do you find the time?' The Queen replied, 'Prince Philip and Prince Charles read in bed. I write my diary. And it's a great deal more honest than anything you'll find in the media.'"

In the decade when I became a biographer—the 1960's—a double revolution in the art took place, the matrix being American universities. First, the availability of sources suddenly increased with the large-scale collecting of archives and the development of photocopying.

Second came the distinction between narrative and analytical-psychological biography. While I myself did not abandon narrative, I have learned from the disciplines of in-depth research. Forget all we ever knew about biography from *The Oxford Dictionary of Quotations*, especially Disraeli's "Read no history: nothing but biography, for that is life without theory." Today in certain quarters biography has become theory without life. As far as possible, the life *story* is ignored; even dates of birth and death may be hard to find. There is instead a wealth of interpretation of the subject's own words, which should eventually lay bare the naked self, the "inner me." Individual lives being incoherent, there must be no attempt at continuous narrative, but everything should be "discontinuous" and open-ended.

In still safeguarding narrative, I accept the need to add to my duties as biographer the roles of interpreter, mediator between other writers' views, and analyst. My chief fear is that the analytical game may become too facile, too seductive.

Biography is too important to become a playground for fantasies, however ingenious; I believe its future is safe with the reading public, who will keep it human, not too solemn.

61

WRITING THE OP-ED ARTICLE

By George W. Earley

Opinions. We all have them, but the difference between yours and mine may well be that I get paid for putting some of mine on paper.

If you live in or near a major city, you've probably seen the market I'm hitting: the newspaper op-ed page.

So-called because its articles appear on the page *op*posite the *edi*torial page, the op-ed page is an ideal market for the beginning writer. But like any other market, it demands that the writer become familiar with editors' needs and requirements for submission.

For the beginning writer, local issues are the best ones to tackle first. Examples of local-interest items can be readily found by reviewing your paper's op-ed page. During one recent two-week period, my local paper, *The Hartford Courant,* carried a mix of serious pieces—abortion, drugs in schools, and state educational reform—and reminiscences— Grandpa vs. the dandelions, Sunday walks in the park, and the Governor's Foot Guard Band. All topics are suited to beginning local writers.

With that as preface, and bearing in mind that the market listing following this article covers specific needs and preferences of a number of papers, let's look at some general requirements.

First, know your market. Make a close study of several dozen local-issue op-ed articles your paper has run. Note the topics covered, the way the articles are structured, and their length. Op-ed pieces generally average about 750 words—a few are shorter and fewer yet are markedly longer. That's tight writing: You'll have to cut and cut and cut again when you first begin doing op-ed pieces. (And when you do get into print, reviewing the published piece against your original manuscript will help you edit your next article.)

Once you feel sufficiently familiar with your target market to be able to write for it, find a topic that's of strong interest to you. The op-ed page is an *opinion* page; if you aren't strongly interested in your topic, it's going to show in your writing and you'll swiftly get a rejection slip.

As your study of them should reveal, op-ed articles generally follow a fairly straightforward three-part format. They open with a statement of opinion, usually on a topical issue, move on to arguments for and against the issue under discussion, and then close with a summing up of the points covered and a restatement of the writer's opinion. You will find variants among different papers; careful study should enable you to tailor this general pattern to your target market.

You don't need formal credentials in your topic . . . but you must have your facts straight! Nothing will kill your reputation as a writer faster than an error-ridden article. Your library can help you get the facts and figures needed to back up an opinion; letters or phone calls to local experts can also elicit useful information and often some good quotes.

With the article done, submission is the next step. Is a query letter needed? Not really. After all, why write a 400-word query letter about a 750-word article? Most papers (see the market listing for exceptions) accept unsolicited manuscripts. However, after you have made two or three sales to your local editor, you might want to ask him if you could discuss new ideas on the phone. I found it useful on several occasions to call my editor and briefly outline an article idea. The go-ahead I received was no guarantee of a sale, but at least I knew that my editor was interested and that no one else had approached him with a similar idea. And cultivating an editor in this way has another advantage. There were times when I sent in an article that was almost salable. Because my editor knew me, I received not a rejection slip, but a letter with comments and suggestions that enabled me to do a salable rewrite. Editors *are* approachable and I have found mine to be very helpful.

After you have developed your skills on local issues for your hometown paper—and especially if you have expertise or special knowledge that would lend itself to pieces submitted outside your local area—you might want to try out-of-town markets. You'll need to research those markets as you did your local ones; your local library, or that of a nearby college, should be able to provide you with a useful sampling of major city newspapers.

Every op-ed submission must be accompanied by a cover letter in which you briefly describe your piece, and indicate any special qualifications you have for writing it. You should also enclose self-addressed, stamped envelopes with all submissions. No SASE, no reply. But keep in mind that many editors will accept photocopied submissions. Just be sure to indicate in your cover letter that the manuscript you're submitting is a Xerox, and that the editor need not return it if he cannot use it. To learn the fate of your article, ask the editor to return a self-addressed postcard on which you've typed the name of your article and the paper to which you sent it. I've been using this submission method for some time now, and find that it works quite well.

One more thing about submissions: Always include your social security number and a daytime telephone number. Both should go on the first page of your manuscript, right below your name and address. Why? Your phone number on your manuscript lets an editor call you to clarify a point or two in an otherwise acceptable manuscript. You could lose a sale if an editor couldn't get in touch with you quickly.

How much will you be paid? Payments range from $25 to $150; the average is about $50, although some papers offer only a flat rate with no increase for subsequent sales. (*The Washington Post* does pay up to $500, but that is for a major [2,500-word] opinion piece.) When a paper lists a payment range of, say, $25 to $75, a first sale will usually bring the lower figure, but you should begin to get more if you continue to sell to that market.

A few other points in closing. Pay attention to those market listings. They're drawn directly from information supplied by the editors of those papers. Don't ignore taboos or seasonal lead times. To do so marks you as less than professional in your approach.

You'll also find that researching an op-ed piece will turn up more data than you can use when you write it. Save everything! Keep a separate file folder for each piece you write, whether it sells or not. Add to those folders any later information you find on your topics. (Also include your submitted manuscript and tear sheets of published pieces.) In time, you may accumulate enough material to do a longer opinion piece for a higher-paying magazine market.

Even rejection can be surmounted. When my op-ed piece on state lotteries was rejected by newspapers in both Connecticut and New York, I resubmitted it—adding a sidebar specific to the Connecticut

318

lottery—to the *Connecticut Weekly* section of the Sunday *New York Times*. They bought it.

Opinions. Everybody has them. I get paid for some of mine, and you can, too!

62

HEADING FOR YOUR FIRST ROUNDUP

By Susan Purdy

As a writer, I wear many hats, both imaginary and real. I've worn a hard hat to get a story about the construction of a movie studio, a cap with MAP CLUB emblazoned in red letters to interview a man who provides maps to the real estate industry, and a plastic rain hat to protect me from the elements as I did field research for a piece on dentistry. But my favorite head covering is the imaginary, ten-gallon cowboy hat I wear while writing roundup articles.

To write a successful roundup article, you have to corral a group of people with an occupation, hobby, or characteristic in common—celebrities, show people, politicians, musicians—and ask them to respond to an interesting question. The roundup format appears in many of the largest national magazines—*Cosmopolitan, McCall's, Good Housekeeping*— which have run roundup articles in the past year on the following: Celebrities were asked, "What's the One Thing You Couldn't Live Without?" Several of the world's great cooks were asked how they diet. And for a roundup piece I wrote for *Good Housekeeping,* I asked some of New York's most influential and powerful men to talk about their mothers.

Roundup articles also appear in most newspapers, regional publications, town shopping newspapers, and Sunday supplements, and provide an easy way for writers to break into print. Editors know that their readers are always interested in what people prominent in a particular field have to say, and by familiarizing yourself with the magazine or newspaper, you can pose a provocative question and sell a roundup article.

How do I come up with a provocative question that will capture an editor's attention? How do I find the right people to ask?

Let's tackle the "question" question first. What piques your interest?

If you had the opportunity to ask almost anyone one question—and as a writer, you do—what would it be? You could ask your local politicians to tell you about the most influential person in their lives, or go down to your community college and ask women who are returning to school after raising a family how it has affected their marriage. You can read your local paper and ask residents how they feel about the sewage plant that is under consideration for their area, or do a roundup of your local clergy. You can find good questions everywhere, if you start thinking like a roundup writer. *Psychology Today* ran an article on "Super Sellers," men and women who are tops in their sales field. Who are the super sellers in your area? Why are they so good? Would the editor of your local paper or regional magazine be interested in them? While shopping for summer clothes this year, I began thinking about what items I should buy in the fall to update my winter wardrobe. (Writers have a tendency to think ahead because of the long lead time required by magazines.) I decided to ask the experts and wrote a roundup article for *Good Housekeeping* last year that included advice from Halston, Geoffrey Beene, and Mary McFadden. Your family and friends are great sources to tap, as are letters to the editor in newspapers, and such advice columns as "Dear Abby."

At a writers conference I attended in Manhattan, editors from national and regional magazines said they were always looking for seasonal material. Holidays like Thanksgiving, Christmas, Valentine's Day lend themselves especially well to roundup articles. Such questions as, "Have you ever spent Thanksgiving (or Christmas) alone?" "What was it like?" and "How did you spend the day?" provide a good focus for an article. Or you might interview the residents in a local nursing home: Elderly people have wonderful—or sad—stories to tell, and you could ask them about the first Christmas they can recall, how they feel the celebration of a holiday has changed since they were young, and other questions that would evoke responses that would be of interest to readers: "How did you trim the Christmas tree?" "Did you make your own ornaments?"—and if so, would they describe how?

A roundup piece for Valentine's Day could include such questions as "What was the most romantic gift you ever received for Valentine's Day?" "Do you think a single rose is more romantic than a bouquet?"

Roundup questions may be serious as well as light, instructive as well as amusing. You might ask lawyers in your city or town, "Do you think a newly married couple should make out a will? Why?" Or a roundup article could deal with such serious questions as, "How did you react when you learned that a member of your family had cancer?" "How did your children react when you and your spouse told them that you were going to be divorced?" "Do you think that a single parent can raise a family successfully?"

Teen-agers are an excellent source of roundup material. Parents as well as pre-teens and young adults might well enjoy reading about problems like, "How do you avoid peer pressure involving drugs, sex, or alcohol?" "If you could change one thing about adults in the world today, what would it be?"

Now you have dozens of questions in mind, and you can't wait to get started. At this point the second HOW comes into play. How do you get to politicians, celebrities, and the experts? Begin in your own backyard. First, query the publications in your area about doing a roundup article of local politicians, singers, theater groups, or business executives on a topic you think will be of interest to local readers. For *Business Connections,* a local magazine, I decided I wanted to question top executives from the banking world, public relations, the aircraft industry, computer sales, real estate, entertainment, and local politicians for a roundup article titled, "Long Island Business People Look Into the Future."

I did not know any of those people personally, but I kept in mind that most people feel flattered when asked for their opinions on a particular subject. For that article, I interviewed the people I'd selected directly, either at their offices or by telephone. That is not always possible. Especially when dealing with celebrities, it is best to go through their public relations or press representatives. For my article on New Year's resolutions—"Promises, Promises"—which appeared in *Good Housekeeping,* I wanted to include some local TV personalities. I called the publicity office of the television station, and identifying myself and the publication I was writing for, I described the questions I wanted to pose for my roundup piece and asked who might be available. (For future reference, I made a note of the name of the publicity person.) From the list she gave me, I chose those celebrities that I thought most suitable for my article.

She took down the question, asked me the deadline (which I always cut by two or three weeks to give me enough time to check and follow up). I always ask for an in-person interview, but if that's not possible, I ask the PR person to mail me the responses, in this way providing me with written proof that the people queried were aware that their responses were for publication.

It sounds simple—and it is—because people in the public eye want to stay there, and writers are an excellent source of free publicity.

I follow the same procedure for political figures, governors or mayors, always dealing with their press secretaries or public relations representatives, who know the officials' schedules and can judge whether they are likely to want to participate in the roundup. When I'm turned down, which happens on occasion, I thank the person I've been in touch with and say I'll call at what may be a more convenient time, leaving the door open for another article.

Some basic information to keep in mind when doing the roundup article:

1. Always get photos of the people you interview. Most people in the entertainment field have "head-shots," glossy 8 × 10 pictures that are available in their press kits. Or, with their permission, you can take your own photos, black and white, to submit with your article.

2. First asking permission, tape the interview, whether in person or over the phone. (You can buy a handy little gadget that attaches to your tape recorder for phone interviews.)

3. Remember, the people you are interviewing do not get paid for their answers. . . . the free publicity is reward enough.

4. Make sure that the publication that runs the piece sends a copy to each person quoted in the article. I always include their names and addresses on a separate sheet of paper when mailing in my roundups and often follow them up with a personal thank-you note.

Now that you have come up with some fantastic questions, have queried the people you wish to include in your article, the only thing left is to write it. *Yes, a roundup is written.* It is not just a compilation of quotes. You need an opening paragraph to prepare the reader for what will follow; lead-ins to the various people interviewed, identifying them and their position; and in most cases, a closing paragraph.

My opening paragraph for "Sons and Mothers" *(Good Housekeeping)* set the mood for the famous sons I interviewed to talk about their mothers:

Ralph Waldo Emerson wrote, "Men are what their mothers made them," and some of New York's most powerful men concur. A mother can help her son attain success by providing nurturing love, guidance, and in many cases, a strong sense of purpose he can emulate. The following men, tops in their fields, have taken time from busy schedules to tell us about this influential person in their lives.

I then led off the piece with New York City Police Commissioner Benjamin Ward, by giving his name, title, the fact that he was one of eleven children, and that his mother Loretta Ward was a great source of inspiration to him. I had interviewed Commissioner Ward in person, so I had pages of quotes to edit before I decided which would be most pertinent to the article.

That's another area in which you "write" the roundup. You must go through each interview and select only the heart. With this roundup, I had interviewed a dozen men, so my space was limited. I wanted the essence of how their mothers had influenced their lives and not pages of uninteresting material. I did not end that roundup with a closing paragraph, because the Governor of New York Mario Cuomo had provided me with an excellent closing quote, and I like to leave my readers with something special to take away when they finish the article. I find this works in most instances, as there is always one quote that lends itself to tying up the piece.

It doesn't matter whether you live in a big city or a small town, the roundup article can be written anywhere about anyone or anything, if you keep in mind that people love to be asked their opinions and are as close to you as a phone call or letter.

63

GETTING INTO TRAVEL WRITING

By Janet Steinberg

"How DID YOU get into travel writing?" is the question I am most frequently asked. "How did you have the guts to tackle the unknown?" How? Literally, by accident.

In the mid-seventies I became a statistic. A split-second accident hurled me into widowhood. Married over half my life (I'd been a teenaged bride), I was now one of the millions of women living alone in America. Grief was the first hurdle, and travel was its conqueror. In those floundering years, I admired the newspaper column of a former schoolmate. When I asked her advice on how to write (and publish) a travel column, she remarked flatly, "Just do it." Little did she realize that her lack of encouragement was the needed shot in the arm that determined me to "just do it."

Innocence (or should I say ignorance?) was another factor in my budding career. Having no knowledge of the complexity of the business, fearing neither competition nor rejection, I started (sans appointment) at the top. The travel editor, not knowing what to do with this lady who appeared before him at the paper's reception desk, did the only thing possible. He smiled, shoved a guidelines sheet into my hand, and graciously disappeared.

Seven days later, that same editor had three pieces by me on his desk. Another week later, I was published. Upon receipt of that first $25 check (frame the photocopy, not the check), I was a professional travel writer.

Eight years, thousands of articles, and thirteen travel-writing awards later, I shall try to share the secrets of success in my writing career. With allowances for individual personality, interests, and style, they should also work for you.

BE NATURAL: Go beyond the sights, the smells, and the cacophony of sounds so overworked by travel writers. Talk to your readers as if you were telling your best friend about the trip. Bubble with enthusiasm; delight in the joys you experienced; weep for the sadness you observed. Keep the human element in your writing.

BE HONEST: Travel writers often receive invitations to be guests of a resort, a hotel, a city, or a country. Puff pieces are out. Likewise, literary prostitution. Those on the take are soon recognized by their readers and by a tightly knit nationwide network of travel writers.

BE FAIR: Advise your readers honestly of any problems or shortcomings but don't try to salve your ego by wiping the destination off the map. When I found a particular hotel to be dirty, I wrote that "roaches romped in dresser drawers." About a tacky tourist trap, I advised, "Save your money, unless a smile on your grandchild's face is worth $30." When establishing the social structure of a particular cruise ship, I merely stated "leisure suits in lieu of tuxedos." Enough was said. Everyone got the picture.

BE FRUGAL: Spend your readers' time and money as if it were your own. Whether their funds and schedules are limited or open-ended, advise them how to get the most out of their travel dollars and days.

BE REAL: Let your readers know that even travel writers have fears. "Sure," I write, "I'm afraid of skyjackers and terrorists. Of course I prayed when our Nepalese plane engine failed, and we turned back to Kathmandu. Certainly an outbreak of meningococcal meningitis in Delhi, prior to my trip there, made me nervous. Undoubtedly I panicked when the Chinese navy encircled our cruise ship, which had unknowingly sailed into the midst of their maneuvers. A cannon at one's porthole is most unsettling."

BE HELPFUL: Tell them how to alleviate those fears; what proper precautions to take. Call the State Department in Washington, D.C., for security alerts; The Center for Disease Control in Atlanta, Georgia, for medical advice; and your tour operator or travel agent for all other unanswered questions or doubts.

BE HUMBLE: Don't become jaded and patronize your readers. Talk *to* them . . . not *over* their heads. Don't try to emerge the *bon vivant* by flaunting how much you know or showing off how many places you've been. A tongue-in-cheek "snob" piece can be fun as long as your readers are in on the joke. Don't use foreign words, local jargon, or complicated dialects to impress. They can be successfully used for local color or mood setting, if accompanied by a simple explanation.

BE A DO-ER: Focus on the "must-do's." Evaluate each destination from the viewpoint of someone who might never have been there before. Focus on places and things tourists *must* see or do before leaving the destination.

BE LIVELY: A travel article must be informative but not boring. Don't try to be a guidebook, listing every available offering. Don't try to be an encyclopedia listing every fact. Your job should be that of the surrogate. Sort through the books and visit the attractions before you write the article. An old song put it best: "You've got to accentuate the positive, eliminate the negative. . . ."

BE PROFESSIONAL: If you're going to be a travel writer, you must travel. I spend approximately half the year on the road. Articles stolen from brochures read just like what they are . . . articles stolen from brochures. Library research is fine as a supplement to travel, not as its replacement. It serves to verify facts and figures that are invariably mixed up by local guides.

BE A PHOTOGRAPHER: Sophisticated photographic skills, though desirable and enviable, are no longer essential. Take it from one who doesn't know a Nikon aperture from a Beethoven overture—all one needs is a good eye and a smart camera. Today's fully automatic equipment gives even amateur photographers a chance to illustrate stories with those one-of-a-kind shots not available from stock files.

BE "OF THE MOMENT": Keep your articles timely. Don't try to sell a Mediterranean cruise after the *Achille Lauro* hijacking . . . or an Eastern European trip immediately following something like the Chernobyl incident. Instead, suggest a Geneva story prior to a summit meeting, or Chamonix, France, just before the 200th anniversary of the first ascent of Mt. Blanc.

BE POSITIVE: Impress upon your readers the importance of protecting themselves against any foreseeable dangers and taking all possible precautions before going on a trip. But by all means they should go on that trip! Never let them forget that it's "the soul afraid of dying that never learns to live."

BE ENTERTAINING: While the primary purpose of a travel article is to inform potential travelers, it also takes thousands of armchair readers to never-never land. Your work can accomplish this feat only if the piece is read from start to finish. Grab your readers with an irresistible lead and don't let go until your very last paragraph takes them back to that engaging lead.

BE SELF-CONFIDENT: You may receive unsolicited advice from well-meaning friends, dishonest rivals, or jealous sharks. Listen to their words, weigh their opinions, pick their brains. But go with your gut. If you have something to do, something to say, then be determined to do it . . . and to say it. After eight years of doing it my way, I'm thoroughly convinced that whatever I'm doing wrong is all right with me.

64

HAVING FUN WRITING HUMOR

By Gene Perret

IRONICALLY, writing and selling humorous magazine pieces follows the classic "good news-bad news" joke form. The good news is that editors want good, funny pieces. "We need good humor," or "We're constantly searching for people who can write humor," editors say. The bad news is that humor is one of the most difficult things to sell to those same editors.

That contradiction may seem as if it were created by a humorist, but it is logical. It's because magazine editors are so selective in buying humor that they're constantly in need of it. If humor were easy to write and sell, they'd have plenty.

Why are the editors so selective? First of all, comedy is an elusive art form. It is to writing what jazz is to music. It's innovative, often rebellious and more often than not, will break tradition rather than follow it. The standard rules might not apply to a humorous piece. Therefore, it can confuse and frighten editors.

With a conventional article, the editor can analyze the form and structure and can grade each piece, calculating whether it will hold the reader's interest. With humor, those hard-and-fast rules become only guidelines. The editor can only guess how effective the article will be.

The basis of judgment changes, too. It's no longer whether the article is well written and well constructed. It's whether the article is entertaining or not. Most editors are less sure of themselves on that ground. Consequently, they're more hesitant about buying.

Secondly, comedy is very subjective. A joke or story is funny only to the person hearing it. That person forms a picture in the mind. If that picture is amusing, the reader laughs; if it isn't, he doesn't. One article can be funny to reader A and not funny to reader B. Since editors are first of all readers, you can see the confusion.

I asked one managing editor how she bought humor for her magazine.

329

She said, "We pass it around to the various editors. If they all laugh, we buy it." If they ALL laugh! That's formidable veto power for a humorist to face.

None of this should discourage the aspiring comedy writer, though. Rather, it should be encouraging for several reasons:

1) Since humor writing is admittedly difficult to sell, it automatically cuts down the competition. If it were easy, everybody would be doing it. Lighter pieces may be a way of reaching editors who have their favorite writers for the more conventional articles.

2) There is a demand for humor. Those magazines that use it often admit that it usually finishes very high in their reader surveys. People enjoy a chuckle. They like comedy in the movies, on TV, and in their reading. And good humor is not easy to find. The demand is high, and the supply is low—that's a situation that every free lancer dreams of.

3) There is probably less rewriting demanded on light pieces than any other type of writing. Why? Because, again, it's an area that is foreign to most editors. They can strengthen a traditional piece with suggestions for rewrites or restructuring, but can they make something funnier? They're writers or journalists and usually not humorists. They leave that fine tuning to the wits. Also, there is less rewriting requested because the piece was basically amusing. If it weren't, it would have been rejected sooner.

4) Comedy is a rewarding type of writing. It's cathartic for the writer as well as the reader. It helps you get many little peeves out of your system and onto the paper. Humor also forces you, by definition, to search out the fun in any topic. Any time I suggest a humor project to a fellow comedy writer, regardless of whether it's a touch project or not, whether it has an unmeetable deadline or not, I always say, "Have fun with it."

Earlier I noted that humor writing was like jazz. It has rules, as jazz does. Music has mathematical rules of scales and rhythms, but sometimes the creativity comes from violating or bending those precepts.

It's difficult to define rules for writing humor. There are almost as many different forms of the art as there are humorists. Erma Bombeck is different from Art Buchwald is different from Stephen Leacock is different from H. Allen Smith. To limit one's style of writing is to restrict the innovation that creates the fun.

One way to create a humorous style is to read and study those

330

humorists you enjoy. Then try to duplicate their style. Within a short time you'll be adding a flair of your own because humor demands that . . . it needs spontaneity. Soon you'll see that their style combined with your variations has created a new and different style.

A humor writer needn't be afraid of experimentation. Comedy has to be unpredictable. If it weren't, it wouldn't be as funny. People don't laugh as hard at a story they've heard before. The surprise element is part of the humor. It's fun writing that says to you, "Try anything."

While there may be few if any rules about the writing of lighter pieces, there are some universal truths about comedy that may keep your humorous writing more salable.

1) The best humor is based on truth. I used to write funny lines for Phyllis Diller. It's hard to imagine anyone more outlandish or bizarre than Phyllis. Yet she would say to me often, "Honey, if the jokes aren't true, don't send them to me." She knew what she was talking about.

Any humor you attempt should be based on a truthful premise. Like Phyllis Diller, you may then distort that truth. You can bend it, twist it, exaggerate it, carry it to extremes—even unbelievable extremes. The basic truth on which it was based remains.

To illustrate, suppose we do a comedy piece on where all the socks go that we lose in the wash. That's basically a truthful premise. Every household has had one unmatched sock show up after the family wash is done. For some reason the other one never does return. From that basic truthful premise you might hypothesize in your article that it goes down through the earth to Australia. You might conjecture that creatures from outer space feed on single socks. You might even suppose that they run off to join some sort of "sock circus." These are all wild, preposterous fantasies, but based on a totally believable, relatively truthful premise.

That's much more effective comedically than any humor based on a false, manufactured premise. For instance, suppose you were to do a hilarious treatise based on the fact that all people who own black dogs as pets are grouches. You may have some funny, plausible stories about people who own black dogs, but the basic premise is flawed. You created the premise to support your funny stories. Whereas in the first instance, you created the outrageous tales based on a believable premise.

Your humor will generally be stronger if it's based on truth.

2) Recognizable humor is usually more fun for a reading audience. Earlier I said that humor is graphic. A joke or story generates a picture in each reader's or listener's mind. If the picture is amusing, they laugh. If they can see themselves in that picture, they laugh harder.

In my lectures I tell the audience that humor is already around them. For example, I say, "If you see a man open the car door for his wife, you know right away either the car is new or the wife is." That line gets a quick response because so many listeners recognize themselves in that scene. The wives see their husbands, and the husbands see themselves. It has a high recognizability factor.

I once read a statement attributed to some vaudeville comic. I don't remember his name, nor do I know if he was a successful comic. I hope he was, because he knew what he was talking about. He said, "A good joke is saying what everybody else is thinking, only you say it better."

The best humor writers look at commonplace, everyday events from a fresh, oblique angle. The topic may be commonplace; the humorist's view of it is original.

3) Remember your readers. Again, the humorist can only suggest. The humorist paints the picture in the reader's mind. The reader then passes judgment on whether that scene is funny or not. You'll score higher if you know what your readers want to see. You do that by knowing who your readers are. Editors admonish us time and time again to "read the magazine." It applies as much in writing humorous pieces as it does in any other writing.

Since humor writing is different from conventional article writing, it also has some slightly different rules for marketing.

"Query first" is almost an absolute in dealing with magazine editors. It's not in selling humor. Editors have told me that they don't want to see a query letter or a proposal for lighter pieces. Why? Because they tell the editor practically nothing about how funny the piece will be. One writer may do a piece about the socks missing from the family wash and make it a masterpiece. Another may use the same premise and never generate a snicker. The value of a humorous piece is the humor. Editors can't tell how funny it is until it's written. So, humor writing will have to be submitted on speculation. Do the piece and then send it to the editors. It's wise to select subjects that have wide appeal—premises that would be of interest to many magazines. As an example, a piece on some aspect of cooking could be sent to all of the family and women's magazines. Then one rejection isn't catastrophic. It just means typing up a new submission envelope.

Try writing humor. The editors claim they want it and need it. We all know the world certainly could use a few more chuckles.

65

HOW TO WRITE GOOD ARTICLE LEADS

By Marshall Cook

IF YOUR article lead doesn't catch the reader's attention immediately, your article doesn't stand a chance in the marketplace. That makes the first words of an article the most important ones you write. And it puts a lot of pressure on you to write them well.

First, your lead should issue a clear invitation to the reader by promising useful or interesting information and an enjoyable reading experience. Never try to trick your readers by promising more than your article will deliver. And there's no use trying to coerce them, either. You can't force your readers to participate in your visions. You can only show them how interesting and exciting those visions are.

Next, your lead should establish the focus of the article by introducing the subject and conveying the main idea or slant.

Finally, your lead should establish the tone of your article. If you plan to take a light, humorous approach, for example, your lead should provoke a chuckle.

Here are seven approaches that can help you create compelling leads.

The startling statement

"Your English teacher lied to you." That's how I started an article on advertising copy writing for an in-house publication. My point was not that English teachers are liars, but that good ad copy often breaks the sacred grammar rules we dutifully learned. "Ad copy often breaks grammar rules" didn't strike me as an especially effective lead, however, so I chose a statement that I hoped would generate more interest.

A study skills article I wrote for *Directions,* a regional college campus magazine, began, "The good grades don't necessarily go to the smartest students." They go, I pointed out, to those who have learned how to study most effectively.

The startling statement should convey the focus or slant quickly while evoking a positive attention and arousing curiosity.

The quote lead

It's often best to let the subjects speak for themselves. Quotation marks around a lead signal readers that the show is about to begin.

My profile of architect Kenton Peters for *Wisconsin Trails* magazine began with Peters' assertion, "We have the fundamental right not to be confronted by ugliness." I thought it a fine quote to lead with, because, though the words are easy to understand, the context isn't clear at once. It should pique the readers' curiosity without befuddling them.

Provide the context, along with attribution for the quote, as quickly as possible. If you leave your readers hanging too long, they may feel manipulated or become confused.

Sometimes the quote can be commonplace and close to home. For my humor piece, "Fraction Action," for *The Milwaukee Journal Green Sheet* (check your local newspapers as potential markets), I quoted my son:

"Hey, Dad. I need help with my homework."
Words to strike terror into any parent's heart.

Your best quotes come from your own sources, because they supply material that has never been in print. Occasionally, however, you may want the richness of allusion that a familiar quote can provide. I've used Mark Twain's, "If you can catch an adjective, kill it," and the immortal advertising slogan, "Plop, plop, fizz, fizz. Oh, what a relief it is," to bring the readers closer to my subjects.

The anecdotal lead

Perhaps the most effective but often the hardest to develop, the anecdotal lead shows rather than tells. The anecdote is a small, human story used to illuminate the point of the whole article.

I began my profile of a thriving acrylics company for *Business Age* magazine with the story of how Jim Lynn started the company with a $200 power saw and a few scraps of wood and plastic in the basement of his home. It provided a simple, human introduction to the complexities of the business and illustrated my theme, that a $2.2 million-a-year business could begin without planning and, indeed, almost by accident.

As with quotes, the best anecdotes come from your own sources. Probe for anecdotes in your interviews. When your subject gives you a generalization such as "You meet the most interesting people in my line of work," your response should be, "Describe some of those interesting people."

It's almost always best to keep yourself out of the article, but it may occasionally be effective to begin with a personal anecdote in order to make contact with your readers. I began my article "Holiday Hassles/ Holiday Happiness" for *Catholic Digest* by describing my 24-hour wait at the Milwaukee airport while my parents, snowbound in Denver, tried to get through for a Thanksgiving visit.

It's all right to make up an anecdote, as long as you make it clear to the reader that you're doing so. For my piece "Personal Publishing," I walked the reader through the experience of submitting a manuscript and having it rejected, to illustrate that the hardest work for the writer sometimes begins when the actual writing is done.

The cliché with a twist

Ordinarily, clichés have no place in your work, and especially not in the lead, where freshness is a must. But a good, hard twist can squeeze new life from a seemingly wrung-out phrase.

I began my article on physical fitness for *Directions* with an old saw with a couple of new teeth: "Caution: College may be hazardous to your health."

I've never forgotten the newspaper article on dieting that began, "Despite all the diets, pills and potions, heft springs eternal" or the baseball story that led with, "Things were so quiet in the Brewers clubhouse last night, you could hear a batting average drop."

Direct address

Often the best approach is the most direct one, a lead that puts the reader directly into the action.

I wanted to begin my description of a Mercury-Marine outboard motor plant for *The Yacht* magazine with the surprising fact that "Many yachts have their beginnings in an aluminum recycling plant in Fond du Lac, Wisconsin." I think I made the lead much stronger by rewriting it in direct address: "Your yacht may have begun as a mound of aluminum cans in Fond du Lac, Wisconsin."

One widely used variation on direct address is the question lead, but be careful here. Writers have overworked this technique, using it as an "if-all-else-fails" catch-all. Especially worn out is the "What do Sylvester Stallone, George Bush and Mother Theresa have in common?" format. Avoid it.

Avoid, too, the rhetorical question, one that clearly manipulates the reader into giving a predetermined response. "Do you want your children to have a good education?" (No, I want my kids to be illiterate bums!)

If the question provokes reader curiosity and introduces a genuine search for answers, it may be an excellent lead.

The narrative lead

For a long time, I thought there were two kinds of writing, "creative" (as in short stories and poetry) and "journalistic" (as in stuff you wrote for money). I've learned better. There are two kinds of writing, all right, writing that works and writing that doesn't. Effective writing uses any appropriate means to tell its story. If description and narration, primary tools of the fiction writer, work best in opening your nonfiction piece, you have both the right and the responsibility to use them.

I began an article on the old Boston Blackie television series for *Airwaves,* a public television programming guide, by describing the opening sequence of each episode, with the mysterious detective's silhouette looming ever-larger at the end of a darkened alley. I did so to try to evoke the rough charm of a 1950s low-budget production.

My profile of National Book Award winner Herbert Kubly for *Wisconsin Trails* began with a panoramic sweep, almost like the opening of a movie, panning from the tiny town of New Glarus, where Kubly grew up, out along a country road to the fourth-generation Kubly family farm. I wanted to show the author's tie to the land and the effect that tie has had on his writing. What better way than to describe that land?

Description for its own sake merely delays the true start of the article and makes the readers impatient—if it doesn't chase them away completely. Effective description must be thematic, revealing the focus of the article.

The comparison lead

Metaphor, simile, and analogy are effective tools for making sense out of nonsense and rendering the abstract concrete. Don't save them for later. Use them in the lead.

337

I've described a Wisconsin street as a carnival, compared a writer's query letter to a job interview, likened the process of scanning a magazine article to standing back to take in an entire mural before moving closer to study details, all to try to shine a light on the darkness of a new subject.

The effective comparison startles readers with new insights, makes them nod in agreement and murmur, "Ah-ha!" As with all good writing, it helps us to see familiar realities in new ways.

These seven lead categories often overlap. A metaphor may arrive wearing quotation marks. Direct address may also twist a cliché. Strict categorization isn't important. Finding the best lead for your article is.

Begin the search early. As you gather material, ask yourself, "What is unique about my subject?" Constantly and consciously look for quotes, anecdotes, and bits of thematic description that might illustrate this uniqueness in a memorable lead.

Trying to write the lead before you're ready can leave you staring into space, too worried about getting off to a good start to get off to any start at all. Work with the material you're comfortable with until lead possibilities begin to emerge.

When you're ready to tackle the lead, write not one but several. Let your imagination play with the idea. See how many possibilities you can generate. Don't be too quick to settle on one. The more choices you give yourself, the more likely you are to discover the best approach.

Finally, never impose a lead on your material. Let the lead emerge from the material.

It's worth the time and effort it takes to craft a compelling lead. It can make the difference between an article that never sees print and one that entertains and informs your readers.

66

OUTLINES THAT SELL BOOKS

By Kenn Oberrecht

UNLESS you're new to the writing business, you probably know that publishers today offer book contracts on the basis of outlines and sample chapters. What might surprise you, however, is the possibility of getting contracts via outlines alone—sans samples. Of the eleven contracts offered me in eight years, seven were based solely on outlines.

The formula I use for writing salable outlines grew mainly out of trial and error and from no small amount of advice from editors, publishers, and others in the book business. If you're where I was a few years ago—on the brink of book publication—perhaps my methods will save you some time and frustration. There are few hard-and-fast rules for outlining, so take what I offer simply as the way one writer outlines and sells his books. The techniques work for me and might put you on the right track.

Page one

Page one is the most important part of my outlines, because this is where I hook or lose editors. It enables them to evaluate my proposal at a glance.

Page one is basically an outline of the outline. After typing my name, address, and phone number in the top left corner, I drop down several spaces and list the main elements of my proposed book. Headings for this list include *Working Title, Alternative Titles, Manuscript Length, Divisions, Completion Time,* and *Illustrations.* Let's examine each.

Titles. As a sales tool, the title is as important as dust-jacket design and paramount to everything else in the book. Spend some time thinking seriously about your title. Jot down the elements of your subject in as few words as possible. Then rearrange these into as many titles as you can think of. List published books in your subject area, both to avoid duplication and to improve on those titles.

Pick your best for a working title, then choose three to twelve others as alternatives, and keep your original list on file.

Manuscript length. If your subject has been written about before, or if you're writing a particular type of book (self-help, how-to, cookbook, biography, etc.), become familiar with related published books, and plan yours to be similar in length to the most successful. It is equally important to be aware of any publisher's current offerings. If a publisher is putting out books of one size, don't jeopardize your chances by offering something considerably longer or shorter.

My first sale was an angling book. Before submitting my outline, I studied other angling books and found that most ranged from 60,000 to 90,000 words. Concurrently, I examined the offerings of several publishers of fishing books and picked my primary target: a house that consistently published books of about 80,000 words. I proposed a book of 75,000 to 85,000 words.

Divisions. Most books are divided into chapters; some are further organized by grouping several related chapters into sections or parts. Your subject will dictate the best arrangement and suitable divisions.

Completion time. Only you can determine how long it will take to write your book, but be careful here, and allow yourself sufficient leeway. If you're an expert on your subject, have files full of supporting material, and can work full time on the project, you might be able to finish your book in a month. Then I would say you could give yourself a three-month deadline, but make it six for safety's sake.

If, on the other hand, you're faced with considerable research and can only work twenty hours a week, you might need six months or more. Add the fudge factor, and agree to deliver in twelve months.

Illustrations. If your book needs illustrations, handle them as you would the text. Find out what the competition is doing, determine what your target publishers want, and make your proposal along those lines. When doing my first book, I found that similar books had from 100 to 150 illustrations, usually black-and-white photographs. In my outline, I proposed 125 photographs.

Text of outline

Subdivisions of this main portion of the outline are grouped under several headings: *Project Description, Style, Length, Markets and Sales Potential, Competing Volumes,* and *Author's Qualifications.*

Project description. This section is next in importance to the page-one summary because, in two or three pages, you distill the essence of the proposed book. The writing must be tight and lively. Be positive and enthusiastic and try to convince the editor that your book will be the best ever written on the subject.

The soundest advice I can give you is to study blurbs on the other books in your subject area. What the blurb writer is trying to do to a potential reader is precisely what you're trying to do to an editor: sell a book.

Style. Each of us has his own style, but most of us work with several styles, adapting them to various subjects and audiences. If you're proposing a textbook, for instance, use an academic style suitable to the field. Psychology books differ in style from history books as much as thrillers differ from romance novels. Further, books on cooking, child rearing, gardening, home improvement, wine, travel, snakes, canoeing, and kazoo playing all differ stylistically, yet they share some similarities.

Keep in mind that popular nonfiction is normally written in an informal, conversational style. It should be grammatically correct, but friendly. Your proposal should clearly demonstrate your ability to write in the style appropriate for the book.

Two paragraphs covered the subject of style in my proposal for a book on the writing craft:

Although *Writing For Real* should prove suitable as a college textbook or supplementary text and will appeal as a popular how-to manual to writers and would-be writers everywhere, it will be neither a stuffy academic tome, nor a formula book written in the too-cute, gee-whiz style favored by some authors these days. Simply, the book will be carefully written and meticulously organized for easy reference.

The subject will be approached seriously and studiously, but not without colorful anecdotes and appropriate humor. Throughout, the purpose will be to inform and motivate the reader, and every effort will be made to entertain him as well.

Length. Mainly, this section deals with the finished book. It's important to envision your book as you will see it on a bookstore shelf. The editor will do so, too.

Take a closer look at some of the books you have already examined in your subject area. Keep in mind that design variations, format, and the use of white space and illustrations can dramatically alter book size. But you should be able to give a reasonable estimate of length and format. Of course, the final decision will be the publisher's.

Markets and sales potential. Although publishers employ people who know more about marketing and sales than the average author does, don't be afraid to address this subject. Your ideas may call the editor's attention to sales possibilities he might otherwise overlook.

Suggest special-interest groups that you think will find your book valuable. Mention similar books that have been marketed successfully by direct mail. If your book seems a natural for one or more book clubs, name them. If you know that a similar book sold 60,000 copies in hardcover, was picked up by two book clubs, serialized in a major periodical, recently sold to a paperback publisher, and you're confident yours will be a better treatment, you can talk specifically, as I did in one of my proposals: "It's not unreasonable to expect hardcover sales to exceed 50,000 copies."

Competing volumes. Make at least one visit to your local library to check the *Subject Guide to Books in Print.* Then, armed with a list of those books most closely related to yours, read, evaluate, and briefly report on as many as possible in your proposal.

Be specific and concise. If you refer to a half-dozen or so books, summarize each in a sentence or two; then demonstrate how yours will excel or improve on them.

If there are no competing volumes, say so. Then explain why your book should be published to fill the obvious void. If you can offer examples of magazine articles on your subject and supporting opinions of well-known experts, all the better.

One of my fishing books was the first in its field. Anticipating criticism of over-specialization, I showed that my subject was as old as fishing itself, that numerous articles had been written about it, and I quoted seven well-known fishing writers. That list of quotations ended up on the back of the dust jacket and was used extensively in promotion and reviews. I'm sure those expert opinions were largely responsible for the contract offer.

Author's qualifications. Here's where you toot your own horn, but with all due modesty. When you're trying to sell a book, your best qualifications are previous books you've had published. But if you're peddling your first book, as all of us once had to, then you'll have to offer other credentials, such as magazine articles you've written, especially those related to your book's subject.

Whether or not you have published anything, be sure to discuss any applicable experience. If you're proposing a book on archery and won the National Field Archery Association Championship three years in a row, that could mean more than previous book sales. Cooking experience might count for more than writing experience in a cookbook proposal.

Everybody is an expert on something, and that expertise can go a long way toward convincing a publisher to offer a book contract.

Contents

Some writers include a table of contents in their outlines; some don't. On the assumption that no editor is going to object to its inclusion, but that some might frown on its omission, I always include one. I also try to outline each chapter in a short paragraph or statement of chapter topics. For example, one chapter of a photography book I currently have in outline form is described this way:

Chapter 20. Communicating With Photographs.
Emphasizes the important communicative aspects of editorial photography and gathers previously discussed principles into a cohesive philosophy. Further convinces the reader of the crucial role photography plays in modern journalism and stresses the ever-present need for effective photographs by magazine and book publishers.

Although my table of contents appears at the end of an outline, this is one of the first sections I start working on. When the project is organized into a workable list of chapters, I know I'm ready to write the outline and send it off to publishers.

Sample chapters

You might need to prepare a sample chapter or two, but that can wait. My feeling is that an editor who has no interest in my idea, or has something similar pending, isn't going to bother reading samples. So why waste money on extra photocopying and postage? And if the idea proves unsalable, preparation of sample chapters will have been a waste of time.

On the other hand, if my proposal sparks interest from the editor, he can always ask for samples. Better yet, he might offer a contract solely on the basis of my outline.

One question I've deliberately left unanswered until now is outline length. I've had good luck with outlines of 10 to 15 double-spaced pages. There's really no set rule for length, other than to make your outline only as long as it must be to cover the proposal and get an editor interested.

If you spend some time on your outline and put your best writing efforts into it, you might soon be doing the most important writing of all: putting your signature on your first book contract.

67

PUNS AND PARODIES PAY OFF

By Selma Glasser

Most writers are unaware of a short form of writing—puns and parodies—that can be a profitable pastime. I have used them to win fabulous awards in prize contests, to write light verse, greeting cards, and other short items. Payment for this type of writing is excellent when you consider how little time, energy, and how few words are required. Besides the amounts one can earn, writing puns and parodies is a delight—a really fun kind of creativity. Puns and parodies usually draw the largest readership, and because of their brevity, pointed revelations, and familiarity, they are long remembered.

What are puns and parodies? Very simply stated—one word or more altered (or not) for sound-alike, humorous, or double-meaning effects that depend heavily on multi-faceted meanings or recognizable qualities. They invariably involve combinations of similar sounds, alliteration, the same or different spellings and often different meanings of the identical word. Ideally, they should be humorous, strike a familiar note, be unique, and original.

You don't have to be quip-witted to compose puns and parodies (notice that "quip-witted" is a parody on the expression "quick-witted"). They're much easier to write than you might think. All that is required is an awareness of popular, recognizable phrases, double meanings of words, and a whimsical mind.

For example, let's take an expression like "Long time no see." Familiar to everyone, right? A sailor (retired) might say: "Long time no sea." An ex-golfer might state: "Long time no tee." And if your TV breaks down in the middle of your favorite show you might quip: "Wrong time no see." Are you beginning to catch on? If imitation is the sincerest form of flattery, why shouldn't takeoffs of popular phrases, words, and proverbs, or *double entendres* appeal to readers, editors, and sponsors of contests? In fact, they do!

345

My earliest initiation, exhilaration, and generous payoff from this form of writing came from a mere four words ending in a pun. A contest called for an answer to the question: "Why is a Stella D'Oro cookie like a trip to the Continent?"

My answer: "They both take dough."

For those few words, I won top prize—a trip to Italy and France.

Another sponsor asked contestants why they wanted to jump back into bed in the morning, I quipped: "Because I'm good for nodding!" Another cash award came my way. When the A.J. Funk Co. of Chicago asked contest entrants to describe their new cleaner, I called their product "funktional," thereby making a pun on the sponsor's own name. A radio show asked listeners to rename Engelbert Humperdinck to win a night on the town with him in New York City. My name was "Howie Sings" (how-he-sings). It was a delightful evening.

Puns are used more and more in greeting card writing. Sometimes even a single word with a double meaning can sell a card.

I liked the slang use of "pad" and thought it had a potential. Here's how I sold it to a major greeting card company:

OUTSIDE: For your birthday, how would you like to share my pad?
INSIDE: There was a real yellow pad enclosed, under which appeared the words: "Enjoy yourself and have a happy birthday."

I sold another card six months prior to St. Patrick's Day (a six-month lead time is standard for holiday and seasonal material). Here's how it went:

OUTSIDE: Know why the Irish parade on St. Patrick's Day?
INSIDE: Cause the calendar sez MARCH! Happy St. Patrick's Day.

For a juvenile market, I wrote this one:

OUTSIDE: Do you know the best way to pass a test?
INSIDE: Just keep walking.

A Bon Voyage card went like this: "I wish you a pleasant trip on your change of place."

A card for a new baby: "Congrats to your newlywet."

Lesson Three of my book, *Glasser Guide to Filler Writing*, called "Pun Fun," has seventeen pages of examples and illustrations. One sample is the word "scales," which may be defined as weighing machines and also something found on fish. Then there are words like "appear," which can be humorously defined as where you fish (a pier), or "campaign" as stomach discomfort of a child at camp (camp pain).

Then there are the parodies or sound-alike words which make for amusing epigrams or definitions. For instance, we can define hayfever as "much achoo about nothing," or spring fever as "loaf at first sight." I once sold a group of puns from A to Z (26) to Hallmark Cards starting with: ALOHA = pullman berth (not an upper), and ending with ZEBRA = brassiere size for an elephant. You can imagine how "way out" the other puns on letters of the alphabet were. I employed a simple rundown on A to Z from ordinary words found in the dictionary, utilizing exaggerated, fun-sounding "take-offs"—and was paid extremely well.

Compiling time-worn clichés and *double entendre* words is the key to successful punning. Searching out these adaptable phrases is a fun sort of hobby in itself. They tend to start your creative juices flowing. The idea is to accumulate an inventory of usable words for unrestrained changes or "plays" on them, a sort of "think tank" that, when utilized productively, pays off.

I overheard a discussion on "problem drinkers," which is a very common phrase. From that one phrase came the title of a light verse I wrote about the newspaper advice-givers, which I titled, "The Problem Thinkers." For many years I listened to the weather forecasters. More times than they care to admit their forecasts are incorrect. After mulling that over in mind, I called my light verse "Weather Flawcasters" and ended it with the fact that they belong to a "Non-Prophet" group. In the summertime when green thumb gardeners are thriving, my garden is never surviving. One light verse I wrote was called "Home Groan." Another time, still on the subject of my failure as a horticulturist, I ended the verse with this line: "I'm thinking of taking REMEDIAL WEEDING."

Sometimes an entire poem or song can be done in parody form, which then would be a sound-alike of the original. Recognizing and appreciating the fact that it's familiar makes it work. For example, my parody of the song "Bye, Bye, Blackbird" (for a Vicks commercial contest) went like this:

> Pack up all my coughing woe,
> Vicks I know makes it go—bye, bye, sore throat.

and ended:

> Take my Vicks for coughing grief
> It assures quick relief, coughing, bye, bye!

This song parody won first prize and was the easiest, most fun of any writing I've done. And all I did was to imitate this well-known song. By adding a new dimension and substituting new words for the old, I came up with a winner.

Familiar phrases and songs are everywhere. My own files are packed with takeoffs on titles of TV shows or plays. Popular sayings, slang words, current expressions, and clichés keep my stock growing. Make your own list of current terminology. Be alert for titles of new books or movies, because the rewards for those puns and parodies can be fantastic, and the thrill of acceptance inestimable.

68

WRITING FOR SYNDICATES

By Valerie Bohigian

JACK ANDERSON, Erma Bombeck, Richard Simmons, Sylvia Porter, and Ann Landers are syndicated writers. They write regular columns familiar to much of newspaper reading America, and they are well rewarded financially for their efforts. For every one of these writers, there are dozens of unknowns also earning steady, though more modest, dollars writing for syndicates. Some of them will build up the kinds of followings that will result in big earnings, book contracts, television and radio spots and lucrative speaking engagements. Other columns will be dropped as national trends and interests change, creating new openings that can be filled by writers who understand how syndicates work and know how to approach this market correctly with fresh, timely ideas. With the right information and the right idea, you can write one of these new columns.

Writing for a syndicate is different from writing for a magazine. A syndicate is not a publication. It is an agency that purchases columns, articles, comic strips, cartoons, photographs, horoscopes, jokes, puzzles, fillers, etc., and sells them to newspapers all around the country and the world. Contributors are paid a percentage—usually 50%—of total sales. (Syndicates occasionally pay a set fee.) Basically, a syndicate seeks to provide first-rate material at reasonable prices to as many newspapers as possible, and tries to stock a little of everything so that if a particular paper calls and asks for a travel column, or an etiquette column, or a humor column, the syndicate has it on hand and can fill the request.

The more newspapers that purchase your column, the more money you earn. Though wide distribution and circulation are important, other factors are equally so: Who buys your column is important. A major metropolitan newspaper will pay $100 for a column, whereas a Peoria paper will pay only $5. This means that if your column appears in such large papers as *The Boston Globe, The New York Daily News,* and *The Los Angeles Times,* you'll earn more than if it appears in fifty small-town papers.

Having your column appear in a small list of large newspapers can be more lucrative than having it appear in a large list of small newspapers. Of course, the ideal situation is to have your column sell to a large list of large and small newspapers. Once you get rolling this can happen. There are about 1,700 newspapers in the United States, and columns like Ann Landers' are bought by about 900 of them on a daily basis. Assuming she were to earn only $5 per paper (and she undoubtedly earns more), that's $4,500 per day!

Most syndicated writers do not earn anywhere near $4,500 per day. Rare is the column that sells to 900 newspapers per day; and rare is the columnist whose columns appear daily. However, there are several beginning columnists whose columns appear once or twice a week in about fifty newspapers. These writers are netting between $200 and $400 per week—not the big time yet, but not bad at all. Who are these people and how can you become one of them?

You have the best chance of becoming syndicated if you are an expert on a subject that is currently popular, not glutted with too many knowledgeable writers, and one that is growing in appeal. Certainly, it doesn't hurt to have an easily recognized name, but it is not crucial: The subject is. Ten years ago, for example, a syndicated column on plant care would not have sold, but now that plants are widely used in homes and offices as major decorating accessories, there are a few successful syndicated columns about plants. Though the authors are not "household names," the information and help they provide is read and used in thousands of households all over the country.

Columns showing people how to cope with various problems are popular today, and they are often written by individuals who have successfully solved these problems, rather than by theorists. For example, there is a lot of current interest in helping the handicapped care for themselves. A recent column on the subject, written by an invalid of many years, is selling widely. The author of this column passes along to her readers useful self-help ideas that she has discovered over the years, and that other disabled people have passed on to her. The handicapped, families of the handicapped, and people in professions relating to the care of the disabled are avid readers of this column.

How-to-cope columns need not deal with disabilities or tragedies; if you're coping successfully with a situation of wide interest, you may have a potential column in your hands. One of the major syndicates just took on as a columnist a mail order specialist who has learned not only how to deal with inflation, unemployment, job security, etc., but more specifically, how to do so by becoming an expert in mail order selling. The problems, pitfalls, and profits awaiting novice entrepreneurs in this field will be covered in this column. Another major syndicate, reflecting the growing interest in religion, has taken on a religion column geared to readers concerned with what they consider a current spiritual crisis in our society.

How-to material is also in demand today. If you know how to do something that most people would like to learn how to do or how to do better, you may have a salable column. Do you have a lot of good information to pass along in the fields of home entertainment, computers, home construction projects, knitting and crocheting, entrepreneurship, animal care? Right now the syndicates are looking for and buying columns in these areas.

Assuming you have a good idea and a concise (columns are generally only a few hundred words each) and readable style, how best to proceed? Though it is not the only way, the best way to begin is to develop a column for your local newspaper. Try to get your local paper to run it for awhile and then submit tear sheets of your columns to the syndicates, either through your local editor or directly. Syndicates respond well to columns that have proven popular in local newspapers.

Whether you're submitting to your local newspaper or to a syndicate, the procedure is the same: Submit an outline of what you have in mind, with six to eight sample columns that will demonstrate to the editors that you have more than just three good shots in your bag. A syndicate's editor can love your column, but its sales force can give it the kiss of death. Make sure, therefore, that your column reveals that it can help many thousands of readers who do not have easy access to the information you can provide, since it is a syndicate's sales department that must ultimately be able to place your work.

Don't get discouraged if you don't have a "hot" item for a column, or if it gets a cold response from a syndicate's editor. The best route to syndicate sales is through a careful study of what the syndicates seem to be selling, new subjects they seem to be taking on, and the writing styles and formats used. Familiarize yourself with all the syndicated newspaper columns you can find. (There are out-of-town newspaper stands in many cities; they can also be found in libraries.) Keep an eye out for trends, and list the specialized information you have to offer and what new ideas syndicates are using. See page 750 for information on the current market needs and requirements of the various syndicates. Also, at a large public library, consult *The Editors and Publishers Syndicate Directory,* which lists all syndicated columns, and *Literary Market Place,* which has a listing of syndicates.

While you're waiting for the right column idea to come along, or for your column to find a home, you might consider trying to sell "one-shots" to the syndicates. One-shots are reportorial pieces that some syndicates buy because they can easily be placed in several newspapers on a one-time basis. One-shots often draw fairly high fees (20¢ to 50¢ per word), and can be on any timely topic ranging from acrophobia to acupuncture. They can also be spin-offs from your already published magazine articles. One-shots not only produce income, but when your big column idea does come along, the editors will know you, and your material will receive special attention. Even though that alone won't make editors buy an unsalable column from you, they will be more likely to comment personally on why your idea won't work or on what you can do to make it more marketable.

Though big syndicates stock a wide variety of material, at a particular time one syndicate may be overstocked with business and fashion-advice columns, or because a key contributor didn't renew his contract, they may have a need for a record/music column. Another syndicate may be very much in the market for a column dispensing fresh business advice or offering money-saving tips. How do you know? You don't. Things change daily and timing can be very important. Unless you have a lot of already produced sample material on hand, or reason to believe that a particular syndicate is in the market for the kind of material you would like to provide, your time is probably best spent sending out a few queries to different syndicates, pitching your idea (for a one-shot or column). When a syndicate expresses interest, you can then follow up with a finished manuscript or several sample columns demonstrating your ability to produce quality with consistency. Always mention your specific qualifications.

The large syndicates sell material to hundreds of newspapers, large and small. There are also several smaller, more specialized syndicates you can try where you won't be competing with established professionals. Try them all, and don't be disheartened by rejections. Several widely syndicated features were turned down many times before being finally accepted. Yours may be, too.

69

HOW TO SHOOT PICTURES TO ILLUSTRATE YOUR ARTICLES

By Daniel R. Hopwood

I BELIEVE that almost any magazine article is more likely to sell if the writer can supply good photographs to illustrate that article, and that writers who do so make more money than writers who don't. It's cheaper, easier, and quicker for the editors to buy articles and photos as a package from one person than it is to assign a photographer to go take pictures or to search for stock photos.

Anyone wanting to do his own magazine photography will need the following things: a 35mm camera (or larger format) with a standard lens, a wide-angle lens, and a telephoto lens; a working knowledge of photography; and a supply of color transparency film (for color shots) and a good black-and-white film (such as Kodak Tri-X). There are hundreds of books about photography, and anyone having questions about the technical side of photography will find books that can answer their questions.

Creating photos is a highly personal form of expression. Your photos must speak to the readers just as your words do; they must convey a visual message to them. The following guidelines will help you present your photos and your articles as a unit, a complete expression of what you are trying to say. Use these twelve tips whenever you take pictures to illustrate an article:

1. *Tone*. Make your photos consistent with the tone of your article. If, for example, your article is about a serious subject like depression, obviously you shouldn't have smiling faces in your pictures. Instead, take pictures of cloudy, overcast days; a person crying; someone all alone; a cemetery, or anything else that says "depression" to you.

2. *When it's easy, don't make it hard*. Many articles are easy to illustrate: I recently did several articles on a sculptor named Peter Toth.

In honor of the American Indian, Toth is giving an Indian sculpture to each of the fifty states. When he was in Kentucky, I found three different magazines interested in an article on him and his work. To do the photos for all three magazines was easy: All I had to do was to follow Toth around for about two hours while he was working on his sculpture. I took over 100 photos all at the same location. I took pictures of Toth at work, his 35-foot-tall wooden sculpture, and shots of some smaller sculptures which he sells to support himself. I didn't need to go anywhere else or come up with any creative ideas to take enough shots for all three magazines. But it's not always that easy.

3. *Be creative*. Some articles just don't lend themselves easily to illustration. But this problem can usually be solved with a little creative thinking. I'm currently writing an article for *Police Product News* on Lizzie Borden, who in 1892 was accused but never convicted of murdering her father and stepmother with an ax. What can I take pictures of for this piece?

After a few minutes of creative thinking, here's what I'm planning: several pictures of a blood-stained ax (since I work for a blood center, this won't be any problem); an ax in a woman's hand; I could go to Fall River, Massachusetts, and take pictures of the house where the murders occurred—it still stands; I could go to Oak Grove cemetery in Fall River and take pictures of the tombstones of Lizzie and her parents; I can get my wife to dress up in one of her great-grandmother's dresses and take a silhouette of her wielding an ax. The possibilities for almost any article are limited only by your imagination.

4. *Slant*. When you take pictures for your articles, try to capture the slant that you are trying to convey. I did an article for *Grit* about Captain John Ritchie, pilot of the *Mississippi Queen* riverboat. The slant of "He's Santa of the *Mississippi Queen*" was that Ritchie, who has a long white beard, looks just like Santa and is constantly so called by the passengers. There were three elements I needed to capture in every picture: (1) Ritchie, (2) looked like Santa, and (3) worked on the riverboat. I shot Ritchie and his beard in the pilot's house, standing in front of the vessel, and holding children on his knee in the ship's library. But, if I shot the Captain driving his car, playing golf or shaving off his beard, I would have strayed from the slant of my article.

5. *Put people in your pictures*. Whatever you are writing about, try, if possible, to photograph people doing something related to the subject.

When I did an article on trouble-shooting the ignition system of the Ford Escort for *Motor Magazine,* I took pictures of ignition parts, spark plug wires and distributors, and I put people in—my wife and kids driving my Escort, my friend Rusty holding parts of the ignition system.

It's important to show that people are involved in the subject of your article. It's often the human element that adds interest to a story. Be sure to get anyone who poses for you to sign a model release, which you can buy at any photography store.

6. *Take many pictures.* Don't try to save money by taking one 12-exposure roll of film. Most professional magazine photographers would be lucky to get two or three publishable shots out of twelve. Many magazines use three or four photos per article. So, shoot two or three 36-exposure rolls for every article. Even if you're not that great with a camera, the law of averages should help you produce several good shots.

7. *Use a tripod.* Whenever you hand-hold a camera, your hand shakes at least some while you are taking the picture. The best way to make sure your photos will be sharp and clear, even in enlargements, is to use a tripod whenever possible. If carefully focused, your pictures will be clear and sharp. You never know when a magazine may want to blow up one of your shots and use it for the cover.

8. *Find the right angles.* Don't just stand in front of your subject and shoot. Stoop down and shoot up at it; climb above it and shoot down at it; go around it; get a close-up; back off and get a wide-angle shot. Finding an unusual angle can make an average shot into a great one.

9. *Think vertical.* Most cameras are made to take pictures horizontally. If you turn your camera ninety degrees, you are now taking a vertical picture. Almost all magazine cover shots and many inside shots are vertical in format. Professional photographers know that editors prefer vertical shots more than horizontal ones.

10. *Direct your photos.* Good marketable magazine photos do not happen by accident, though many beginning photographers act as if that were so. As the photographer, you must control all the elements that make up a picture. Pretend you are a motion picture director, and

356

tell everybody concerned with your picture what to do. If the background is cluttered, either remove the clutter or take the picture another place. If the lighting is bad, you must bring in better lighting (open the curtains, turn on more lights, use a flash) or go where the light is better. Tell the models what to do. Don't settle for anything less than perfection with your photos.

11. *Captions.* Before you send your photos in, write a caption for each one. A caption is simply a one- or two-sentence description of the picture, who is in it, or what is going on in the picture. Don't just say, "This is a picture of Norman Dyson." Tell the editor what Norman Dyson is doing. Keep your captions specific and to the point.

12. *Study the magazine.* This probably the most important tip of all: Look carefully through several back issues of the magazine you are aiming for to get a feel for the kinds of photos they use. Also, write and ask for their photographers' guidelines. What have they bought in the past is a key to what they will buy in the future.

The writer who also does photography has several advantages over the writer who just writes: He makes more money. He improves his chances of making a sale by supplying tailor-made photos to illustrate his article, rather than making the editor search for some photos that fit the piece. He expresses himself in both words and photography. And he gets a thrill from seeing his article *and* photography grace the pages of a national magazine. For the magazine article writer, it doesn't get much better than that.

70

TRICKS OF THE NONFICTION TRADE

By Donald M. Murray

UNDER the apprentice system still practiced in most crafts, a beginner has the opportunity to work beside an experienced worker and pick up small but significant tricks of the trade. Few of us, however, observe a writer at the workbench turning a phrase, cutting a line or reordering a paragraph so that a meaning runs easy and runs clear. Here are a few of the tricks I've picked up during more than forty years of trying to make writing look easy.

Before writing

An effective piece of writing is a dialogue between the writer and the reader, with the writer answering the reader's questions just before they are asked. Each piece usually has five or six questions that must be answered if the reader is to be satisfied.

I brainstorm and polish the questions first, then put them in the order the reader will ask them. For example, if I am doing a piece on diabetes, I list such questions as:

- What is diabetes?
- How can I tell if I have it?
- What's the latest treatment?
- Do I have to give myself shots?
- Where can I get that treatment?
- How dangerous is diabetes?

Then I reconsider, refine, and reorder the questions:

1. *Lead:* What's the latest treatment for diabetes?
2. How dangerous is diabetes?
3. What is diabetes?
4. How can I tell if I have it?

5. Do I have to give myself shots? No. New treatment.
6. Where can I get it?

As I write, I may have to reorder the questions if I "hear" the reader ask the question earlier than I expected, but that doesn't happen very often. It is also helpful to write these questions down before revising a draft—especially a confusing one. Just role-play a reader and put down the questions you would ask, combining them if necessary, and then put them in order. This trick will help you understand what readers want to know and when they want to know it.

Professional writers, however, don't wait until they have a completed draft to read what they have written. They learn to pay attention to lists, collections of information, partially drafted sentences and paragraphs, abandoned pages, notes, outlines, phrases, code words that constitute the kind of writing they do on the notebook page and in their heads before the first draft.

Reading those fragments, the writer discovers a revealing or organizing specific around which an article can be built, a pattern of action or argument on which a meaning may be hung, a voice that tells the writer what he or she feels about the subject and that may be used to communicate that feeling to the reader.

Many writers write everything at the same distance from the subject. It becomes an unconscious habit. Academic writers may stand too far back from the subject, so that the reader feels detached and really doesn't become involved with the content. Magazine writers usually move in close, many times getting too close, so that readers are lost in the details of a particular person and are not able to understand the significance of the piece.

The writer should use an imaginary zoom lens before writing the first draft and decide the proper distance for this particular article, the point from which the reader will see the piece clearly, understand its context, and care about the subject. The writer may stand back and put the winning play in the context of all Army-Navy football games or move in close and tell the story of the game in terms of the winning play itself, concentrating on the fifty seconds that made the difference.

Leads and endings
The first line, the first paragraph, the first ten lines of an article establish its direction, dimensions, voice, pace. "What's so hard about

359

the first sentence is that you're stuck with it," says Joan Didion. "Everything else is going to flow out of that sentence. And by the time you've laid down the first *two* sentences, your options are all gone." It's worth taking time to get those sentences right.

The more complicated the subject the more time you may need to spend on the lead to make sure that you are giving the readers the information they need to become interested right away. You can't start too far back with background, and you can't plunge into the middle of the story so that the readers do not know what they are reading. You have to start at the right point in the right way, and the more time you spend drafting new leads, and then refining the leads you choose, the faster you will be able to write the whole piece. Most of the major problems in writing an article are solved when the right lead is found.

When I worked as writing coach at *The Boston Globe,* I found that the best writers usually knew where they would end. They had a quote, an anecdote, a scene, a specific detail with which they would close. It would sum up the piece by implication. The good writer has a sense of direction, a destination in mind. The best endings are rarely written to solve the problems of a piece that just trails off. The best endings are usually seen by the writer as waiting just ahead for the draft to take the writer and the reader there.

The right voice
Experienced writers rarely begin a first draft until they hear in their heads—or on the page—a voice that may be right. Voice is usually the key element in effective writing. It is what attracts the reader and communicates to the reader. It is that element that gives the illusion of speech. Voice carries the writer's intensity and glues together the information that the reader needs to know. It is the music in writing that makes meaning clear.

Writers keep rehearsing possible first lines, paragraphs, or endings, key scenes or statements that will reveal how what is to be said may be said best. The voice of a piece of writing is the writer's own voice, adapted in written language to the subject and audience. We speak differently at a funeral or a party, in church or in the locker room, at home or with strangers. We are experienced with using our individual voices for many purposes. We have to learn to do this same thing in

360

writing, and to hear a voice in our head that may be polished and developed on the page.

The voice is not only rehearsed but practiced. We should hear what we're writing as we write it. I dictate most of my writing and monitor my voice as I'm speaking so that the pace, the rhythm, the tone support what I'm trying to say. Keep reading aloud as you draft and edit. To train yourself to do this, it may be helpful, if you use a word processor, to turn off the screen and write, listening to what you're saying as you're saying it. Later you can read it aloud and make the changes you need to develop a voice that the reader can hear.

Put your notes away before you begin a draft. What you remember is probably what should be remembered; what you forget is probably what should be forgotten. No matter; you'll have a chance to go back to your notes after the draft is completed. What is important is to achieve a draft which allows the writing to flow.

Planning allows the writer to write fast without interruptions, putting a space or TK (to come) in the text for the quote or the statistic that has to be looked up later. There are some writers who proceed slowly, but most of us learn the advantage of producing a draft at top speed when the velocity forces unexpected connections and makes language twist and spin and dance in ways we do not expect.

When you finish your daily stint or if you are interrupted during the fast writing, stop in the middle of a sentence so you can return to the text and start writing again at a point when you know what you have to say. It's always a good idea to stop each day before the well is drained dry, when you know what you'll try to deal with the next day. This is the best way to overcome the inertia we all suffer when returning to a draft. If we know how to finish a sentence, the chances are the next sentence will rise out of that one, and we'll be writing immediately.

Planning is important, but it isn't writing. You want to be free enough in writing a draft to say more than you expect to say. Writers do not write what they already know as much as they write to know. Edward Albee echoes many writers when he says, "I write to find out what I'm thinking about." Writing is an act of thinking, and the process of writing adds two and two and comes up with seven.

An effective article usually has one dominant theme or message; everything in it should advance that meaning. Other meanings collect around the dominant one, but in the process of revision, the writer must make sure that everything in the piece relates to the main idea, cutting what does not move the reader forward.

The inexperienced writer cuts a piece of writing by compression and produces a package of tight language that can be difficult to understand and is rarely a pleasure to read. The professional writer selects those parts that most efficiently and effectively advance the meaning and then develops them fully so that the reader understands the significance of the anecdote, the full strength of the argument.

Writing in which the meaning is not clear often occurs because writers bury the most important information. One way to make an article clear is to look at the most significant paragraphs and move the sections around so that the most important information is at the end of the paragraph, the next most important at the beginning, and the least most important in the center of the paragraph.

We need important information at the beginning to attract the reader, but what the reader remembers is usually at the end of the paragraph. This pattern doesn't work for every paragraph, and shouldn't. But it is a way of clarifying a complicated and significant paragraph, and the same rule may be applied to an entire piece of writing.

I find that I am a more efficient editor of my own draft if I read it three times and have a specific goal for each reading. *First,* I read it to see if I have all the information I need. Do I have the facts, statistics, quotations, anecdotes I need to construct an accurate, persuasive article? And do I understand that information? If I don't have the information or understand it I must stop my editing and deal with these problems.

Second, I read for organization. Does the article, as I have mentioned earlier, answer the readers' questions in the order they will ask them? Does the article flow naturally from beginning to end, with each part of the article fitting what has gone before and leading to what follows?

Third, I read the article line by line, listening both to what is said and how it is said, making sure, by reading it aloud, that my voice carries the meaning to the reader. I hope that my articles will be accurate and have the illusion of speech, the rhythm, music, and ease of an ideal conversation.

Those are a few of the tricks of the nonfiction trade. Try them out to see if they work for you. Collect others from your writer friends, and become aware of those devices that you have used to make your meaning clear, so that you will be able to call on them as you continue your lifelong course in learning how to write.

71

MAKING A NAME IN POETRY

By X. J. Kennedy

As poets know only too well, trying to sell poetry to paying magazines and book publishers is a rough task, often impossible. Even giving away poems may be difficult: Some little magazines that pay in free copies can be choosey. And as John Ciardi once observed, it is hard for poets to prostitute their talents. There just aren't that many buyers around.

It would be hypocritical for me to claim that for a poet to see print shouldn't matter. Of course it matters. If you write poems, having them accepted helps convince you that you are right to believe in yourself. Disappointments notwithstanding, just being published once in a while encourages a poet to stick to what William Butler Yeats glumly called "this sedentary trade."

That poems are hard to peddle isn't terribly depressing—to poets who live for the pleasure of making poems. "Well, so Editor X has bounced my sublime ode," they'll tell themselves. "The benighted creep." But to writers who aren't yet widely published and who fiercely crave to be, writers who live not necessarily to write good poems but to see their names in print, this difficulty leads to chagrin.

Writing poetry is radically different from writing articles, stories, or fillers. Most moneymaking writers—that is, writers who aren't poets— scout for a likely market. Then, they often shrewdly adapt their product to suit that market's needs. Their lives make sense: They can supply a demand. Poets, however, if they are serious about writing good poems, have to think differently.

Poetry is probably the one field of writing in which it is a mistake to try to psych out editors. In fact, specific marketing advice can sometimes harm the novice poet by enticing him to pursue fashions. The poet's best hope is to sound like *nobody* else: The finest, most enduring poetry constructs a new marketplace of it own.

Excellent poems are like better mousetraps: Build one, said Emer-

364

son, and the world will beat a path to your door. It always amazes me how quickly a good, original book of poetry becomes known: W. D. Snodgrass's *Heart's Needle,* for instance, a book acclaimed soon after publication and laden with a Pulitzer, despite the fact that its author had published relatively little before.

Evidently, it is much simpler to chase after fashions than to transform yourself into a fine poet, the likes of whom the world hasn't seen before. It is easy to advise anyone whose poetic ambition goes no further than to achieve publication. To such a person, I'd suggest the following strategies:

1. Center your poem on your experience, your family, your everyday concerns—however drab. If you write a poem about your cousin's case of AIDS, you will surely find an editor who will accept it, no matter how bad it may be, for he fears that if he doesn't, you will think him a coarse, unfeeling swine who won't sympathize with your cousin. I'm serious!

2. Write in the first person, in the present tense. Not long ago, Peter Davison, poetry editor for *The Atlantic,* remarked that most of the poems he currently receives are like that. Some other, less discriminating editors mistakenly believe that the present tense lends everything a kind of immediacy.

3. Brainstorm, force your unconscious to yoke together disparate things. In the midst of a dull poem on your grandfather's old antimacassar, throw in a mention of something completely far-out and unexpected, such as a fur-lined frying pan.

4. Include a dash of violent realism, preferably straight out of current news. If you can relate your workaday world to, say, war-torn Nicaragua, you've got it made.

5. Give your poem a snappy title to catch an editor's eye. With a little more brainstorming, you can readily invent titles of poems for which many editors, the dolts, will be pushovers: "Contracting Chicken-pox in a First Kiss," "A Lesbian Mother Tells Her Daughter the Facts of Life." Titles like that either promise something interesting, or else reek of Significance with a capital S.

6. Don't, whatever you do, write in traditional forms. To do so will only slow your rate of production. Even worse, you might reveal your

365

lack of skill. Traditional forms, such as sonnets and blank verse, which held sway over English-speaking poetry for five centuries (up until about 1960), can still nourish wonderful poems—as witness recent work by Seamus Heaney, Derek Walcott, Gjertrud Schnackenberg, and Timothy Steele. But remember, I'm not talking about quality. If you write in traditional forms, you had better be good. In rhymed metrical stanzas, mediocre poetry tends to look shoddy in an obvious way, while bad poetry looks really horrible. On the other hand, bad poems in open forms (or "free verse") tend to seem passable. And—I hate to say this, but it's true—mediocre poems in open forms look like most poems appearing nowadays in respectable places.

7. Study an annual that lists poetry markets such as the *International Directory of Little Magazines and Small Presses* (found in the reference section of many libraries). Then zero in on the less competitive markets, like *Superintendent's Profile & Pocket Equipment Directory,* a monthly for highway superintendents and directors of departments of public works. Although it uses only poems about snowplowing and road repairing, the magazine prints two out of every three poems it receives.

If indeed all you care about is becoming a widely published poet, those hints may be as good as any. What I hope, of course, is that you will ignore all those suggestions.

For a poet who cares about the art of poetry, merely to be published isn't enough. The first time you see your name in print, it may seem to scintillate on the page like a Fourth of July sparkler. Karl Shapiro once recalled the joy of seeing rows of his own book on a shelf, "saying my golden name from end to end." But after you see it a few times, your own name may not prove especially interesting. At the moment, the problem for a poet in this country isn't to get published. A couple of thousand markets now publish poetry, some of whose editors have no taste. And anyone who can't get published can, for $200, start his own little magazine and generously heap his own work with acceptances. Unfortunately, the problem, in this time of dwindling attention spans, is to find attentive readers.

Poets whose work is widely published may still be widely ignored. The poetry star system that produced household names like Robert Frost, Dylan Thomas, and E.E. Cummings passed away twenty years ago, so there is no longer much point in a poet's trying for celebrity. The celebrity that a poet may attain isn't the tenth part of one percent of the celebrity that a rock songwriter can attain from a single video. If you are going into the poetry writing business, you might as well forget about fame and fortune and seek other rewards.

Some writers think that bringing out that first collection of poems will be an experience far superior to beholding the beatific vision. This view is distorted. Publishing a book can be a lot of fun, but it may not transform your life. Having published a volume of poetry, you, unlike Michael Jackson or Madonna, can walk the streets and not be over-whelmed by autograph-seekers. Moreover, you can publish a book of poems and continue to suffer from any ailment or lacks that afflicted you.

Poetic fame, like sea water, isn't worth thirsting for. Poets, if they are any good, compete for space in books not only with their peers but with the giants of the ages. They race not only with John Ashbery and Tess Gallagher, to name two deservedly admired contemporaries, but with John Milton and Emily Dickinson. Let them not imitate the plumage of any currently acclaimed poet. Let them discover their own natures, however disappointing the discovery, and stay faithful to whoever they may be.

At the risk of appearing to hold myself up as a sterling example, I shall recall that as a whitehat in the Navy back in the early fifties, just beginning to fool around writing poems, I made plenty of mistakes. (One mistake was trying to write like Dylan Thomas, an attempt that rendered my work thick, fruitcake-like, and impenetrable.) One mistake I didn't make was to crave premature publication. I resigned myself to just writing, piling up poems, not showing them to anybody. Pigheadedly, I believed that one day an editor would print my work, or some of it. At least that attitude kept up my morale: I didn't have to cope with the rejection slips I would certainly have received. And when I finally started licking stamps and getting poems rejected, I was a little (but not a whole lot) more competent.

For a poet, there can be no greater luxury than to work as a complete unknown. When you are an undiscovered gem, there isn't the least bit of pressure on you to publish, to become better and better and stun your critics, to win prizes, and all that debilitating responsibility. All you need care about is writing good poems. Too many college sophomores

367

and also a few grandparents who have never read any poetry other than Hallmark greeting card verse assume that if their first stumbling efforts don't get published, they have failed miserably. But that Sylvia Plath won a noteworthy prize when she was a college student, that Amy Clampitt published her first book in middle age and won immediate accolades, doesn't mean that they should feel any grim duty to succeed. America is full of excellent poets who have had their poems published for years, despite the fact that they receive little notice. Luckily for our poetry, they persist.

Nowadays, lust for hasty fame takes root early. The other day I was talking with a bunch of fourth-graders in a public library in Quincy, Massachusetts, and a lad of ten asked me again and again—insistently rephrasing the question—how you get poems published. I wanted to tell him, Kid, forget it. I'll bet your stuff at the moment, while it may show flickers of something good, is not much good yet; you will be smart to shelve your ambition for another ten or fifteen years. But, too craven to hit him with the hard truth, I pointed out how rare it is to publish poems in nationwide places when you are ten. Myra Cohn Livingston in her wonderful book *The Child as Poet* tells some horror stories about fledgling poets whose parents goaded them into print at an early age.

All right, call me a sourpuss. I'm trying to dash a little cold water on the notion, so dear to many unpublished writers, that publication is the be-all and end-all of existence. This attitude makes such people push-overs for racketeers: for contests that charge forty-dollar entrance fees, accept everything, then try to sell the contestants a bound volume containing their supposedly winning work for $38.95, or $62.95 for the gold-edged edition. It makes them suckers for vanity publishers who, appealing to their pride and frustration, urge them to subsidize an edition of their own poems, which will sell to nobody, or to practically nobody, unless they themselves sell the copies, and which no reviewer in a national magazine would touch with a thirty-foot flagpole.

Letting oneself be the victim of such con games is all right if seeing your name in print is your one aim. And with any luck, sheer, tireless stamp-licking will result in *some* kind of publication. But sometimes, if viewed as fortresses to be stormed and overpowered, poetry magazines tend to resist. I can recall when, as poetry editor for the *Paris Review,* I kept getting a tide of manuscripts from a poet who had published little but whose name must have been known to every poetry editor. His manuscripts came in *daily* showing the wrinkles of many previous rejections. Always folded and refolded sixteen times, sometimes looking as if they'd been given a fresh press with a steam iron, always in envelopes saying Biltmore and Statler and Hilton (pilfered, it seemed, from writing desks in hotel lobbies). If only the contributor had devoted as much time to learning to write as he spent stuffing envelopes!

Why is it that hundreds of thousands of people want to be poets? I don't know, but I have a hunch. In this anonymous society in which we feel like zip codes or social security numbers, writing a poem and publishing it is one way to stand up on your hind legs and sass the universe. A printed poem proclaims, "I exist." There is something powerfully appealing in the thought that you can seize paper and pencil in an odd moment and scrawl a few lines that might make you immortal in anthologies. Immortality is all very well, but it is more interesting to think about the problems of writing good poetry. You don't need to publish a thousand poems in order to become immortal; you need publish only one poem, if it is good enough.

Literary history is full of cases of great poets who garnered no fame or praise or significant publication in their lifetimes. Gerard Manley Hopkins, whose strange masterpiece "The Wreck of the Deutschland" was rejected by a small Jesuit magazine, showed his poems to only a tiny handful of correspondents. Emily Dickinson, after local newspaper editors rewrote the few items she submitted to them, evidently said the hell with them and stitched her poems into little packets that she stashed away in her attic, as is well known. Hopkins and Dickinson, to be sure, were superb poets whose work refused to die. But my point is that they placed quality first and bravely turned their backs upon celebrity.

Sometimes, when I look at the current spate of forgettable poems, I think it would be a great idea if literary magazines were to declare a moratorium on by-lines for a few years. Just suppose every poem were printed anonymously. By and by, of course, the real original poets would be recognized by the character of their work, as surely as "The Pearl" poet of the Middle Ages. But the great mass of poems, undistinguished and forgettable, would slip into oblivion. And there would be fewer of them, since people who now publish poems in order to boost their egos would have no reason to.

I think it is a good idea for young poets to start having their poems published in the very smallest magazines, those read by few people. If in later years they should decide that their maiden works were poor, they can comfort themselves with the knowledge that practically nobody will have read them. Most poets I have known have come to regard their first works as pretty embarrassing. John Ciardi, who won a prize in a student writing contest at the University of Michigan, once told me he longed to burgle his found manuscript from the library and burn it.

Those poets willing to try the most onerous route of all—growing in depth and in skill—might cultivate an aloof coolness toward publication. No formula, no market tip, no advice from me or anybody else will help you write a great poem. But you can take action. You can try reading. Most poets do too little of that. Talk to any editor of a poetry magazine, and you will learn that the would-be contributors usually outnumber paying subscribers by at least five to one. Many poets want to heap their outpourings upon the world, expecting the world to take them gladly. Too impatient to read other poets, they never find out how poetry is written, and they keep repeating things that have already been done well, and so do not need redoing.

If you haven't been published and deserve to be, you might make a personal anthology of poems you admire—the dozen or twenty poems you'd swear by. This task will concentrate your attention, make you aware of your own standards, and reveal your nature to you. I made such a anthology once and learned to my surprise that the poems I most cherish in all of literature are religious ones. You might also try writing a lot—and throwing most of it away. Delmore Schwartz said that a poet is wise to write as much, and to publish as little, as possible.

Keats put it beautifully in a letter to a friend: "I should write for the mere yearning and fondness I have for the beautiful, even if my night's labors should be burnt every morning and no eye shine upon them." That is, I think, a noble attitude. Rejections—or critical attacks—could not thwart a Keats; they simply had no great power over him. For a poet, the only sure reward is the joy of making a poem. Any reward besides—fame, prizes, publication—is like money found in the street. If you see a silver dollar gleaming on the sidewalk, you pick it up. But you need not roam the streets desperately looking for that gleam.

370

72

POETIC DEVICES

By William Packard

THERE is a good story about Walter Johnson, who had one of the most natural fast balls in the history of baseball. No one knows how "The Big Train" developed such speed on the mound, but there it was. From his first year of pitching in the majors, 1907, for Washington, Walter Johnson hurtled the ball like a flash of lightning across the plate. And as often as not, the opposing batter would be left watching empty air, as the catcher gloved the ball.

Well, the story goes that after a few seasons, almost all the opposing batters knew exactly what to expect from Walter Johnson—his famous fast ball. And even though the pitch was just as difficult to hit as ever, still, it can be a very dangerous thing for any pitcher to become that predictable. And besides, there were also some fears on the Washington bench that if he kept on hurtling only that famous fast ball over the plate, in a few more seasons Walter Johnson might burn his arm out entirely.

So, Walter Johnson set out to learn how to throw a curve ball. Now, one can just imagine the difficulty of doing this: here is a great pitcher in his mid-career in the major leagues, and he is trying to learn an entirely new pitch. One can imagine all the painful self-consciousness of the beginner, as Johnson tried to train his arm into some totally new reflexes—a new way of fingering the ball, a new arc of the elbow as he went into the wind-up, a new release of the wrist, and a completely new follow-through for the body.

But after awhile, the story goes, the curve ball became as natural for Walter Johnson as the famous fast-ball pitch, and as a consequence, Johnson became even more difficult to hit.

When Walter Johnson retired in 1927, he held the record for total strike-outs in a lifetime career (3409), and he held the record for total pitching of shut-out games in a lifetime career (110)—records which have never been equaled in baseball. And Walter Johnson is second only to the mighty Cy Young for total games won in a lifetime career.

Any artist can identify with this story about Walter Johnson. The determination to persist in one's art or craft is a characteristic of a great artist and a great athlete. But one also realizes that this practice of one's craft is almost always painstakingly difficult, and usually entails periods of extreme self-consciousness, as one trains oneself into a pattern of totally new reflexes. It is what Robert Frost called "the pleasure of taking pains."

The odd thing is that this practice and mastery of a craft is sometimes seen as an infringement on one's own natural gifts. Poets will sometimes comment that they do not want to be bothered with all that stuff about metrics and assonance and craft, because it doesn't come "naturally." Of course it doesn't come naturally, if one hasn't worked to make it natural. But once one's craft becomes second nature, it is not an infringement on one's natural gifts—if anything, it is an enlargement of them, and an enhancement and a reinforcement of one's own intuitive talents.

In almost all the other arts, an artist has to learn the techniques of his craft as a matter of course.

The painter takes delight in exploring the possibilities of his palette, and perhaps he may even move through periods which are dominated by different color tones, such as viridian or Prussian blue or ochre. He will also be concerned, as a matter of course, with various textural considerations such as brushing and pigmentation and the surface virtue of his work.

The composer who wants to write orchestra music has to begin by learning how to score in the musical notation system—and he will play with the meaning of whole notes, half notes, quarter notes, eighth notes, and the significance of such tempo designations as *lento, andante, adagio,* and *prestissimo.* He will also want to explore the different possibilities of the instruments of the orchestra, to discover the totality of tone he wants to achieve in his own work.

Even so—I have heard student poets complain that they don't want to be held back by a lot of technical considerations in the craft of poetry.

That raises a very interesting question: Why do poets seem to resist learning the practice and mastery of their own craft? Why do they protest that technique *per se* is an infringement on their own intuitive gifts, and a destructive self-consciousness that inhibits their natural and magical genius?

I think a part of the answer to these questions may lie in our own modern Romantic era of poetry, where poets as diverse as Walt Whitman and Dylan Thomas and Allen Ginsberg seem to achieve their best effects with little or no technical effort. Like Athena, the poem seems to spring full blown out of the forehead of Zeus, and that is a large part of its charm for us. Whitman pretends he is just "talking" to us, in the "Song of Myself." So does Dylan Thomas in "Fern Hill" and "Poem in October." So does Allen Ginsberg in "Howl" and "Kaddish."

But of course when we think about it, we realize it is no such thing. And we realize also, in admiration, that any poet who is so skillful in concealing his art from us may be achieving one of the highest technical feats of all.

What are the technical skills of poetry, that all poets have worked at who wanted to achieve the practice and mastery of their craft?

We could begin by saying that poetry itself is language which is used in a specific way to convey a specific effect. And the specific ways that language can be used are expressed through all of the various poetic devices. In "The ABC of Reading," Ezra Pound summarized these devices and divided them into three categories—phonopoeia (sight), melopoeia (sound), and logopoeia (voice).

SIGHT

The image is the heart and soul of poetry. In our own psychic lives, we dream in images, although there may be words superimposed onto these images. In our social communication, we indicate complete understanding of something when we say, "I get the picture"—indicating that imagistic understanding is the most basic and primal of all communications. In some languages, like Chinese and Japanese, words began as pictures, or ideograms, which embodied the image representation of what the word was indicating.

It is not accidental that our earliest record of human civilization is in the form of pure pictures—images of bison in the paleolithic caves at Altamira in Northern Spain, from the Magdalenian culture, some 16,000 years B.C. And there are other records of stone statues as pure

373

images of horses and deer and mammoths, in Czechoslovakia, from as far back as 30,000 years B.C.

Aristotle wrote in the "Poetics" that metaphor—the conjunction of one image with another image—is the soul of poetry, and is the surest sign of genius. He also said it was the one thing that could not be taught, since the genius for metaphor was unaccountable, being the ability to see similarities in dissimilar things.

Following are the principal poetic devices which use image, or the picture aspect of poetry:

image—a simple picture, a mental representation. "That which presents an intellectual and emotional complex in an instant of time." (Pound)

metaphor—a direct comparison. "A mighty fortress is our God." An equation, or an equivalence: A = B. "It is the east and Juliet is the sun."

simile—an indirect comparison, using "like" or "as." "Why, man, he doth bestride the narrow world/Like a Colossus..." "My love's like a red, red rose."

figure—an image and an idea. "Ship of state." "A sea of troubles." "This bud of love."

conceit—an extended figure, as in some metaphysical poetry of John Donne, or in the following lines of Shakespeare's Juliet:

> Sweet, good-night!
> This bud of love, by summer's ripening breath,
> May prove a beauteous flower when next we meet...

SOUND

Rhythm has its source and origin in our own bloodstream pulse. At a normal pace, the heart beats at a casual iambic beat. But when it is excited, it may trip and skip rhythm through extended anapests or hard dactyls or firm trochees. It may even pound with a relentless spondee beat.

In dance, rhythm is accented by a drumbeat, in parades, by the cadence of marching feet, and in the night air, by churchbell tolling.

These simple rhythms may be taken as figures of the other rhythms of the universe—the tidal ebb and flow, the rising and setting of the sun, the female menstrual cycles, the four seasons of the year.

Rhythm is notated as metrics, but may also be seen in such poetic devices as rhyme and assonance and alliteration. Following are the poetic devices for sound:

assonance—rhyme of vowel sounds. "O that this too too solid flesh would melt..."

alliteration—repetition of consonants. "We might have met them dareful, beard to beard, And beat them backward home."

rhyme—the sense of resonance that comes when a word echoes the sound of another word—in end rhyme, internal rhyme, perfect rhyme, slant or imperfect rhyme, masculine rhyme, or feminine rhyme.

metrics—the simplest notation system for scansion of rhythm. The most commonly used metrics in English are:

iamb $(\smile{'})$
trochee $({'}\smile)$
anapest $(\smile\smile{'})$
dactyl $({'}\smile\smile)$
spondee $({'}{'})$

VOICE

Voice is the sum total of cognitive content of the words in a poem. Voice can also be seen as the signature of the poet on his poem—his own unmistakable way of saying something. "Only Yeats could have said it that way," one feels, in reading a line like:

That is no country for old men...

Similarly, Frost was able to endow his poems with a "voice" in lines like:

Something there is that doesn't love a wall...

Following are the poetic devices for voice:

denotation—literal, dictionary meaning of a word.

connotation—indirect or associative meaning of a word. "Mother" means one thing denotatively, but may have a host of other connotative associations.

personification—humanizing an object.

diction—word choice, the peculiar combination of words used in any given poem.

syntax—the peculiar arrangement of words in their sentence structures.

rhetoric—"Any adornment or inflation of speech which is not done for a particular effect but for a general impressiveness..." (Eliot)

persona—a mask, an assumed voice, a speaker pretending to be someone other than who he really is.

375

So far these are only words on a page, like diagrams in a baseball book showing you how to throw a curve ball. The only way there can be any real learning of any of these devices is to do endless exercises in notebooks, trying to master the craft of assonance, of diction shifts, of persona effects, of successful conceits, of metrical variations.

Any practice of these craft devices may lead one into a period of extreme self-consciousness, as one explores totally new reflexes of language. But one can trust that with enough practice they can become "second nature," and an enhancement and reinforcement of one's own intuitive talents as a poet.

73

FORM AND EXPERIMENTATION
IN POETRY

By Liz Rosenberg

THE WAR between poetic form and poetic license has been raging for a long time and continues to this day. In 1668 the poet John Milton threw down one gauntlet, in his blank verse poem *Paradise Lost:* "This neglect of Rhyme so little is to be taken for a defect, though it may seem so perhaps to vulgar Readers, that it rather is to be esteem'd an example set, the first in English, of ancient liberty recover'd to Heroic Poem from the troublesome and modern bondage of Rhyming."

Three hundred years later Robert Frost dropped the other glove in his now-famous scorn of unrhymed verse: "I'd as soon play tennis with the net down."

Rhyme has been the chief net over which the opposing sides slug it out, maybe because it is the most instantly noticeable musical aspect of English poetry and poetic form, though by no means the only formal element available to the poet. Anglo-Saxon poetry, which was highly regimented, depended upon a certain number of stressed beats per line, and alliteration. Chinese poetry uses pitch. Other formal elements have held precedence at various times—the controlled musicality of Sapphic verse, syllabics, cinquains, haikus, William Carlos Williams's "variable foot," and so on. Between structure and freedom the pendulum swings widely and regularly, one way, then another. We tend to think of our own time as the absolute reign of free verse: unrhymed, unmetered, personal, brief, as jumpy as a gesture by James Dean—yet there are already signs of a swing leading the other way, in poems one feels an urge to call "verse"—the formal, rhymed, structured and ornamented work of poets like Amy Clampitt, Philip Booth, Gertrude Schnackenberg, and others.

As we draw closer to the end of the twentieth century, I suspect that the tendency both to poetic structure and poetic freedom will grow more exaggerated. Ends of centuries produce extremes, as witness

Alfred, Lord Tennyson on the one hand and Walt Whitman on the other, at the end of the nineteenth century. That these two poets had a great interest in and admiration for one another's work should come as no surprise. It's at both ends of the spectrum—extreme formal control, extreme poetic freedom—that the poet is pushing at boundaries, struggling to discover the necessities of the craft. It is exactly this pitched battle, *in extremis,* that produces great art, this pushing against limits, exploration of what is possible. The poet must write only according to internal necessity. The danger lies with those caught in the middle, like Dante's souls forever caught in the ante-chambers of hell, following first one flag and then another. This is the only mistake one can make in regard to poetic form: to allow the form to choose you. And it is as easy, as we have all lately discovered, to be the stooge of free verse as of formal verse. The worst one can do is to write in a particular form out of habit, intimidation, or laziness. There is an equal slackness in the doggerel rhyme of greeting cards or the nebulous free-form of Rod McKuen and his imitators. What one feels lacking in both is the tension of discovery, of necessity. And these are achieved only by a continual questioning of the status quo, by relentless experimentation and invention.

By "experimentation" I don't necessarily mean those finger exercises that are the stock in trade of many creative writing workshops. I'm not sure it's a good idea to get in the habit of just fooling around with poetry this way. It encourages a small kind of achievement; it puts a great emphasis on competence and cleverness, whereas great poetry is more like an explosion, built up under great pressure over a long period. One might practice with some of the tools of poetry—to sharpen musical and linguistic skills—but the poem, the thing itself, is not much good diluted.

Poets who practice with exercises must have a deep, nearly inexhaustible well of vital material. In this case, it will be impossible for anything the poet writes not to turn to poetry. But there is a frigidity in most poetic exercise, a sense of withholding that is deadly to real art. Poets shouldn't write villanelles or sonnets the way we are told we "should" write bread-and-butter letters or thank-you notes to Aunt Claire. This again is an encouragement to fall into the trap of thinking about form as somehow prescribed and habitual, as something one "really ought to do," rather than something one must do, having exhausted all other possibilities. It is only when this internal combustion

378

forces one into new forms that something strange and lovely takes place.

"New" forms proceed from an intuition of potentialities, of something lurking around the corner, a sense that what *is* is not enough. "Mine deeper, that's the ticket!" wrote Melville, and his remains the one true battle cry of all art. Experimentation is as natural to poetry as breathing is to life. If one were content with the old forms, with things-as-they-are, and with things-as-they-have-been-said, one could not write poetry at all.

Invention is the almost incidental by-product of this constant chafing against what is, an emergence into discovery. Invention need not be new to the world; it need only be genuinely new and fresh to the writer, who discovers his or her form alone, in solitude, after many failures and much self-doubt. It is absurd to imagine that Robert Frost did not grope his way toward the lyrical, rhyming, colloquially American language that evolved as his own. All of the so-called traditional or classical poets were wildly inventive and outrageous in their day. Milton, with his thundering blank verse, is only one example. Dante dropped from the "acceptable" elevated language of great poetry—Latin—to the mundane Italian spoken by street vendors, fishwives, soldiers, and farmers, and he did it against the advice and imprecations of his friends. Shakespeare careens from blank verse to formal sonnets to prose, all within a single play, and anyone who believes that his verse was written in strict iambic pentameter has a tin ear: "Howl, howl, howl, howl!" or "Bare ruined choirs, where late the sweet birds sang."

Invention is playful, but it is not merely play. My one objection to Frost's famous remark on free verse is that poetry seems to me an infinitely more important and complex "game" than tennis. Invention is the one true genius child of necessity, and it comes with the kind of passion and power that we may imagine first breathed life into the planets and spun them, the impulse that is always behind birth and creation. It is not strange, but familiar and fundamental to the very fact of our existence. Perhaps this is why great "new" poetry feels at the same time shocking and yet inevitable. There is nothing alien or rarefied about poetry, in whatever form. It is indeed at its best when it is closest to the mundane mysteries, when it is fresh with its own discoveries, with invention, and therefore brings us close to the common, creative wellspring of all being.

74

LIGHT VERSE

By Robert Wallace

A FEW YEARS ago, John Updike, heir to generations of great light verse poets (Dorothy Parker, Franklin P. Adams, Phyllis McGinley, E. B. White, Ogden Nash, Morris Bishop, Richard Armour among them) called light verse "a dying art." He added, "I write no light verse now." (It is hard to remember that Updike's first book was light verse.)

That glum conclusion was no great surprise to those who had watched the shrinking of markets to a mere handful—*The New Yorker* stopped printing light verse in the 1960's—and the dwindling of marketable forms to the clever, topical quatrains:

TAX HANG-UP
For those inclined to play
It fast and loose
Sometimes a tax loophole
Ends up a noose.

Light verse has been in the shadows for twenty years or more. It would be easy to see as its tombstone the fat anthology *The Best of Modern Humor* (Mordecai Richler, ed., Knopf, 1983), which is *entirely prose*. 542 big pages, going back to 1922, and not a shred, not even a single line of Dorothy Parker or Ogden Nash!

But, in Mark Twain's phrase, the report of its death would be "greatly exaggerated."

As long as there is laughter and as long as there is verse, someone will always be bringing the two together. Both fill deep needs. A comic tradition that includes Chaucer, Shakespeare, Pope, and Byron isn't about to vanish. What *has* happened, however, needs understanding before we can see the way ahead clearly.

We are victims, I think, of a distinction made in 1867 by an English light verse poet, Frederick Locker-Lampson. He distinguished between "poetry"—that high, serious art—and what he called, coining the phrase, "light verse." He saw it as "another kind of poetry . . . which, in its more restricted form, has somewhat the same relation to the poetry of lofty imagination and deep feeling, that the Dresden China Shepherds and Shepherdesses of the last century bear to the sculpture of Donatello and Michael Angelo."

Though Locker-Lampson meant the term light verse as praise, this Victorian distinction has turned into a villainous Mr. Hyde, dividing poetry (seriousness) from mere light verse (humor). Joined to the Frankenstein of the twentieth-century's obsession with criticism (which essentially holds that no ordinary reader can really read a poem, novel, or play on his or her own), this distinction has been devastating. Laughter has been read out of the emotions proper for literature. Poetry, struggling under the weight of what can only be called *heavy* verse, has lost touch with the general reader. And light verse, isolated, trivialized, has fallen into the shadows. Ogden Nash doesn't even appear in the 1456 pages of that other could-be tombstone, *The Norton Anthology of Modern Poetry!*

Among the hopeful signs are three anthologies: *The Oxford Book of English Light Verse* (Kingsley Amis, ed., 1978), *The Oxford Book of American Light Verse* (William Harmon, ed., 1979), *The Penguin Book of Light Verse* (Gavin Ewart, ed., 1980). The magazine *Open Places* recently devoted a whole issue—222 pages—to humor, half of it verse. And there is *Light Year,* the annual of light verse and funny poems, which I edit. In its first three issues (totaling 626 pages) are poems by 306 poets, among them beginners as well as many of the finest writers in America: Richard Wilbur, Marge Piercy, X. J. Kennedy, Donald Hall, John Ciardi, May Swenson, Roy Blount Jr., Richard Armour—and John Updike!

And there is this most interesting straw-in-the-wind: as I write, Shel Silverstein's *A Light in the Attic* was on *The New York Times Book Review*'s hardcover best seller list for more than two-and-a-half years. That's a record. If only 10% of the "graduates" of *A Light in the Attic* can be persuaded to go on to other funny poems, there will be a very large, lively, paying audience once again. Perhaps there's gold in them thar hills.

Light verse—maybe we'd better call them *funny poems*?—is coming out of the shadows, and may well be in for a revival.

If I'm even partly right, what can a writer of funny poetry expect? What should he or she do differently, if anything? What will the funny poems of the immediate future be like? Here's some practical advice from the poet-and-editor's crystal ball:

Funny poetry will show a great variety in both subject and form, and will be more sophisticated, more honest, and—often at least—more serious. It will, in short, be more like what it really is: poetry.

1) Freed of the trivializing restrictions, it will find a range of subjects much broader than baldness, going on a diet, jogging, postal rate increases, and such foibles. It will be more topical, less moralizing, and often sillier and just plain merrier. There will be room again for things like Don Marquis's wonderful *archy & mehitabel*. It will, having the space, be peopled with more real and interesting characters. Look for poems like Katharyn Machan Aal's

HAZEL TELLS LAVERNE

last night
im cleanin out my
howard johnsons ladies room
when all of a sudden
up pops this frog
musta come from the sewer
swimmin aroun an tryin ta
climb up the sida the bowl
so i goes ta flushm down
but sohelpmegod he starts talkin
bout a golden ball
an how i can be a princess
me a princess
well my mouth drops
all the way to the floor
an he says
kiss me just kiss me
once on the nose
well i screams
ya little green pervert
an i hitsm with my mop
an has ta flush
the toilet down three times
me
a princess

2) Though epigrammatic quatrains will thrive—like Robert N. Feinstein's

THE OWL

Though I don't wish to seem too fanatical,
I consider the owl ungrammatical.
"To-whit, to-who" he sits and keens;
"To-whit, to-*whom*" is what he means.

—funny poems will often be longer, and both more varied and more daring in form. Look for more free verse, and for poems in complex forms like villanelle and sestina again. Whatever's happening in poetry will be happening in funny poetry. Visual poems, concrete poems, even funny "prose" poems like George Starbuck's

JAPANESE FISH

Have you ever eaten a luchu? It's poisonous like fugu, but it's cheaper and you cook it yourself.

You cut it into little squares as fast as possible but without touching the poison-gland. But first, you get all the thrill you can out of the fact that you're going to do it. You sit around for hours with your closest friends, drinking and telling long nostalgicky stories. You make toasts. You pick up your knives and sing a little song entitled "We who are about to dice a luchu." And then you begin.

3) It will be more sophisticated—often as corny, but probably cleverer. No doubt, sometimes, sexier. It will be less inclined to "nudge" the reader to be sure he gets the point. Titles will be less "cute," more functional, as in Michael Spence's

PROGRAMMING DOWN ON THE FARM

As all those with computers know,
Input-output is called I/O.
But farmers using these machines
See special letters on their screens.
So when they list a chicken fence
To "Egg Insurance and Expense,"
Into what file would it go?
Of course to EIE I/O.

4) It will be more honest and exact, more realistic. Puffy comic exaggeration—"[something or other] makes me tear my hair"—will vanish, as will banal (and untrue) generalities like "A man will stand for anything / Without a fight or fuss, / Except a lady or a lass / Upon a

383

crowded bus." Understatement will turn out to work better, as in Edward Willey's

FAMILY ECCENTRIC

Marie is bald and doesn't
give a damn. To prove it
she often spits in public
and hates to wear a hat.

I hope she changes
for the better before
she learns to talk.

5) It will often be closer to serious poetry, able to mingle the amusing with the lyrical, as in my

MYTH, COMMERCE, AND COFFEE
ON UNITED FLIGHT #622 FROM
CLEVELAND TO NORFOLK

Clouds, like bird-tracked snow,
spread to dawn-sun five miles below,

while businessmen (& poets) flow
on air streams, to and fro.

Now, of course, we know
Icarus *could* have made a go,

formed Attic Airways Co.,
expanded, advertised, and so

have carried Homer and Sappho
from Athens to Ilo

on reading tours—with, below,
clouds spread out like bird-tracked snow.

Or to mingle the amusing with the genuinely thoughtful—which is to say that it will have simply become poetry again!—as in Howard Nemerov's

POETICS

You know the old story Ann Landers tells
About the housewife in her basement doing the wash?
She's wearing her nightie, and she thinks, "Well hell,
I might's well put this in as well," and then
Being dripped on by a leaky pipe puts on
Her son's football helmet; whereupon
The meter reader happens to walk through

384

And "Lady," he gravely says, "I sure hope your team wins."

A story many times told in many ways,
The set of random accidents redeemed
By one more accident, as though chaos
Were the order that was before creation came.
That is the way things happen in the world:
A joke, a disappointment satisfied,
As we walk through doing our daily round,
Reading the meter, making things add up.

6) And one other, by no means the least consideration: funny poets may expect far more, and better paying, markets than they're used to. That's happening now.

75

PASSION AND THE MODERN POET

By Dick Allen

I KEEP coming back to passion. It is something all of us have felt, of course, but the severe and sustained passion of the poet is unique. The poet has a passionate need to create lines that seem to stand still but actually tremble and hover a lifetime in the mind: hummingbird lines.

"Batter my heart, three person'd God . . ." (John Donne). . . . "The seal's wide spindrift gaze toward paradise" (Hart Crane). . . . "Downward to darkness, on extended wings" (Wallace Stevens). . . . "You do not do, you do not do" (Sylvia Plath)—these and hundreds of other lines are in my mind daily. It is against them and the poems which sustain them that I measure my own work and the work of my contemporaries.

I do not mean to say that writing poetry is solely a matter of creating memorable lines, "touchstones" as Matthew Arnold called them. Rather, I am saying that the intensity of feeling they contain, their balance and art, is something toward which poets daily strive. The journey of the poet to a place and time when he may have a chance to write great poetry derives in large part from a passion of remembering. That is why the first test of a poet lies in the extent of his love for poetry itself. Virtually every publishing poet I know is a compulsive reader of past and present poetry. There is no quicker way to sort out hobbyist poets from poets who seem to have a chance at doing important work than by asking what they are reading.

The poet who answers that he regularly reads Shakespeare's sonnets, and such poets as Dante, Goethe, Pushkin, Keats, Whitman, Rilke, Akmatova, Montale, and Robert Lowell reveals that he honors and learns from the continuing tradition of poetry. The poet who reads his contemporaries, who subscribes to (or reads in libraries) such magazines as *Poetry, The Hudson Review, The New Yorker, The Atlantic*

Monthly, The American Poetry Review, and many large and small literary periodicals does likewise.

Let's assume that a poet sets out to read, say, the works of Robert Hayden and Adrienne Rich, Richard Howard's translation of Baudelaire's *Les Fleurs du Mal* and Anthony Hecht's *The Hard Hours.* What then?

The dominant mode of twentieth-century poetry is the short personal lyric, usually written in free verse. It is this mode that most college poetry workshops teach and that magazines most frequently publish. Learning to write a passable poem in this mode is not enormously difficult. Technique can be taught to any relatively talented poet. With technique, the poet can write and probably publish the standard contemporary American poem: a lyric that is essentially good, interesting personal journalism, written more or less rhythmically.

I don't mean to disparage such poetry. Just as writing the well-rhymed sonnet was a criterion for measuring a poet's ability in past generations, writing the intense and crafted personal lyric has become the late twentieth-century criterion. As in previous times, poets usually begin with trying to master a way of expression that seems most acceptable to the age in which they live.

The key technical principles for twentieth-century writers, poets included, are the two well-known admonitions of "Show, don't tell" and "Be specific." A great deal of the tension in modern verse derives from the poet's holding back what he or she would otherwise say outright, holding it back so that it will come into the reader's mind as a painting does, as does music, the thought or feeling seeming to have jumped distance and be born from the reader's own sensibility rather than impressed upon it.

"Be specific" forces the beginning poet really to observe the world around him or her and to search for precise words to describe what is seen. A passion for observation is also a passion for knowing and rendering life intensely. In fact, much of contemporary poetry has assumed—consciously or unconsciously on the part of poets—a duty to keep words alive and thus the ideas and feelings they evoke.

With "Show, don't tell" and "Be specific" in mind, the poet unlocks his or her experience. These admonitions intensify the poet's daily doings, meditations, conversations, and memories. What would otherwise be a dull walk on a gray day may turn into one in which the poet notices a small lightning bolt-shaped crack in a neighbor's kitchen windowpane, or how a haphazard arrangement of crocuses and tulips scattered on a suburban lawn makes it look as if the flower clumps were shot there by random cannon bursts. If the neighbor has been going through troubles recently, such imagery may connote it. To think vaguely of a past, lost love but then focus on the pattern of the towel wrapped around her as she stepped from a steamy shower makes that love seem alive in time.

My favorite definition of poetry comes from critic Fred B. Millett's *Reading Poetry:* "Poetry is language measured and supercharged." Supercharged relates to lyric poetry's intensity, which is a matter of many elements. "Language measured" reminds us that anyone serious about writing poetry should train himself in writing in a variety of meters. Knowledge of meter gives the poet maximum freedom; some poems wish to be iambic, or trochaic, or in lines of few or many feet. If a poet can write only free verse, that poet is cut off not only from the past, but from the challenge of writing in many of poetry's greatest traditional forms and modes.

Similarly, the poet who cannot write a decent rhymed poem is not one to be trusted as solidly grounded in the art. If you balk at this, remember that a prevalent kind of rhyming in our century is "slant" or "eye" rhyme. When the poet learns that "window" can be rhymed not only with "snow" but with "threw" and even with "now" or maybe even "blue," enormous possibilities open.

Since a contemporary poem is often valued for its interest—its interesting words, experiences—beginning poets who wish to do other than rake their lives to the coals in the "confessional" manner of Sylvia Plath are sometimes helped by being reminded that the contemporary personal lyric does not have to be an exact rendering of an actual event. "I" poems are not usually literal renderings; the "I" can easily be a persona.

If a poem comes from a train ride to Cleveland but works better when set on a train ride from Montreal, so be it. If "blue chair" works better than the "orange couch" on which a poet actually sat, the fictional aspect of writing allows use of the latter when it will create an emotionally truer and richer poem.

Based on actual experience or not, a great stress of contemporary poetry is on "honesty." The "honest" personal lyric is valued because, reading it, we are reminded that no matter how formula TV shows would convince us differently, each different human life is a remarkably varied and vivid reflection on our own lives. Stereotypes and clichés are clumsy clay representations of the actual wonders and nuances to be seen and felt and heard by those who would truly know that living is more ripples than plains.

When a poet speaks of honesty, what she means is that the best lyrics contain elements that convince the reader that their feeling is not artificial. A poem must not seem to be a hiding place, or counterfeit the "proper" responses to situations with falsifying sentiment. The poet who writes only that she felt bad but resigned when she broke up with her boyfriend, yet does not show how she actually drew his picture in lipstick on her mirror and spat on it is not being honest with her readers. Her consequent poem will almost surely be hollow.

A continual lifetime involvement with reading poetry and with studying technique, as well as an open attitude toward writing poetry can take poets a long way; they cannot, however, give us much poetry that seems to matter ultimately. Good personal journalism and conversation written in free verse lyric poem form, fine descriptive vignettes—if the poet cannot do more she or he will remain at the best marvelously minor.

Everything else being equal, it is the content of the poem that causes it to change lives. In the twentieth century, a misplaced emphasis on "how a poem means" has misled too many poets into writing and teaching as if poetry were primarily a matter of aesthetics. Deep down, the best poets know it isn't, that their passionate intensity comes from a need to communicate deeply felt truths about the world or to tell stories concerning it in words, lines, images, musical throbs that simultaneously seem to hold still and vibrate.

Degrees of passion for subject material and the necessity to deal with ideas as well as feelings divide minor poets from major poets, and craftsmen from geniuses. Content crudely handled in verse has ruined hundreds of thousands of poems; yet without significant content a poet's work will be thin.

It is my conviction that contemporary poetry of the highest order—and who would strive for less?—requires a desperate need to be continually involved with the edges of experience, never to stop trying to write about the great subjects—love, religion, death, who we are, what is our purpose here, how shall we live; to have a living engagement with science and politics, and as many other matters as possible; and then to spend weeks, months, years honing individual works that laugh and shimmer, sob and stare.

76

EVERYONE WANTS TO BE PUBLISHED, BUT...

By John Ciardi

At a recent writers' conference I sat in on a last-day session billed as "Getting Published." Getting published was, clearly, everyone's enthusiasm. The hope of getting published will certainly do as one reason for writing. It need not be the only, nor even the best, reason for writing. Yet that hope is always there.

Emily Dickinson found reasons for writing that were at least remote from publication. Yet even she had it in mind. She seems to have known that what she wrote was ahead of its time, but she also seemed to know that its time would come. If Thomas H. Johnson's biography of her is a sound guide, and I believe it is, she spent her last ten years writing her "letters to the future." The letters, to be sure, were addressed to specific friends; yet they were equally addressed *through* her friends to her future readers. As Hindemith spent ten years composing his quartets and then ten more creating the terms by which they were to be assessed critically, so Emily spent ten years writing her poems (1776 of them, if I recall the right number), and then ten more years stating the terms for their reception.

Even she, then, had an audience (which is to say, publication) in mind. Nor do I imply that the desire to publish is an ignoble motive. Every writer wants to see himself in print. No writer, to my knowledge, has ever been offended when his published offerings were well received. The desire to publish becomes ignoble only when it moves a writer to hack and hurry the work in order to get it into print.

Poetry, of course, is relatively free of commercial motive. Every generation has its Edgar Guest. Ours, I suppose, is Rod McKuen. These are writers whose remouthing of sentiments catches some tawdry emotional impulse in commercial quantities. Yet such writers—or so I have long suspected—must come to believe seriously in the inanities they write. I doubt that they have sold out to the dollar sign: more tragically, they have sold out to themselves.

Such writers aside, it is hard to imagine that anyone would think to bribe a poet to write a bad poem. It would follow then (all temptation to cheat being out of the equation) that the only reason for writing a poem is to write it as well as one possibly can. Having so written it, one would naturally like to see it published.

I was, accordingly, in sympathy with the conference members—but I was also torn. For I had just spent days reading a stack of the manuscripts these people had submitted, and I had found nothing that seemed worthy of publication. I sat by, thinking that session on getting published was an exercise in swimming in a mirage. I even suspected a few of those present of drowning in their mirages.

Then one of the hard-case pros on the conference staff delivered a statistic. "You want to get published?" he said. "Fine. Look at the magazines. What are they publishing? The answer is, roughly, 98 percent nonfiction and not quite half of one percent poetry. Yet of the manuscripts submitted at this conference, seventy-six are poetry and only two are nonfiction." He paused. "Now you tell me," he said, "where are you going to get published?"

The hard case, as it happened, was a successful nonfiction writer for the large-circulation magazines; he had dismissed from consideration the literary quarterlies that do publish poetry, sometimes without payment, but sometimes with an "honorarium." To the quarterlies, I would certainly add our two excellent poetry tabloids, *The American Poetry Review* and *Poetry Now*.

For poetry does get published, though not on terms that would be attractive to the big-circulation pros. Poets *qua* poets do not run into serious income tax problems. So be it. If a little is all one asks, then a little is enough. I have never known of anyone who turned to poetry in the expectation of becoming rich by it. Were I to impersonate the hard-case pro at that conference, I could argue that a writer writes as an alcoholic drinks—which is to say, compulsively, and for its own sake. An alcoholic expects no special recognition for being helpless in his compulsion: Why should a poet expect money and recognition for his compulsion?

The fact is that the good poets do generally find their rewards and recognitions. Ego being what it is (and the poet's ego more so), any given poet may think his true merit has been slighted. For myself, whatever I have managed to make of my writing (and it has been a love affair, not a sales campaign), I have always felt that my own satisfaction (or at least the flickering hope of it) was a total payment. Whatever else came has always struck me as a marvelous bonus. And there have been bonuses—grants, prizes, even a small, slow rain of checks. How could I fail to rejoice in that overflow of good? I wish it to every writer, and wish him my sense of joy in it.

But there is more to it. The hard case's manuscript count stayed with me. Can seventy-six poets and two nonfiction writers be called a writers' conference? He hadn't mentioned fiction, and I never learned how many fiction manuscripts had been turned in. But why, I asked myself, would seventy-six turn to poetry and only two to nonfiction? All writing is writing; all of it is part of one motion. I have enjoyed trying different sorts of writing. This present piece, for example, is nonfiction. It is part of the same exploration that poems take me on.

I asked myself the question, but I know I already had the answer —at least part of it—from the poems I had read and criticized. The poems had been bad, and I had fumbled, as one must, at trying to say why I thought they were bad. I wished on that last day that the conference were just starting and that I had ahead of me another chance to identify the badness of the poems. But perish that thought: I was emotionally exhausted.

Yet on that last day the reason so few of the conference members had turned to nonfiction seemed clear to me. Even to attempt nonfiction a writer must take the trouble of acquiring some body of information. The poems I had read lacked anything that could be called a body of information. The writers seemed to have assumed that their own excited ignorance was a sufficient qualification for the writing of poetry.

I wanted to go back and say to my conferees, "Your poems care nothing about the fact!" Isn't that another way of saying they were conceived in ignorance? Not one of the poets I read had even tried to connect fact A to fact B in a way to make an emotional experience of the connection. The writing lacked *thingness* and a lover's knowledge of thing.

Consider these lines by Stanley Kunitz (the italics are mine):

> Winter that *coils* in the thickets now,
> Will *glide* from the fields, the *swinging* rain
> Be *knotted* with flowers. On every bough
> A bird will *meditate* again.

393

The diction, the rhyming, the rhythmic flow and sustainment are effortless, but how knowledgeably things fall into place! Winter *coils* in the thickets because that snow that lies in shade is the last to melt, thinning down to scrolls of white by the last thaw. Winter will then *glide* from the fields—and what better (continuous, smooth) motion for the run-off of the last melt? The *swinging* rain (what word could better evoke our sense of April showers?) will then be *knotted* (as if) with flowers while birds (as if) *meditate* on every bough. The rain, of course, will not literally be knotted with flowers, nor will birds, literally, meditate. Yet what seems to be a scientific inaccuracy is of the central power of metaphor. Metaphor may, in fact, be conceived as an exactly felt error.

Metaphor is supposed to state the unknown in terms of the known. It is supposed to say X equals Y. Yet when we say "John is a lion," we do not think of John with a mane, with four clawed paws, nor with a pompon tipped tail. We extract from "lion" the emotional equivalent we need and let the rest go. The real metaphoric formula is X does-and-does-not-equal Y. Kunitz understands this formula. His knowledge of it is part of his qualification as a master poet.

There is more. More than can be parsed here. But note how the italicized words *hearken* to one another, each later term being summoned (by some knowledge and precision in the poet) by what went before. The italicized words form what I will dare to call a chord sequence by a composer who has mastered musical theory.

The passage, that is to say, is empowered by a body of knowledge of which I could find no trace in the poets I had been reading at the conference. My poets had been on some sort of trip. Their one message was "I feel! I feel!" Starting with that self-assertive impulse (and *thing* be damned), they then let every free association into the poem. They were too ignorant even to attempt a principle of selection.

I do not imply that I know what any given poem's principle of selection ought to be. To find the principle that serves best and to apply it in a way to enchant the reader is the art and knowledge of the poet. Everything in a good poem must be *chosen* into it. Even the accidents. How else could it be when one stroke of the pen will slash a thing out forever? All that has not been slashed out, it follows, is chosen in.

Ignorance, as nearly as I could say it (too late), was what had really stifled the poems I had read. The writers had not cared enough to learn their own art and use their eyes.

They will, I suppose, get published. Some of them somewhere. But have they earned the right to publication? I ask the question not to answer it. It is every writer's question to ask for himself.

77

WRITING POETRY FOR CHILDREN

By Myra Cohn Livingston

I NEVER intended to write poetry for children. It was a complete accident, and even today I marvel that it happened at all. I was eighteen, in college, and writing what I considered far more important—poetry about love! My instructor at Sarah Lawrence College, Katherine Liddell, had given us an assignment; we were to use alliteration and onomatopoeia. I turned in some verses. "These," she said to me in her converted closet-conference room, reeking with the odor of Sano cigarettes, "would be wonderful for children. Send them to *Story Parade*" (a magazine for boys and girls published by Simon & Schuster). I grudgingly followed her instructions—the accompanying letter, the self-addressed stamped envelope. Several weeks later the envelope came back. I threw it onto a pile of papers and three weeks later became so angry with Miss Liddell's folly, that I ripped it open to confront her with her error. I caught my breath. The editor had carefully clipped three of the poems, and there was a letter accepting these for publication.

It took me eleven years for my first book, *Whispers and Other Poems,* written when I was a freshman, to be accepted for publication by the same editor, Margaret K. McElderry, who had seen the manuscript when I was in college and encouraged me to continue writing. I know now that during the war years few new books were published, and certainly poetry for children was far down on the list of desired manuscripts. In those days, I read *The Writer* religiously, hoping to find someone who would want my work, and collected a sheaf of rejection slips.

But I did not write and never have consciously written *for* children. I cannot understand why the world appeared to me from the start as through the eyes of a child—of my own childhood—or why, even today, most of the poetry I write comes out that way. The only clue I have is that, even as an anthologist, I am drawn to (or write) those poems that speak to the subjects, emotions, and thoughts of children in a diction they understand.

My own poems have often been called "deceptively simple"; the first review of *Whispers* scathingly accused me of writing about "simple, everyday things," as though this were some sort of evil. Perhaps this is because many adults forget that to the child, these very things are what pique his curiosity, engage his attention. As the poet-in-residence for our school district, in my visits to schools and libraries throughout this country, and in teaching courses for teachers at U.C.L.A. Extension, I note that today's child is very different, in many respects, from the child I was, or that my children are, but that many things remain eternal. Children may know more facts, be more worldly wise, but the curiosity, wonder and fresh way of looking, the joys and pains and doubts, seem just as they always were.

I would like to suggest that anyone who wishes to write poetry that children might enjoy face up to a few basics about this vocation. The climate today is far more receptive to poetry than it was a number of years ago when the English—Walter de la Mare, Robert Louis Stevenson, and A. A. Milne—dominated the field. America has given us Elizabeth Madox Roberts, David McCord and Harry Behn, to mention but a few—and there are many exciting middle-aged and young poets publishing today whose work is excellent. We no longer have to take second place to the English, but we do have to recognize that poetry is still somewhat of a stepchild in juvenile literature. Children, themselves, are more apt to read a story in a picture book than to read poetry, for most adults and teachers feel uncomfortable about presenting it. Even Mother Goose is not as well known as once she was. And poetry demands an involvement of the emotions, whether it be laughter or wonder or a more serious way of viewing the world.

The crisis we seem to face now is the mistaken notion that *anyone* can write a poem. The Poets-in-the-Schools program, in many areas, has too often, in my opinion, fostered undisciplined writing, that which John Ciardi has called "a spillage of raw emotion." Any word or series of words written down are called "poems." This, as I see it, is a great disservice to the children who are falsely praised, but it also applies to older aspiring poets. Many of the high school and college students have had no real discipline. Metrical feet, scansion, forms are

397

unknown. Of course, we do not want didactic, sing-song verse, the moralizing of a Henley's "Invictus" or the elusive fairies of Rose Fyleman. What we do need is true poetry that takes into account the interests and yearnings of the young and leads them toward a process of humanization.

In offering suggestions to the person who wishes to write such poetry, I would ask that he ask himself if anything of the child remains in him—a way of looking, tasting, smelling, touching, thinking; if he is in touch with the contemporary child and his way of viewing the world, if he is truly comfortable with children. I would also suggest that he make the commitment to learn the basics of writing in disciplined forms and meters. One cannot, for example, attempt a limerick without knowing how to use the iambus and anapest correctly, nor even free verse without knowing why it *is* free verse.

Another, and perhaps more elusive point, is that the writer understand and believe that poetry for children is not second-best; there is a tendency on the part of many to feel that a so-called children's poet is one who has failed in writing adult poetry, or that it is "easy" to do. The poet who writes for children exclusively is a sort of second-class citizen.

Although I have spent almost twenty years sharing with young people poetry ranging from Mother Goose to T.S. Eliot, it is difficult to give any definite answer as to what sort of poetry children like best. We know through experience that levity is always high on the list, and humor is important, for it counters the view of poems as soul-building messages in high-flown diction. But many a child prefers the more serious. The more a young person is exposed to poetry, the more refined is his taste in this, as in all arts. I would hope that any writer aspiring to publish poetry would not write for what he thinks is the juvenile market, but rather concentrate on his own strengths. The word-play of David McCord is something that comes naturally to his art; curiosity and a love for nature are intrinsic to Harry Behn's work; and Elizabeth Madox Roberts wrote about experiences of her own as a child.

My own poetry has gone through a series of changes. Trained in the traditional rhyme/meter school, I have at times broken away to free verse, knowing that the force of what I wished to say had to dictate the form. Yet I do not feel I could have made this break without a sure knowledge of the disciplines, taught to me by Robert Fitzgerald and Horace Gregory. I know that there are many who would take issue with me, who feel that anything one wishes to put down, if arranged in a certain order, is a poem.

This change may best be shown by contrasting my first published poem, "Whispers," to later work:

> Whispers
> tickle through your ear
> telling things you like to hear.
>
> Whispers
> are as soft as skin
> letting little words curl in.
>
> Whispers
> come so they can blow
> secrets others never know.

Most of my verse in *Whispers, Wide Awake, Old Mrs. Twindlytart* and *The Moon and a Star* was written in traditional forms. But in *A Crazy Flight* (published in 1969), what I wanted to say suddenly refused to be confined by rhyme. The need to use repetition and a freer form of expression asserted itself in a poem that also picked up some current speech patterns of the children I was then teaching:

THE SUN IS STUCK

> The sun is stuck.
> I mean, it won't move.
> I mean, it's hot, man, and we need a red-hot
>   poker to pry it loose,
> Give it a good shove and roll it across the sky
> And make it go down
> So we can be cool,
> Man.

Yet, *The Malibu,* my poem inspired by the moon landing and America's concerns with litter, combined both the rhyming couplet and some elements of free verse:

Hey moonface,
man-in-the-moonface,

do you like the way
we left your place?

can you stand the view
of footprints on you?

is it fun to stare
at the flags up there?

did you notice ours
with the stripes and stars?

does it warm you to know
we love you so?

moonface,
man-in-the-moonface,

thanks a heap for the rocks.

In *The Way Things Are,* the meter follows a child's pattern with a different rhyme pattern, in "Growing: For Louis."

It's tough being short.

Of course your father tells you not to worry,
But everyone else is giant, and you're just the
way you were.
And this stupid guy says, "Hey shorty, where'd
you get the long pants?"
Or some smart beanpole asks how it feels to
be so close to the ants?
And the school nurse says to tell her again how
tall you are when you've already told her.
Oh, my mother says there's really no hurry
And I'll grow soon enough.

But it's tough being short.

(I wonder if Napoleon got the same old stuff?)

But the rhymed couplet creeps up again and again in *4-Way Stop* (published in 1976):

OCEAN AT NIGHT

Mother Wave sings soft to sleep
the fish and seaweed of the deep

black ocean, and with quiet hands
pats to peace her tired sands,

her kelp and driftwood; fills her shoals
with gleaming tides, and gently pulls

across her bed the pale moonlight.
And this is night. And this is night.

Throughout these later books are outcroppings of free verse with which I am still experimenting, but there is an inherent pull that constantly draws me back to the containment of fixed forms. I have finally begun to tackle the haiku and cinquain, most demanding in their use of words:

Even in summer
bees have to work in their orange
and black striped sweaters.

Like any other poet, I feel that the most important factor in my poetry writing is not that I set out to write in any given form, but that I must find the right form for the subject matter. For this is when —and only when—the poem "comes right" for me.

What is right for me is not so for everybody. There are no surefire methods, although I do believe that one must know the basics and rules before breaking them. Even children need these rules, for without them, they flounder and grow dissatisfied with what they are doing. What we all have in common is that we are still learning, and, I hope, growing and changing.

78

ROLES IN COLLISION:
A PLAY BEGINS

By Jeffrey Sweet

MY SON CAME BACK from his visit to a department store Santa Claus with a handout from an elf—one of those infernal little plastic doodads containing three tiny BB's. On the floor of the container is a picture pocked by three shallow indentations. The object is to tip the container to and fro so as to propel the three BB's into the three indentations and thus complete the picture (in this case—a juggler with three balls overhead).

I had better things to do. So of course I picked up the game. More than half an hour evaporated as I jiggled and jostled and cussed. Finally, after countless near-misses, I had two of the three BB's snugly placed. Only one to go. I held my breath and tapped gingerly. And, with lazy grace, the third BB rolled across the face of the picture and settled into the third indentation with a plop.

There was something very familiar about that plop. It is with a similar sound that I find that the premises of my plays usually come together. After analogous jiggling, jostling, and tapping in my imagination, some small element drops into place, and I suddenly know how I'm going to be spending the next several months. Mind you, this is not primarily a matter of luck (though luck is never entirely absent in writing). Just as there is skill (however trivial) involved in the BB game, there is skill involved in taking images, hunches, and impulses that have lodged in one's mind and manipulating them into an arrangement that is sufficient grounds for typing "Act One" onto a piece of paper.

Different dramatists arrive at their starting points in different ways. Many rely on instinct and intuition, but I've always held to the belief that when performing surgery you're more likely to have a successful outcome if the lights are on in the operating room so you can see your tools. I'd like to share a tool that I've found of particular use in building plays.

I had long ago been fascinated by the blacklisting of entertainers that occurred during the McCarthy era and wanted to find a way to deal with the subject dramatically. A friend of mine named Kate Draper had told me that her father Paul had been among those blacklisted in the fifties, so I asked her if we could arrange to get together so that I could fire a few questions at her. She was agreeable, and soon after, in a local coffee shop, she told me how her father, a famous dancer, had seen his career all but destroyed when someone accused him of being a Communist. After she had shared details of her family's ordeal and answered all of my prepared questions, the conversation shifted to chat about what was going on in our lives at the moment. She had good news. She had just been cast in a Broadway musical. Idly, I asked how she thought her father would react if it turned out that the director of the musical had been one of those who had cooperated with the House Committee on Un-American Activities, one of the forces responsible for the blacklist.

"The director didn't," said Kate.

"I know," I said. "I'm asking 'if.' "

She paused for a second, then replied, "He probably wouldn't say much of anything. He tends not to talk too much about those days."

My reaction was, "That's not dramatic."

This led me to wonder what would make it dramatic. The answer, of course, was if the father had quite a strong reaction indeed. Plop. There was the premise of my play. A year or so later, my play *The Value of Names* opened at the Actors Theatre of Louisville and has since been staged by a number of other companies and been published.

Thinking about the matter later, I realized that what I did when I asked Kate that question was construct the dilemma that would result if two important roles in her life—those of actress and daughter—were to come into conflict. This dilemma—the conflict between two or more of a central character's roles—is the dynamic element in most of the plays I write as well as those I admire.

Everybody plays several roles. Among the ones I count in my personal repertoire: my son's father, my wife's husband, my father's son, my mother's son, my agent's client, my students' teacher, and so on. Frequently, these roles come into conflict. For instance, as any dedi-

403

cated writer who is married knows, there inevitably come times when your spouse asks, "Are you married to me or your work?" How one responds to this question may determine whether one retains the role of husband and wife or takes on the challenge of the new role of a divorced person.

Characters in plays, too, must choose between roles. Their choices and the resulting fates are the stuff of drama.

Let's dive into the deep and look at *Hamlet*. Shakespeare loads him with several conflicting roles. Hamlet is simultaneously the ghost's appointed avenger, Gertrude's son, Claudius's nephew, Ophelia's boyfriend, Rosencrantz and Guildenstern's schoolmate, and so on. The impossibility of being all of these things at the same time and the choice he has to make between these roles are what make the action of the play possible. One of the many things Hamlet and the audience discover is that his role as avenger ultimately supersedes all of the other roles. Because he embraces this role and the attendant responsibility, Gertrude is poisoned, Claudius is stabbed, Ophelia drowns, Rosencrantz and Guildenstern are executed, and Hamlet himself dies.

In Sophocles' *Antigone,* the title character must choose between two mutually exclusive roles. Creon, the king of Thebes, has refused to allow the slain rebel Polyneices the dignity of funeral rites and has decreed that anybody contravening his order is to be executed. Antigone's dilemma is that she is both a citizen of Thebes (and thereby bound to obey Theban law) and Polyneices' sister (and thereby bound by family obligation to give her brother a proper funeral). The play centers on her determination that her role as sister takes precedence over her role as citizen. In burying her brother she condemns herself to death.

Much has been written about why one experiences a catharsis watching tragedy. How is it that witnessing the destruction of heroes produces in the audience not a profound depression but a kind of elation? My theory is that this feeling is a result of our knowledge that Hamlet, Antigone, Iphigenia, Romeo and Juliet, Macbeth, and Medea (to name but a few) meet and embrace their true natures. "To thine ownself be true" is an injunction few in real life have the courage to fulfill, and there is something liberating about seeing characters who, in full knowledge of the frequently cataclysmic consequences, choose to be their truest selves.

But this business of characters choosing their true selves is not limited to classical tragedy. Neil Simon's *The Odd Couple* is a comedy in which characters, again, have to determine their real roles. Felix and Oscar must battle their way to the understanding that their relationship is more truly that of good friends than bad roommates. The title character in Molière's *Tartuffe* meets his deserved comeuppance when he gives free rein to his usually-hidden lecherous nature. At the end of Ibsen's *A Doll House,* Nora walks out on her marriage having resolved to put aside the degrading part of Torvald's "doll-wife" in favor of the role of a mature and self-respecting adult.

I have found this construct useful not only for the analysis of others' plays, but for the synthesis of my own. Before I begin to write a script, I ask myself a number of questions about my central character's options. A play depicts the actions taken by the central character or characters. It is not enough, however, to know what my protagonist does. I have to know what my protagonist chooses *not* to do. After all, the choice of one road necessarily implies the rejection of at least one other. If a character's choice is to have any tension or resonance, the case for the road not taken must be very strong. In the case of *The Value of Names,* Norma, the daughter, knows that if she chooses to stay in the cast of the play being directed by her father's enemy, she puts her relationship with her father at risk. If she resigns from the play, she jeopardizes her career. It is the difficulty of the choice that attracted me to the story.

Because Norma ultimately decides to stay with the play, Benny, her father, then is faced with a choice: either to accept and forgive what he sees as a betrayal or to hold fast to his bitterness and, in essence, blacklist his daughter from his affections. During the writing of the play I found that this choice became the central question of the piece.

To summarize the process, what started as my speculation about which choice Paul Draper would make in a hypothetical situation led me to wonder which choice my character Norma would make if confronted over this issue by her father Benny, which, in turn, led me to wonder which choice Benny would make in reaction to Norma's choice.

I am not suggesting that one should blithely appropriate the private lives of friends. (As I hope I've established, my play, though derived from a speculation about how Kate and her father would handle a certain situation, is in no meaningful way a reflection of Kate's rela-

405

tionship with her father.) But everybody lives with contradictions in his or her life. Most of us are fairly nimble about keeping these contradictions from coming to too much of a head. But drama is found in the exploration of these contradictions, in asking what would happen if push were indeed to come to shove.

Get into the habit of this kind of speculation, and you may also find the third BB dropping into place in your imagination.

79

TEN GOLDEN RULES FOR PLAYWRIGHTS

By Marsha Norman

Budding playwrights often write to ask me advice on getting started—and succeeding—in writing plays. The following are a few basics that I hope aspiring playwrights will find helpful.—M.N.

1. Read at least four hours every day, and don't let anybody ask you what you're doing just sitting there reading.

2. Don't write about your present life. You don't have a clue what it's about yet. Write about your past. Write about something that terrified you, something you *still* think is unfair, something that you have not been able to forget in all the time that's passed since it happened.

3. Don't write in order to tell the audience how smart you are. The audience is not the least bit interested in the playwright. The audience only wants to know about the characters. If the audience begins to suspect that the thing onstage was actually written by some other person, they're going to quit listening. So keep yourself out of it!

4. If you have characters you cannot write fairly, cut them out. Grudges have no place in the theatre. Nobody cares about your grudges but you, and you are not enough to fill a house.

5. There must be one central character. One. Everybody write that down. Just one. And he or she must want something. And by the end of the play, he or she must either get it or not. Period. No exceptions.

6. You must tell the audience right away what is at stake in the evening, i.e. how they know when they can go home. They are, in a sense, the jury. You present the evidence, and then they say whether it seems true to them. If it does, it will run, because they will tell all their friends to come see this true thing, God bless them. If it does not seem true to them, try to find out why and don't do it any more.

7. If, while you are writing, thoughts of critics, audience members or family members occur to you, stop writing and go read until you have successfully forgotten them.

8. Don't talk about your play while you are writing it. Good plays are always the product of a single vision, a single point of view. Your friends will be helpful later, after the play's direction is established. A play is one thing you can get too much help with. If you must break this rule, try not to say what you have learned by talking. Or just let other people talk and you listen. Don't talk the play away.

9. Keep pads of paper near all your chairs. You will be in your chairs a good bit (see Rule 1), and you will have thoughts for your play. Write them down. But don't get up from reading to do it. Go right back to the reading once the thoughts are on the paper.

10. Never go to your typewriter until you know what the first sentence is that day. It is definitely unhealthy to sit in front of a silent typewriter for any length of time. If, after you have typed the first sentence, you can't think of a second one, go read. There is only one good reason to write a play, and that is that there is no other way to take care of it, whatever it is. There are too many made-up plays being written these days. So if it doesn't spill out faster than you can write it, don't write it at all. Or write about something that does spill out. Spilling out is what the theatre is about. Writing is for novels.

80

GUIDELINES FOR
THE BEGINNING PLAYWRIGHT

By Louis E. Catron

YEARS OF teaching playwriting probably have been more educational for me than for my students. Several hundred young playwrights have taken one or more of my classes since I first started teaching at the College of William and Mary in 1966, and they have taught me that writing a play can be simplified—maybe not made "easy," but certainly "easier"—if certain boundaries are imposed.

We began experimenting with guidelines because so many playwrights were expending too much creative energy chasing nonproductive fireflies. We found that these limitations help playwrights over difficult hurdles. More, they are highly important for the overall learning process.

To be sure, for some writers the very idea of imposed limits appears to be a contradiction in significant terms. How, they ask, can I do creative writing if you fence me in?

Their objections have merit. Limitations often inhibit the creative mind, and many creative people expend a great deal of effort seeking clever ways of circumventing the rules. Certainly I've had students react to the guidelines with the fervor of a bull to a red flag and we've had to arm wrestle about the rules.

Nonetheless, imposition of limitations is a way of life in all creative arts. Theatre is no exception. As a play director, for example, I have found that one key portion of my job is establishing parameters of character for actors, holding these walls tightly in place during rehearsals, and encouraging the performers to create depth within those limitations.

We're talking about the contrast between the casual and sloppy meandering of a Mississippi River versus a tightly confined Colorado. The former changes directions so often that it confuses even experienced riverboat captains, but the latter is held so tightly in direction that it cuts the Grand Canyon. Discipline is essential for the creation of beauty.

The beginning playwright is encouraged to accept the following guidelines to write his or her first play. Later plays can be more free. Indeed, deliberately breaking selected guidelines later will help you better understand the nature of dramatic writing. For now, however, let these guidelines help you in your initial steps toward learning the art and craft of playwriting.

1. *Start with a one-act play.* A full-length play isn't merely three times longer and therefore only three times more difficult. And that a one-act is simpler doesn't mean it is insignificant. The one-act play can be exciting and vibrantly alive, as has been shown by plays such as *No Exit* (Sartre), *Zoo Story* (Albee), *The Maids* (Genet), *the Dumb Waiter* (Pinter) and *The Madness of Lady Bright* (Wilson).

Starting with the one-act lets the writer begin with a canvas that is easily seen at a glance, instead of a mural that covers such a huge space perception doesn't grasp it all.

The one-act typically has only a few characters, is an examination of a single dramatic incident, and runs about half an hour in length. It usually stays within one time frame and one place. Because there are fewer complexities, you'll be able to focus more upon the actual writing, and you'll have less concern about a number of stage problems which come with full-length plays.

2. *Write about something you care about.* Writing manuals usually tell the beginner to write "about what you know best." I think that can lead a beginner to think in terms of daily, mundane events. Better, I believe, is for the beginner to *care;* if the playwright is involved with the subject, that interest will pull an audience along.

3. *Conflict is essential to drama.* Quibble me no quibbles about plays which may not have conflict. For *your* first play, there should be conflict. Drama is the art of the showdown. Force must be opposed by force, person (or group) by person (or group), desire by desire.

If there's no conflict, the dramatic qualities are lost. The result may still hold the stage, but the odds against it are increased. More important, even if the one-act has no conflict and yet holds the stage, the playwright hasn't learned that all-significant lesson about showing conflict. You'll want to know that when you write more.

4. *Let there be emotion.* People *care,* in your first play, I hope; people feel strongly, whether it is love or hate, happiness or despair. If you are able to get them emotional, your characters more than likely are going to be active and going somewhere. The audience will care more about emotional people than those dull-eyed, unfeeling dramatic deadbeats.

5. *Stay within the "realistic" mode.* Realism deals with contemporary people, the sort who might live next door, in their contemporary activities, and with selective use of ordinary speech. It avoids the aside and the soliloquy. It is quite comfortable inside the traditional box set. Realism is selective, and sometimes critical, in its presentation of objective facts.

Realism is the familiar mode you've seen most often: it dominates television, and only a handful of movies break away from realism. No doubt you've also seen it on stage more than any other mode. Because you know it best, your first play will be easier to write if you stay in realism. Expressionism, absurdism, symbolism, epic: avoid these for your first experience with playwriting.

(Examples of realism would be full-length plays like *Ghosts* or *A Doll's House,* both by Ibsen, or one-acts like *Ile* and other sea plays by O'Neill. More recent plays tend to be eclectic—primarily but not totally realistic, like the full-length *Death of a Salesman,* by Arthur Miller, or the one-act *Gnadiges Fraulein* by Tennessee Williams.)

6. *Limit the number of characters.* Too many characters and you may lose some: they'll be on stage but saying and doing nothing, so you'll send them off to make dinner or fix the car while you focus on the remaining characters you like better. Consider eliminating those who are dead.

Strenuously avoid "utilitarian" characters—those people who make minor announcements (in older drawing-room plays they say little more than, "Dinner is served"), or deliver packages or messages (Western Union's delivery boy, remember, is as much a relic as the butler). Such characters tend to be flat and no fun for playwright, performer or audience.

Some utilitarians are confidants, on stage to serve as ears so the protagonist will be able to speak inner thoughts without resorting to the soliloquy. The confidant in this sort of case turns out to be about as vital as a wooden listening post.

Confidants, by the way, are easily recognized: their faces are covered with a huge question mark. They seem to be asking questions eternally, without any apparent interest in question or answer. The playwright uses the confidant to get to the answer. If such a person is necessary, let the character be more than a pair of ears.

Just how many characters should be in the play?

Three is a good number for the first play. The triangle is always helpful; three characters allow development of good action and conflict and variety. More, and there's the risk of excess baggage; less, and the characters may quickly become thin and tired.

7. *Keep them all on stage as long as you can.* All too often I've seen plays developing potentially exciting situations, only to be deflated by the exit of a prime character. The audience will feel let down—promised excitement evaporated through the swinging door.

A flurry of activity with entrances and exits is deceptive. There may be a feeling of action but in truth there's only movement of people at the door. The more such business, often the less the drama: in class we begin to comment jokingly about wanting a percentage of the turnstile concession.

The beginning writer needs to learn to keep all characters alive and actively contributing to the play's action. So, then, you need to try to keep them all on stage as long as you possibly can. If you have a character who keeps running out, perhaps he ought to be eliminated.

You needn't invent a supernatural force to keep them in the same room, by the way, although I've seen my student writers come up with fascinating hostage or kidnap situations and locked doors in order to justify keeping everyone present. All of that is clever, but all you need is action that involves all the characters.

8. *No breaks: no scene shifts, no time lapses.* Just as some playwrights have people leaving when stage action is growing, so also are there authors who cut from the forthcoming explosion with a pause to shift scenery or to indicate a passage of time. There is a break in the action and that always is disappointing. Such lapses are all too often barriers to the play's communication with the audience.

If you have in mind a play that takes place first in an apartment, then in a grocery store, then in a subway, you have let the motion pictures

412

overly influence your theatrical concept. It just won't wash, not in a one-act stage play; with so many sets and breaks producers will shy away from your script. (Yes, yes, you can cite this or that exception, but we're talking about a beginner's first play, not a script by someone with an established reputation.)

Reduce the locales to the *one* place where the essential action occurs, and forget the travelogue. So also with the jumps in time: find the *single* prime moment for these events to take place.

Later you can jump freely in time and space, as Miller does so magnificently in *After the Fall.* Your first play, however, needs your concentrated attention on action, not on inventive devices for jumping around through time and space.

9. *Aim for a thirty-minute play.* One-act plays are delightfully free of the restrictions placed upon full lengths, and can run from only a few minutes to well over an hour. The freedom is heady stuff for a beginning writer.

Aim for around half an hour. Less than that and you probably only sketched the characters and action; much longer, and you might exhaust your initial energies (and your audience!). Your goal, of course, is to be sure you achieve adequate amplification; too many beginners start with a play only eight or ten minutes long, and it seems full of holes. Your *concept* should be one that demands around half an hour to be shown.

10. *Start the plot as soon as you can.* Let the exposition, foreshadowing, mood and character follow the beginning of the plot (the point of attack). Get into the action quickly, and let the other elements follow.

11. *Remember the advantage of the protagonist-antagonist structure.* Our era of the anti-hero apparently has removed the protagonist from the stage. Too bad. The protagonist is a very handy character indeed, and the protagonist-antagonist structure automatically brings conflict which, you recall, is essential for drama.

The protagonist is the "good guy," the one with whom we sympathize and/or empathize, the central character of the play. A better definition: *The one whose conscious will is driving to get a goal.* The antagonist stands firmly in the way. Both should be equal forces at the beginning of

413

the play: if one is obviously stronger, the conflict is over quickly and so should the play be.

(If you do not fully understand the personality of a true protagonist, look at Cyrano in Hooker's translation of Edmond Rostand's *Cyrano de Bergerac*. Cyrano is so strongly a conscious will moving actively that it takes several antagonists to balance him.)

12. *Keep speeches short.* Long speeches often grow boring. Sometimes they are didactic; the playwright delivering The Play's Message. Always they drag the tempo. But the worst sin of a long speech is that it means the playwright is thinking just of that one character and all the others are lying about dead.

Short speeches—quick exchanges between characters—on the other hand keep all of them alive and make the play appear to be more crisp and more vital. The play will increase in pace and you'll automatically feel a need to increase the complications.

How long is "short"? Let the dialogue carry but one idea per speech. Or, to give you another answer, let your ear "listen" to the other characters while one is talking, and see who wants to interrupt. A third answer: try to keep the speeches under, say, some twenty words.

One grants the effectiveness of the "Jerry and the Dog" speech in Albee's *Zoo Story*. It makes a nice exception to this guideline. But there are very few such examples, and there are many more examples of plays where the dialogue is rich and effective because the playwright disciplined the talky characters.

13. *Complications are the plot's heartbeat.* John wants Mary. Mary says fine. Her family likes the idea. Her dog likes John. His parrot likes Mary and the dog. So John and Mary get married. They have their 2.8 kids, two cars, a dishwasher, and they remember anniversaries. Happiness.

Interesting? Not very. Dramatic? Hardly.

John wants Mary. Mary is reluctant, wondering if John simply is in love with love. John is angry at the charge. Mary apologizes. John shows full romanticism. Mary worries again. Mary's grandmother advises Mary to take John to see what love really is by visiting Mary's older sis who everyone knows is happy in marriage. Mary and John visit. Sis and her husband Mike are having a violent fight; mental cruelty; damning accusations. Sis gets John to help her and he unwillingly does; Mike pulls John to his side; Mary yells at John for causing trouble.

That's the first ten minutes.

I think you'll grant it has more potential than the first sketch. *Complications* keep it vital, moving, alive. *A play depends upon conflict for its dramatic effect, and complications are the active subdivision of the basic conflict.*

So, then: the traditional baker's dozen—thirteen guidelines which will help you with your first play. They will help you avoid pitfalls which have lamed so many playwrights, and they will give you a basic learning experience which will help you with future plays.

81

HOW TO SELL YOUR TELEVISION SCRIPT

By RICHARD A. BLUM

MARKETING a television script requires strategy, determination, and a realistic understanding of the industry. The marketplace is extremely competitive, and even the best projects written by established professionals might end up on the shelf. Still, an *excellent* original script—submitted to the right person at the right time—might suddenly break through all barriers. The key word is *excellent*. It makes no sense to submit a script unless you feel that it is in the most polished form (even then it will be subject to rewrites), and that it represents the highest calibre of your creative potential. One might think producers are inclined to see the masterpiece lurking behind a rough draft script. More likely, they'll focus on the weaknesses, compare it to top submissions, and generalize about the writer's talents. So, if you feel uncertain about the professional quality of a work, hold off submitting it. Your next work might show you off to better advantage.

Since unsolicited scripts tend to be lost or "misplaced" by production companies, it's a good idea to have a sufficient number of copies. The *minimum* number you will need is three—one for your files, one for submission, and one for inevitable rewrites. More realistically, you'll probably want additional copies for two or three producers, an agent or two, and your own reserve file for unanticipated submissions. Incidentally, fancy covers and title designs are totally unnecessary. Three inexpensive brads can be punched through the left hand margins of the manuscript. Scripts are usually printed or photocopied to avoid the smudged look of carbons.

The Writers Guild

The Writers Guild of America protects writers' rights, and establishes minimum acceptable arrangements for fees, royalties, credits, and so on. You are eligible to join the Guild as soon as you sell your first project to a signatory company (one who has signed an agreement with the Guild). A copy of your contract is automatically filed and you will then be invited to join the membership. Before you sell the new project, you *have* to be a member of the Guild; otherwise, no signatory company can hire you.

The one-time membership fee for Writers Guild of America, West (Los Angeles) is $1,500, plus 1% of yearly earnings as a writer (or $25 quarterly, if you earn less than $1,000 as a writer). The membership fee for Writers Guild of America, East (New York) is $1,000. Dues are $62 per year, plus 1½% of annual earnings as a writer.

Any writer can register a story, treatment, series format, or script with the Writers Guild of America. The service was set up to help writers establish the completion dates of their work. It doesn't confer statutory rights, but it does supply evidence of authorship which is effective for ten years (and is renewable after that). If you want to register a project, send one copy with the appropriate fee ($15 for nonmembers; $5 for members) to: Writers Guild of America West, Registration Service, 8955 Beverly Blvd., Los Angeles, CA 90048, or Writers Guild of America East, Inc., 555 West 57th Street, New York, NY 10019.

You can also register dramatic or literary material with the U.S. Copyright Office—but most television writers rely on the Writers Guild. The Copyright Office is mainly used for book manuscripts, plays, music or lyrics, which the Writers Guild will not register. For appropriate copyright forms (covering dramatic compositions), write to: Register of Copyrights, Library of Congress, Washington, D.C. 20540.

The release form or waiver

If you have an agent, there is no need to bother with release forms. But if you're going to submit a project without an agent, you'll have to send to the producer or the production company for a release form—or waiver—in advance. (Addresses of selected production companies are listed at the end of this chapter.) Most production companies will return your manuscript without it. The waiver states that you won't sue the production company and that the company has no obligations to you. That may seem unduly harsh, but consider the fact that millions of dollars are spent on fighting plagiarism suits, and that hundreds of ideas are being developed simultaneously and coincidentally by writers, studios, and networks.

The waiver is a form of self-protection for the producer who wants to avoid unwarranted legal action. But it also establishes a clear line of communication between the writer and producer. So rest assured, if legal action is warranted, it can be taken.

The cover letter

When you prepare to send out your project, draft a cover letter that is addressed to a *person* at the studio, network, or production company. If you don't know who is in charge of program development, look it up in the trade papers, or telephone the studio receptionist. If she says, "Mr. So-and-So handles new projects," ask her to *spell* "Mr. So-and-So." That courtesy minimizes the chance of embarrassment, and maximizes the chance that the project will wind up at the right office.

The letter you write should sound professional. There's no need to offer apologies for being an unsold writer, or to suggest that the next draft will be ten times better than this one. If a cover letter starts off with apologies, what incentive is there to read the project?

Here's the tone a cover letter might have:

Dear_____

I've just completed a mini-series called FORTUNES, based on the book by Frank Tavares. I've negotiated all TV and film rights to the property, which is a dramatic adventure series about a family caught in the California Gold Rush. I think you'll find the project suitable for the mini-series genre. It's highly visual in production values and offers unusual opportunities for casting.

I look forward to your reaction. Thank you for your cooperation.

Sincerely,

The letter doesn't say I'm an unsold writer in the midwest or that Frank Tavares is my friend and let me have the rights for a handshake. Nor does it take the opposite route, aggressively asserting that it is the best project the studio will ever read. There's no need for such pretentions. The cover letter sets the stage in a simple and dignified manner. The project will have to speak for itself.

Submitting a script

Independent producers represent the widest span of marketing potential for the free-lance writer. If one producer turns down an idea,

418

there are many others who might still find it fresh and interesting. However, the smaller independent producer is not likely to have the financial resources to compete with the development monies available at the network or studio.

Production companies do have that bargaining power. The distinction between smaller independents and larger production companies is their relative financial stability and current competitive strength on the airwaves. Production companies form and dissolve according to the seasonal marketing trends and network purchases. The more successful production companies have become mini-studios in their own right, with a great number of programs on the air and in development. Some of the more recognizable entities are M. T. M. Enterprises (Mary Tyler Moore), Embassy TV (Norman Lear), and Lorimar Productions (Lee Rich).

The major motion picture studios are in keen competition with production companies. Only six major film studios have aggressive and viable television divisions: Columbia Pictures—TV; Paramount Pictures—TV; Metro-Goldwyn-Mayer (M.G.M.)—TV; 20th Century-Fox—TV; Universal—TV; and Warner Brothers—TV. (Addresses at the end of this chapter.) They represent highly fertile ground for program development; strong deals can be negotiated by agents for the right project.

At the top of the submission ladder is the network oligarchy: ABC, CBS, NBC. Once a project is submitted at this level, there's no turning back. If a project is "passed" (*i.e.,* turned down), it's too late to straddle down the ladder to independent producers. *Their* goal is to bring it back up to the networks (who in turn must sell to the sponsors).

The closer the project comes to the network, the more limited the number of buyers. As the submission moves up the ladder, it faces stiffer competition and fewer alternatives. So you see that the marketplace is highly competitive, although not totally impenetrable. Your submission strategy will depend on knowing the marketplace trends and organizing a campaign to reach the most appropriate people and places.

There's no better way to stay on top of marketing and personnel changes than reading the trade papers—*Daily Variety* (1400 N. Cahuenga Blvd., Hollywood, CA 90028) and the *Hollywood Reporter* (6715 Sunset Blvd., Hollywood CA 90028). The trades reflect the daily

419

pulse of the entertainment industry on the West Coast. Moreover, each paper offers a weekly compilation of production activities ("TV Production Chart," "Films in Production," etc.), which lists companies, addresses, phone numbers, and producers for shows in work. A careful scrutiny of those lists will provide helpful clues to the interests and current activities of independent producers, production companies, and studios.

A similar resource is the "Television Market List," published regularly in the *Writers Guild of America Newsletter* (8955 Beverly Blvd., Los Angeles, CA 90048). It lists all current shows in production or pre-production, and identifies the story consultant or submission contact for each show. The WGA's market list states whether or not a show is "open" for submissions, and whom to contact for assignments. A careful reading of these and other publications, such as *Ross Reports Television* (40–29 27th St., Long Island City, NY 11101), a monthly magazine that lists new television programs and their producers, can help bring you closer to making knowledgeable and practical decisions about marketing your own projects and scripts.

In the network marketplace, you have a choice of submitting a script to a great number of places at the same time or sending it selectively to a few individuals. The specific strategy depends on the needs of the marketplace at the time. You should determine which producers and production companies are particularly interested in the type of project you have developed.

Options, contacts, and pay scales

If a producer is interested in a project he or she will propose a *deal, i.e.*, the basic terms for a contract. If you have no agent, now is the time to get one. *Any* agent will gladly close the deal for the standard 10% commission. An attorney would be equally effective, or if you have an appropriate background, you might want to close the deal yourself. The need for counsel depends on the complexity of the proposed deal, and the counter-proposals you wish to present.

On the basis of your discussions, a *Deal Memo* is drawn up which outlines the basic points of agreement—who owns what, for how long, for how much, with what credits, royalties, rights, and so on. The deal memo is binding, although certain points may be modified if both parties initial it. The *Contract* is based on the terms of the deal memo and is the formal legal document. If you're dealing with a producer who is a signatory to the Writers Guild (most established producers are), the contract will adhere to the terms of the Minimum Basic Agreement (M.B.A.) negotiated by the Writers Guild of America.

A producer can either option your work, purchase it outright, or assign you to write new material. If the property is *optioned,* the producer pays for the right to shop it around (which means the project can be submitted by the producer to a third party, e.g., the network). During the option period, you can't submit the project to anyone else. Typically, option money is relatively small; perhaps $1,500 or $2,500 for a six-month period. But the writer will be paid an additional sum of money if the producer elicits interest and moves the project forward. If the producer fails to exercise the option (*i.e.,* if the option expires), the rights revert back to the writer.

A *Step Deal* is the most common form of agreement between producers and free-lance writers. It sets forth fees and commitments for story and teleplay in several phases. The first step is at the *story* stage. When the writer turns in a treatment, the producer pays for it—at least 30% of the total agreed upon compensation—but the producer does not have to assign that writer to do the script. If the writer *is* retained, the producer exercises the *first draft* option. When that draft of the script is turned in, the writer receives a minimum of 40% of the total agreed upon compensation. Now the producer has the final option—putting the writer to work on the *final draft*. Once that script is received, the writer is entitled to the balance of payment. The *Step Deal* is a form of protection for the producer who can respond to the quality of content, the inviolability of delivery dates, and the acceptability of the project to the networks. It also guarantees the writer that his or her work will be paid for, whether there is a cut-off or a go-ahead on the project.

How to get an agent

A good agent is one with a respectable track record, a prestigious list of clients, and a reputation for fairness in the industry. There is no magical list of good agents, although the Writers Guild does publish a lists of agents who are franchised by the Guild. (Send $1.00 to Writers Guild West, *Attn: Agency List,* 8955 Beverly Blvd., Los Angeles, CA 90048.) Names and addresses of literary and dramatic agents appear in *Literary Market Place* (Bowker), available in most libraries. A list of

421

agents can also be obtained by sending a stamped, self-addressed envelope to Society of Authors' Representatives, 39½ Washington Square South, New York, NY 10012.

If you have no agent representing you, it's difficult to get projects considered by major producers. One of the best ways is to submit your work to an agent who already represents a friend, a professor, a long-lost uncle in the industry. If you are recommended by someone known to the agency, it makes you less of an unknown commodity. If you have no contact, make a list of possible agents for your project, and prioritize them in your submission status file. You might send the project to one top agency for consideration, or to a select number of agencies at the same time.

A brief cover letter might introduce you as a free lancer looking for representation on a specific project. If you don't get a response within six to eight weeks, you can follow up with a phone call or letter, and submit the project to the next agent on your list. Don't be discouraged if you get no response at first; just keep the project active in the field. If the script or presentation is good enough, you might eventually wind up with some positive and encouraging response from the agency.

If an agent is interested in your work, he or she will ask to represent it in the marketplace. If the work sells, the agent is entitled to 10% commission for closing the deal. If the work elicits interest but no sale, you have at least widened your contacts considerably for the next project.

The larger agencies offer an umbrella of power and prestige, but that elusive status is seriously undermined by the sheer size of the agency itself. Many clients inevitably feel lost in an overcrowded stable, and newcomers can hardly break into that race. In contrast, a smaller literary agency provides more personalized service, and is more open to the work of new talent. If you're going to seek representation, the smaller agency is the likely place to go. But don't be fooled by the label "small." Many of these agencies are exceptionally strong and have deliberately limited their client roster to the cream of the crop. In fact, many smaller agents have defected from executive positions at the major agencies. So you'll have to convince them you're the greatest writer since Shakespeare came on the scene—and that your works are even more salable.

How do you prove that you have the talent to be a star talent? It's all in the writing. If your projects look professional, creative, and stylistically effective, you're on the right track. Indeed, you can call yourself a writer. If the artistic content is also marketable and you back it up with determination and know-how, you might just become a *selling* writer.

And that is the "bottom line" for success in the television industry.

Networks, Studios and Production Companies

(Note: New submissions should be addressed to the Head of Program Development.)

NETWORKS

ABC-TV
4151 Prospect Ave.
Los Angeles, CA 90027
or, 1330 Ave. of the Americas
New York, NY 10019

CBS-TV
7800 Beverly Blvd.
Los Angeles, CA 90036
or, 51 West 52nd St.
New York, NY 10019

NBC-TV
3000 W. Alameda
Burbank, CA 91523
or, 30 Rockefeller Plaza
New York, NY 10020

MAJOR STUDIOS

Columbia Pictures-TV
3000 Colgems Sq.
Burbank, CA 91505

MGM-TV
10202 W. Washington Blvd.
Culver City, CA 90230

Paramount Pictures-TV
5555 Melrose Ave.
Los Angeles, CA 90038

20th Century Fox-TV
10201 W. Pico Blvd.
Los Angeles, CA 90064

Universal Studios-TV
100 Universal City Plaza
Universal City, CA 91608

Warner Bros.-TV
4000 Warner Blvd.
Burbank, CA 91505

SELECTED INDEPENDENT
PRODUCTION COMPANIES

Embassy Television Corp.
100 Universal City Pl.
Universal City, CA 91608

Lorimar Productions
3970 Overland Ave.
Culver City, CA 90230

M.T.M. Enterprises
4024 Radford Ave.
Studio City, CA 91604

Aaron Spelling Productions
1041 N. Formosa
Los Angeles, CA 90046

423

82

THE S-N-A-P-P-E-R TEST FOR PLAYWRIGHTS

By Lavonne Mueller

WHENEVER I finish a play, I check to see that I have applied to it every point from what I call the "S-N-A-P-P-E-R Formula." Here is my "Snapper" checklist.

Secret

Everyone loves to hear a secret. Have the main characters in your play tell something about themselves that is revealing and intimate.

In my play *The Only Woman General,* Olive Wiggins tells us that when she was in combat, she couldn't tell the winning from the losing; all battles seemed the same.

The secret Anne reveals (but only to her diary) in *The Diary of Anne Frank* is the physical change in her body that turns her into a woman. Willy Loman, in Arthur Miller's *Death of a Salesman,* tells Ben about his life insurance policy and also what his funeral will be like:

They'll come from Maine, Massachusetts, Vermont, New Hampshire! All the old timers with strange license plates.

In Tennessee Williams' *The Glass Menagerie,* Laura tells the Gentleman Caller her secret humiliation when she was going to school with a brace on her leg:

My seat was in the back row. I had to go clumping all the way up the aisle with everyone watching.

How would *Death of a Salesman* change, for example, if Willy's secret was that he wanted to be an artist? How would *The Glass Menagerie* change if the secret Laura confides to the Gentleman Caller was that she had successfully hid from the world the brace on her leg?

Names

Give your characters interesting names. Names can define a
character. They can also function ironically and humorously. A cowboy
in my play *Little Victories* is called Double Ugly because he's been in a
fight that cut his face in two places. In *The Only Woman General,* the
woman general is ironically named Olive—olive for peace.

Big Daddy in Tennessee Williams's *Cat on a Hot Tin Roof* is the head
of a wealthy household, and not only does he command obedience and
servitude, but the humorous overtones of his name add an ironic dimension. Big Daddy's sons are Gooper and Brick—the first is simpering, the
second headstrong.

How would *Cat on a Hot Tin Roof* change if Tennessee Williams had
named Big Daddy Herbert or Leslie or reversed the names of his sons?

If you wrote a one-act play about a dermatologist, would you want to
call him Sam Lumpkin?

Action

Every play must have action. Drama is like a boxing match. Two
characters go at each other until one is shoved up against the wall. Or
knocked out. The image of a boxing match is actually used by author
Shirley Lauro in her excellent play, *Open Admissions.* Ms. Lauro states:
"The audience's experience from the start should be as if they had
suddenly tuned in on the critical round of a boxing match."

In *Little Victories,* Joan wishes to be a successful general. She has to
convince her adjutants that she is competent. She is constantly being
pressured by them. In desperation, she uses many tricks of common
sense that she learned as a farm girl. Her main goal is always a source of
action: Joan pulls soldiers out of mudholes with the same skill she used
on her cows. Because she can't read, she uses the lines in the palm of
her hand as a map. She struggles to win over her troops. Action.

Make sure your main character wants something, and make sure
somebody is keeping him/her from getting it. In *Cat on a Hot Tin Roof,*
Big Daddy wants a son from Brick. Brick is obstinate. They struggle.
Action!

Props

Props can be very effective. They are visual messages to the audience, and they are an extension of the character's personality. Try to

425

think of props that are genuinely important to the development of your play. You don't want to use a prop that is gratuitous.

In my play *Breaking the Prairie Wolf Code,* Helen, a pioneer woman, takes a tea set with her on the westward journey. At every wagon stop, she has tea to remind herself of a former gentility. As the trip progresses, parts of the tea set are broken and lost. I use this prop to show graphically the hardships of the journey.

Hamlet speaks to the skull of Yorick. The Moor in *Othello* uses a handkerchief as proof of his suspicions of Desdemona's infidelity. In *The Diary of Anne Frank,* Anne tapes pictures of movie stars on the wall of her small hiding space. In Eugene O'Neill's *Long Day's Journey into Night,* Mary's faded wedding dress is her one tangible connection to the past.

It's hard to imagine these plays without their classic props. What if Hamlet delivered his monologue to a rock instead of Yorick's skull? What if Anne Frank had pictures of food instead of movie stars on her wall?

Plot

Plot is as important to a dramatist as it is to a novelist. The attention of the audience is held by a clear, strong story line. Shakespeare is a master of storytelling. We want to know, for example, what will happen to Romeo and Juliet. What will happen to Lear after he's turned over his power to his children?

The plot is closely related to what we call "the dramatic question." This question is something an audience wants answered. In *Hamlet,* the dramatic question is: Will Hamlet avenge his father? The answer to that dramatic question keeps each person interested enough to come back after the intermissions.

The plot/dramatic question does not have to be complex. In *Little Victories,* the question is simply: How will Joan win the battle? In the musical *A Chorus Line,* the plot/dramatic question is simply: Who will get chosen for the chorus line?

If you think of a question to ask on stage, it becomes easier to structure a plot around it. In *Breaking the Prairie Wolf Code,* my question is simply: Will the wagon train get to California? After I came up with the question, I began to imagine all the things that could prevent this journey and make it more difficult. I invented obstacles and characters to "hang" on the story line of my dramatic question.

Ending

Give your characters a well-planned exit. They've come to the end of their tale, and it's very effective if they can leave the stage with some relevant words or actions.

Again, in *Little Victories,* the drama ends when Joan tells Susan that she must reach into the future and find somebody who can help her. Joan takes Susan's hand and points it to the audience, saying: "Take the dark."

In *Cat on a Hot Tin Roof,* Maggie says to Brick at the end of the play: "Oh, you weak, beautiful people who give up so easily. You need somebody to hand your life back to you like something gold."

Anne's father in *The Diary of Anne Frank* reads a last line from her diary entry: "In spite of everything I still believe that people are really good at heart."

How would *Cat on a Hot Tin Roof* change if the ending line were Brick's—perhaps saying that he didn't know if he had the strength to go on?

How would *The Diary of Anne Frank* change if her last diary entry were that people are basically corrupt?

Relatives

Let the characters tell us something about their relatives or background. It helps us to understand how they came to be the people they are.

Esther Bibbs, an ex-slave on the wagon train in *Breaking the Prairie Wolf Code,* tells us:

I used to make this pea soup for the Fenchler family. They were my marsters in Georgia. My folks was took to the South from Africa and sold into the Fenchler family, ya know. Course the North whupped the South and they made the Constitution signed. That's why I'm free—here in the west.

In *Death of a Salesman,* Willy tells us that his father lived for many years in Alaska and was an adventurous man. Willy adds: "We've got quite a little streak of self-reliance in our family."

Mary, in *Long Day's Journey into Night,* tells us that she was in a convent school for girls when she was young:

At the Convent I had so many friends. Girls whose families lived in lovely homes.

How would *Death of a Salesman* change if Willy's father had been a college professor? How would *Long Day's Journey into Night* change if Mary had gone to a public school?

Now you know the formula. It works for me, and it can work for you. Don't mail out your script until you give it the S-N-A-P-P-E-R test. And after you do so and send it off, begin immediately to think of your next play. Don't wait for the mail. Let your mind work on new ideas. The following test may help get your imagination rolling again. It is not meant to be an indicator of your creativity, but only a vector to point the way to your creative potential.

How's Your I. Q. (Imagination Quotient)?

(Give yourself 5 points for each YES answer. Give yourself 2 points for each SOMETIMES answer.)

1. When I see a person for the first time, I always observe the color of his eyes and hair.
YES   SOMETIMES   NO

2. I like to think about a person's name and how it is appropriate or not appropriate for that person.
YES   SOMETIMES   NO

3. I would definitely laugh (to myself) if I became acquainted with a Japanese man named John Smith.
YES   SOMETIMES   NO

4. When I look at a cloud in the sky, I often see more than just a cloud.
YES   SOMETIMES   NO

5. When I'm observing the behavior of animals, I am often reminded of certain human characteristics.
YES   SOMETIMES   NO

428

6. If I came across an empty food tray in a cafeteria, I would find it fun to *guess* by the leftovers what kind of person belonged to that tray.
YES   SOMETIMES   NO

7. If a person sits across from me on a bus or train or airplane for any length of time, I like to guess the occupation of that person by his appearance.
YES   SOMETIMES   NO

8. I find it fun to sit in an outdoor restaurant or park bench for long periods of time just to peoplewatch.
YES   SOMETIMES   NO

9. When I go into a person's house, I like to observe how that person added his own personality to the house by means of furniture, art objects, and color scheme.
YES   SOMETIMES   NO

10. If I see a person reading a particular book, I imagine what kind of person he is by the book he is reading.
YES   SOMETIMES   NO

11. If I observe a person carrying a large, wrapped box, I often imagine quite a few things that could be inside that box.
YES   SOMETIMES   NO

12. When someone I don't know is on the phone, I try to imagine what that person is like from the tone of his voice.
YES   SOMETIMES   NO

13. When I am at a large function such as a ball game, concert, or picnic, I often like to strike up a conversation with someone next to me because I find it interesting to know what they are thinking or what they might say to me.
YES   SOMETIMES   NO

14. If I see a movie I really like, I like to imagine what happens to the main character after the movie ends.
YES   SOMETIMES   NO

15. I always see variety in a rainy day. Rainy days are not all alike.
YES   SOMETIMES   NO

16. If I am outside and hear a jet going over, I like to imagine what the inside of the jet looks like and the people on it and what they might be doing at that instant.
YES   SOMETIMES   NO

17. I like to look at other people's picture albums and piece together their lives from the various photos.
YES   SOMETIMES   NO

18. I like to try strange and exotic foods just for the experience.
YES   SOMETIMES   NO

19. Whenever I go through a department store or grocery store, I have a strong desire to "touch" things so that I can feel as well as see objects.
YES   SOMETIMES   NO

20. An interesting smell such as that of perfume or food or flowers can suddenly bring back a memory to me.
YES   SOMETIMES   NO

WHAT IS YOUR IMAGINATION SCORE?

100–80 = Excellent
 79–60 = Very Good
 59–40 = Average
Below 40 = You need to be more observant about ways to improve your imagination.

83

CONFLICT: THE HEARTBEAT
OF A PLAY

By D. R. Andersen

EVERY PLAYWRIGHT is a Dr. Frankenstein trying to breathe life into a page for the stage. In a good play, the heartbeat must be thundering. And the heartbeat of a play is conflict.

Simply put, conflict exists when a character wants something and can't get it. Conflict may sometimes be internal—as when a character struggles to choose between or among opposing desires. For example, Alma in Tennessee Williams's *Summer and Smoke* longs to yield to her sexual yearnings but is prevented by the repressed and conventional side of her nature.

Conflict in drama may also be external—as when a character struggles against another *character* (Oscar and Felix in Neil Simon's *The Odd Couple*); against *society* (Nora in Ibsen's *A Doll's House*); against *nature* (the mountain climbers in Patrick Meyers' *K2*); or against *fate* (Sophocles' *Oedipus*).

In most plays, the conflict is a combination of internal and external struggles. In fact, internal conflict is often externalized for dramatic impact. In Philip Barry's *Holiday,* for instance, the hero's inner dilemma is outwardly expressed in his attraction to two sisters—one who represents the safe but boring world of convention, and the other who is a symbol of the uncertain but exciting life of adventure.

Granted that a conflict may be internal or external; that a character may be in conflict with another character, society, nature or fate; and that most plays are a combination of internal and external conflict, many plays that have these basic elements of conflict do not have a thundering heartbeat. Why? These plays lack one, some, or all of the five magic ingredients of rousing, attention-grabbing-and-holding conflict.

The five magic ingredients

I. *Never let your audience forget what your protagonist wants.*

You can achieve this in a number of ways. Often the protagonist or another character states and periodically restates in dialogue what is at stake. Or in some plays, he explains what he wants directly to the audience in the form of a monologue. As you read or watch plays you admire, take note of the obvious and ingenious techniques playwrights use to tell the reader or audience what the characters' goals are.

Sometimes the method used to keep your audience alerted to your protagonist's goal/concern/need is a direct reflection of the protagonist's personality. In the following three short passages from my play *Graduation Day,*[1] a mother and father with very traditional values have a conversation while waiting to meet their rebellious daughter, who has told them she has a big surprise. Notice how the protagonist—Mrs. Whittaker—nervously and comically manipulates the conversation, reminding her husband and the audience of her concern for her daughter Jane:

MRS. WHITTAKER
(Knocking on the door)
Jane. Jane. It's Mom and Dad.
(Pause)
No answer. What should we do, Tom?
MR. WHITTAKER
Let's go in.
MRS. WHITTAKER
Suppose we find Jane in a compromising situation?
MR. WHITTAKER
Nobody at Smith College has ever been found in a compromising situation.

*   *   *

MRS. WHITTAKER
Tom, you know, this was my freshman room.
MR. WHITTAKER
Of course, I know.
MRS. WHITTAKER
And Jane's. It was Jane's freshman room too, Tom. Remember?

*   *   *

MR. WHITTAKER
Mary, you get in the craziest moods at these reunions. I may never bring you back again.

---

1. First produced by Playwrights Horizons in New York, starring Polly Holliday.

432

MRS. WHITTAKER
Do you know why you fell in love with me, Tom?

MR. WHITTAKER
I fell in love with you the minute I saw you eat pancakes.

MRS. WHITTAKER
That's a sound basis for a relationship. Tom, where do you suppose Jane is? And more frightening, what do you suppose she wants to tell us? She said just enough on the phone to suggest that she's going to be bringing a boy here for us to meet.

MR. WHITTAKER
A man, Mary, a man.

MRS. WHITTAKER
Oh, God. I never even considered that possibility. Suppose Jane brings a fiancé—our age—like Pia Zadora did.

MR. WHITTAKER
Don't you want Jane to live her own life?

MRS. WHITTAKER
No. Especially not her own life. Practically anyone else's. But not her own.

MR. WHITTAKER
What *do* you want for Jane?

MRS. WHITTAKER
I don't see why Jane can't fall in love with a plain Harvard Business School student, let's say. Someone who'll be steady and dependable.

And so it goes. The protagonist discusses a number of topics, but she inevitably leads the conversation back to her overriding concern. Mrs. Whittaker's desire to see her daughter do the right thing and marry wisely is always uppermost in the mind and conversation of the character.

In this one act, a comic effect is achieved by having Mrs. Whittaker insistently remind the audience what she wants. Once you have clearly established what a character wants, you can then write powerful and often hilarious scenes in which the audience, already knowing the character's point of view, is able to anticipate his reaction.

II. *Show your protagonist struggling to achieve what he wants.*

This principle is, of course, the basic writing advice to *show,* not tell, and it was a major concern for me when I was writing *The House Where I Was Born.*[2]

The plot: A young man, Leo, has returned from the Vietnam War, a psychosomatic mute because of the atrocities he witnessed. He comes back to a crumbling old house in a decaying suburb, a home populated

---

2. First produced by Playwrights Horizons in New York.

433

by a callous stepfather; a mother who survives on aphorisms and by bending reality to diminish her despair; a half-crazy aunt; and a grandfather who refuses to buckle under to the pressures from his family to sell the home.

I set out to dramatize Leo's painful battle to free himself of memories of the war and to begin a new life. However, each time I worked on the scene in the play when Leo first comes home, his dialogue seemed to trivialize his emotions.

Then it occurred to me that Leo should not speak at all during the first act; that his inability to speak would *show* an audience his suffering and pain far better than his words could.

At the end of the third act, when Leo regains some hope, some strength to go on, every speech I wrote for him also rang false. The problem, I eventually realized, was that as playwright, I was *telling* the audience that a change had taken place, instead of *showing* the change as it took place.

In the final draft, I solved this dramatic problem by having Leo, who had loved music all his life, sit down at the piano and begin playing and singing Christmas carols while his surprised and relieved family joined in.

First silence, then singing, served my play better than mere telling.

III. *Create honest, understandable, and striking obstacles against which your protagonist must struggle.*

Many plays fail because their characters' problems seem too easily solved. I wrestled with this issue when I was writing *Oh Promise Me!*[3] a play that takes place in a private boarding house for the elderly. The play's original title was *Mr. Farner Wants a Double Bed.* The plot involved the attempt of an elderly man and woman—an unmarried couple—to share a double bed in a rooming house run by a repressed and oppressive owner. I wanted to explore contemporary attitudes toward the elderly, particularly as they concerned sexuality.

The more I played with the idea, the more I repeatedly heard an inner voice saying, "Chances are the couple could find some place to live where nobody cared if they were married or not." This voice—like the

---

3. Winner of the Jane Chambers Memorial Playwriting Award.

audience watching a play without an honest, understandable, convincing obstacle for the protagonist—kept saying, "So what?"

The writer's response: "Suppose, instead of a man and a woman, the couple is two men." Here was a real obstacle: Two elderly, gay men, growing feeble, want to sleep together in a double bed under the roof of an unsympathetic and unyielding landlord.

Suddenly, the play was off and running.

IV. *In the final scene or scenes, make sure your protagonist achieves what he wants; comes to understand that there is something* else *he wants; or accepts (defiantly, humbly, etc.) that he cannot have what he wants.*

If we spend time in the theater watching a character battle for something, we want to know the outcome—whatever it may be.

In my psychological thriller *Trick or Treat,*[4] Kate, a writer in her forties, has been badly burned in a love affair and is unable to decide whether to accept or reject a new relationship. She is involved at present with Toby, a younger man, but—as the following dialogue reveals—she insists on keeping him at a cool distance.

KATE
That does it, Toby. We're getting out of this place.
TOBY
Okay. Tomorrow we'll check into the local Howard Johnson's.
KATE
I want to go home—to New York—to my own apartment.
TOBY
Okay. Okay. If you insist. Besides, Howard Johnson's is not to be entered into lightly.
KATE
Huh?
TOBY
It's an old college rule. You'd never shell out for a room at Howard Johnson's—unless you were *very* serious about the girl.
KATE
I'll remember that. The day I agree to check into a Howard Johnson's—you'll know I've made a serious commitment to our relationship.

In the course of the play, Kate faces a number of trials—including a threat to her life—as she tries to expose the fraudulent leader of a

___
4. First produced by the Main Street Theater, New York, New York.

435

religious cult. Through these trials—with Toby by her side—Kate comes to realize that she's ready to forget the past and give herself over to a new relationship. This critical decision is humorously expressed in the last seconds of the play:

KATE

Do you love me, Toby?

TOBY

Yes, I do. I found that out tonight . . . when I thought I might be losing you forever. Do you love me?

KATE

Yes. And I can prove it.

TOBY

How?

KATE

Take me to Howard Johnson's—please! Take me to Howard Johnson's!

The curtain falls and the audience knows that the heroine has made an unequivocal decision.

V. *Make sure that the audience ultimately sympathizes with the protagonist's yearning to achieve his goal, however outlandish his behavior.*

This may be the most important of the five magic ingredients of conflict. It may also be the most elusive. To oversimplify, in a good play, the protagonist must be very likable and/or have a goal that is universal.

In the plays I've had produced, one character seems to win the sympathy of the audience hands down. In my romantic comedy *Funny Valentines*,[5] Andy Robbins, a writer of children's books, is that character. Andy is sloppy, disorganized, and easily distracted, and—this is his likable trait—he's painfully aware of his shortcomings and admits them openly. Here's Andy speaking for himself:

ANDY

Judging by my appearance, you might take me to be a complete physical and emotional wreck. Well, I can't deny it. And it's gotten worse—much worse—since Ellen left. You know that's true.

---

5. Published by Samuel French; winner of the Cummings/Taylor Playwriting Award; produced in Canada under the title *Drôles de Valentins*.

436

Andy is willing to admit his failings to old friends and strangers alike. Here he's talking to an attractive young woman he's just met.

ANDY

You don't have to be consoling just because I haven't finished a book lately. I won't burst into tears or create a scene. No. I lied. I might burst into tears—I'm warning you.

ZAN

I didn't mean to imply . . . (*She laughs.*)

ANDY

Why are you laughing?

ZAN

You stapled your shirt.

ANDY

What's so odd about that? Millions of derelicts do it every day.

ZAN

And your glasses are wired together with a pipe cleaner.

ANDY

I didn't think twine would be as attractive.

In addition to liking Andy, audiences seem to sympathize with his goal of wanting to grow up and get back together with his collaborator and ex-wife, Ellen.

Whether you're wondering where to find an idea for a one-act play or beginning to refine the rough draft of a new full-length work or starting rehearsals of one of your plays, take your cue from the five magic ingredients of conflict. Whatever your experience as a playwright and whatever your current project, understanding the nature of dramatic conflict and how to achieve it will prove invaluable at every point in the writing and staging process.

* * *

Five exercises for creating dramatic conflict

Try these exercises to develop your skill in handling conflict.

1. Choose five plays you like. Summarize each in one sentence, stating what the protagonist wants. For example, Hamlet wants to avenge his father's murder.
2. Write one page of dialogue in which character A asks character B to do something that character B doesn't want to do. Have character A

437

make a request in three different ways, each showing a different emotion—guilt, enthusiasm, humility, anger.

3. Write a speech in which a character talks to another character and conveys what he wants without explicitly stating his goal.
4. Choose a famous play you enjoy. Rewrite the last page or two so that the outcome of the conflict for the protagonist is entirely different from the original.
5. Flip through today's newspaper until you find a story about a person—famous or unknown—who interests you. Then summarize the story in one sentence, stating what the person wants. For example: X wants to save an endangered species of bird. Next list the obstacles the person is facing in trying to get what he wants:
   • A developer wants to build a shopping mall where the remaining members of the endangered species live.
   • Pollution from a nearby factory is threatening the birds' food supply.

Finally, write several short scenes in which X (the protagonist) confronts the people (the antagonists) who represent the cause of each obstacle. (In this example, the antagonist would be the developer or the owner of the factory.) Decide which of the scenes you've written is the most dramatically satisfying. Identify the reasons you think it is the best scene.

84

CREATING TELEVISION STORIES AND CHARACTERS

By Stewart Bronfeld

CREATING stories and the characters in them is what script writing is really all about. The rest — the technology, the business, the timing and the luck—are also found in a thousand other activities of life. But when, in the matrix of a blank page, a story starts to emerge which never before existed, and characters are born and develop who never lived before that moment, something very special is happening. It is part craft, part art and (there's no other word) part magic.

The magic of the creative process remains basically mysterious, like any other kind of birth. The art is a product of the artist's personality and thus differs with each person. But the craft is based on experience, common sense and professional techniques and *can* be learned and practiced.

Principles and rules and fashions of playcraft change but one bedrock truth remains constant: *the basis of effective drama is conflict.* Learn this and you learn a lot. Sophocles knew it. Shakespeare knew it. And the writer of the script for that popular TV series you saw last Tuesday knew it. The conflict of man against man, man against woman, man against nature, man against himself—the clang of two opposing forces coming against each other makes for drama. The conflict may be Big and Important—the numberless masses tearing down the mighty regime of the Czar in *Dr. Zhivago*. Or it may be small and wistful—a fat, homely butcher and a plain neighborhood girl making a clumsy grab at a chance for love in *Marty*.

Consider one of the most successful motion pictures of all time, *Gone With the Wind*. Along with her skill for recreating a colorful time and place and sheer storytelling art, Margaret Mitchell built her story with such effective dramatic conflicts that both the book and the movie are still very much alive (and making money) today. While the Civil

War itself was not directly one of the conflicts (for conflict implies two opposing forces and the North almost never appears in her work), it served as a suitable backdrop for the interplays of strong dramatic conflicts with which the author fashioned her story and characters:

The Old South versus the emerging reality of a new and different world.

Rhett Butler, who could have any woman he wanted—*except* the one he wanted most.

Scarlett O'Hara, beautiful enough to attract any man *she* wanted—except the one she wanted most.

Ashley Wilkes, torn between wanting Scarlett and needing Melanie.

These characters, with their frustrations and longings, could have become no more than soap opera figures— just as *Macbeth* could have become no more than a murder melodrama. The difference, in both cases, was that the authors had the gift of imparting life to their characters and meaning to their conflicts. Thus audiences *cared;* they still do.

Examine any good story and you will discover the conflict that motivates the main character(s) and moves the plot along. One of Somerset Maugham's most enduring stories is *Of Human Bondage,* whose very title highlights the conflict of the young surgeon fighting against his imprisoning love for a worthless girl. But just as enduring, if not as deep, are Laura Lee Hope's children's books about the Bobbsey Twins, each of which gets the kids into some conflict which, happily, is resolved in the final pages.

Sometimes if you look carefully you find the same basic conflict in widely different stories. In *Tom Sawyer,* it is wanting to be good to a loved one (Aunt Polly) versus the pull of adventure with wilder companions. The same conflict (in a dog instead of a boy) is the basis for the drama in *The Call of the Wild.* And, in essence, nearly the same conflict is at the heart of the story of the opera *Carmen.*

The knowledge that conflict makes for drama is a nuts-and-bolts tool which writers can use—especially when they sit at their writing desk caught up in a conflict of their own, namely, "I've got a rough idea of a plot but I don't know what to do with it." First, *think of the plot in terms of the conflict or conflicts involved.* If you cannot identify any, you probably do not have the basis for a very strong story idea. This in itself is an accomplishment, for it can save hours of work, reams of paper and pangs of disappointment later.

What contributes drama to the plot is not the conflict itself, but rather what the character does and how he or she does it in response to that conflict. People are naturally more interested in people than they are in circumstances. What engages their attention is not so much the adventure as the adventurer, not the danger so much as how the people react to what is menacing them, not the surprise ending, but how the characters in the story are affected by, and respond to, the surprise.

This simple but fundamental fact that people are primarily interested in people is the basis for another important tool of scriptcraft: *characterization,* the development in a character of specific personality traits. Examine most successful movies and television series and you will find they often have one thing in common: a well-drawn central character (or characters) whose personality traits are clearly defined. These traits may be good ones or bad ones, but they are distinctive. Early in a movie, over the weeks in a TV series, these characteristics become familiar to the viewer. They add a dimension of depth and reality to the character. Another (and perhaps paramount) reason for the enduring success of *Gone With the Wind* is the author's skillful use of characterization; Rhett Butler and Scarlett O'Hara were so vividly conceived and depicted that millions of readers and viewers have found it impossible to believe they are not real people.

On television, the mortality rate of new programs is appalling. Not many new shows survive a season's journey through the ratings mine field. Half-hour comedies are especially popular with viewers, and so smoke pours out the stacks of the Hollywood fun factories day and night as they churn out an endless assembly line of new shows, in which "wacky" characters do "wacky" things—and get "wacky" ratings and disappear. Sometimes, before they expire, they are desperately switched from one time slot to another, scrambling around the network's program schedule like escaped hamsters.

Why do so few of them take root and prosper? The answer, I think, is that they are sitcoms, or situation comedies—which means their emphasis is on ever-zanier "situations," with the people in them seldom developed beyond the cartoon character stage. But there *are* half-hour comedies that become popular successes with longtime runs and high ratings. While they also may be called sitcoms in the trade, these shows might be more accurately called "charcoms," for their humor

441

comes not from artificially contrived "situations," but from artfully created characterization.

Among them was one of the most successful television series of all time, *The Mary Tyler Moore Show,* which ended only because the star grew tired of the weekly grind. The program immediately became a top success on the rerun circuit and established something of a record for the price paid for syndication rights. The secret of the show's success was clearly the effective characterization established by the original creators and skillfully followed by all the subsequent script writers. The funny situations almost always resulted from, or were related to, the regular cast's character traits, which were familiar to every viewer. Proof of the power of good characterization is the fact that no less than three of the show's characters were spun off into successful series of their own: Rhoda, Phyllis and Lou Grant.

What makes this kind of "charcom" so successful is also what makes many dramatic series attain great popularity while their competition regularly arrives and departs. This includes action-adventure shows. *Kojak,* for example, was a tremendous hit, and still is, in its syndication afterlife. But *Kojak* was never really about cops-and-robbers and drug busts; it was primarily about Lieutenant Theo Kojak.

Therefore, whether you are writing a script for a television series, a single original teleplay or a movie, a prime factor to consider is the importance of character creation. Even when you feel your plot is the paramount consideration in a particular script, your characters should never be mere puppets manipulated to suit it. It does not always take a full-scale portrait to make a character come alive; sometimes a few well drawn strokes can do it.

The best and strongest plots, however, are those that evolve naturally, even inevitably, out of the characterization. These stories have more impact, because they are more believable. There is good reason for this. In the lives of most of us, very few important things happen for totally external reasons; what happens to us is often the result of what we do—and what we do is often the result of what we are. That is true of you and me and your potential viewers. If it is also true of your characters in what you make happen to them, they will be perceived not as concoctions, but as living characters with a dimension of depth and reality. Thus your story will not merely gain the attention of the audience; it will make some impact upon them. There's a difference; it means they will *care* about what they are watching. And, as producers, directors and story editors well know, when an audience feels an involvement, it shows in the ratings and at the box office.

Let us see an example of plot developing out of characterization. Jane is a timid young woman, terrified of asserting herself, due in large part to her overbearing mother. She is constantly driven to gain her mother's approval, seldom succeeding. A situation arises at work wherein problems are causing the company's management to consider going out of business. Jane, who has a keen and analytic mind, has diagnosed the problems and feels she has a solution that may save the company. The frantic meetings of the managers behind closed doors are getting louder each day.

Conflict: Jane's desire to offer her solution, thus possibly becoming a heroine, getting her reward and making her mother proud of her—versus her inability to push herself into the councils of upper management and possibly be rebuffed and humiliated. It's not *Hamlet,* but it is the basis for an interesting human drama with which the audience can identify.

The point is that the characterization I created for Jane does not function merely as a kind of outer garment she wears as she makes her way through the plot; the plot evolves directly out of her characterization. If I changed the kind of person Jane is, my plot would no longer work. The two—characterization and plot—are welded together.

Some writers may have an intuitive ability to create a fully defined character as they go along; however, it cannot hurt (and will always help) to write a detailed sketch or profile of any major character first. Creatively, the more you "know" about a character the more you contribute to his or her reality in the script. Practically, facets of the character's personality will often strongly suggest plot ideas. (When one of my characters is especially well defined, I occasionally become aware that he or she is really writing the scene, while I follow along at the typewriter, interested and even curious to find out what will happen next.)

However, writers do vary in both their skill and their inclination for characterization. For some writers, formulating a plot is paramount, and the people caught up in the action are merely vehicles to advance the story line. Obviously, if a plot is compelling enough, viewers will

443

be interested in what is happening even though they are not particularly interested in those to whom it happens. Many movies and television series attest to this. While I believe a more memorable story will evolve out of characterization, I would much rather see a script with an intriguing plot moving at a well-orchestrated pace even though with cardboard characters, than one with vividly sketched characters whose personalities are fascinating, but *nothing really happens.*

There is a test the script writer should apply to his or her work as it proceeds to be sure that there is a consistent plausibility to the characters and the plot. The test is *motivation.* Motivation makes the difference between actions seeming real or staged. People are not robots; they generally do what they do for a reason. Sensible people act from sensible reasons and fools act from foolish reasons. The writer looks at each action of the main characters and asks, "Would this particular person do this, in this particular circumstance?"

The movies of the thirties and forties, mostly ground out by writers on a weekly salary, were often written as fast as they were typed, and frequently had no time to bother with motivation. Now they live on mainly at 2:30 A.M. on television and there is a reliable way to identify them in the TV listings: the word *decides.* "An heiress decides to run off with her gardener . . ." "A millionaire decides to take a slum kid into his household . . ." Whenever you see the word *decides* in a movie listing, you know that the only motivation involved is that it was Thursday and the script was due in the producer's office by Friday. When you look over your script after a cooling-off period, try to be objective enough to note whether your character "decides" to do something just because, solely for plot purposes, you want him to. If he does, if proper motivation is lacking, it is a sign that the scene (or possibly a larger segment of the script) requires rethinking and rewriting.

There is another element in any kind of story, one not so susceptible to definite guidelines. I refer to *theme.* Writers generally are writers because they have an inclination (or perhaps an impulse) to communicate. But the reason any individual writes any particular story must vary, not only with each writer but with each story he or she writes. We all have different interests, different outlooks on life and different matters we consider important; if these motivate us when we sit down to do our communicating—our writing—our work will reflect a theme.

444

In a story, plot is what happens. Theme is the larger framework of meaning in which it happens. Larger stories have larger themes, and lesser stories have lesser themes. In the powerfully written and expansively produced *The Godfather,* the theme was that evil is self-consuming. In a program I saw last night in a half-hour comedy series, the theme was the importance of good friends later in life.

Do not confuse a theme with a "message." The writer should not be trying to make a commentary on his or her theme, only to *air* it. Reflection on the meaning should rest with the viewer.

Do all writers have themes for their stories? The answer is, not all the time (and not always consciously). But a theme is an asset to any literary work. First, it elevates the story because there is some central meaning to it all. Then, it assures a better, more unified construction to the script, for it provides a general reference point to guide the direction of the plot and the development of the characters.

Herman Melville wrote, "To produce a mighty book, you must choose a mighty theme." You will find, however, that when it happens, it is more as though the mighty theme chose *you*.

85

PEOPLE I HAVE KNOWN

By Katherine Paterson

How do you build your characters?" It's a familiar question to those of us who write fiction and, I suspect, one of the most uncomfortable. When someone asks me about "building characters," I'm tempted to remind him that characters are people, not models you put together with an erector set. You don't "build" people, you get to know them.

All human beings are born on a certain day in a particular place and from two parents. These are all givens. When I am beginning a book, the central character is little more than an uneasy feeling in the pit of my stomach. I spend a long time trying to understand who this person is—where he or she was born, when, and from whom.

When I was trying to start *Jacob Have I Loved,* I knew the protagonist was a girl of about fourteen, who was eaten up with jealousy for a brother or sister. That was all I had to go on in the beginning. When I discovered, quite by accident, that she lived on a tiny island in the middle of the Chesapeake Bay, I was well on my way to getting to know her.

(Incidentally, anyone who has written fiction knows that such revelatory accidents are a way of life for writers. This one involved a Christmas gift book about the Chesapeake Bay which I happened to read because I was desperate for reading material on the 29th of December. Time after time, writers stumble blindly upon the very secrets that will serve to unlock the story they are currently struggling with.)

Anyhow, as I discovered, life on a Chesapeake Bay island is different from life anywhere else in America. On Tangier and Smith (the islands upon which I modeled my imaginary island of Rass), there are families that have lived on the same narrow bits of land since well before the Revolutionary War. The men of the island earn their living crabbing in the warmer months and oystering in the colder. For island people, all of life is organized about the water that surrounds them and even today cuts them off from the rest of our country. The speech of the people is unlike that of those in nearby Maryland or Virginia. Scholars think it may resemble the Elizabethan speech of colonial America. The islands were converted to Methodism in the 18th century and remain strongly religious communities. I could go on, but you can see how being born and spending her formative years on such an island would affect the growth of Louise Bradshaw. She could be molded by her adaptation to her environment or by her rebellion against it. Either way, the place is of vital significance to the person she is and will become.

When a character is born is another revealing point. You can see this in life. My husband and I were born at the height of the depression. Our older boy was born soon after Kennedy was assassinated. Our younger daughter was born the year both Martin Luther King and Robert Kennedy were killed. When I am trying to get to know a character, I always ask what was happening in the world when this person was born and what effect these events might have had on his life.

Usually, I determine the date of birth of all of my central characters, not just the protagonist. This was crucial to the story in my novel *Come Sing, Jimmy Jo*. James was born in 1973, and his mother was born in 1959. "But that means . . !" Yes, it means that Keri Su was fourteen when James was born. If I know that, I can begin to understand some of the problems that have always existed between them—why almost from birth James has looked to his grandma for mothering rather than his mother.

This leads directly to the question of parentage. When I first began writing *Jimmy Jo,* I assumed that Keri Su was James's mother, and Jerry Lee was his father. The fact that Jerry Lee was ten years older than his wife explained to some extent why he was the more responsible parent of the two. After all, he was already a grownup when the boy was born.

But the better I got to know this family, the more I realized that there was something there that they weren't telling. Gradually, I got a picture of Keri Su, a thirteen-year-old girl from the West Virginia hills. The mountain boyfriend who has made her pregnant has run away and joined the navy to escape the wrath of the girl's hard-drinking father. Now all of the father's anger is directed toward his daughter. She runs away with nowhere to run and happens into a tiny mountain town where the Johnson Family Singers are performing at one of the local churches.

447

The girl loves music, and she hangs around until the Johnsons, especially Grandma and Jerry Lee, realize the extent of her desperation and take her under their wings. She is a good-looking, spunky kid with a powerful singing voice, and Jerry Lee, with a mixture of admiration and pity and affection, marries her. James, the child that is born so soon afterwards, is a Johnson heart and soul, made so by the love of Jerry Lee and Grandma, who share with him the special love they have for one another.

What happens, then, to the rest of the family members? There is brother Earl, who was a young adolescent when Keri Su joined the family. He has always resented Jerry Lee, who is older, wiser, nicer, and, as Earl sees it, much their mother's favorite. Now his brother has married a girl Earl's own age, a girl, who under different circumstances, he might have liked to take out himself. Earl is jealous of the position Keri Su immediately achieves in the family and at the same time is attracted to her despite himself.

And what about Grandpa? He seems to take his wife for granted, but perhaps he, too, feels a wistful twinge when he sees how she dotes on Jerry Lee and on the fatherless child that their son has totally accepted as his own. Doesn't blood count for something? Grandpa wonders. Like most mountain men, he puts a lot of stock in good blood. He likes the boy and all, but it's not as if James were really his grandson.

So far nothing I've said is actually in the book. It is all in the background to the story—the life these people lived before they entered the pages of this particular book. But I have to know all of these things about the characters or run the risk that my characters will be as separate and inanimate as Barbie and Ken. If you let *living* people into a story, they will move each other. If you put in *constructed* characters, you'll have to do the moving yourself. The reader won't be fooled. He'll be able to tell which is which.

When it comes to deciding what about these people will actually be revealed on the printed page, I am guided, of course, by the story I want to tell, but also, quite particularly, by point of view. *Jacob Have I Loved* is written in the first person. The only point of view the reader is given is that of Louise, who is so jealous of her sister that she is blind to the affection that her parents, Call, the Captain, and even her sister have for her. Now I am not Louise. I can see what she cannot, and it breaks my heart to realize how much her mother loves her and to know how little Louise can understand or trust that love.

A wise reader will be aware of the narrowness of Louise's vision, but since I write principally for children and young people, I know that many of my readers will assume that Louise's badly skewed view is the correct view. I suppose I could have written the book differently to give Louise's mother and even sister Caroline a sporting chance, but then the power of Louise's jealousy would have been diminished. It would have been a different, and, I believe, weaker story.

Again, in *Come Sing, Jimmy Jo,* the story is told wholly from James's viewpoint. He's never been told about his origins, but that doesn't mean he doesn't feel the uneasiness of the other family members when the past is referred to.

Often children will ask me about the parents in my books. "Why are they so mean?" is a question I've gotten more than a few times about Jesse Aarons's parents in the book, *Bridge to Terabithia.* I use the occasion to try to help young readers understand point of view. All the parents in my stories are seen from their children's point of view, and it has been my experience that children are very seldom fair in their judgments of their parents. I hope I've sent all my questioners home to take another, more objective look not only at my book, but at their own parents, most of whom, I dare say, are like the parents in *Bridge to Terabithia,* doing the best they can under trying circumstances.

Characters are like people in another way. Some of them are very easy to get to know, others more difficult. Maime Trotter, the foster mother in *The Great Gilly Hopkins,* simply arrived one day full grown. She was so powerfully herself that the other characters in the book came to life responding to her immense loving energy. Gilly, who had spent her time before the book began cynically manipulating the people about her, had to learn how to reckon with a force greater than her own anger.

The actual appearance of one of the most important characters in *The Great Gilly Hopkins* takes up less than two pages of the text. She is Gilly's mother—the unwed flower child who gave Gilly up to foster care years before the book opens. Yet what she actually is and what Gilly dreams she is (two different things, as you might suspect) combine to help shape the troubled and troubling child, whom we first meet in the back seat of the social worker's car on the way to yet another foster home.

There is, finally, something mysterious about the life of one's characters. In my secret heart, I almost believe that one of these days I'll meet Jesse Aarons walking toward me on a downtown street. I'll recognize him at once, although he will have grown to manhood, and I'll ask him what he's been doing in the years since he built that bridge across Lark Creek.

On the second thought, I probably won't ask. I'll smile and he'll nod, but I won't pry. Years ago he let me eavesdrop on his soul, but that time is past. He is entitled to his privacy now. Still, I can't help wondering.

86

REMEMBERING HOW IT WAS

By Lois Lowry

I REMEMBER hitting my daughter once. Swatting her right across the seat of her jeans with a wire coat hanger, when she was nine years old.

It was back in the days when little girls still wore dresses to school, and mothers still ironed them. I had ironed a whole week's worth of those cotton, starched, puffed-sleeved horrors, placed them on hangers, and asked her to take them to her room.

And she did. When I entered her room later, I found her sprawled on her bed with a book, and all seven freshly-ironed dresses in a heap on the floor where she had deposited them.

Naturally I swatted her on the behind with the nearest available weapon.

But my point is not confession or absolution. My point is this: recently I mentioned the incident to my daughter—who is now twenty-five and has a child of her own—and asked her if she remembered it.

"*Remember* it?" she replied. "How could I *not* remember the time my own mother beat me unmercifully around the head and shoulders with a blunt instrument?"

Memory, we should bear in mind, is a subjective thing.

It always amazes me when I hear people say, as many do, that they don't remember their own childhood. What time is my doctor's appointment? What was the name of the librarian I met at that last convention? Those things I forget. But childhood? I have only to press the mental key that calls up each year: 1941 (nursery school: I snitched a blue crayon and wrote my name on my cot during naptime; Pearl Harbor, and my father in uniform, letting me try on his major's cap; my green wicker rocking chair; a book about penguins); 1945 (the fourth-grade bully named Gene; the stain on the blanket under my cat after she gave birth to kittens in the attic); 1948 (the green jumper and white blouse I wore, my first day in seventh grade; the three maids giggling together in the kitchen of our Tokyo home; "Kerria Japonica": the room I shared with my sister during a spring vacation in the Fujiya Hotel, where each room was named for a flower).

Each detail appears, and with it come back the emotions. Humiliation, at four, caught stealing a crayon. Anger at Allen, the boy across the street, who borrowed and lost my penguin book. Fear of the boy Gene, who terrorized the fourth grade. Sudden and frightening awareness, watching my cat lick her firstborn litter, that birth involves blood.

For me it is all there, and I can call it back. If that were not so, I could not write for children.

Some years ago, when working on an article about medical hypnosis, I interviewed a doctor who suggested that it would be helpful if he were to hypnotize me. I agreed, and sat there, relaxed, while he talked in a steady voice; I watched, feeling no pain, as he inserted a needle into the back of my hand.

Then he suggested that I would be regressing in age: now fifteen; now ten; now five.

"Now that you are five," his droning voice said, "where do you find yourself? What are you experiencing?"

"In my grandparents' backyard," I said without hesitation. "Barefoot, standing under the big pine tree; I can feel the dry needles under my feet. I can smell my grandmother's roses. I can hear a mourning dove."

"You're a good subject," he said, later. "Wasn't that amazing, how all those sensations came back from the time you were five?"

"But I do that all the time, without hypnosis," I told him. "If I'm writing about a five-year-old, I *remember* being five. And I can feel those pine needles, smell the roses, hear the mourning dove."

"Well," he said huffily, "somehow, then, you've mastered the art of self-hypnosis."

But I don't think it's self-hypnosis at all. For me it is simply memory, a phenomenon with which I seem to be richly endowed. And what a blessing it is for one who chooses to write for kids! Each day, sitting here at work, I call upon it constantly.

Anastasia Krupnik is a character who has now appeared in six of my books and is currently making her way through the manuscript pages of a seventh. She is fictional. She is not me. I never had her freckles, her astigmatism, her family, or what my mother would have referred to as her "smart alec mouth." But I have used my own memories again and again as I have created her and moved her through the incidents that appear on those pages.

Anastasia is ten in the first book, whose title bears her name. Writing it—specifically, writing a scene in her school classroom—I thought back, remembering my own anger at a supposed classroom injustice: for me, it was the day that the drawing of the class mural began. It was to be a mural across one entire wall, depicting a wagon train heading west.

I had looked forward to the mural so. At ten I prided myself on my drawing ability, and I had planned, in my mind, the creation of the stalwart pioneer figures: the gaunt sunbonneted mothers holding babies; the carefree children running beside the covered wagons, loyal dogs at their heels. I would draw a girl my own age, I would even make her look a little like me, skinny and blonde—turning with a look of irritated surprise as a brother pulled at her pigtails.

But my teacher took me aside in the midst of the classroom excitement as the paper was being unrolled and tacked across the wall, the art materials brought from the supply closet.

"You know," she said with a kind smile, "you draw better than anyone else in the class."

Of course I knew. But humility was appropriate, and I hung my head shyly. Inside myself, I glowed.

"And because of that," she went on, "I'm assigning you to the very hardest part of the mural."

A tiny gremlin of suspicion began to gnaw inside me where the glow had been, and I looked up at her.

"I want you to do all eight oxen for us," she explained. "All the children can draw people pretty well. But I know that no one but you will be able to draw oxen."

Oxen? Had I heard her correctly? Yes. Oxen.

And so I obediently, diligently, conscientiously, drew oxen for a week, while the other kids did the people. I researched oxen, practiced oxen, and completed oxen; and even today, forty years later, I'd bet you anything that they were the best-rendered, most anatomically-accurate oxen any ten-year-old ever presented in crayon on a twenty-foot-long strip of white paper.

But oh, how I remember my resentment of the moment. Writing of Anastasia, I recreated not the moment itself, but the emotions of it. I had Anastasia's teacher, Mrs. Westvessel, assign the writing of a poem to her fourth-grade students. I tried to recapture the joy of the assignment:

. . . when Mrs. Westvessel announced one day in the fall that the class would begin writing poetry, Anastasia was the happiest she had ever been in school.
Somewhere, off in a place beyond her own thoughts, Anastasia could hear Mrs. Westvessel's voice. She was reading some poems to the class; she was talking about poetry and how it was made. But Anastasia wasn't really listening. She was listening instead to the words that were appearing in her own head, floating there and arranging themselves into groups, into lines, into poems.

. . . and the bitter disappointment of its outcome:

An F. Anastasia had never had an F in her entire life. She kept looking at the floor. Someone had stepped on a red crayon once; the color was smeared into the floor forever.
"Iworkedveryhardonthatpoem," whispered Anastasia to the floor.
"Speak up, Anastasia."
Anastasia lifted her head and looked Mrs. Westvessel in the eye. "I worked very hard on that poem," she said in a loud, clear voice.

In a later book, Anastasia is twelve. I punched my mental button to the memory section marked "12" and saw myself standing in front of a mirror, yanking a comb through tangled hair which seemed to have taken on, at puberty, characteristics of seaweed marinated in Wesson Oil. And I wrote:

. . . .Vaguely she remembered the fairy tale of Rapunzel, who had been locked in a tower, and who had hung her long hair from the window so that her lover could climb up. That was kind of neat.
But that Anastasia ran her fingers through her own hair, which had begun to be pretty long—halfway down her back—but she realized that it needed washing again. Yuck. If a lover tried to climb her greasy hair, he would slide back down.

Another book, and now she was thirteen. Almost unbidden (because surely I have repressed it; my mother is such a gracious and charming

454

lady now, at eighty) came this memory: me, thirteen, glaring at her as she appeared from her bedroom, dressed to attend a mother/daughter school event with me. I could hear my own voice: "You're not going to wear *that,* are you?" and see her look of surprise and hurt, as she stared down at her best dress. And I wrote:

"Well, I used to like you a whole lot. I thought you were really a neat mother. You used to be fun. But lately—"
"Yes? Go on. Tell me about lately."
"Well, your clothes, for example. They're embarrassing. You always wear jeans. I don't even like to walk beside you on the street because you don't look like a regular mother."

Now about the bludgeoning of my daughter. The details of memory, as I pointed out, are subjective. They are subjective because they depend upon the emotions. If my daughter remembers that I beat her mercilessly with a heavy wooden weapon, it is because she remembers not the weapon (and it *was* a wire hanger) but the overwhelming and terrifying astonishment of being physically attacked by a usually pleasant, soft-spoken mother.

And perhaps my fourth-grade teacher would be able to document that it was only six oxen, not eight; and that she let me draw a couple of people as well.

But in writing, it is not the veracity of the details that matters. As fiction writers, we lie about those anyway. The truth of the feelings is the only essential thing.

If you do not, or cannot remember those feelings, don't fake them; they're too strong, too powerful to be faked even by the best of tricksters at typewriters. And young readers are masters of phoniness-detection.

If your youth doesn't come back for you, call upon yesterday instead. Remember your rage and frustration standing at the Hertz desk in Boise after being told that they have no record of your reservation made three weeks before, and no car either? And then the clerk saying, "Have a nice day"? Use it, that memory. Apply that same pressure-cooker anger to your fictional adolescent who has just been cut from the basketball squad, or grounded for a month by his parents.

I use yesterday's—and this morning's—emotions myself, adding them to the stockpile of those that come from the past. Recently, for a short story called "Splendor," I created two sisters, thirteen- and fourteen-years-old. Writing the scene where the younger has just acquired a very special new dress, I called back the old jealousies that I remembered from my own adolescent relationship with my own older sister, and wrote:

Back upstairs, she hung the dress carefully in her closet, and looked with pleasure at the burst of color it provided there in contrast to the clothes of her ordinary life. Beside it hung an outgrown brown jumper of Angela's, and next to that Angela's old plaid skirt. It was a closet full of leftovers, Becky thought, a *life* full of leftovers—until the dress changed everything.

But for a separate scene, I used other, more recent memories as well. I remembered a very few years back, when my husband, children, and I went every Thanksgiving to the home of a brother and sister-in-law. The sister-in-law was Wonder Woman. She could do anything, and did. Every Thanksgiving there were new accomplishments to admire: a hand-hooked rug, a newly papered room, a promotion in her professional field, a new and faster finish time in the Boston Marathon. Finally, one Thanksgiving, instead of the usual turkey, she had roasted a goose. Helping her clean up after dinner, I removed a pan swimming with goose grease from the oven.

"What would you like me to do with this?" I asked her, holding it carefully so that it wouldn't drip on the vinyl floor which she had, of course, installed herself.

"Why don't you take some of it home with you?" she suggested.

I stood there for quite a while, staring at several quarts of thick yellow grease, before I finally said, "What for? What would I do with it?"

She was hanging up a dish towel. It was probably handwoven. And she replied cheerfully, "Make soap."

I sulked all the way home, two hours by car. Every now and then I muttered, "Make soap."

I didn't. Didn't make soap, that is. And I didn't save the goose grease, either. But I saved the memory. And I used it when the younger sister, Becky, thrilled with her new, expensive dress, feels that same frustrating, antagonistic rivalry.

"Mine only cost ten dollars," Angela said smugly.

"Well, you *made* yours. Not all of us can sew," muttered Becky. Or sing, she

456

thought, or cook, or play the piano, or get all A's in school. Angrily she listed her sister's accomplishments in her mind. "Not all of us are perfect."

I suppose that psychologically, using painful memories fictionally is a way of getting over them. Personally, I think it's a good way of getting even. And pragmatically, it's a nifty way of getting published.

87

HOW TO MAKE BELIEVE

By Anne Lindbergh

When I was a child, I expected a good book to be like summer vacation: endless. Unfortunately, even the best books, like summer vacation, came to a sudden stop. This seemed outrageously unfair. The author had opened a door into a new world, letting me through to meet people who had obviously existed before the story took place and would go on existing after I had closed the book. He was there to record events, and had no business wandering off in pursuit of other activities. My ambition at the time was to become an author myself and continue the stories abandoned by C. S. Lewis, or E. B. White.

I had forgotten this ambition by the time I went to college. Attending lectures on "Great Books" rather than joining workshops in creative writing, I tried to write in the style of Virginia Woolf and turned out grim, meandering fiction for the next ten years. Toward the end of that period, a friend came to me claiming that my latest short story had given him a headache. "I don't believe you'd enjoy reading it either, if you hadn't written it yourself," he grumbled. "Why not write the sort of thing you like to read?"

What did I like to read? Children's books, on the sly. Although the puritan in me naggingly asked what enjoyment had to do with it, I sat down to write *Osprey Island*. Instinctively, I gave my first book a structure similar to that of the books I had loved as a child. This meant one adventure and usually one day per chapter, ending safely at bedtime. It also meant a book where the author tells you how every character is reacting to every other character, whenever possible. By the middle of page two in *Osprey Island,* I told my readers what each of the three children and one parent was thinking. I soon added the remaining three parents, a doctor, and a dog. Even my own opinion was carefully included:

But it was obvious that while the children were on the island, they would have to fend for themselves. If they waited a whole month to be rescued, what would they eat? Where would they sleep? How would they stay warm?

Five books later, I was asked to lead a workshop on writing fiction for children. Never having led a workshop or taught anything at all, I went to the library and found several manuals on the subject. I read them carefully, taking notes. Before long I was horrified. It was the first I had ever heard of "P.O.V." (point of view), and I suspected there wasn't one in my books. "Conflict" had been emphatically stressed by all the manuals and seemed to involve psychological problems unfamiliar to my characters. And if it was true that children couldn't handle the complexity of flashbacks, I was in real trouble.

Thoroughly intimidated myself, I set out to intimidate the writers in my workshop. It wasn't hard. When I mentioned point of view, they were baffled. When I moved on to conflict, they turned green. One rebellious student asked me to explain the conflict in *Goodnight Moon*. "Fear of the dark?" I suggested glibly.

I grew fond of my students, however, and had second thoughts. I remembered the day in a high school biology class when I told the teacher desperately, "I can't find the esophagus, but I'm still sure it's a frog." Was I discouraging future authors by throwing unfamiliar terms at them? At the next session, I qualified the strict rules that I had imposed during the first workshops. If children liked their stories, they were doing something right; it was that simple. I told them that P.O.V. was often a matter of fashion, and that while some writers felt comfortable with first-person-singular narratives, others (including Newbery Award winners) stuck to the "old-fashioned," universal or omniscient point of view. I told them that if children couldn't handle flashbacks, it was the author's fault. (Who said flashbacks have to be complex?) I told them that conflict, as far as I was concerned, was whatever made the reader turn the page.

As long as the author doesn't bore, confuse, or lose the reader, a story works. But remember that unless a book is required reading for school, a child has only one motive to continue reading: the desire to find out what happens next. He didn't choose the book because it was a best seller, or because he was embarrassed at a dinner party to admit that he had never read it.

I took another look at *Osprey Island*. I ached to rewrite it, loosening the style and tightening the structure. Still, children had liked it. Why? Probably because I had taken my friend's advice and written the sort of thing that I liked to read: an adventure heavily dosed with magic, but with real characters with whom I could identify, so that the story seemed to be happening to me.

"Real" is the key word. The farther I venture into make-believe, the more important reality becomes for me as a writer: make-believe must be believable. The children in *Osprey Island* travel by magic on Sunday afternoons, but on weekdays they lead ordinary lives. Once the magic has delivered them to the island they are still ordinary children with ordinary needs, so they have to plan carefully before leaving home. This planning provides the practical details that inspire belief:

> When the children said the magic words that Sunday, it seemed more natural to find themselves in a patch of ferns. In fact, they weren't really thinking about the magic at all; they were thinking about the things they had brought with them. Charles had his knapsack, Amy had her sketchbook and Lizzie was carrying her mother's kettle and a home-made cherry pie.

Real children get hungry, catch colds, and quarrel. Bearing this in mind, I let August Brown make himself a sandwich before going off to spend the day with the time travelers of Pineapple Place. Zannah, in *The Hunky-Dory Dairy,* is sent back to her own time from the nineteenth-century farm after sneezing into the applesauce. Dawn and her brother Marcus are so busy bickering over a spilled milkshake at the beginning of *The Shadow on the Dial* that Mr. Bros and his magical Removers Van nearly escape their attention.

Children occasionally want to know why there is magic in so many of my stories. I tell them that once I started, it became a habit I couldn't break.

Paradoxically, I started using magic in *Osprey Island* because the situation in which I put my characters was not believable. What parents, I asked myself, would allow young children to camp by themselves on a faraway island? I couldn't include the parents as chaperones because the moment trouble arose, they would insist on taking charge. How about a shipwreck? The parents could go down with the boat while the children were washed ashore with the dog. But what children would enjoy an adventure knowing that their parents had just drowned?

460

I didn't want any brooding orphans on Osprey Island. Should I make the children older?

Thrashing about for a believable solution, I thought of magic. My original plan was to use it as a taxi: Magic would take the children to the island in Chapter One and bring them back at the end of the book. But it seemed a pity to let the taxi wait there with its motor running. The instantaneous slip from one place or time to another by means of a magic painting, or window, or sundial, offered tempting possibilities. Why not let the children use it to explore? My habit was formed and developed fast. The children in *Osprey Island* travel back and forth repeatedly, returning home for a sandwich, a change of clothes, or simply to baffle the grownups in the story.

Meals, clean laundry, and other reminders of everyday life are essential in order to fasten my fantasies to reality, but before entering into fantasy at all I like to give the reader a long introduction to my characters and their surroundings. If Bailey, of *Bailey's Window,* had marched straight upstairs on his first day at the farm, painted a snow scene on his bedroom wall, and stepped out of August into March, a reader might hold back doubtfully—might even close the book. I wanted to convince my readers of the total believability of the farm, the children who lived there, and the long, hot summer. I wanted them to meet the parents and the dogs. I wanted them to smoulder with indignation at Bailey's tricks. When Bailey jumped through the painted window into knee-deep snow I wanted readers to jump, too—not for a whimsical change of scene, but to keep an eye on Bailey and make sure he gets what's coming to him.

Unfortunately, it took me thirty-two pages to accomplish this, and the resulting discussions with my editor were endless. Why, I was asked, if I promise magic on the book flap does it take me five chapters to deliver? "Who's promising?" was my answer. "Let the magic come as a surprise."

When I read *Bailey's Window* now, I am surprised that my readers are willing to bear with me (and the obnoxious Bailey) until Chapter Five. The story seems to meander. Again, I wish I could tighten a bit here, loosen a bit there. But it worked.

With each new book I try to bring in the magic a little closer to the beginning. This is a matter of setting, rather than of structure. Planning for the window to be painted or the sundial to be turned in Chapter One

461

is not enough. It's more important to create a setting so real that when magic crops up, the reader will be too off guard to step back.

Most important of all, the reality of the setting must be sustained. Make-believe is not to be taken lightly. Once you have your reader's trust, it is a betrayal to imply that the magic is a joke, a fairy tale, or a dream. As a child I could not forgive Alice's sister (or, indirectly, Lewis Carroll) for the words:

"It was a curious dream, dear, certainly: but now run in to your tea; it's getting late." So she sat on, with closed eyes, and half believed herself in Wonderland.

Why not whole belief? Why shouldn't Alice have her tea and Wonderland too?

88

WRITING FOR YOUNG ADULTS

By Norma Fox Mazer

Writing for young adults today is particularly satisfying. These young people are going through the most intensely felt time of their lives. They are a devoted audience and, once caught by one of your books, they will read all of them and wait impatiently for the next one to appear. To write for this audience, it's not necessary to know their slang or the latest fad. It is important to understand their fears, dreams and hopes, but it is vital to know your *own* point of view: what you, the writer, think, feel, fear, understand and believe. You cannot write a deeply felt, satisfying book without a point of view on your material.

The storyteller brings order to events that in life might be random, purposeless, even meaningless. It's this sense of orderliness and meaning that makes the novel so satisfying. But to create that order, the writer should be aware of certain rhythms and patterns. To begin with, a story needs those simple classic elements: a beginning, a middle, and an ending. Most books have a beginning and an ending of sorts, but a great many fall down in the middle. If the writer flounders, the reader gets the sense of the writer's despair: I've come this far—what do I do now?

There are two things I think will help the new writer. One is to work with a unity of opposites as the foundation for your story—two characters locked together but intent on opposite goals. In my novel *Taking Terri Mueller,* Phil and Terri are father and daughter; that is their essential unity. They are further united by the deep love between them, and this, in turn, is reinforced by their life style, which isolates them from other people. This is the background of the struggle that ensues between them. Terri is determined to know the truth about her past. Phil is equally determined that she should not. There they are, united, unable and unwilling to get away from each other, and wanting completely different things.

463

When you first come up with an idea for a novel, test it by asking yourself a few questions: What is the basic unity? (It does not have to be two people. The unity of a character and an animal, or a character and nature, such as a landslide or a hurricane, is just as valid.) What is the opposition? Can I put the idea of the story into a paragraph that will suggest the unity of opposites? *Taking Terri Mueller* began with a single sentence. "A girl has been kidnapped by her own father."

When a writer works with a powerful unity of opposites, there are scenes that almost demand to be written. Long before I knew how I would develop the story to the point at which a confrontation about Phil's lying takes place between Terri and Phil, I knew that scene had to be written. All I had to do was work my way through the story toward that point. This key scene comes about midway through the novel, when the reader has been fully engaged with Terri's struggles and her father's painful desire to keep her ignorant of the truth.

The second thing I find helpful in writing a novel is to think in threes. Three is a magic number. Human beings respond to threes. A story must rise and fall three times to satisfy the reader. When I'm planning, I often divide the book into three sections. Then each section can also be divided twice into three parts. And in most chapters, there is a threefold rise and fall. Let me give one illustration from the key chapter in *Taking Terri Mueller:*

Terri and her father Phil have a close, affectionate and trusting relationship. Her only other relative is her Aunt Vivian. Now it's time for Aunt Vivian's once-a-year visit, a wonderful event to which Terri looks forward all year.

She wants to make the most of the visit, yet it's marred almost from the beginning. Three things happen. First, Vivian dislikes Nancy, Phil's new girlfriend, creating a strained atmosphere. Secondly, Terri sees a wallet snapshot of her aunt, who is said to have no other family, with two young boys. And finally, Terri overhears a conversation between her father and her aunt that strongly suggests there are secrets between them.

There are other ways to use the rhythm of three. For instance, a working rule of thumb for fixing a character in the reader's mind is to repeat something about that character three times. Although it needn't be a physical characteristic, the obvious and old example is the mole on the nose. Use a bit of subtlety in repeating the detail—certainly don't say it the same way each time—but within the first five or six chapters, working in the "mole" helps the reader visualize the character, especially if the detail can be used to shed light on the character's personality or state of mind.

In a description of Terri, I work on her appearance, but also on her state of mind.

She was a tall girl with long hair that she sometimes wore in a single braid down her back. . . . She was quiet and watchful and didn't talk a lot, although she liked to talk, especially to her father, with whom she felt she could talk about anything.

The end of that description reveals something much more important than that Terri has long hair: her trust in her father. That he betrayed this trust is one of the central themes of the book. In the next chapter, Nancy thinks Terri is older than she is. Terri says, "You only thought so . . . because I'm tall." Thus, through dialogue, I repeat one of the points of Terri's description. And through narration we also learn that Terri is almost always the tallest girl in her class. But what's important here is not Terri's height, but her emotional maturity. And this is reinforced when Nancy says that it isn't Terri's being tall—but her poise—that made her think Terri was older.

In creating characters, remember that key word—create. You are not making a real human being, but an illusion of a human being. It would be impossible, confusing, and boring to put down on paper all the elements that go into any one actual person. Your job as a writer is to make your readers believe. Therefore, on the one hand your character needs a certain consistency, and on the other hand those very contradictions that are part of being human.

It's good to give your readers a sense of how your characters look, but what's basic are words and actions. What the characters say. What the characters do. I, the author, tell you, the reader, that Terri is a warmhearted girl, but if what you see her do is trip up a little old lady, then you know I'm lying to you. When I'm struggling with a character, I remind myself of the basic dictum: show, don't tell. I wanted to show Terri's longing for a family. Rather than say it, I showed Terri looking at a friend's family snapshots. Terri's interest and eagerness bring home to the reader her underlying sense of isolation and loneliness.

I've been speaking here of the young adult novel, and yet most of the

465

things I'm saying should apply to any novel. Still, the young adult novel stands in a class by itself. Briefly, I'd like to mention what, in general, distinguishes the young adult novel from any other novel.

The first and most obvious point is the age of the protagonist. Nearly always, the main character is going to be a person the same age or slightly older than the people in your audience. In the young adult novel, there tends to be a very close identification between the reader and the protagonist. A reader wrote me recently, "I hope you know your book describes my life." Literally, it couldn't have, since story, setting, and characters were all products of my imagination. Yet this reader believed in the reality of the world I created. To achieve this sense of verisimilitude, when you write you cannot stand above or to one side of the character, you cannot comment as an older, "wiser" adult, but you must see and report the world through your protagonist's eyes. This limitation, more than anything else, makes the difference between a novel written for this audience and one written for an adult audience.

Although it's important to recognize who your audience is, it's simply death to allow a patronizing attitude to creep into your writing. Your readers deserve your best. The one time I focus on the fact that I'm writing for teenagers is in the early stages when I'm searching for the right idea. Clearly, some book ideas are better than others.

I consider this early stage of writing the novel, which is really an almost non-writing stage, the most important. Concept is all. A silly or unimportant concept can mean months of wasted work.

Questions: Is the idea about young people? Is there an opportunity for the characters to work out their own problems and destinies? Is there a chance for consideration of some serious subjects? Is there also a place for the playful scene or character? I like to achieve a balance. Even in *Taking Terri Mueller,* which is about the terribly serious problem of childnapping, there are a few funny scenes with her father, a scattering of amusing dialogues with her girlfriend.

There are rewards in writing for young adults. There is hardly a subject or an idea that can't be tackled. I have written short stories, serious realistic novels, a time fantasy and, in *Taking Terri Mueller,* a mystery.

Perhaps the first real lesson I learned about writing was that not only did I have something to say, but, whether I recognized it or not, it was

466

there, inside me, waiting to be said. I'm convinced this is true for everyone. Each of us has a unique point of view on the world; the struggle is to get in touch with that uniqueness and bring it into our writing.

My method is to write a first draft in which I spill out everything. The inner censor is banished. I do not allow myself to ponder over the "right" word, to search for the felicitous phrase or struggle for the beautifully constructed sentence. For me, a first draft means putting the truth of a story before all else. It means digging down for all those unique, but what-if-no-one-else-agrees-with-me thoughts, bringing them into the light and onto paper.

Then there is your audience. Is there another group of readers who are quite so enthusiastic, who are ready to laugh and cry over your book, who will cheer you on and write to you in droves? What can compare with the thrill of receiving a letter like the one that came in my mail from a girl in Pennsylvania: "Once I began to read about Terri, I could not get my eyes away from the book."

Each time I approach the writing of a new young adult novel I wonder, "Can I do it again? Will I do this story justice? Will I write a book readers will enjoy? What does this story mean? And aren't there enough books in the world already?"

No, not as long as there are readers and writers. Not as long as there are people like me, like you, like all of us who, like the writer Katha Pollitt, believe that we "go to fiction for the revelation of character, the rich presentation of lived life and the daily clutter of things."

89

A SENSE OF AUDIENCE

By Jill Paton Walsh

I FEEL DISTINCTLY uneasy about giving practical, down-to-earth advice about writing for children. There are many things in the world, like riding a bicycle, which one may be well able to do, about which one cannot offer a coherent explanation; in one sense one does not know how to do it, even while bowling along the road! Writing for children may be very like riding a bike.

Certainly in the case of the bike, if you become too self-conscious about it you fall off at once; and a similar Catch-22 really does apply to writing for children; if you think that because your audience is young, something special needs doing, or not doing, then you probably can't do it at all. I would like to pursue the heavy metaphor about bike riding a little further, because much of the advice about writing for children that one reads is like exhortations to remember your balance when riding. It is so often telling people to think deliberately about their audience, the vocabulary, the market, whereas, I believe, the sense of audience really is like a sense of balance: If you need to think about it, you haven't got it, and you can't get it by wrinkling your brows and thinking about it harder, because to do it properly you need to be thinking about something else, rather as the cyclist, unaware of how to ride, thinks about which way to take into town.

Let me elaborate on this a little further, though enough about the bike, I promise. I once read an article advising people to "*write for children as though they were your equals.*" Does that startle you as much as it did me? Children *are* my equals. Many of them, in time, will turn out to be my superiors—in brain power, in sensitivity, in warmth of heart. By and large, I believe, one generation is pretty much like another, and belonging to an older one gives no ground for claiming superior status.

But, perhaps you won't feel easy with this statement. Perhaps you think that claiming to think of children as equals is a sign of lack of sophistication, or a form of swank, in the way that Damon Runyon was swanking when he said he had never met a boring person. If that is how you are reacting as you read these words, then my down-to-earth advice is that you should ask yourself whom you *do* think of as your equals, and write for them; they are your natural audience. For them you will be able to write without, metaphorically speaking, putting on a funny hat, adopting a curious vocal tone, or limiting your vocabulary.

I have often wondered in the course of what is now a twenty-year career as a children's writer, why some people instinctively take children seriously, and others—including some published writers for children—simply fool about, and I have arrived at a contentious theory, which is that it depends what sort of childhood you had. If you have half forgotten your own; if it was happy and uneventful, and nothing painful or dangerous happened, or if it tested you much until you reached your teens, then, when you write, your characters will be teen-agers or older. I was a child in the war; I think of childhood as the most important formative time of life. I don't think about children when I write; I just assume without thinking that some of the readers will be children and that things had best be told as simply as possible, because everyone, including me, prefers it that way.

You must by now be wondering what I do think about when working, and the answer is, the subject. Day and night, at the typewriter, off the typewriter, waiting at the bus stop, lying in the bath, while washing up, dusting, eating, I recommend thinking consciously about the *book*. Or, more accurately perhaps, having book-shaped thoughts about the subject. Not just any subject, either; not something concocted from worldly-wise assessments of publishers' stated needs, or deductions about what sells based on reading what has sold. Not something that someone thinks there ought to be a book about. But something that moves your mind to enthusiasm. That gives you that glow of real interest. I realize that this sounds wildly impractical—the other kind of advice sounds so *sensible;* and of course I am thinking, in what I say, only about fiction—nonfiction may be different, or may not, I don't know enough about writing it to say—but however airy-fairy it sounds, it has always worked for me. I write about things that move me deeply, I never try to write commercially salable work, I try to write the best book I possibly can about this wonderful subject; and I honestly think that the best book you can write is your best prospect of publication and commercial success. It is also your best prospect of noncommercial success—of that letter from a child who has never managed to finish a book until he reads yours, or who has read what you say about the war and found a sudden sympathy for a dreadful grandpa, or who just wants you to look at the picture he has drawn for you, of a scene in your book.

When I ask myself if my method is successful, I think of the flaws and shortcomings in my books—none of us can write as well as we wish we could—and then I remember the hundreds of loving letters I have received from children all over the world, and I feel like the most lucky and successful person I can possibly imagine.

Of course, it's all very well for me to tell you to burn with enthusiasm for your subject. Most people do that readily for their first book. But most first books don't get published. Keeping oneself supplied indefinitely with burning enthusiasms to make books out of is a problem for published and unpublished writers alike. And here comes my most practical piece of advice, my only really useful suggestion—do as I do, keep a notebook.

A notebook is not a diary, and doesn't have to be written in every day, or contain a note of anything dull. And everyone's notebook would contain a different balance of items. A notebook is a record of the activity of that part of your mind that produces ideas. Writing is a split personality activity: a "producer," which creates a huge output of thought and story and description, and a "controller," which carves and squashes and selects, and constructs a book from the raw material thrown up by the "producer." In my experience, the "controller" is easy to advise and improve and teach, and is sitting in your conscious mind, where you can talk to it. The notebook is an attempt to talk to the producer down in the unconscious depths, where it all comes from.

So what's in the notebook? Mine contains a good deal of description. I like places and often get ideas for books just from some interesting place. But I might come back from a week at the seaside with nothing in the notebook except a few sentences about the exact color of a breaking wave, and a list of the types of seaweed on a lee shore. I often try to write very exact descriptions of unusual weather, sky formations, effects of the light, and so on. The notebook entries are fragmentary and short, but in the year of the drought, for example, I made a lot of

470

such notes. Three years ago I wrote a novel set in the summer of the Plague, when it didn't rain for three and a half months, and I reaped the benefit.

The next most frequent entry is fragments of overheard conversation, especially in any regional or highly demotic voice. I eavesdrop ruthlessly, wherever I am. Catching the tune of real voices—the English don't speak standard English—is terribly difficult. Months and months before I began work on *Gaffer Samson's Luck,* I had noted two children talking about a mouse their cat had caught: "What did you do with that?" "She put that in the bin, haven't she . . . ." The local children in my book never say "it." But if you don't eavesdrop, how will you know?

I also clip newspapers for stories that catch my attention, as in the item about a forest fire started deliberately to provide a rare bird with the hot pine cones it needed to nest; the fire went out of control and destroyed a small North American town. Hundreds of such fascinating possible starting points are printed free in the papers—local papers especially—every week. I clip or note the ones I like.

Finally I list reactions to the books I am reading, and sometimes make notes of states of mind—especially of frames of mind about the book I am writing; there is some comfort in looking back and seeing how gloomy I was about the last one, which is now in print and doing nicely, when I am feeling suicidal about the current one.

The point about a writer's notebook is writing it, of course—not reading it. I never read mine. I don't even, very often, consult it. If you went back and copied one of those exact descriptions, or conversations, directly into a book the words would be sure to stick out like a sore thumb. The tone of voice would be all wrong. But I find I can remember things I noted down, as I remembered the dusty surface of rivers and ponds in the year of the drought, all the way through till I needed that little detail. Perhaps your memory is marvelous anyway. But writing in a notebook regularly has an astonishing effect on your attention; things you would have no reason to notice, aspects of the world for which you have no present use, and which would normally float past you on the tide of weeks and days, will collect in your notebook. You will be like a child gathering handfuls of unremarkable special pebbles from a beach, and it will gradually enhance your powers of attention, and the vividness and realism with which you can write.

For really, writers have no special expertise. The only claim we have

471

on the reader's time is that we have learned more, thought more, looked more carefully at some aspect of the human context, the human predicament, than most people have time for. There is a teaching method for very young children called "Look and Say." Look comes before Say. Otherwise what shall we have to tell each other stories *about*?

90

STORYTELLING: THE OLDEST AND NEWEST ART

By Jane Yolen

SOME time ago I received one of those wonderful letters from a young reader, the kind that are always signed mysteriously "Your fiend." This one had an opening that was an eye-opener. It read:

Dear Miss Yolen:
I was going to write to Enid Blyton or Mark Twain, but I hear they are dead so I am writing to you...

Of course I answered immediately—just in case. After all, I did not want that poor child to think that all the storytellers were dead. Because that was what the three of us—Enid Blyton, Mark Twain, and Miss Yolen—had in common. Not style. Not sense. Not subject. Not "message or moral." The link was clear in the child's mind just as it was in mine. Blyton, Twain, and Yolen. We were all storytellers.

Nowadays most of the storytellers *are* dead. Instead, we are over-loaded with moralists and preachers disguised as tale tellers. Our medium has become a message.

So I want to talk to you today about the art of and the heart of storytelling; about tales that begin, go somewhere, and then end in a satisfying manner. Those are the tales that contain their own inner truth that no amount of moralizing can copy. The Chinese, the *New York Times* reported in 1968, were recruiting "an army of proletarian storytellers" who were ordered to fan out into the countryside and "disseminate the thoughts of Chairman Mao." They told the kind of stories that end: "As a result, the evil wind of planting-more-water-melons-for-profit was checked." These tales waste no time in getting their message across. But they are sorry excuses for stories. As Isaac Bashevis Singer has said: "In art, truth that is boring is not true."

Storytelling may be the oldest art. The mother to her child, the hunter to his peers, the survivor to his rescuers, the priestess to her

473

followers, the seer to his petitioners. They did not just report, *they told a tale*. And the better the tale was told, the more it was believed. And the more it was believed, the truer it became. It spoke to the listener because it spoke not just to the ears but to the heart as well.

These same stories speak to us still. And without the story, would the tale's wisdom survive?

The invention of print changed the storyteller's art, gave it visual form. Since we humans are slow learners, it took a while to learn that the eye and ear are different listeners. It took a while to learn the limits and the limitlessness of two kinds of tellers—the author and the illustrator—in tandem. And it has taken us five centuries, dating from Gutenberg, to throw away the tale at last.

Children, the last audience for the storytellers who once entertained all ages, are finding it hard to read the new stories. Their literature today is full of realism without reality, diatribes without delight, information without incantation, and warning without wisdom or wit. And so the children—and the adults they grow into—are no longer reading at all. The disturbing figure I heard only last month is that 48% of the American people read no book at all in the past five years.

And so I dare. I dare to tell tales in the manner of the old storytellers. I do not simply retell the old tales. I make up my own. I converse with mermaids and monsters and men who can fly, and I teach children to do the same. It is the only kind of teaching I allow in my tales.

What of these stories? There is a form. First, a story has a beginning, an opening, an incipit. Sometimes I will use the old magical words "Once upon a time." Sometimes I vary it to please my own ear:

Once many years ago in a country far to the East....

There was once a plain but goodhearted girl....

In ancient Greece, where the spirits of beautiful women were said to dwell in trees....

Once on the far side of yesterday....

In the time before time, the Rainbow Rider lives....

Once upon a maritime, when the world was filled with wishes the way the sea is filled with fishes....

474

But always a story begins at the beginning. That is surely a simple thing to remember. Yet my husband begins reading any book he picks up in the middle and, if he likes it, he will continue on. He says it does not matter where he begins, with modern books—and he is right. If stories and books no longer start at the beginning, why should the reader? And if, as Joyce Cary says, "... reading is a creative art subject to the same rules, the same limitations, as the imaginative process...," then a story that begins in the middle and meanders around and ends still in the middle encourages that kind of reading.

Now I am not saying that a story has to move sequentially in time to have a beginning. One does not have to start with the birth of the hero or heroine to start the story at the beginning. Still, there must be a reason, a discernible reason, for starting a tale somewhere and not just the teller's whim. The person who invented the words "poetic license" should have his revoked.

What of the story's middle? First it should not be filled with middle-age spread. But also, it should not be so tight as to disappear. Do you remember the nursery rhyme:

> I'll tell you a story
> About Jack O'Nory,
> And now my tale's begun.
> I'll tell you another
> Of Jack and his brother,
> And now my tale is done.

Where is the middle of that story? It should be the place in the tale that elicits one question from the reader—*what then*? The middle is the place that leads the reader inevitably on to the end.

Is that not a simple task? I run a number of writers' groups and conferences, and all persuasions of writers have passed through. There are the naive novices who think that children's books must be easier to write because they are shorter and the audience less discriminating. There are the passable writers, almost-pros who have had a story or two published in religious magazines and are ready to tackle a talking animal tale or—worse—a talking prune story where inanimate objects converse on a variety of uninteresting subjects. And there are the truly professional writers whose combined publications make a reasonable backlist for any publishing company. And they all have trouble with the middles of stories.

475

The problem is one of caring. Too few writers today care enough about storytelling. If they should happen in the throes of "inspiration" to come upon a beginning and an ending, then they simply link the two together, a tenuous lifeline holding two climbers onto a mountain.

Of course the middle *is* the mountain. It is the most important part of the book, the tale, the story. It is where everything important occurs. Perhaps that is why so few people do it well.

What of the end? Ecclesiastes says: "Better is the end of a thing than the beginning thereof." An overstatement perhaps. But if the end is not *just* right, and is not filled with both inevitability and surprise, then it is a bad ending.

Adults are quite willing to forgive bad endings. I saw only recently a review of an adult book that said, in essence, the ending is silly, unconvincing, and weak, but the book is definitely worth reading. Children will not forgive a weak ending. They demand a rounding off, and they are very vocal in this demand. I remember reading a story of mine in manuscript to my daughter, then age seven. It was a tale about three animals—a sow, a mare, and a cow—who, tired of men and their fences, decided to live together. When I finished reading, with great feeling and taking the dialogue in special voices, I looked up at my audience of one. She looked back with her big brown eyes.

"Is that all?" she asked.

"Well, that's all in this story," I said, quickly adding "Would you like another?"

She tried again. "Is that all that happens?"

"Well, they just...I mean they...yes, that's all."

She drew in a deep breath. "That *can't* be all," she said.

"Why?" I asked, defeated.

"Because if that's all, it's not a story."

And she was right. I have not yet worked out a good ending for that story, though I am still trying. G.K. Chesterton noted this about fairy tale endings, which are sometimes bloodier than an *adult* can handle. He wrote: "Children know themselves innocent and demand justice. We fear ourselves guilty and ask for mercy."

But lots of stories can still have a beginning, a middle, and an end and not be right. If they are missing that "inner truth," they are nothing. A tale, even a small children's tale filled with delight, is still saying something. The best stories are, in Isak Dinesen's words, "a statement of our existence." Without meaning, without metaphor, without reaching out to touch the human emotion, a story is a pitiable thing; a few rags upon a stick masquerading as life.

I believe this last with all my heart. For storytelling is not only our oldest art, it is our oldest form of religion as well; our oldest way of casting out demons and summoning angels. Storytelling is our oldest form of remembering; remembering the promises we have made to one another and to our various gods, and the promises given in return; of recording our human-felt emotions and desires and taboos.

The story is, quite simply, an essential part of our humanness.

91

WRITING FOR YOUNG PEOPLE

AN EMOTIONAL DÉJÀ VU

BY CHARLOTTE ZOLOTOW

THE MORE I TRY to analyze children's books or children's minds, or the fusion of feelings and events that goes into writing for them, the more I realize what a mystery children's thoughts are, and what a mystery the whole process of writing for them is. Part of it is the imagery and events and feelings that are completely individual; part of it the dreamlike, almost Jungian, merging of thoughts, feelings, fantasies, and desires that are universal.

A friend of mine on the brink of divorce told me of a recurring dream: She opened a door in her house and discovered a room she never knew was there. Her dream haunted me, and I would remember it at odd times. It had such evocative power that years later I used it in my book *Someday,* where a little girl is dreaming of lovely things she would like to have come true.

Last week, Andrea, a small girl who lives on my street, rang my bell and asked if she could go through my house again. "I haven't been upstairs in a long time," Andrea said. And she climbed upstairs humming under her breath and disappeared. When her mother came to collect her, I said, "She's upstairs. She wanted to go through my house." Andrea's mother began to laugh. "Ever since she read *Someday,* she's been searching for a new room in our house. I guess she thinks since you wrote the book, she'll find it here."

What a fusion! Of my friend's dream, with her unconscious telling her of unknown new things ahead; of my own inability to forget the dream, of having it turn up years later as I was writing a book about a little girl's wish fulfillment, and then its effect on the little girl next door, who wasn't even born when my friend dreamed her dream. There's a continuity, a flow of something unexplainable, a lovely, slow, rich mystery that lies at the core of life.

It is this mystery that flows through much writing for young children, although on the surface the stories may seem to be about very ordinary things.

Some writers for children deal with the most exaggerated kinds of events. Most of my books are about ordinary, daily events: relationships between children and adults, brothers and sisters, mothers and daughters, mothers and sons, fathers and sons, and fathers and daughters—and the infinite variety of personal encounters out of which emotions arise.

Emotions, *feelings* don't change. A child's emotions are similar to those an adult experiences—anger, jealousy, loneliness, loss, hate, and love—but adults have found ways to buffer themselves against the intensity of a child's emotions, emotions that can be aroused by the most ordinary situations. Adults have learned to camouflage—through religion or withdrawal or resignation or humor or cynicism; to protect themselves from the full impact of their feelings. They have memory to help them. As children, they have felt everything before, but children have no way of understanding that sad, wise, eternal truth: "This, too, shall pass." To adults the phrase can bring comfort; but to children, it would destroy the meaning, the moment of the experience itself. And for both good and bad experiences, the more fully we feel them, the more fully we live. In a way, children live more fully, more completely than we do. They are the true existentialists of the world.

So how and why does one write for the very young? For me it is an emotional *déja vu*. My adult anger or grief or joy is intensified by its familiarity. I have felt this way before. I remember not only childhood events themselves but the feelings those long-ago events evoked. They are the same feelings I experience again as an adult. And now when I experience a sense of loss or change or love or hate, I can remember the events of childhood that gave me grief or pleasure long ago, and see the kinds of events that give grief or pleasure to the children around me, who recognize and understand these happenings. The emotion they arouse is intensified by the fact that as an adult I am reexperiencing it.

A grown person's unrequited love evokes the same misery as a child's when his big brother or sister goes off without him. The loss of a job to another person can awaken the same feeling of anger a small child gets when a dog he wanted is given to someone else. We adults are no different from the children we were—only more experienced and defen-

479

sive and better able to disguise our feelings from others (if not from ourselves).

Children experience keenly feelings that arise from events that to the adult seem unimportant. But to know and remember this is to respect a child's feelings in a way that will lead to greater understanding.

When a friend of mind read *The Name of the Rose,* by Umberto Eco, she told me I *must* read it. With her increasing enthusiasm and urging, my irritation grew. Later, I realized that the second she said, "You must read it," resistance built up in me: I knew I was *not* going to read it, even though I value my friend's judgment and taste. As I examined my ornery reaction, I realized that my childish resistance to what others urge upon me is much the same resistance that some children have to certain books. In a way, it's an intrusion on our privacy. For reading is a very private affair, and that's why TV will never replace it! I have so much I want to read and reread that I want to select what fills my own emotional needs, needs that are often different from or unknown to even my closest friends.

It was not that way when I was an adolescent, or in my middle years, when I had a wide, all-encompassing, greedy desire to read everything. But when I think back, I do remember as a child wanting to read certain books over and over again, and others not at all. I think that's because very young children—like adults—want to read books that help them sort out their own most acute needs, their own questions about life.

I remember a small girl at the dinner table listening for as long as she could to adults discussing politics, and then, suddenly breaking in by saying, "Now let's talk about me." Selfish? No. Self-centered? Yes. It is intelligent to be self-centered. Being "centered" is good; it describes a healthy psychological or physical state, and this self-interest and self-knowledge help you understand the interests and needs of others. That is what little children are doing; that is why they choose certain books over others. For each book is a world into which they are trying to fit their own perception and feelings. And that is why it is good that there are so many different kinds of books being written for children today: If they don't like one, they will like another. *They* must be allowed to find the ones that answer some need of their own.

In the hundreds of letters I've received over the years from children and parents, there are two comments that please me the most. One is from the child who writes, "How do you know about me?" And the other is from the parent who complains that when he finishes reading the book out loud to the child, the child turns to the front of the book and asks to hear it again.

The reason the child thinks the book is about him or wants to hear it over and over again is that he is facing or feeling or trying to clarify something he recognizes about himself in the book. For young children this is often the most ordinary, daily event. They want to understand *why* their parents or peers do a certain thing, why they respond to it in a way that perplexes them and the people around them. They want to know that their experience exists in other people, that they are not alone. It is themselves they search for.

My first published book, *The Park Book,* illustrated by H. A. Rey, originally published in 1944, was reissued in 1986. I am especially pleased to have my early books reissued, because the emotions in these books are valid for children today. The children of the thirties, forties, fifties, sixties, and seventies felt as children do now when they are lonely or frightened, or angry or happy. Although events change from period to period, in both the world and personal history, emotional reactions are the same.

I've been talking so far almost entirely about the picture book. I've skipped over that adolescent, middle-years period when we want to plunge into all things great and small, specific and abstract; into experiences we've had, might have, will never have, but want to have vicariously through the books we read. Adolescence is that strange time of life when we have matured physically, but our experience and understanding and independence lag behind. Despite increased sexual education and open discussion and television dramas to which young people are constantly exposed today, they still suffer from not knowing how to talk to each other, or how to deal with the violence and dissipation and contradicting moral behavior of their peers and adults. They are capable of understanding more than most books before the fifties gave them credit for. Not only capable, hungry, too. They need books that deal with protagonists their own age, facing their own struggles and conflicts and joys and desires.

But how does an editor find such books? There is a certain would-be author who will ask us what kind of book we are looking for. I can write anything, they say, just tell us what themes, what trends, you want. An editor can't assign authors to write books. No genuine piece of writing

481

ever happens without the author's total emotional belief and involvement in what he or she is writing about. It must germinate inside his own unconscious and consciousness and emotions if it is to be a truly fine book.

Some authors write out of great happiness, and theirs are warm, exciting, loving books; other books come out of some bad and troubled experiences in the author's own development. Any writer honest enough to recall and put on paper the full story of his or her turbulent adolescence—or any segment of it—will have a book intense and rich and true for any reader, young or old. Fine books like *The Catcher in the Rye* or *I Never Promised You a Rose Garden* or *My Sweet Charlie*, all published originally for adults decades ago, are read and cherished by young people everywhere. Excellent writers such as Patricia Windsor, Louise Lawrence, Mollie Hunter, Paul Zindel, M. E. Kerr, and Adrienne Jones have written magnificent books that are read by both young people and adults with equal absorption and satisfaction.

When these books are written, coming as they do from the emotional experiences of the individual writer, they often deal with issues and ideas or evoke feelings and doubts and dilemmas that have not been dealt with before in young people's fiction. Often because it is so new in content and breaks new ground, a book has a hard time making its way. And often, too, those first startling revelations of a unique reaction to experiences previously untried in books for the young are books of passion and belief, not books that pander to the public.

An editor has to be open to new ideas, new ways of writing, new styles, new approaches, new thoughts, new directions, in content and form. But, of course, we are often fallible. Sometimes it's tempting to advise an author to cut a scene, which, however effectively written, we feel might arouse the anxiety or anger of some part of the reading public. Words or scenes may shock, but the editor's criteria must be how necessary to the reality of the story these words and scenes are. When such things are thrown into a story simply for shock value, that is bad writing, and no good writer resorts to it.

When Maurice Sendak's *Where the Wild Things Are* first came out, there was an outcry from angry adults, but the monsters that horrified some adults, the children took to their hearts immediately. They recognized their honesty as an expression of a small child's rage.

Other writers deal with similar themes in different fashion. Mine is

482

down-to-earth, everyday, ordinary events. *The Hating Book* is an example. The episodes or desires that evoke the reader's emotions are accessible to young children: a broken pencil, a friend not sitting next to you on the school bus. But the emotion of anger toward someone you really liked is there, not because I knew of two little girls who quarreled, not because I knew about their quarrel with their best friend, but because at the age of fifty when I wrote that book, I had just had a quarrel with a friend across the street. My anger and hurt and hate poured out; when I sat down at the typewriter, full of adult rage, that was familiar from previous times going back to my childhood when I had experienced it. As I said at the beginning, we are not all that different, adults and children. Emotionally, we experience the same feelings. That is what makes us, whatever nationality, whatever age, adult and child alike, more human than otherwise. That is why so many children identify with the book I sat down to write, angry at my friend across the street, and began it with, "I hate, hate, hated my friend." How do you know about me, the children write and ask. I don't. I only know about myself.

92

CREATING SUSPENSE IN THE YOUNG ADULT MYSTERY

By Joan Lowery Nixon

CREATING SUSPENSE in the young adult mystery novel is not just a matter of keeping the reader guessing: Suspense calls for all the nail-biting emotional responses of anxiety, excitement, and fear, as readers live through the viewpoint of the main character.

Young adult readers are impatient. They'll often read the first few lines of a book, and if it doesn't intrigue them, they'll put the book down and reach for another; so suspense must begin in the first few paragraphs, as in my book *The Kidnapping of Christina Lattimore:*

> I don't like the way he's looking at me.
> It's a kind of creepy look as though the two of us shared some kind of secret, and it's making me uncomfortable.

The story might begin with an immediate, fully written scene of terror, as in *The Dark and Deadly Pool:*

> Moonlight drizzled down the wide glass wall that touched the surface of the hotel swimming pool, dividing it into two parts. The wind-flicked waters of the outer pool glittered with reflected pin-lights from the moon and stars, but the silent water in the indoor section had been sucked into the blackness of the room.
> I blinked, trying to adjust my eyes to the darkness, trying to see the edge of the pool that curved near my feet. I pressed my back against the wall and forced myself to breathe evenly. I whispered aloud, "Mary Elizabeth Rafferty, there is nothing to be afraid of here! Nothing!" But even the sound of my own wobbly words terrified me.

It's not enough just to capture the attention and interest of young adult readers; the author has to keep them in suspense throughout the entire story, and there are a number of ways in which this can be done.

1. *Challenge readers with a situation that is completely new and different.* Many of us fondly remember stories from our childhood that involved buried treasure, trunks in attics, and secret passages. But those stories are familiar to today's adolescent mystery fans, too, and unless you can come up with an original, unusual twist, you'd better develop a plot based on your own ideas. Ask yourself an intriguing question and challenge yourself to find the answer.

What if a thirteen-year-old girl, who has been shot during a robbery, wakes from a semi-comatose state four years later to find that she is the only eyewitness to the unsolved crime? (*The Other Side of Dark*)

What if a girl with a serious illness has given up hope and decides not to fight for her life? Suppose her life were in danger from an unexpected direction— wouldn't she instinctively, automatically fight to live? (*The Specter*)

2. *Take a sudden, unexpected turn, making good use of the element of surprise.* In *The Seance,* another of my mysteries, the girls' nervousness during the seance builds to terror, resulting in a scene of panic, in which the candles—the only light in the house—are extinguished. During those few minutes of darkness, before a lamp is plugged in and turned on, one of the girls—Sara—disappears. It's a "locked room mystery" until readers are led to suspect that one of the other girls present must have been involved in Sara's disappearance. When it's revealed that the main character, Lauren, is the one who is responsible, it comes as a total surprise. From this point, the story shifts, and Lauren becomes a potential murder victim.

3. *Throw suspicion on someone whom the main character has trusted.* In *The Ghost of Now,* Angie's brother has been struck by a hit-and-run driver. She tries to unravel the events of that night and comes to suspect that her brother's accident had really been attempted murder. As Angie uncovers information that may lead to the identity of the killer, she confides in Del, a boy she's begun to care for. Then one night Del says something that arouses Angie's suspicions, and she begins to be afraid that Del might be the one who tried to kill her brother.

4. *Let readers know something that the main character hasn't found out yet.* In the novel of detection, a crime has been committed, and the

485

identity of the criminal must be discovered by both the main character and the readers. In the novel of suspense, someone is out to do away with the main character—who may or may not know the identity of this person—but readers know what is planned and watch the main character head into danger, ignorant of what awaits.

I combined these two forms in *The Stalker*. Every odd-numbered chapter is written in the form of *detection*, from the viewpoint of Jennifer, whose best friend's mother has been murdered. Circumstantial evidence points to the friend, but Jennifer enlists the help of a retired police detective to help her prove Bobbie's innocence. Every even-numbered chapter is written in the form of *suspense*, in the mind of the murderer. The murderer's identity is unknown to both Jennifer and to readers, but readers are aware that he presents an ever-growing danger to Jennifer.

5. *Let the main character become aware of some information but keep it from the reader for a while*. While you must play fair with readers by eventually giving them every clue, there is no reason you can't heighten suspense by showing your reader that your main character knows something but is not yet ready to divulge it. In Chapter One of *The Stalker*, Jennifer, still in shock with news of the murder, questions her grandmother.

"Where is Bobbie? Did they say?"
"Good question. Police don't know where she is. Looks like she up and run away. Nobody on God's earth knows where that girl's gone off to."
Jennifer clutched the (freshly ironed) shirts to her chest, ducking into the smell of starch and scorch so that Grannie couldn't see her face. "I'll start supper," she mumbled, and hurried from the room.
Where was Bobbie? Suddenly, surely, Jennifer knew.

The chapter ends as the police question Jennifer, who is so angry that she keeps her knowledge from them, too.

There was a pause. The detective with the pad and pen leaned toward her just a fraction. The other one did, too. It was coming—the question Jennifer had expected, had been afraid of.
"Jennifer," he said, "do you know where Bobbie Trax is now?"
Jennifer looked at him without blinking, as steadily as she could manage. She gripped the arms of her chair so tightly that her fingers ached as she answered, "No, I don't."

It is not until Chapter Three, when Jennifer is on her way to join Bobbie, that readers are made aware of what Jennifer has known all along.

6. *Tantalize readers by hinting at other kinds of secrets that are up to them to uncover.* In *A Deadly Game of Magic,* Lisa and three companions seek refuge from a storm in a nearby house. From the beginning, Lisa, who is intuitive, feels uncomfortable in this house, sensing that though they thought they were alone, there is some other presence in the house with them; her fear zeros in on a room at the end of the bedroom wing—the only room in which the door stands open. Throughout the story an unseen person again and again attempts to lure them toward that room, but each time they manage to avoid entering it. While readers begin to suspect what might be in that room, the final clue isn't given until the last paragraph in the book, and readers must figure out the answer themselves.

7. *Let readers see your main character make a mistake, or choose a totally wrong course of action, as a result of a personality flaw.* In *The Stalker,* Jennifer has been characterized as loyal and loving, but impulsive and stubborn, too. Readers are well aware that she should stay away from the scene of the crime, but her impatient single-mindedness causes her to make the wrong choice. Without telling her detective-partner, Jennifer goes alone to the scene, placing herself in immediate danger.

8. *Description of the setting can help to create and maintain suspense.* Highly visual writing through active picturesque verbs is the essential tool here. In *The Ghosts of Now,* an empty house holds such an important place in the story that it deserves the detailed description which begins:

The Andrews place squats alone at the end of an empty, quiet street. Maybe it's because of the overlarge lot that surrounds it; maybe it's because the house looks like an unkempt, yellowed old man who badly needs a barber, but I feel that the other houses on the block have cringed away from this place, tucking in their tidy porches and neat walkways and dropping filmy curtains over blank eyes. . . .

Someone once lived in this house and loved it, and for a few moments I feel sad that it should be so neglected, left alone to die.

But the house is not dead.

There are small rustlings, creakings, and sounds barely loud enough to be heard as the house moves and breathes with the midday heat. I feel that it's watching me, waiting to see what I'll do. Or could someone be watching, listening, just as I listen?

9. *Sub-mysteries can aid suspense*. A sudden shadow on the porch, which is accounted for in the next chapter; a character whose actions are so peculiar that they frighten your main character; an aunt who is frantic to keep something hidden—such sub-mysteries tie in with the central mystery to be solved and heighten suspense. Sometimes they can do double duty by serving as red herrings. In *The Kidnapping of Christina Lattimore*, Christina, upstairs in bed and doing her home-work, thinks she is alone in the house, until:

Maybe there was the click of a doorknob downstairs. If there was, I didn't notice it. I hold my breath and listen as I become aware that softly, very softly, through the thick plush carpeting on the stairway, footsteps are padding, pat-ting, like little slaps with a power puff. And they are coming up the stairs!

Christina, preparing to defend herself, discovers it's only her father's secretary, Rosella, and relaxes. But as they talk, Rosella's inconsistent, nervous behavior arouses Christina's suspicions.

10. *A peculiar character can add suspense whenever he or she appears*. In *The Seance*, the daily life of Ila Hughes, grandmother of one of Lauren's friends, is built around superstitions, some of them creepy, such as the cat she has buried inside the walls of her house to keep the devil away. And her hobby?

My glance fell on something that made me automatically step back. On the mantel, on a level with my eyes, was a row of little gray skulls!
There was a chuckle close to my ear, and Mrs. Hughes touched my shoul-ders, moving me forward again. "Those are my little birds," she said, laughing. "Aren't they precious? Little bird skulls. I began finding them in the Thicket years ago."

11. *Old tricks can still be used*. We're all familiar with the *time is running out* technique, but it can still be effective. And so can the technique of *making the readers—but not the main characters—aware that someone is sneaking toward the house or slowly turning the knob on the bedroom door*. Pull out all the stops. Readers of young adult mysteries love it.

12. *Each chapter ending should be so intriguing that readers can't close the book.* These last sentences can whet curiosity or be downright terrifying, but their job is to lead readers from one chapter into the next, nonstop:

From *The Other Side of Dark:*

If I shot Jarrod, wouldn't it be self-defense? And wouldn't it end the trials and the questions and the badgering and the harassment and the nightmares and the worries and the years and years of fear?
Carefully I aim the gun.

From *A Deadly Game of Magic:*

I would have liked to comfort her. I would have loved it if someone had tried to comfort me. All I could do was lean against the door, hoping it would hold me. My legs were wobbly. My mind seemed to tremble as much as my body, but one thought came through clearly. "Whatever Sam saw," I said, "is still in this house. And like it or not, we're trapped in here with it."

To keep readers from becoming exhausted, you must have the suspense in your mystery build and peak, drop and build again. The valleys are a good place for humor, for development of the relationships between the main character and her family and friends, for her moments of introspection and attempts to handle the non-mystery problems that are part of her life.

But it's those peaks of suspense that will cause your readers to write, "I just couldn't put your book down. When is your next mystery coming out?"

93

MESSAGES BELONG IN TELEGRAMS

By Connie C. Epstein

Sam Goldwyn, driving force of Metro-Goldwyn-Mayer, once said, "If you want to send a message, send a telegram." Although he is not usually thought of as a source of good advice for children's authors, his remark is one the aspiring writer for the young would do well to take to heart. Message writing is usually bad writing, and children's books appear to be especially vulnerable to it. In fact, it may be the reason children's writing is often considered a lesser art.

Katherine Paterson, a Newbery Medal winner, expressed her feelings about message writing very cogently: When an interviewer asked her, "What are you trying to do when you write for children?," he was clearly disappointed when she answered that she was simply trying to write as good a story as she possibly could. She concluded, "He seemed to share the view of many intelligent, well-educated, well-meaning people that while adult literature may aim to be art, the object of children's books is to whip the little rascals into shape."

What is message writing? After all, every writer has a point of view, and without it a book is boringly bland. My definition is that the message writer believes in one or more universal truths that hold for everyone, whatever the circumstances. The artistic writer, on the other hand, is interested in people as individuals, the way each behaves and why. She or he describes them as clearly as possible and then trusts the reader to draw the appropriate conclusions from the actions of the characters.

All kinds of messages have shown up in children's books ever since children's writing was first considered a form of its own. At first, proper manner, good habits, and virtuous behavior were a prime concern. Today's writers continue to worry about virtuous behavior, but the problems have changed. Instead of thumb-sucking, stories deal

490

now with the terrors of drug addiction. Or writers may feel they should instill proper attitudes toward social problems such as racism, sexism, and ageism.

Some of the early children's cautionary tales seem startling, to say the least, in this day and age. There is the famous *Struwwelpeter (Slovenly Peter)* by Heinrich Hoffman, published in Germany in 1845. It was considered a great advance in the development of children's books, for it used the technique of comic exaggeration, a largely missing ingredient until then. Still, to cure Little Suck-a-Thumb of his bad habit, the tailor cuts off his thumb with his shears. The illustration shows the blood dripping down, and the caption reads, "That made little Conrad yell."

I learned good table manners from a book that had dropped the violence but retained both the preaching and the humor. Certainly it pulled no punches when it advised on right and wrong. This Manual of Manners for Polite Infants was titled *Goops and How to Be Them* by Frank Gelett Burgess, first published in 1900, a collection of verses about a strange subculture of bald, round-headed beings. The opening poem read:

> The Goops they lick their fingers,
> And the Goops they lick their knives;
> They spill their broth on the tablecloth—
> Oh, they lead disgusting lives!
> The Goops they talk while eating,
> And loud and fast they chew;
> And that is why I'm glad that I
> Am not a Goop—are you?

We recited these lines in a chorus whenever any one of the three children in our family made a slip at the dinner table and, strangely, thought they were funny rather than irritating. Perhaps the silliness was a relief in contrast to the parental lecture. Anyway, the priggishness didn't offend us and apparently doesn't offend children today, for I find to my surprise that the book is still in print.

Humor, in fact, has saved many a morality tale. One that I was most closely connected with was *The Chocolate Touch* by Patrick Skene Catling, a modern variation on the legend of King Midas (Morrow). In it, everything the hero touches turns to chocolate, and it preaches the evils of greed unabashedly, but a number of the effects are really very funny. In retrospect, I think it was more popular with children than with critics, so much so that Morrow brought out a new reillustrated edition with considerable success.

Judging from the manuscripts submitted to children's book editors, I would say that the temptation to pass along a constructive message to children continues unabated. Everyone who cares about young people these days worries about the problems of addiction to alcohol and drugs. This topic turns up constantly. Sometimes the concern takes such precedence over characterization that we get dialogue like the following:

> "If Sandy hadn't messed with drugs, she'd still be alive. . . ."
> "Well, it won't ever happen to me," Tommy answered.
> "I'm sure Sandy thought it would never happen to her."
> "I guess you're right. After all, a lot of famous people have overdosed—Janis Joplin, Jimmy Hendrix."

I can't believe that any two teen-agers ever talked to each other this way, and I doubt that any other reader would be convinced, either. Unfortunately, drug addiction is not solved so simply, and this whole story loses credibility because the writer has clearly put the message before characters and plot, a reverse of writing priorities.

Because this writer has taken his message so seriously, the reader cannot take him seriously—certainly not as an author. Adult writing-in-progress rarely suffers from the disease of wishful thinking in quite so virulent a form, with the possible exception of religious work, in which the message is truly the medium. To master their craft, children's fiction writers must constantly guard against wishful thinking and not play their characters false, or they always will be considered lesser artists.

Some people are surprised that a topic as unpleasant as drug addiction appears in juvenile writing at all, but the extent of this modern plague has pretty well settled the question. Regrettably, it is part of the scene for teen-agers in most large urban areas. More to the point is the artistry with which the subject is handled. When believable characters and plot are created, the problem falls into perspective.

The danger is the "single-issue novel," narrated in first person so that it is limited to the scope of one, sometimes immature, sensibility. All too often, the characters in such a story are defined entirely in terms of their attitude toward the problem—in this case addiction. It is their only topic of conversation and the sole motive for their actions. If characters and plot are given proper priority, however, then the problem is only one part of the whole, and the story is probably not considered a problem novel at all.

The present-day problem novel seems to me simply the latest form of message writing. Even now when we smile about the Goops of the past, children's fiction is still afflicted with obvious messages.

Manuscripts written for little children usually do not get entangled with complicated social problems, but they sometimes try even more earnestly to instruct in good behavior. In one manuscript I saw last year entitled *The Little Ice Cream Truck Who Hated Snowballs,* a personalized truck explained to a group of children the dangers of throwing things at moving vehicles. Perhaps this concept would work visually as an animated television commercial for Good Humor sticks, but between covers it seems a thinly disguised tract.

Another recent example carried the title *Aunti-Pollution and the Bubble-Gum Mess.* Aunti-Pollution was a turtle who stepped on a wad of gum and needed the help of all her animal friends to make her clean again. Pollution is of crucial importance today, but presenting it in terms of do's and don'ts for the young runs the risk of turning them off with a lecture or, at the least, of making them always uncertain exactly how the word *anti* is spelled.

When messages dominate a story, all the characters are likely to be stick figures, but one type suffers especially: the villain. Adventure tales desperately need a good, credible villain to make them work properly, yet all too often the writer wants to shield child readers from evil and cannot bring himself to describe wrong-doing with conviction or, for that matter, with understanding. In fact, the villain in this kind of story may be more important to its success than the hero, and you should be sure to develop him or her with just as much or even more care.

Of course, citing examples of what not to do is much easier than offering advice on good technique. Recently the children's writer Beverly Cleary had the following to say about messages:

There are those who feel that a children's book must *teach* a child. I am not one of them. Children prefer to learn what is implicit in a story, to discover what they need to know. As a child I was tired of being taught when there was so much room for improvement in adults.

493

These remarks were made in acceptance of an award for her story, *Ramona and Her Mother,* in which Mrs. Cleary did reluctantly allow there was a message. She didn't know it was there until she had finished the book (which is a good thing to remember: let the characters grow naturally and the moral will emerge of itself), and then the message turned out to be for adults, not for children at all. Ramona learns at last that though she has done exasperating things like squeezing out an entire tube of toothpaste, her mother does love her. So Mrs. Cleary concluded, "If there are any adults in the audience who feel that a book for children *must* have a moral, here it is: Children need to be told in words that their parents love them."

In other words, the child's point of view should be paramount. Try to imagine how the *child* in your dramatic situation would feel, and relate adult reactions to this feeling. If you are truly seeing the world through the eyes of children, you can hardly send them a message about it at the same time. Perhaps the biggest challenge for the children's writer is the leap in point of view that must always take place. From memory, instinct, and observation, the writer is always re-creating another, slightly different sensibility. The adult writer is frequently able to take the far easier course of writing from his or her personal reactions and perspective.

Children's writing is said to have come of age in the United States since World War II, for in that period it came to be recognized as a distinct area of publishing with formal standards of its own. Those who care agree that children deserve the finest writing and resent the notion that it is in any way a lesser art. But until we remember to use Western Union, not children's books, for our messages, I suspect they won't be completely accepted in the mainstream. Sam Goldwyn was a smart man, and we should listen to him.

494

94

WRITING NONFICTION BOOKS FOR YOUNG READERS

By James Cross Giblin

Where do you get the ideas for your nonfiction books?" is often the first thing I'm asked when I speak to writers. My usual reply is, "From anywhere and everywhere."

I've found a good place to start in the search for ideas is with your own interests and enthusiasms. It also helps if you can make use of personal experience. For example, the idea for my *The Skyscraper Book* (Crowell) really had its beginnings when I was a child, and loved to be taken up to the observation deck of the Terminal Tower, the tallest building in my home city of Cleveland.

Years later, after I moved to New York, I rented an apartment that was just a few blocks away from the Flatiron Building, one of the city's earliest and most striking skyscrapers. No matter how many times I passed the building, I always saw something new when I looked up at the carved decorations on its surface.

Although I had edited many books for children, I'd never thought of writing for a young audience until I was invited to contribute a 500-word essay to *The New York Kid's Book.* I chose the Flatiron Building as my topic because I wanted to find out more about it myself.

That piece led to an expanded magazine article (for *Cricket*) called "Buildings That Scrape the Sky," and then to *The Skyscraper Book.* In the latter I was finally able to tell the story behind Cleveland's Terminal Tower, the skyscraper that had fascinated me forty years earlier.

Besides looking first to your own interests and knowledge, you should also be open to ideas that may come your way by luck or chance. The idea of *Chimney Sweeps* (Crowell) literally came to me out of the blue when I was flying to Oklahoma City on business.

The plane stopped in Chicago and a tall, rangy young man carrying what I thought was a musical instrument case took the seat next to me. We started to talk, and I discovered that the man—whose name was Christopher Curtis—was a chimney sweep, and his case contained samples of the brushes he manufactured at his own small factory in Vermont. He was on his way to Oklahoma City to conduct a seminar for local sweeps on how to clean chimneys more efficiently.

Chris went on to tell me a little about the history of chimney sweeping and its revival as a profession in the last decade, because of the energy crisis. In turn, I told him I was a writer of children's books, and that he'd fired my interest in chimney sweeps as a possible subject.

We exchanged business cards, and a month or so later I wrote to tell him that I'd followed up on the idea and had started researching the book on chimney sweeps. I asked him if he'd be willing to read the manuscript for accuracy. He agreed to do so and volunteered to supply photographs of present-day sweeps that could be used (and were) as illustrations in the book.

According to an old English superstition, it's lucky to meet a chimney sweep. Well, meeting Christopher Curtis was certainly lucky for me!

Evaluating an idea

Once you have an idea for a book, the next step is to decide whether or not it's worth pursuing. The first thing I do is check R. R. Bowker's annual *Subject Guide to Children's Books in Print,* available in the reference department of most libraries, to see what else has been written on the subject. With *Chimney Sweeps,* there was nothing at all. In the case of *The Skyscraper Book,* I discovered that there were several books about *how* skyscrapers are constructed, but none with a focus on *why* and *by whom* they're constructed, which was the angle of the book I wanted to write. There may be many books on a given subject, but if you find a fresh or different slant, there'll probably be room in the market for yours, too.

Another thing to weigh when evaluating an idea is the matter of levels: A subject worth treating in a book usually has more than one. For instance, when I began researching *Chimney Sweeps,* I soon realized that besides the obvious human and social history, the subject also touched on economic and technological history. Weaving those different levels together made the book more interesting to write—and I believe it makes it more interesting for readers also.

496

A third important factor to consider is what age group to write the book for. That decision has to be based on two things: the nature of the subject and a knowledge of the market for children's books. I aimed *Chimney Sweeps* at an older audience, because I felt that the subject required more of a sense of history than younger readers would have. At the same time, I kept the text as simple and compact as possible, because I knew that there's a much greater demand today for children's nonfiction geared to the upper elementary grades than there is for Young Adult nonfiction.

After you've checked out your idea and decided what slant to take with it, and what age group to write for, it's time to begin the research. An entire article could be devoted to research methods alone. The one thing I feel it's safe to say after writing seven books is that each project requires its own approach, and you have to discover it as you go along.

When I was researching *The Scarecrow Book* (Crown, 1980), I came up against one stone wall after another. It seemed no one had ever bothered to write anything about scarecrows. Research became a matter of following up on the skimpiest of clues. For example, a brief mention in a magazine article that the Japanese had a scarecrow god led me to the Orientalia Division of the Library of Congress, where a staff member kindly translated a passage from a Japanese encyclopedia describing the god and its relation to Japanese scarecrows.

The Skyscraper Book presented the opposite problem. There was so much background material available on skyscrapers that I could easily have spent ten years researching the subject and never come to the end. Choices had to be made early on. I settled on the eight or ten New York skyscrapers I wanted to discuss and sought detailed information only on those. I did the same thing with skyscrapers in Chicago and other cities around the country.

Chimney Sweeps opened up the exciting area of primary source material. On a visit to the Economics Division of the New York Public Library, I discovered the yellowing transcripts of early 19th-century British investigations into the deplorable living and working conditions of child sweeps.

Fireworks, Picnics, and Flags: The Story of The Fourth of July Symbols (Clarion) introduced me to the pleasures of on-site research. I had spent two days at beautiful Independence National Historical Park in Philadelphia. I toured Independence Hall, visited the rented rooms nearby where Thomas Jefferson drafted the Declaration of Independence, and watched a group of third-grade youngsters touch the Liberty Bell in its pavilion. I won't soon forget the looks of awe on their faces.

Whenever I go out on a research expedition, I always take along a supply of 4 × 6-inch cards. At the top of each one, I write the subject for handy reference when I file the cards alphabetically in a metal box. I also write the title, author, publisher, and date of the book I'm reading so that I'll have all that information on hand when I compile the bibliography for my book. Then I go on to jot down the facts I think I might be able to use.

I try to check each fact against at least two other sources before including it in the text. Such double-checking can turn up myths that have long passed as truths. For instance, while researching *Fireworks, Picnics, and Flags,* I read two books that said an old bell-ringer sat in the tower of Independence Hall almost all day on July 4, 1776. He was waiting for word that independence had been declared so that he could ring the Liberty Bell.

At last, in late afternoon, a small boy ran up the steps of the tower and shouted, "Ring, Grandfather! Ring for Liberty!" The old man did so at once, letting all of Philadelphia know that America was no longer a British colony. It makes a fine story—but according to the third source I checked, it simply isn't true.

By no means will all of the facts I find appear in the finished book. Only a small part of any author's research shows up in the final manuscript. But I think a reader can feel the presence of the rest beneath the surface, lending substance and authority to the writing.

Picture research

With most of my books, I've gathered the illustrations as well as written the text, and this has led me into the fascinating area of picture research. On *The Scarecrow Book,* for example, I discovered the resources of the Prints and Photographs Division of the Library of Congress, where I located several stunning photographs of Southern scarecrows taken during the 1930s. Later, in a back issue of *Time* magazine, I came across a story about Senji Kataoka, a public relations officer with the Ministry of Agriculture in Tokyo, whose hobby was taking pictures of scarecrows. Over the years, the article said, Mr.

Kataoka had photographed more than 2000 examples in the countryside around Tokyo.

I decided to follow up on this lead, remote as it might prove to be. From the Japanese consulate in New York I obtained the address of the Ministry of Agriculture in Tokyo, and wrote Mr. Kataoka there. Six weeks later his answer arrived in neatly printed English, along with eight beautiful color snapshots of scarecrows. I wrote back saying I needed black-and-white photos for the book and Mr. Kataoka immediately mailed me a dozen, four of which were used in the chapter on Japanese scarecrows. Another appeared on the jacket. When I asked Mr. Kataoka how much he wanted for his photos, he said just a copy of the book.

Experiences such as these have taught me several important things about doing picture research. The first is: Never start with commercial photographic agencies. They charge high reproduction fees which are likely to put you in the red if your contract states that you are responsible for paying such costs.

Instead, try non-profit sources like U.S. government agencies, which provide photographs for just the cost of the prints; art and natural history museums, which charge modest fees; and national tourist offices, which will usually give you photographs free of charge, asking only that you credit them as the source.

Other good sources of free photos are the manufacturers of various products. Their public relations departments will be happy to send you high quality photographs of everything from tractors to inflatable vinyl scarecrows in return for an acknowledgment in your book.

Selling

Writers often ask me if they should complete all the research for a nonfiction book before trying to sell the idea to a publisher. That's usually not necessary. However, if you're a beginner you should do enough research to make sure there's sufficient material for a book. Then you'll need to write a full outline and draft one or two sample chapters. After that, you can send query letters to publishers and ask if they'd like to look at your material.

If a publisher is interested, you should be prepared to rewrite your sample chapters several times before being offered a contract. That happened to me with my first book, *The Scarecrow Book,* and looking back now I'm glad it did. For it helped me and my collaborator, Dale Ferguson, to sharpen the focus of that book.

Of course it's different after you become an established author. Then both you and your editors know what you can do, and generally a two- or three-page proposal describing your new book idea will be enough for the publisher to make a decision.

Once you have your contract for the book in hand, you can proceed with the writing of the manuscript. Some authors use electric type-writers, others have turned to word processors. I write longhand in a spiral notebook and mark in the margins the date each passage was drafted. That encourages me as I inch through the notebook, working mainly on Saturdays and Sundays and during vacations from my full-time editorial job.

Achieving a consistent personal voice in a nonfiction book takes me at least three drafts. In the first, I get down the basic material of the paragraph or section. In the second, I make certain the organization is logical and interesting, and I then begin to smooth out those spots where the style of the original research source may be too clearly in evidence. In the third draft, I polish the section until the tone and voice are entirely mine.

After I deliver to the editor the completed manuscript and the il-lustrations I've gathered, I may heave a sigh of relief. But chances are my work won't be over. The editor may feel that extensive revisions are necessary; sections of the manuscript may have to be reorganized, others rewritten. Perhaps the editor will want me to compile a bibliogra-phy, or a glossary of unfamiliar words used in the text.

At last everything is in place, and a year or so later—during which time the manuscript has been copyedited, designed, and set in type— the finished book arrives in the mail. That's an exciting moment, fol-lowed by a few anxious weeks as you wait for the first reviews to appear. The verdict of the critics isn't the final one, though. There's yet another stage in the life of any children's book: the reaction of young readers.

Perhaps a boy will come up to me after a library talk and tell me that he was inspired to find out more about the skyscrapers in his city after reading *The Skyscraper Book.* Or a girl will write to say that the chapter on a day in the life of a climbing boy in *Chimney Sweeps* made her cry. It's only then that I know I'm on the way toward achieving my goal—to write lively, accurate, and entertaining books for young people.

95

WRITING BIOGRAPHIES FOR CHILDREN

By Gloria Kamen

LAYER BY LAYER, stroke by stroke, the painter builds an image on canvas. A biographer does so with words, creating a portrait that either enhances, distorts, or defines. What both must never lose sight of is the essential character of their subject. It is careful attention to detail that helps do this.

If you are thinking of writing a biography for children, be prepared to go on a treasure hunt for details with special appeal to young readers. They may make the difference between an acceptable book and a *good* one.

Your starting place for research will be the library reference department, with *Books in Print,* which will show at a glance how many books there are on your subject, and when they were published. Then check the shelves for older books in both the adult and children's biography sections. If, as I did when researching the life of Charlie Chaplin, you find several substantial volumes about your subject, it would appear to be simply a matter of editing and condensing to come up with a 70-page children's book. But I was especially interested—and I believed my young readers would be also—in the events of Chaplin's childhood, for it was those events that later shaped his art and had a lot to do with his creation of "the little tramp." Most of the adult biographies about him either concentrated on his rise to fame or went into great detail about his films. But how did Chaplin feel when, for example, his mother was taken to an asylum, leaving him alone to roam the streets of Victorian London? What was it like to be in an orphanage, to be taken out of school to start working at age eight? Chaplin, I discovered, wrote most poignantly about all this in his autobiography. His own words were invaluable when I came to write about his childhood—which brings me to the subject of autobiographies as a primary source of information.

As reference material, autobiographies are extremely useful, *but* be

501

on guard against their pitfalls. Like a painter's self-portrait, an autobiography will tell you as little or as much as the author intended. It is up to you, the writer, to decide on the accuracy of the portrait. To do this, as with paintings or photos, one should compare them with those done by others. Chaplin, in his mid-seventies when he wrote his autobiography, did not have all his facts correct, and, as with most of us, had no desire to confess his faults or explain his failures in print. There were painful periods in his life that he either omitted or dismissed with a sentence. We learn little, for example, of the famous pantomimist's feelings about the introduction of sound to motion pictures, of his anxiety that it might mean the end of his movie career. He merely mentions that there was a seven-year gap in which he couldn't think of a scenario for a new film. *Modern Times,* the hybrid film, half silent, half talking, was his compromise.

When I read Fiorello La Guardia's autobiography, *The Making of an Insurgent,* I was disappointed to find the writing self-conscious and a little dull. Remembering him as the outspoken, wisecracking mayor of the New York City of my childhood, I had expected witty, lively anecdotes and a feisty, sardonic style. It was in the books written by his associates that I found the flavor of the man, who once told a reporter that "he had an obligation to get his facts straight *before* he distorted them." His own self-portrait was entirely misleading.

For my biography of Rudyard Kipling, I took copious notes from his book, *Something About Myself, For My Friends Known and Unknown.* As the title implies, he was trying to present what he considered to be an honest portrait of himself. The facts were there. His feelings and prejudices, on the other hand, could be found elsewhere: in his poetry, his fiction, and in his personal letters. Many of his letters were as free and informal as conversation, and, as such, useful in taking the place of made-up dialogue. Letters, particularly in the 19th century, were a kind of recorded dialogue between friends and family, replaced, alas, in today's world by voices on the telephone.

There was one letter Kipling wrote to his son in boarding school that was clearly meant to both amuse and reprimand him. It was reproduced in toto in the book, *O, Beloved Kids,* and went as follows:

HOW WOOD YU LICK IT IF I ROTE YOU A LETER AL FUL OF
MIS SPELT WURDS? I NO YU KNO KWITE WEL HOWE TO SPEL
ONLI YU WONTE TAIK THE TRUBBLE TO THINCK?

As I read it, the stiff-collared, walrus-moustached Kipling turned into a loving and concerned parent for me, and, I hope, for my readers.

How to use dialogue is a chronic problem for biographers, especially if the subject of the biography and those who knew him best are long since dead. If you have a strong commitment to veracity, as I do, there are ways of getting around the use of fake dialogue. Newspaper and magazine interviews may provide direct quotes, as I found, for example, when I discovered a report of Kipling's angry words about small-town small talk in America in an old Vermont newspaper. In his autobiography he recalled his parting words to his nursemaid and Hindu bearer when he left Bombay:

"Come back, baba," said Ayah, daubing her eyes.
"Yes, I will come back and I'll be a burra sahib bahadur," Ruddy answered in Hindi.

It was a touching piece of authentic dialogue that would have been all but impossible for me to make up. Without it, I would have described his departure and his feelings, those shared by any child in similar circumstances. Writing about emotions can be done without putting words in the person's mouth. Readers can accept joy, relief, or anxiety that is wordless. But hold onto those special quotes you come across, which will help enliven your book:

"Please, Ruddy," said Mrs. Kipling, "don't let Trix forget me." Kipling recalled his mother's words on his way to England, unaware that he and his sister, Trix, would not see their parents again for five years.
So each morning (on board ship) Ruddy asked three-year-old Trix, who answered, somewhat puzzled, that she "bemembered Momma."

Set yourself a reasonable limit for completing your research after which writing should begin. By putting your material in chronological order: birth and family, childhood, schooling, young adulthood, etc., you will have the facts ready to jog your memory as you go along. It is only after you begin to write that the gaps in your research will clearly show. Make a note of them, but continue to write while you seek out additional information.

It is easy to say *Begin* . . . but where? How? What should be kept in and what left out? For the writer of adult biographies, this last item may

503

not be as crucial. It becomes primary when you write for children. You cannot indulge in the luxury of wordiness. The "on the one hand, but on the other" style of adult biographers will not do for juveniles. Information must also be made comprehensible and have some relevance to a child. Adult "gossip" of disappointing love affairs, nasty court cases, political squabbles don't belong in the book, unless they carry the story to some new conclusion or give some insight into the personality of the man or woman. I briefly mentioned Kipling's court case with his brother-in-law because it was the main reason for abandoning the house he loved in Vermont and moving to England. But I did not go into Chaplin's affairs or paternity court case.

The writer of juvenile biographies must squarely face the reason he chose that man or that woman as a subject. What will be conveyed through telling his or her life story? I do not mean a flat-out message, but rather the underlying one. The things you stress—courage, talent, persistence—should come through anecdotes, humor, and through glimpses of the person's strengths and shortcomings. It is then that I am most mindful of being a storyteller as well as a biographer, for biographies share many of the characteristics of novels. I like to think of them as novels coming directly from life, but with certain constraints: Characters and events are set out for you and cannot be changed. You are free as any writer, however, to interpret them. Like a novelist, you must breathe life back into your people and events. There were, no doubt, some crises, some resolutions, that made your subject interesting to you.

Keeping in mind the age level of your intended audience, you could begin your story with an event leading to this crisis, especially one happening at the age of your readers. Chaplin is twelve when my book begins. From here I used flashbacks to his infancy and his parents' early marriage. In the case of Kipling, I started the book just before he is to be sent halfway around the world to go to school. Some background on Ruddy's life as a little sahib in India was necessary to show the tremendous wrench this change had on him.

Because eight- to eleven-year-olds are expected to have only a limited knowledge of history or foreign cultures, it is necessary, somewhere along the way, to add the essential background information in your book. It must not slow down the narrative or be placed in indigestible

504

chunks inside the story. Researching this information may lead you to some interesting reading. You may find yourself absorbed in books on the history and religions of India, on Hollywood and the "silent film" era, or on New England fisheries. One thing leads to another, one subject, one idea to another . . . so, write on!

96

EDITOR TO WRITER

By Joan Kahn

I'LL START OFF with some don'ts—don't pay any attention (or much attention) to anything I'm about to say if you're a genius. If you're a genius *you'll* know where you're going and what you're going to do. Though I don't think I've known very many geniuses and maybe—oh, well—

And don't pay any attention (or much attention) to anything I'm about to say if you feel that writing a book is a snap and that all you need is some spare time and a word processor.

Otherwise—and I'll stick to novels, mystery or non-mystery—I think the first thing you should do is try to write a book to please yourself. If you're bored with what you've embarked on, stop as soon as you realize that, and go off and do something else for a while. Often, when you come back and look at what you've been working on, you'll think, "Hey, that isn't too bad, all it needs is etc., etc." Or sometimes you'll tear it up, throw it away, and start out in another direction.

Oh, another very important thing: If you're just embarking on your novel, I hope you've been reading other people's novels, lots of them, and that you feel what you're working on isn't something everyone else has already done—that your book will have *your* observations and your point of view; that you're not going to be just an echo.

After you've decided you do like what you're working on, keep at it. The opening of a novel *is* very important—but the end of the book is *much* more important—and a good ending is much harder to come by. Much. When you have completed your book, reread it. Because you're not writing the book just for yourself, you're hoping that other people will want to read it, preferably a lot of other people. As you reread it, *try* to look at it dispassionately and see if you think you've accomplished what you set out to do, or if you've made things not clear enough for your potential readers. Everything might have seemed clear and compelling while you were at work, but no one else can get into your head.

I find that a number of authors, alas, are so careless, or so stupidly smug, that they don't (apparently, considering the state of their manuscripts) bother to go back over what they're sending out into the world. And, considering how tough it is (in most cases) to get published, you should do everything *you* can to help your book before you send it on its way.

I'd better say at this point that though I can and do consider incomplete nonfiction manuscripts, because I feel that with evidence of the author's writing ability, his idea for the book, and an outline, it's safe to move ahead, I don't think an editor can help a novel *while it's coming into being.* A good novelist, the best novelists I've known—and I know some very good ones—knows that the book, however carefully he plans, will choose its own path, will change about, its people will change, in many instances, as he writes. After the book has been completed and the editor can see the whole picture, only then, I feel, can the editor be helpful in suggesting modifications, if any are needed.

Once you have given birth to your novel, a novel that pleases you, the next step is finding a publisher and the publisher's editor for your book. As is perhaps already evident, *I* don't want to see anything but the completed manuscript of a novel. Many other editors disagree with me. One of the things I do feel strongly about is that publishers should read unagented manuscripts with the same care that they read agented ones—if the manuscripts are good, of course. I'll look at *any* manuscript submitted to me. A really bad piece of work can be dismissed very quickly (and sometimes such bad pieces come in via agents!). The beginning author, especially an author who doesn't have writing friends or a good local librarian to advise him, may have trouble figuring out where he'd like to send his manuscript.

I wish (and someday I hope it will be common publishing practice) that on the copyright page of every book published, where there now is information about the Library of Congress number, etc., there will be—it can be in small type—the editor's name. So that if an author far away from available knowledge of the publishing world picks up a book he admires—a book of poetry (if he wants to write poetry), a book on the Roman emperors (if that's a subject he wants to write about), a sensitive

507

novel about a girl's sixteenth birthday (if that's what he's thinking about), or a blood-and-thunder shoot-'em-up (if that's where he's heading)—he can say to himself, "I think *that* editor would respond to my work, why don't I try him?"

An inexperienced author may need a lawyer's advice on his contract, and an author can certainly be helped by a good agent who not only can advise him financially, but can help him also by sending his manuscript on, if the first publishing house he sends it to doesn't respond. And a good agent can be a friend, and even a soothing nanny if things get rough. But sometimes a beginning author may find it hard to get a good agent. Still, no one ever said it was easy in the world of the arts, and of all the arts, the art of writing is probably the least difficult one. Hang in there. And, once you *have* published a book, I recommend joining the Authors Guild (234 W. 44th, NYC 10036) and (if it's a mystery) the Mystery Writers of America (236 W. 27th, NYC 10001).

I have just said that the writing world isn't the toughest, but after you've found your publisher and your editor, there are the book buyers (or the book borrowers from libraries) to think about. *Very* important people—actually the people you have to think about *right* after you've thought about how you feel about the book. If they want to read your book, that's all anyone can ask.

After hearing about all these things to contend with you may wonder why bother. Because you want to. And, if what you want to write is a mystery—a word of encouragement. Mystery readers read more than any other kind of fiction reader—they are (I think) more intelligent—and if you plan on writing a mystery, though you have to do a lot of homework so that the police work, the medical aspects, etc., are sound, you don't have to worry, "What *is* my theme?" It's just a matter of life and death—not unimportant elements. Plus giving your readers a chance to use their deductive skills, which I think they enjoy. But remember—the ending, as I said earlier, of any novel is *especially* important in a mystery. You can't cheat at all on your way to the solution. And, your people, as in any novel, have to be real. *You* have to know them thoroughly—or you won't have a book worth writing.

Work hard—and good luck. Luck is *very* much a part of the picture.

97

A LITERARY AGENT'S PERSPECTIVE

By Anita Diamant

IN THIS AGE of proliferating conglomerates, the publishing industry has followed suit: The former cottage industry has indeed become big business. The business department, the sales and marketing departments are apt to influence the acceptance of a manuscript by the publishing house. And so literary agents, following the trends, often become interested primarily in projects bearing the promise of a six-figure advance. Where does this leave the great majority of writers and would-be writers? Is it impossible for them to secure representation?

It is true that conservatively 75% of all manuscripts are sold through agents today, but it is also a fact that there remain many bona fide agents who are more interested in representing a writer than only in securing huge advances. I can think of no greater pleasure than to place a first novel that indubitably will bring a relatively small advance. And it is important and rewarding for an agent to be an integral part of building a successful career for a new writer. Does this mean that every agent will take on any project that is sent in to him or her? Of course, we have to be discriminating, and obviously we will all take on manuscripts and ideas that appeal to us and would seem to bear the promise of a sale. I would like to start by assuring writers that it is possible even for a neophyte to obtain representation by a professional agent; but a good deal depends upon the way in which the work is presented and of course on the feasibility of selling the material.

The author-agent relationship is a very personal one. There must be complete trust and respect between the writer and the agent. This is true financially as well as editorially. The agent receives all monies due the writer, deducts a percentage, and then sends the balance to the writer. This should be done as soon as the publisher's check has cleared, but I must admit that I have heard numerous stories about an undue length of time that elapses before the writer is paid by the agent.

All of this can be avoided if a writer secures a reference before deciding to have a particular agent represent him or her.

I also feel that an agent must have enough background in the publishing world to be able to offer some editorial assistance to a writer. I do not mean that it is an agent's job to edit or rewrite, but an agent should know whether a proposal is sufficiently effective; whether plot, style, and characterization are successful; whether a theme is handled with clarity. If there are problems, the agent should be willing and able to indicate where the problems lie and perhaps offer suggestions that would help correct them. Your agent should also be your friend. This does not mean that an agent should take the place of your psychiatrist, your attorney, or your financial adviser, although we generally listen carefully to problems in all these areas.

The value of agents obviously is their knowledge of the markets, of the changing editorial staffs, and, of course, the close contact with all of the people who are in the field at any one time. And this is certainly a changing scene: This past year has seen enormous changes in ownership of the large publishing companies and in the hiring and firing of editorial personnel. It is very often important to think not solely of the suitable publishing house for a project, but also of the editor who will be most empathic and whose interests are somewhat analogous to the material presented.

The question inevitably rises, "Is it necessary for a writer to have an agent?" Of course, there are always manuscripts submitted directly to publishers, which sell, but the fact remains that many houses simply will not read unsolicited manuscripts, and in the case of a book project, I would certainly advise a writer to get an agent, if it is at all possible. All successful agents work on a commission basis—from 10% to 15% on domestic sales, 15% to 20% on foreign sales—and this is how the agent makes a livelihood.

An agent will also know how best to handle a property. If it is a book project, the question arises whether it should be a hardcover book, a paperback, or perhaps it would be best to sell to a hard/soft firm. Since in the case of most book contracts, the writer must give up 50% of the monies secured on a softcover deal by a hardcover publisher, it is often advisable to sell both hard- and softcover rights to a publisher who offers this arrangement, in which case there will not be a 50% split on the softcover sale.

There is always the question of multiple submissions or auctions. Not every work should be auctioned; if we feel there is a particularly appropriate publisher or editor for a certain idea, we would rather give first crack at the work to that editor. We're told by many top editors today that they are really annoyed by auctions of books that are not top properties, and it seems totally unfair and a waste of time for them to read a manuscript that is also being read by a great many other editors simultaneously. Hence, the agent's decision on how the work should be presented becomes of the utmost importance.

An agent also often assumes the role of an arbiter—between the publisher and the writer and also, more importantly, between two writers on a project. We were asked recently to handle a manuscript that had been contracted for by a major publishing house, but later rejected because of the arguments between the writers. We resold the material for a larger advance and made a very good deal with the former publisher to pay back only a portion of the money advanced. However, we spent endless hours again trying to get the parties to agree to accepting responsibility for the share each had in the manuscript. At this moment, everything is signed and we hope the new publisher will receive a satisfactory revision and the work can get underway.

Now, how does a writer go about finding an agent? First, through recommendation from other writers, perhaps from a publisher. However, three good sources are the lists offered by The Society of Authors' Representatives (39½ Washington Square South, New York, NY 10012); The Independent Literary Agents Association (55 Fifth Avenue, New York, NY 10003); and *Literary Market Place,* published by R. R. Bowker Co., available in the reference department of most good public libraries. Also, there are always agents who speak at writers' conferences and even to writers' groups.

Once you decide on having an agent, you must write a good, selling query letter, indicating just what the idea may be, outlining the idea, as well as including something about your own background and authority for writing the book; your general vita; any previous publications you have had, and why you feel there is a market for this idea. DO NOT send manuscripts, and by all means make certain that you are approaching the agent who handles the kind of material you are writing. *Literary Market Place* indicates in the agents' section the type of manuscripts the agent will accept.

When we read a query letter that is intelligently written, we will ask to see either a proposal and sample chapters, or we may even ask to see the entire manuscript. We have been fortunate in finding even best-selling writers this way, the most notable of whom was V. C. Andrews, whose novels have sold over 30 million copies in this country alone. Consequently, even though realistically an agent will prefer to handle a writer who already has a track record, it is unrealistic for us not to take a chance at reading something that evokes our interest.

Each time I speak at a writers' conference, I am bombarded with requests for my address, and I realize that this will bring in numerous proposals and a good deal of mail. But I have found several very good writers through these conferences, and I would advise writers who are not living near the major markets to attend writers' conferences, for this gives them an opportunity to meet and talk to agents and editors and in this way make a professional contact.

Often writers ask me whether it is necessary to sign a contract with an agent. Many agents do require contracts, but I personally do not feel this is necessary, for like a marriage, the relationship between writer and agent is good only if they can work amicably together. If not, then a divorce is inevitable. Also, all book contracts have an agency clause stipulating that the agent has the right to negotiate for the author, and all monies due will be sent directly to the agent.

However, if problems develop between you and your agent, first discuss the situation with him or her. If this does not resolve the problem, send a registered letter detailing your complaints and stating that you are hereby ending your agreement. Even though there may not be a termination clause in your agreement with your agent, most agents will release a client if there is a bona fide reason for disagreement.

We find that writers today are shopping for agents as they might publishers. This is certainly legitimate, but we do resent having to take the time to read manuscripts if we have not been given them exclusively. And frankly, many agents have told me that they simply will not read anything if they know it has been given to many other agents. It is far better to select an agent, give that person a specified time to respond to the project and to your letter, and if you are not satisfied at that point, go on to seek another agent. After all, personalities do not always mesh, and you may be happier with one agent representing you than another.

It's important for the writer to be able to keep in touch with his agent, who, upon the writer's request, must make available a record of where a manuscript has been sent and what the rejections have been. Many writers ask whether it is advisable to seek an attorney as well as an agent, or perhaps in lieu of an agent. If an attorney has been dealing with literary properties, he can of course be very helpful, but the average attorney does not know the practices of the trade, and we find (as do publishers) that the average lawyer simply does not know what is negotiable in a contract and what must remain intact. Since agents spend so many hours attempting to sort out these problems, they are more knowledgeable about them. Recently, a deal was almost killed because of the inappropriate interference of an attorney who did not understand that his client must assume responsibility for what he presents in his manuscript.

The publishing business has become exceedingly complex, and it is because of the nature of the changes that I feel it is so important for a writer to find representation with a well-established agent. A good agent knows what rights must be protected for a writer in a contract and which houses offer better contracts than others. It is an interesting fact that in selling a manuscript, we find it easier to obtain a higher advance for a writer when the idea is so exciting that many publishers want it, than for a writer who has published many books but whose sales record is not very good. The first question editors ask when we submit an idea by a published writer is how many copies his or her last book sold. The fact is that editors are looking almost exclusively for book ideas that will sell in big numbers.

Since agents receive publishers' lists of their forthcoming books, we are also in a position to advise our writers whether they are zeroing in on an idea that has been presented before, and perhaps we can save the writer time in trying to work out that particular idea. The agent must be constantly in touch with the market, and this is where a writer receives the greatest benefit from that representation.

In spite of the fact that publishers prefer best sellers and blockbusters to anything of a literary nature, the market is still open for well-written, fresh works, and any legitimate agent will welcome the submission of a work that has a *good sales potential* or reveals a writer with a future.

Certainly, any writer who has the urge, the ability, and the time to pursue such a career should not be discouraged at this time. It was George Sand who once said, "The trade of authorship is a violent and indestructible obsession."

98

ERASING THE BLUE-PENCIL BLUES

By David Petersen

IF YOU'VE ever felt that too many of the magazine articles you've strived so diligently to create have wound up getting edited too harshly, then I don't need to tell you about the Blue-Pencil Blues. You know the ailment well, even if you've not heard the term before. While I'd never say that you should consider this potentially debilitating malady a blessing, I *will* suggest that your writing can benefit from it.

During more than a decade of straddling the publishing fence as both a free lancer and a magazine editor, I've identified five nonfiction problem areas that I feel comprise the most common reasons editors bring out their blue pencils. The good news is that by learning to recognize and weed out these troublemakers, you can significantly reduce the need for editing and—a delightful spin-off—increase sales.

Here, then, are what I perceive to be the five primary reasons editors edit—along with a few tips to help you eliminate them from your writing.

1. *Editors edit for grammar, punctuation, spelling, and all the other nuts and bolts that hold a manuscript together, but that too many free lancers too often fail to tighten.*

Many aspiring wordsmiths feel so blessed with talent that they think they needn't bother with the more mundane details of the writer's craft—things such as submitting clearly typed manuscripts free of punctuation errors, pronouns that disagree in number, misspellings, and the like. Some of these writers do show budding talent, but anyone who believes that just a good yarn is enough to win consistently at the free-lancing game is setting himself up for a fall.

The reality is that few magazine editors have the time or inclination to take on serious cosmetic surgery, no matter how beautiful the hidden message may be. Sloppily prepared pieces, peppered with mechanical glitches that could easily have been caught and corrected by the writer, are rarely going to sell—and the few that do are bound to be heavily edited.

The self-evident remedy, therefore, is to make sure that your copy is road-ready; that nary a screw that you can detect is left jangling loose for an editor to spot and tighten. If *you* don't take care of the mechanical essentials and your editors have to, consider their tinkering a blessing rather than a curse.

2. *Editors edit for style.*

No two publications speak with exactly the same voice. A serious free lancer knows this and—while making no attempt to parrot every stylistic inflection of a magazine—will avoid submitting seriously off-key articles. You wouldn't, for example, use a stiff, academic style in an article bound for a magazine whose voice is as informal and conversational as *The Mother Earth News,* but many free lancers have—only to be rejected or heavily edited for their trouble.

A submission written in a voice that's gratingly off-key tells an editor that the writer a) hasn't bothered to familiarize himself with the publication (a cardinal and surprisingly common free lancer's sin); or b) is unable to recognize a magazine's style when he sees it. An off-key article is far less likely to sell and, if it does, is certain to be returned to bring it into editorial harmony. So, familiarize yourself with your target publication's voice, and pitch your style accordingly.

3. *Editors edit for length.*

When I queried one of my favorite magazines about an article idea not long ago, the editors gave me a green light to submit the piece on speculation, but stipulated that I hold the length to around 1,500 words. Had I sent them the 2,500 tome I generated on the first draft (rather than the 1,500 words I eventually trimmed it to), I could hardly have taken umbrage had they cut the piece to the requested length—or even rejected it. The moral: When an editor is helpful enough to indicate a preferred length for an article, don't exceed it.

But many times you don't have a specified length to shoot for. What then? Here's a procedure that has worked well for me as a free lancer—and *with* me as an editor.

Begin by studying a few recent issues of the target magazine to determine the average word count of several articles similar in style and scope to the one you plan to submit. Next, send an SASE for writer's guidelines (which will probably suggest minimum and maximum lengths for different kinds of articles). Finally, a query. And in that query, suggest a length for your article based on what you've learned by studying the guidelines and the magazine itself. This procedure will significantly improve your chances of getting a go-ahead from the editor. If the editor is interested in your proposal but wants more or fewer words than you've suggested, he can say so in his response.

4. *Editors edit for accuracy and completeness.*

Consider this scenario: You've written and submitted an article in which you quote a fellow named Stewart. The piece sells, is published, and all is well . . . until the day the publication's editor sends you a copy of a letter received from Mr. Stewartt (two t's). No matter that the extra "t" is a somewhat unusual spelling; Mr. Stewartt is upset that you got his name wrong—and the editors are also upset because they feel compelled to print Stewartt's letter along with an apology. How eager do you think they'll be to purchase more of your work?

The most common inaccuracies are dates, figures, quotations, professional titles, and the names of persons and places. The free-lancing war is won or lost through many small battles. Verify, verify, verify!

Hand-in-hand with accuracy goes completeness. Never assume that readers will have sufficient foreknowledge of your topic to fill in informational blanks for themselves. When in doubt, err on the side of providing too much detail rather than too little.

5. *Editors edit for clarity.*

Clarity is the cornerstone of effective communication—and effective communication is the foundation of good writing. To achieve clarity, polish each of your manuscripts until you think it shines, then ask a reliable friend who's willing to play the part of candid literary critic to read it and point out any hazy spots. If your critic is confused by a passage, fails to chuckle at a joke you thought was an absolute knee-slapper, or otherwise misses a point you've tried to make, it's a fair bet that other readers—including editors—will have the same trouble. (If you don't have someone to read your work for you, the next best critic is *time*. The longer you can afford to let a piece rest after you've "completed" it, the more objective you'll be when you return to it for further editing.)

516

Sure, a good editor can shine up your slightly hazy prose for you—that's part of what he's trained and paid to do. But a serious writer won't expect him to, won't want him to, won't give him the need to. To increase sales and minimize editing, polish your product until even the filmiest patches of fog disappear. Then polish some more.

And there you have it—the five kinds of problems that most frequently prompt editors to reject or heavily edit manuscripts . . . along with a few suggestions for eliminating them from your writing.

Of course, all this talk of how to minimize having your work altered assumes that you'll be dealing with competent editors. A fair assumption, I believe. Slovenly and unqualified editors are as scarce as fur on a fish and as ephemeral as Hailey's comet. In general, you can trust career blue-pencilers to be skilled professionals dedicated to making their publications the best they can be by making their free-lance contributors perform at their best. Both are essential.

When an editor improves my words without making them sound more like his than mine, I'm unabashedly grateful. But as much as I appreciate the help, I nonetheless set my sights on leaving no loose nuts and bolts to tighten, no fat to trim away, no murky prose to clarify, no inaccuracies to correct or blanks to fill in, and no off-key voice to bring my article into line with the magazine's style. I don't always succeed, but I always try. That's my duty as a writer.

And when I'm sitting on the other side of the editorial desk, I try to make every article I work with as good as it can be without destroying the writer's voice or betraying the style of my magazine. That's my duty as an editor.

I've never known a sadistic editor, and the unqualified are few and far between. In the majority of cases, therefore, the most effective way to avoid the feeling that your work is being edited too severely by others is to bear down a little harder with your own blue pencil.

517

99

INSIDE THE EDITOR'S OFFICE

BY PATRICIA TOMPKINS

THE EDITOR'S OFFICE. If you've never been inside one, perhaps you've imagined what it is like: a plush, spacious room, with framed photographs on paneled walls; behind a vast teak desk and leather chair, a panoramic view of the city. Outside the door to this center of serene efficiency sits a secretarial sentinel. The elusive editor is out having lunch with a writer.

For the novice free-lance writer, the editor's office may seem like an inner sanctum, a place where only writers with the right password are admitted. But you'll be closer to reality—and closer to getting inside the office—if you imagine the following: a typewriter and possibly a word processor on a little table; mismatched chairs crowded around a gray metal desk, with calendars, memos, and page layouts taped on plaster walls; through the venetian blinds, a view of a parking lot. On the littered desk, alongside an overflowing in-box, are a salad in a plastic container and a mug of cold coffee. The phone rings while the editor is down the hall, trying to fix the photocopying machine. The editor's office, in short, is usually about as glamorous as that of a free-lance writer. (I'm writing this at my "desk"—a folding card table.)

Having set the scene, let's look at what the editor does in that office. First, understand that an editor is a working professional, often overworked and underpaid, in a wonderful, competitive business. That could describe a free-lance writer, too. Well, an editor is not so very different from you. But sometimes the mutual interests of writers and editors get lost in the shuffle of manuscripts. Aspiring contributors often forget that editors can be writers' greatest allies. The following guidelines, drawn from my experience as a copy editor for a monthly city magazine, apply to most publications and will enable you to improve your chances of selling articles. These three basics will help you reach your most important reader—the editor:

(1) Show your familiarity with the magazine to which you send your proposal or query.
(2) Communicate your enthusiasm for your subject in your query letter.
(3) Understand what an editor does and expects from free-lance writers.

The clues to what the editor is looking for appear in every issue. Study several recent issues of the magazine and obtain a copy of its writers guidelines. If your public library has back issues, you may also want to look at several copies from the past year and five years ago. Note any changes in format, content, and staff.

A thorough reading includes advertisements, which give a sense of the magazine's audience. And look at the staff list. The magazine I work for lists numerous contributing editors and identifies the subjects they cover. If there is already a regular columnist on wine, you may have a tough time selling your article on wine to the editor. But regular contributors are not necessarily permanent, and the magazine may buy free-lance material as well.

Once you've done your research and are confident your proposal suits the magazine, introduce yourself in your query letter. Remember: first impressions count, and you are competing with many others; to get the editor's attention, your letter must stand out. This doesn't mean typing in red ink on purple paper; it means writing an engaging, informative letter. Perhaps you're aiming at a local publication and are tempted to skip a letter and simply telephone the editor. Your idea is so good, you think, the editor will naturally say yes. And you'll save a month waiting for a reply by getting an instant assignment. No, you won't. The editor is not sitting around waiting for unsolicited proposals by telephone from unfamiliar callers. If you're a writer, write a letter; put your idea on paper so the editor can assess it at a convenient time.

Two weeks may pass before the editor has time to look at your letter. Why? Partly because most editors can't spend their days reading; they're busy putting out a magazine. Consider an average day in the editor's office: Arrives at nine o'clock; a glance through the mail reveals that two manuscripts due today didn't arrive. Assistant calls in sick. Editor writes final headlines and captions for three articles; associate art director asks for two lines to be cut from an article to fit layout. Desk lamp burns out; no spare bulbs around. Appointment at ten with writer to discuss work needed on feature story. Meets with editorial staff at eleven to discuss possibilities for the next issue, three months away. Eats lunch at desk while returning phone calls. Writer delivers assignment and spends fifteen minutes pitching another article idea. Editor looks at an assigned article that arrived in the day's mail. Calls printer to find out why galleys are late; writer calls wanting to update her piece. Fact-checker brings in manuscript full of errors; copy editor asks how to handle a writer who refuses her suggested changes. Interview at four with potential summer intern. Discusses illustrations for cover story with art director. Selects five letters to the editor for inclusion in next issue. Leaves at six to spend half an hour at a press preview party.

Generally, the day doesn't allow time to read unsolicited manuscripts or queries. The editor I work for coordinates editorial production with two senior editors and manages a staff of two full-time assistants supplemented by six part-time helpers (free-lance copy editors and proofreaders, plus interns) in a noisy, crowded room next to her office. Rarely does she have ten minutes alone and uninterrupted at her desk—not exactly ideal reading conditions.

One assistant weeds out the inappropriate queries each week and passes along more hopeful prospects to the editor, who then reviews them, along with recent fiction submissions. When does she read? At home in the evening and on the weekends when, much as she loves her job, she wouldn't mind doing something else. Under these circumstances, she appreciates a clear, concise query, one with enthusiasm for and knowledge of the subject and the magazine.

Keep in mind that your query is one of dozens in limbo (make that hundreds or thousands for popular national publications). Although no one likes form rejection letters, they are time-savers. Unfortunately, they don't convey how close you may have come to acceptance. The difference between a positive and a negative response to a query is often a matter of timing and luck—good and bad. Once I proposed an idea for a new column in a monthly magazine; it seemed a natural, given the publication's audience. No, thanks. I still thought my idea was sound, so twelve months later, I tried again; this time the answer was yes. Why? The proposal was the same; so was the editor, but—unknown to me—he was planning a change in format, and my suggestion now solved a problem.

No can mean the editor already has a related story in the works. I've seen two pieces on the same subject arrive simultaneously; both took a similar approach to their subject. (The one chosen was by a writer long established with the magazine.) *No* can also mean the editor has a backlog of good material ready; she knows your article would sit on hold for many months—frustrating for the writer when payment is on publication, impractical for the editor when payment is on acceptance.

Suppose the editor says *yes*—on speculation—and gives you guidelines on the desired focus, length, and deadline. These guidelines are made to avoid wasting your time and the editor's. Follow them. The magazine's production schedule won't collapse if your piece is late, but the delay will be passed along to the copy editor, art department, printer, and proofreader. (The tendency to ignore basic directions is one reason editors ask new writers to submit work on speculation, rather than on assignment.) Turn your work in on time; it will save you the trouble of thinking up novel excuses for being late.

A problem even more common than missing deadlines is submitting a manuscript that is longer than requested. A maximum of 2,000 words doesn't mean that you should write 2,500 or 3,000. But isn't that the editor's job—to edit stories to the right length? No, it isn't. The right length is the requested or assigned length. The editor has other pieces competing for space and attention. Although the magazine may vary in length from issue to issue, the amount of advertising sold, not the length of articles, usually determines an issue's size. Holding to the assigned length can be an aid to keep your piece focused.

If you've done your job, the editor can concentrate on hers: critically examining the article and seeing if its parts work well together. Are the transitions adequate? Is the subject covered adequately, or is vital material missing? Does the piece start fast and finish slow? Will it inform or entertain readers? In asking such questions, the editor exercises her skills creatively, making murky prose lucid.

Once your article is accepted, the fact-checker, copy editor, and proofreader will be looking at your work closely. (With a small staff, one person may handle all three tasks.) The fact-checker verifies the statistics, the spelling of names, and the accuracy of quotes. These details are checked with primary sources when possible, usually not with the writer. Just a few misspelled names will cast doubt on your reliability;

substantial discrepancies and errors may put your piece in jeopardy. Check your manuscript for accuracy before submitting it.

The proofreader and copy editor will be alert to other types of errors. No one will reject a manuscript if it has a dangling participle and uses "which" where "that" is correct, but the fewer mistakes, the more professional you will look. The copy editor will ask for clarification of cryptic and confusing passages. If you're a local writer, include your home and work phone numbers, along with your name and address, on the first page of your manuscript so an editor can get in touch with you easily.

It's natural to assume your writing is perfectly clear when you know the topic. The copy editor helps ensure that everything will be clear to readers, too. I've found most writers appreciate careful editorial attention to their work, but some regard copy editors as meddlers and hacks, critics who can't write. Avoid this superiority complex and cooperate. All writers' work receives the same scrutiny. You might be surprised and encouraged if you saw the deletions and revisions on most manuscripts by the time they're ready for the typesetter. Only rarely does what appears in the magazine exactly match what the editor received in manuscript form. An acceptable manuscript doesn't have to meet impossible criteria of perfection before an editor will accept it, but the less time the editorial staff has to spend cutting and polishing your manuscript, the better they'll like it.

When you have the published version of your work in hand, compare it with your original copy. Over a period of several weeks or months between writing and publication, you may be better able to see alterations as improvements. Think of editing as a writing lesson. If you're pleased with the results, send a note of thanks to the editor.

At its best, the editor-writer relationship is a partnership of peers. If you use common sense and courtesy and treat the editor as an ally, you'll be two steps ahead of the crowd.

100

WHAT EVERY WRITER NEEDS TO KNOW ABOUT
LITERARY AGENTS

By Ellen Levine

Q. *At what stage in their careers should writers look for an agent—
or will a good agent find them?*

A. Most agents prefer to begin a working relationship with a writer
when there is a book-length work to market, rather than articles or
short stories. Some agents prefer writers who already have publication
credits, perhaps magazine publication of shorter work. However, a
writer who has never published before, but who is offering a book
which deals with a unique or popular topic may also have an excellent
chance of securing an agent. Quite a number of agents are actively
looking for new writers, and they comb the little magazines for talented
writers of fiction. They also read general interest and specialty magazines for articles on interesting subjects, since they might contain the
seeds for books. Some agents visit writers conferences and workshops
with the express purpose of discovering talented authors who might be
interested in representation.

Q. *How does a writer go about looking for a legitimate agent?*

A. Writers can obtain lists of agent members from two professional
organizations—The Society of Authors' Representatives (SAR) or The
Independent Literary Agents Association (ILAA)— by writing to these
organizations at (for SAR) 39½ Washington Square South, New York,
New York 10012 and (for ILAA) 21 W. 26th St., New York, NY 10010.
Writers can also obtain a more complete list of agents by checking the
"Agents" section of *Literary Market Place* (LMP), available from R. R.
Bowker, 205 E. 42nd St., New York, NY 10017, or as a reference work
at the local library. Finally, the Authors Guild at 234 W. 44th St., New
York, NY 10036 will supply a list of agents.

Q. *How important is it for an agent to be a member of SAR or ILAA?*

A. It is not essential for a good agent to belong to either organization, but membership is very helpful and adds credibility and professionalism to the agency. These organizations schedule meetings to discuss issues and problems common to the industry and their members work together to solve them. Expertise is often shared; panels and seminars are regularly scheduled, often including key publishing personnel. There are also certain codes of professional ethics, which members of each group subscribe to. This, of course, is to the writer's advantage.

Q. *Do literary agents specialize in particular types of material—novels, plays, nonfiction books, short stories, television scripts? Are there some categories that agents could not profitably handle that could better be marketed by the authors?*

A. Most of the agents' listings in LMP specify which kind of material the agency handles. A few agencies do have certain areas of specialization such as screenplays, or children's books, as well as more general fiction and nonfiction.

Q. *Should a writer query an agent (or several agents) before sending him or her his manuscript(s)?*

A. It is acceptable for a writer to query more than one agent before sending material, but it should be made clear to the agent that the writer is contacting several agents at one time. It is even more important for the writer to clarify whether he plans to make multiple submissions of a manuscript. Most agents prefer to consider material on an exclusive basis for a reasonable period of time, approximately four to eight weeks.

Q. *What do agents look for before accepting a writer as a client?*

A. An agent usually takes on a new client based on his or her enthusiasm for that writer's work and a belief that it will ultimately be marketable.

Q. *Once an agent has agreed to take a writer on as a client, what further involvement can the agent expect and legitimately ask of the writer?*

524

A. It may take longer to place the work of a new author, and the client should be patient in the process. If the writer has made contact with a specific editor or knows that there is interest in the work from a specific publisher, he or she should inform the agent. The writer should feel free to continue contacts with book editors with whom he or she has worked, and to discuss ideas with magazine editors.

Q. *Do most agents today ask for proposals, outlines, synopses, etc., of a book-length work before taking on the job of reading and trying to market the whole book? Do agents ever prepare this type of material, or is that solely the author's function?*
A. This varies among agents. A popular procedure for consideration of material from a prospective client is the request of an outline or proposal and the first 50 or 100 pages. If the book is complete, some agents might request the completed manuscript. It is common practice to submit a nonfiction work on the basis of one or more chapters and a synopsis or outline. The extent of the sample material needed is often based on the writer's previous credentials. It is generally the author's job to prepare the outline and the agent's to prepare the submission letter or the "pitch."

Q. *When, if ever, are multiple queries or submissions allowable, acceptable, desirable? By agent or by author?*
A. If an author is working without an agent, multiple submissions to publishers are acceptable only if the author informs the publisher that the book is being submitted on that basis. However, this can sometimes backfire since those publishers who will read unsolicited manuscripts may not care to waste the staff's reading time on a manuscript that is on simultaneous submission to five other publishers. Multiple queries with one-at-a-time submissions upon receipt of a favorable reply are probably more effective for a relatively new author. However, if a writer has a nonfiction project that is obviously very desirable or timely (an inside story, a current political issue), it is of course expedient to proceed with a multiple submission. This should be done carefully, informing all the participants of the deadline, ground rules, and so on. Agents must judge each project individually and decide on the appropriate procedure. If more than one publisher has expressed an interest in a specific writer or project, a multiple submission is not

only appropriate, it is fair and in the author's best interest if there are competitive offers. If a book is very commercial, an auction may well be the result of a multiple submission. If other factors, such as a guaranteed print order or publicity plans are important, a multiple submission without the necessity of taking the highest bid may bring the best results. If an agent routinely makes multiple submissions of all properties, credibility may be lost. If this practice is reserved for the projects which warrant it, the procedure is more effective. It is usually not appropriate to send out multiple copies of a promising first novel. It may be for the inside story of last week's Congressional investigation.

Q. *What business arrangements should a writer make with an agent? Are contracts common to cover the relationship between author and agent? How binding should this be and for what period of time?*

A. Author-agent business arrangements vary among agencies. Some agents will discuss commission, expenses, and methods of operation with their authors, and this informal verbal agreement is acceptable to both parties. Others will write letters confirming these arrangements. Several agencies require contracts defining every detail of the business arrangements, and others require formal, but less extensive contracts. Written agreements often contain a notification of termination clause by either party with a period varying from 30 days to a full year. A few of the agency agreements require that the agency continue to control the subsidiary rights to a book even after the author and agent have parted. Most agents include what is known as an "agency clause" in each book contract the author signs, which provides for the agency to receive payments for the author due on that book for the complete life of the contract, whether or not the author or agent has severed the general agency agreement. In a few cases this clause will contain the provision mentioned above (compulsory representation of the author's retained subsidiary rights). It is important for a writer to discuss these and all aspects of the agency's representation at the beginning of the relationship. In addition to understanding clearly commission rates and expenses he or she will be required to pay, a writer might want to discuss such matters as expectations for consultation on marketing, choice of publishers, the number of submissions to be made, frequency of contact with agent, and so on. *Poets and Writers, Inc.* at 201 West

54th Street, New York, NY 10019 has published a helpful handbook entitled *Literary Agents: A Writer's Guide* ($5.95), which addresses these issues. Commissions vary among agents. The range is often between 10% and 20%. Some agencies may vary the commission for different rights, charging 10% or 15% for domestic sales and 15% or 20% for foreign sales. Certain agencies have different rates for different authors, depending upon the length of time the author has been with the agency, the size of the publishing advance, or the amount of editorial and preparatory work the agent must do before marketing the book. Some agents work more extensively in an editorial capacity than others and may make detailed suggestions and ask for revisions before marketing a work.

Q. *Can a writer express a preference to the agent concerning the particular publishing house or kind of house he would prefer for his book?*

A. Writers should share with their agents any preferences or ideas they may have about their work, including which publishers would be most appealing, and in which format they envision their books. However, writers should not be dismayed if their agents feel in some cases that a particular preference may be unrealistic or inappropriate.

Q. *How much of the business side of publishing does the writer need to deal with, once he is in the hands of a competent agent?*

A. An agent acts as a writer's business representative for his publishing affairs. Most agents do not act as a writer's overall financial manager, and if an author begins to earn a substantial income, he or she may be well-advised to consult with a C.P.A. and/or tax attorney. The prudent writer, while entrusting his business affairs to his or her agent, will want to stay informed about these matters.

Q. *How much "reporting" can a writer legitimately expect from the agent who has agreed to handle his work?*

A. This would depend on the agent's individual style and the writer's need and preference. Many agents keep clients informed about the progress of submissions by sending copies of rejection letters; others do not, and will give the writer a summary periodically. A writer should be kept informed of all important events and conversations with editors and co-agents about his or her work; for instance, a favorable *Publishers Weekly* review that has come in, a substantial delay in publication, a paperback auction date that has been set. On the other hand, writers should not expect daily contact with an agent as an established routine.

Q. *What involvement, if any, should a writer have in the contract that the agent makes with a publisher? Does he have the right, responsibility to question the terms, change them, insist on higher royalty rates, advertising, etc., or is this left entirely to the agent, along with the sale of substantial rights?*

A. It is the agent's responsibility to consult with the author before accepting any of the basic terms of an offer such as the advance, royalties, subsidiary rights, and territories granted. If the author has any particular reasonable requests which he or she would like to include in the contract, such as approval or consultation on the jacket design, it is the author's responsibility to let the agent know before the start of negotiations. The choice of an agent should imply the author's trust and confidence in the agent's expertise in negotiating the contract and securing the best possible financial and legal terms for the author. Authors should read contracts carefully and ask questions about any provisions, if necessary. However, it is not reasonable for an author to ask for changes in every clause or expect provisions that are extremely difficult to obtain, particularly for authors who have not had best sellers. For instance, advertising guarantees in contracts are not common for new authors. If the author has chosen a skillful agent, he or she should have confidence in the agent's explanation of what is or is not feasible in a contract with a particular publisher.

Q. *If an agent feels that he cannot place a manuscript and the author feels that it is marketable, or, at least, worthy of publication, can the author try to sell it on his own?*

A. If this happens on occasion and the agent has no objection, the author should feel free to try after discussing what he or she plans to do. The agent will want to be informed so that no prior obligation, such as an option requirement, is breached. If the author's agent repeatedly feels that the author's manuscripts cannot be placed, perhaps it is time for the author and agent to re-examine their relationship and discuss a change.

Q. *What services, other than the marketing of the manuscripts, negotiating the terms of their publishing contracts and related business arrangements may authors reasonably expect from their agents?*

A. In addition to marketing manuscripts, agents often help authors in formulating book ideas, passing along book ideas from editors when appropriate, and making introductions to appropriate editors if the author is between projects and free of contract obligations. Agents also follow up on various details of the publication process, such as production schedules, publicity, promotion, suggestions of other writers who might offer a quote for the jacket. The agent should also disseminate reviews, quotes, and information on subsidiary rights sales such as reprint and book club sales. Agents also examine royalty statements and, when necessary, obtain corrected statements.

Authors should not expect an agent to act as a secretary, travel agent, or bank. On the other hand, it is inevitable that a more personal bond may often form in the author/agent relationship, and in certain cases, agents do become involved to varying extents in friendships with their clients. In fact, hand-holding, "mothering" and counseling are not unfamiliar to many agents in dealing with certain authors. This is really a function of the agent's personality and often a conscious decision about how personally involved with his or her clients that particular agent wishes to be. A client should not expect that agent to solve his or her personal problems routinely.

Q. *How would you sum up the major role the agent plays in selling an author's work?*

A. If a manuscript is marketable, a good agent can short-circuit the random process of submissions by knowledge of the market, publishers, and the tastes and personalities of specific editors. However, an agent cannot place unsalable work. An agent can also be effective in the choice of marketing strategy for a particular work—should the book be sold as a trade paperback? Is a "hard-soft" deal best for the project? Would the author best be served by an auction, or would select individual submissions with editorial meetings be best?

529

PART IV

Where to Sell

This year's edition of THE WRITER'S HANDBOOK includes an extensive, completely revised and updated list of markets, and writers at all levels of experience should be encouraged by the number and variety of opportunities available to them. Editors, publishers, and producers rely on free lancers for a wide range of material—from articles and fiction to play scripts, opinion essays, how-to and children's books—and are very receptive to the work of talented newcomers.

Beginning free lancers will find that the field of specialized publications—including travel, city and regional magazines, and those covering such fields as health, science, consumer issues, sports, hobbies and crafts—remains one of the best markets. Editors of these magazines are in constant need of authoritative articles (for which the payment is usually quite high), and writers with experience in and enthusiasm for a particular field—whether it's gardening, woodworking, mountain climbing, car repair, or chess—will find their knowledge particularly helpful, as there is usually at least one publication devoted to every one of these areas. Such interests and activities can generate more than one article, if a different angle is used for each magazine, and the writer keeps the audience and editorial content firmly in mind.

The market for technical, computer, health, and personal finance writing is also very strong, with articles on these topics appearing in almost every publication on the newsstands today. For these subjects, editors are looking for writers who can translate technical material into lively, readable prose—often the most important factor in determining a sale.

While some of the more established markets may seem difficult to break into, especially for the beginner, there are thousands of lesser-known publications where editors will consider submissions from first-time free lancers. City and regional publications offer some of the best opportunities, since these editors generally like to work with local writers, and often use a wide variety of material, from features to fillers. Many newspapers accept op-ed pieces, and are most receptive to

531

pieces on topics not covered by syndicated columnists (politics, economics, and foreign affairs); pieces with a regional slant are particularly welcome here.

It is important for writers to keep in mind the number of opportunities that exist for nonfiction, because the paying markets for fiction are somewhat limited. Many general-interest and women's magazines do publish short stories; however, beginners will find these markets extremely competitive, with their work being judged against that of experienced professionals. We highly recommend that new writers look into the small, literary, and college publications, which always welcome the work of talented beginners. Payment is usually only in copies, but publication in literary journals can lead to recognition by editors of larger circulation magazines, who often look to the smaller publications for new talent. A growing number of regional, specialized, and Sunday magazines use short stories, and are particularly interested in local writers.

The market for poetry in general-interest magazines continues to be tight, and the advice for poets, as for fiction writers, is to try to get established and build up a list of publishing credits by submitting material to literary journals. Poets should look also to local newspapers, which often use verse, especially if it relates to holidays or other special occasions.

New playwrights will find that community, regional, and civic theaters and college dramatic groups offer the best opportunities for staged production in this competitive market. Indeed, many of today's well-known playwrights received their first recognition in regional theaters, and aspiring writers who can get their work produced by one of these have taken a dramatic step toward breaking into this field. In addition to producing plays and giving dramatic readings, many theaters also sponsor competitions or new play festivals.

Though a representative number of television shows are included in this section of the HANDBOOK, writers should be aware of the fact that this market is inaccessible without an agent, and most writers break into it only after a careful study of the medium, and a long apprenticeship.

While the book publishing field remains competitive, beginners should be especially encouraged by the many first novels published over the past few years, with more editors than ever before seeking out new works of fiction. An increasing number of publishers are broadening their nonfiction lines, as well, and editors at many hardcover and paperback houses are on the lookout for new authors, especially those with a knowledge of or training in a particular field. And writers of juvenile and young adult books will be encouraged to hear that in response to a growing audience of young readers and increased sales, many publishers are reevaluating—and often expanding—their lists of children's books.

Small presses across the country continue to flourish—in fact, they are currently publishing more books by name authors, and more books on important subjects, than at any time in recent years, according to *The New York Times*—offering writers an attractive alternative for their manuscripts.

All information in these lists concerning the needs and requirements of magazines, book publishing companies, and theaters comes directly from the editors, publishers, and directors, but editors move and addresses change, as do requirements. No published listing can give as clear a picture of editorial needs and tastes as a careful study of several issues of a magazine, and writers should never submit material without first thoroughly researching the prospective market. If a magazine is not available in the local library, write directly to the editor for a sample copy (often sent free or at a small cost). Contact the publicity department of a book publisher for an up-to-date catalogue or a theater for a current schedule. Many companies also offer a formal set of writers guidelines, available for an SASE upon request.

ARTICLE MARKETS

The magazines in the following list are in the market for free-lance articles of many types. Unless otherwise stated in these listings, a writer should submit a query first, including a brief description of the proposed article and any relevant qualifications or credits. A few editors want to see samples of published work, if available. Manuscripts must be typed double-space on good white bond paper (8½ × 11), with name, address, and telephone number at the top left- or right-hand corner of the page. Do not use erasable or onion skin paper, since it is difficult to work with, and always keep a copy of the manuscript, in case it is lost in the mail. Submit photos or slides only if the editor has specifically requested them. A self-addressed envelope with sufficient postage to cover the return of the manuscript or the answer to a query should accompany all submissions. Response time may vary from two to eight weeks, depending on the size of the magazine and the volume of mail it receives. If an editor doesn't respond within what seems to be a reasonable amount of time, it's perfectly acceptable to send a polite inquiry. Many publications have writer's guidelines, outlining their editorial requirements and submission procedures; these can be obtained by sending a self-addressed, stamped envelope (SASE) to the editor. Also, be sure to ask for a sample copy: Editors indicate the most consistent mistake free lancers make is failing to study several issues of the magazine to which they are submitting material.

GENERAL-INTEREST PUBLICATIONS

ALCOHOLISM & ADDICTION MAGAZINE—P.O. Box 31329, Seattle, WA 98103. Neil Scott, Ed. Articles on all aspects of alcoholism: treatment, legislation, education, prevention, and recovery. Send SASE for guidelines.

ALLIED PUBLICATIONS—1776 Lake Worth Rd., Lake Worth, FL 33460. Carol Bowling, Assistant Ed. Articles, to 800 words, on business, careers, management, foreign travel, fashion, beauty, and hairstyling. Photos; cartoons. Pays 5¢ a word, extra for photos and cartoons, on publication. Guidelines. Publishes *Trip & Tour, Management Digest, Modern Secretary, Woman Beautiful,* and *Home.*

THE AMERICAN LEGION MAGAZINE—Box 1055, Indianapolis, IN 46206. Michael D. LaBonne, Ed. Articles, 750 to 1,800 words, on current world affairs, public policy, and subjects of contemporary interest. Pays $100 to $1,000, on acceptance. Query.

AMERICAN VISIONS, THE MAGAZINE OF AFRO AMERICAN CULTURE—The Visions Foundation, Rm. A1040, National Museum of American History, Smithsonian Institution, Washington, DC 20560. Madelyn Bonsignore, Ed.-at-Large. Articles, 1,500 to 4,000 words, and columns, 1,500 to 3,000 words, on people and events that contribute significantly to black culture and black heritage. Pays from $200 to $1,000, on publication. Query first.

AMERICAS—OAS, General Secretariat Bldg., 1889 F St., NW, Washington, DC 20006. A. R. Williams, Man. Ed. Features, to 2,500 words, on life in Latin America and the Caribbean. Wide focus: anthropology, the arts, travel, science and development, etc. No political material. Query. Pays from $200, on publication.

AMTRAK EXPRESS—140 E. Main St., Suite 11, Huntington, NY 11743. Christopher Podgus, Ed. General-interest articles on business, health, books, sports, personal finance, life style, entertainment, travel (within Amtrak territory), technology, and science for Amtrak travelers. Submit seasonal material three to six months in advance. Pays on publication, $300 to $700 for 1,800- to 3,000-word manuscripts; $250 to $600 for department pieces of 1,500 to 2,500 words. Query with published clips.

ARRIVAL—48 Shattuck Sq., Suite 194, Berkeley, CA 94704. William Katovsky, Ed. Articles, interviews, and essays, 500 to 5,000 words, on American culture. Pays varying rates, on publication. Query first.

THE ATLANTIC—8 Arlington St., Boston, MA 02116. William Whitworth, Ed. In-depth articles on public issues, politics, social sciences, education, business, literature, and the arts, with emphasis on information rather than opinion. Ideal length: 3,000 to 6,000 words, though short pieces (1,000 to 2,000 words) are also welcome. Pays $1,000 to $7,000, on acceptance.

BETTER HOMES AND GARDENS—1716 Locust St., Des Moines, IA 50336. David Jordan, Ed. Articles, to 2,000 words, on home and family entertainment, building, decorating, food, money management, health, travel, pets, and cars. Pays top rates, on acceptance. Query.

CAPPER'S—616 Jefferson St., Topeka, KS 66607. Nancy Peavler, Ed. Articles, 300 to 500 words: human-interest, personal experience for women's section, historical. Pays varying rates, on publication.

CHATELAINE—Maclean Hunter Bldg., 777 Bay St., Toronto, Ont., Canada M5W 1A7. Mildred Istona, Ed. Articles, 2,500 words, for Canadian women, on current issues, personalities, medicine, psychology, etc. Pays $750 for personal-experience pieces, from $1,000 for articles, on acceptance.

THE CHRISTIAN SCIENCE MONITOR—One Norway St., Boston, MA 02115. Roderick Nordell, Feature Ed. Articles on arts, travel, education, food, sports, science, and lifestyle; interviews. Pays varying rates.

CLASS—27 Union Sq. W., New York, NY 10003. W. Franklin Joseph, Ed. Articles, to 2,500 words, of interest to the Third World population living in the U.S., and inhabitants of the Caribbean Islands. Pays 5¢ to 20¢ a word, after acceptance. Query.

COSMOPOLITAN—224 W. 57th St., New York, NY 10019. Helen Gurley Brown, Ed. Guy Flatley, Man. Ed. Articles, to 4,500 words, and features, to 2,500 words, on issues affecting young career women. Pays $1,500 to $2,500 for full-length articles, less for features, on acceptance. Query.

COUNTRY—5400 S. 60th, Greendale, WI 53129. Dan Johnson, Assoc. Ed. Articles, 500 to 1,000 words, for a rural audience. Taboos: tobacco, liquor, and sex. Pays $125 to $200, on acceptance. Query.

COUNTRY JOURNAL—P.O. Box 8200, Harrisburg, PA 17105. John Randolph, Ed.-in-Chief; David Sleeper, Man. Ed. Articles, 2,000 to 2,500 words, for country and small-town residents; practical, informative pieces on contemporary rural life. Pays about $400, on acceptance. Query.

COUNTRY LIVING—224 W. 57th St., New York, NY 10019. Mary Roby, Man. Ed. Articles, 1,000 to 1,500 words, on decorating, crafts, cooking, real estate, and antique-related topics. Pays $300 to $400, on acceptance.

DAWN—628 N. Eutaw, Baltimore, MD 21201. Bob Matthews, Exec. Ed.

Illustrated feature articles, 1,500 words, on subjects of interest to black families. Pays $100, on publication. Query.

DIVERSION MAGAZINE—60 E. 42nd St., Suite 2424, New York, NY 10165. Stephen N. Birnbaum, Ed. Dir. Articles, 1,200 to 3,000 words, on travel, sports, hobbies, entertainment, food, etc. Photos. Pays from $350, on publication. Query.

EBONY—820 S. Michigan Ave., Chicago, IL 60605. Herbert Nipson, Exec. Ed. Articles, with photos, on blacks: achievements, civil rights, etc. Pays from $150, on publication. Query.

THE ELKS MAGAZINE—425 W. Diversey Pkwy., Chicago, IL 60614. Fred D. Oakes, Exec. Ed. Articles, 3,000 words, on business, sports, and topics of current interest; for non-urban audience with above-average income. Informative or humorous pieces, to 2,500 words. Pays $150 to $500 for articles, on acceptance. Query.

ELLE—551 Fifth Ave., New York, NY 10176. Joan Harting, Sr. Ed. Articles, varying lengths, for fashion-conscious women, ages 20 to 50. Topics include beauty, fashion, careers, fitness, travel, and life styles. Pays top rates, on publication. Query required.

EM: EBONY MAN—1270 Ave. of the Americas, New York, NY 10020. Alfred Fornay, Exec. Ed. Articles of interest to black men. Mostly staff-written; query required.

EQUINOX—7 Queen Victoria Rd., Camden East, Ont., Canada K0K 1J0. Jody Morgan, Assistant Editor. Articles, 3,000 to 6,000 words, on popular geography, wildlife, astronomy, science, the arts, travel, and adventure. Pays $1,250 to $2,000, on acceptance.

ESQUIRE—1790 Broadway, New York, NY 10019. David Hirshey, Articles Editor. Articles, 250 to 7,000 words, for intelligent adult audience. Pays $250 to $1,500, on acceptance. Query.

ESSENCE—1500 Broadway, New York, NY 10036. Susan L. Taylor, Ed.-in-Chief. Provocative articles, 1,500 to 3,000 words, about black women in America today: self-help, how-to pieces, careers, health, celebrity profiles, and political issues. Pays varying rates, on acceptance. Query first.

FAMILY CIRCLE—110 Fifth Ave., New York, NY 10011. Susan Ungaro, Articles Ed. Articles, to 2,500 words, on marriage, family, child-rearing, consumer affairs, financial affairs, social issues, travel, and humor. Pays top rates, on acceptance. Query.

FORD TIMES—One Illinois Center, 111 E. Wacker Dr., Suite 1700, Chicago, IL 60601. Thomas A. Kindre, Ed. Articles for a family audience, particularly geared to ages 18 to 35: topical pieces (trends, life styles); profiles; first-person accounts of unusual vacation trips or real-life travel adventures; unusual sporting events or outdoor activities; food and cooking; humor. Bright, lively photos desired. "Road Show": travel and dining anecdotes; pays $50, on publication. Payment for articles, 1,200 to 1,700 words, is $550 to $800; $400 for 800 to 1,200 words; and $250 for short pieces (500 to 800 words), on acceptance. Query with SASE required for all but humor and anecdotes.

FRIENDLY EXCHANGE—Locust at 17th, Des Moines, IA 50336. Adele Malott, Ed. Articles, 1,000 to 2,000 words, of interest to the active Western family, on travel, leisure, health, safety, consumerism, heritage, and education. Photos. Pays $400 to $800, extra for photos. Query preferred. Guidelines.

536

FRIENDS—30400 Van Dyke, Warren, MI 48093. Michael Brudenell, Ed. Articles for owners of Chevrolet vehicles on travel and leisure with emphasis on reader service. Photos required. Pays from $300, extra for photos. Query Karel Bond or Shannon Mrock.

GENTLEMEN'S QUARTERLY—350 Madison Ave., New York, NY 10017. Eliot Kaplan, Man. Ed. Articles, 1,500 to 4,000 words, for a male audience, on politics, personalities, life styles, trends, grooming, sports, travel, business. Columns, 1,000 to 2,500 words: "Private Lives" (essays by men on life); "All about Adam" (nonfiction by women about men); "Games" (sports); "Health"; and "Humor"; also columns on fitness, nutrition, investments, music, wine and food. Pays $750 to $3,000, on acceptance. Query with clips.

GLAMOUR—350 Madison Ave., New York, NY 10017. Ruth Whitney, Ed.-in-Chief; Judith Coyne, Art. Ed. Articles on careers, health, psychology, interpersonal relationships, etc.; editorial approach is "how-to" for women, 18 to 35. Fashion and beauty material staff-written. Pays from $1,000 for 1,500- to 2,000-word articles, from $1,500 for longer pieces, on acceptance.

GLOBE—5401 NW Broken Sound Blvd., Boca Raton, FL 33431. Donald McLachlan, Assoc. Ed. Factual articles, 500 to 1,000 words, with photos: exposes, celebrity interviews, consumer and human-interest pieces. Pays $50 to $1,500.

GOOD HOUSEKEEPING—959 Eighth Ave., New York, NY 10019. Joan Thursh, Articles Ed. Personal-experience articles, 2,500 words, on an inspirational, unique, or trend-setting event; personal medical pieces dealing with an unusual illness, treatment, and result. Short essays, 750 to 1,000 words, on family life or relationships. Pays top rates, on acceptance. Queries preferred. Guidelines.

GOOD READING MAGAZINE—Litchfield, IL 62056 Peggy Kuethe, Assoc. Ed. Articles, 500 to 1,000 words with B&W photos, on current subjects of general interest: travel, business, personal experiences, relationships. Pays $10 to $100.

GRIT—208 W. Third St., Williamsport, PA 17701. Alvin Elmer, News Ed. Articles, to 500 words, on religion, communities, jobs, recreation, families and coping. Pays 12¢ a word, extra for photos, on acceptance.

HARPER'S BAZAAR—1700 Broadway, New York, NY 10019. Anthony Mazzola, Ed.-in-Chief. Articles on topics of interest to women: food, career, finance, beauty, health, and travel. Query required.

HARPER'S MAGAZINE—666 Broadway, New York, NY 10012. No unsolicited articles or queries. Considers manuscripts submitted through an agent only.

INQUIRER MAGAZINE—*Philadelphia Inquirer,* P.O. Box 8263, 400 N. Broad St., Philadelphia, PA 19101. Fred Mann, Ed. Local-interest features, 500 to 7,000 words. Profiles of national figures in politics, entertainment, etc. Pays varying rates, on publication. Query.

INSIDE MAGAZINE—226 S. 16th St., Philadelphia, PA 19102. Jane Biberman, Editor. Articles, 1,000 to 3,000 words, on Jewish issues and the arts. Query required. Pays $75 to $600, after acceptance.

LADIES' HOME JOURNAL—100 Park Ave., New York, NY 10017. Articles on contemporary subjects of interest to women. Personal-experience and regional pieces. Queries only (with SASE) to Exec. Ed. Jan Goodwin or Beth

Weinhouse and Roberta Grant, Sr. Eds. Fiction and poetry through literary agents only. Not responsible for unsolicited manuscripts.

LIFE—Time-Life Bldg., Rockefeller Center, New York, NY 10020. Jeff Weelwright, Sr. Ed. General-interest articles, 3,000 to 5,000 words. Pays varying rates, on acceptance. Query. Rarely buys free-lance material.

MCCALL'S—230 Park Ave., New York, NY 10169. A. Elizabeth Sloan, Ed. Andrea Thompson, Art. Ed. Interesting, unusual, and topical narratives; reports on health, home management, social trends relating to women of all ages, 1,000 to 3,000 words. Humor. Human-interest stories. Pieces for VIP-ZIP and regional sections: consumer, travel, crafts. Pays top rates, on acceptance.

MADEMOISELLE—350 Madison Ave., New York, NY 10017. Michelle Stacy, Articles Ed. Articles, 2,000 to 3,000 words, on subjects of interest to single women in their 20's. Pays from $1,750, on acceptance. Query.

MARRIAGE & FAMILY LIVING—St. Meinrad, IN 47577. Kass Dotterweich, Man. Ed. Articles, 1,500 to 2,000 words, on husband-wife and parent-child relationships. Pays 7¢ a word, on acceptance. Query.

MD MAGAZINE—3 East 54th St., New York, NY 10022. A. J. Vogl, Ed. Articles, 750 to 2,500 words, for doctors, on the arts, history, other aspects of culture. Fresh angle required. Pays from $200 to $700, on acceptance. Query

METROPOLITAN HOME—750 Third Ave., New York, NY 10017. Service and informational articles for residents of houses, co-ops, lofts, and condominiums, on real estate, equity, wine and spirits, collecting, trends, travel, etc. Pays varying rates. Query.

MODERN MATURITY—3200 East Carson St., Lakewood, CA 90712. Ian Ledgerwood, Ed. Articles on careers, workplace, human interest, living, finance, relationships, and consumerism, for persons over 50 years, to 2,000 words. Photos. Pays $500 to $3,000, extra for photos, on acceptance.

MOTHER EARTH NEWS—105 Stoney Mt. Rd., Hendersonville, NC 28791. Articles, with photos, on alternative life styles, for rural and urban readers: home improvements, how-to's, indoor and outdoor gardening, family pastimes, etc. Also, self-help, health, food-related, ecology, energy and consumerism pieces. Pays varying rates, on acceptance. Send for writers' guidelines.

MOTHER JONES—1663 Mission St., San Francisco, CA 94103. Doug Foster, Ed. Investigative articles, political essays, cultural analyses. Pays $750 to $2,000, after acceptance. Query.

MS.—119 W. 40th St., New York, NY 10018. Address Manuscript Ed. Articles relating to women's roles and changing lifestyles; general interest, how-to, self-help, profiles. Pays varying rates, on acceptance. Query with SASE required.

NATIONAL ENQUIRER—Lantana, FL 33464. Articles, of any length, for mass audience; topical news, the occult, how-to, scientific discoveries, human drama, adventure, personalities. Photos. Pays from $325. Query; no unsolicited manuscripts accepted.

NATIONAL EXAMINER—5401 NW Broken Sound Blvd., Boca Raton, FL 33431. Cliff Linedecker, Assoc. Ed. Celebrity interviews and human-interest pieces, 500 to 1,000 words. Must be well documented. Pays varying rates, on acceptance. Query required.

NATIONAL GEOGRAPHIC MAGAZINE—17th and M Sts. N.W., Washington, DC 20036. Wilbur E. Garrett, Ed. First-person, general-interest, heavily-illustrated articles on science, natural history, exploration, and geographical regions. Query required.

NEW WOMAN—215 Lexington Ave., New York, NY 10016. Pat Miller, Ed. "Read the magazine in order to become familiar with our needs before querying." Articles on new lifestyles. Features on financial and legal advice, building a business, marriage, relationships, surviving divorce, innovative diets. Pays varying rates, on acceptance. Query.

THE NEW YORK TIMES MAGAZINE—229 W. 43rd St., New York, NY 10036. Address Articles Ed. Timely articles, approximately 4,000 words, on new items, forthcoming events, trends, culture, entertainment, etc. Pays $350 to $500 for short pieces, $1,000 to $2,500 for major articles, on acceptance. Query with clips.

THE NEW YORKER—25 W. 43rd St., New York, NY 10036. Robert A. Gottlieb, Ed. Factual and biographical articles, for "Profiles," "Reporter at Large," "Annals of Crime," "Onward and Upward with the Arts," etc. Pays good rates, on acceptance. Query.

NEWSWEEK—444 Madison Ave., New York, NY 10022. Phyllis Malamud, My Turn Ed. Original opinion essays, 1,000 to 1,100 words, for "My Turn" column: must contain verifiable facts. Submit manuscript with SASE. Pays $1,000, on publication.

OMNI—1965 Broadway, New York, NY 10023-5965. Patrice Adcroft, Ed. Articles, 2,500 to 3,000 words, on scientific aspects of the future: space, machine intelligence, ESP, origin of life, future arts, lifestyles, etc. Pays $750 to $3,500, less for short features, on acceptance. Query.

PARADE—750 Third Ave., New York, NY 10017. Fran Carpentier, Articles Ed. National Sunday newspaper supplement. Factual and authoritative articles, 1,000 to 1,500 words, on subjects of national interest: health, education, consumer and environmental issues, science, the family, sports, etc. Profiles of well-known personalities and service pieces. No fiction, poetry, games or puzzles. Photos with captions. Pays from $1,000. Query.

PD—*St. Louis Post Dispatch*, 900 N. Tucker Blvd., St. Louis, MO 63101. Robert Duffy, Ed. Articles, 1,500 to 2,000 words, on lifestyles, arts, science, and history; profiles. Pays to $150, on publication. Query.

PENTHOUSE—1965 Broadway, New York, NY 10023-5965. Claudia Valentino, Man. Ed. Peter Bloch, Exec. Ed. General-interest or controversial articles, to 5,000 words. Pays from 20¢ a word, on acceptance.

PEOPLE IN ACTION—Box 10010, Ogden, UT 84409. Marjorie H. Rice, Ed. Features, 1,200 words, on nationally noted individuals in the fine arts, literature, entertainment, communications, business, sports, education, etc.: must exemplify positive values. Manuscripts should be accompanied by high-quality color transparencies. Query. Pays 15¢ a word, on acceptance.

PEOPLE WEEKLY—Time-Life Bldg., Rockefeller Center, New York, NY 10020. Hal Wingo, Ass't. Man. Ed. Considers article proposals only, 3 to 4 paragraphs, on timely, entertaining, and topical personalities. Pays good rates, on acceptance. Most material staff written.

PLAYBOY—919 N. Michigan Ave., Chicago, IL 60611. John Rezek, Articles Ed. Sophisticated articles, 4,000 to 6,000 words, of interest to urban men. Humor: satire. Pays to $3,000, on acceptance. Query.

PLAYGIRL—801 Second Ave., New York, NY 10017. Nancie S. Martin, Ed.-in-Chief. "We publish feature articles, to 2,500 words, of all sorts: interviews with top celebrities; essays on relationships; informative pieces on health, sexuality, careers, and current trends. We publish erotic fantasies (6 to 8 typewritten pages) written from a woman's point of view, in 'Readers' Fantasy Forum' (only a first name byline will be used). In 'The Men's Room' and 'The Women's Room' we use 1,000-word pieces that take a humorous look at different aspects of daily life and relationships from a male or female perspective.

"The common thread to all material published in PLAYGIRL—besides, of course, good writing and scrupulous accuracy—is a fresh, inquisitive attitude. We are not interested in 'formula' articles. We seek to provide women with an informative, entertaining approach to the world, speaking to their strengths rather than their insecurities.

"Prospective contributors are advised to read several issues of the magazine before submitting queries to appropriate department editor. Also enclose an SASE with each submission, or it will not be returned. Our rates of payment vary." Guidelines.

PRIME TIMES—Suite 120, 2802 International Ln., Madison, WI 53704. Joan Donovan, Exec. Ed. Articles, 500 to 2,500 words, for dynamic, young to middle-aged audience. Departments, 850 to 1,000 words. Pays $125 to $750, on publication. Query.

PSYCHOLOGY TODAY—1200 17th St. N.W., Washington, DC 20036. Address Manuscripts Ed. Most articles assigned to researchers in the social sciences. Query.

READER'S DIGEST—Pleasantville, NY 10570. Kenneth O. Gilmore, Ed.-in-Chief. Unsolicited manuscripts will not be read or returned. General-interest articles already in print and well-developed story proposals will be considered. Send reprint or query to any editor on the masthead.

REDBOOK—224 W. 57th St., New York, NY 10019. Annette Capone, Ed.-in-Chief. Karen Larson, Sr. Ed. Articles, 1,000 to 3,500 words, on subjects related to relationships, sex, current issues, marriage, the family, and parenting. Pays from $750, on acceptance. Query.

ROLLING STONE—745 Fifth Ave., New York, NY 10151. Magazine of modern American culture, politics, and art. Query; "rarely accepts free-lance material."

THE ROTARIAN—1600 Ridge Ave., Evanston, IL 60201. Willmon L. White, Ed. Articles, 1,200 to 2,000 words, on international social and economic issues, business and management, human relationships, travel, sports, environment, science and technology; humor. Pays good rates, on acceptance. Query.

SATELLITE ORBIT—P.O. Box 53, 9440 Fairview Ave., Boise, ID 83707. Julia Leigh, Sr. Ed. Television-related articles, 1,500 to 2,000 words; personality profiles; and articles of interest to the satellite TV viewer. Query with clips. Pays varying rates, on acceptance.

THE SATURDAY EVENING POST—1100 Waterway Blvd., Indianapolis, IN 46202. Ted Kreiter, Exec. Ed. Family-oriented articles, 1,500 to 3,000 words: humor, preventive medicine, destination-oriented travel pieces (not personal experience), celebrity profile, the arts, and sciences. Pieces on sports and home repair (with photos). Photo essays. Pays varying rates, on publication. Queries preferred.

SAVVY—3 Park Ave., New York, NY 10016. Analyn Swan, Ed. Profiles of successful women in all fields, and articles that relate to women, 3,000 words. Shorter, 800 to 1,200 words, service pieces on money and management topics. Pays on publication. Query.

SELF—350 Madison Ave., New York, NY 10017. Valorie Griffith Weaver, Ed. Articles for women of all ages, with strong how-to slant, on self-development. Pays from $700, on acceptance. Query.

STAR—660 White Plains Rd., Tarrytown, NY 10591. Topical articles, 50 to 800 words, on human-interest subjects, show business, lifestyles, the sciences, etc., for family audience. Pays varying rates.

SUCCESS—342 Madison Ave., New York, NY 10175. Scott DeGarmo, Ed.-in-Chief. Profiles of successful executives, entrepreneurs; management science, psychology, behavior, and motivation articles, 500 to 3,500 words. Query.

SUNDAY MORNING MAGAZINE—*Worcester Sunday Telegram,* 20 Franklin St., Worcester, MA 01613. Anne Murray, Editor. Articles on business, politics, sports, life styles, the arts, history—regional tie-in is preferred. Pays varying rates, on publication.

SUNDAY PUNCH—*San Francisco Chronicle,* 901 Mission St., San Francisco, CA 94103. Peter Y. Sussman, Ed. "Lively, revealing, reflective general-interest features, to 2,200 words." Pays on publication.

SUNDAY WOMAN PLUS—King Features Syndicate, 235 E. 45th St., New York, NY 10017. Merry Clark, Ed. General-interest articles, 1,000 to 1,200 words, and profiles, 1,200 words, on a wide range of topics. Study magazine before querying. Pays from $50 to $500, on acceptance.

TOWN & COUNTRY—1700 Broadway, New York, NY 10019. Address Features Dept. Considers one-page proposals for articles. Rarely buys unsolicited manuscripts.

TRAVEL & LEISURE—1120 Ave. of the Americas, New York, NY 10036. Pamela Fiori, Ed.-in-Chief. Articles, 800 to 3,000 words, on destinations and leisuretime activities. Regional pieces for regional editions. Pays $600 to $3,000, on acceptance. Query.

TROPIC—*The Miami Herald,* One Herald Plaza, Miami, FL 33132. Tom Shroder, Assoc. Ed. Essays and articles on current trends and issues, light or heavy, 1,000 to 4,000 words, for sophisticated audience. Pays $200 to $1,000, on publication. Query.

TV GUIDE—Radnor, PA 19088. Andrew Mills, Ass't Man. Ed. Short, light, brightly-written pieces about humorous or offbeat angles of television. Pays on acceptance. Query.

US MAGAZINE—One Dag Hammarskjold Plaza, New York, NY 10017. Chris Connelly, Man. Ed. Articles, 800 to 3,000 words, on timely general-interest, entertainment, life style, and related topics. Pays from $500, on publication. Query with published clips required.

USA WEEKEND—P.O. Box 500W, Washington, DC 20044. Janice Lloyd, Fitness Ed.; Amy Eisman, Celebrities/Entertainment Ed.; Ron Schoolmeester,

Travel/Food/Books Ed. Short articles, 100 to 1,000 words, on celebrities, athletes, etc. Query required.

VANITY FAIR—350 Madison Ave., New York, NY 10017. Tina Brown, Ed. Articles. Pays on acceptance. Query.

VILLAGE VOICE—842 Broadway, New York, NY 10003. David Herndon, Man. Ed. Articles, 500 to 2,000 words, on current or controversial topics. Pays $75 to $450, on acceptance. Query.

VISTA—2355 Salzedo St., Suite 301, Coral Gables, FL 33134. Renato Perez, Man. Ed. Newspaper supplement for Hispanic Americans. Articles, 2,000 words, on job advancement, bilingualism, immigration, the media, fashion, education, medicine, sports, and food. Profiles of Hispanic Americans in unusual jobs, 100 words. Pays $500 for features, $50 for profiles, on acceptance. Queries are required.

VOGUE—350 Madison Ave., New York, NY 10017. Amy Gross, Features Ed. Articles, to 1,500 words, on women, entertainment and the arts, travel, medicine and health. General features. Query.

VOLKSWAGEN'S WORLD—Volkswagen of America, Troy, MI 48099. Marlene Goldsmith, Ed. Articles, 600 to 1,000 words, for Volkswagen owners: profiles of well-known personalities; inspirational or human-interest pieces; travel; humor. Photos. Pays $150 per printed page, on acceptance. Query. Guidelines on request.

WASHINGTON POST MAGAZINE—*The Washington Post,* 1150 15th St., NW, Washington, DC 20071. Stephen L. Petranek, Man. Ed. Personal-experience essays, profiles and general-interest pieces, to 5,000 words, on business, arts and culture, politics, science, sports, education, children, relationships, behavior, etc. Pays from $250, after acceptance.

WEEKLY WORLD NEWS—600 S. East Coast Ave., Lantana, FL 33462. Joe West, Ed. Human-interest news pieces, about 500 to 1,000 words, involving human adventure, unusual situations. Pays $125 to $500, on publication.

WOMAN'S DAY—1515 Broadway, New York, NY 10036. Rebecca Greer, Articles Ed. Articles, 500 to 3,500 words, on subjects of interest to women: marriage, education, family health, child rearing, money management, interpersonal relationships, changing lifestyles, etc. Dramatic first-person narratives about women who have experienced medical miracles or other triumphs. "Reflections": short, provocative personal essays, 1,000 to 1,500 words, humorous or serious, dealing with concerns of interest and relevance to women. Pays $2,000 for essays, top rates for articles, on acceptance.

WOMAN'S WORLD—177 N. Dean St., Englewood, NJ 07631. Gerry Hunt, Sr. Ed. Articles, 600 to 1,800 words, of interest to middle-income women between the ages of 18 and 60, on love, romance, careers, medicine, health, psychology, family life, travel, dramatic stories of adventure or crisis. Pays $300 to $750, on acceptance. Query.

WORKING WOMAN—342 Madison Ave., New York, NY 10173. Anne Mollegen Smith, Ed. Articles, 1,000 to 2,500 words, on business and personal aspects of working women's lives. Pays from $400, on acceptance.

CURRENT EVENTS, POLITICS

AFRICA REPORT—833 U.N. Pl., New York, NY 10017. Margaret A.

Novicki, Ed. Well-researched articles by specialists, 1,000 to 4,000 words, with photos, on current African affairs. Pays $150 to $250, on publication.

AMERICAN LAND FORUM—See *The New American Land.*

THE AMERICAN LEGION MAGAZINE—Box 1055, Indianapolis, IN 46206. Michael D. LaBonne, Ed. Articles, 750 to 1,800 words, on current world affairs, public policy, and subjects of contemporary interest. Pays $100 to $1,000, on acceptance. Query.

AMERICAN POLITICS—810 18th St., NW, Suite 802, Washington, DC 20006. Grant Oliphant, Ed. Articles, 1,200 to 2,500 words, on issues, trends and figures in American politics; political perspectives on business, entertainment, science, and health. Pay varies, 30 days after publication. Query.

THE AMERICAN SCHOLAR—1811 Q St., N.W., Washington, DC 20009. Joseph Epstein, Ed. Nontechnical articles and essays, 3,500 to 4,000 words, on current affairs, the American cultural scene, politics, arts, religion and science. Pays $450, on acceptance.

THE AMICUS JOURNAL—Natural Resources Defense Council, 122 E. 42nd St., Rm. 4500, New York, NY 10168. Peter Borrelli, Ed. Investigative articles related to national and international environmental policy. Pays on acceptance.

THE ATLANTIC—8 Arlington St., Boston, MA 02116. William Whitworth, Ed. In-depth articles on public issues, politics, social sciences, education, business, literature, and the arts, with emphasis on information rather than opinion. Ideal length: 3,000 to 6,000 words, though short pieces (1,000 to 2,000 words) are also welcome. Pays $1,000 to $7,000, on acceptance.

CANADIAN AQUACULTURE—4611 William Head Rd., Victoria, BC Canada, V8X 3W9. Peter Chettleburgh, Ed. Articles related to Canadian fish farming: in-depth analyses of political and resource issues 1,200 to 2,000 words. Pays varying rates, on publication. Query first.

COMMENTARY—165 E. 56th St., New York, NY 10022. Norman Podhoretz, Ed. Articles, 5,000 to 7,000 words, on contemporary issues, Jewish affairs, social sciences, community life, religious thought, cultural activities. Pays about 20¢ a word, on publication.

COMMONWEAL—15 Dutch St., New York, NY 10038. Peter Steinfels, Ed. Catholic. Articles, to 3,000 words, on political, social, religious and literary subjects. Pays 3¢ a word, on acceptance.

THE CRISIS—260 Fifth Ave., New York, NY 10001. Fred Beauford, Ed. Articles, to 1,500 words, on the arts, civil rights, and the problems and achievements of blacks and other minorities. Pays $75 to $500.

DOSSIER—3301 New Mexico Ave., N.W., Suite 310, Washington, DC 30016. Nancy Smith, Ed. Sophisticated investigative pieces, personality profiles, service articles, etc., 1,000 to 2,500 words, with a Washington, D.C. slant. Pays from 10¢ a word, on acceptance. Query

ENVIRONMENT—4000 Albemarle St., N.W., Washington, DC 20016. Jane Scully, Man. Ed. Articles, 2,500 to 6,500 words, on environmental, scientific and technological policy and decision-making issues. Pays $75 to $300, on publication. Query.

FOREIGN POLICY JOURNAL—11 Dupont Circle, N.W., Suite 900, Washington, DC 20036. Charles William Maynes, Ed. Articles, 3,000 to 5,000 words, on international affairs. Honorarium, on publication. Query.

FOREIGN SERVICE JOURNAL—2101 E St. N.W., Washington, DC 20037. Stephen R. Dujack, Ed. Articles on American diplomacy, foreign affairs and subjects of interest to Americans representing U.S. abroad. Pays 2¢ to 10¢ a word, on publication. Query.

THE FREEMAN—Foundation for Economic Education, Irvington-on-Hudson, NY 10533. Brian Summers, Sr. Ed. Articles, to 3,500 words, on economic, political and moral implications of private property, voluntary exchange, and individual choice. Pays 10¢ a word, on publication.

INQUIRER MAGAZINE—*Philadelphia Inquirer,* P.O. Box 8263, 400 N. Broad St., Philadelphia, PA 19101. Fred Mann, Ed. Local-interest features, 500 to 7,000 words. Profiles on national figures in politics, entertainment, etc. Pays varying rates, on publications. Query.

IRISH AMERICA—114 E. 28th St., New York, NY 10016. Patricia Harty, Man. Ed. Articles, 1,000 words, of interest to Irish-American audience; preferred topics include history and politics. Pay 7¢ a word, after publication. Query.

MIDSTREAM: A MONTHLY JEWISH REVIEW—515 Park Ave., New York, NY 10022. Joel Carmichael, Ed. Articles, reviews on Jewish topics. Pays 5¢ a word, after publication.

MOMENT—3000 Connecticut Ave. N.W., Suite 300, Washington, DC 20008. Charlotte Anker, Ed. Sophisticated articles, 2,000 to 4,000 words, on Jewish political, social, literary, and religious issues. Pays on publication. Query.

MOTHER JONES—1663 Mission St., San Francisco, CA 94103. Doug Foster, Ed. Investigative articles, political essays, cultural analyses. Pays $750 to $2,000, after acceptance. Query.

THE NATION—72 Fifth Ave., New York, NY 10011. Victor Navasky, Ed. Articles, 1,500 to 2,500 words, on politics and culture from a liberal/left perspective. Pays $75 per published page, to $300, on publication. Query.

THE NEW AMERICAN LAND (formerly *American Land Forum*)—1516 P St., NW, Washington, DC 20005. Sara Ebenreck, Ed. Articles, 2,500 words, on U.S. land issues, achievements, leadership profiles, or land use topics. Pays $15 to $300. Guidelines.

THE NEW YORK TIMES MAGAZINE—229 W. 43rd St., New York, NY 10036. Address Articles Ed. Timely articles, approximately 4,000 words, on new items, forthcoming events, trends, culture, entertainment, etc. Pays $350 to $500 for short pieces, $1,000 to $2,500 for major articles, on acceptance. Query with clips.

THE NEW YORKER—25 W. 43rd St., New York, NY 10036. Robert A. Gottlieb, Ed. Factual and biographical articles, for "Profiles," "Reporter at Large," "Annals of Crime," "Onward and Upward with the Arts," etc. Pays good rates, on acceptance. Query.

NEWSWEEK—444 Madison Ave., New York, NY 10022. Phyllis Malamud, My Turn Ed. Original opinion essays, 1,000 to 1,100 words, for "My Turn" column: must contain verifiable facts. Submit manuscript with SASE. Pays $1,000, on publication.

NUCLEAR TIMES—1601 Connecticut Ave., NW, Suite 300, Washington, DC 20009. Elliott Negin, Ed. Terse, timely news articles, to 1,500 words, on the nuclear disarmament movement, the arms race, nuclear weapons and nuclear war. Pays 12¢ a word, on publication.

POLITICAL WOMAN—4521 Campus Dr., #254, Irvine, CA 92715. Sally Corngold, Ed. Well-documented, nonpartisan political articles, 1,000 to 3,000 words, for "thinking women." Pays $25 to $1,000, on publication.

PRESENT TENSE—165 E. 56th St., New York, NY 10022. Murray Polner, Ed. Serious reportage and political journalism, 2,000 to 3,000 words, on contemporary developments concerning Jews worldwide. Pays $100 to $250, on publication. Query.

THE PROGRESSIVE—409 E. Main St., Madison, WI 53703. Erwin Knoll, Ed. Articles, 1,000 to 3,500 words, on political, social problems. Light features. Pays $75 to $300, on publication.

PUBLIC CITIZEN MAGAZINE—P.O. Box 19404, Washington, DC 20036. Bimonthly. Catherine Baker, Ed. Investigative reports and articles of timely political interest, for members of Public Citizen: consumer rights, health and safety, environmental protection, safe energy, tax reform and government and corporate accountability. Photos, illustrations. Pays to $500.

THE QUALITY REVIEW—253 W. 73rd St., New York, NY 10023. Brenda Niemand, Man. Ed. Articles, 2,000 to 4,000 words, that "analyze the relationship of quality to public policy, global business, and growing concerns about competitiveness." Articles should be nontechnical and include case studies for illustration. Pays varying rates, on acceptance. Query.

ROLL CALL: THE NEWSPAPER OF CAPITOL HILL—317 Mass. Ave. N.E., Washington, DC 20002. Sidney Yudain, Ed. Factual, breezy articles with political or Congressional angle: Congressional historical and human-interest subjects, political lore, etc. Political satire and humor. Pays on publication.

THE ROTARIAN—1600 Ridge Ave., Evanston, IL 60201. Willmon L. White, Ed. Articles, 1,200 to 2,000 words, on international social and economic issues, business and management, human relationships, travel, sports, environment, science and technology; humor. Pays good rates, on acceptance. Query.

TROPIC—*The Miami Herald,* One Herald Plaza, Miami, FL 33132. Tom Shroder, Assoc. Ed. Essays and articles on current trends and issues, light or heavy, 1,000 to 4,000 words, for sophisticated audience. Pays $200 to $1,000, on publication. Query.

VFW MAGAZINE—Broadway at 34th, Kansas City, MO 64111. Magazine for Veterans of Foreign Wars and their families. James K. Anderson, Ed. Articles, 1,000 words, on current issues, solutions to everyday problems, personalities, sports, etc. How-to and historical pieces. No poetry. Pays 5¢ to 10¢ a word, extra for photos, on acceptance.

VILLAGE VOICE—842 Broadway, New York, NY 10003. David Herndon, Man. Ed. Articles, 500 to 2,000 words, on current or controversial topics. Pays $75 to $450, on acceptance. Query.

THE WASHINGTON MONTHLY—1711 Connecticut Ave., N.W., Washington, DC 20009. Charles Peters, Ed. Investigative articles, 1,500 to 5,000 words, on politics, government and the political culture. Pays 10¢ a word, on publication. Query.

WASHINGTON POST MAGAZINE—*The Washington Post,* 1150 15th St., NW, Washington, DC 20071. Stephen L. Petranek, Man. Ed. Personal-experience essays, profiles and general-interest pieces, to 5,000 words, on business, arts and culture, politics, science, sports, education, children, relationships, behavior, etc. Pays from $250, after acceptance.

REGIONAL AND CITY PUBLICATIONS

ADIRONDACK LIFE—P.O. Box 97, Rt. 86, Jay, NY 12941. Jeffrey G. Kelly, Ed. Features, to 3,000 words, on outdoor activities: hiking, camping, canoeing, etc.; arts and crafts, wilderness, business, life styles, and history in the upstate New York region. Pays $100 to $400, on publication.

ALASKA—808 E. St., Anchorage, AK 99501. Articles, 1,500 words, on life in Alaska and northwestern Canada. Pays on acceptance.

ALOHA, THE MAGAZINE OF HAWAII—P.O. Box 3260, Honolulu, HI 96801. Rita Ariyoshi, Ed. Articles, 1,500 to 4,000 words, on the life, customs, and people of Hawaii and the Pacific. Pays 10¢ a word, on publication. Query first.

AMERICAN WEST—3033 N. Campbell Ave., Tucson, AZ 85719. Mae Reid-Bills, Man. Ed. Articles, 2,500 to 3,000 words, and department pieces, 900 to 1,000 words, that celebrate the West, past and present; emphasis on travel. Pays $200 to $800, on acceptance. Query required.

ARIZONA HIGHWAYS—2039 W. Lewis Ave., Phoenix, AZ 85009. Merrill Windsor, Ed. Articles, 2,000 words, on travel in Arizona; pieces on adventure, nature, arts and crafts, humor, life styles, nostalgia, history, archaeology. Pays 35¢ to 50¢ a word, on acceptance. Query first.

ARKANSAS TIMES—Box 34010, Little Rock, AR 72203. Mel White, Ed. Articles, to 6,000 words, on Arkansas history, people, travel, politics. All articles *must* have strong AR orientation. Pays $100 to $500, on acceptance.

ATLANTA—6255 Barfield Rd., Atlanta, GA 30328. Neil Shister, Ed. Articles, 2,500 words, on Atlanta subjects or personalities. Pays $600 to $1,000, on publication. Query.

THE ATLANTIC ADVOCATE—P.O. Box 3370, Gleaner Bldg., Prospect St., Fredericton, N.B., Canada E3B 5A2. Harold P. Wood, Ed. Well-researched articles on Atlantic Canada and general-interest subjects. Pays to 8¢ a word, on publication.

ATLANTIC CITY MAGAZINE—1637 Atlantic Ave., Atlantic City, NJ 08401. Ronnie Polaneczky, Ed. Lively articles, 500 to 5,000 words, on Atlantic City and Southern New Jersey: casinos, business, personalities, environment, local color, crime, for locals and tourists. Pays $100 to $600, on publication. Query.

AUSTIN MAGAZINE—P.O. Box 4368, Austin, TX 78765. Laura Tuma, Man. Ed. Profiles, civic affairs and general-interest articles, 750 to 3,000 words, with local business focus. Query preferred. Pays $75 to $400, on publication.

AVENUE—145 E. 57th St., New York, NY 10022. Joan Kron, Ed. Articles, 2,000 to 2,500 words, for Upper East Side New Yorkers, and residents of affluent zip codes around the country. Profiles of people in business and the arts, food, fashion. Pays $400 to $500, on publication. Query required.

BALTIMORE MAGAZINE—26 S. Calvert St., Baltimore, MD 21202. Alan Sea, Man. Ed. Articles, 500 to 3,000 words, on people, places, and things in the Baltimore metropolitan area. Consumer advice, investigative pieces, profiles, humor, and personal-experience pieces. Payment varies, on publication. Query required.

BEACON MAGAZINE—*Akron Beacon Journal,* 44 E. Exchange St., Akron, OH 44328, Articles of varying lengths, on business, science, life styles, sports, politics, arts, and history: A Northeast Ohio tie-in is required. Photos. Pays $50 to $400, on publication. Query.

BIRMINGHAM—2027 First Ave., N., Birmingham, AL 35203. Ray Martin, Man. Ed. Personality profiles and nostalgia pieces, 8 double-spaced typed pages, with strong Birmingham tie. Pays $50 to $175, on publication.

BOCA RATON—J E S Publishing, 114 NE 2nd St., Boca Raton, FL 33432. Shirley Bartley, Ed. Articles, 800 to 3,000 words, on Florida topics, personalities, and travel. Pays $175 to $500, on publication. Query with clips required.

BOSTON GLOBE MAGAZINE—*The Boston Globe,* Boston, MA 02107. Ande Zellman, Ed. General-interest articles, interviews, and profiles, 2,500 to 5,000 words. Pays from $750. Query required.

BOSTON MAGAZINE—300 Massachusetts Ave., Boston, MA 02115. David Rosenbaum, Ed. Informative, entertaining features, 1,000 to 4,000 words, on Boston area personalities, institutions and phenomena. Pays $250 to $1,200, on publication. Query Betsy Buffington, Man. Ed. or Janice Brand, Service Features Ed.

BOSTONIA—10 Lenox St., Brookline, MA 02146. Articles, 1,800 words, on politics, the arts, travel, food and wine; life style essays, 1,200 words. Regional (Boston/New England) angle required. Pays $150 to $800, on publication. Query.

BUFFALO SPREE MAGAZINE—Box 38, Buffalo, NY 14226. Johanna Shotell, Ed. Articles, to 1,800 words. Pays $75 to $100, $25 for poetry, on publication.

BURLINGTON MAGAZINE—333 S. Union St., Burlington, VT 05401. Tim Etchells, Ed. Articles with Burlington area tie-in. Pays varying rates, on acceptance.

CALIFORNIA—11601 Wilshire Blvd., Los Angeles, CA 90025. Lisa Blansett, Asst. Ed. Features with a California focus, on politics, business, environmental issues, ethnic diversity, travel, style, fashions, restaurants, the arts, and sports. Service pieces, profiles, and well-researched investigative articles. Pays $500 to $2,500 for features, $250 to $500 for shorter articles, on acceptance. Query first.

CAPE COD LIFE—P.O. Box 222, Osterville, MA 02655. Brian F. Shortsleeve, Pub. Articles, 2,000 words, on current events, business, nautical history, art, and gardening. Pays 10¢ per word, after publication. Query first.

CAPITOL, THE COLUMBUS DISPATCH SUNDAY MAGAZINE—Columbus, OH 43216. T. R. Fitchko, Ed. General-interest, essays, humorous articles, to 3,000 words. Pays varying rates, on publication.

CHARLOTTE MAGAZINE—P.O. Box 36639, Charlotte, NC 28236. Diane Clemens, Ed. Articles, 500 to 750 words, 1,200 words, and features from 1,600 words, of interest to young, affluent professionals in the Charlotte area. Pays 10¢ a word, 30 days after publication. Queries preferred.

CHESAPEAKE BAY MAGAZINE—1819 Bay Ridge Rd., Annapolis, MD 21403. Betty D. Rigoli, Ed. Articles, 8 to 10 typed pages, related to the

Chesapeake Bay area. Profiles. Photos. Pays $75 to $125, on publication. Query first.

CHICAGO—303 E. Wacker Dr., Chicago, IL 60601. Don Gold, Ed.-in-Chief. Articles, 1,000 to 5,000 words, related to Chicago. Pays varying rates, on acceptance. Query.

CHICAGO HISTORY—Clark St. at North Ave., Chicago, IL 60614. Russell Lewis, Ed. Articles, to 4,500 words, on urban political, social and cultural history. Pays to $250, on publication. Query.

CINCINNATI MAGAZINE—35 E. Seventh, Suite 300, Cincinnati, OH 45202. Laura Pulfer, Ed./Pub. Articles, 1,000 to 3,000 words, on Cincinnati people and issues. Pays $75 to $100 for 1,000 words, on acceptance. Query with writing sample.

CLINTON STREET QUARTERLY—Box 3588, Portland, OR 97208. Lenny Dee, Ed. Articles and creative non-fiction: "eclectic blend of politics, culture, humor and art." Regional distribution. Pays $50 to $200, on publication.

COLORADO BUSINESS—5951 S. Middlefield Rd., Littleton, CO 80123. Ann Feeney, Ed. Articles, to 1,500 words, on banking, real estate, transportation, manufacturing, etc. in Colorado. Pays 10¢ a word, on publication. Query.

COLORADO HOMES & LIFESTYLES—Suite 154, 2550 31st St., Denver, CO 80216. Ania Savage, Man. Ed. Articles on topics related to Colorado: travel, fashion, design and decorating, gardening, luxury real estate, art, celebrity lifestyles, people, food and entertaining. Pays to 20¢ a word, on acceptance. Query.

COLORADO OUTDOOR JOURNAL—P.O. Box 432, Florence, CO 81226. Chas S. Clifton, Man. Ed. Articles, 1,000 to 1,500 words, and features, 1,250 to 3,000 words, on hunting, fishing, camping, conservation, backpacking, shooting, non-technical mountaineering, Colorado history, cross-country skiing, outdoor photography, cooking and travel. Pays on publication. Query required.

CONNECTICUT—Communications International, P.O. Box 6480, Bridgeport, CT 06606. Dale B. Salm, Man. Ed. Features (from 2,500 words) and columns (1,800 to 2,500 words) on health, education, politics, people, business, and the arts, with a Connecticut tie-in. Pays up to $600, on publication. Query.

CONNECTICUT TRAVELER—2276 Whitney Ave., Hamden, CT 06518. Elke P. Martin, Man. Dir. Articles, 500 to 1,200 words, on travel and tourist attractions in New England. B&W photos, Pays $50 to $175, on publication. Query.

THE COURIER JOURNAL MAGAZINE—*The Courier Journal*, 525 W. Broadway, Louisville, KY 40202. Jimmy Pope, Ed. Articles on such topics as life styles, science, religion, sports, and arts; profiles (500 to 3,000 words): a regional angle is required. Pays from $50, on publication. Query.

THE COVENTRY JOURNAL—P.O. Box 124, Andover, CT 06232. Bill Cisowski, Ed. Articles, to 2,000 words, about the Eastern Connecticut region: historical, how-to gardening, travel, and events. "Yankee-type" fiction. Pays $50 to $250, on acceptance.

CRAIN'S DETROIT BUSINESS—1400 Woodbridge, Detroit, MI 48207. Peter Brown, Ed. Business articles, 500 to 1,000 words, about Detroit, for Detroit business readers. Pays $75 to $150, on acceptance. Query required.

CREATING EXCELLENCE—New World Publishing, P.O. Box 2084, S.

Burlington, VT 05403. David Robinson, Ed. Self-help and inspirational articles, profiles and essays related to Northern Vermont and Vermonters. "We want to accent the positive." Pays $75 to $250, on acceptance. Query.

D—3988 N. Central Expressway, Suite 1200, Dallas, TX 75204. Ruth Fitzgibbons, Ed. In-depth investigative pieces on current trends and problems, personality profiles, and general-interest articles on the arts, travel, and business, for upper-class residents of Dallas. Pays $350 to $500 for departments, $800 to $1,200 for features. Written queries only.

DALLAS LIFE MAGAZINE—*The Dallas Morning News,* Communications Center, Dallas, TX 75265. Melissa Houtte, Ed. Well-researched articles and profiles, 1,000 to 3,000 words, with photos, on contemporary issues, personalities, or subjects of strictly Dallas-related interest; short humor features, also Dallas-related, 500 to 750 words. Pays 10¢ and up a word, on acceptance. Query.

DALLAS MAGAZINE—1507 Pacific Ave., Dallas TX 75201. D. Ann Shiffler, Ed. Features, 2,500 words, on business and businesses in Dallas. Department pieces, 1,500 words. Pays $100 to $600, on acceptance. Query required.

DELAWARE TODAY—P.O. Box 4440, Wilmington, DE 19807. Peter Mucha, Ed. Service articles, profiles, news features, on topics of local interest. Best bets for out-of-state writers are articles on finance, high-tech consumer items or cars. No fiction, humor, poetry. Pays $75 to $125 for department pieces, $125 to $300 for features, on publication. Query required; enclose writing sample.

DETROIT MAGAZINE—*Detroit Free Press,* 321 W. Lafayette Blvd., Detroit, MI 48231. Articles, 500 to 1,500 words, with a Detroit-area or Michigan focus, on issues, lifestyles. Personality profiles; essays; humor. Pays $100 to $500.

DETROIT MONTHLY—1400 Woodbridge, Detroit, MI 48207. Susan Wyland, Ed. Articles on Detroit-area people, issues, life styles and business. Payment varies. Query with clips required.

DOWN EAST—Camden, ME 04843. Davis Thomas, Ed. Articles, 1,500 to 2,500 words, on all aspects of life in Maine. Photos. Pays to 10¢ a word, extra for photos, on acceptance. Query.

ERIE & CHAUTAUQUA MAGAZINE—Charles H. Strong Bldg.. 1250 Tower La., Erie, PA 16505. Kim Kalvelage, Man. Ed. Feature articles, to 2,500 words, on issues of interest to upscale readers in the Erie, Warren, and Crawford counties (PA), and Chautauqua (NY) county. Investigative pieces. Pays $35 per published page, on publication. Query preferred, with writing samples. Buys all rights. Guidelines available.

FLORIDA GULF COAST LIVING—1311 N. Westshore Blvd., Suite 109, Tampa, FL 33607. Milana Petty, Ed. Articles, 750 to 1,200 words, for the active home buyer on the Gulf Coast: Home-related articles, moving tips, financing, etc. Pays 7¢ to 10¢ a word, on acceptance. Query.

FLORIDA KEYS MAGAZINE—Box 818, 2111 O/S Hwy., Marathon, FL 33050. Address David Ethridge. Articles, 1,000 to 4,000 words, on the Florida Keys: history, environment, natural history, profiles, etc. Photos. Pays varying rates, on publication. Query preferred.

FLORIDA MAGAZINE—The Orlando Sentinel, 633 N. Orange St., Orlando, FL 32801. Lisa Velders, Ed. Articles, 1,000 to 3,000 words, with a local focus on arts, history, politics, sports, science and business. Pays varying rates, on publication.

FLORIDA TREND—Box 611, St. Petersburg, FL 33731. Richard Edmonds, Ed. Articles, to 2,000 words, on Florida business and businesspersons. Photos. Query.

GEORGIA JOURNAL—Agee Publishers, Inc., Athens, GA 30603. Jane M. Agee, Ed. Articles, 1,200 words, on people, events, travel, etc. in and around GA. Poetry, to 20 lines. Pays $20 to $35, on acceptance.

GO: THE AUTHENTIC GUIDE TO NEW ORLEANS—1033 Pleasant St., Suite D, New Orleans, LA 70115. Katherine Dinker, Ed. Articles, 2,000 words, on local events of interest to visitors. Pays $150, on publication. Query.

GOLD COAST LIFE MAGAZINE—4747 N. Ocean Dr., Ft. Lauderdale, FL 33308. Fern Matthews, Ed. Articles, from 1,000 words, on life styles of southeastern Florida. Pays $50 to $250, on publication.

GOLDEN YEARS—233 E. New Haven Ave., Melbourne, FL 32902-0537. Carol Brenner Hittner, Ed. Controlled-circulation monthly for Florida residents over the age of 50. Pieces on unique hobbies, beauty and fashion, sports, and travel, 500 words. Pays 10¢ a word, on publication.

GREAT LAKES TRAVEL & LIVING—108 W. Perry St., Port Clinton, OH 43452. David G. Brown, Ed. Features, 3,500 words, and shorts, 250 to 1,000 words, about events and locations, personalities, home and lifestyle, food, and history in the Great Lakes region. Pays $100 to $300 for features, on publication. Query first.

GULFSHORE LIFE—2975 S. Horseshoe Dr., Naples, FL 33942. Lynn Walker, Man. Ed. Articles, 950 to 3,500 words, on personalities, travel, sports, business, investment, nature, in southwestern Florida. Pays $50 to $300. Query.

HIGH COUNTRY NEWS—Box 1090, Paonia, CO 81428. Betsy Marston, Ed. Articles on environmental, land management, energy and natural resource issues; profiles of western innovators; pieces on western politics. B & W photos. Pays $2 to $4 per column inch, on publication, for 750-word roundups and 2,000-word features. Query first.

HONOLULU—36 Merchant St., Honolulu, HI 96813. Brian Nicol, Ed. Features highlighting life in the Hawaiian islands—politics, sports, history, people, events are all subjects of interest. Pays $400, on acceptance. Columns and department pieces are mostly staff-written. Queries are required.

HUDSON VALLEY MAGAZINE—Box 429, Poughkeepsie, NY 12602. R. B. Dandes, Ed. Profiles, investigative articles, and features on the businesses, arts and resources of the region. Pays $75 to $150, on publication, for features of 1,200 to 1,500 words; queries are required.

ILLINOIS ENTERTAINER—2200 E. Devon, Suite 192, Des Plaines, IL 60018. Bill Dalton, Ed. Articles, 500 to 1,500 words, on local and national entertainment and leisure time activities in the greater Chicago area. Personality profiles; interviews, reviews. Photos. Pays varying rates on publication. Query preferred.

ILLINOIS TIMES—Box 3524, Springfield, IL 62708. Fletcher Farrar, Jr., Ed. Articles, 1,000 to 2,500 words, on people, places and activities of Illinois, outside the Chicago metropolitan area. Pays 4¢ a word, on publication. Query required.

550

IMAGE—*San Francisco Examiner,* 110 Fifth St., San Francisco, CA 94103. Articles, 1,200 to 4,000 words, on life styles, issues, business, history, events, and people in northern California. Query first. Pays varying rates.

INDIANAPOLIS MAGAZINE—32 E. Washington St., Indianapolis, IN 46204. Nancy Comiskey, Ed. Articles on almost any topic—health, business, sports, people, etc.—must have a regional tie-in. Lengths vary (to 12 pages). Pays $40 to $300, on publication. Query first.

INDIANAPOLIS MONTHLY—8425 Keystone Crossing, Indianapolis, IN 46240. Deborah Paul, Ed.-in-Chief; Sam Stall, Assoc. Ed. Articles, 1,000 words, on health, sports, politics, business, and Indiana personalities. All material must have a regional focus. Pays varying rates, on publication.

INQUIRER MAGAZINE—*Philadelphia Inquirer,* 400 N. Broad St., Philadelphia, PA 19101. Fred Mann, Ed. Articles, 1,500 to 2,000 words, and 3,000 to 7,000 words, on politics, science, arts and culture, business, life styles and entertainment, sports, health, beauty, psychology, education, religion, home and garden, and humor. Short pieces, 200 to 800 words, for "Our Town" department. Pays varying rates. Query.

INSIDE CHICAGO—2501 W. Peterson Ave., Chicago, IL 60659. Deborah Loeser, Exec. Ed. Articles of varying lengths related to life in Chicago. Query with ideas for departments (art, design, music, film, performance, etc.). Pays from $100, on acceptance.

THE IOWAN MAGAZINE—Mid-America Publishing Corp., 214 9th St., Des Moines, IA 50309. Charles W. Roberts, Ed. Quarterly for educated, affluent Iowans. Articles, 1,000 to 3,000 words, on the business, arts, people and history of Iowa, with photos, if available. Query first. Pays $100 to $400, on publication.

ISLAND LIFE—P.O. Box X, Sanibel Island, FL 33957. Joan Hooper, Ed. Articles, 500 to 1,200 words, with photos, on unique or historical places, wildlife, architecture, fashions, home decor, cuisine, on barrier islands off Florida's S.W. Gulf Coast. Pays 3¢ a word, on publication. SASE necessary.

JACKSONVILLE MAGAZINE—P.O. Box 329, Jacksonville, FL 32201. Carolyn Carroll, Ed. Articles of interest to the Northeast Florida community: strong regional slant a must. Pays $100 to $300, on acceptance. Query required.

JACKSONVILLE TODAY—P.O. Box 5610, 1032 Hendricks Ave., Jacksonville, FL 32247-5610. Carole Caldwell, Ed. Informative and lively articles related to Jacksonville and other North Florida cities: life styles, health, behavior, business, politics and the arts are all good topics. Profiles are also used. Payment is made on publication: $200 to $400 for features (2,000 to 3,000 words); $150 to $200 for departments (1,500 to 2,000 words). Query.

KANSAS!—Kansas Dept. of Economic Development, 400 W. 8th Ave., 5th fl., Topeka, KS 66603-3957. Andrea Glenn, Ed. Quarterly. Articles of 5 to 7 typed pages on the people, places, history and events of Kansas. Color slides. Pays $75 to $150, on acceptance. Query.

LAKE SUPERIOR MAGAZINE—325 Lake Ave. S., #100, Duluth, MN 55802. Paul Hayden, Ed. Articles with unusual twists on regional subjects; historical pieces that highlight the people, places and events that have affected the Lake Superior region. Pictorial essays. Pays to $200, after publication. Query first.

LONG ISLAND'S NIGHTLIFE MAGAZINE—1770 Deer Park Ave., Deer

Park, NY 11729. Bill Ervolino, Ed. Articles, 600 to 1,500 words, on entertainment, leisure, personalities. Photos. Pays $50 to $95, on publication. Query preferred.

THE LOOK—P.O. Box 272, Cranford, NJ 07016. John R. Hawks, Pub. Articles, 1,500 to 3,000 words, for readers age 16 to 26, on life styles in New Jersey. Query. Pays $30 to $200, on publication.

LOS ANGELES MAGAZINE—1888 Century Park E., Los Angeles, CA 90067. Lew Harris, Exec. Ed. Articles, to 3,000 words, of interest to sophisticated, affluent southern Californians, preferably with local focus on a life style topic. Pays from 10¢ a word, on acceptance. Query.

LOS ANGELES READER—12224 Victory Blvd., N. Hollywood, CA 91606. Anita Newman, Ed. Articles, 750 to 2,500 words, on subjects relating to the Los Angeles/Southern California area; special emphasis on entertainment, feature journalism, and the arts. Pays $25 to $250, on publication. Query preferred.

LOS ANGELES TIMES MAGAZINE—*The Los Angeles Times,* Times Mirror Sq., Los Angeles, CA 90053. Michael Parrish, Ed. General-interest news features, photo spreads, profiles, and interviews focusing on people and events of interest in Southern California, to 5,000 words; columns to 750 words. Pays to $2,000, on acceptance. Query required.

LOUISIANA JOURNAL—5615 Corporate Blvd., 4th Floor, Baton Rouge, LA 70808. Elizabeth Carpelan, Ed. Articles, 1,000 to 6,000 words, on political, economic, and social issues affecting the state. Pays 10¢ a word, on publication.

LOUISVILLE—One Riverfront Plaza, Louisville, KY 40202. Betty Lou Amster, Ed. Articles, 1,000 to 2,000 words, on community issues, personalities, and entertainment in the Louisville area. Photos. Pays from $50, on acceptance. Query; articles on assignment only. Limited free-lance market.

MAGAZINE OF THE MIDLANDS—*Omaha World Herald,* World Herald Sq., Omaha, NE 68102. Tim Anderson, Ed. "We use articles on a wide range of topics—from business to religion—but a Midwest tie-in is absolutely required." Pays $25 to $150, on publication. Query.

MAGNETIC NORTH—c/o Thorn Books, Franconia, NH 03580. Jim McIntosh, Ed. Well-researched, offbeat articles, 500 to 1,500 words, for residents and visitors to New Hampshire's White Mountains. Pays $50 to $150, on publication. Query with SASE.

MAINE LIFE—8 St. Pierre St., Lewiston, ME 04240. Bradbury D. Blake, Assoc. Pub. Articles, 150 to 3,000 words, about traveling, places to see, and things to do in Maine. Of particular interest are unusual or little known spots. Features cover contemporary social, political, economic, and environmental topics. Pays 8¢ a word, on publication.

MARYLAND—Dept. of Economic and Community Development, 45 Calvert St., Annapolis, MD 21401. Bonnie Joe Ayers, Ed. Articles, 800 to 2,200 words, on Maryland subjects. Pays varying rates, on acceptance. Query preferred. Guidelines available.

MAUIAN MAGAZINE—P.O. Box 10669, Lahaina, Maui, HI 96761. Joe Harabin, Ed. Informative, thought-provoking, upbeat articles, 500 to 5,000 words, about any aspect of life and times on Maui—past, present, or future. Pays $50 to $500, on publication.

MEMPHIS—MM Corp., Box 256, Memphis, TN 38101. Larry Conley, Ed.

Articles, 1,500 to 4,000 words, on a wide variety of topics related to Memphis and the Mid-South region: politics, education, sports, business, etc. Profiles; investigative pieces. Pays $75 to $1,000, on publication. Query. Guidelines available.

MIAMI/SOUTH FLORIDA MAGAZINE—P.O. Box 140008, Coral Gables, FL 33114-0008. J. P. Faber, Man. Ed. Features, 1,500 to 2,500 words, and department pieces, 900 to 1,300 words, on a variety of subjects related to South Florida. Pays $75 to $400, 15 days before publication.

MICHIANA—*The South Bend Tribune,* Colfax at Lafayette, South Bend, IN 46626. Bill Sonneborn, Ed. Articles, 300 to 3,000 words, on the people, places and events in the Northern Indiana and Southern Michigan area. Photos. Pays $50 to $125, on publication. Query.

MICHIGAN BUSINESS—Cranbrook Center, Suite 302, 30161 Southfield Rd., Southfield, MI 48076. Ron Garbinski, Ed. Business news and features on Michigan businesses. Query. Pay varies, on publication.

MICHIGAN LIVING—17000 Executive Plaza Dr., Dearborn, MI 48126. Len Barnes, Ed. Travel articles, 500 to 1,500 words, on tourist attractions and recreational opportunities in the U.S. and Canada, with emphasis on Michigan: places to go, things to do, costs, etc. Color photos. Pays $100 to $350, extra for photos, on acceptance.

MICHIGAN: THE MAGAZINE OF THE DETROIT NEWS—Evening News Assn., 615 W. Lafayette Blvd., Detroit, MI 48231. Cynthia Boal-Janssens, Ed. Articles, from 750 words, on business, politics, arts and culture, science, people, sports and education, etc., with a Michigan slant. Cover articles, to 3,000 words. Some fiction. Pays $200 to $650, on publication.

THE MICHIGAN WOMAN—P.O. Box 1171, Birmingham, MI 48012. Betsy Hull, Ed. Articles, 750 words, highlighting the achievements and contributions of Michigan women in helping others enjoy more fulfilling careers and personal lives. Pays 10¢ a word, on publication. Query first.

MID-ATLANTIC COUNTRY—P.O. Box 246, Alexandria, VA 22313. Jim Scott, Ed. Articles, 2,000 words, related to life in the Mid-Atlantic region: travel, home, food, gardening, antiques, history, architecture, and entertaining. Photos. Pays from $3.50 per column inch, on publication. Query.

MID-SOUTH MAGAZINE—*The Commercial Appeal,* 495 Union, Box 334, Memphis, TN 38101. Scott Hill, Ed. Articles, to 1,500 words, with a regional tie-in. Pays to $200, on publication. Query.

MID-WEST OUTDOORS—111 Shore Dr., Hinsdale, IL 60521. Gene Laulunen, Ed. Articles, 1,500 words, with photos, on where, when, and how to fish within 500 miles of Chicago. Pays $25, on publication.

MILWAUKEE—312 E. Buffalo, Milwaukee, WI 53202. Charles Sykes, Ed. Profiles, investigative articles, and historical pieces, 3,000 to 4,000 words; local tie-in a must. Pays $300 to $500, on publication. Query required.

MPLS. ST. PAUL—12 S. 6th St., Ste. 1030, Minneapolis, MN 55402. Sylvia Paine, Man. Ed. In-depth articles, features, profiles and service pieces, 400 to 3,000 words, with Mpls.–St. Paul focus. Pays to $600.

MONTANA MAGAZINE—P.O. Box 5630, Helene, MT 59604. Carolyn Cunningham, Ed. Where-to-go items, regional profiles, photo essays. Montana-oriented only. B & W prints, color slides. Pays $75 to $350, on publication. Query first.

MYRTLE BEACH MAGAZINE—P.O. Box 1474, N. Myrtle Beach, SC 29598. Toby Beckham, Ed. Features, 1,500 to 2,500 words; articles, 500 to 1,500 words. Must have a local angle and be geared for residents, not tourists, in the area. Pays from $75 for features, from $35 for topical features, on publication.

NEVADA—Capitol Complex, Carson City, NV 89710. Kirk Whisler, Ed. Articles, 500 to 700 or 1,500 to 1,800 words, on topics related to Nevada—history, profiles, travel, and places—with photos. Pay varies, on publication.

THE NEVADAN—*The Las Vegas Review-Journal,* Box 70, Las Vegas, NV 89125—0070. A.D. Hopkins, Ed. Feature articles, to 3,000 words, on social trends in Southern Nevada. Pieces, 2,000 words, on history in Nevada, Southwest Utah, Northeast Arizona, and Death Valley area of California, accompanied by B & W photos. Pays $100, extra for photos, on publication. Query.

NEW ENGLAND GETAWAYS—21 Pocahontas Dr., Peabody, MA 01960. Address Assoc. Ed. Features, 1,500 to 2,500 words, "designed to lure travelers to specific regions of New England. We are looking for specific, informational articles that will motivate the reader to explore New England and will supply the tools (addresses, phone numbers, hours of business) to make the trip easy." Pays $150 to $300, on publication.

NEW ENGLAND MONTHLY—P.O. Box 446, Haydenville, MA 01039. Paul Keegan, Assoc. Ed. Articles on politics, arts, business, education, crime and nature; a regional angle is a must, and a strong accent on reportage is preferred. Pays from $1,000 for features (3,000 to 4,000 words), on acceptance. Include published clips with query.

NEW HAMPSHIRE PROFILES—90 Fleet St., Portsmouth, NH 03801. Lynn Harnett, Ed. Articles, 500 to 2,500 words, on New Hampshire people, events, arts, and life styles. Pays $100 to $300, on publication. Query in writing.

NEW HAVEN BUSINESS DIGEST—375 Orange St., New Haven, CT 06510. Kin Hanson, Ed. Feature articles, 1,500 to 2,000 words, on New Haven area businesses. Pays $2.75 per published inch, $10 per photo, on publication. Query required.

NEW JERSEY MONTHLY—7 Dumont Place, Morristown, NJ 07960. Larry Marscheck, Ed. Patrick Sarver, Man. Ed. Articles, profiles, and service pieces, 2,000 to 3,000 words; department pieces on health, business, education, travel, sports, local politics, and arts, 1,200 to 1,800 words, with New Jersey tie-in. Pays $450 to $750, on acceptance. Query first. Send for guidelines.

NEW JERSEY REPORTER—The Center for Analysis of Public Issues, 16 Vandeventer Ave., Princeton, NJ 08542. Rick Sinding, Ed. In-depth articles, 2,000 to 6,000 words, on New Jersey politics and public affairs. Pays $100 to $250, on publication. Query required.

NEW MEXICO MAGAZINE—Joseph M. Montoya Bldg., 1100 St. Francis Dr., Santa Fe, NM 87503. Address Ed. Articles, 250 to 2,000 words, on New Mexico subjects. Pays about 12¢ a word, on acceptance.

NEW ORLEANS MAGAZINE—Box 26815, New Orleans, LA 70186. Sherry Spear, Ed. Articles, 3 to 15 triple-spaced pages, on New Orleans area people and issues. Photos. Pays $50 to $300, extra for photos, on publication. Query.

NEW YORK—755 Second Ave., New York, NY 10017. Edward Kosner, Ed. Laurie Jones, Man. Ed. Feature articles of interest to New Yorkers. Pays from $850 to $3,500, on acceptance. Query required; not responsible for unsolicited material.

NEW YORK ALIVE—152 Washington Ave., Albany, NY 12210. Mary Grates Stoll, Ed. Articles aimed at developing knowledge of and appreciation for New York State. Features, 3,000 words maximum, on lifestyle, sports, travel and leisure, history and the arts. Pays $200 to $350. Query preferred.

NORTH DAKOTA HORIZONS—P.O. Box 2467, Fargo, ND 58108. Sheldon Green, Ed. Quarterly. Articles, about 3,000 words, on the people, places and events that affect life in North Dakota. Photos. Poetry. Pays $75 to $300, on publication.

NORTHCOAST VIEW—Blarney Publishing, Box 1347, Eureka, CA 95502. Scott K. Ryan, Damon Maguire, Eds. Local news articles, 8 to 10 pages. Pays $5 per typed page, on publication.

NORTHEAST MAGAZINE—*The Hartford Courant,* 285 Broad St., Hartford, CT 06115. Lary Bloom, Ed. Articles and short essays that reflect the concerns of Connecticut residents, 750 to 3,000 words. Pays $250 to $1,000, on acceptance.

NORTHERN LIGHTS—Box 8084, Missoula, MT 59807-9962. Dan Whipple, Ed. Thoughtful articles, 500 to 1,500 words, about the West. "We're open to virtually any subject as long as it deals with our region (the Rocky Mountains) in some way." Pays to 10¢ a word, on publication.

NORTHWEST LIVING—130 Second Ave. S., Edmonds, WA 98020. Archie Satterfield, Ed. Lively, informative articles, 400 to 1,000 words, on the natural resources of the Northwest: homes, gardens, people, travel, history, etc. Color photos essential. Pays $50 to $400, on acceptance. Query required.

NORTHWEST MAGAZINE—*The Sunday Oregonian,* 1320 SW Broadway, Portland, OR 97201. Jack R. Hart, Ed. Articles on regional issues (1,000 to 3,000 words); life styles (1,000 to 2,500 words); travel and recreation (1,000 to 2,000 words); science and business topics, and profiles (1,000 to 3,000 words); and personal essays (800 to 1,000 words). A regional tie-in is *required.* Pays $75 to $500, on acceptance. Query. Guidelines.

OHIO MAGAZINE—40 S. Third St., Columbus, OH 43215. Ellen Stein Burbach, Man. Ed. Profiles of the people, cities and towns of Ohio; pieces on its historic sites, tourist attractions, little-known spots. Lengths and payment vary. Query.

OK MAGAZINE—*Tulsa World,* 315 S. Boulder Ave., Tulsa, OK 74102. Personality profiles, life style articles, and stories on people, places and things in Oklahoma, 250 to 1,000 words. Pays on publication. Photos.

OKLAHOMA TODAY—Box 53384, Oklahoma City, OK 73152. Sue Carter, Ed. Travel articles; profiles, history and arts articles. All material must have regional tie-in. Queries for 1,000- to 2,000-word articles are preferred. Pays $100 to $300, on acceptance. Send SASE for guidelines.

ORANGE COAST—245-D Fisher, Suite 8, Costa Mesa, CA 92626. Janet Eastman, Ed. Articles of interest to educated, affluent Southern Californians. Pieces, 1,000 to 1,500 words, for regular departments: "Profile," "Coasting" (op-ed), "Media," "Business" (hard news about the regional business community), and "Nightlife." Feature articles run 1,500 to 2,500 words. Query. Pays $150 for features, $100 for columns, on acceptance. Guidelines are available.

ORLANDO MAGAZINE—P.O. Box 2207, Orlando, FL 32802. Nancy Long, Features Ed. Articles and profiles, 1,000 to 1,500 words, related to Central Florida. Photos a plus. Pays $50 to $150, on acceptance. Query required.

PD—*St. Louis Post-Dispatch,* 900 N. Tucker Blvd., St. Louis, MO 63101. Robert W. Duffy, Ed. Profiles, personal-experience pieces and investigative articles, 3,000 to 4,000 words: politics, science, life styles and entertainment, psychology, etc. Pays $125 to $150, on publication. No unsolicited manuscripts. Query.

PENNSYLVANIA MAGAZINE—Box 576, Camp Hill, PA 17011. Albert E. Holliday, Ed. General-interest features with a Pennsylvania tie-in, accompanied by illustrations. Pays to 10¢ a word, usually on acceptance. Query preferred.

PHILADELPHIA—1500 Walnut St., Philadelphia, PA 19102. Bill Tonelli, Articles Ed. Articles, 1,000 to 5,000 words, for sophisticated audience, relating to Philadelphia area. Pays on publication. Query.

PHOENIX METRO MAGAZINE—4707 N. 12th St., Phoenix, AZ 85014. Fern Stewart Welch, Ed. Dir. Articles, 1,000 to 3,000 words, on topics of special interest to Phoenix-area residents. Pays $75 to $300 for features, on publication. Query.

PITTSBURGH—4802 Fifth Ave., Pittsburgh, PA 15213. Bruce Van Wyngarden, Ed. Articles, 850 to 3,000 words, with western Pennsylvania slant. 3- to 4-month lead time. Pays after publication.

THE PITTSBURGH PRESS SUNDAY MAGAZINE—*The Pittsburgh Press,* 34 Blvd. of the Allies, Pittsburgh, PA 15230. Ed Wintermantel, Ed. Well-written, well-organized, in-depth articles of local or regional interest, 1,000 to 3,000 words, on issues, trends or personalities. No hobbies, how-to's or "timely events" pieces. Pays $100 to $400, extra for photos, on publication. Query.

PITTSBURGH PREVIEW—1112 S. Braddock Ave., Suite 203, Pittsburgh, PA 15218. Kimberly Flaherty, Ed. Career-oriented articles for women, preferably with a local slant. Pays $25 to $300, on publication. Query required.

PORTLAND MONTHLY—154 Middle St., Portland, ME 04101. Colin Sargent, Sen. Ed. Articles on local people, fashion, culture, trends, commercial and residential real estate. Pays on publication. Query preferred.

PRIME TIMES—Senior World, Inc., 121 Mercer St., Seattle, WA 98109. Anthony E. Thein, Pub./Ed. Articles to address active, affluent residents of King County, WA, ages 55 to 70. Pays $50 to $75, on publication.

ROCKFORD MAGAZINE—211 W. State St., Box 197, Rockford, IL 61101. Penny Christianson, Man. Ed. Feature articles, 3,000 words, and fillers, 400 to 1,000 words, on local events, arts and entertainment, nostalgia and history as well as pieces on how national trends or news affect the Midwest. Pays 10¢ a word, on publication. Query first.

RURAL LIVING—P.O. Box 15248, Richmond, VA 23227-0648. Richard G. Johnstone, Jr., Ed. Features, 1,000 to 1,500 words, on people, places, historic sites in Virginia and Maryland's Eastern Shore. Queries are preferred. Pays $100 to $150, on publication.

RURALITE—P.O. Box 558, Forest Grove, OR 97116. Address Editor or Feature Editor. Articles, 800 words, of interest to a primarily rural and small-town audience in Oregon, Washington, Idaho, Nevada, and Alaska. Upbeat articles; biographies, local history and celebrations, self-help, etc. Humorous articles and animal pieces. No sentimental nostalgia. Pays $30 to $100, on acceptance. Queries are preferred.

SACRAMENTO MAGAZINE—P.O. Box 2424, Sacramento, CA 95811. Ann McCully, Man. Ed. Features, 2,500 words, on a broad range of topics related to the region. Department pieces, 1,200 to 1,500 words. Pays to $200, on acceptance. Query first.

SAN DIEGO MAGAZINE—4206 W. Point Loma Blvd., P.O. Box 85409, San Diego, CA 92138. Winke Self, Man. Ed. Articles, 1,500 to 3,000 words, on local personalities, politics, life styles, business, history, etc., relating to San Diego area. Photos. Pays $250 to $600, on publication.

SAN DIEGO READER—P.O. Box 80803, San Diego, CA 92138. Jim Holman, Ed. Articles, 2,500 to 10,000 words, on the San Diego region. Pays $500 to $2,000, on publication.

SAN FRANCISCO BUSINESS TIMES—325 Fifth St., San Francisco, CA 94107. Donald L. Keough, Ed. Business-oriented articles, about 20 column inches. Limited freelance market. Pays $75 to $100, on publication. Query.

SAN FRANCISCO FOCUS—680 Eighth St., San Francisco, CA 94103. Mark Powelson, Ed. Service features, profiles of local newsmakers, and investigative pieces of local issues, 2,500 to 3,000 words. Pays $250 to $750, on publication. Query required.

SAN FRANCISCO: THE MAGAZINE—45 Belden Place, San Francisco, CA 91404. Maggie Canon, Ed. "Our readership is upscale, and we want articles on the people, places, power, and issues of the San Francisco Bay area." Pays varying rates, half on acceptance, half on publication. Query required.

SOUTH CAROLINA WILDLIFE—P.O. Box 167, Columbia, SC 29202. Tom Poland, Man. Ed. Articles, 1,000 to 3,000 words, with regional outdoors focus: conservation, natural history and wildlife, recreation. Profiles, natural history. Pays from 10¢ a word. Query.

SOUTH FLORIDA HOME & GARDEN—P.O. Box 140008, Coral Gables, FL 33114-0008. Erica Rauzin, Ed. Features, 800 to 1,000 words, and department pieces, 400 to 800 words, about South Florida interior design, architecture, landscaping, gardening, cuisine and home entertaining. Must focus on the Key West to Melbourne area. Pays $50 to $300, extra for photos, before publication.

SOUTHERN—P.O. Box 3418, 201 E. Markham, Suite 200, Little Rock, AR 72203. Linton Weeks, Ed. "We rely 99 and 44/100ths percent purely on free-lance material, and our goal is to explore all facets of the contemporary South. In all cases, we look for a strong Southern angle. Articles for the main section of the magazine run 1,000 to 6,000 words, and encompass hard journalism, profiles, essays, first-person adventure pieces, history, personal-service features." Pays to $2,000, on acceptance.

SOUTHERN OUTDOORS—No. 1, Bell Rd., Montgomery AL 36141. Larry Teague, Ed. How-to articles, 400 to 600 words or 1,500 to 2,000 words, on hunting and fishing, for fishermen and hunters in the 16 southern states. Pays 15¢ a word, on acceptance. Query.

SOUTHWEST ART—9 Greenway Plaza, Suite 2010, Houston, TX 77219. Susan McGarry, Ed. Articles on the artists, museums, galleries, history and art trends west of the Mississippi. Particularly interested in representational or figurative arts. Pays $300, on acceptance, for manuscripts of 1,800 to 2,200 words. Query.

THE STATE: DOWN HOME IN NORTH CAROLINA—P.O. Box 2169, Raleigh, NC 27602. W. B. Wright, Ed. Articles, 600 to 2,000 words, on people, history, and places in North Carolina. Photos. Pays $15 to $50, on acceptance.

SUN MAGAZINE—*The Baltimore Sun,* 501 N. Calvert St., Baltimore, MD 21278. *"Sun Magazine* focuses primarily on people," writes Editor Susan Bauer, who wants to see queries for articles—with a regional slant—on politics, life styles, sports, the arts, and profiles (1,500 to 3,000 words). Pays $125 to $400, on publication.

SUNDAY—*Chicago Tribune,* 435 N. Michigan Ave., Chicago, IL 60611. Mary Knoblauch, Ed. Unique, compelling articles, from 3,000 words, on a wide variety of subjects (from politics and people to arts and travel (1,500 words). Pays from $1,000, on publication. Query first.

SUNDAY ADVOCATE MAGAZINE—Capital Publishing, Box 588, Baton Rouge, LA 70821. Larry Catalanello, Ed. Articles, to 4 typed pages, on local topics. Pays $50 to $150, on publication. Limited market.

SUNDAY MAGAZINE—*The Houston Post,* 4747 SW Freeway, Houston, TX 77001. Martha Liebrum, Ed. Articles on Texas- and Houston-related topics, including politics, sports, life styles, arts and sciences. Pays $75 to $400, on acceptance.

SUNDAY MAGAZINE—*The Minneapolis Star & Tribune,* 425 Portland Ave., Minneapolis, MN 55488. Leonard Witt, Ed. Articles, 500 to 3,000 words, with a regional slant. "Read and study our magazine and then query before submitting material." Pays $50 to $600, on publication.

SUNDAY MAGAZINE—*Providence Sunday Journal,* 75 Fountain St., Providence, RI 02902. Alan Rosenburg, Ed. Profiles, personal-experience pieces, New England features, 1,000 to 1,500 words. Pays $75 to $350, on publication. Query.

SUNDAY PUNCH—*San Francisco Chronicle,* 901 Mission St., San Francisco, CA 94103. Peter Y. Sussman, Ed. "Lively, revealing, reflective general-interest features, to 2,200 words." Pays on publication.

SUNSET MAGAZINE—80 Willow Rd., Menlo Park, CA 94025. William Marken, Ed. Western regional. Queries not encouraged.

SUNSHINE MAGAZINE—*The News/Sun-Sentinel,* P.O. Box 14430, 101 North New River Dr. E., Ft. Lauderdale, FL 33302. John Parkyn, Ed. Articles, 1,000 to 4,000 words, on topics of interest to South Floridians. Pays to 25¢ a word, on acceptance. Query. Guidelines.

TALLAHASSEE MAGAZINE—P.O. Box 12848, Tallahassee, FL 32317. William Needham, Ed. Articles, 800 to 1,100 words, with a positive outlook on the life, people, and history of the North Florida area. Pays 10¢ a word, on publication. Query.

TEXAS HIGHWAYS MAGAZINE—State Dept. of Highways and Public Transportation, 11th and Brazos, Austin, TX 78701-2483. Frank Lively, Ed. Texas history, scenic and travel features, 200 to 1,800 words. Pays $150 to $800, on acceptance, extra for photos. Guidelines.

TEXAS MONTHLY—P.O. Box 1569, Austin, TX 78767. Gregory Curtis, Ed. Features, 2,500 to 5,000 words, and departments, to 2,500 words, on Texas-related topics, for an educated audience. Query required; guidelines available. Pay varies, on acceptance.

558

THIRD COAST—P.O. Box 592, Austin, TX 78767. Kate Berger, Man. Ed. Articles, 1,000 to 1,500 words, on business, arts, architecture, growth, politics, education, etc., in Austin. Pays from 10¢ a word, after publication.

TIMELINE—1985 Velma Ave., Columbus, OH 43211-2497. Christopher S. Duckworth, Ed. Articles, 1,000 to 6,000 words, on the history and natural history of Ohio, and related regional or national topics—political, economic, and social history—aimed at lay readers in the Midwest. Pays $100 to $900, on acceptance. Query.

TOLEDO MAGAZINE—*The Sunday Blade,* 541 Superior St., Toledo, OH 43660. Sue Stankey, Ed. Profiles and articles, with a regional slant, on topics from history to life styles. Pays $50 to $500, on publication. Query.

TORONTO LIFE—59 Front St. E., Toronto, Ont., Canada M5E 1B3. Marq De Villiers, Ed. Articles, 1,500 to 4,500 words, on Toronto. Pays $1,000 to $2,500, on acceptance. Query.

TRISTATE MAGAZINE—*The Cincinnati Enquirer,* 617 Vine St., Cincinnati, OH 45201. Alice Hornbaker, Ed. Local stories about people, places and things in Ohio, Northern Kentucky, and Indiana, to 1,500 words. Pays $125 to $500, on publication. Photos. Query first.

TROPIC—*The Miami Herald,* One Herald Plaza, Miami, FL 33132. Gene Weingarten, Ed. General-interest articles, 750 to 3,000 words, for South Florida readers. Pays $200 to $1,000, on acceptance. Send SASE.

TWIN CITIES READER—600 First Ave. N., Minneapolis, MN 55403. Susie E. Wilson, Ed.-in-Chief. Articles, 2 to 4 printed pages, on cultural phenomena, city politics, and general-interest subjects, for local readers aged 25 to 44. Pays to $3 per inch, on publication.

UPSTATE MAGAZINE—*Democrat & Chronicle,* 55 Exchange St., Rochester, NY 14614. Peggy Moran, Acting Ed. Features, to 2,400 words, of interest to readers in Upstate New York: life styles, arts, sciences, etc. Profiles, humorous essays. Pays to $400, on publication. Query.

VALLEY MAGAZINE—16800 Devonshire, Suite 275, Granada Hills, CA 91344. Anne Framroze, Ed. Articles, 1,000 to 3,000 words, on celebrities, issues, education, health, business, dining and entertaining, etc., in the San Fernando Valley. Pays $100 to $500, within 8 weeks of acceptance.

VERMONT LIFE—61 Elm St., Montpelier, VT 05602. Tom Slayton, Editor-in-Chief. Articles, 500 to 3,000 words, about Vermont subjects only. Photos. Pays 20¢ a word, extra for photos. Query required.

THE VIRGINIAN—P.O. Box 2828, Staunton, VA 24401. Hunter S. Pierce, IV, Man. Ed. Articles, 1,000 words, relating to VA, WV, MD, NC, and DC.

WASHINGTON—901 Lenora, Seattle, WA 98121. David Fuller, Man. Ed. Articles, varying lengths, on the people and places of Washington State. Payment varies. Query required.

WASHINGTON POST MAGAZINE—*The Washington Post,* 1150 15th St., NW, Washington, DC 20071. Stephen L. Petranek, Man. Ed. Personal-experience essays, profiles and general-interest pieces, to 6,000 words, on business, arts and culture, politics, science, sports, education, children, relationships, behavior, etc. Pays from $300, on acceptance.

THE WASHINGTONIAN—1828 L. St. N.W., Suite 200, Washington, DC

20036. John Limpert, Ed. Helpful, informative articles, 1,000 to 4,000 words, on Washington-related topics. Pays 30¢ a word. Query.

WE ALASKANS—*Anchorage Daily News,* Box 6616, Anchorage, AK 99502. Kathleen McCoy, Ed. Articles and profiles, 2,000 to 4,000 words, on Alaskan topics. Regional angle is required. Pays to $300, on publication. Query.

THE WEEKLY, SEATTLE'S NEWS MAGAZINE—1931 2nd Ave., Seattle, WA 98101. David Brewster, Ed. Articles, 700 to 4,000 words, with a Northwest perspective. Pays $75 to $800, three weeks after publication. Query.

WEST MICHIGAN MAGAZINE—7 Ionia St. SW, Grand Rapids, MI 49503. Dotti Clune, Ed. Articles, to 2,000 words, on the people, places, issues and events of the region. Pays varying rates on publication.

WESTERN SPORTSMAN—P.O. Box 737, Regina, Sask., Canada S4P 3A8. Rick Bates, Ed. Informative articles, to 2,500 words, on outdoor experiences in Alberta and Saskatchewan. Photos. Pays $40 to $325, on publication.

WESTWAYS—Box 2890, Terminal Annex, Los Angeles, CA 90051. Mary Ann Fisher, Ed. Articles, 1,000 to 1,500 words, and photo essays, on western U.S., Canada, and Mexico: history, contemporary living, travel, personalities, etc. Photos. Pays from 20¢ a word, extra for photos, 30 days before publication. Query.

WISCONSIN—*The Milwaukee Journal Magazine,* Newspapers, Inc., Box 661, Milwaukee, WI 53201. Alan Borsuk, Ed. Articles, 500 to 2,000 words, on business, politics, arts, science, personal finance, psychology, entertainment, health, etc. Personal-experience essays and investigative articles. Pays $75 to $500, on publication. Query.

WISCONSIN TRAILS—P.O. Box 5650, Madison, WI 53705. Geri Nixon, Man. Ed. Articles, 1,500 to 3,000 words, on regional topics: outdoors, life style, events, adventure, travel; profiles of artists and craftsmen, and regional personalities. Pays $100 to $300, on acceptance and on publication. Query.

WORCESTER MAGAZINE—P.O. Box 1000, Worcester, MA 01614. Steven Jones-D'Agostino, Man. Ed. Articles, to 1,500 words, on the arts, entertainment, fashion, events, and issues specific to Central Massachusetts. Pays $1.00 to $1.50 per column inch, on publication. Query required.

YANKEE—Dublin, NH 03444. Judson D. Hale, Ed. Articles, to 3,000 words, with New England angle. Photos. Pays $150 to $800 (average $500 to $600), on acceptance.

YANKEE HOMES—Main St., Dublin, NH 03444. Jim Collins, Ed. Articles, 200 to 1,500 words, on New England real estate, housing, and living. Pays $50 to $500, on acceptance. Queries required.

YANKEE MAGAZINE'S TRAVEL GUIDE TO NEW ENGLAND AND ITS NEIGHBORS—Main St., Dublin, NH 03444. Elizabeth Doyle, Ed. Articles, 500 to 2,000 words, on unusual activities, attractions, places to visit in New England, New York State, and Atlantic Canada. Photos. Pays $50 to $300, on acceptance. Query with outline and writing samples.

TRAVEL ARTICLES

AAA WORLD—8111 Gatehouse Rd., Falls Church, VA 22047. Clyde T. Linsley, Jr., Man. Ed. Articles, 600 to 1,500 words, on automotive and travel concerns. Pays $200 to $800, on acceptance. Query.

ACCENT—P.O. Box 10010, Ogden, UT 84409. Robyn C. Walker, Editor. Articles, 1,200 words, about destinations in the U.S. Must include transparencies. Query. Pays 15¢ a word, on acceptance.

ADVENTURE ROAD—Citicorp Publishing, 641 Lexington Ave., New York, NY 10022. Marilyn Holstein, Ed. Official publication of the Amoco Motor Club. Articles, 1,500 words, on destinations in North America, Mexico, and the Caribbean. Photos. Pays $400 to $850, on acceptance. Query required.

AIRFAIR INTERLINE—25 W. 39th St., New York, NY 10018. Ratu Kamlani, Ed. Travel articles, 1,000 to 2,500 words, with photos, on shopping, sightseeing, and dining, for airline employees. Prices, discount information, and addresses must be included. Pays $75, after publication.

ARIZONA HIGHWAYS—2039 W. Lewis Ave., Phoenix, AZ 85009. Richard G. Stahl, Man. Ed. Informal, well-researched travel articles, 2,000 to 2,500 words, focusing on a specific city or region in Arizona and environs and including anecdotes, historical references, etc. Pays 35¢ to 50¢ a word, on acceptance. Query required. Guidelines available.

CALIFORNIA HIGHWAY PATROLMAN—2030 V. St., Sacramento, CA 95818. Carol Perri, Ed. Articles, on transportation safety, California history, travel, topical consumerism, humor, general items, etc. Photos a plus. Pays 2½¢ a word, extra for black-and-white photos, on publication. Guidelines.

CARIBBEAN TRAVEL AND LIFE—606 N. Washington St., Alexandria, VA 22314. Veronica Gould Stoddart, Ed. Lively, informative articles, 500 to 2,500 words, on all aspects of travel, leisure, recreation, and culture in the Caribbean, Bahamas, and Bermuda, for upscale, sophisticated reader. Photos. Pays $75 to $550, after acceptance. Query.

CHARTERING MAGAZINE—P.O. Box 755, Jensen Beach, FL 33457. Antonia Thomas, Ed. Articles on chartered yacht vacations, 1,000 to 1,800 words. Query first. Pays varying rates, on publication.

CHEVRON USA ODYSSEY—Rm. 3188, 575 Market St., San Francisco, CA 94105. Mark Williams, Ed. Quarterly. Articles, 700 to 1,600 words, on travel and leisure activities in the United States and Canada. Color slides. Pays about 25¢ to 30¢ a word, on acceptance; $125 to $400 for slides, on publication.

COLORADO HOMES & LIFESTYLES—Suite 154, 2550 31st St., Denver, CO 80216. Ania Savage, Man. Ed. Travel articles on cities, regions, establishments in Colorado; roundups and travel pieces with unusual angles, 1,200 to 3,000 words. Pays 10¢ to 25¢ a word, on acceptance. Query.

CONNECTICUT TRAVELER—2276 Whitney Ave., Hamden, CT 06518. Elke P. Martin, Man. Dir. Articles, 500 to 1,200 words, on travel and tourist attractions in New England. Pays $50 to $225, on acceptance. Query first with SASE.

DISCOVERY—Allstate Motor Club, 3701 W. Lake Ave., Glenview, IL 60025. Claire McCrea, Ed. Articles, 1,000 to 2,500 words, on travel topics that explore continental North America and its people. Photos on assignment only. Pays $500 to $850, on acceptance. Query and published samples required.

EARLY AMERICAN LIFE—Box 8200, Harrisburg, PA 17105. Frances Carnahan, Ed. Travel features about historic sites and country inns, 1,000 to 3,000 words. Pays $50 to $400, on acceptance. Query.

ENDLESS VACATION: THE MAGAZINE FOR INTERNATIONAL VACATIONERS—Box 80260, Indianapolis, IN 46280. Helen A. Wernle, Ed. Travel features, to 2,000 words; international scope. Pays on acceptance. Query preferred. Guidelines.

FAMILY CIRCLE—110 Fifth Ave., New York, NY 10011. Susan Ungaro, Articles Ed. Travel articles, to 2,000 words. Destination pieces should appeal to a national audience and focus on affordable activities; prefer area roundups, theme-oriented travel pieces or first person family vacation stories. Pay rates vary, on acceptance. Query first.

FARM FAMILY AMERICA—1999 Shepard Rd., St. Paul, MN 55116. George Ashfield, Ed. Quarterly travel and recreation magazine for American farm families. Articles, 1,000 to 1,500 words. Pays $250 to $500, on acceptance. Query.

FORD TIMES—One Illinois Center, 111 E. Wacker Dr., Suite 1700, Chicago, IL 60601. Lauren R. Reskin, Man. Ed., Thomas A. Kindre, Ed. Articles, 500 to 1,500 words, on current trends, life styles, profiles, places of interest, travel, outdoor activities, food, and humor, appealing to drivers aged 18 to 35. Pays from $550 for 1,200- to 1,500-word articles, on acceptance. Query with SASE required.

FREQUENT FLYER—888 Seventh Ave., New York, NY 10019. Coleman Lollar, Ed. Articles, 1,000 to 3,000 words, on all aspects of frequent business travel, international trade, aviation, etc. No pleasure travel or personal experience pieces. Pays $100 to $500, on acceptance. Query required.

GREAT LAKES TRAVEL & LIVING—108 W. Perry St., Port Clinton, OH 43452. David G. Brown, Ed. Features, 3,500 words, and shorts, 250 to 1,000 words, about off-the-beaten path destinations, events, or locations in the Great Lakes Region (MN, WI, IL, OH, MI, western PA and NY). Pays $100 to $300, on publication. Query first.

INTERNATIONAL LIVING—824 E. Baltimore St., Baltimore, MD 21202. Bruce Totaro, Ed. Newsletter. Short pieces and features, 200 to 2,000 words, with useful information on investing, shopping, travel, employment, and life styles overseas. Pays 10¢ a word within a month of publication.

THE ITINERARY—Box 1084, Bayonne, NJ 07002. Robert S. Zywicki, Ed. Articles, 750 to 1,500 words, relating specifically to travel for the disabled: how-to features, new product pieces, interviews, etc. Black-and-white photos showing disabled individuals in travel-related experiences also welcome. Pays $50 to $100, extra for photos, on publication. Query.

MICHIGAN LIVING—Automobile Club of Michigan, 17000 Executive Plaza Dr., Dearborn, MI 48126. Len Barnes, Ed. Informative travel articles, 500 to 1,500 words, on U.S., Canadian tourist attractions and recreational opportunities; special interest in Michigan. Photos. Pays $100 to $300, extra for photos, on acceptance.

MID-ATLANTIC COUNTRY—P.O. Box 246, Alexandria, VA 22313. Jim Scott, Ed. Travel articles, 1,500 words, on destinations in the Mid-Atlantic region (VA, MD, DE, WV, NC, NJ, PA, and DC). Strong on history, architecture, regional lore, weekend "tours." Pays from $3.50 per column inch, on publication. Query first.

THE MIDWEST MOTORIST—12901 N. Forty Drive, St. Louis, MO 63141. Jean Kennedy, Man. Ed. Articles, 1,000 to 1,500 words, with photos, on travel, transportation and consumerism. Pays $50 to $200, on acceptance or publication.

NATIONAL GEOGRAPHIC—17th and M Sts., N.W. Washington, D.C. 20036. Wilbur E. Garrett, Ed. Publishes first-person articles on human geography, exploration, natural history, archeology, and science. Half staff written; half by recognized authorities and published authors. Does not review manuscripts.

NATIONAL GEOGRAPHIC TRAVELER—National Geographic Society, 17th and M Sts., NW, Washington, DC 20036. Joan Tapper, Ed. Articles, 1,500 to 4,000 words, that highlight specific places. Query with 1–2 page proposal, resume, and published clippings required. Pays $1 a word, on acceptance.

NATIONAL MOTORIST—One Market Plaza, Suite 300, San Francisco, CA 94105. Jane Offers, Ed. Illustrated articles, 500 or 1,100 words, for California motorists, on motoring in the West, car care, roads, personalities, places, etc. Photos. Pays from 10¢ a word, extra for photos, on acceptance.

NEW ENGLAND GETAWAYS—21 Pocahontas Dr., Peabody, MA 01960. Martha E. Ruch, Assistant Ed. Features, 1,500 to 2,500 words, designed to lure travelers to New England; include specific information such as addresses, phone numbers, hours of business, etc. Pays $150 to $300, on publication.

NEW WOMAN—215 Lexington Ave., New York, NY 10016. Armchair travel pieces; personal experience and "what I learned from this experience" pieces, 2,000 to 3,000 words. Pays $500 to $2,000, on acceptance. Query required.

NEW YORK DAILY NEWS—220 E. 42nd St., New York, NY 10017. Harry Ryan, Travel Ed. "Most of our articles (600 to 1,200 words) involve practical trips that the average family can afford. We use all types of travel articles, ranging from experiences to service-oriented pieces that tell readers how to make a certain trip, how to read the fine print in brochures, how to deal with emergencies, take advantage of bargain rates, etc. This is not the place for the 'How I Spent My Summer Vacation' type of article. On occasion, we run 'Short Hops,' pieces on trips within 300 miles of New York City." Pays $100 to $200, on publication; extra for B&W photos.

THE NEW YORK TIMES—229 W. 43rd St., New York, NY 10036. Nora Kerr, Travel Ed. Considers queries only; include writer's background, description of proposed article. No unsolicited manuscripts or photos. Pays on acceptance.

NORTHWEST—1320 S.W. Broadway, Portland, OR 97201. Travel articles, 800 to 1,000 words, that focus on the central overall psychological experience—the article should give the reader an idea of what unique experiences he might encounter by taking the trip. All material must pertain to the Northwest (Oregon, Washington, Idaho, and Montana). Include details about where to go, what to see, plans to make, with specific information about reservations, ticket purchases, etc. Pays $150 to $250, on acceptance. Query. Guidelines available.

NORTHWEST LIVING—130 Second Ave. South, Edmonds, WA 98020-3588. Terry W. Sheely, Ed. Articles, 400 to 1,500 words, on regional travel and natural resources. Color slides or B & W prints. Query with SASE required.

NORTHWEST MAGAZINE—*The Sunday Oregonian,* 1320 SW Broadway, Portland, OR 97201. Articles, 1,500 to 2,000 words, on regional travel destinations. Pays $175 to $250, on acceptance. Guidelines.

OFF DUTY MAGAZINE—3303 Harbor Blvd., Suite C-2, Costa Mesa, CA 92626. Bruce Thorstad, U.S. Ed. Travel articles, 1,800 to 2,000 words, for active duty military Americans (aged 20 to 40) and their families, on U.S. regions or cities. Military angle essential. Pieces with focus on an event or activity, with sidebars telling how-to and where-to. Photos. Pays from 13¢ a word, extra for photos, on acceptance. Query required. Send for guidelines. European and Pacific editions. Foreign travel articles for military Americans and their families stationed abroad. Send SASE for guidelines. Limited market.

THE ORIGINAL NEW ENGLAND GUIDE—Historical Times, Inc., 2245 Kohn Rd., Box 8200, Harrisburg, PA 17105. Howard Crise, Ed. Annual. Articles, to 1,000 words, of interest to visitors in New England: special events, sightseeing, travel destinations, and activities. Pays to 15¢ a word, on acceptance. Query with clips preferred.

SACRAMENTO MAGAZINE—P.O. Box 2424, Sacramento, CA 95811. Nancy Martini, Ed. Destination-oriented articles in the Sacramento area (or within a 6-hour drive), 1,000 to 1,500 words. Pay varies, on acceptance. Query first.

TEXAS HIGHWAYS MAGAZINE—State Dept. of Highways and Transportation, 11th and Brazos, Austin, TX 78701-2483. Frank Lively, Ed. Travel, historical, cultural, scenic features on Texas, 1,000 to 1,800 words. Pays $400 to $800, on acceptance, extra for photos. Guidelines available.

TOURS & RESORTS—World Publishing Co., 990 Grove St., Evanston, IL 60201-4370. Robert Meyers, Ed. Features on international vacation destinations, to 1,500 words. Also essays, nostalgia, how-tos, humor, and profiles. Service articles, 800 to 1,500 words, for "Travel Views." Pays $125 to $500, on acceptance. Query.

TRANSITIONS ABROAD—18 Hulst Rd., Box 344, Amherst, MA 01004. Martha Yoder, Man. Ed. Articles, to 2,000 words, for travelers overseas; work, study, travel, budget tips. Include practical, first-hand information. B & W photos a plus. Pays on publication. Send SASE for guidelines and editorial schedule.

TRAVEL AGE WEST—100 Grant Ave., San Francisco, CA 94108. Donald Langley, Man. Ed. Articles, 800 to 1,000 words, with photos, on any aspect of travel useful to travel agents, including names, addresses, prices, etc.; news or trend angle preferred. Pays $2.00 per column inch, after publication.

TRAVEL AND LEARNING ABROAD—P.O. Box 1122, Brattleboro, VT 05301. Douglas I. Grube, Ed. Articles, to 1,500 words, for people of all ages participating in or planning learning trips (exchange or study abroad programs), as well as independent international travel. Pays varying rates, on publication. Query. Guidelines available.

TRAVEL & LEISURE—1120 Ave. of the Americas, New York, NY 10036. Pamela Fiori, Ed.-in-Chief. Articles, 800 to 2,500 words, on destinations and leisuretime activities. Regional pieces for regional editions. Pays $600 to $2,000, on acceptance. Query; articles on assignment.

TRAVEL HOLIDAY—Travel Bldg., Floral Park, NY 11001. Scott Shane, Ed. Informative, lively features, 1,400 to 1,600 words, on foreign and domestic travel to well-known or little-known places; featurettes, 1,000 to 1,200 words, on special-interest subjects: museums, shopping, smaller cities or islands, special aspects of destination. Pays from $250 for featurettes, $400 for features, on acceptance. Query with published clips.

TRAVEL SMART—Dobbs Ferry, NY 10522. Short pieces, 250 to 1,000 words, about interesting, unusual and/or economical places: give specific details on hotels, restaurants, transportation, and costs. Pays to $100, on publication.

TRAVEL SMART FOR BUSINESS—Dobbs Ferry, NY 10522. H. J. Teison, Ed. Articles, 200 to 1,000 words, for company executives and business travel managers, on lowering travel costs and increasing travel convenience. Pays on publication.

VISTA/USA—Box 161, Convent Station, NJ 07961. Exxon Travel Club. Kathleen M. Caccavale, Ed. Travel articles, 1,500 to 2,500 words, on North America, Hawaii, Mexico, and the Caribbean. "Flavor of the area, not service, oriented." Pays from $600, on acceptance. Query with writing sample and outline. Limited market.

VOLKSWAGEN'S WORLD—Volkswagen of America, Inc. P.O. Box 3951, 888 W. Big Beaver, Troy, MI 48007-3951. Marlene Goldsmith, Ed. Travel articles on unique places, to 750 words. Pays $150 per printed page, on acceptance. Query.

WESTWAYS—P.O. Box 2890, Terminal Annex, Los Angeles, CA 90051. Mary Ann Fisher, Exec. Ed. Travel articles on where to go, what to see, and how to get there, 1,500 words. Domestic travel articles are limited to Western U.S., Canada, and Hawaii; foreign travel articles are also of interest. Quality color photos should be available. Pays 20¢ a word, 30 days before publication.

WOMAN TRAVELER MAGAZINE—P.O. Box 6117, New York, NY 10150. Jeanine Moss, Ed./Pub. Detailed travel advice about America's major business cities from a woman's point of view: hotels with skirt hangers, hairdryers, fitness facilities, light cuisine; restaurants comfortable for a woman alone, good for entertaining; some vacation travel. Costs and specific details a must. Pays from $200, on publication. Query required.

YANKEE MAGAZINE'S TRAVEL GUIDE TO NEW ENGLAND AND ITS NEIGHBORS—Main St., Dublin, NH 03444. Elizabeth Doyle, Ed. Articles, 500 to 2,000 words, on unusual activities, restaurants, places to visit in New England, New York, and Atlantic Canada. Photos. Pays $50 to $300, on acceptance. Query with outline and writing samples.

INFLIGHT MAGAZINES

Inflight magazines are published by commercial airlines for their passengers, and use a wide variety of general-interest articles, as well as travel pieces on the airlines' destinations.

ABOARD—North-South Net, Inc., 777 41st St., P.O. Box 40-2763, Miami Beach, FL 33140. Ana C. Mix, Ed. Inflight magazine of nine Latin American international airlines. Articles, with photos, on Chile, Panama, Paraguay, Dominican Republic, Ecuador, El Salvador, Bolivia, Venezuela, and Honduras. Pieces on science, sports, home, fashion, and gastronomy, 1,200 to 1,500 words. Pays $150, on acceptance and on publication. Query required.

AMERICA WEST AIRLINES MAGAZINE—Skyword Marketing, Inc., 7500 N. Dreamy Draw Dr., Suite 236, Phoenix, AZ 85020. Michael Derr, Ed. Articles, 750 to 2,000 words, celebrating entrepreneurism and the Southwest region. Pays from $250 to $750, on publication. Query required. Send for guidelines.

AMERICAN WAY—P.O. Box 619616, MD 2G23, DFW Airport, TX 75261-9616. Charles Marsh, Ed. American Airlines' inflight magazine. Features, 1,500 to 1,750 words, on health, business, the arts, etc.; profiles of people and places. Photos. Pays from $450, on acceptance. Query articles editor.

CONTINENTAL—Brighton Inflight Group, 901 Mopac Expressway S., Ste. 350, Austin, TX 78746. Charles J. Lohrmann, Ed. "Concise, thought-provoking" queries for business, sports, and life style articles, and profiles. "Facts, figures, and accuracy" are essential, as is a national/international focus. Features run to 2,000 words. Pay varies, on publication. Query.

ECHELON—Halsey Publishing Co., 12955 Biscayne Blvd., N. Miami, FL 33181. Debra Silver, Ed. Inflight magazine for Butler Aviation International. Pays one month prior to publication. Query with SASE required.

MIDWAY—Skies Publishing Co., Plaza West, Suite 310, 9600 SW Oak St., Portland, OR 97223. Robert Patterson, Ed. Articles, 1,200 to 1,500 words, of interest to business travelers. Pays $200 to $400, on publication. Queries preferred.

NORTHWEST (formerly *Northwest Orient*)—East/West Network, 34 E. 51st., New York, NY 10022. Bill McCoy, Ed. Features, 1,500 to 3,000 words, on travel, business, sports, entertainment, media, and profiles. Pays from $300, on acceptance. Query with clips required.

PACE—338 N. Elm St., Greensboro, NC 27401. Davis A. March, Ed. Piedmont Airlines inflight magazine. Articles of interest to business travelers; economic reports, business management and communication. Travel pieces to Piedmont destination cities. Pays varying rates, on acceptance.

PAN AM CLIPPER—East/West Network, 34 E. 51st St., New York, NY 10022. Dick Kagan, Ed. Monthly inflight for Pan Am Airlines. Interviews, profiles, and travel pieces on Pan Am destinations, varying lengths. Pays varying rates, on acceptance. Very limited market.

PRESIDENTIAL AIRWAYS MAGAZINE—338 N. Elm St., Greensboro, NC 27401. Davis March, Ed. Articles, 3,000 to 4,000 words, on business, travel, leisure, and the Southeast region. Pays to $50, on acceptance. Query preferred.

PSA MAGAZINE—Pacific Southwest Airlines, East/West Network, 5900 Wilshire Blvd., Los Angeles, CA 90036. Al Austin, Ed. Articles on personalities, environment, sports, arts, business in the CA, NV, OR, WA, and AZ region. Calendar listings; business trends; regular columns: restaurants, saloons, show business, finance, sports, health. Write for guidelines.

SKY—12955 Biscayne Blvd., North Miami, FL 33181. Lidia de Leon, Ed. Delta Air Lines' inflight magazine. Articles on business, lifestyle, high tech, sports, the arts, etc. Color slides. Pays varying rates, on acceptance. Query.

SOUTHWEST SPIRIT—Southwest Airlines, East/West Network, 5900 Wilshire Blvd., Suite 800, Los Angeles, CA 90036. Gabrielle Cosgriff, Ed. Articles, 1,000 to 2,500 words, on business, arts and lifestyles in the Southwest. Pays $350 to $450, on acceptance. Guidelines.

UNITED—United Airlines, East/West Network, 34 East 51st St., New York, NY 10022. Jonathan Black, Ed. Features on executive life styles and business. Regular columns on travel, sports, driving, personal finance; art portfolios; high-level new products of interest to executives. Guidelines.

USAIR—600 Third Ave., New York, NY 10016. Richard Busch, Ed. Articles, 1,500 to 3,000 words, on travel, business, sports, entertainment, food, health, and other general-interest topics. No downbeat or extremely controversial subjects. Pays $350 to $800, on acceptance. Query first.

VIS A VIS—East/West Network, 34 E. 51st St., New York, NY 10022. Fred R. Smith, Ed. First-person articles, 600 to 700 words, for departments: "Face to Face" (profiles), "Take Your Clubs" (golf resorts), and "The Royal Life" (luxury vacations). Pays varying rates, on acceptance. Query.

WOMEN'S PUBLICATIONS

BEAUTY DIGEST—126 Fifth Ave., New York, NY 10011. Linda Stasi, Ed. Reprints and original pieces, 1,800 to 2,500 words, on beauty, health, exercise, self-help, for women. Pays varying rates, on publication.

BLACK ELEGANCE—Go Stylish Publications, 475 Park Ave., S., New York, NY 10016. Sharyn J. Skeeter, Ed. Articles, 1,000 to 2,000 words, for upscale black women, on beauty, fashion, relationships, home design, etc. Pays $150 to $225, on publication. Query.

BRIDAL GUIDE—441 Lexington Ave., New York, NY 10017. Suzanne Kresse, Ed.-in-Chief. Features, 500 to 20,000 words, on wedding planning, remarriage, honeymoons, ethnic traditions, and unusual and celebrity weddings. Photos. Pays $100 to $400, on publication. Guidelines.

BRIDE'S—350 Madison Ave., New York, NY 10017. Andrea Feld, Copy and Features Ed. Articles, 1,000 to 3,000 words, for engaged couples or newlyweds, on communication, sex, housing, finances, careers, remarriage, step-parenting, health, birth control, pregnancy, babies, religion, in-laws, relationships, and wedding planning. Pays $300 to $800, on acceptance.

CAPPER'S—616 Jefferson St., Topeka, KS 66607. Nancy Peavler, Ed. Human interest, personal experience, historical articles, 300 to 500 words. Pays varying rates, on publication.

CHATELAINE—Maclean Hunter Bldg., 777 Bay St., Toronto, Ont., Canada M5W 1A7. Mildred Istona, Ed. Articles, 2,500 words, on controversial subjects and personalities of interest to Canadian women. Pays $750 for personal-experience pieces, from $1,000 for articles, on acceptance.

COMPLETE WOMAN—1165 N. Clark, Chicago, IL 60610. Mary James, Assoc. Ed. Articles, 800 to 1,800 words, with practical advice for women on careers, health, personal relationships, etc. Inspirational profiles of successful women. Pays varying rates, on publication.

COSMOPOLITAN—224 W. 57th St., New York, NY 10019. Helen Gurley Brown, Ed. Guy Flatley, Man. Ed. Roberta Ashley, Exec. Ed. Betty Nichols Kelly, Fiction and Books Ed. Articles, to 5,000 words, and features, 2,000 to 3,000 words, on issues affecting young career women. Pays from $1,500 for full-length articles, $750 to $1,500 for short stories, on acceptance.

COUNTRY WOMAN (formerly *Farm Woman*)—P.O. Box 643, Milwaukee, WI 53201. Eleanor Jacobs, Man. Ed. Personal-experience, humor, service-oriented articles, and how-to features, to 1,000 words, of interest to country women. Pays $40 to $250, on acceptance.

ELLE—551 Fifth Ave., New York, NY 10176. Joan Harting, Sr. Ed. Articles, varying lengths, for fashion-conscious women, ages 20 to 50. Subjects include beauty, health, careers, fitness, travel, and life styles. Pays top rates, on publication. Query required.

ESSENCE—1500 Broadway, New York, NY 10036. Susan L. Taylor, Ed.-in-Chief. Provocative articles, 1,500 to 3,000 words, about black women in America today: self-help, how-to pieces, careers, health, celebrity profiles and political issues. Pays varying rates, on acceptance. Query.

EXECUTIVE FEMALE—1041 Third Ave., New York, NY 10021. Mary Elizabeth Terzella, Ed. Features, 6 to 12 pages, on managing people, time, and careers, for women in business. Articles, 6 to 8 pages, for "More Money," "Horizons," "Profiles," and "Entrepreneur's Corner." Pays varying rates, on publication. Limited market.

FAMILY CIRCLE—110 Fifth Ave., New York, NY 10011. Susan Ungaro, Articles Ed. Ellen Stoianoff, Sen. Ed., Leah Breier, Health Ed. Articles, to 2,500 words, on marriage, family, child-rearing, consumer affairs, social and political issues, travel, humor, health and fitness. Query required.

FLARE—777 Bay St., Toronto, Ont., Canada M5W 1A7. Dianne Rinehart, Assoc. Ed. Service articles, 1,500 to 3,000 words, on health, careers, relationships, and contemporary problems; articles on home decor, food, and entertaining for Canadian women aged 18 to 34. Profiles, 750 to 1,500 words, of up-and-coming Canadians. Pays on acceptance. Query.

GLAMOUR—350 Madison Ave., New York, NY 10017. Ruth Whitney, Ed.-in-Chief. Barbara Coffey, Man. Ed. Rona Cherry, Exec. Ed. Janet Chan, Senior Ed. How-to articles, from 1,500 words, on careers, health, psychology, interpersonal relationships, etc., for women aged 18 to 35. Fashion and beauty pieces staff-written. Submit queries to Judeth Welderholt Coyne, Articles Ed. Pays from $1,500.

GOOD HOUSEKEEPING—959 Eighth Ave., New York, NY 10019. Joan Thursh, Articles Ed. Naome Lewis, Fiction Ed. "Most of the articles in every issue are free-lance written. We'll read queries for personal experience stories that tell readers about some inspirational, unique or trend-setting event; personal medical stories that detail an unusual illness, treatment, and result; short, essay-type reminiscences in which the author reflects on some aspect of family life or relationship; medical and health articles." Avoid topics covered by contributing editors (food, beauty, fashion, travel, crafts, decorating, and nutrition)." Short pieces run 750 to 1,500 words; articles from 2,500 words. Ideas on subjects of practical interest to women for "Better Way." Pays top rates, on acceptance.

HARPER'S BAZAAR—1700 Broadway, New York, NY 10019. Anthony Mazzola, Ed.-in-Chief. Articles, 1,500 to 2,000 words, for active, sophisticated women. Topics include the arts, world affairs, food, wine, travel, families, education, personal finance, careers, health, and sexuality. No unsolicited manuscripts; query first with SASE. Payment varies, on acceptance.

IDEALS—Nelson Place at Elm Hill Pike, P.O. Box 141000, Nashville, TN 37214-1000. Romona Richards, Ed. Articles, 600 to 800 words. Send for guidelines.

LADIES' HOME JOURNAL—100 Park Ave., New York, NY 10017. Myrna Blyth, Ed.-in-Chief. Articles of interest to women. Send queries with outlines to Jan Goodwin, Exec. Ed.; Roberta Grant and Beth Weinhouse, Sr. Eds.

MCCALL'S—230 Park Ave., New York, NY 10169. Andrea Thompson, Ed. Articles, 1,000 to 3,000 words, on current issues, human interest, family relationships. Pays top rates, on acceptance.

MADEMOISELLE—350 Madison Ave., New York, NY 10017. Kate

White, Exec. Ed., Articles; Eileen Schnurr, Fiction Ed. Articles, 1,200 to 3,500 words. Pays $800 to $1,000 for short articles, and $1,750 for full-length articles, on acceptance.

THE MICHIGAN WOMAN—P.O. Box 1171, Birmingham, MI 48012. Betsy Hull, Ed. Articles, to 2,000 words, that highlight the achievements of Michigan women. Pays 10¢ a word, on publication. Query required.

MODERN BRIDE—One Park Ave., New York, NY 10016. Mary Ann Cavlin, Ed. Articles, from 1,500 words, for bride and groom, on wedding planning, financial planning, juggling career and home, etc. Pays on acceptance.

MS. MAGAZINE—One Times Sq., New York, NY 10036. Address Manuscript Editor. Articles relating to women's roles and changing lifestyles; general interest, self-help, how-to, profiles. Pays varying rates. Query with SASE. Accepts very little free-lance material.

NA'AMAT WOMAN—200 Madison Ave., 18th fl., New York, NY 10016. Judith Sokoloff, Ed. Articles on Jewish culture, women's issues, social and political topics, and Israel, 1,500 to 2,500 words. Pays 8¢ a word, on publication. Query.

NEW BODY—888 Seventh Ave., New York, NY 10106. Constance Boze, Ed. Lively, readable service-oriented articles, 1,000 to 2,000 words, by writers with background in health field: exercise, nutrition, and diet pieces for women aged 18 to 40. Pays $100 to $300, on publication. Query.

NEW WOMAN—215 Lexington Ave., New York, NY 10016. Pat Miller, Ed./Pub. Self-help/inspirational articles, on psychology, relationships, money, careers. Travel features, with personal discovery angle. Lifestyle, health, and fitness features. Profiles of celebrities, business women. Pays to $1 a word, on acceptance. Query.

PLAYGIRL—801 Second Ave., New York, NY 10017. Nancie S. Martin, Ed.-in-Chief. Articles, to 2,500 words, on health, sexuality, trends, and careers; interviews with top celebrities; essays on relationships, to 2,500 words. Erotic fantasies (6 to 8 typed pages) from a woman's point of view. Query appropriate department editor after studying several issues. Pay varies.

POLITICAL WOMAN—4521 Campus Dr., Ste. 388, Irvine, CA 92715. Articles, 1,000 to 3,000 words, on national and international events, politics, and current events. Pays $25 to $1,000, on publication. Address Sally Corngold, Ed.

REDBOOK—224 W. 57th St., New York, NY 10019. Gini Kopecky, Articles Ed. Articles for women ages 25 to 40. Pays to $850 for short shorts, to 9 typed pages; $750 for personal-experience pieces, 1,000 to 2,000 words, on solving problems in marriage, family life, or community, for "Young Mother's Story." Query for articles only. SASE required.

SAVVY—3 Park Ave., New York, NY 10016. Mary H. J. Farrell, Senior Editor. Sophisticated articles on money and career for successful women; topical features and profiles of interesting women, 2,500 to 3,000 words. Short pieces for "Money," "Manager," and "Smart Talk" sections. Query with SASE and published clips. Guidelines. Payment negotiable.

SELF—350 Madison Ave., New York, NY 10017. Valerie Griffith Weaver, Ed. Articles for women of all ages, with strong how-to slant, on self-development. Pays from $700, on acceptance. Query.

SLIMMER—801 Second Ave., New York, NY 10017. Rhonda J. Wilson, Exec. Ed. Articles, 2,500 words, and columns, 1,000 words, on nutrition, fitness, beauty, skin care, diet, exercise, fashion, travel, and sports, for women aged 18 to 40. Pays $200 to $300 for features, $100 to $150 for columns, 30 days after acceptance. Query required.

SUNDAY WOMAN PLUS—235 E. 45th St., New York, NY 10017. Merry Clark, Ed. Articles, 1,000 to 1,200 words, on topics of interest to the North American family: lifestyles, relationships, careers, businesses, and money management. Pays $150 to $500, on acceptance. Query required.

VIRTUE—P.O. Box 850, Sisters, OR 97759. Becky Durost-Fish, Ed. Articles, 1,000 to 1,500 words, on the family, marriage, self-esteem, working mothers, opinions, food, decorating. Pays 10¢ per word, on publication. Query required.

VOGUE—350 Madison Ave., New York, NY 10017. Address Features Ed. Articles, to 1,500 words, on women, entertainment and the arts, travel, medicine and health. General features. No unsolicited manuscripts. Query first. Pays good rates, on acceptance.

WEIGHT WATCHERS MAGAZINE—360 Lexington Ave., New York, NY 10017. Nelly Edmondson, Articles Ed. Articles on nutrition and health. Pays from $250, on acceptance. Query with clips required. Guidelines.

WOMAN—1115 Broadway, New York, NY 10010. Sherry Amatenstein, Ed. Personal-experience and how-to pieces, 1,000 to 2,000 words, for women who want to better their relationships, careers or lifestyles. Profiles of women business owners for "Be Your Own Boss." Short interviews with successful women for "Woman in the News." Pays $25 to $200, on acceptance. Query.

WOMAN'S DAY—1515 Broadway, New York, NY 10036. Rebecca Greer, Articles Ed. Articles, 500 to 3,500 words, on subjects of interest to women: marriage, education, family health, child rearing, money-management, relationships, careers, changing life styles, etc. "Although we're primarily interested in articles that will help women improve their lives, we also welcome dramatic narratives about women who have experienced medical miracles, survived a disaster—provided they have reader identification. We also use short provocative personal essays, 1,200 to 1,500 words, humorous or serious, for 'Reflections' page." Query first. Pays top rates, upon acceptance.

WOMAN'S WORLD—177 N. Dean St., Englewood, NJ 07631. Gerry Hunt, Sr. Ed. Articles, 600 to 1,800 words, of interest to middle-income women between the ages of 18 and 60, on love, romance, careers, medicine, health, psychology, family life, travel, dramatic stories of adventure or crisis. Dramatic, first-person accounts, 1,200 to 1,500 words, for "Turning Point," on how a woman's life has changed, either through an outside influence or through a change in her own way of thinking. "These pieces must be full of emotion and very sympathetic, and must have a definite turning point: a peak at which the woman makes a decision regarding the change. No miraculous recoveries from disease, please." Query first. Pays $300 to $750, $500 for "Turning Point," on acceptance. Query.

WOMEN IN BUSINESS—9100 Ward Parkway, Box 8728, Kansas City, MO 64114. Margaret E. Horan, Ed. American Business Women's Assn. Features, 1,000 to 1,500 words, for working women between 35 and 55 years. No profiles. Pays on acceptance. Written query required.

WOMEN'S CIRCLE—Box 689, Seabrook, NH 03874. Marjorie Pearl, Ed.

Success stories of home-based female entrepreneurs. How-to articles for craft and needlework projects. Unique money saving ideas and interesting hobbies. Pays varying rates, on acceptance.

WOMEN'S SPORTS AND FITNESS—501 Second Ave., Suite 400, San Francisco, CA 94107. Martha Nelson, Ed. How-to's, profiles, and sports reports, 500 to 3,000 words, for the active woman. Health, fitness, and sports pieces. Photos. Pays from $50, on publication.

THE WORKBASKET—4251 Pennsylvania, Kansas City, MO 64111. Roma Jean Rice, Ed. Instructions and models for original knit, crochet, and tat items. How-to's on crafts and gardening, 400 to 1,200 words, with photos. Pays 7¢ a word for articles, extra for photos, on acceptance; negotiable rates for instructional items.

WORKING MOTHER—230 Park Ave., New York, NY 10169. Olivia Buehl, Ed. In-depth articles, 800 to 1,500 words, for working mothers, on child care, home management, the work world, single mothers, etc. Pays varying rates, on acceptance. Query first with detailed outline.

WORKING WOMAN—342 Madison Ave., New York, NY 10173. Julia Kagan, Exec. Ed. Articles, 1,000 to 2,500 words, on business and personal aspects of working women's lives. Pays from $400, on acceptance.

HOME AND LIFESTYLE PUBLICATIONS

THE AMERICAN ROSE MAGAZINE—P.O. Box 30,000, Shreveport, LA 71130. Harold S. Goldstein, Ed. Articles on home rose gardens: varieties, products, etc. Pays in copies.

AMERICANA—29 W. 38th St., New York, NY 10018. Sandra Wilmot, Ed. Articles, 1,000 to 2,500 words, with historical slant: restoration, crafts, food, antiques, travel, etc. Pays $350 to $600, on acceptance. Query.

BETTER HEALTH & LIVING—800 Second Ave., New York, NY 10017. Sharon Schwartzman, Man. Ed. Articles, 2 to 35 typed pages, on healthful living; shorter items and tips. Pays $50 to $100 for short tips, from $500 for features, 90 days after acceptance. Query preferred.

BETTER HOMES AND GARDENS—1716 Locust St., Des Moines, IA 50336. David Jordan, Ed. Articles, to 2,000 words, on home and family entertainment, money management, health, travel, pets, and cars. Pays top rates, on acceptance. Query.

BLACK FAMILY MAGAZINE—1180 Sunrise Valley Dr., Suite 320, Reston, VA 22091. Evelyn Ivery, Ed. Articles, 2,000 words, on health, education, finance, tips for home decorating and repair; profiles. Short stories; fillers. Pays from $300 for features, $25 for fillers. Queries preferred.

BON APPETIT—5900 Wilshire Blvd., Los Angeles, CA 90036. Barbara Fairchild, Sr. Ed. Articles on fine cooking (menu format or single focus), cooking classes, and gastronomically-focused travel. Query, with samples of published work. Pays varying rates, on acceptance.

THE CHRISTIAN SCIENCE MONITOR—One Norway St., Boston, MA 02115. Roderick Nordell, Features Ed. Keith Henderson, Home and Family Page. Phyllis Hanes, Food Ed. Articles on lifestyle trends, women's rights, family, parenting, consumerism, fashion, and food. Pays varying rates, on acceptance.

CONSUMERS DIGEST—5705 N. Lincoln Ave., Chicago, IL 60659. John Manos, Ed. Articles, 500 to 3,000 words, on subjects of interest to consumers: products and services, automobiles, health, fitness, consumer legal affairs, and personal money management. Photos. Pays from 30¢ a word, extra for photos, on publication. Buys all rights. Query with resume and published clips.

THE COOK'S MAGAZINE—2710 North Ave., Bridgeport, CT 06604. Sheila Lowenstein, Ed. Articles on trends in home and restaurant food and cooking. Query with three- to four-sentence outline, published clips, and sample recipe (for writing and recipe style). Pays $200 to $375, 60 days after publication. SASE required.

COUNTRY LIVING—224 W. 57th St., New York, NY 10019. Mary Roby, Man. Ed. Articles, 1,000 to 1,500 words, on decorating, crafts, cooking, real estate, and antique-related topics. Pays $300 to $400, on acceptance.

FARM & RANCH LIVING—5400 S. 60th St., Greendale, WI 53129. Bob Ottum, Man. Ed. Articles, 2,000 words, on rural people and situations; nostalgia pieces, profiles of interesting farms and farmers, ranches and ranchers. Poetry. Pays $15 to $400, on acceptance and on publication.

FARM FAMILY AMERICA—1999 Shepard Rd., St. Paul, MN 55116. George Ashfield, Ed. Articles, 1,200 to 1,500 words, on life style, activities, and travel-related subjects of interest to farmers and farm families across the U.S. Pays $350 to $700, on publication. Query first.

FARMSTEAD MAGAZINE—Box 111, Freedom, ME 04941. Heidi N. Brugger, Man. Ed. Articles, 700 to 2,500 words, on organic home gardening, country living, livestock and marketing for the small farmer, wood heat, how-to, and homestyle recipes. Pays 5¢ a word, on publication. Query preferred.

FLOWER AND GARDEN MAGAZINE—4251 Pennsylvania, Kansas City, MO 64111. Rachel Snyder, Ed.-in-Chief. How-to articles, to 1,200 words, with photos, on indoor and outdoor home gardening. Pays 7¢ a word, on acceptance. Query preferred.

FOOD & WINE—1120 Ave. of the Americas, 9th fl., New York, NY 10036. Ila Stanger, Ed.-in-Chief. Warren Picower, Man. Ed. Current culinary or beverage ideas for dining and entertaining at home and out. Submit detailed proposal.

FRIENDLY EXCHANGE—Locust at 17th, Des Moines, IA 50336. Adele Malott, Ed. Features, 1,000 to 2,500 words, for young, active families who live in the western half of the U.S. Subjects include domestic travel, camping, health, culture, personal finance, consumer information, and food. Photos. No poetry, fiction, cartoons. Pays $400 to $800, extra for photos. Query preferred.

GARDEN—The Garden Society, Botanical Garden, Bronx, NY 10458. Ann Botshon, Ed. Articles, 1,000 to 2,500 words, on botany, horticulture, ecology, agriculture. Photos. Pays to $300, on publication. Query.

GARDEN DESIGN—1733 Connecticut Ave., NW, Washington, DC 20009. Susan Frey, Ed.-in-Chief. Articles, 500 to 1,000 words, on classic and contemporary examples of residential landscape, garden art, history and design; interviews. Pays $300, on publication. Query.

HARROWSMITH—The Creamery, Ferry Rd., Charlotte, VT 05445. Tom Rawls, Man. Ed. Investigative pieces, 4,000 to 5,000 words, on ecology, energy, health, gardening, do-it-yourself projects, and the food chain. Short pieces for

"Screed" (opinions); and "Gazette" (news briefs). Pays $500 to $1,500 for features, from $50 to $600 for department pieces, on acceptance. Query required. Send SASE for guidelines.

THE HERB QUARTERLY—P.O. Box 275, Newfane, VT 05345. Jeanne Turner, Assoc. Ed. Articles, 2,000 to 10,000 words, on herbs: practical uses, cultivation, gourmet cooking, landscaping, herb tradition, unique garden designs, profiles of herb garden experts, practical how-to's for the herb businessperson. Include garden design when possible. Pays on publication. Send for writers' guidelines.

HOME MAGAZINE—P.O. Box 92000, Los Angeles, CA 90009. Channing Dawson, Ed. Articles of interest to homeowners: architecture, remodeling, decorating, how-to's, project ideas, landscaping, taxes, insurance, conservation and solar energy. Pays varying rates, on acceptance. Query with 50- to 200-word summary.

THE HOMEOWNER—3 Park Ave., New York, NY 10016. Joe Carter, Ed. Articles, 500 to 1,500 words, with photos, on do-it-yourself home improvement and remodeling projects. Pays $100 to $150 per printed page, on acceptance. Query.

HOMEOWNERS—The Personal Marketing Co., 8520 Sweetwater, Ste. F57, Houston, TX 77037. Theresa Seegers, Man. Ed. Short articles, 200 to 500 words, on buying and selling real estate, mortgages, investment, home improvement, interior design, etc. Pays 10¢ to 20¢ a word, on acceptance. Query. Newsletter.

HORTICULTURE—755 Boylston St., Boston, MA 02116. Steven Krauss, Man. Ed. Authoritative, well-written articles, 1,200 to 3,000 words, on all aspects of gardening and horticulture. Pays competitive rates. Query.

HOUSE AND GARDEN—350 Madison Ave., New York, NY 10017. Louis O. Gropp, Ed.-in-Chief. Shelley Wanger, Articles Ed. Articles on decorating, architecture, gardens, the arts. Query. Rarely buys unsolicited manuscripts.

HOUSE BEAUTIFUL—1700 Broadway, New York, NY 10019. Carol Cooper Garey, Dir. Copy/Features. Service articles related to the home. Pieces on architecture, design, travel and gardening mostly staff-written. Pays varying rates, on acceptance. Send for writer's guidelines. Query with detailed outline.

HOUSTON HOME & GARDEN—5615 Kirby, Suite 600, P.O. Box 25386, Houston, TX 77265. Diane Stafford, Ex. Ed. Articles on interior design, regional gardening, cooking, art, architecture, health, fitness, and travel. Limited freelance market. Query.

LIFE IN THE TIMES—Times Publishing Co., Springfield, VA 22159. Barry Robinson, Ed. Travel articles, 900 to 1,400 words; features on food, 500 to 1,000 words; and short, personal-experience pieces, 750 words, of interest to military people and their families around the world. Pays from $25 to $150 for short pieces, to $350 for general-interest features, on acceptance.

LOG HOME GUIDE FOR BUILDERS & BUYERS—Exit 447, I-40, Hartford, TN 37821. Articles, 500 words, on building new, or restoring old, log homes, especially with solar or alternative heating systems, as well as pieces on decorating or profiles of interesting builders of old homes. Pays 15¢ a word, extra for photos, on publication. Limited market.

METROPOLITAN HOME—750 Third Ave., New York, NY 10017. Service and informational articles for metropolitan dwellers in apartments, houses, co-ops, lofts and condos. Pays varying rates. Query.

MILITARY LIFESTYLE MAGAZINE—1732 Wisconsin Ave., N.W., Washington, DC 20007. Hope Daniels, Ed. Articles, 800 to 2,000 words, for military families in the U.S. and overseas, on lifestyles; pieces on issues of interest to military families; fiction. Pays $100 to $400, on publication. Query.

THE MOTHER EARTH NEWS—105 Stoney Mt. Rd., Hendersonville, NC 28791. Bruce Woods, Ed. Articles on country living: home improvement and construction, how-to's, indoor and outdoor gardening, crafts and projects. etc. Also self-help, health, food-related, ecology, energy, and consumerism pieces; profiles. Pays from $100 per published page, on acceptance. Address Submissions Ed.

NATIONAL GARDENING MAGAZINE—180 Flynn Ave., Burlington, VT 05401. Katherine Anderson, Ed. Articles, 500 to 2,500 words: how-to pieces on food gardens and orchards, general-interest pieces for gardeners. Pays $75 to $450, extra for photos, on acceptance. Query preferred.

NEW AGE—342 Western Ave., Brighton, MA 02135. Gail Whitney, Ed. Assistant. Features, 2,000 to 4,000 words; columns, 750 to 1,500 words; short news items, 50 words; and first-person narratives, 750 to 1,500 words, for readers who take an active interest in holistic health, personal and spiritual growth, social responsibility, and contemporary social issues. Pays varying rates. Query first.

THE NEW HOMEOWNER—Castlewood Corp., 222 Keswick Ave., 2nd Floor, Glenside, PA 19038. Articles on resources, homecare, interior design, and decorating, of varying lengths, for the affluent new homeowner. Pays varying rates, on acceptance.

NEW SHELTER—See *Rodale's Practical Homeowner.*

1001 HOME IDEAS—3 Park Ave., New York, NY 10016. Ellen Frankel, Ed. General-interest articles, 500 to 2,000 words, on home decorating, furnishings, antiques and collectibles, food, household tips, crafts, remodeling, gardening. How-to and problem-solving decorating pieces. Pays varying rates, on acceptance. Query.

RODALE'S PRACTICAL HOMEOWNER (formerly *New Shelter*)—33 E. Minor St., Emmaus, PA 18098. Articles on contemporary home management: how-to, total home design, home improvement, with emphasis on energy efficiency, new products, materials and technologies. Query with SASE required; address Man. Ed.

SELECT HOMES—3835 W. 30th Ave., Vancouver, B.C., Canada V6S 1W9 (Western edition); 1450 Don Mills Rd., Don Mills, Ont., M3B 2X7 (Eastern edition). How-to articles, 750 to 1,200 words, on home improvement, decorating, and maintenance; profiles of building and renovation projects. "What's available" pieces (compact furnaces, hardwood flooring, etc.). Pays $200 to $500, on acceptance. Query (include international reply coupons) Pam Withers, Western Ed. or Jim Adair, Eastern Ed. Guidelines.

WORKBENCH—4251 Pennsylvania, Kansas City, MO 64111. Robert N. Hoffman, Ed. Illustrated how-to articles on home improvement and woodworking, with detailed instructions, energy conservation and alternatives, manufactured housing. Pays from $125 per printed page, on acceptance. Send SASE for writers' guidelines.

574

YOUR HOME MAGAZINE—P.O. Box 10010, Ogden, UT 84409. Marjorie H. Rice, Ed. Upbeat articles, 1,000 to 1,200 words, with color transparencies, for renters and homeowners on the latest trends and styles in home decor: renovating, decorating, remodeling; garden/patio/outdoor articles; Profiles of exotic and beautiful houses; short home/garden humor pieces. Pays 15¢ a word, $35 for color photos, on acceptance. Query with SASE.

SPORTS, OUTDOORS, RECREATION

AAA WORLD—AAA Headquarters, 8111 Gatehouse Rd., Falls Church, VA 22047. Douglas Damerst, Ed. Automobile and travel concerns, including automotive travel, maintenance and upkeep, 750 to 1,500 words. Pays $300 to $600, on acceptance. Query with clips.

AERO—P.O. Box 6050, Mission Viejo, CA 92690. Mary F. Silitch, Ed. Articles, 1,000 to 4,000 words, for owners of high performance single- and twin-engine planes, relating to ownership, piloting, and use; pieces on favorite fly-in travel spots. Photos. Pays $75 to $250, on publication.

THE AMERICAN FIELD—222 W. Adams St., Chicago, IL 60606. William F. Brown, Ed. Yarns about hunting trips, bird-shooting; articles to 1,500 words, on dogs and field trials, emphasizing conservation of game resources. Pays varying rates, on acceptance.

AMERICAN FORESTS—1516 P St., N.W., Washington, DC 20005. Bill Rooney, Ed. Well-documented articles, to 2,000 words, with photos, on recreational and commercial uses and management of forests. Photos. Pays on acceptance.

AMERICAN HANDGUNNER—Suite 200, 591 Camino de la Reina, San Diego, CA 92108. Cameron Hopkins, Ed. Semi-technical articles on shooting sports, gun repair and alteration, handgun matches and tournaments, for lay readers. Pays $100 to $500, on publication. Query.

AMERICAN HUNTER—470 Spring Park Pl., Suite 1000, Herndon, VA 22070. Tom Fulgham, Ed. Articles, 1,400 to 2,000 words, on hunting. Photos. Pays on acceptance.

AMERICAN LAND FORUM—See *The New American Land.*

AMERICAN MOTORCYCLIST—American Motorcyclist Assn., Box 6114, Westerville, OH 43081-6114. Greg Harrison, Ed. Articles and fiction, to 3,000 words, on motorcycling: news coverage, personalities, tours. Photos. Pays varying rates, on publication. Query.

THE AMERICAN RIFLEMAN—470 Spring Park Pl., Suite 1000, Herndon, VA 22070. Bill Parkerson, Ed. Factual articles on use and enjoyment of sporting firearms. Pays on acceptance.

THE AMICUS JOURNAL—Natural Resources Defense Council, 122 E. 42nd St., Rm. 4500, New York, NY 10168. Peter Borrelli, Ed. Investigative articles and poetry related to national and international environmental policy. Pays on acceptance. Query required.

ARCHERY WORLD—319 Barry Ave. S., Ste. 101, Wayzata, MN 55391. Richard Sapp, Ed. Articles, 1,000 to 2,000 words, on all aspects of bowhunting, with photos. Pays from $250, extra for photos, on publication.

THE ATLANTIC SALMON JOURNAL—1435 St. Alexandre, Suite 1030, Montreal, Quebec, Canada H3A 2G4. Joanne Eidinger, Ed. Material related to

Atlantic salmon: Conservation, ecology, travel, politics, biology, etc. How-to's, anecdotes, cuisine. Articles, 1,500 to 3,000 words. Pays $100 to $350, on publication.

ATV SPORTS (formerly *Three Wheeling*)—Box 2260, Costa Mesa, CA 92628. Bruce Simura, Ed. Articles, 1,000 to 1,500 words, related to three- and four-wheel all-terrain vehicles. Pays $60 per printed page, on publication. Query.

BACKPACKER MAGAZINE—1515 Broadway, New York, NY 10036. John A. Delves, Ed. Articles, 250 to 3,000 words, on backpacking, technique, kayaking/canoeing, mountaineering, alpine/nordic skiing, health, natural science. Photos. Pays varying rates. Query.

THE BACKSTRETCH—19363 James Couzens Hwy., Detroit, MI 48235. Ruth LeGrove, Man. Ed. United Thoroughbred Trainers of America. Feature articles, with photos, on persons involved with thoroughbred horses. Pays after publication.

BASEBALL ILLUSTRATED—See *Hockey Illustrated*.

BASKETBALL ANNUAL—See *Hockey Illustrated*.

BASSIN'—15115 S. 76th E. Ave., Bixby, OH 74008. Andre Hinds, Exec. Ed. Articles, 1,200 to 2,000 words, on how-to and where-to bass fish, for the average fisherman. Pays $175 to $250, on acceptance.

BASSMASTER MAGAZINE—B.A.S.S. Publications, P.O. Box 17900, Montgomery, AL 36141. Dave Precht, Ed. Articles, 1,500 to 2,000 words, with photos, on freshwater black bass and striped bass. "Short Casts" pieces, 400 to 800 words, on news, views, and items of interest. Pays $200 to $400, on acceptance. Query.

BAY & DELTA YACHTSMAN—2019 Clement Ave., Alameda, CA 94501. Bruce Todd, Ed. Humorous features, satire and cruising stories. Must have Northern California tie-in. Photos and illustrations. Pays varying rates.

BC OUTDOORS—#202, 1132 Hamilton St., Vancouver, B.C., Canada V6B 2S2. George Will, Ed. Articles, to 1,500 words, on fishing, hunting, conservation and all forms of non-competitive outdoor recreation in British Columbia and Yukon. Photos. Pays from 10¢ to 15¢ a word, extra for photos, on acceptance.

BICYCLE GUIDE—711 Boylston St., Boston, MA 02116. Theodore Costantino, Ed. "Our magazine covers all aspects of cycling—racing, touring, sport riding, product reviews, and technical information—from an enthusiast's perspective. We depend on free lancers for touring articles and race coverage." Queries are preferred. Pays varying rates, on publication.

BICYCLING—33 E. Minor St., Emmaus, PA 18098. James C. McCullagh, Ed. Articles, 500 to 2,500 words, on recreational riding, training, equipment, racing and touring, for serious cyclists. Photos, illustrations. Pays $25 to $600, on publication. Guidelines available.

BIKEREPORT—Bikecentennial, P.O. Box 8308, Missoula, MT 59807. Daniel D'Ambrosio, Ed. Accounts of bicycle tours in the U.S. and overseas, interviews, personal-experience pieces, humor and news shorts, 1,200 to 2,500 words. Pays $25 to $65 per published page.

BIRD WATCHER'S DIGEST—P.O. Box 110, Marietta, OH 45750. Mary B. Bowers, Ed. Articles, 600 to 2,500 words, for bird watchers: first-person accounts; how-to's; pieces on endangered species; profiles. Cartoons, fillers. Pays to $50 for articles, $25 for reprints, $5 for fillers, $10 for cartoons, on publication.

BOAT PENNSYLVANIA—Pennsylvania Fish Commission, P.O. Box 1673, Harrisburg, PA 17105-1673. Articles, 200 to 2,500 words, with photos, on boating in Pennsylvania: motorboating, sailing, waterskiing, canoeing, kayaking, and rafting. No pieces on fishing. Pays $50 to $300, on acceptance. Query.

BOATING—One Park Ave., New York, NY 10016. Doug Schryver, Ed. Illustrated articles, 1,000 to 2,000 words, on power boating. Pays good rates, on acceptance. Query.

BOW & ARROW HUNTING—Box HH, 34249 Camino Capistrano, Capistrano Beach, CA 92624. Roger Combs, Ed. Articles, 1,200 to 2,500 words, with photos, on bowhunting; profiles and technical pieces. Pays $50 to $300, on acceptance. Same address and requirements for *Gun World*.

BOWHUNTER MAGAZINE—3720 S. Calhoun St., Fort Wayne, IN 46807. M. R. James, Ed. Informative, entertaining features, 500 to 5,000 words, on bow and arrow hunting. Fillers. Photos. Pays $25 to $300, on acceptance. Study magazine first.

BOWLERS JOURNAL—101 E. Erie St., Chicago, IL 60611. Mort Luby, Ed. Trade and consumer articles, 1,200 to 2,200 words, with photos, on bowling. Pays $75 to $200, on acceptance.

BOWLING—5301 S. 76th St., Greendale, WI 53129. Dan Matel, Ed. Articles, to 1,500 words, on amateur league and tournament bowling. Profiles. Pays varying rates, on publication.

CALIFORNIA ANGLER—1921 E. Carnegie St., Suite N, Santa Ana, CA 92705. Tom Waters, Ed. How-to and where-to articles, 2,000 words, for freshwater and saltwater anglers in California: travel, new products, fishing techniques, profiles. Photos. Pays $50 to $300, on acceptance. Query first.

CAR AND DRIVER—2002 Hogback Rd., Ann Arbor, MI 48105. Don Sherman, Ed. Articles, to 2,500 words, for enthusiasts, on car manufacturers, new developments in cars, etc. Pays to $1,500, on acceptance.

CAR CRAFT—8490 Sunset Blvd., Los Angeles, CA 90069. Cameron Benty, Ed. Articles and photofeatures on unusual street machines, drag cars, racing events; technical pieces; action photos. Pays from $150 per page, on publication.

CASCADES EAST—716 N.E. 4th St., P.O. Box 5784, Bend, OR 97708. Geoff Hill, Ed./Publisher. Articles, 1,000 to 2,000 words, on outdoor activities, (fishing, hunting, backpacking, rafting, skiing, snowmobiling, etc.), history, and scenic tours in Cascades region of Oregon. Photos. Pays 3¢ to 10¢ a word, extra for photos, on publication.

CHESAPEAKE BAY MAGAZINE—1819 Bay Ridge Ave., Annapolis, MD 21403. Betty Rigoli, Ed. Technical and how-to articles, to 1,500 words, on boating, fishing, conservation, in Chesapeake Bay. Photos. Pays $85 to $125, on publication.

CITY SPORTS MAGAZINE—P.O. Box 3693, San Francisco, CA 94119. Jane McConnell, Ed/Northern California. Peg Moline, Ed/Southern California, 1120 Princeton Dr., Marina Del Rey, CA 90291. Will Balliett, Ed/New York, 140 N. 22nd St., NY, NY 10011. Articles, 1,700 to 3,000 words, on sports for active lifestyles. Pays $50 to $450, on publication. Query.

577

CORVETTE FEVER—Box 44620, Ft. Washington, MD 20744. Pat Stivers, Ed. Articles, 500 to 2,500 words, on Corvette repairs, swap meets, and personalities. Corvette-related fiction, about 700 lines, and fillers. Photos. Pays 10¢ a word, on publication.

CRUISING WORLD—524 Thames St., Newport, RI 02840. George Day, Ed. Articles on sailing, 1,000 to 2,500 words: technical and personal narratives. No fiction, poetry, or logbook transcripts. 35mm slides. Pays $100 to $600, on acceptance. Query preferred.

CYCLE MAGAZINE—5706 Corsa Ave., Ste. 200, Westlake Village, CA 91362. Paul Gordon, Exec. Ed. Articles, 6 to 20 manuscript pages, on motorcycle races, history, touring, technical pieces; profiles. Photos. Pays on publication. Query.

CYCLE NEWS—2201 Cherry Ave., Box 498, Long Beach, CA 90801. Jack Mangus, Ed. Technical articles on motorcycling; profiles and interviews with motorcycle newsmakers. Pays $2 per column inch, on publication.

CYCLE WORLD—1499 Monrovia Ave., Newport Beach, CA 92663. Paul Dean, Ed. Technical and feature articles, 1,500 to 2,500 words, for motorcycle enthusiasts. Photos. Pays $100 to $200 per page, on publication. Query.

CYCLING U.S.A.—U.S. Cycling Federation, 1750 E. Boulder St., Colorado Springs, CO 80909. Diane Fritschner, Ed. Articles, 500 to 1,500 words, on bicycle racing. Pays 10¢ a word, on publication. Query first.

CYCLIST—20916 Higgins Ct., Torrance, CA 90501. John Francis, Ed. Articles on all aspects of bicycling: touring, travel and equipment. Query required.

DIVER MAGAZINE—#295, 10991 Shellbridge Way, Richmond, B.C., V6X 3C6, Canada. Neil McDaniel, Ed. Well-illustrated articles, 1,000 to 2,000 words, on dive regions, with up-to-date service information for Scuba divers in the U.S. and Canada; features on aquatic life, history, equipment, underwater photography, interviews, personal experience, humor, and travel destinations. Pays $2.50 per column inch, extra for photos, after publication. Query first with international reply coupons.

EASTERN HORSE WORLD—P.O. Box 249, Huntington Sta., NY 11746. Diana DeRosa, Ed. Horse-related articles of varying lengths of interest to owners, trainers, and riders. Pays on publication. Query.

ENVIRONMENTAL ACTION—1525 New Hampshire Ave., NW, Washington, DC 20036. News and features, varying lengths, on a broad range of political and/or environmental topics: energy, toxics, self-sufficiency, etc. Book reviews; environmentally-related consumer goods. Pays $75 to $125 for features, extra for photos, on publication. Query required.

FIELD & STREAM—1515 Broadway, New York, NY 10036. Duncan Barnes, Ed. Articles, 1,500 to 2,500 words, with photos, on hunting, fishing. Fillers, 350 to 900 words. Cartoons. Pays from $450 for articles with photos, $250 to $350 for fillers, $100 for cartoons, on acceptance. Query in writing on articles.

FINS AND FEATHERS—401 N. Third St., Minneapolis, MN 55401. Dave Greer, Ed. Articles, 2,000 to 2,500 words, on a wide variety of recreational activities, including hunting, fishing, camping, and environmental issues. Pays $100 to $500, on publication. Query.

FISHING WORLD—51 Atlantic Ave., Floral Park, NY 11001. How-to articles for fresh- and saltwater sport fishermen, 1,000 to 3,000 words, with color transparencies. Pays $100 to $300, on acceptance. Query.

THE FLORIDA HORSE—P.O. Box 2106, Ocala, FL 32678. F. J. Audette, Publisher. Articles, 1,500 words, on Florida thoroughbred breeding and racing. Pays $100 to $150, on publication.

FLY FISHERMAN—Box 8200, Harrisburg, PA 17105. John Randolph, Ed. Articles, to 3,000 words, on how to and where to fly fish. Fillers, to 100 words. Pays from $35 to $400, on acceptance. Query.

FLYING MAGAZINE—1515 Broadway, New York, NY 10036. Richard Collins, Ed.-in-Chief. Articles, 1,500 words, on personal flying experiences. Pays varying rates, on acceptance.

FOOTBALL DIGEST—Century Publishing Co., 990 Grove St., Evanston, IL 60201. Michael K. Herbert, Ed. Profiles of pro stars, "think" pieces, 1,500 words, aimed at the pro football fan. Pays on publication.

FOOTBALL FORECAST—See *Hockey Illustrated*.

FUR-FISH-GAME—2878 E. Main St., Columbus, OH 43209. Tom Glass, Ed. Illustrated articles, 800 to 2,500 words, preferably with how-to angle, on hunting, fishing, trapping, dogs, camping or other outdoor topics. Some humorous or where-to articles. Pays $40 to $150, on acceptance.

GAME AND FISH PUBLICATIONS—P.O. Box 741, Marietta, GA 30061. Publishes outdoors magazines for 37 states. Articles, 2,000 to 2,500 words, on hunting and fishing. How-to's, where-to's, and adventure pieces. Profiles of successful hunters and fishermen. No hiking, caneoing, camping, or backpacking pieces. Pays $150 for state-specific articles, $200 to $300 for multi-state articles, on publication.

GOAL—650 Fifth Ave., 33rd fl., New York, NY 10019. Stu Hackel, Exec. Ed. Official magazine of the National Hockey League. Player profiles and trend stories, 1,000 to 1,800 words, for hockey fans with knowledge of the game and players, by writers with understanding of the sport. Pays $100 to $200, before publication. Query.

GOLF DIGEST—5520 Park Ave., Trumbull, CT 06611. Jerry Tarde, Ed. Instructional articles, tournament reports, and features on players, to 2,500 words. Fiction, 1,000 to 3,000 words. Poetry, fillers, humor, photos. Pays varying rates, on acceptance. Query preferred.

GOLF ILLUSTRATED—3 Park Ave., New York, NY 10016. Al Barkow, Editor. David Earl, Managing Ed. Golf-related features, 1,000 to 2,000 words: instruction, profiles, photo essays, travel, technique, nostalgia, opinion. Pays $750 to $1,500, on acceptance. Query preferred.

GOLF JOURNAL—Golf House, Far Hills, NJ 07931. Robert Sommers, Ed. U.S. Golf Assn. Articles on golf personalities, history, travel. Humor. Photos. Pays varying rates, on publication.

GOLF MAGAZINE—380 Madison Ave., New York, NY 10017. James Frank, Exec. Ed. Articles of 1,500 words, with photos, on golf. Shorts, to 500 words. Pays $500 to $1,000 for articles, $75 to $150 for shorts, on publication.

GREAT LAKES SAILOR—572 W. Market St., P.O. Box 591, Akron, OH 44309. Drew Shippey, Ed. Articles, 2,500 to 3,000 words, profiles, trip tips, how-to pieces, and human-interest stories for sailors who race or cruise on the Great Lakes. Pays to 20¢ a word, on publication. Query required. Guidelines.

THE GREYHOUND REVIEW—National Greyhound Assn., Box 543, Abilene, KS 67410. Tim Horan, Man. Ed. Articles, 1,000 to 10,000 words, pertaining to the greyhound racing industry: how-to, historical nostalgia, interviews. Pays $40 to $150, on publication.

GUN DIGEST AND HANDLOADER'S DIGEST—4092 Commercial Ave., Northbrook, IL 60062. Ken Warner, Ed. Well-researched articles, to 5,000 words, on guns and shooting, equipment, etc. Photos. Pays from 10¢ a word, on acceptance. Query.

GUN DOG—P.O. Box 35098, Des Moines, IA 50315. Bob Wilbanks, Man. Ed. Features, 1,000 to 2,500 words, with photos, on bird hunting: how-to's, where-to's, dog training, canine medicine, breeding strategy. Fiction. Humor. Fillers. Pays $50 to $150 for fillers and short articles, $150 to $350 for features, on acceptance.

GUN WORLD—See *Bow & Arrow Hunting.*

GUNS & AMMO—8490 Sunset Blvd., Los Angeles, CA 90069. E. G. Bell, Jr., Ed. Technical and general articles, 1,500 to 3,000 words, on guns, ammunition, and target shooting. Photos, fillers. Pays from $150, on acceptance.

HANG GLIDING—U.S. Hang Gliding Assn., P.O. Box 500, Pearblossom, CA 93553. Gilbert Dodgen, Ed. Articles and fiction, 2 to 3 pages, on hang gliding. Pays to $50, on publication. Query.

HOCKEY ILLUSTRATED—355 Lexington Ave., New York, NY 10017. Stephen Ciacciarelli, Ed. Articles, 2,500 words, on hockey players, teams. Pays $125, on publication. Query. Same address and requirements for *Baseball Illustrated, Wrestling World, Pro Basketball Illustrated, Pro Football Illustrated, Basketball Annual* (college), *Baseball Preview, Baseball Forecast, Pro Football Preview, Football Forecast,* and *Basketball Forecast.*

HORSE & RIDER—941 Calle Negocio, San Clemente, CA 92672. Ray Rich, Ed. Articles, 500 to 3,000 words, with photos, on Western riding and general horse care: training, feeding, grooming, etc. Pays varying rates, before publication. Buys all rights. Guidelines.

HORSEMAN—25025 I45 N., Ste. 390, Spring, TX 77380. David T. Gaines, Ed. Instructional articles, to 2,500 words, with photos, for Western trainers and riders. Pays to $350, on acceptance.

HORSEMEN'S YANKEE PEDLAR—785 Southbridge St., Auburn, MA 01501. Nancy L. Khoury, Pub. News and feature-length articles, about horses and horsemen in the Northeast. Photos. Pays $2 per published inch, on publication. Query.

HORSEPLAY—Box 130, Gaithersburg, MD 20877. Cordelia Doucet, Ed. Articles, to 3,000 words, on eventing, show jumping, horse shows, dressage, driving and fox hunting, for horse enthusiasts. Pays 9¢ a word, after publication.

HOT BIKE—2145 W. La Palma, Anaheim, CA 92801. Tod Knuth, Ed. Articles, 250 to 2,500 words, with photos, on motorcycles. Event coverage on high performance street and track and sport touring motorcycles, with emphasis on Harley Davidsons. Pays $50 to $100 per printed page, on publication.

HOT ROD—8490 Sunset Blvd., Los Angeles, CA 90069. Jeff Smith, Ed. How-to pieces and articles, 500 to 5,000 words, on auto mechanics, hot rods, track and drag racing. Photo-features on custom or performance-modified cars. Pays to $250 per page, on publication.

HUNTING—8490 Sunset Blvd., Los Angeles, CA 90069. Craig Boddington, Ed. How-to articles on practical aspects of hunting. At least 15 photos required with articles. Pays $250 to $400, for articles, on acceptance.

INSIDE RUNNING & FITNESS—9514 Bristlebrook Dr., Houston, TX 77083. Joanne Schmidt, Ed. Articles, fiction, and fillers on running, cycling, and aerobic fitness in Texas. Pays $35 to $100, $10 for photos, on acceptance.

KEEPIN' TRACK OF VETTES—P.O. Box 48, Spring Valley, NY 10977. Shelli Finkel, Ed. Articles of any length, with photos, relating to Corvettes. Pays $25 to $200, on publication.

KITPLANES—P.O. Box 6050, Mission Viejo, CA 92690. Dave Martin, Ed. Articles, geared to the growing market of aircraft built from kits by home craftsmen, on all aspects of design, construction and performance, 1,000 to 4,000 words. Pays $100 to $300, on publication.

LAKELAND BOATING—1921 St. John's Ave., Highland Park, IL 60035. Brian Callaghan, Ed. Articles for powerboat and sailboat owners on the Great Lakes and major inland rivers, on long distance cruising, short trips, maintenance, equipment, history, and environment. Photos. Pays on publication. Query first. Guidelines.

MICHIGAN OUT-OF-DOORS—P.O. Box 30235, Lansing, MI 48909. Kenneth S. Lowe, Ed. Features, 1,500 to 2,500 words, on hunting, fishing, camping and conservation in Michigan. Pays $75 to $150, on acceptance.

MID-WEST OUTDOORS—111 Shore Dr., Hinsdale, IL 60521. Gene Laulunen, Ed. Articles, 1,500 words, with photos, on where, when and how to fish in the Midwest. Fillers, 200 to 500 words. Pays $15 to $35, on publication.

MOTOR TREND—8490 Sunset Blvd., Los Angeles, CA 90069. Mike Anson, Ed. Articles, 250 to 2,000 words, on autos, racing, events, and profiles. Photos. Pay varies, on acceptance. Query.

MOTORCYCLIST—8490 Sunset Blvd., Los Angeles, CA 90069. Art Friedman, Ed. Articles, 1,000 to 3,000 words. Action photos. Pays varying rates, on publication. Query.

MOTORHOME MAGAZINE—29901 Agoura Rd., Agoura, CA 91301. Bob Livingston, Ed. Articles, to 2,000 words, with color slides, on motorhomes; travel and how-to pieces. Pays to $500, on acceptance.

MUSCULAR DEVELOPMENT—Strength and Health Publishing, P.O. Box 1707, York, PA 17405. Jan Dellinger, Ed. Articles, 5 to 10 typed pages, on competitive body building and powerlifting for serious weight training athletes. Pays $50 to $200, extra for photos, on publication. Query.

NATIONAL PARKS MAGAZINE—1015 31st St., NW, Washington, DC 20007. Michele Strutin, Ed. Articles, 1,000 to 2,000 words, on natural history, wildlife, outdoors activities, travel and conservation as they relate to national parks: illustrated features on the natural, historic and cultural resources of the National Park System. Pieces about legislation and other issues and events related to the parks. Pays $100 to $400, on acceptance. Query. Send for guidelines.

NATIONAL RACQUETBALL—P.O. Drawer 6126, Clearwater, FL 33528. Sigmund Brouwer, Ed. Articles, 800 to 1,200 words, on health and conditioning. How-to's. Profiles. Fiction. Material must be related to racquetball. Pays $25 to $150, on publication. Photos.

NATIONAL WILDLIFE AND INTERNATIONAL WILDLIFE—8925 Leesburg Pike, Vienna, VA 22184. Mark Wexler, Man. Ed., *National Wildlife*. Jon Fisher, Man. Ed. *International Wildlife*. Articles, 1,000 to 2,500 words, on wildlife, conservation, environment; outdoor how-to pieces. Photos. Pays market rates, on acceptance. Query.

NAUTICAL QUARTERLY—Pratt St., Essex, CT 06426. Joseph Gribbins, Ed. In-depth articles, 3,000 to 7,000 words, about boats and boating, U.S. and foreign. Pays $500 to $1,000, on acceptance. Query.

THE NEW AMERICAN LAND (Formerly *American Land Forum*)—1516 P St., NW, Washington, DC 20005. Sara Ebenreck, Ed. Articles, 2,500 words, on U.S. land issues, achievements, leadership profiles, or land use topics. Pays $15 to $300. Guidelines.

NORTHEAST OUTDOORS—P.O. Box 2180, Waterbury, CT 06722-2180. Debora Nealley, Ed. Articles, 500 to 1,800 words, preferably with B/W photos, on camping in Northeast U.S.: recommended private campgrounds, camp cookery, recreational vehicle hints. Stress how-to, where-to. Cartoons. Pays to $80, on publication. Send for guidelines.

NORTHEAST RIDING—225 Palisado Ave., Windsor, CT 06095. Paul Essenfeld, Pub. Motorcycle-related articles, 500 to 1,000 words, for motorcyclists in the Northeast. Pays negotiable rates, on publication.

OFFSHORE—220 Reservoir St., Needham Hts., MA 02194. Rich Booth, Man. Ed. Articles, 1,000 to 3,000 words, on boats, people, and places along the New England coast. Photos. Pays from 5¢ to 10¢ a word, on acceptance.

ON TRACK—17165 Newhope St., "M", Fountain Valley, CA 92708. Jeremy Shaw, Edit. Dir. Features and race reports, 500 to 2,500 words. Pays $3 per column inch, on publication.

OUTDOOR AMERICA—1701 N. Ft. Myer Dr., Suite 1100, Arlington, VA 22209. Quarterly publication of the Izaak Walton League of America. Articles, 1,500 to 2,000 words, on natural resource conservation issues and outdoor recreation; especially fishing, hunting and camping. Pays from to 15¢ a word, for features, on publication. Query Articles Ed. with published clippings.

OUTDOOR LIFE—380 Madison Ave., New York, NY 10017. Clare Conley, Ed. Articles on hunting, fishing and related subjects. Pays top rates, on acceptance. Query.

OUTSIDE—1165 N. Clark St., Chicago, IL 60610. John Rasmus, Ed. "We publish well-written, original articles on all aspects of the outdoors. In particular, we look for solid seasonal service pieces; profiles of outdoor personalities, regions, wildlife; adventures-oriented sports pieces with a national appeal; indepth pieces on outdoor life styles, sciences, activities, and important environmental issues (2,000 to 4,000 words). Department pieces: "Dispatches" (outdoor news and events, 200 to 700 words); "Review" (1,000 to 1,500 words); "Field Notes" (coming events, etc., 1,000 to 1,500 words); "Law of the Land" (legal or political issues (1,500 to 2,000 words); "Destinations" (activity-oriented travel ideas, 1,500 words). Pays $500 to $1,500 for features, $100 to $750 for departments, on publication. Query with clips required.

PENNSYLVANIA ANGLER—Pennsyvania Fish Commission, P.O. Box 1673, Harrisburg, PA 17105-1673. Address Editor. Articles, 250 to 2,500 words, with photos, on freshwater fishing in Pennsylvania. Pays $50 to $200 on acceptance. Must send SASE with all material. Query.

PENNSYLVANIA GAME NEWS—Game Commission, Harrisburg, PA 17110-9797. Bob Bell, Ed. Articles, to 2,500 words, with photos, on outdoor subjects, except fishing and boating. Photos. Pays from 5¢ a word, extra for photos, on acceptance.

PERFORMANCE HORSEMAN—Gum Tree Corner, Unionville, PA 19375. Miranda Lorraine, Articles Ed. Factual how-to pieces for the serious western rider, on training, improving riding skills, all aspects of care and management, etc. Pays from $300, on acceptance.

PETERSEN'S FISHING—8490 Sunset Blvd., Los Angeles, CA 90069. Robert Robb, Ed. Articles, 2000 words, on fishing in North America. "We're a semi-technical publication, and articles have a how-to focus. Profiles, unusual techniques, and product reviews will also be considered. We prefer to be queried first." Pays $300 to $400, on acceptance. Guidelines.

PGA MAGAZINE—100 Avenue of the Champions, Palm Beach Gardens, FL 33418. Articles, 1,500 to 2,500 words, on golf-related subjects. Pays $300 to $500, on acceptance. Query.

PLEASURE BOATING—1995 N.E. 150th St., North Miami, FL 33181. Robert Ulrich, Ed. Articles, 1,000 to 2,000 words, on fishing and recreational boating, covering the coastline from Texas to New York harbor. Pays varying rates, on publication. Query first. Study sample copies.

POPULAR LURES—15115 S. 76th E. Ave., Bixby, OK 74008. Andre Hinds, Exec. Ed. Articles, 1,200 to 1,500 words, on tackle and techniques for catching all freshwater and saltwater fish, primarily bass, trout, catfish, crappie, walleye and salmon. Pays $175 to $225, on acceptance.

POPULAR SCIENCE—380 Madison Ave., New York, NY 10017. C. P. Gilmore, Ed.-in-Chief. Factual articles, 300 to 2,000 words, with photos and illustrations, on advances in science and technology, new products in electronics, cars, tools; recreational or do-it-yourself projects for home, shop, and yard. Pays varying rates, on acceptance. Query.

POWERBOAT—15917 Strathern St., Van Nuys, CA 91406. Randy Scott, Ed. Articles, to 1,500 words, with photos, for powerboat owners, on outstanding achievements, water-skiing, competitions; technical articles on hull developments; how-to pieces. Pays about $300, on acceptance. Query.

PRACTICAL HORSEMAN—Gum Tree Corner, Unionville, PA 19375. Miranda D. Lorraine, Articles Ed. How-to articles on English riding, training, and horse care. Pays on publication. Query.

PRIVATE PILOT—P.O. Box 6050, Mission Viejo, CA 92690. Steve Kimball, Ed. True-experience pieces and technically-based aviation articles, 1,000 to 4,000 words, for aviation enthusiasts. Photos. Pays $75 to $250, on publication. Query.

PRO BASKETBALL ILLUSTRATED—See *Hockey Illustrated*.

PRO FOOTBALL ILLUSTRATED—See *Hockey Illustrated*.

PURE BRED DOGS/AMERICAN KENNEL GAZETTE—51 Madison Ave., New York, NY 10010. Marion Lane, Exec. Ed; Judy Hartop, Sen. Ed. Articles, 1,000 to 2,500 words, relating to pure-bred dogs. Pays from $100 to $300, on publication. Queries preferred.

RIDER—29901 Agoura Rd., Agoura, CA 91301. Tash Matsuoka, Ed. Articles, with photos, to 3,000 words, with emphasis on travel, touring, commuting, and camping motorcyclists. Pays $100 to $500, on publication. Query.

ROAD RIDER MAGAZINE—P.O. Box 6050, Mission Viejo, CA 92690. Bob Carpenter, Ed. Articles, to 1,500 words, with photos or b&w illustrations, on motorcycle touring. Pays from $150, on publication. Query.

RUNNER'S WORLD—Rodale Press, 33 E. Minor St., Emmaus, PA 18098. Bob Wischnia, Sr. Ed. Well-researched articles and columns, varying length. Pays on acceptance. Query.

SAIL—Charlestown Navy Yard, 100 First Ave., Charlestown, MA 02129. Keith Taylor, Ed. Articles, 1,500 to 3,500 words, features, 1,000 to 1,500 words, with photos, on sailboats, equipment, racing, and cruising. How-to's on navigation, sail trim, etc. Pays $75 to $1,000 on publication. Writers' guidelines sent on request.

SAILING—125 E. Main St., Port Washington, WI 53074. William F. Schanen, III, Ed. Features, 700 to 1,500 words, with photos, on cruising and racing; first-person accounts; profiles of boats and regattas. Query for technical or how-to pieces. Pays varying rates, 30 days after publication. Writer's guidelines sent on request.

SAILING WORLD—111 East Ave, Norwalk, CT 06851. John Burnham, Ed. Articles, 8 to 10 typed pages, on sailboat racing and cruising, regatta reports, equipment, techniques. Photos. Pays $150 per published page, on publication. Query.

SCORE, CANADA'S GOLF MAGAZINE—287 MacPherson Ave, Toronto, Ont., Canada M4V 1A4. Lisa A. Leighton, Man. Ed. Articles, 800 to 3,500 words, on travel, golf equipment, golf history, personality profiles of prominent professionals. Fillers, 25 to 100 words. Pays $10 to $25 for fillers, $125 to $600 for features, on assignment and publication. Query with published clips.

SEA—P.O. Box 1579, Newport Beach, CA 92663. Cathi Douglas, Man. Ed. Articles, 200 to 900 words, about cruising destinations, profiles of boating personalities, nautical navigation and seamanship. News and features, 800 to 3,500 words, on the marine environment, for West Coast boaters. Query. Payment varies, on publication.

SEA KAYAKER—1670 Duranleau St., Vancouver, BC, Canada, V6H 3S4. John Dowd, Ed. Articles, 400 to 2,000 words, on ocean kayaking. Fiction. Pays 10¢ a word, on publication. Query with international reply coupons.

SHOTGUN SPORTS—Box 340, Lake Havasu City, AZ 86403. Frank Kodl, Ed. Articles with photos, on trap and skeet shooting and hunting with shotguns. Pays $25 to $200, on publication.

SIERRA—730 Polk St., San Francisco, CA 94109. Jonathan F. King, Ed. Articles, 1,000 to 2,500 words, on environmental and conservation topics, hiking, backpacking, skiing, rafting, cycling. Book reviews and children's dept. Photos. Pays from $75 to $500, extra for photos, on acceptance. Query.

SKI MAGAZINE—380 Madison Ave., New York, NY 10017. Dick Needham, Ed. Articles, 1,300 to 2,000 words, for experienced skiers: profiles, humor, "it-happened-to-me" stories, and destination pieces. Short, 100 to 300 words, news items for "Ski Life" column. Equipment and racing articles are staff written. Query first (with clips) for articles. Pays from $200, on acceptance.

SKI RACING—Box 1125, Rt. 100, Waitsfield, VT 05673. Gary Black, Jr.,

Pub. Interviews, articles, and how-to pieces on national and international nordic and alpine ski competitions. Photos. Pays varying rates.

SKIING—One Park Ave., New York, NY 10016. Bill Grout, Ed. Personal adventures on skis, from 2,500 words (no first-time-on-skis stories); profiles and interviews, 50 to 300 words. Pays $150 to $300 per printed page, on acceptance.

SKIN DIVER MAGAZINE—8490 Sunset Blvd., Los Angeles, CA 90069. Bonnie J. Cardone, Exec. Ed. Illustrated articles, 500 to 2,000 words, on scuba diving activities, equipment and dive sites. Pays $50 per published page, on publication.

SKYDIVING—P.O. Box 1520, Deland, FL 32721. Michael Truffer, Ed. Timely news articles, 300 to 800 words, relating to sport and military parachuting. Fillers. Photos. Pays $25 to $200, extra for photos, on publication.

SNOWMOBILE—319 Barry Ave., S., Ste. 101, Wayzata, MN 55391. Dick Hendricks, Ed. Articles, 700 to 2,000 words, with b&w and color photos, related to snowmobiling: races and rallies, trail rides, personalities, travel. How-to's; humor; cartoons. Pays to $450, on publication. Query.

SNOWMOBILE WEST—P.O. Box 981, Idaho Falls, ID 83402. Steve Janes, Ed. Articles, 1,200 words, with photos, on snowmobiling in the western states. Pays to $100, on publication.

SOCCER AMERICA MAGAZINE—P.O. Box 23704, Oakland, CA 94623. Lynn Berling-Manuel, Ed. Articles, to 1,000 words, on soccer: news, profiles, coaching tips. Pays $25 to $100 for features, within 60 days of publication. Query.

SOUTH CAROLINA WILDLIFE—P.O. Box 167, Columbia, SC 29202. John E. Davis, Ed. Articles, 1,000 to 3,000 words, with regional outdoors focus: conservation, natural history and wildlife, recreation. Profiles, how-to's. Pays on acceptance.

SPORT MAGAZINE—119 W. 40th St., New York, NY 10018. Neil Cohen, Ed. Query.

THE SPORTING NEWS—P.O. Box 56, 1212 N. Lindbergh Blvd., St. Louis, MO 63132. Tom Barnidge, Ed.-in-Chief. Articles, 1,000 to 1,500 words, on baseball, football, basketball, hockey, and other sports. Pays $150 to $500, on publication.

SPORTS AFIELD—250 W. 55th St., New York, NY 10019. Tom Paugh, Ed. Articles, to 3,000 words, on hunting, fishing, camping and related subjects (cooking, collectibles); nature pieces, outdoor humor and history; photos and art stories; guns, sporting dog and fishing where-to-go features; and some fiction. "The best place for new writers to break in is by submitting short items for our monthly Almanac section." Pays top rates. Query first.

SPORTS AFIELD SPECIALS—250 W. 55th St., New York, NY 10019. Well-written, informative fishing and hunting articles, 2,000 to 2,500 words, with photos, with primary focus on how-to techniques: include lively anecdotes, and good sidebars, charts. Pays to $450 for features, on acceptance. Query.

SPORTS ILLUSTRATED—1271 Ave. of the Americas, New York, NY 10020. Rob Fleder, Articles Ed. No unsolicited material.

SPUR MAGAZINE—P.O. Box 85, Middleburg, VA 22117. Address Ed.

Dept. Articles, 300 to 5,000 words, on Thoroughbred racing, breeding, polo and steeplechasing. Profiles of people and farms. Historical and nostalgia pieces. Pays $50 to $250, on publication. Query.

STOCK CAR RACING—P.O. Box 715, Ipswich, MA 01938. Dick Berggren, Ed. Articles, to 6,000 words, on stock-car drivers, races, and vehicles. Photos. Pays to $350, on publication.

SURFER MAGAZINE—Box 1028, Dana Point, CA 92629. Steve Pezman, Pub. Paul Holmes, Ed. Articles, 500 to 5,000 words, on surfing, surfers, etc. Photos. Pays 10¢ to 15¢ a word, $10 to $600 for photos, on publication.

SURFING—P.O. Box 3010, San Clemente, CA 92672. David Gilovich, Ed. Bill Sharp, Assoc. Ed. First-person travel articles, 1,500 to 2,000 words, on surfing locations; knowledge of sport essential. Pays varying rates, on publication. Query.

TENNIS—5520 Park Ave., P.O. Box 0395, Trumbull, CT 06611-0395. Alex McNab, Ed. Instructional articles, features, profiles of tennis stars, 500 to 2,000 words. Photos. Pays from $100 to $500, on publication. Query.

TENNIS, U.S.A.—3 Park Ave., New York, NY 10016. Liza DeLuca, Man. Ed. Articles, 750 to 1,000 words, on local and sectional, and national tennis personalities and news events. Pays $50 to $75, on publication. Query; uses very little free-lance material.

TENNIS WEEK—6 E. 39th St., Ste. 800; New York, NY 10016. Eugene L. Scott, Pub. Robin Serody, Ed. In-depth, researched articles, from 1,000 words, on current issues and personalities in the game. Pays $100, on publication. Query.

THREE WHEELING—See *ATV Sports.*

TRAILER BOATS—20700 Belshaw Ave., P.O. Box 5427, Carson, CA 90249-5427. Jim Youngs, Ed. Technical and how-to articles, 500 to 2,000 words, on boat, trailer or tow vehicle maintenance and operation, skiing, fishing, cruising. Fillers; humor. Pays 7¢ to 10¢ a word, on publication. Query.

TRAILER LIFE—29901 Agoura Rd., Agoura, CA 91301. Bill Estes, Ed. Articles, to 2,500 words, with photos, on trailering, truck campers, motorhomes, hobbies and RV lifestyle. How-to pieces. Pays to $500, on acceptance. Send for guidelines.

TURF AND SPORT DIGEST—26 W. Pennsylvania Ave., Towson, MD 21204. Allen L. Mitzel, Jr., Ed. Articles, 1,500 to 4,000 words, on national turf personalities, racing nostalgia, and handicapping. Pays $75 to $200, on publication. Query.

VELO-NEWS—Box 1257, Brattleboro, VT 05301. Geoff Drake, Ed. Articles, 500 to 2,000 words, on bicycle racing. Photos. Pays $2.75 per column inch, extra for photos, on publication. Query.

VOLKSWAGEN'S WORLD—Volkswagen of America, Troy, MI 48007. Marlene Goldsmith, Ed. Articles, 1,000 words, related to Volkswagen cars and their owners. Color slides necessary. Pays $150 per printed page, on acceptance. Query.

THE WALKING MAGAZINE—711 Boylston St., Boston, MA 02116. Bradford Ketchum, Ed. Articles, 1,500 to 3,000 words, for recreational and fitness walkers, in fitness, health, equipment, nutrition, travel, adventure, famous walkers, and other walking-related topics. Short pieces, 500 to 1,500 words, and essays for "Ramblings." Pays $500 to $1,000 for features, $100 to $350 for departments. Guidelines.

WASHINGTON FISHING HOLES—P.O. Box 32, Sedro Woolley, WA 98284. Detailed articles, with specific maps, 800 to 1,500 words, on fishing holes in Washington. Local Washington fishing how-to's. Photos. Pays on publication. Query. Send SASE for guidelines.

THE WATER SKIER—P.O. Box 191, Winter Haven, FL 33882. Duke Cullimore, Ed. Offbeat articles on waterskiing. Pays varying rates, on acceptance.

THE WESTERN BOATMAN—P.O. Box 7980, Colorado Springs, CO 80933. Randy Witte, Ed. Articles, around 1,500 words, with photos, on care and training of horses. Pays from $150, on acceptance.

THE WESTERN HORSEMAN—P.O. Box 7980, Colorado Springs, CO 80933. Randy Witte, Ed. Articles, around 1,500 words, with photos, on care and training of horses. Pays from $150, on acceptance.

WESTERN OUTDOORS—3197-E Airport Loop, Costa Mesa, CA 92626. Timely, factual articles on fishing and hunting, 1,500 to 1,800 words, of interest to western sportsmen. Pays $300 to $500, on acceptance. Query. Guidelines.

WESTERN SALTWATER FISHERMAN—See *California Angler.*

WESTERN SPORTSMAN—P.O. Box 737, Regina, Sask., Canada S4P 3A8. Rick Bates, Ed. Articles, to 2,500 words, on outdoor experiences in Alberta and Saskatchewan; how-to pieces. Photos. Pays $75 to $325, on publication.

WIND SURF—P.O. Box 561, Dana Point, CA 92629. Drew Kampion, Ed. Articles on all aspects of windsurfing. Pays 10¢ to 20¢ a word, on publication.

WINDRIDER—P.O. Box 2456, Winter Park, FL 32790. Terry L. Snow, Pub./Ed. Features, instructional pieces, and tips, by experienced boardsailors. Fast action photos. Pays $50 to $75 for tips, $100 to $250 for features, extra for photos. Send for guidelines first.

THE WOMAN BOWLER—5301 S. 76th St., Greendale, WI 53129. Bill Krier, Ed. Profiles, interviews, and news articles, to 1,000 words, for women bowlers. Pays varying rates, on acceptance. Query with outline.

WOMEN'S SPORTS AND FITNESS—501 Second St., Ste. 400, San Francisco, CA 94107. Martha Nelson, Ed. How-to's, profiles, and sports reports, 500 to 2,500 words, for active women. Fitness, recreation, adventure-travel, psychology, nutrition and health pieces. Pays from $25, on acceptance.

WRESTLING WORLD—See *Hockey Illustrated.*

YACHT RACING & CRUISING—See *Sailing World.*

YACHTING—P.O. Box 1200, 5 River Rd., Cos Cob, CT 06807. Roy Attaway, Ed. Articles, 2,000 words, on recreational power and sail boating. How-to and personal-experience pieces. Photos. Pays $250 to $450, on acceptance. Query.

YOGA JOURNAL—2054 University Ave., Berkeley, CA 94704. Stephan Bodian, Ed. Articles, 1,200 to 3,000 words, on holistic health, consciousness, spirituality, and yoga. Pays $50 to $150, on publication.

AUTOMOTIVE PUBLICATIONS

AAA WORLD—AAA Headquarters, 8111 Gatehouse Rd., Falls Church, VA 22047. Douglas Damerst, Ed. Automobile and travel concerns, including automotive travel, maintenance and upkeep, 750 to 1,500 words. Pays $300 to $600, on acceptance. Query preferred.

AMERICAN MOTORCYCLIST—American Motorcyclist Assn., Box 6114, Westerville, OH 43081-6114. Greg Harrison, Ed. Articles and fiction, to 3,000 words, on motorcycling: news coverage, personalities, tours. Photos. Pays varying rates, on publication. Query.

ATV SPORTS (formerly *Three Wheeling*)—Box 2260, Costa Mesa, CA 92628. Bruce Simura, Ed. Articles, 1,000 to 1,500 words, related to three- and four-wheel all-terrain vehicles. Pays $60 per printed page, on publication. Query.

CAR AND DRIVER—2002 Hogback Rd., Ann Arbor, MI 48105. Don Sherman, Ed. Articles, to 2,500 words, for enthusiasts, on car manufacturers, new developments in cars, etc. Pays to $1,500, on acceptance.

CAR CRAFT—8490 Sunset Blvd., Los Angeles, CA 90069. Cameron Benty, Ed. Articles and photofeatures on unusual street machines, drag cars, racing events; technical pieces; action photos. Pays from $150 per page, on publication.

CORVETTE FEVER—Box 44620, Ft. Washington, MD 20744. Pat Stivers, Ed. Articles, 500 to 2,500 words, on Corvette repairs, swap meets, and personalities. Corvette-related fiction, about 700 lines, and fillers. Photos. Pays 10¢ a word, on publication.

CYCLE MAGAZINE—5706 Corsa Ave., Ste. 200, Westlake Village, CA 91362. Paul Gordon, Exec. Ed. Articles, 6 to 20 manuscript pages, on motorcycle races, history, touring, technical pieces; profiles. Photos. Pays on publication. Query.

CYCLE NEWS—2201 Cherry Ave., Box 498, Long Beach, CA 90801. Jack Mangus, Ed. Technical articles on motorcycling; profiles and interviews with motorcycle newsmakers. Pays $2 per column inch, on publication.

CYCLE WORLD—1499 Monrovia Ave., Newport Beach, CA 92663. Paul Dean, Ed. Technical and feature articles, 1,500 to 2,500 words, for motorcycle enthusiasts. Photos. Pays $100 to $200 per page, on publication. Query.

HOT BIKE—2145 W. La Palma, Anaheim, CA 92801. Tod Knuth, Ed. Articles, 250 to 2,500 words, with photos, on motorcycles. Event coverage on high performance street and track and sport touring motorcycles, with emphasis on Harley Davidsons. Pays $50 to $100 per printed page, on publication.

HOT ROD—8490 Sunset Blvd., Los Angeles, CA 90069. Jim Smith, Ed. How-to pieces and articles, 500 to 5,000 words, on auto mechanics, hot rods, track and drag racing. Photo-features on custom or performance-modified cars. Pays to $250 per page, on publication.

KEEPIN' TRACK OF VETTES—P.O. Box 48, Spring Valley, NY 10977. Shelli Finkel, Ed. Articles of any length, with photos, relating to Corvettes. Pays $25 to $200, on publication.

MOTOR TREND—8490 Sunset Blvd., Los Angeles, CA 90069. Mike Anson, Ed. Articles, 250 to 2,000 words, on autos, racing, events, and profiles. Photos. Pay varies, on acceptance. Query.

MOTORCYCLIST—8490 Sunset Blvd., Los Angeles, CA 90069. Art

Friedman, Ed. Articles, 1,000 to 3,000 words. Action photos. Pays varying rates, on publication. Query.

NORTHEAST RIDING—225 Palisado Ave., Windsor, CT 06095. Paul Essenfeld, Pub. Motorcycle-related articles, 500 to 1,000 words, for motorcyclists in the Northeast. Pays negotiable rates, on publication.

POPULAR SCIENCE—380 Madison Ave., New York, NY 10017. C. P. Gilmore, Ed.-in-Chief. Factual articles, 300 to 2,000 words, with photos and illustrations, on advances in science and technology, new products in electronics, cars, tools; recreational or do-it-yourself projects for home, shop, and yard. Pays varying rates, on acceptance. Query.

RIDER—29901 Agoura Rd., Agoura, CA 91301. Tash Matsuoka, Ed. Articles, with photos, to 3,000 words, with emphasis on travel, touring, commuting, and camping motorcyclists. Pays $100 to $500, on publication. Query.

ROAD RIDER MAGAZINE—P.O. Box 6050, Mission Viejo, CA 92690. Bob Carpenter, Ed. Articles, to 1,500 words, with photos or b&w illustrations, on motorcycle touring. Pays from $150, on publication. Query.

STOCK CAR RACING—P.O. Box 715, Ipswich, MA 01938. Dick Berggren, Ed. Articles, to 6,000 words, on stock-car drivers, races, and vehicles. Photos. Pays to $350, on publication.

THREE WHEELING—See *ATV Sports.*

VOLKSWAGEN'S WORLD—Volkswagen of America, P.O. Box 3951, Troy, MI 48007. Marlene Goldsmith, Ed. Articles, 1,000 words, related to Volkswagen cars and their owners. Color slides necessary. Pays $150 per printed page, on acceptance. Query.

FITNESS MAGAZINES

AMERICAN FITNESS (formerly *Aerobics & Fitness*)—15250 Ventura Blvd., Suite 310, Sherman Oaks, CA 91403. Peg Angsten, Ed. Articles, 500 to 1,500 words, on exercise, health, sports, nutrition, etc. Illustrations, photos, cartoons.

AMERICAN HEALTH: FITNESS OF BODY AND MIND—80 Fifth Ave., New York, NY 10011. Address Editorial Dept. Features, 1,000 to 3,000 words, on recent developments in nutrition and exercise. Pays from $125 per manuscript page, on acceptance. Query required.

BETTER HEALTH AND LIVING—800 Second Ave., New York, NY 10017. Laura L. Vitale, Man. Ed. Articles, 2 to 35 manuscript pages, on healthful living; shorter items and tips. Pays $50 to $100 for short tips, to $1,000 for features, 90 days after acceptance. Query preferred.

HEALTH—3 Park Ave., New York, NY 10016. Articles, 800 to 2,500 words, on fitness. Pays $150 to $1,200, on acceptance. Query.

INSIDE RUNNING & FITNESS—9514 Bristlebrook Dr., Houston, TX 77083. Joanne Schmidt, Ed. Articles, fiction, and fillers on running and aerobic fitness in Texas. Pays $35 to $100, $10 for photos, on acceptance.

MUSCULAR DEVELOPMENT—Strength and Health Publishing, P.O. Box 1707, York, PA 17405. Jan Dellinger, Ed. Articles, 5 to 10 typed pages, geared to serious weight training athletes, on any aspects of competitive body building and powerlifting. Photos. Pays $50 to $200, on publication. Query.

NEW BODY—888 Seventh Ave., New York, NY 10106. Constance Boze, Ed. Well-researched, service-oriented articles, 1,000 to 2,000 words, on exercise, nutrition, diet and health for women aged 18 to 35. Writers should have some background in or knowledge of the health field. Pays $250 to $500, on publication. Query.

THE PHYSICIAN AND SPORTSMEDICINE—4530 W. 77th St., Minneapolis, MN 55435. Cindy Christian Rogers, Features Ed. News and feature articles, 500 to 3,000 words, on fitness, sports, and exercise. Medical angle necessary. Pays $150 to $900, on acceptance. Guidelines.

SLIMMER—801 Second Ave., New York, NY 10017. Rhonda J. Wilson, Exec.Ed. Articles, 2,500 words, and columns, 1,000 words, on nutrition, fitness, beauty, skin care, diet, exercise, and sports, for women aged 18 to 40. Pays $200 to $300 for features, $100 to $150 for columns, 30 days after acceptance. Query required.

VEGETARIAN TIMES—P.O. Box 570, Oak Park, IL 60603. Paul Obis, Pub. Articles, 750 to 3,000 words, on health, nutrition, exercise and fitness. Pays $25 to $300, on publication.

VIM & VIGOR—2040 W. Bethany Home Rd., Suite 105, Phoenix, AZ 85015. Leo Calderella, Ed. Positive articles, with accurate medical facts, on health and fitness, 1,200 words. Pays $250 to $350, on publication.

THE WALKING MAGAZINE—711 Boylston St., Boston, MA 02116. Bradford Ketchum, Ed. Articles, 1,500 to 3,000 words, on fitness, health, equipment, and nutrition. Pays $500 to $1,000 for features, $100 to $350 for department pieces. Guidelines.

WEIGHT WATCHERS MAGAZINE—360 Lexington Ave., New York, NY 10017. Nelly Edmondson, Articles Ed. Articles on nutrition and health. Pays from $250, on acceptance. Query with clips required. Guidelines.

WOMEN'S SPORTS AND FITNESS—501 Second St., Suite 400, San Francisco, CA 94107. Martha Nelson, Ed. How-to's, profiles, and sports reports, 500 to 3,000 words, for the active woman. Health, fitness, and sports pieces. Photos. Pays from $50, on publication.

YOGA JOURNAL—2054 University Ave., Berkeley, CA 94704. Stephan Bodian, Ed. Articles, 1,200 to 3,000 words, on holistic health, spirituality, yoga, and transpersonal psychology; "new age" profiles; interviews. Pays $50 to $150, on publication.

CONSUMER/PERSONAL FINANCE

BETTER HOMES AND GARDENS—1716 Locust St., Des Moines, IA 50336. Margaret V. Daly, Money Management, Automotive and Features Ed. "We run to twelve articles on finance each year. They cover any and all topics that would be of interest to our audience of eight million households, primarily homeowning, family-oriented, middle-income people. Some of the articles we've run are 'Health Insurance: Seven Common Gaps,' 'Fifteen Mutual Funds That Let You Start Small,' and 'Answers to the Questions Most Asked of Financial Planners.' We prefer to see queries first, but will look at complete manuscripts (750 to 1,000 words). Payment runs roughly from 75¢ to $1.00 a word, on acceptance. We buy all rights." Address N.Y. office: 750 Third Ave., New York, NY 10017.

COMPLETE WOMAN—1165 N. Clark, Chicago, IL 60610. Mary James, Associate Ed. Articles, addressed to a general audience, which cover broad-based financial planning (for taxes, retirement, etc.) rather than highly specific investment vehicles. Readers are working women, 25–50, who want to improve and enrich all aspects of their lives. Query first. Payment rates for articles of 1,800 to 2,000 words vary, on publication.

CONSUMERS DIGEST—5705 N. Lincoln Ave., Chicago, IL 60659. John Manos, Ed. Articles, 500 to 3,000 words, on subjects of interest to consumers: products and services, automobiles, travel, health, fitness, consumer legal affairs, and personal money management. Photos. Pays from 30¢ a word, extra for photos, on acceptance. Buys all rights. Query with resume and published clips.

DIVERSION MAGAZINE—60 E. 42nd St., New York, NY 10165. *Diversion* is a monthly travel and leisure magazine read by 180,000 physicians across the country, and editors welcome proposals, 100 to 150 words in length. Enclose samples of published work when submitting article ideas. Articles run from 1,000 to 1,200 words; payment is $350, on publication. Send for a copy of the edtitorial guidelines.

FAMILY CIRCLE—110 Fifth Ave., New York, NY 10011. Susan Ungaro, Articles, Ed. "We publish a money management feature in every issue, and are particularly interested in well-written, easy-to-understand articles on investing, real estate and financial planning. Articles should be geared to our typical reader: an educated, middle- to upper-middle class woman in her 30s, 40s, and 50s, who is a home owner looking for other ways to invest her spare cash. Almost seventy percent are working women. 'Should You Refinance Your Mortgage Now,' 'How to Cut Car Insurance Costs,' and 'Twelve Ways to Secure Your Financial Future' are a few of the recent articles we've run. Always send a query with sample clips before submitting complete manuscripts (1,000 to 2,000 words). Payment rates are $1.00 a word, on acceptance."

GEICO DIRECT—1999 Shepard Rd., St. Paul, MN 55116. Jane A. Kennedy, Managing Ed. "We have a department titled 'Money-Wise,' in which we use four to five capsule pieces on various money matters. The topics are general, and each runs about five paragraphs. Our audience is made up of government and military employees, as well as general insurance policy holders. We prefer to be queried first; payment is made on acceptance."

GOLDEN YEARS—233 E. New Haven Ave., Melbourne, FL 32902-0537. Carol Brenner Hittner, Ed. "We consider articles on pre-retirement and retirement planning and real estate—topics of particular interest to our readers, most of whom are over 50 and affluent. Payment for manuscripts (to 500 words) is 70¢ per column line, on publication.

THE KIWANIS MAGAZINE—3636 Woodview Trace, Indianapolis, IN 46468. Chuck Jonak, Exec. Ed. "Although the majority of our readers are older small-business owners and professionals—or retirees from the same areas—we also have a large percentage of younger readers, so we'd like to see articles on financial planning for younger families in a variety of areas, as well as pieces on financial planning for retirees and small business owners. Articles should be in the 2,500- to 3,000-word range; a 300-word sidebar is always helpful. Payment, on acceptance, is $400 to $1,000. Query first."

MARRIAGE & FAMILY LIVING—St. Meinrad, IN 47577. Kass Dotterweich, Managing Ed. In demand here are articles, 1,500 to 2,000 words, on taxes, retirement planning, real estate, or other financial matters of interest to Christian couples. Payment is 7¢ a word, on acceptance. Query first.

MODERN MATURITY—3200 E. Carson St., Lakewood, CA 90712. Ian Ledgerwood, Ed. "We consider queries from free-lancers on a wide range of financial topics—almost anything is a possibility, but it mustn't be too technical. Articles (1,500 to 2,000 words) should be directed to our readers, who are age 50 and over. Payment ranges up to $2,500 for 2,000-word manuscripts."

MONEY—Time-Life Bldg., New York, NY 10020. Landon Jones, Man. Ed. Articles on personal finance: how to earn more money, invest more profitably, spend more intelligently and more pleasurably, save more prudently, and enhance your career. Pays on acceptance and publication. Query.

THE MONEYPAPER—Two Madison Ave., Larchmont, NY 10538. Vita Nelson, Ed. and Pub. "*The Moneypaper* covers all aspects of money and money management. We do consider complete manuscripts. Payment is $75 on publication."

MONEYPLAN MAGAZINE—3500 Western Ave., Highland Park, IL 60035. Margaret Mucklo, Ed. "Ninety-five percent of our magazine is written by free lancers. We use articles on taxes, insurance, real estate, retirement, automobiles, leisure, and employment—all with a financial planning/money management slant. The magazine is purchased by financial institutions to distribute to their high-balance and multi-account customers. Articles should not advocate specific investments, especially those not offered by banks and savings & loans institutions. Our purpose is to provide practical financial planning information to a general audience, so articles must cross age and education lines and emphasize the broad application. Articles run from 375 to 600 words or 1,000 to 1,200 words, 1,300 to 1,600 for cover stories. Query first, with a brief description of the article idea and credentials. Payment is made 30 days after acceptance; rates range from $100 to $600."

PHYSICIANS FINANCIAL NEWS—BMI/McGraw-Hill, McGraw-Hill Healthcare Group, 800 Second Ave., New York, NY 10017. Joseph Lisanti, Senior Ed. Articles, about 1,000 words, for doctors on personal and professional money management: personal finance and investment topics, non-clinical medical economic topics (Medicare reimbursements, HMOs, medical marketing, etc.). Pays $400, after acceptance. Query required.

SAVVY—3 Park Ave., New York, NY 10016. Address Business Editor. "We are looking for articles on women in finance-related jobs (banking, brokerages, insurance, etc.), and personal money management. Topics covered in the money management column range from accounting quirks in annual reports to how to buy the best auto insurance. Recent issues featured a stock investment column on Nike, Inc., an article on how to get a second mortgage, and a Q & A piece on questions most frequently asked about IRAs. We always prefer to see queries first. Payment (for 800- to 1,000-word manuscripts) is made on acceptance and varies, depending on the writer's abilities and experience— usually starting at $650 an article."

SELF—350 Madison Ave., New York, NY 10017. Pamela Bayless, Sr. Ed., Money/Careers. "We seek articles on money strategies for our readers, most of whom are women in their 20s and 30s. More than half of them are single, nearly three-quarters have some college education and most are employed—about 40% in secretarial/clerical occupations. In recent months, we've published 'Four New Options in Banking,' 'A Snap Course in Mutual Funds,' 'How to Profit From Our Cheaper U.S. Dollar,' and 'A Shy Shopper's Guide to Bargaining.' Always query first, keeping it to one page whenever possible; read back issues first for content and style. Payment for articles of 1,500 to 2,000 words is on acceptance and varies with the writer's experience. A writer's first piece for *Self* might earn him $800; rates would escalate for subsequent sales."

SUNDAY WOMAN PLUS—235 E. 45th St., New York, NY 10017. Merry Clark, Ed. Articles on financial planning that would interest the broad range of people who read *Sunday Woman,* the weekly newspaper supplement distributed throughout the U.S. and Canada. Recent issues carried pieces on how to make money at home, and women and retirement planning. Submit query or completed manuscript (1,000 to 1,500 words). Payment—$50 to $500—is on acceptance.

SUNDAY SHOPPER—2929 S. Industrial Rd., Las Vegas, NV 89109. Howard Bernard, Ed. Articles, 200 to 1,000 words, that will help readers in their budgeting and shopping activities. Pays $50 to $100.

SYLVIA PORTER'S PERSONAL FINANCE MAGAZINE—380 Lexington Ave., New York, NY 10017. Greg Daugherty, Exec. Ed. Well-researched articles on investing, taxes, financial planning, real estate, entrepreneurship, etc. Pays on acceptance. Query.

WOMAN'S DAY—1515 Broadway, New York, NY 10036. Rebecca Greer, Articles Ed. "We use free-lance articles that are fresh and authoritative and that do not conflict with our 'Money Facts' column. Pieces should appeal to a broad range of women." Ms. Greer prefers to see queries for articles of varying lengths (to 3,000 words). Top rates are paid, on acceptance.

PROFESSIONAL/TRADE PUBLICATIONS

ACCESSORIES MAGAZINE—50 Day St., Norwalk, CT 06854. Reenie Brown, Ed. Dir. Articles, with photos, for women's fashion accessories buyers and manufacturers. Profiles on retailers, designers, and manufacturers, and merchandising and marketing articles on accessories. Pays $75 to $100 for short articles, from $100 to $300 for features, on publication. Query.

ACROSS THE BOARD—845 Third Ave., New York, NY 10022. Nancy Boas, Assoc. Ed. Articles, to 5,000 words, on a variety of topics of interest to business executives; straight business angle not required. Pays $100 to $750, on publication. Query required.

ALTERNATIVE ENERGY RETAILER—P.O. Box 2180, Waterbury, CT 06722. Ed Easley, Ed. Feature articles, 2,000 words, for retailers of alternative energy products—wood, coal and fireplace products and services. Interviews with successful retailers, stressing the how-to. B/W photos. Pays $200, extra for photos, on publication. Query first.

AMERICAN BANKER—One State Street Plaza, New York, NY 10004. William Zimmerman, Ed., Patricia Stanza, Features Ed. Articles, 1,000 to 3,000 words, on banking and financial services, human resources, management techniques. Pays varying rates, on publication. Query preferred.

AMERICAN BAR ASSOCIATION JOURNAL—750 N. Lake Shore Dr., Chicago, IL 60611. Robert Yates, Assoc. Ed. Practical articles, to 3,000 words, that will help lawyers in small firms better their practices. Pays from $500 for features, $25 for shorts, on acceptance. Query.

AMERICAN BICYCLIST—80 Eighth Ave., Suite 305, New York, NY 10011. Konstantin Doren, Ed. Articles, 1,500 to 2,800 words, on sales and repair practices of successful bicycle and moped dealers. Photos. Pays from 9¢ a word, extra for photos, on publication. Query.

AMERICAN CLAY EXCHANGE—P.O. Box 2674, La Mesa, CA 92044-0700. Susan N. Cox, Ed. Thoroughly-researched articles to 1,000 words, for collectors and dealers of American-made pottery, with emphasis on antiques and collectibles. Pays $5 for fillers, up to $100 for features, on acceptance.

AMERICAN COIN-OP—500 N. Dearborn St., Chicago, IL 60610. Ben Russell, Ed. Articles, to 2,500 words, with photos, on sucessful coin-operated laundries: management, promotion, decor, maintenance, etc. Pays from 6¢ a word, $6 per B & W photo, two weeks prior to publication. Query. Send SASE for guidelines.

AMERICAN DEMOGRAPHICS—P.O. Box 68, Ithaca, NY 14851. Cheryl Russell, Ed. Articles, 1,500 to 3,000 words, on demographic trends and business demographics for strategists in industry, government, and education. Pays $300, on publication. Query.

AMERICAN FARRIERS JOURNAL—63 Great Rd., Maynard, MA 01754. Susan G. Philbrick, Ed. Articles, 800 to 5,000 words, on horse handling, equine lameness, hoof care, tool selection, and general farriery issues. Pays 30¢ per published line, extra for photos, on publication. Query.

AMERICAN MEDICAL NEWS—535 N. Dearborn St., Chicago, IL 60610. Flora Johnson Skelly, Ass't. Exec. Ed. Features, 1,000 to 3,000 words, and news pieces, 200 to 1,000 words, of interest to physicians across the USA: "socio-economic angle is preferred; no 'clinical breakthrough' pieces are used." Queries are required. Pays $50 to $1,000, on acceptance.

AMERICAN PAINTING CONTRACTOR—2911 Washington Ave, St. Louis, MO 63103. Paul B. Stoecklein, Ed. Technical articles, to 2,500 words, with photos, on challenging industrial maintenance painting, for contractors and architects.

THE AMERICAN SALESMAN—424 N. Third St., Burlington, IA 52601-5524. Barbara Boeding, Ed. Articles, 900 to 1,200 words, on techniques for increasing sales. Pays 3¢ a word, on publication.

ARCHITECTURE—1735 New York Ave., N.W., Washington, DC 20006. Donald Canty, Ed. Articles, to 3,000 words, on architecture, urban design. Book reviews. Pays $100 to $500, extra for photos. Query.

AREA DEVELOPMENT MAGAZINE—525 Northern Blvd., Great Neck, NY 11021. Tom Bergeron, Ed. Articles for top executives of manufacturing companies, on industrial and office facility planning. Pays $40 per manuscript page. Query.

ART BUSINESS NEWS—60 Ridgeway Plaza, P.O. Box 3837, Stamford, CT 06905. Jo Yanow Schwartz, Ed. Articles, 1,000 words, for art dealers and framers, on trends and events of national importance to the art industry, and relevant business subjects. Pays $75 plus, on publication. Query preferred.

ART MATERIAL TRADE NEWS—6255 Barfield Rd., Atlanta, GA 30328. Charles C. Craig, Ed. Articles, from 800 words, for dealers, wholesalers, and manufacturers of artist materials; must be specific to trade. Pays to 15¢ a word, on publication. Query.

ASSOCIATION & SOCIETY MANAGER—1640 Fifth St., Santa Monica,

CA 90401. Helene Kass, Ed. Features, 1,500 to 2,200 words, geared to people who run nonprofit membership societies and associations: "should emphasize methods of organization management, procedures for increasing membership, conducting meetings, and related topics." Pays 10¢ a word, after acceptance.

AUTOMATION IN HOUSING & MANUFACTURED HOME DEALER— P.O. Box 120, Carpinteria, CA 93013. Don Carlson, Ed. Articles, 500 to 750 words, on various types of home manufacturers and dealers. Query required. Pays $300, on acceptance for articles with slides.

AUTOMOTIVE EXECUTIVE—8400 Westpark Dr., McLean, VA 22102. Joe Phillips, Man. Ed. National Automobile Dealers Assn. Articles, 750 to 2,500 words, on management of automobile and heavy-duty truck dealerships and general business and automotive issues. Photos. Pays on publication. Query.

BANKING WEEK—1 State Plaza, New York, NY 10004. William Zimmerman, Ed. Articles, 3 to 5 typed pages, on important news and trends in the banking industry; profiles of interesting bankers. Payment varies, on acceptance. Queries are required.

BARRISTER—American Bar Assn., 750 N. Lake Shore Dr., Chicago, IL 60611. Anthony Monahan, Ed. Articles, to 3,500 words, on legal and social affairs, for young lawyers. Pays to $700, on acceptance.

BARRON'S—200 Liberty St., New York, NY 10281. Alan Abelson, Ed. National-interest articles, 1,200 to 2,500 words, on business and finance. Query.

BETTER BUSINESS—235 East 42nd St., New York, NY 10017. John F. Robinson, Pub. Articles, 10 to 12 double-spaced pages, for the small business/minority business markets. Query.

BLACK ENTERPRISE—130 Fifth Ave., New York, NY 10011. Earl G. Graves, Ed. Articles on money, management, careers, political issues, entrepreneurship, high technology, and lifestyles for black professionals. Profiles. Pays on acceptance. Query.

BOATING INDUSTRY—850 Third Ave., New York, NY 10022. Olga Badillo-Sciortino, Ed. Articles, 1,000 to 1,500 words, on marine management, merchandising and selling, for boat dealers. Photos. Pays varying rates, on publication. Query first.

BUILDER—Hanley-Wood, Inc., 655 15th St., N.W., Suite 475, Washington, DC 20005. Frank Anton, Ed. Articles, to 1,500 words, on trends and news in home building: design, marketing, new products, etc. Pays negotiable rates, on acceptance. Query.

BUSINESS AGE MAGAZINE—P.O. Box 11597, Milwaukee, WI 53211. Margaret Brickner, Ed. Articles, 1,000 to 2,000 words, on how to operate a small business effectively; departments include accounting, finance, personnel management, taxes, etc. Query first. Guidelines.

BUSINESS AND COMMERCIAL AVIATION—Hangar C-1, Westchester Co. Airport, White Plains, NY 10604. John W. Olcott, Ed. Articles, 2,500 words, with photos, for pilots, on use of private aircraft for business transportation. Pays $100 to $500, on acceptance. Query.

BUSINESS ATLANTA—6255 Barfield Rd., Atlanta, GA 30328. Barrie S. Rissman, Ed. Articles, 1,000 to 4,500 words, with Atlanta or "deep South" business angle, strong marketing slant that will be useful to top Atlanta executives and business people. Pays $300 to $800, on publication. Query with clippings.

BUSINESS MARKETING—220 E. 42nd St., New York, NY 10017. Bob Donath, Ed. Articles on selling, advertising, and promoting products and services, for marketing executives. Pays competitive rates, on acceptance. Query only.

BUSINESS MONTH (formerly *Dun's Business Month*)—488 Madison Ave., New York, NY 10022. John Van Doorn, Ed.-in-Chief. Articles, to 5,000 words: profiles of CEOs, in-depth reports on large corporations, trends in corporation management, the economy, finance. Pays to $1 a word, on publication.

BUSINESS SOFTWARE MAGAZINE—M & T Publishing, 501 Galveston Dr., Redwood City, CA 94063. Nancy Beckus, Man. Ed. Software applications for business-oriented audience; tips and techniques using popular software; reviews of new products; case studies of corporate users. Pays to $500, before publication. Query.

BUSINESS SOFTWARE REVIEW—9100 Keystone Crossing, Indianapolis, IN 46240. Dennis Hamilton, Ed.-in-Chief. Articles, 300 to 3,000 words, on the computer business, centering on management software: productivity, profitability, return-on-investment. Pays $50 to $500, on publication. Query.

THE BUSINESS TIMES—544 Tolland St., E. Hartford, CT 06108. Mark D. Isaacs, Ed. Articles on Connecticut businesses and corporations, for Connecticut executives. Pays $2 per column inch, on publication. Query.

BUSINESS TODAY—P.O. Box 10010, 1720 Washington Blvd., Ogden, UT 84409. Karen E. Hill, Ed. Articles, 1,200 words; profiles of businessmen and women. Pays 15¢ a word, $35 for color photos, on acceptance. Query.

BUSINESS VIEW—P.O. Box 9859, Naples, FL 33941. Eleanor K. Sommer, Pub. Innovative articles and columns, 750 to 1,500 words, on business, economics, finance; profiles of business leaders; new trends in technology and advances in management techniques. Real estate and banking trends. Southwest Florida regional angle a must. Pays $75 to $200, on publication. Query.

CALIFORNIA BUSINESS—4221 Wilshire Blvd., Suite 400, Los Angeles, CA 90010. S. C. Gwynne, Ed. Articles, 1,200 to 3,000 words, on business and econometric issues in California. Pays varying rates, on acceptance. Query.

CALIFORNIA HORSE REVIEW—P.O. Box 2437, Fair Oaks, CA 95628. Jennifer Forsberg Meyer, Ed. Articles, 1,000 to 3,000 words, for professional horsemen, on training; how-to pieces, features. Pays $35 to $125, on publication.

CALIFORNIA LAWYER—555 Franklin St., San Francisco, CA 94102. Thomas K. Brom, Ed. Articles, 2,500 to 3,000 words, for attorneys in California, on legal subjects (or the legal aspects of a given political or social issue); how-to's on improving techniques in law practice. Pays $250 to $750, on acceptance. Query.

CAMPGROUND MANAGEMENT—11 N. Skokie Hwy., #205, Lake Bluff, IL 60044. Mike Byrnes, Ed. Detailed articles, 500 to 2,000 words, on managing recreational vehicle campgrounds. Photos. Pays $50 to $200, after publication.

CANADIAN AQUACULTURE—4611 William Head Rd., Victoria, BC Canada, V8X 3W9. Peter Chettleburgh, Ed. Articles related to Canadian fish farming: profiles of fish farmers; technical, how-to articles geared to making farms more profitable and efficient; in-depth analyses of political and resource issues, 1,200 to 2,000 words. Pays varying rates, on publication. Query first.

CASHFLOW—6255 Barfield Rd., Atlanta, GA 30328. Richard Gamble, Ed. Articles, 1,250 to 2,500 words, for treasury managers in public and private institutions: cash management; investments; domestic and international financing; credit and collection management; developments in law, economics, and tax. Pays $125 per published page, on publication. Query.

CERAMIC SCOPE—3632 Ashworth N., Seattle, WA 98103. Michael Scott, Ed. Articles, 800 to 1,500 words, on retail or wholesale business operations of hobby ceramic studios. Photos. Pays 10¢ a word, extra for photos, on publication. Query.

CHEESE MARKET NEWS—Gorman Publishing Co., 8750 W. Bryn Mawr, Chicago, IL 60631. Jerry Dryer, Ed. Articles, to 2,500 words, on innovative dairies, dairy processing operations, marketing successes, new products, for milk handlers, and makers of dairy products. Fillers, 25 to 150 words. Pays $25 to $300, $5 to $25 for fillers, on publication.

CHEMICAL WEEK—1221 Ave. of the Americas, New York, NY 10020. Patrick P. McCurdy, Ed.-in-Chief. News pieces, to 200 words, on chemical business. Pays $11 per column inch, on acceptance. Query.

CHINA, GLASS & TABLEWARE—P.O. Box 2147, Clifton, NJ 07015. Amy Stavis, Ed. Case histories and interviews, 1,500 to 2,500 words, with photos, on merchandising of china and glassware. Pays $50 per page, on publication. Query.

CHRISTIAN BOOKSELLER—190 N. Westmonte Dr., Altamonte Springs, FL 32714. Nancy Sabbag, Ed. Articles, 800 to 1,200 words, for Christian booksellers, on management, display, and promotion. Interviews with Christian authors. Photos. Pays $20 to $150, on publication. Query.

CLEANING MANAGEMENT—15550-D Rockfield, Irvine, CA 92718. R. Daniel Harris, Jr., Pub. Articles, 1,000 to 1,500 words, on managing efficient cleaning and maintenance operations. Photos. Pays 10¢ a word, extra for photos, on publication.

COLLEGE STORE EXECUTIVE—P.O. Box 1500, Westbury, NY 11590. Catherine Orobona, Ed. Articles, 1,000 words, for college store industry only; news; profiles. No general business or how-to articles. Photos. Pays $2 a column inch, extra for photos, on acceptance. Query.

THE COMICS JOURNAL—Comics Journal, Inc., 4359 Cornell Rd., Agoura, CA 91301. Kim Fryer, Man. Ed. Criticism, essays on comic books, interviews with comics professionals, 700 to 4,000 words. Include graphics. Pays 1½¢ a word, on publication.

COMPUTER CONSULTANT—208 N. Townsend St., Syracuse, NY 13202. Articles, to 2,500 words, on innovative sales techniques, and tips for increasing profitability for computer consultants. Pays varying rates, on publication. Query required.

COMPUTER DECISIONS MAGAZINE—10 Mulholland Dr., Hasbrouck Hgt., NJ 07604. Mel Mandell, Ed. Articles, 800 to 4,000 words, on generic uses of computer systems. Pays $30 to $100 per printed page, on acceptance. Query.

COMPUTER GRAPHICS WORLD—119 Russell St., Littleton, MA 01460. Tom McMillan, Man. Ed. Articles, 1,000 to 5,000 words, on computer graphics technology, applications, and products. Photos. Pays $100 per printed page, on publication. Query.

COMPUTER PRODUCT SELLING—Lebhar-Friedman, 425 Park Ave., New York, NY 10022. Betty Taylor, Exec. Ed. Features, 1,200 words, for computer salespeople. How-to and professional development articles and new product applications and reviews; industry news. Query required. Pays 30¢ a word, on publication.

CONCRETE INTERNATIONAL: DESIGN AND CONSTRUCTION—Box 19150, 22400 W. Seven Mile Rd., Detroit, MI 48219. Robert E. Wilde, Ed. Articles, 6 to 15 double-spaced pages, on concrete construction and design, with drawings and photos. Pays $100 per printed page, on publication. Query.

CONTACTS—17 Myrtle Ave., Troy, NY 12180. George J. Yamin, Ed. Articles, 300 to 1500 words, on management of dental laboratories, lab techniques, and equipment. Pays from 7¢ a word, on acceptance.

CONTRACTORS MARKET CENTER—Box 2029, Tuscaloosa, AL 35403. Robert Ruth, Ed. Features, 500 to 1,500 words, for contractors who use heavy equipment; success stories. Pays $10 to $50, on acceptance.

CONVENIENCE STORE NEWS—254 W. 31st St., New York, NY 10001. Denise Melinsky, Ed. Features and news items, 500 to 750 words, for convenience store owners, operators, and suppliers. Photos, with captions. Pays $3 per column inch, extra for photos, on publication. Query.

COOKING FOR PROFIT—P.O. Box 267, Fond du Lac, WI 54935. Bill Dittrich, Ed. Practical how-to articles, 1,000 words, on commercial food preparation, energy management; case studies, etc. Pays $75 to $250, on publication.

CRAIN'S CHICAGO BUSINESS—740 Rush St., Chicago, IL 60611. Dan Miller, Ed. Business articles about the Midwest exclusively. Pays $10.25 per column inch, on acceptance.

CREATING EXCELLENCE—New World Publishing, P.O. Box 2084, S. Burlington, VT 05403. David Robinson, Ed. Self-help and inspirational articles, profiles, and essays related to Northern Vermont and Vermont business. Queries are required. Payment is $75 to $250, on acceptance.

CREDIT AND COLLECTION MANAGEMENT BULLETIN—Bureau of Business Practice, 24 Rope Ferry Rd., Waterford, CT 06386. Russell Case, Ed. Interviews, 500 to 1,250 words, for commercial and consumer credit managers, on innovations, successes and problem solving. Query.

D & B REPORTS—299 Park Ave., New York, NY 10171. Patricia W. Hamilton, Ed. Articles, 1,500 to 2,500 words, for top management of smaller businesses: government regulations, export opportunities, employee relations; how-to's on cash management, sales, productivity; profiles; etc. Pays on acceptance.

DAIRY HERD MANAGEMENT—P.O. Box 2400, Minnetonka, MN 55343. Edward Clark, Ed. Articles, 500 to 2,000 words, with photos, on dairy finance, production, and marketing. Pays on acceptance. Query.

DEALERSCOPE MERCHANDISING—North American Publishing Co., 401 N. Broad St., Philadelphia, PA 19108. Neil Spann, Ed. Articles, 750 to 3,000 words, for dealers and distributors of audio, video, personal computers for the home, office; satellite TV systems for the home; major appliances on sales, marketing and finance. How-to's for retailers. Pays varying rates, on publication. Query with clips first.

DENTAL ECONOMICS—P.O. Box 3408, Tulsa, OK 74101. Dick Hale, Ed. Articles, 1,200 to 3,500 words, on business side of dental practice, patient and staff communication, personal investments, etc. Pays $100 to $250, on acceptance.

DOMESTIC ENGINEERING—135 Addison St., Elmhurst, IL 60126. Stephen J. Shafer, Ed. Articles, to 3,000 words, on plumbing, heating, air conditioning, and process piping. Photos. Pays $20 to $35 per printed page, on publication.

DRAPERIES & WINDOW COVERINGS—P.O. Box 13079, North Palm Beach, FL 33408. Katie Renckens, Ed. Articles, 1,000 to 2,000 words, for retailers, wholesalers, designers and manufacturers of draperies and window coverings. Profiles, with photos, of successful businesses in the industry. Pays $150 to $250, after acceptance. Query.

DRUG TOPICS—680 Kinderkamack Rd., Oradell, NJ 07649. Valentine A. Cardinale, Ed. News items, 500 words, with photos, on drug retailers and associations. Merchandising features, 1,000 to 1,500 words. Pays $100 to $150 for news, $200 to $400 for features, on acceptance. Query for features.

DUN'S BUSINESS MONTH—See *Business Month*.

EARNSHAW'S INFANTS & CHILDREN'S REVIEW—393 Seventh Ave., New York, NY 10001. Christina Gruber, Ed. Articles on retailers, retail promotions, and statistics for children's wear industry. Pays $50 to $200, on publication. Query. Limited market.

ELECTRICAL CONTRACTOR—7315 Wisconsin Ave., Bethesda, MD 20814. Larry C. Osius, Ed. Articles, 1,000 to 1,500 words, with photos, on construction or management techniques for electrical contractors. Pays $100 per printed page, before publication. Query.

EMERGENCY—P.O. Box 159, Carlsbad, CA 92008-0032. Laura Gilbert, Assoc. Ed. Features, to 3,000 words, and department pieces, to 1,000 words, of interest to paramedics, emergency medical technicians, and ambulance drivers: disaster management, advanced first-aid, medical assessment, etc. Pays $100 to $400 for features, $50 to $250 for department pieces. Photos are a plus. Queries preferred; guidelines available.

EMPLOYEE SERVICES MANAGEMENT—NESRA, 2400 S. Downing, Westchester, IL 60153. Joan Price, Ed. Articles, 800 to 2,500 words, for human resource, fitness, and employee service professionals.

ENGINEERED SYSTEMS—7314 Hart St., Mentor, OH 44060. Robert L. Schwed, Ed. Articles, case histories, on business management and legal issues related to hvac and refrigeration engineering systems in large buildings or industrial plants. Pays $4.75 per column inch, $12 per illustration, on publication. Query.

ENTRÉE—825 Seventh Ave., New York, NY 10019. Terence Murphy, Ed. Articles, 100 to 2,500 words, on trends and people in better housewares industry, both retailers and manufacturers. Pays from $400, on acceptance. Query.

EXECUTIVE REPORT—Riverview Publications, 3 Gateway Ctr., Pittsburgh, PA 15222. John M. McCarty, Ed. Articles, 600 to 2,500 words, on business news in western Pennsylvania. Pays 10¢ a word, on publication. Query first.

EXPORT MAGAZINE—386 Park Ave. South, New York, NY 10016. Robert Weingarten, Ed. Articles, 1,000 to 1,500 words, on the business of agents and distributors who import products in foreign countries. Pays $300 to $350, with photos, on acceptance. Query preferred.

FACT: THE MONEY MANAGEMENT MAGAZINE—305 E. 46th St., New York, NY 10017. Daniel M. Kehrer, Ed.-in-Chief. No unsolicited material.

FARM JOURNAL—230 W. Washington Sq., Philadelphia, PA 19105. Practical business articles on growing crops and producing livestock. Pays $50 to $500, on acceptance. Query required.

FENCE INDUSTRY/ACCESS CONTROL—6255 Barfield Rd., Atlanta, GA 30328. Bill Coker, Ed./Assoc. Pub. Articles on fencing and access control industry; interviews with dealer-erectors; on-the-job pieces. Photos. Pays 10¢ a word, extra for photos, on publication. Query.

FINANCIAL WORLD—1450 Broadway, New York, NY 10018. Douglas McIntyre, Pub. Articles on international business and financial topics. Query required. Pays on publication.

THE FISH BOAT—P.O. Box 2400, Covington, LA 70434. William A. Sarratt, Ed. Articles on commercial fishing, seafood marketing and processing. Short items on commercial fishing and boats. Pays varying rates.

FITNESS MANAGEMENT—P.O. Box 1198, Solana Beach, CA 92075. Edward H. Pitts, Ed. Authoritative features, 750 to 2,500 words, and news shorts, 100 to 750 words, for owners, managers, and program directors of fitness centers. Content must be in keeping with current medical practice: no fads. Pays 8¢ a word, on publication. Query.

FLORIST—29200 Northwestern Hwy., P.O. Box 2227, Southfield, MI 48037. Susan Nicholas, Man. Ed. Articles, to 2,000 words, with photos, on retail florist business improvement. Photos. Pays 8¢ a word.

FLOWERS &—Teleflora Plaza, Suite 260, 12233 W. Olympic Blvd., Los Angeles, CA 90064. Marie Moneysmith, Exec. Ed. Articles, 1,000 to 3,500 words, with how-to information for retail florists. Pays from $400, on acceptance. Query first with clips.

FOOD MANAGEMENT—747 Third Ave., New York, NY 10017. Donna Boss, Ed. Articles, on food service in healthcare, schools, colleges, prisons, business and industry. Trends and how-to pieces, with management tie-in. Pays to $500. Query.

FOREIGN TRADE—8208 W. Franklin, Minneapolis, MN 55426. John Freivalds, Ed. Articles and interviews, 1,700 to 2,100 words, on topics related to international trade that examine problems managers have faced, and deal with how they solved them. Pays $400, on publication. Guidelines.

THE FOREMAN'S LETTER—24 Rope Ferry Rd., Waterford, CT 06386. Carl Thunberg, Ed. Interviews, with photos, with top-notch supervisors and foremen. Pays 8¢ to 12¢ a word, extra for photos, on acceptance.

FRANCHISE—747 Third Ave., New York, NY 10017. Michael J. McDermott, Ed. "The Business Magazine of Franchising seeks articles, 1,200 to 1,500 words, on franchise-related business topics." Queries are required. Pays varying rates, on publication.

GARDEN DESIGN—1733 Connecticut Ave., NW, Washington, DC 20009. Susan Frey, Ed. Association of American Landscape Architects. Articles, 1,500 to 2,000 words, on classic and contemporary examples of residential landscape, garden, art, history, and design. Interviews. Pays $300, on publication. Query.

GLASS DESIGN—310 Madison Ave., New York, NY 10017. Charles Cumpston, Ed. Articles, 1,200 to 1,500 words, on building projects and glass/metal dealers, distributors, storefront and glazing contractors. Pays varying rates, on publication.

GLASS NEWS—P.O. Box 7138, Pittsburgh, PA 15213. Liz Scott, Man. Ed. Articles, to 1,500 words, on developments in glass manufacturing, glass factories, types of glass. Personality profiles. Pays 5¢ to 10¢ a word, on publication. Query with SASE.

GOLF SHOP OPERATIONS—5520 Park Ave., Box 395, Trumbull, CT 06611-0395. Nick Romano, Ed. Articles, 200 to 800 words, with photos, on successful golf shop operations; new ideas for merchandising, display, bookkeeping. Short pieces on golf professionals. Pays $175 to $250, on publication. Query with outline.

GRAPHIC ARTS MONTHLY—249 W. 17th St., New York, NY 10011. Roger Ynostroza, Ed. Technical or business-oriented articles, 1,500 to 2,000 words, on printing industry. No profiles. Pays 10¢ a word, on publication. Query.

GREENHOUSE MANAGER—P.O. Box 1868, Fort Worth, TX 76101. Jim Bates, Man. Ed. How-to articles, success stories, 500 to 1,800 words, accompanied by color slides, of interest to professional greenhouse growers. Profiles. Pays $50 to $300, on acceptance. Query required.

HARDWARE AGE—Chilton Way, Radnor, PA 19089. Rick Carter, Man. Ed. Articles on merchandising methods in hardware outlets. Photos. Pays on acceptance.

HARDWARE MERCHANDISER—7300 N. Cicero Ave., Chicago, IL 60646. Pamela C. Taylor, Ed. Articles, to 1,000 words, with photos, on merchandising in hardware and discount stores. Pays on acceptance.

HARVARD BUSINESS REVIEW—Harvard Graduate School of Business Administration, Boston, MA 02163. Query Editors on new ideas about business management of interest to senior executives. Pays on publication.

HEALTH FOODS BUSINESS—567 Morris Ave., Elizabeth, NJ 07208. Mary Jane Dittmar, Ed. Articles, 1,500 words, with photos, on managing health food stores. Shorter pieces on trends, research findings, preventive medicine, alternative therapies. Interviews with doctors and nutritionists. Brief items for "Quote/Unquote" (include source). Pays on publication. Query. Send for guidelines.

HEATING/PIPING/AIR CONDITIONING—2 Illinois Cntr., Chicago, IL 60601. Robert T. Korte, Ed. Articles, to 5,000 words, on heating, piping and air conditioning systems in industrial plants and large buildings; engineering information. Pays $60 per printed page, on publication. Query.

HIGH TECH MARKETING—1460 Post Rd. East, Westport, CT 06880. Candice Port, Ed. Feature-length articles, 9 to 15 pages, on the marketing of high-tech products. Pays 20¢ to 30¢ a word, on acceptance. Query required.

HIGH TECHNOLOGY BUSINESS—214 Lewis Wharf, Boston, MA 02110. Mary H. Frakes, Man. Ed. "Our mission is to cover the latest developments in technology, with special emphasis on the companies and the marketplace in which the technology is being introduced. Articles submitted to us must be interesting, understandable, and above all useful to a busy reader who wants to know what is important in technology." Payment is $75 to $2,000, on acceptance, for manuscripts of 300 to 3,000 words. Query.

HOSPITAL GIFT SHOP MANAGEMENT—7628 Densmore, Van Nuys, CA 91406. Barbara Feiner, Ed. Articles, 750 to 2,500 words, with managerial tips and sales pointers; hospital and merchandise profiles. Pays $10 to $100, on acceptance. Query required.

HOSPITAL SUPERVISOR'S BULLETIN—24 Rope Ferry Rd., Waterford, CT 06386. Michele Dunaj, Ed. Interviews, articles with nonmedical hospital supervisors on departmental problem solving. Pays 12¢ a word. Query.

HOSPITALS—211 E. Chicago Ave., Suite 700, Chicago, IL 60611. Frank Sabatino, Ed. Articles, 500 to 800 words, for hospital administrators. Pays varying rates, on acceptance. Query.

INC.—38 Commercial Wharf, Boston, MA 02110. George Gendron, Ed. Feature articles about how owners and managers of small companies solve common problems. Pays to $1,500, on acceptance. Query.

INCENTIVE TRAVEL MANAGER—1640 Fifth St., Santa Monica, CA 90401. Helene Kass, Ed. Articles, 1,500 to 2,500 words, on methods of organizing and implementing employee motivational travel programs. Queries are required. Pays 10¢ a word, after acceptance.

INCOME OPPORTUNITIES—380 Lexington Ave., New York, NY 10017. Stephen Wagner, Ed. Helpful articles, 1,000 to 2,500 words, on how to make money full or part-time; how to run a successful small business, improve sales, etc. Pays varying rates, on acceptance. Query.

INDUSTRIAL DESIGN—330 W. 42nd St., New York, NY 10036. Annetta Hanna, Man. Ed. Articles to 2,000 words, on product development, design management, graphic design, design history, fashion, art, and environments for designers and marketing executives. Profiles of designers and corporations that use design effectively. Pays $250 to $600, on publication.

INFOSYSTEMS—25W550 Geneva Rd., Hitchcock Bldg., Wheaton, IL 60188. Wayne L. Rhodes, Ed. How-to articles, 6 to 8 pages, for managers in the data processing field. Pays negotiable rates, on publication. Query.

INSTANT & SMALL COMMERCIAL PRINTER—P.O. Box 368, Northbrook, IL 60065. Dan Witte, Ed. Articles, 3 to 5 typed pages, for owners and/or managers of printing businesses specializing in retail printing: case histories, how-to's, technical pieces, interesting ideas. Opinion pieces, 1 to 2 typed pages. Photos. Pays $150 to $200 ($25 to $50 for opinion pieces), extra for photos, on publication. Query preferred.

INTV JOURNAL—80 Fifth Ave., Suite 501, New York, NY 10011. William Dunlap, Man. Ed. Features and short pieces on trends in independent television. Pays to $500, after publication. Query.

JEMS, THE JOURNAL OF EMERGENCY SERVICES—215 S. Highway 101, Ste. 100, Box 1026, Solana Beach, CA 92075. Rick Minerd, Ed. Articles, 1,500 to 3,000 words, for providers and administrators of emergency medical care. Pays 10¢ per word, on publication. Query first. Guidelines.

KIDS FASHIONS—71 W. 35th St., Suite 1600, New York, NY 10001. Larry Leventhal, Ed. Articles, 1,000 to 2,000 words, with photos, on retailing and merchandising of children's apparel. Pays from $250 for articles with photos;

from $150 for "how-to" and consultation pieces, on acceptance. Queries preferred.

LOS ANGELES BUSINESS JOURNAL—3345 Wilshire, #207, Los Angeles, CA 90010. David Yochum, Ed. Features articles on specific industries in the five-county Los Angeles area, stressing the how-to, trends and analysis. Pays on publication.

LOS ANGELES LAWYER—Box 55020, Los Angeles, CA 90055. Susan Pettit, Ed. Journalistic features, 12 to 16 pages, and consumer articles, 8 to 12 pages, on legal topics. Pays $200 to $600, on acceptance. Query required.

LOTUS—P.O. Box 9123, Cambridge, MA 02139. Chris Brown, Sr. Ed. Articles, 1,500 to 2,000 words, for business and professional people using Lotus software. Query with outline required. Payment varies, on acceptance.

LP-GAS MAGAZINE—131 W. First St., Duluth, MN 55802. Zane Chastain, Ed. Articles, 1,500 to 2,500 words, with photos, on LP-Gas dealer operations: marketing, management, etc. Photos. Pays to 15¢ a word, extra for photos, on acceptance. Query.

MACHINE DESIGN—Penton Publications, 1100 Superior Blvd., Cleveland, OH 44114. Robert Aronson, Exec. Ed. Articles to 10 typed pages, on design-related topics for engineers. Pays varying rates, on publication. Submit outline or brief description.

MAGAZINE DESIGN & PRODUCTION—4551 W. 107th St., Suite 343, Overland Park, KS 66207. Maureen Waters, Man. Ed. Articles, 6 to 10 typed pages, on magazine design and production: printing, typesetting, computers, layout, etc. Pays $100 to $200, on acceptance. Query required.

MANAGE—2210 Arbor Blvd., Dayton, OH 45439. Doug Shaw, Ed. Articles, 1,500 to 2,200 words, on management and supervision for first-line and middle managers. Pays 5¢ a word.

MANUFACTURED HOMES MAGAZINE—P.O. Box 354, Bremerton, WA 98310. Sandra E. Haven, Ed. Well-researched articles on all aspects of buying and owning a mobile home; humorous reflection; "Reader Projects"; and cartoons. All material *must* be related to *today's* manufactured homes and lifestyle. Photos. Pays to 7¢ a word, on acceptance. Query first. Guidelines available.

MANUFACTURING SYSTEMS—Hitchcock Bldg., Wheaton, IL 60188. Tom Inglesby, Ed. Articles, 500 to 2,000 words, on computer and information systems for industry executives seeking to increase productivity in manufacturing firms. Pays 10¢ to 20¢ a word, on acceptance. Query required.

MEDICENTER MANAGEMENT—1640 5th St., Santa Monica, CA 90401. Rebecca Morrow, Ed. Articles, 1,500 to 3,000 words, on the business of practicing medicine: in-office testing, controls, customer relations, equipment development, advertising and marketing, joint ventures, etc. Payment varies, on acceptance. Query required.

MEMPHIS BUSINESS JOURNAL—4515 Poplar, Suite 322, Memphis, TN 38117. Barney DuBois, Ed. Articles, to 2,000 words, on business, industry trade, agribusiness and finance in the Mid-South trade area. Pays $80 to $200, on acceptance.

MINIATURES DEALER—Clifton House, Clifton, VA 22024. Geraldine Willems, Ed. Articles, 1,000 to 1,500 words, on advertising, promotion, merchandising of miniatures and other small business retailer concerns. Pays to $200, on publication.

MIX MAGAZINE—2608 Ninth St., Berkeley, CA 94710. David Schwartz, Ed. Articles, varying lengths, for professionals, on audio, video, and music entertainment technology. Pays 10¢ a word, on publication. Query required.

MODERN HEALTHCARE—740 N. Rush St., Chicago, IL 60611. Clark Bell, Ed. Features on management, finance, building design and construction, and new technology for hospitals, health maintenance organizations, nursing homes, and other health care institutions. Pays $7 per column inch, on publication. Query.

MODERN TIRE DEALER—P.O. Box 5417, 110 N. Miller Rd., Akron, OH 44313. Lloyd Stoyor, Ed. Merchandising management and service articles, 1,000 to 1,500 words, with photos, on independent tire dealers and retreaders. Pays $200 to $300, on publication.

MONEY MAGAZINE—Time & Life Bldg., New York, NY 10020. Landon Jones, Man. Ed. Articles on various aspects of personal finance and investment. Welcomes article suggestions. Pays $2,500 and up for major articles.

MONEY MAKER—5705 N. Lincoln Ave., Chicago, IL 60659. John Manos, Ed. Informative jargon-free articles, to 4,000 words, for beginning to sophisticated investors, on investment opportunities, personal finance, and low-priced investments. Pays 25¢ a word, on acceptance. Query for assignment.

THE MONEYPAPER—2 Madison Ave., Larchmont, NY 10538. Vita Nelson, Ed. Financial news and money-saving ideas, especially those of interest to women. Brief, well-researched articles on personal finance, money management: saving, earning, investing, taxes, insurance and related subjects. Features on women's attitudes toward money and personal experiences in solving money management problems. Pays $75 for articles, on publication. Query with resume and writing sample.

NATIONAL BEAUTY SCHOOL JOURNAL—3839 White Plains Rd., Bronx, NY 10467. Mary Jane Tenerelli, Ed. Articles, 1,500 to 2,000 words, on running a cosmetology school: teaching techniques and problems, new procedures. Pays $150, on publication.

NATIONAL FISHERMAN—21 Elm St., Camden, ME 04843. James W. Fullilove, Ed. Articles, 200 to 2,000 words, aimed at commercial fishermen and boatbuilders. Pays from $3.00 per inch, extra for photos, on publication. Query preferred.

NATION'S BUSINESS—1615 H St. NW, Washington, DC 20062. Robert Gray, Ed. Articles, 1,500 to 2,000 words, "that provide direct guidance on the day-to-day operation of a business; reports on strategies and techniques used by successful business people; up-to-date information on Washington developments of interest to business people; and personal advice in such areas as finance, taxes, and health." Query first with one-page outline. Payment is 30¢ to 40¢ a word, after acceptance. Guidelines.

NEW BUSINESS—P.O. Box 3312, Sarasota, FL 34230. Business-related articles of regional/general interest. Pays $75 to $225, on publication. Query.

NEW CAREER WAYS NEWSLETTER—67 Melrose Ave., Haverhill, MA 01830. William J. Bond, Ed. How-to articles, 1,500 to 2,000 words, on new ways to succeed in business careers. Pays varying rates, on publication. Query with outline.

NEW HAVEN BUSINESS DIGEST—375 Orange St., New Haven, CT 06510. Kim Hanson, Ed. Feature articles, 1,500 to 2,000 words, on successful New Haven-area businesses and owners. Pays $2.75 per published inch, on publication. Query required.

NORTHERN HARDWARE—2965 Broadmoor Valley Rd., Suite B, Colorado Springs, CO 80906. Edward Gonzales, Ed. Articles, 800 to 1,000 words, on unusual hardware and home center stores and promotions in Northwest and Midwest. Photos. Pays 8¢ a word, extra for photos, on publication. Query.

NURSINGWORLD JOURNAL—470 Boston Post Rd., Weston, MA 02193. Shirley Copithorne, Ed. Articles, 500 to 1,000 words, for nurses and nurse educators, on all aspects of nursing. B&W photos. Pays from 25¢ per column inch, on publication.

ONLINE ACCESS GUIDE—53 W. Jackson Blvd., Chicago, IL 60604. Elias F. Crim, Ed. Features, 2,500 words, and columns, 1,500 words, on business applications of online services for users of informational service systems. Queries are required. Pays $500 to $1,500.

OPPORTUNITY MAGAZINE—6 N. Michigan Ave., Suite 1405, Chicago, IL 60602. Jack Weissman, Ed. Articles, 900 words, on sales psychology, sales techniques, self-improvement. Pays $20 to $40, on publication.

OPTIONS—7628 Densmore Ave., Van Nuys, CA 91406. Barbara Feiner, Ed. Articles, 1,000 to 3,000 words, on practice management and related business topics for physicians in transition. Queries are required. Pays $50 to $200, on acceptance.

THE OSHA COMPLIANCE LETTER—See *The Safety Compliance Letter.*

PAPERBOARD PACKAGING—7500 Old Oak Blvd., Cleveland, OH 44130. Mark Arzoumanian, Ed. Articles, any length, on corrugated containers, folding cartons and setup boxes. Pays on publication. Query with outline.

PC WEEK—800 Boylston St., Boston, MA 02199. David DeJean, Exec. Ed. Features, 1,500 to 2,500 words, for volume buyers of PC's and related equipment and software within large organizations; corporate strategy profiles; reviews of PC-related products. Pays $500 to $1,000, on acceptance. Query required.

PET BUSINESS—5400 NW 84th Ave., Miami, FL 33166. Linda Mills, Ed. Brief documented articles on animals and products found in pet stores; research findings; legislative/regulatory actions. Pays $4 per column inch, on publication; $10 to $20 for photos.

PETS/SUPPLIES/MARKETING—One E. First St., Duluth, MN 55802. David D. Kowalski, Ed. Articles, 1,000 to 1,200 words, with photos, on pet shops, and pet and product merchandising. Pays 10¢ a word, extra for photos. No fiction or news clippings. Query.

PHOTO MARKETING—3000 Picture Pl., Jackson, MI 49201. Perry Washburn, Man. Ed. Business articles, 1,000 to 3,500 words, for owners and managers of camera stores or photo processing labs. Pays $150 to $500, extra for photos, on publication.

PHYSICAL THERAPY JOB NEWS—470 Boston Post Rd., Weston, MA 02193. Shirley Copithorne, Ed. Articles, case studies, and profiles, 1,500 to 2,500 words, of interest to professional and student physical therapists. Payment is $25 to $100, on publication. Guidelines.

605

PHYSICIANS FINANCIAL NEWS—BMI/McGraw-Hill, McGraw-Hill Healthcare Group, 800 Second Ave., New York, NY 10017. Joseph Lisanti, Senior Ed. Articles, about 1,000 words, for doctors, on personal and professional money management: personal finance and investment topics, nonclinical medical economic topics (Medicare reimbursements, HMOs, medical marketing, etc.). Pays $400, after acceptance. Query required.

P.O.B.—P.O. Box 810, Wayne, MI 48184. Jeanne M. Helfrick, Assoc. Ed. Technical and business articles, 1,000 to 4,000 words, for professionals and technicians in the surveying and mapping fields. Technical tips on field and office procedures and equipment maintenance. Pays $150 to $400, on acceptance.

POLICE PRODUCT NEWS—P.O. Box 847, Carlsbad, CA 92008. F. McKeen Thompson, Ed. Reviews of new products and equipment, and profiles of people in the law enforcement profession, 1,000 to 3,000 words. Pays from $100 to $300, on acceptance.

POOL & SPA NEWS—3923 West Sixth St., Los Angeles, CA 90020. News articles for the swimming pool, spa, and hot tub industry. Pays from 8¢ to 12¢ a word, extra for photos, on publication. Query first.

THE PRESS—302 Grote St., Buffalo, NY 14207. Janet Tober, Mary Lou Vogt, Eds. Quarterly. Short profiles, 800 to 1,200 words, on cartoonists and industry and advertising personalities for advertising executives at newspapers and ad agencies. Pieces on unusual hobbies or occupations. Travel articles. Humor. Pays 10¢ a word, on acceptance.

PRIVATE PRACTICE—Box 12489, Oklahoma City, OK 73157. Cindy Wickersham, Asst. Ed. Articles, 1,500 to 2,000 words, on state or local legislation affecting medical field. Pays $250 to $350, on publication.

PROFESSIONAL OFFICE DESIGN—111 Eighth Ave., New York, NY 10011. Muriel Chess, Ed. Articles, to 1,500 words, on space planning and design for offices in the fields of law, medicine, finance, accounting, advertising, and architecture/design. Pays competitive rates, on publication. Query required.

RADIO ELECTRONICS—500-B Bi-County Blvd., Farmingdale, NY 11735. Brian C. Fenton, Man. Ed. Technical articles, 1,500 to 3,000 words, on electronic equipment. Pays $50 to $500, on acceptance.

REAL ESTATE TODAY—National Association of Realtors, 430 N. Michigan Ave., Chicago, IL 60611. Articles on all aspects of residential, finance, commercial-investment, and brokerage-management real estate, to 2,000 words. Query required. Pays in copies.

RESORT & HOTEL MANAGEMENT—P.O. Box A, Del Mar, CA 92014. Articles, 1,000 to 1,500 words, on successful resort and hotel operation and management.

ROOFER MAGAZINE—P.O. Box 06253, Fort Myers, FL 33906. Mr. Shawn Holiday, Ed. Technical and nontechnical articles, 500 to 1,500 words, on roofing-related topics: new roofing concepts, energy-saving ideas, pertinent issues, industry concerns. No business or computer articles. Pays negotiable rates, on publication.

RV BUSINESS—29901 Agoura Rd., Agoura, CA 91301. Katherine Sharma, Exec. Rd. Articles, 1,500 to 2,500 words, on manufacturing, financing, selling and servicing recreational vehicles. Articles on legislative matters affecting the industry. Pays varying rates.

THE SAFETY COMPLIANCE LETTER (formerly *The OSHA Compliance Letter*)—24 Rope Ferry Rd., Waterford, CT 06386. Laurie Beth Roberts, Ed. Interview-based articles, 800 to 1,250 words, for safety professionals, on solving OSHA-related safety and health problems. Pays to 15¢ a word, on acceptance, after editing. Query.

SALES & MARKETING MANAGEMENT—Bill Communications, Inc., 633 Third Ave., New York, NY 10017. Robert H. Albert, Ed. Short and feature articles for sales and marketing executives of medium to large corporations. Pays varying rates, on acceptance. Query required.

SALTWATER DEALER—One Bell Rd., Montgomery, AL 36117. Dave Ellison, Ed. Articles, 300 to 1,250 words, for merchants who carry saltwater tackle and marine equipment—business focus is required, and writers should provide practical information for improving management and merchandising. Payment varies, on acceptance. Queries are required.

SECRETS OF WINNERS—157 Whooping Loop, Altamonte Springs, FL 32701. Fred C. Kibler, Ed. Profiles of successful entrepreneurs, how-to articles on starting a business, and articles on tax tips for business people, 1,500 to 2,500 words. Queries are required. Pays 10¢ a word, on acceptance.

SECURITY MANAGEMENT—1655 N. Ft. Myer Dr., Suite 1200, Arlington, VA 22209. Mary Alice Crawford, Pub. Articles, 2,500 to 3,000 words, on legislative issues related to security; case studies of innovative security applications; management topics: employee relations, training programs, etc. Pays 10¢ a word, on publication. Query.

SELLING DIRECT—6255 Barfield Rd., Atlanta, GA 30328. Robert S. Rawls, Ed. Articles, 400 to 1,800 words, for independent salespersons selling to homes, stores, industries, and businesses. Pays 10¢ a word, on publication.

SIGN BUSINESS—P.O. Box 985, Broomfield, CO 80020. Stephanie H. Walters, Ed. Articles on general business topics as well as pieces specifically targeted to the sign business. Pays $20 per typed page, on acceptance.

SNACK FOOD MAGAZINE—131 W. First St., Duluth, MN 55802. Jerry Hess, Ed. Articles, 600 to 1,500 words, on trade news, personalities, promotions, production in snack food manufacturing industry. Short pieces; photos. Pays 12¢ to 15¢ a word, $15 for photos, on acceptance. Query.

SOFTWARE NEWS—1900 W. Park Dr., Westborough, MA 01581. Edward J. Bride, Ed. Technical features, 1,000 to 1,200 words, for computer literature audience, on how software products can be used. Pays about $500 to $750, on publication. Query preferred.

SOUTHERN LUMBERMAN—P.O. Box 1627, Franklin, TN 37064. Nanci P. Gregg, Ed. Articles, 500 to 750 words, on pine and hardboard sawmill operations, interviews with industry leaders, and how-to and technical pieces with emphasis on increasing production and efficiency. Queries are required. Pays $150 to $250, on publication.

SOUVENIRS AND NOVELTIES—Suite 226–27, 401 N. Broad St., Philadelphia, PA 19108. Articles, 1,500 words, quoting souvenir shop managers on items that sell, display ideas, problems in selling, industry trends. Photos. Pays from $1 per column inch, extra for photos, on publication.

SUCCESSFUL FARMING—1716 Locust St., Des Moines, IA 50336. Loren Kruse, Ed. Articles, to 2,000 words, for farming families, on all areas of business farming: money management, marketing, machinery, soils and crops, livestock, and buildings. Pays from $300, on acceptance. Query required.

TEXTILE WORLD—4170 Ashford-Dunwoody Rd. N.E., Suite 420, Atlanta, GA 30319. L. A. Christiansen, Ed. Articles, 500 to 2,000 words, with photos, on manufacturing and finishing textiles. Pays varying rates, on acceptance.

TOURIST ATTRACTIONS AND PARKS—Suite 226–27, 401 N. Broad St., Philadelphia, PA 19108. Chuck Tooley, Ed. Articles, 1,500 words, on successful management of parks and leisure attractions. News items, 250 and 500 words. Pays 7¢ a word, on publication. Query.

TRAILER/BODY BUILDERS—1602 Harold St., Houston, TX 77006. Paul Schenck, Ed. Articles on engineering, sales, and management ideas for truck body and truck trailer manufacturers. Pays from $100 per printed page, on acceptance.

TRAINING, THE MAGAZINE OF HUMAN RESOURCES DEVELOPMENT—50 S. Ninth St., Minneapolis, MN 55402. Jack Gordon, Ed. Articles, 1,000 to 2,500 words, for managers of training and development activities in corporations, government, etc. Pays to 15¢ a word, on acceptance. Query.

THE TRAVEL AGENT—825 7th Ave., New York, NY 10019. Michael Kahn, Ed. Articles, 1,500 words, with photos, on travel trade, for travel agents. Pays $50 to $75, on acceptance.

TRAVELAGE SOUTHEAST—555 N. Birch Rd., Ft. Lauderdale, FL 33304. Marylyn Springer, Ed. Articles, 1,500 to 2,000 words, for travel agents and other travel industry personnel. Interviews, some travel articles. Pays $1.50 per column inch, on publication.

TRAVEL BUSINESS MANAGER—51 Monroe St., #1501, Rockville, MD 20850. Eleanor Alexander, Ed. Articles and features, 1,000 to 1,800 words, on management and strategic issues in the travel industry. Pays $200 to $500, on publication. Query required. Send SASE for guidelines.

TRUCKER/USA—P.O. Box 2029, Tuscaloosa, AL 35403. Claude Duncan, Ed. Features, 250 to 1,000 words, for longhaul truck drivers. Pays $10 to $50, on acceptance.

VENDING TIMES—545 Eighth Ave., New York, NY 10018. Arthur E. Yohalem, Ed. Feature and news articles, with photos, on vending machines. Pays varying rates, on acceptance. Query.

VIEW—80 Fifth Ave., Suite 501, New York, NY 10011. Kathy Haley, Ed. Features and short pieces on trends in the business of television programming (network, syndication, cable and pay). Profiles. Pays to $400, after publication. Query.

VIRGINIA BUSINESS—600 E. Broad St., Richmond, VA 23219. James Bacon, Ed. Articles, 1,000 to 2,500 words, related to the business scene in Virginia. Pays varying rates, on acceptance. Query required.

WESTERN INVESTOR—400 S.W. Sixth Ave., Suite 1115, Portland, OR

97204. Business and investment articles, 800 to 1,200 words, about companies and their leaders listed in the *Western Investor* data section. Pays from $50, on publication. Query first.

WINES & VINES—1800 Lincoln Ave., San Rafael, CA 94901. Philip E. Hiaring, Ed. Articles, 1,000 words, on grape and wine industry, emphasizing marketing and production. Pays 5¢ a word, on acceptance.

WOMEN IN BUSINESS—9100 Ward Parkway, Box 8728, Kansas City, MO 64114. Publication of the American Business Women's Association. Margaret E. Horan, Ed. Features, 1,000 to 2,000 words, for career women from 25 to 55 years old; no profiles. Pays 15¢ a word, on acceptance. Query.

WOOD 'N ENERGY—P.O. Box 2008, Laconia, NY 03247. Jason Perry, Ed. Profiles and interviews, 1,000 to 2,500 words, with retailers and manufacturers of alternative energy equipment. Pays $150 to $250, on acceptance. Query.

WOODSHOP NEWS—Pratt St., Essex, CT 06427-1122. Ian C. Bowen, Ed. "We're a monthly newspaper devoted to finding and reporting news for and about people who work with wood. Features, business stories, profiles, and how-to pieces, 1 to 3 typed pages, are needed." Pays $2 an inch, on publication. Queries are preferred.

WORLD OIL—Gulf Publishing Co., P.O. Box 2608, Houston, TX 77252. T. R. Wright, Jr., Ed. Engineering and operations articles, 3,000 to 4,000 words, on petroleum industry exploration, drilling or producing. Photos. Pays from $50 per printed page, on acceptance. Query.

WORLD SCREEN NEWS—80 Fifth Ave., Suite 501, New York, NY 10011. Claire Poole, Man. Ed. Features and short pieces on trends in the business of international television programming (network, syndication, cable and pay). Pays to $500, after publication.

WORLD WASTES—6255 Barfield Rd., Atlanta, GA 30328. Bill Wolpin, Pub., Toni O'Neal, Man. Ed. Case studies, 1,000 to 2,000 words, with photos, of refuse haulers, landfill operators, resource recovery operations and transfer stations, with solutions to problems in field. Pays from $100 per printed page, on publication. Query preferred.

YOUNG FASHIONS—370 Lexington Ave., New York, NY 10017. Marc Richards, Ed. Articles, 2,000 to 4,000 words, that help store owners and department store buyers of children's clothes with merchandising or operations; how-to pieces. Payment varies, on acceptance. Query required.

COMPANY PUBLICATIONS

Company publications (also called house magazines or house organs) are excellent, well-paying markets for writers at all levels of experience. Hundreds of these magazines are published, usually by large corporations, to promote good will, familiarize readers with the company's services and products, and interest customers in these products. Always read a house magazine before submitting an article; write to the editor for a sample copy (offering to pay for it) and the editorial guidelines. Stamped, self-addressed envelopes should be enclosed with any query or manuscript. This list includes only a sampling of publications in this large market.

THE COMPASS—Mobil International Aviation and Marine Sales, Inc., 150 E. 42nd St., New York, NY 10017. R. G. MacKenzie, Ed. Articles, to 3,500 words, on the sea and deep sea trade. Photos. No fiction. Pays to $250, on acceptance. Query.

FORD NEW HOLLAND NEWS (formerly *New Holland, Inc.*)—New Holland, PA 17557. Gary Martin, Ed. Articles, to 1,000 words, with strong photo support, on production agriculture, research, and rural human interest. Pays on acceptance. Query.

FRIENDS, THE CHEVY OWNERS' MAGAZINE—30400 Van Dyke, Warren, MI 48093. Herman Duerr, Exec. Ed. Feature articles, 800 to 1,200 words, travel-related with specific focus; outdoor/adventure oriented; lifestyle; celebrity profiles; entertainment. Chevrolet tie-in preferred. Pays $300, extra for photos, on acceptance. Query.

THE FURROW—Deere & Company, John Deere Rd., Moline, IL 61265. George R. Sollenberger, Ed. Articles and humor, to 1,500 words; researched agricultural-technical features; rural social- and economic-trend features. Pays to $1,000, on acceptance.

INLAND—Inland Steel Co., 30 W. Monroe, Chicago, IL 60603. Sheldon A. Mix, Man. Ed. Imaginative articles, essays, commentaries, of any length, of special interest in Midwest. Pays varying rates, on acceptance.

THE MODERN WOODMEN—Modern Woodmen of America, Mississippi River at 17th St., Rock Island, IL 61201. Gloria Bergh, Manager, Public Relations. Family- and community-oriented, general-interest articles; some quality fiction. Photos. Pays from $50, on acceptance. Publication not copyrighted.

NEW HOLLAND, INC.—See *Ford New Holland News.*

RAYTHEON MAGAZINE—141 Spring St., Lexington, MA 02173. Robert P. Suarez, Ed. Articles by assignment only. Pays $1,000 to $1,250, on acceptance, for articles 800 to 1,200 words. Query with writing sample.

ASSOCIATIONS, ORGANIZATIONS

CALIFORNIA HIGHWAY PATROLMAN—2030 V St., Sacramento, CA 95818. Carol Perri, Ed. Articles, with photos, on transportation safety, California history, travel, consumerism, humor, general items, etc. Photos. Pays 2½¢ a word, extra for black-and-white photos, on publication.

CATHOLIC FORESTER—425 W. Shuman Blvd., Naperville, IL 60566. Barbara Cunningham, Ed. Official publication of the Catholic Order of Foresters, a fraternal life insurance company for Catholics. Articles and fiction that appeal to Middle America, to 2,000 words; no sex or violence. Pays 5¢ a word, on acceptance.

COLUMBIA—Box 1670, New Haven, CT 06507. Elmer Von Feldt, Ed. Journal of the Knights of Columbus. Articles, 2,500 to 3,500 words, on a wide variety of topics of interest to K. of C. members, their families, and the Catholic layman: current events, religion, education, art, etc. Must include substantial quotes from a variety of sources, and *must* be illustrated with color transparencies. Pays to $750, on acceptance.

THE ELKS MAGAZINE—425 W. Diversey Pkwy., Chicago, IL 60614. William J. Balles, Exec. Ed. Articles, 3,000 words, on business, sports, and topics of current interest; for non-urban audience with above-average income. Informative or humorous pieces, to 2,500 words. Pays $150 to $500 for articles, on acceptance. Query.

FIREHOUSE—33 Irving Pl., New York, NY 10003. Janet Kimmerly, Exec. Ed. Articles, 500 to 2,000 words: on-the-scene accounts of fires, trends in firefighting equipment, controversial fire service issues, and life styles of firefighters. Pays $100 to $200, on publication. Query.

FOCUS—Turnkey Publishing, 5332 Thunder Creek Rd., Suite 105, Austin, TX 78759. Greg Farman, Ed. Magazine of the North American Data General Users Group. Articles, 700 to 4,000 words, on Data General computers. Photos a plus. Pays to $100, on publication. Query required.

GEOBYTE—P.O. Box 797, Tulsa, OK 74101. Ken Milam, Man. Ed. Quarterly publication of the American Association of Petroleum Geologists. Articles, to 20 typed pages, on computer applications in exploration and production of oil, gas, and energy minerals. Pays varying rates, on acceptance. Query first.

KIWANIS—3636 Woodview Trace, Indianapolis, IN 46268. Chuck Jonak, Exec. Ed. Serious and light articles on a variety of topics of interest to an intelligent male audience—current business; humanitarian, youth, and community issues; family relations; recreation; consumer trends; education; etc. Readership is becoming increasingly international, and articles should reflect this, taking into account information from various regions of the world. Queries are preferred. Pays $400 to $1,000 for 2,000- to 3,000-word manuscripts, on acceptance.

THE LION—300 22nd St., Oak Brook, IL 60570. Robert Kleinfelder, Senior Ed. Official publication of Lions Clubs International. Articles, 800 to 2,000 words, and photo essays, on Club activities. Pays from $50 to $400, including photos, on acceptance. Query.

NRA NEWS—See *Restaurants USA.*

OPTIMIST MAGAZINE—4494 Lindell Blvd., St. Louis, MO 63108. James E. Braibish, Ed. Articles, to 1,500 words, on activities of local Optimist club, and techniques for personal and club success. Pays from $100, on acceptance. Query.

RESTAURANTS USA (formerly *NRA News*)—311 First St., N.W., Washington, DC 20001. Publication of the National Restaurant Association. Sylvia Rivchun, Ed. Articles, 2,500 to 3,500 words, on the food service and restaurant business. Pays $350 to $750, on acceptance. Query.

THE ROTARIAN—1600 Ridge Ave., Evanston, IL 60201. Willmon L. White, Ed. Articles, 1,200 to 2,000 words, on international social and economic issues, business and management, human relationships, travel, sports, environment, science and technology; humor. Pays good rates, on acceptance. Query.

WOODMEN OF THE WORLD MAGAZINE—1700 Farnam St., Omaha, NE 68102. Leland A. Larson, Ed. Publication of the Woodmen of the World Life Insurance Society. Articles on history, travel, sports, do-it-yourself projects, science, etc. Photos. Pays 5¢ a word, extra for photos, on acceptance.

RELIGIOUS AND DENOMINATIONAL

ADVANCE—1445 Boonville Ave., Springfield, MO 65802. Gwen Jones, Ed. Articles, 1,200 words, slanted to ministers, on preaching, doctrine, practice; how-to-do-it features. Pays 3¢ to 4¢ a word, on acceptance.

AGLOW MAGAZINE—P.O. Box I, Lynnwood, WA 98046-1557. Gwen Weising, Ed. First-person articles and testimonies, 1,000 to 2,000 words, that encourage, instruct, inform or entertain Christian women of all ages, and relate to the work of the Holy Spirit. Should deal with contemporary issues. Pays 8¢ to 10¢ a word, on acceptance. Queries are required.

AMERICA—106 W. 56th St., New York, NY 10019. George W. Hunt, S.J., Ed. Articles, 1,000 to 2,500 words, on current affairs, family life, literary trends. Pays $75 to $150, on acceptance.

AMERICAN BIBLE SOCIETY RECORD—1865 Broadway, New York, NY 10023. Clifford P. Macdonald, Man. Ed. Material related to work of American Bible Society: translating, publishing, distributing. Pays on acceptance. Query.

AMIT WOMAN—817 Broadway, New York, NY 10003. Micheline Ratzerdorfer, Ed. Articles, 1,000 to 2,000 words, of interest to Jewish women: Middle East, Israel, history, holidays, travel. Pays to $50, on publication.

ANNALS OF ST. ANNE DE BEAUPRÉ—P.O. Box 1000, St. Anne de Beaupré, Quebec, Canada G0A 3C0. Roch Achard, C.Ss.R., Ed. Articles, 1,100 to 1,200 words, on Catholic subjects and on St. Anne. Pays 2¢ to 4¢ a word, on acceptance.

BAPTIST LEADER—American Baptist Churches, USA, P.O. Box 851, Valley Forge, PA 19482-0851. L. Isham, Ed. Practical how-to or thought-provoking articles, 1,200 to 1,600 words, for local church education lay leaders and teachers. B & W photos a plus.

THE B'NAI B'RITH INTERNATIONAL JEWISH MONTHLY—1640 Rhode Island Ave., NW, Washington, DC 20036. Marc Silver, Ed. Original, lively articles, 500 to 3,000 words, on trends, politics, personalities, and culture of the Jewish community. Fiction, 1,000 to 4,000 words. Pays 10¢ to 25¢ a word, on publication. Query.

BREAD—6401 The Paseo, Kansas City, MO 64131. Karen De Sollar, Ed. Church of the Nazarene. Devotional, Bible study and Christian guidance articles, to 1,200 words, for teen-agers. Religious short stories, to 1,500 words. Pays from 3¢ a word for prose, on acceptance.

BRIGADE LEADER—Box 150, Wheaton, IL 60189. Steve Neideck, Man. Ed. Inspirational articles, 1,000 to 1,800 words, for Christian men who help boys. Pays $60 to $150. Query only.

CATECHIST—2451 E. River Rd., Dayton, OH 45439. Patricia Fischer, Ed. Informational and inspirational articles, 1,200 to 1,500 words, for Catholic teachers, coordinators, and administrators in religious education programs. Pays $25 to $75, on publication.

CATHOLIC DIGEST—P.O. Box 64090, St. Paul, MN 55164. Address Articles Ed. Articles, 2,000 to 2,500 words, on Catholic and general subjects. Fillers, to 300 words, on instances of kindness rewarded, for "Hearts Are Trumps"; accounts of good deeds, for "People Are Like That." Pays from $200 for original articles, $100 for reprints, on acceptance; $4 to $50 for fillers, on publication.

CATHOLIC FORESTER—425 W. Shuman Blvd., Naperville, IL 60566. Barbara Cunningham, Ed. Official publication of the Catholic Order of Foresters. General-interest articles and fiction, to 3,000 words; "Our purpose is to entertain and inform. No sex or violence." Religious angle not essential. Pays from 5¢ a word, on acceptance.

CATHOLIC LIFE—35750 Moravian Dr., Fraser, MI 48026. Robert C. Bayer, Ed. Articles, 600 to 1,200 words, on Catholic missionary work in Hong

Kong, India, Latin America, Africa, etc. Photos. No fiction or poetry. Pays 4¢ a word, extra for photos, on publication.

CATHOLIC NEAR EAST MAGAZINE—1011 First Ave., New York, NY 10022. Michael Healy, Ed. Articles, 1,000 to 1,800 words, on places, people, religious history, sacred ritual, artistic heritage, living culture, and faith traditions of the Balkans, Near East, Middle East, and India. Special interest in Eastern Catholic churches. Color photos illustrate all articles. Pays 10¢ a word, on publication. Query with SASE.

CATHOLIC TWIN CIRCLE—6404 Wilshire Blvd., Suite 900, Los Angeles, Ca 90048. Mary Louise Frawley, Ed. Articles and interviews of interest to Catholics, 1,000 to 2,000 words, with photos. Strict attention to Catholic doctrine required. Enclose SASE. Pays 10¢ a word, on publication.

CHARISMA/CHRISTIAN LIFE—190 N. Westmonte Dr., Altamonte Springs, FL 32714. Howard Earl, Sr. Ed. Charismatic/Evangelical Christian articles, 1,000 to 2,000 words, for developing the spiritual life. Photos. Pays varying rates, on publication.

THE CHRISTIAN CENTURY—407 S. Dearborn St., Chicago, IL 60605. James M. Wall, Ed. Ecumenical. Articles, 1,500 to 2,500 words, with a religious angle, on political and social issues, international affairs, culture, the arts. Poetry, to 20 lines. Photos. Pays about $25 per printed page, extra for photos, on publication.

CHRISTIAN HERALD—Chappaqua, NY 10514. Dean Merrill, Ed. Interdenominational. Articles, personal-experience pieces, to 1,500 words, on biblically-oriented topics. Short verse. Pays from 10¢ a word for full-length features, from $10 for short pieces, after acceptance. Query first.

CHRISTIAN SINGLE—127 Ninth Ave. N., Nashville, TN 37234. Cliff Allbritton, Ed. Articles, 600 to 1,200 words, on leisure activities, inspiring personal experiences, for Christian singles. Humor. Pays 5¢ a word, on acceptance. Query. Send SASE for guidelines.

CHRISTIANITY TODAY—465 Gundersen Dr., Carol Stream, IL 60188. Harold Smith, Man. Ed. Doctrinal, social issues and interpretive essays, 1,500 to 3,000 words, from evangelical Protestant perspective. Pays $300 to $500, on acceptance. Query required.

CHURCH ADMINISTRATION—127 Ninth Ave. N., Nashville, TN 37234. Gary Hardin, Ed. Southern Baptist. How-to articles, 1,500 to 1,800 words, on administrative planning, staffing, organization and financing. Pays 5¢ a word, on acceptance. Query.

CHURCH & STATE—8120 Fenton St., Silver Spring, MD 20910. Joseph L. Conn, Man. Ed. Articles, 600 to 2,600 words, on religious liberty and church-state relations issues. Pays varying rates, on acceptance. Query.

CHURCH EDUCATOR—Educational Ministries, 2861-C Saturn St., Brea, CA 92621. Robert G. Davidson, Ed. Articles, 200 to 3,000 words, with a "person-centered" approach to Christian education; articles on youth programs. How-to's for adult and juvenile Christian education. Pays 3¢ a word, on publication.

THE CHURCH HERALD—6157 28th St. SE, Grand Rapids, MI 49506. John Stapert, Ed. Reformed Church in America. Articles, 500 to 1,500 words, on Christianity and culture, politics, marriage and home. Pays $40 to $125, on acceptance.

THE CHURCH MUSICIAN—127 Ninth Ave. N., Nashville, TN 37234. W. M. Anderson, Ed. Articles for spiritual enrichment, testimonials, human-interest pieces, and other subjects of interest to music directors, pastors, organists, pianists, choir coordinators, and members of the music council in local churches. No clippings. Pays to 5¢ a word, on acceptance. Same address and requirements for *Glory Songs* (for adults) and *Opus One* and *Opus Two* (for teen-agers).

THE CIRCUIT RIDER—P.O. Box 801, Nashville, TN 37202. Keith Pohli, Ed. Articles for United Methodist Pastors, 800 to 1,600 words. Pays $25 to $100, on acceptance. Query, with SASE, preferred.

COLUMBIA—Box 1670, New Haven, CT 06507. Elmer Von Feldt, Ed. Knights of Columbus. Articles, 2,500 to 3,500 words, for Catholic families. Must be accompanied by color photos or transparencies. No fiction. Pays to $750 for articles and photos, on acceptance.

COMMENTARY—165 E. 56th St., New York, NY 10022. Norman Podhoretz, Ed. Articles, 5,000 to 7,000 words, on contemporary issues, Jewish affairs, social sciences, religious thought, culture. Serious fiction: book reviews. Pays on publication.

COMMONWEAL—15 Dutch St., New York, NY 10038. Peter Steinfels, Ed. Catholic. Articles, to 3,000 words, on political, religious, social and literary subjects. Pays 3¢ a word, on acceptance.

CONFIDENT LIVING—Box 82808, Lincoln, NE 68501. Norman A. Olson, Man. Ed. Articles, to 1,500 words, on relating biblical truths to daily living. Photos. Pays 4¢ to 10¢ a word, extra for photos, on acceptance. No simultaneous submissions or reprints. SASE required.

DAILY MEDITATION—Box 2710, San Antonio, TX 78299. Ruth S. Paterson, Ed. Inspirational nonsectarian articles, 650 to 2,000 words. Fillers, to 350 words; verse, to 20 lines. Pays ½¢ to 1½¢ a word for prose, 14¢ a line for verse, on acceptance.

DECISION—Billy Graham Evangelistic Association, 1300 Harmon Pl., Minneapolis, MN 55403. Roger C. Palms, Ed. Articles, Christian testimonials, 1,800 to 2,000 words. Poems, 4 to 20 lines, preferably free verse; narratives, 500 to 1,000 words. Pays varying rates, on publication.

THE DISCIPLE—Box 179, St. Louis, MO 63166. James L. Merrell, Ed. Articles on Christian living; devotionals, 150 words. Poetry; short humor. Pays $10 to $35 for articles, $2 to $10 for poetry, on publication.

DISCOVERIES—6401 The Paseo, Kansas City, MO 64131. Middler Editor. Fiction for children, grades 3 to 6, 400 to 500 words, defining Christian experiences and demonstrating Christian values and beliefs. Pays 3½¢ a word for first rights, 2¢ a word for second rights, on acceptance. Query.

ENGAGE/SOCIAL ACTION MAGAZINE—100 Maryland Ave. NE, Washington, DC 20002. Lee Ranck, Ed. Articles, 1,800 to 2,000 words, on social issues for concerned persons of faith. Pays $75 to $100, on publication.

THE EPISCOPALIAN—1201 Chestnut St., Philadelphia, PA 19107. Judy Foley, Man. Ed. Articles to 2,000 words, that show Episcopalians solving problems; action stories; profiles. Pays $25 to $100, on publication.

THE EVANGEL—901 College Ave., Winona Lake, IN 46590. Vera Bethel, Ed. Free Methodist. Personal-experience articles, 1,000 words. Short, devotional items, 300 to 500 words. Fiction, 1,200 words, on Christian solutions to problems. Serious poetry, 8 to 12 lines. Pays $25 for articles, $35 to $40 for fiction, $5 for poetry, on publication. Return postage required.

EVANGELICAL BEACON—1515 E. 66th St., Minneapolis, MN 55423. George Keck, Ed. Evangelical Free Church. Articles, 250 to 1,750 words, on religious topics; testimonials; pieces on current issues from an evangelical perspective; short inspirational and evangelistic devotionals. Pays 3¢ to 4¢ a word, on publication. Send SASE for writers' guidelines.

FAITH TODAY—Box 8800, Sta. B, Willowdale, Ont., Canada M2K 2R6. Brian C. Stiller, Ed.; Audrey Dorsch, Man. Ed. Articles, 1,500 words, on current issues relating to the church in Canada. Pays negotiable rates, on publication. Queries are preferred.

THE FUNDAMENTALIST JOURNAL—2220 Langhorne Rd., Lynchburg, VA 24514. Deborah Huff, Ed. Articles, 500 to 2,500 words, that examine matters of contemporary interest to all Fundamentalists: news articles, profiles, family living, and human-interest pieces; moral and religious issues; Bible studies. Payment varies and is made on publication.

THE GEM—Box 926, Findlay, OH 45839. Marilyn Rayle Kern, Ed. Articles, 300 to 1,600 words, and fiction, 1,000 to 1,600 words; true-to-life experiences of God's help, of healed relationships, and of growing maturity in faith. For adolescents through senior citizens. Pays $15 for articles and fiction, $7.50 to $10 for fillers, after publication.

GLORY SONGS—See *The Church Musician.*

GROUP, THE YOUTH MINISTRY MAGAZINE—Box 481, Loveland, CO 80539. Joani Schultz, Ed. Dir. Interdenominational magazine for leaders of high-school-age Christian youth groups. Articles, 500 to 1,700 words, about successful youth groups or youth group projects. Short how-to pieces, to 300 words, for "Try This One"; tips and news items, to 500 words, for "News, Trends, and Tips." Pays to $150 for articles, $15 to $25 for department pieces, on acceptance. Guidelines available.

GUIDE—Review and Herald Publishing Co., 55 W. Oak Ridge Dr., Hagerstown, MD 21740. Stories and articles, 1,000 to 2,000 words for Christian youth, ages 10 to 14. Pays 3¢ to 4¢ a word, on acceptance.

GUIDEPOSTS—747 Third Ave., New York, NY 10017. True first-person stories, 250 to 1,500 words, stressing how faith in God helps people cope with life. Anecdotal fillers, to 250 words. Pays $100 to $400, $10 to $50 for fillers, on acceptance.

HIS MAGAZINE—See *U (University) Magazine.*

HOME LIFE—127 Ninth Ave. N., Nashville, TN 37234. Mary P. Darby, Ass't. Ed. Southern Baptist. Articles, preferably personal-experience, and fiction, to 2,000 words, on Christian marriage, parenthood, and family relationships. Human-interest pieces, 200 to 500 words; cartoons and short verse. Pays to 5¢ a word, on acceptance.

INSIDE—226 S. 16th St., Philadelphia, PA 19102. Jane Biberman, Ed. Articles, 1,500 to 3,000 words, and fiction, 2,000 to 3,000 words, of interest to Jewish men and women. Pays $100 to $500, on acceptance. Query.

INSIGHT—55 West Oak Ridge Dr., Hagerstown, MD 21740. Christopher Blake, Ed. Seventh-day Adventist. Personal-experience narratives, articles and humor, to 1,500 words, for high school students. Parables; shorts; poetry. Pays 10¢ to 15¢ a word, extra for photos, on acceptance. Query.

INTERACTION—See *Teachers Interaction*.

KEY TO CHRISTIAN EDUCATION—8121 Hamilton Ave., Cincinnati, OH 45231. Virginia Beddow, Ed. Articles, on teaching methods, and success stories, for workers in Christian education. Pays varying rates, on acceptance.

LIBERTY MAGAZINE—6840 Eastern Ave. N.W., Washington, DC 20012. Roland R. Hegstad, Ed. Timely articles, to 2,500 words, and photo essays, on religious freedom and church-state relations. Pays 6¢ to 8¢ a word, on acceptance. Query.

LIGHT AND LIFE—901 College Ave., Winona Lake, IN 46590. Robert Haslam, Ed. Fresh, lively articles about practical Christian living, and sound treatments of vital issues facing the Evangelical in contemporary society. Pays 4¢ a word, on publication. Query.

LIGUORIAN—Liguori, MO 63057. Rev. Norman J. Muckerman, Ed. Francine O'Connor, Man. Ed. Catholic. Articles and short stories, 1,500 to 2,000 words, on Christian values in modern life. Pays 10¢ to 12¢ a word, on acceptance. Buys all rights.

LIVE—1445 Boonville Ave., Springfield, MO 65802. John T. Maempa, Adult Ed. Sunday school paper for adults. Fiction, 1,500 to 2,000 words, and articles, 1,000 to 1,500 words, on applying Bible principles to everyday living. Pays 2¢ to 3¢ a word, on acceptance. Send SASE for guidelines first.

LIVING WITH CHILDREN—127 Ninth Ave. N., Nashville, TN 37234. SuAnne Bottoms, Ed. Articles, 800, 1,450 or 2,000 words, on parent-child relationships, told from a Christian perspective. Pays 5¢ a word, after acceptance.

LIVING WITH PRESCHOOLERS—127 Ninth Ave., N., Nashville, TN 37234. SuAnne Bottoms, Ed. Articles, 800, 1,450 or 2,000 words, and fillers, to 300 words, for Christian families. Pays 5¢ a word, on acceptance.

LIVING WITH TEENAGERS—127 Ninth Ave. N., Nashville, TN 37234. Articles, told from a Christian perspective for parents of teenagers; first-person approach preferred. Poetry, 4 to 16 lines. Pays 5¢ a word, on acceptance.

THE LOOKOUT—8121 Hamilton Ave., Cincinnati, OH 45231. Mark A. Taylor, Ed. Articles, 1,000 to 1,500 words, on families and people overcoming problems by applying Christian principles. Inspirational or humorous shorts, 500 to 800 words; fiction. Pays 4¢ to 6¢ a word, on acceptance.

THE LUTHERAN—8765 W. Higgins Rd., Chicago, IL 60631. Edgar R. Trexler, Ed. Articles, to 2,000 words, on Christian ideology, personal religious experiences, family life, church, and community. Pays $100 to $400, on acceptance. Query.

MARRIAGE AND FAMILY LIVING—Division of Abbey Press, St. Meinrad, IN 47577. Kass Dotterweich, Man. Ed. Expert advice, personal-experience articles, 1,500 to 2,000 words, on marriage and family relationships. Family humor, 1,000 to 2,000 words. Pays 7¢ a word, on acceptance.

MATURE LIVING—127 9th Ave. N., Nashville, TN 37234. Jack Gulledge, Ed. General-interest pieces, travel articles, nostalgia and fiction, 900 words, for Christian senior adults 60 years and older. Also, profiles recognizing a senior adult for an accomplishment or interesting or unusual experience, 25 lines; must include a B/W action photo. Brief, humorous items for "Cracker Barrel."

Pays 5¢ a word, $25 for profiles, $5 for "Cracker Barrel," on acceptance. Buys all rights.

MATURE YEARS—201 Eighth Ave. S., Nashville, TN 37203. Jack Gilbert, Ed. United Methodist. Articles on retirement or related subjects, 1,500 to 2,000 words. Humorous and serious fiction, 1,500 to 1,800 words, for adults. Poetry, to 14 lines. Pays 4¢ a word, 50¢ a line for poetry, on acceptance.

MESSENGER OF THE SACRED HEART—661 Greenwood Ave., Toronto, Ont., Canada M4J 4B3. Articles and short stories, about 1,500 words, for American and Canadian Catholics. Pays from 2¢ a word, on acceptance.

MIDSTREAM—515 Park Ave., New York, NY 10022. Jewish-interest articles and book reviews. Fiction, to 3,000 words, and poetry. Pays 5¢ a word, after publication.

MODERN LITURGY—160 E. Virginia St., #290, San Jose, CA 95112. Ken Guentert, Ed. Creative material for worship services; religious parables, to 1,000 words; how-to's, essays on worship, 750 to 1,600 words. Plays. Poetry. Pays in copies.

MOMENT—3000 Conn. Ave., Suite 300, Washington, DC 20008. Charlotte Anker, Man. Ed. Sophisticated articles and some fiction, 2,000 to 5,000 words, on Jewish topics. Pays $150 to $400, on publication.

MOMENTUM—National Catholic Educational Assn., Suite 100, 1077 30th St., NW, Washington, DC 20007-3852. Patricia Feistritzer, Ed. Articles, 500 to 1,500 words, on outstanding programs, issues and research in education. Book reviews. Pays 2¢ a word, on publication. Query.

MOODY MONTHLY—820 N. La Salle Dr., Chicago, IL 60610. Mike Umlandt, Man. Ed. Articles, 1,200 to 1,800 words, on the Evangelical Christian experience in school, the home and the workplace. Pays 10¢ to 15¢ a word, on acceptance. Query.

THE NATIONAL CHRISTIAN REPORTER—See *The United Methodist Reporter.*

NEW ERA—50 E. North Temple, Salt Lake City, UT 84150. Brian Kelly, Ed. Articles, 150 to 3,000 words, and fiction, to 3,000 words, for young Mormons. Poetry; photos. Pays 5¢ to 10¢ a word, 25¢ a line for poetry, on acceptance. Query.

NEW WORLD OUTLOOK—475 Riverside Dr., Rm. 1351, New York, NY 10115. George M. Daniels, Ed. Articles, 1,500 to 2,500 words, on Christian missions, religious issues and public affairs. Pays on publication.

OBLATES MAGAZINE—15 S. 59th St., Belleville, IL 62222. Address Jacqueline Lowery Corn. Articles, 500 to 600 words, for middle-age to older Catholics, which inspire, uplift, and motivate through positive Christian values in relation to everyday life. Inspirational poetry, to 16 lines. Pays $75 for articles, $25 for poems, on acceptance. Guidelines.

OPUS ONE AND OPUS TWO—See *The Church Musician.*

OUR FAMILY—Box 249, Battleford, Sask., Canada SOM OEO. Nestor Gregoire, Ed. Articles, 1,000 to 3,000 words, for Catholic families, on modern society, family, marriage, and current affairs. Fiction, 1,000 to 3,000 words. Humor; verse. Pays 7¢ to 10¢ a word for articles and fiction, 75¢ to $1 a line for poetry, on acceptance. Send SAS with *international reply coupons* for guidelines.

617

OUR SUNDAY VISITOR—Huntington, IN 46750. Robert Lockwood, Ed. In-depth features, 1,000 to 1,200 words, on the Catholic Church in America today. Pays $150 to $250, on acceptance.

PARISH FAMILY DIGEST—Noll Plaza, Huntington, IN 46750. Louis F. Jacquet, Ed. Articles, 750 to 900 words, fillers, and humor, for Catholic families and parishes. Pays 5¢ a word, on acceptance.

PARTNERSHIP—Christianity Today, Inc., 465 Gundersen Dr., Carol Stream, IL 60188. Sharon Donohue, Man. Ed. Articles, 500 to 2,000 words, related to marriage, for men and women who wish to fortify their relationship. Cartoons, humor, fillers. Pays $50 to $300, on acceptance. Queries are required.

PENTECOSTAL EVANGEL—1445 Boonville Ave., Springfield, MO 65802. Richard Champion, Ed. Assemblies of God. Religious personal-experience and devotional articles, 500 to 1,500 words. Verse, 12 to 30 lines. Pays 4¢ a word, on publication.

PRESBYTERIAN SURVEY—341 Ponce de Leon Ave. NE, Atlanta, GA 30365. Vic Jameson, Ed. Articles, to 1,500 words, of interest to members of the Presbyterian Church or ecumenical individuals. Pays to $200, on acceptance. Query.

PRESENT TENSE—165 E. 56th St., New York, NY 10022. Murray Polner, Ed. Serious articles, 2,000 to 3,000 words, with photos, on news concerning Jews throughout the world; first-person encounters and personal-experience pieces. Literary-political reportage. Contemporary themes only. Pays $200 to $300, on publication. Query.

THE PRIEST—200 Noll Plaza, Huntington, IN 46750. Articles, to 2,500 words, on life and ministry of priests, current theological developments, etc., for priests, permanent deacons, and seminarians. Pays $35 to $100, on acceptance.

PURPOSE—616 Walnut Ave., Scottdale, PA 15683-1999. James E. Horsch, Ed. Articles, 350 to 1,200 words, on Christian discipleship themes, with good photos; pieces of history, biography, science, hobbies, from a Christian perspective. Fiction, 1,200 words, on Christian problem solving. Poetry, 3 to 12 lines. Pays to 5¢ a word, to $1 per line for poetry, on acceptance.

QUEEN—26 S. Saxon Ave., Bay Shore, NY 11706. James McMillan, S.M.M., Ed. Publication of Montfort Missionaries. Articles and fiction, 1,000 to 2,000 words, relating to the Virgin Mary. Poetry. Pays varying rates on acceptance.

THE QUIET HOUR—850 N. Grove Ave., Elgin, IL 60120. John A. Barbous, Ed. Short devotionals. Pays $15, on acceptance. Queries are required.

THE RECONSTRUCTIONIST—270 W. 89th St., New York, NY 10024. Dr. Jacob Staub, Ed. Articles and fiction, 2,000 to 3,000 words, relating to Judaism. Poetry. Pays $18 to $36, on publication.

ST. ANTHONY MESSENGER—1615 Republic St., Cincinnati, OH 45210. Norman Perry, O.F.M., Ed. Catholic. Articles, 2,500 to 3,500 words, on personalities, major movements, education, family, and social issues. Human-interest pieces. Humor. Fiction. Pays 12¢ a word, on acceptance. Query on nonfiction.

ST. JOSEPH'S MESSENGER—P.O. Box 288, Jersey City, NJ 07303. Sister Ursula Maphet, Ed. Inspirational articles, 500 to 1,000 words, and fiction, 1,000 to 1,500 words. Verse, 4 to 40 lines. Query first.

SEEK—8121 Hamilton Ave., Cincinnati, OH 45231. Eileen H. Wilmoth, Ed. Articles and fiction, to 1,200 words, on inspirational and controversial topics and timely religious issues. Christian testimonials. Pays up to 3¢ a word, on acceptance.

SHARING THE VICTORY—8701 Leeds Rd., Kansas City, MO 64129. Skip Stogsdill, Ed. Articles, interviews, and profiles, to 800 words, for coed Christian athletes and coaches in high school and college. Pays from $75, on publication. Queries required.

SIGNS OF THE TIMES—P.O. Box 7000, Boise, ID 83707. Kenneth J. Holland, Ed. Feature articles on Christians who have performed community services; current issues from a Biblical perspective; health, home, marriage, human-interest pieces; inspirational articles, 500 to 2,000 words. Pays 12¢ to 15¢ a word, on acceptance. Seventh-day Adventists.

SISTERS TODAY—The Liturgical Press, St. John's Abbey, Collegeville, MN 56321. Sister Mary Anthony Wagner, O.S.B., Ed. Articles, 500 to 3,500 words, on Roman Catholic theology, religious issues for women and the Church. Poetry, to 34 lines. Pays $5 per printed page, $10 per poem, on publication. Send articles to Editor at St. Benedict's Convent, St. Joseph, MN 56374. Send poetry to Sister Audrey Synnott, R.S.M., 1437 Blossom Rd., Rochester, NY 14610.

SOCIAL JUSTICE REVIEW—3835 Westminster Pl., St. Louis, MO 63108. Rev. John H. Miller, C.S.C., Ed. Articles, 2,000 to 3,000 words, on social problems in light of Catholic teaching and current scientific studies. Pays 2¢ a word, on publication.

SPIRITUAL LIFE—2131 Lincoln Rd. N.E., Washington, DC 20002-1199. Christopher Latimer, O.C.D., and Steven Payne, O.C.D., Co-editors. Professional religious journal. Religious essays, 3,000 to 5,000 words, on spirituality in contemporary life. Pays from $50, on acceptance. Guidelines.

SPIRITUALITY TODAY—7200 W. Division St., River Forest, IL 60305. Richard Woods, O.P., Ed. Quarterly. Biblical, liturgical, theological, ecumenical, historical, and biographical articles, 4,000 words, about the challenges of contemporary Christian life. No poetry. Pays from 1¢ a word, on publication. Guidelines available.

STANDARD—6401 The Paseo, Kansas City, MO 64131. Address Ed. Articles, 300 to 1,500 words: true experiences; poetry to 20 lines; fiction, 800 to 1,700 words, with Christian emphasis but not preachy; fillers, puzzles, cryptograms of Scripture verses or inspiring quotes, cartoons in good taste. Pays 3½¢ a word, on acceptance.

SUNDAY DIGEST—850 N. Grove Ave., Elgin, IL 60120. Articles, 900 to 1,500 words, on Christian faith in contemporary life; inspirational and how-to articles; free-verse poetry. Anecdotes, 500 words. Pays 10¢ a word, on acceptance.

SUNDAY SCHOOL COUNSELOR—1445 Boonville Ave., Springfield, MO 65802. Sylvia Lee, Ed. Articles, 1,000 to 1,500 words, on teaching and Sunday school people, for local Sunday school teachers. Pays 3¢ to 5¢ a word, on acceptance.

SUNSHINE MAGAZINE—Litchfield, IL 62056. Address Ed. Inspirational articles, to 600 words. Short stories, 1,000 words and juveniles, 400 words. No heavily religious material or "born-again" pieces. Pays varying rates, on acceptance.

TEACHERS INTERACTION (formerly *Interaction*)—1333 S. Kirkwood Rd., St. Louis, MO 63122. Martha S. Jander, Ed. Articles, 800 to 1,200 words; how-to pieces, to 100 words, for Lutheran volunteer church school teachers. Pays $10 to $35, on publication. Limited free-lance market.

TEENS TODAY—Church of the Nazarene, 6401 The Paseo, Kansas City, MO 64131. Karen De Sollar, Ed. Short stories that deal with teens demonstrating Christian principles, 1,200 to 1,500 words. Pays 3¢ a word, on acceptance.

THEOLOGY TODAY—Box 29, Princeton, NJ 08542. Craig Dykstra, Ed. Articles, to 3,500 words, or to 1,500 words, on theology, religion and related social issues. Literary criticism. Pays $50 to $100, on publication.

U MAGAZINE (formerly *His Magazine*)—P.O. Box 1450, Downers Grove, IL 60515. Verne Becker, Ed. First-person pieces, to 2,000 words, on Christian living in college, for a student audience. Pays 2¢ to 7¢ a word, on acceptance.

THE UNITED CHURCH OBSERVER—85 St. Clair Ave. E., Toronto, Ont., Canada M4T 1M8. Factual articles, 1,500 to 2,500 words, on religious trends, human problems, social issues. No poetry. Pays after publication. Query.

UNITED EVANGELICAL ACTION—P.O. Box 28, Wheaton, IL 60189. Don Brown, Ed. National Assn. of Evangelicals. News-oriented expositions and editorials, 750 to 1,000 words, on current events of concern and consequence to the evangelical church. Pays about 7¢ to 10¢ a word, on publication. Query with writing samples required.

THE UNITED METHODIST REPORTER—P.O. Box 660275, Dallas, TX 75266–0275. Spurgeon M. Dunnman III, Ed. John Lovelace, Man. Ed. United Methodist. Religious features, to 500 words. Religious verse, 4 to 12 lines. Photos. Pays 4¢ a word, on publication. Send for guidelines. Same address and requirements for *The National Christian Reporter* (interdenominational).

UNITED SYNAGOGUE REVIEW—155 Fifth Ave., New York, NY 10010. Ruth M. Perry, Ed. Articles 1,000 to 1,200 words, on issues of interest to the conservative Jewish community. Pays after publication. Query.

UNITY MAGAZINE—Unity School of Christianity, Unity Village, MO 64065. Pamela Yearsley, Ed. Inspirational and metaphysical articles, 500 to 1,500 words. Pays 5¢ to 9¢ a word, on acceptance.

VIRTUE—P.O. Box 850, Sisters, OR 97759. Articles and fiction for Christian women. Query only, except for pieces for "One Woman's Journal" and "In My Opinion."

VISTA—P.O. Box 50434, Indianapolis, IN 46250–0434. Articles and adult fiction, on current Christian concerns and issues. First-person pieces, 750 to 1,500 words. Opinion pieces from an Evangelical perspective, 500 to 750 words. Pays from 3¢ a word.

THE YOUNG SALVATIONIST—The Salvation Army, 799 Bloomfield Ave., Verona, NJ 07044. Robert R. Hostetler, Ed. Articles 1,000 to 1,200 words, teaching the Christian view to everyday living, for teen-agers. Short shorts, first-person testimonies, 600 to 800 words. Pays 3¢ to 5¢ a word, on acceptance. SASE required. Guidelines.

THE YOUNG SOLDIER—The Salvation Army, 799 Bloomfield Ave., Verona, NJ 07044. Robert R. Hostetler, Ed. For children 6 to 12. Must carry a definite Christian message, or teach a Biblical truth. Fiction, 800 to 1,000 words. Some poetery. Fillers, puzzles, etc. Pays 3¢ a word, $3 to $5 for fillers, puzzles, on acceptance. Guidelines.

ACCENT ON LIVING—P.O. Box 700, Bloomington, IL 61702. Raymond C. Cheever, Pub./Ed. Articles, 250 to 1,000 words, about physically disabled people—their careers, recreation and sports, self-help devices, and ideas that can make daily routine easier. Good photos a plus. Pays 10¢ a word, on publication. Query.

AEROBICS & FITNESS—See *American Fitness.*

AIM PLUS—Arthritis Information Magazine, 45 W. 34th St., New York, NY 10001. Tim Moriarty, Ed.; Gayle Turim, Assoc. Ed. Well-researched articles, 800 to 1,500 words, about arthritis, how to cope with it physically and emotionally; new treatments; exceptional people, etc. Also, articles on general health and general-interest pieces. Pays $400 to $750, on acceptance. Query required. Guidelines.

AMERICAN BABY—249 W. 17th St., New York, NY 10011. Judith Nolte, Ed. Articles 1,000 to 2,000 words, for new or expectant parents, on prenatal infant care. Pays varying rates, on acceptance.

AMERICAN FITNESS (formerly *Aerobics & Fitness*)—15250 Ventura Blvd., Suite 310, Sherman Oaks, CA 91403. Peg Angsten, Ed. Articles, 500 to 1,500 words, on exercise, health, sports, nutrition, etc. Illustrations, photos, cartoons.

AMERICAN HEALTH: FITNESS OF BODY AND MIND—80 Fifth Ave., New York, NY 10011. Address Editorial Dept. Features, 1,000 to 3,000 words, on recent developments in nutrition, exercise, medicine, prevention and psychology. Shorter news items on similar topics: medical advances, consumer health, and life styles. Pays from $125 per manuscript page, on acceptance. Query required.

AMERICAN JOURNAL OF NURSING—555 W. 57th St., New York, NY 10019. Mary B. Mallison, R.N. Articles 1,500 to 2,000 words, with photos, on nursing. Query.

AMERICAN MEDICAL NEWS—535 N. Dearborn St., Chicago, IL 60610. Flora Johnson Skelly, Ass't Exec. Ed. Features, 1,000 to 3,000 words of interest to physicians across the country. Socio-economic angle preferred. No pieces on clinical treatments or research. Query required. Pays $50 to $1,000, on acceptance.

ARTHRITIS TODAY—The Arthritis Foundation, 1314 Spring St., NY, Atlanta, GA 30309. Cindy Thompson, Ed. Self-help, how-to, and inspirational articles (1,000 to 2,500 words); "slice-of-life" fiction (750 to 2,500 words), and short fillers (100 to 250 words) to help people with arthritis live more productive, independent and pain-free lives. Pays from $350, on acceptance. Query.

BESTWAYS—1501 S. Sutro Terrace, P.O. Box 2028, Carson City, NV 89701. Barbara Bassett, Ed. Articles, 1,500 to 2,000 words, on health, food, life styles, exercise, nutrition. Pays from $150, on publication. Query.

CHILDBIRTH EDUCATOR—249 W. 17th St., New York, NY 10011. Marsha Rehns, Ed. Articles, 2,000 words, on maternal and fetal health, childcare, child development, and teaching techniques for teachers of childbirth and baby care classes. Pays $500, on acceptance. Query with detailed outline.

DANCE EXERCISE TODAY—2437 Morena Blvd., 2nd fl., San Diego, CA 92110. Patricia Ryan, Ed. Practical articles, 1,000 to 3,000 words, on new programs, business tips, nutrition, sports medicine, and dance exercise techniques. Payment negotiable, on acceptance. Query preferred.

EAST WEST: THE JOURNAL OF NATURAL HEALTH & LIVING—17 Station St., Box 1200, Brookline, MA 02147. Features, 1,500 to 2,500 words, on holistic health, natural foods, the environment, etc. Material for "Body," "Healing," "In the Kitchen," and "Beauty and Fitness." Interviews. Photos. Pays 7¢ to 12¢ a word, extra for photos, on publication.

EXPECTING—685 Third Ave., New York, NY 10017. Evelyn A. Podsiadlo, Ed. Articles, 700 to 1,800 words, for expectant mothers. Pays $150 to $350, on acceptance.

HEALTH—3 Park Ave., New York, NY 10016. Articles, 800 to 2,500 words, on medicine, nutrition, fitness, emotional and psychological well-being. Pays $150 to $1,200, on acceptance. Query.

HEALTH PROGRESS—4455 Woodson Rd., St. Louis, MO 63134. Judy Cassidy, Ed. Journal of the Catholic Health Association. Features, 1,500 to 2,000 words, on hospital management and administration, medical-moral questions, technological developments and their impacts, nursing, and financial and human resource management. Pays by arrangement. Query.

HIPPOCRATES—475 Gate Five Rd., Ste. 100, Sausalito, CA 94965. John Kiefer, Editorial Coordinator. Articles, 850 to 5,000 words, on health and medicine; pieces for "Food," "Sports," "Drugs," "Mind," "Family," and "Housecalls" departments. Pays 50¢ to 80¢ a word, on acceptance. Query required.

HOSPITALS—211 E. Chicago Ave., Chicago, IL 60611. Frank Sabatino, Ed. Articles, 800 to 1,500 words, for hospital administrators, on financing, staffing, coordinating, and providing facilities for health care services. Pays varying rates, on acceptance. Query.

LET'S LIVE—P.O. Box 74908, Los Angeles, CA 90004. Debra A. Fields, Man. Ed. Articles, 800 to 1,050 words, on preventive medicine and nutrition, alternative medicine, diet, exercise, recipes, and natural beauty. Pays $150, on publication. Query.

MUSCULAR DEVELOPMENT—Strength and Health Publishing, P.O. Box 1707, York, PA 17405. Jan Dellinger, Ed. Articles, 5 to 10 typed pages, geared to serious weight training athletes, on any aspects of competitive body building and powerlifting. Photos. Pays $50 to $200, on publication. Query.

NEW BODY—888 Seventh Ave., New York, NY 10106. Constance Boze, Ed. Well-researched, service-oriented articles, 1,000 to 2,000 words, on exercise, nutrition, diet and health for women aged 18 to 35. Writers should have some background in or knowledge of the health field. Pays $250 to $500, on publication. Query.

NURSING 88—1111 Bethlehem Pike, Springhouse, PA 19477. Maryanne Wagner, Ed. Most articles are clinically oriented, and assigned to nursing experts. No poetry. Pays $25 to $350, on publication. Query.

NURSING HOMES—Centaur & Co., 5 Willowbrook Ct., Potomac, MD 20854. William D. Magnes, Ed.-in-Chief. Articles 1,000 to 2,500 words, of interest to administrators, managers, and supervisory personnel in nursing homes; human-interest, academic and clinical pieces; book reviews, 250–300 words. Pays $50 for articles, $30 for reviews, on acceptance. Photos, graphics welcome.

NURSING LIFE—1111 Bethlehem Pike, Springhouse, PA 19477. Tony DeCrosta, Man. Ed. Articles, 12 to 15 double-spaced pages, by nurses, lawyers, management consultants, psychologists, with practical, inspirational, and humorous advice for staff nurses. Pays negotiable rates, on publication. Query.

NURSINGWORLD JOURNAL—470 Boston Post Rd., Weston, MA 02193. Eileen Devito, Man. Ed. Articles, 500 to 1,500 words, for and by nurses and nurse-educators, on aspects of current nursing issues. Pays from 25¢ per column inch, on publication.

PATIENT CARE—690 Kinderkamack Rd., Oradell, NJ 07649. Robert L. Edsall, Ed. Articles on medical care, for physicians. Pays varying rates, on publication. Query; all articles assigned.

THE PHYSICIAN AND SPORTSMEDICINE—4530 W. 77th St., Minneapolis, MN 55435. Cindy Christian Rogers, Features Ed. News and feature articles, 500 to 3,000 words, on fitness, sport, and exercise. Medical angle necessary. Pays $150 to $900, on acceptance. Guidelines.

A POSITIVE APPROACH—1600 Malone, Municipal Airport, Millville, NJ 08332. Ann Miller, Ed. Articles, 500 words, on all aspects of the positive-thinking disabled/handicapped person's private and business life. Well-researched articles of interest to the visually and hearing impaired, veterans, the arthritic, and all categories of the disabled and handicapped, on interior design, barrier-free architecture, gardening, wardrobe, computers, and careers. Pays 10¢ a word, on publication.

RECOVERY—P.O. Box 31329, Seattle, WA 98103. Neil Scott, Ed. Articles, to 1,500 words, for recovering alcoholics, on how to meet the challenge of sobriety. First-person recovery stories, with helpful how-to's for others, 500 to 1,000 words. Poetry and fillers. Send SASE for complete guidelines.

RN MAGAZINE—Oradell, NJ 07649. Articles, to 2,000 words, preferably by R.N.s, on nursing, clinical care, etc. Pays 10¢ to 15¢ a word, on acceptance. Query.

RX BEING WELL—800 Second Ave., New York, NY 10017. Mark Deitch, Ed. Articles, to 2,000 words, providing authoritative information on disease prevention, and current medical topics. No personal-experience pieces. Most articles co-authored by doctors. Pays from $500, a few weeks after acceptance. Query with SASE.

RX HOME CARE—P.O. Box 2178, Santa Monica, CA 90406–2178. Les Plesko, Ed. Articles, 1,500 to 2,000 words, on marketing aspects of home health care and rehabilitation equipment. Pays 12¢ a word, on acceptance. Query first.

VEGETARIAN TIMES—P.O. Box 570, Oak Park, IL 60603. Paul Obis, Pub. Articles, 750 to 3,000 words, on health, nutrition, exercise and fitness, meatless food, etc. Personal-experience and historical pieces, profiles. Pays $25 to $300, on publication.

VIBRANT LIFE—55 W. Oak Ridge Dr., Hagerstown, MD 21740. Features 1,000 to 2,800 words, on total health: physical, mental, and spiritual. No disease-related articles or manuscripts geared to people over 50. Seeks upbeat articles on how to live happier and healthier lives; Christian slant. Pays $150 to $450, on acceptance.

VIM & VIGOR—2040 W. Bethany Home Rd., Suite 105, Phoenix, AZ 85015. Leo Calderella, Ed. Positive articles, with accurate medical facts, on health and fitness, 1,200 words. Pays $250 to $350, on publication.

THE WALKING MAGAZINE—711 Boylston St., Boston, MA 02116. Bradford Ketchum, Ed. Articles, 1,500 to 3,000 words, on fitness, health, equipment, nutrition, travel and adventure, famous walkers, and other walking-related topics. Shorter pieces, 500 to 1,500 words, and essays for "Ramblings" page. Photos welcome. Pays $500 to $1,000 for features, $100 to $350 for department pieces. Guidelines.

YOUR HEALTH—1720 Washington Blvd., Box 10010, Ogden, UT 84409. Karen E. Hill, Ed. Articles, 1,200 words, on individual health care needs: prevention, treatment, fitness, nutrition, etc. Photos required. Pays 15¢ a word, after acceptance. Guidelines.

EDUCATION

AMERICAN SCHOOL & UNIVERSITY—401 N. Broad St., Philadelphia, PA 19108. Dorothy Wright, Ed. Articles and case studies, 1,200 to 1,500 words, on design, construction, operation and management of school and college facilities. Payment varies.

CAPSTONE JOURNAL OF EDUCATION—P.O. Box Q, Tuscaloosa, AL 35487. Alexia M. Kartis, Asst. Ed. Articles, to 5,000 words, on contemporary ideas in educational research.

CHANGE—4000 Albemarle St. N.W., Suite 500, Washington, DC 20016. Reports, 1,500 to 2,000 words, on programs, people and institutions of higher education. Intellectual essays, 3,000 to 5,000 words, on higher education today. Payment varies.

CLASSROOM COMPUTER LEARNING—Peter Li, Inc., 2169 Francisco Blvd. E., Suite A-4, San Rafael, CA 94901. Holly Brady, Ed. Articles, to 3,000 words, for teachers of grades K–12, related to uses of computers in the classroom: human-interest and philosophical articles, how-to pieces, software reviews, and hands-on ideas. Payment varies, on acceptance.

ELECTRONIC EDUCATION—Electronic Communications, 1311 Executive Center Dr., Suite 220, Tallahassee, FL 32301. Cindy Whaley, Man. Ed. Articles, to 1,000 words, for K–12 educators and administrators, on the uses of technology in education. Fillers. Query. Pays $100 to $200, on publication.

FOUNDATION NEWS—1828 L St. N.W., Washington, DC 20036. Arlie W. Schardt, Ed. Articles, to 2,000 words, on national or regional activities supported by, or of interest to, grant makers. Pays to $1,500, on acceptance. Query.

HOME EDUCATION MAGAZINE—P.O. Box 1083, Tonasket, WA 98855. Mark J. Hegener, Ed. Positive, informative articles, 1,500 words, on alternative education, including home schooling, alternative and community schools, cooperative learning, and other educational options. Pays after publication.

THE HORN BOOK MAGAZINE—Park Sq. Bldg., 31 St. James Ave., Boston, MA 02116. Anita Silvey, Ed. Articles, 600 to 2,800 words, on books for young readers, and related subjects, for librarians, teachers, parents, etc. Pays $25 per printed page, on publication. Query.

INDUSTRIAL EDUCATION—31600 Telegraph Rd., Suite 200, Birmingham, MI 48010. Kelley Harding, Ed. Educational and instructional articles, 1,000 to 1,500 words, for secondary and post-secondary technical education classes. Photos and drawings. Pays $30, on publication.

INSTRUCTOR—HBJ Publications, 7500 Old Oak Blvd., Cleveland, OH 44130. How-to articles on elementary classroom teaching, and computers in the classroom, with practical suggestions and project reports. Pays varying rates, on acceptance.

JOURNAL OF CAREER PLANNING & EMPLOYMENT—62 Highland Ave., Bethlehem, PA 18017. Patricia A. Sinnott, Man. Ed. Articles 3,000 to 4,000 words, on topics related to college, career planning, placement, and recruitment. Pays $200 to $400, on acceptance. Query first with clips. Guidelines available.

KEY TO CHRISTIAN EDUCATION—8121 Hamilton Ave., Cincinnati, OH 45231. Virginia Beddow, Ed. Articles, 600 to 2,000 words, on Christian education; tips for teachers in the local church. Pays varying rates, on acceptance.

LEARNING 88/89—1111 Bethlehem Pike, Springhouse, PA 19477. Charlene Gaynor, Ed. How-to, why-to, and personal-experience articles, to 3,000 words, for teachers of grades K–8. Tested classroom ideas for curriculum roundups, to 600 words. Pays to $300, on acceptance. Query.

MEDIA & METHODS—1429 Walnut St., Philadelphia, PA 19102. Michele Sokoloff, Ed. Articles, 1,200 to 1,500 words, on media, technologies, and methods used to enhance instruction and learning in junior and senior high school classrooms. Pays $25 to $75, on publication. Query.

THE MINORITY ENGINEER—44 Broadway, Greenlawn, NY 11740. James Schneider, Ed. Articles, 1,000 to 3,000 words, for college students, on career opportunities in engineering, scientific and technological fields; techniques of job hunting; developments in and applications of new technologies. Interviews. Profiles. Pays 10¢ a word, on publication. Query. Same address and requirements for *The Woman Engineer.*

PHI DELTA KAPPAN—8th and Union St., Box 789, Bloomington, IN 47402. Robert W. Cole, Jr., Ed. Articles, 1,000 to 4,000 words, on educational research, service, and leadership; issues, trends, and policy. Pays from $250, on publication.

SCHOOL ARTS MAGAZINE—50 Portland St., Worcester, MA 01608. David W. Baker, Ed. Articles, 800 to 1,000 words, on art education with special application to the classroom. Photos. Pays varying rates, on publication.

SCHOOL SHOP—Box 8623, Ann Arbor, MI 48107. Alan H. Jones, Pub./ Exec. Ed. Articles, 1 to 10 double-spaced typed pages, for teachers and administrators in industrial, technical, and vocational educational fields, with particular interest in classroom projects and computer uses. Pays $25 to $150, on publication. Guidelines.

TEACHER UPDATE—P.O. Box 469, Belmont, MA 02178. Nick Roes, Ed. Original suggestions for classroom activities. Each page should have a unifying theme, preferably related to specific monthly issue. Pays $20 per published page, on acceptance. Readers are mostly preschool teachers.

TEACHING AND COMPUTERS—Scholastic, Inc., 730 Broadway, New York, NY 10003. Mickey Revenaugh, Ed. Articles, 300 to 500 words, for computer-using teachers in grades K–8. Payment varies, on acceptance.

TODAY'S CATHOLIC TEACHER—26 Reynolds Ave., Ormond Beach, FL 32074. Ruth A. Matheny, Ed. Articles, 600 to 800 words and 1,200 to 1,500 words, on Catholic education, parent-teacher relationships, innovative teaching, teaching techniques, etc. Pays $15 to $75, on publication.

WILSON LIBRARY BULLETIN—950 University Ave., Bronx, NY 10452.

Milo Nelson, Ed. Articles, 2,500 to 3,000 words, on libraries, communications, and information systems. News, reports, features. Pays from $250, extra for photos, on acceptance.

THE WOMAN ENGINEER—See *The Minority Engineer.*

FARMING AND AGRICULTURE

ACRES USA—10008 E. 60 Terrace, Kansas City, MO 64133. Articles on biological agriculture. Pays 6¢ a word, on publication. Query required.

AMERICAN BEE JOURNAL—51 N. Second St., Hamilton, IL 62341. Joe M. Graham, Ed. Articles on beekeeping, for professionals. Photos. Pays 75¢ per column inch, extra for photos, on publication.

BEEF—1999 Shepard Rd., St. Paul, MN 55116. Paul D. Andre, Ed. Articles on beef cattle feeding, cowherds, stocker operations, and related phases of the cattle industry. Pays to $300, on acceptance.

BUCKEYE FARM NEWS—Ohio Farm Bureau Federation, 35 E. Chestnut St., Columbus, OH 43216. George Robey, Man. Ed. Articles and humor, to 1,000 words, related to agriculture. Pays on publication. Query.

THE EVENER—See *Rural Heritage.*

FARM & RANCH LIVING—5400 S. 60th St., Greendale, WI 53129. Bob Ottum, Man. Ed. Articles, 2,000 words, on rural people and situations; nostalgia pieces; profiles of interesting farms and farmers, ranches and ranchers. Poetry. Pays $15 to $400, on acceptance and on publication.

FARM FAMILY AMERICA—1999 Shepard Rd., St. Paul, MN 55116. George Ashfield, Ed. Articles 1,200 to 1,500 words, covering life styles, activities, and travel-related subjects of interest to farmers and farm families. Pays $350 to $700, on publication. Query first.

FARM FUTURES—Plaza East Office Center, 330 E. Kilbourn Ave., Suite 200, Milwaukee, WI 53202. Claudia Waterloo, Ed. Articles, to 1,500 words, on marketing of agricultural commodities, farm business issues, management success stories, and the use of commodity futures and options by agricultural producers. Query with outline.

FARM INDUSTRY NEWS—1999 Shepard Rd., St. Paul, MN 55116. Joe Degnan, Ed. Articles for farmers, on new products, buying, machinery, equipment, chemicals, and seeds. Pays $175 to $400, on acceptance. Query required.

FARM JOURNAL—Washington Sq., Philadelphia, PA 19105. Earl Ainsworth, Ed. Articles, 500 to 1,500 words, with photos, on the business of farming, for farmers. Pays 20¢ to 50¢ a word, on acceptance. Query.

FARM SUPPLIER—Mt. Morris, IL 61054. K. McMillan, Ed. Articles, 600 to 1,800 words, preferably with color photos, on retail farm trade products: feed, fertilizer, agricultural chemicals, etc. Photos. Pays $100 to $200 on acceptance.

FLORIDA GROWER & RANCHER—1331 N. Mills Ave., Orlando, FL

32803. Frank H. Abrahamson, Ed. Articles and case histories on farmers, growers and ranchers. Pays on publication. Query; buys little freelance material.

THE FURROW—Deere & Company, John Deere Rd., Moline, IL 61265. George Sollenberger, Exec. Ed. Specialized, illustrated articles on farming. Pays to $1,000, on acceptance.

GURNEY'S GARDENING NEWS—Gurney Seed and Nursery Co., 2nd and Capitol, Yankton, SD 57079. Pattie Vargas, Ed. Practical articles on specific gardening topics and gardener profiles, 1,000 words. Children's section and "News from Gurney Gardeners." Pays 10¢ a word. Write for themes and guidelines first, then query.

HARROWSMITH—Camden House Publishing Ltd., Camden East, Ont., Canada KOK 1J0. Wayne Grady, Ed. Articles, 250 to 4,000 words, on country life, homesteading, husbandry, organic gardening and alternative energy with a Canadian slant. Pays $100 to $1,500, on acceptance. Query.

HARROWSMITH/USA—The Creamery, Ferry Rd., Charlotte, VT 05445. Tom Rawls, Man. Ed. Investigative pieces, 4,000 to 5,000 words, on ecology, energy, health, gardening, do-it-yourself projects, and the food chain. Short pieces for "Screed" (opinions), and "Gazette" (news briefs). Pays $500 to $1,500 for features, $50 to $600 for department pieces, on acceptance. Query required. Send SASE for guidelines.

NORDEN NEWS—601 W. Cornhusker Hwy., Lincoln, NE 68501. Gary Svatos, Ed. Technical articles, 1,200 to 1,500 words, and clinical features, 500 words, on veterinary medicine. Photos. Pays $200 to $250, $100 for shorter pieces, extra for photos, on publication.

THE OHIO FARMER—1350 W. Fifth Ave., Columbus, OH 43212. Andrew L. Stevens, Ed. Articles on farming, rural living, etc., in Ohio. Pays $20 per column, on publication.

PEANUT FARMER—P.O. Box 95075, Raleigh, NC 27625. Sid Reynolds, Ed. Articles, 500 to 1,500 words, on production and management practices in peanut farming. Pays $50 to $350, on publication.

PENNSYLVANIA FARMER—704 Lisburn Rd., Camp Hill, PA 17011. John R. Vogel, Ed. Articles on farmers in PA, NJ, DE, MD, and WV; farm operations and successful farm management concepts.

RURAL HERITAGE (formerly *The Evener*)—P.O. Box 287, Marion, IA 52302. Allan Young, Ed./Pub. How-to and feature articles, 300 to 2,500 words, related to draft horses, mules, and oxen. Pays 3¢ to 10¢ a word, $5 to $25 for photos, on acceptance. Queries preferred.

SHEEP! MAGAZINE—Box 329, Jefferson, WI 53549. Dave Thompson, Ed. Articles, to 1,500 words, on successful shepherds, woolcrafts, sheep raising and sheep dogs. B/W photos. Pays $2 per column inch, extra for photos, on publication.

SMALL ACREAGE MANAGEMENT—Rt. 1, Box 143, Silex, MO 63377. Kelly Klober, Ed. Articles, 500 to 800 words, on land uses for small farm owners. Pays 1¢ to 3¢ a word, on publication. Query.

SMALL FARMER'S JOURNAL—438 Soup Creek Rd., Reedsport, OR 97467. How-to's, humor, practical work horse information, livestock and produce marketing, and articles appropriate to the independent family farm. Pays negotiable rates, on publication. Query first.

SUCCESSFUL FARMING—1716 Locust St., Des Moines, IA 50336. Loren Kruse, Man. Ed. Articles on farm management, production, marketing, and machinery; also farm personalities, health and leisure topics. Pays varying rates, on acceptance.

WALLACES FARMER—#501, 1501 42nd St., W. Des Moines, IA 50265. Monte Sesker, Ed. Features, 600 to 700 words, on farming in IA, MN, NE, KS, ND and SD; methods and equipment; interviews with farmers. Pays 4¢ to 5¢ a word, on acceptance. Query.

THE WESTERN PRODUCER—Box 2500, Saskatoon, Saskatchewan, Canada S7K 2C4. Attn. Man. Ed. Articles, to 1,000 words, on agricultural and rural subjects, preferably with a Canadian slant. Photos. Pays from 10¢ a word, $15 for b&w photos and cartoons, on acceptance.

ENVIRONMENT, CONSERVATION, WILDLIFE, NATURAL HISTORY

AMERICAN FORESTS—1516 P St. NW, Washington, DC 20005. Bill Rooney, Ed. Well-documented articles, to 2,000 words, with photos, on recreational and commercial uses and management of forests. Photos. Pays on acceptance.

AMERICAN LAND FORUM—See *The New American Land.*

THE AMICUS JOURNAL—National Resources Defense Council, 122 E. 42nd St., Rm. 4500, New York, NY 10168. Peter Borrelli, Ed. Investigative articles related to national and international environmental policy. Pays on acceptance.

ANIMAL KINGDOM—New York Zoological Society, Bronx, NY 10460. Eugene J. Walter, Jr., Ed.-in-Chief. Articles, 1,000 to 2,500 words, with photos, on natural history, ecology and animal behavior, preferably based on original scientific research. No articles on pets. Pays $250 to $750, on acceptance.

THE ATLANTIC SALMON JOURNAL—1435 St. Alexandre, Suite 1030, Montreal, Quebec, Canada H3A 2G4. Joanne Eidinger, Ed. Material related to Atlantic salmon: Conservation, ecology, politics, biology, etc. How-to's, anecdotes. Articles, 1,500 to 3,000 words; short fillers and poetry, 50 to 100 words. Pays $100 to $350, on publication.

ENVIRONMENTAL ACTION—1525 New Hampshire Ave., NW, Washington, DC 20036. News and features, varying lengths, on a broad range of political and/or environmental topics: energy, toxics, self-sufficiency, etc. Book reviews; environmentally-related consumer goods. Pays 7¢ to 10¢ a word, extra for photos, on publication. Query required.

EQUINOX—7 Queen Victoria Rd., Camden East, Ont., Canada K0K 1J0. Jody Morgan, Ass't. Ed. Articles, 3,000 to 6,000 words, on popular geography, wildlife, astronomy, science, and adventure. Department pieces, 300 to 500 words, for "Nexus" (science and medicine) and "Habitat" (man-made and natural environment). Pays $1,250 to $2,000 for features, $100 to $300 for short pieces, on acceptance.

HARROWSMITH/USA—The Creamery, Ferry Rd., Charlotte, VT 05445. Tom Rawls, Man. Ed. Investigative articles, 4,000 to 5,000 words, on ecology, energy, and the food chain. Pays $500 to $1,500 for features, on acceptance. Query first.

INTERNATIONAL WILDLIFE—See *National Wildlife.*

THE LOOKOUT—Seamen's Church Institute, 50 Broadway, New York, NY 10004. Carlyle Windley, Ed. Factual articles on the sea. Features, 200 to 1,500 words, on the merchant marines, sea oddities, etc. Photos. Pays $25 to $100, on publication.

NATIONAL GEOGRAPHIC MAGAZINE—17th and M Sts. N.W., Washington, DC 20036. Wilbur E. Garrett, Ed. First-person, general-interest, heavily-illustrated articles on science, natural history, exploration, and geographical regions. Query required.

NATIONAL PARKS MAGAZINE—1015 31st St., NW, Washington, DC 20007. Michele Strutin, Ed. Articles, 1,000 to 2,000 words, on natural history, wildlife, outdoors activities, travel and conservation as they relate to national parks: illustrated features on the natural, historic and cultural resources of the National Park System. Pieces about legislation and other issues and events related to the parks. Pays $100 to $400, on acceptance. Query. Send for guidelines.

NATIONAL WILDLIFE and **INTERNATIONAL WILDLIFE**—8925 Leesburg Pike, Vienna, VA 22184. Mark Wexler, Man. Ed., *National Wildlife*. Jon Fisher, Man. Ed. *International Wildlife*. Articles 1,000 to 2,500 words, on wildlife, conservation, environment; outdoor how-to pieces. Photos. Pays market rates, on acceptance. Query.

NATURAL HISTORY—American Museum of Natural History, Central Park West at 79th St., New York, NY 10024. Alan Ternes, Ed.-in-Chief. Informative articles, to 3,000 words, by experts, on anthropology and natural sciences. Pays $800 for features, on acceptance. Query.

THE NEW AMERICAN LAND (formerly *American Land Forum*)—1516 P St., NW, Washington, DC 20005. Sara Ebenreck, Ed. Articles, 2,500 words, on U.S. land issues, achievements, leadership profiles, or land use topics. Pays $15 to $300. Guidelines.

OCEANS—2001 W. Main St., Stamford, CT 06902. Michael Robbins, Ed. Articles, to 5,000 words, with photos, or marine life, oceanography, marine art, undersea exploration, seaports, conservation. Pays on acceptance. Query. Guidelines available.

OUTDOOR AMERICA—1701 N. Ft. Myer Dr., Suite 1100, Arlington, VA 22209. Quarterly publication of the Izaak Walton League of America. Articles, 1,500 to 2,000 words, on natural resource conservation issues and outdoor recreation; especially fishing, hunting and camping. Pays from to 15¢ a word, for features, on publication. Query Articles Ed. with published clippings.

SEA FRONTIERS/SEA SECRETS—3979 Rickenbacker Causeway, Virginia Key, Miami, FL 33149. Jean Bradfisch, Exec. Ed. Illustrated articles, 500 to 3,000 words, on scientific advances related to the sea, biological, physical, chemical, or geological phenomena, ecology, conservation, etc., written in a popular style for lay readers. Send SASE for guidelines. Pays $50 to $300, on acceptance. Query.

SIERRA—730 Polk St., San Francisco, CA 94109. James Keough, Ed. Articles, 1,000 to 2,500 words, on environmental and conservation topics. Book reviews and children's dept. Photos. Pays from $200 to $500, extra for photos, on acceptance. Query.

SMITHSONIAN MAGAZINE—900 Jefferson Dr., Washington, DC 20560. Marlane A. Liddell, Articles Ed. Articles on natural history, physical science, etc. Query.

SPORTS AFIELD—250 W. 55th St., New York, NY 10019. Tom Paugh, Ed. Articles, 2,000 words, with quality photos, on hunting, fishing, natural history, personal experiences, new hunting/fishing spots. How-to pieces; humor; fiction. Pays top rates, on acceptance.

MEDIA AND THE ARTS

AHA! HISPANIC ARTS NEWS—Assoc. of Hispanic Arts, 200 East 87th, New York, NY 10028. Dolores Prida, Ed. Interviews and book reviews with Hispanic authors, to 500 words. Pays on publication. Query required.

AIRBRUSH ACTION—317 Cross St., Lakewood, NJ 08701. Articles, 500 to 3,000 words, on airbrush and art-related topics. Pays $75 to $300, on publication. Query.

THE AMERICAN ART JOURNAL—40 W. 57th St., 5th Floor, New York, NY 10019. Jane Van N. Turano, Ed. Quarterly. Scholarly articles, 2,000 to 10,000 words, on American art of the 17th through 20th centuries. Photos. Pays $200 to $400, on acceptance.

AMERICAN FILM—3 E. 54th St., New York, NY 10022. Peter Biskind, Ed. Feature articles, 2,500 to 4,000 words, on film and television. Profiles; news items; reports. Columns, 100 to 1,500 words. Photos. Pays from $50 to $1,500. Query preferred.

AMERICAN INDIAN ART MAGAZINE—7314 E. Osborn Dr., Scottsdale, AZ 85251. Roanne P. Goldfein, Man. Ed. Detailed, specific articles, 10 typed pages, on American Indian arts—painting, carving, beadwork, basketry, textiles, ceramics, jewelry, etc. Pays varying rates for articles, on publication. Query.

AMERICAN THEATRE—355 Lexington Ave., New York, NY 10017. Jim O'Quinn, Ed. Features, 500 to 4,000 words, on the theatre and theatre-related subjects. Payment negotiable, on publication. Query.

ART & ANTIQUES—89 Fifth Ave., New York, NY 10003. Judith Cressy, Man. Ed. Personal narratives, informatively related to a particular kind of art or antique; investigative subjects and feature related to arts/antiques, 1,500 words. Pays 50¢ a word, on publication. Query in writing only.

ART GALLERY INTERNATIONAL—P.O. Box 52940, Tulsa, OK 74152. Debra Carter Nelson, Ed. Articles on artists and collecting, 1,000 to 1,500 words. Pays 10¢ a word or $50 a page, on publication. Query first.

ARTSATLANTIC—P.O. Box 848, Charlottetown, P.E.I., Canada C1A 7L9. Joseph Sherman, Ed. Articles, 800 to 2,500 words, on visual, performing and literary arts, crafts in Atlantic Canada. Also, "idea and concept" articles of universal appeal. Pays from 10¢ per word, on publication. Query.

BLUEGRASS UNLIMITED—Box 111, Broad Run, VA 22014. Peter V. Kuykendall, Ed. Articles, to 3,500 words, on bluegrass and traditional country music. Photos. Pays 6¢ to 8¢ a word, extra for photos.

BROADCASTER—7 Labatt Ave., Toronto, Ont., Canada M5A 3P2. Daphne Lavers, Ed. Articles, 500 to 2,000 words, on communications business in Canada. Pays from $250, on publication. Query.

CLAVIER MAGAZINE—200 Northfield Rd., Northfield, IL 60093. Barbara Kreader, Ed. Practical articles, 2,000 words, for keyboard performers and teachers. Fiction and poetry. Pays $35 to $45 per column inch, on publication.

DANCE MAGAZINE—33 W. 60th St., New York, NY 10023. William Como, Ed.-in-Chief. Features on dance, personalities, techniques, health issues, and trends. Photos. Query; limited free-lance market.

DANCE TEACHER NOW—University Mall, Suite 2, 803 Russell Blvd., Davis, CA 95616. Martin A. David, Ed. Articles, 1,500 to 2,500 words, for professional dance teachers and dancers, on practical aspects of a dance teacher's professional life, and political or economic issues related to the dance profession. Profiles on teachers or schools. Must be thoroughly researched. Pays $50 to $300, on acceptance.

DARKROOM PHOTOGRAPHY—9021 Melrose Ave., Suite 203, Los Angeles, CA 90069. Richard Senti, Ed. Articles on post-camera photographic techniques, 1,000 to 2,500 words, with photos, for all levels of photographers. Pays $100 to $500. Query.

DESIGN GRAPHICS WORLD—Communications Channels, 6255 Barfield Rd., Atlanta, GA 30328. James J. Maivald, Ed. Articles, 1,500 to 2,000 words, on news, trends, and current methods of engineering architecture, computer graphics, reprographics, and related design fields. Pays on publication. Query required.

THE DRAMA REVIEW—School of the Arts, New York Univ., 721 Broadway, New York, NY 10003. Richard Schechner, Ed. Quarterly journal of performance. Essays, interviews, letters, and editorials on all aspects of theatre, drawing from anthropology, performance theory, ethology, psychology, and politics. Pays 2¢ a word, on publication.

DRAMATICS—3368 Central Pkwy., Cincinnati, OH 45225. Don Corathers, Ed. Articles, 1,000 to 3,500 words, on the performing arts: theater, puppetry, dance, mime, one-act plays, etc. Emphasis on performance skills for high school and college student actors. Pays $25 to $200, on acceptance.

THE ENGRAVERS JOURNAL—26 Summit St., Box 318, Brighton, MI 48116. Michael J. Davis, Man. Ed. Articles, varying lengths, on topics related to the engraving industry. Pays $60 to $175, on acceptance. Query first.

EXHIBIT—1776 Lake Worth Dr., Lake Worth, FL 33460. Chas Brunk, Ed. Articles, to 800 words, with color transparencies, on fine arts, techniques, new movements, profiles of artists. Query.

FILM QUARTERLY—Univ. of California Press, 2120 Berkeley Way, Berkeley CA 94720. Ernest Callenbach, Ed. Film reviews, historical and critical articles, production projects, to 5,000 words. Pays on publication. Query.

FLUTE TALK—Instrumentalist Publishing Co., 200 Northfield Rd., Northfield, IL 60093. Polly Hansen, Ed. Articles, 6 to 12 typed pages, on flute performance and pedagogy; flute-related poetry; fillers; photos and line drawings. Thorough knowledge of the instrument a must. Pays $45 per page, on publication. Queries preferred.

FRETS—20085 Stevens Creek, Cupertino, CA 95014. Phil Hood, Ed. Articles, 750 to 3,000 words, for musicians, on acoustic string instruments, instrument making and repair, music theory and technique. Covers jazz, folk, bluegrass, classical, etc. Profiles of musicians and instruments. Pays $175 to $350, on acceptance. Query.

FUNCTIONAL PHOTOGRAPHY—210 Crossways Park Dr., Woodbury, NY 11797. David A. Silverman, Sr. Ed. Articles on use of photography and other image-making processes in science, medicine, research, etc. Photos. Pays varying rates, on publication. Query.

GLASS STUDIO—Publication Development, Box 23383, Portland, OR 97223. Pat Watters, Assoc. Ed. Articles, 1,500 to 2,500 words, for professional glass artists: profiles, techniques, business tips, etc. Pays $50 to $300, on publication. Query with SASE.

GUITAR PLAYER MAGAZINE—20085 Stevens Creek, Cupertino, CA 95014. Tom Wheeler, Ed. Articles, 1,500 to 5,000 words, on guitarists, guitars, and related subjects. Pays $75 to $300, on acceptance. Buys one-time and reprint rights.

HIGH FIDELITY—825 Seventh Ave., New York, NY 10019. Michael Riggs, Ed. Articles, 2,000 to 3,000 words, on stereo equipment, video equipment, and classical and popular recorded music. Pays on acceptance. Query.

HOME VIEWER MAGAZINE—Home Viewer Publications, 11 N. 2nd St., Philadelphia, PA 19106. Bruce Apar, Ed. Feature articles, reviews, celebrity interviews, commentary on home video/audio and all forms of popular entertainment. Pays from $100 for features, $35 for reviews, on publication. Query.

HORIZON—P.O. Drawer 30, Tuscaloosa, AL 35402. Articles 1,500 to 3,500 words, on art, film, literature, photography, dance, music, theater, and other cultural happenings. Pays from $300 on publication. Query Senior Editor.

INTERNATIONAL MUSICIAN—Suite 600, Paramount Bldg., 1501 Broadway, New York, NY 10036. Kelly L. Castleberry II, Ed. Articles, 1,500 to 2,000 words, for professional musicians. Pays varying rates, on acceptance. Query.

JAZZIZ—P.O. Box 8309, Gainesville, FL 32605. Michael Jarrett, Ed. Feature articles on jazz: interviews, profiles, concept pieces. Departments include "Reviews," "Videos," and "Audio." Emphasis on new releases. Pays varying rates, on acceptance. Query.

KEYBOARD MAGAZINE—20085 Stevens Creek, Cupertino, CA 95014. Dominic Milano, Ed. Articles, 1,000 to 5,000 words, on keyboard instruments and players. Photos. Pays $125 to $500, on acceptance. Query.

MEDIA HISTORY DIGEST—c/o Editor & Publisher, 11 W. 19th St., New York, NY 10011. Hiley H. Ward, Ed. Articles, 1,500 to 2,000 words, on the history of media for wide consumer interest. Puzzles and humor related to media history. Pays varying rates, on publication. Query.

MODERN DRUMMER—870 Pompton Ave., Cedar Grove, NJ 07009. Ronald L. Spagnardi, Ed. Articles, 500 to 2,000 words, on drumming; how-to's, interviews. Pays $50 to $500, on publication.

MUSIC MAGAZINE—P.O. Box 96, Station R, Toronto, Ont., Canada M4G 3Z3. Articles, with photos, on musicians, conductors, and composers, for all classical music buffs. Pays $150 to $800, on publication. Query required. Guidelines.

MUSICAL AMERICA—825 Seventh Ave., New York, NY 10019. Shirley Fleming, Ed. Authoritative articles, 1,000 to 1,500 words, on classical music subjects. Pays around 15¢ a word, on acceptance.

NEW ENGLAND ENTERTAINMENT—P.O. Box 735, Marshfield, MA 02050. Paul J. Reale, Ed. News features and reviews on arts and entertainment in New England. Light verse. Pays $10 to $25, $1 to $2 for verse, on publication.

OPERA NEWS—The Metropolitan Opera Guild, 1865 Broadway, New

York, NY 10023. Jane L. Poole, Man. Ed. Articles, 600 to 2,500 words, on all aspects of opera. Pays 13¢ a word for articles, on publication. Query.

PERFORMANCE—1020 Currie St., Fort Worth, TX 76107. Don Waitt, Pub./Ed.-in-Chief. Reports on the touring industry: concert promoters, booking agents, concert venues and clubs, as well as support services, such as lighting, sound and staging companies. Pays 35¢ per column line, on publication.

PETERSEN'S PHOTOGRAPHIC—8490 Sunset Blvd., Los Angeles, CA 90069. Bill Hurter, Ed. Articles and how-to pieces, with photos, on still, video, studio and darkroom photography, for beginners and advanced amateurs. Pays $60 per printed page, on publication.

PHOTOMETHODS—One Park Ave., New York, NY 10016. Lief Ericksenn, Ed. Articles, 1,500 to 3,000 words, on innovative techniques in imaging (still, film, video), working situations, and management. Pays from $75, on publication. Query.

PLAYBILL—71 Vanderbilt Ave., New York, NY 10169. Joan Alleman, Ed.-in-Chief. Sophisticated articles, 700 to 2,000 words, with photos, on theater and subjects of interest to theater-goers. Pays $100 to $500, on acceptance.

POPULAR PHOTOGRAPHY MAGAZINE—One Park Ave., New York, NY 10016. Sean Callahan, Ed. How-to articles, 500 to 2,000 words, for amateur photographers. Query first with outline and photos.

PREVUE—P.O. Box 974, Reading, PA 19603. J. Steranko, Ed. Lively articles on films and filmmakers; entertainment features and celebrity interviews. Length: 4 to 25 pages. Pays varying rates, on acceptance. Query with clips.

PROFESSIONAL STAINED GLASS—270 Lafayette St., Rm. 701, New York, NY 10012. Chris Peterson, Man. Ed. Practical articles of interest to stained glass professionals. No historical articles. Pays $100 to $150, on publication. Query required.

ROLLING STONE—745 Fifth Ave., New York, NY 10151. Articles on American culture, art, and politics. Query required. Rarely accepts free-lance material.

SOAP OPERA DIGEST—254 W. 31st St., New York, NY 10001. Lynn Davey, Man. Ed. Features, to 1,500 words, for people interested in daytime and nighttime soaps. Pays from $225, on acceptance. Query with clips.

SUN TRACKS—Box 2510, Phoenix, AZ 85002. Andy Van De Voorde, Music Ed. Music section of *New Times*. Long and short features, record reviews and interviews. Pays $15 to $150, on publication. Query.

TECHNICAL PHOTOGRAPHY—210 Crossways Park Drive, Woodbury, NY 11797. David A. Silverman, Sr. Ed. Features, 8 to 10 double-spaced pages, on applications and techniques of imaging for staff image producers. Some material on audio-visuals, film, and video. Pays varying rates, on publication. Query.

THEATRE CRAFTS MAGAZINE—135 Fifth Ave., New York, NY 10010. Patricia MacKay, Ed. Articles, 500 to 2,500 words, for professionals in the business, design, and production of theatre, film, video, and the performing arts. Pays on acceptance. Query.

VIDEO MAGAZINE—460 W. 34th St., New York, NY 10001. Judith Hudnutt Sawyer, Ed.-in-Chief. How-to and service articles on home video equipment, technology, and programming. Interviews and human-interest features related to non-broadcast television, from 800 to 2,500 words. Pays varying rates, on acceptance. Query.

VIDEOMAKER—P.O. Box 4591, Chico, CA 95927. Bradley Kent, Ed. Authoritative, how-to articles geared at amateur video camera users: instructionals, innovative applications, tools and tips, industry developments, new products, etc. Pays varying rates, on publication. Queries preferred.

HOBBIES, CRAFTS, COLLECTING

AMERICAN CLAY EXCHANGE—P.O. Box 2674, La Mesa, CA 92044-0700. Susan N. Cox, Ed. Articles, from 400 words, for collectors and/or dealers of American-made pottery, with an emphasis on antiques and collectibles. Photos. Pays from $5 for short items, to $100 for thoroughly-researched articles, on acceptance. Buys all rights.

ANTIQUE MONTHLY—P.O. Drawer 2, Tuscaloosa, AL 35402. Articles, 750 to 1,200 words, on the exhibition and sales (auctions, antique shops, etc.) of decorative arts and antiques more than 100 years old, with photos or slides. Pays varying rates, on publication. Query.

THE ANTIQUE TRADER WEEKLY—Box 1050, Dubuque, IA 52001. Kyle D. Husfloen, Ed. Articles, 1,000 to 2,000 words, on all types of antiques and collectors' items. Photos. Pays from $5 to $150, extra for photos, on publication. Query preferred. Buys all rights.

ANTIQUES & AUCTION NEWS—P.O. Box 500, Mount Joy, PA 17552. Weekly newspaper. Factual articles, 600 to 1,500 words, on antiques, collectors, and collections. Photos. Pays $12.50 to $15, on publication.

ANTIQUEWEEK—P.O. Box 90, Knightstown, IN 46148. Tom Hoepf, Ed. Articles, 500 to 1,500 words, on antiques, collectibles, restorations, genealogy. Auction and show reports. Photos. Pays from $1 per inch, $75 to $125 for in-depth articles, on publication. Query.

AOPA PILOT—421 Aviation Way, Frederick, MD 21701. Magazine of the Aircraft Owners and Pilots Assn. Thomas A. Horne, Ed. Articles, to 2,500 words, with photos, on general aviation for beginning and experienced pilots. Pays to $750.

THE AUTOGRAPH COLLECTOR'S MAGAZINE—P.O. Box 55328, Stockton, CA 95205. Joe Kraus, Ed. Articles, 100 to 1,500 words, on all areas of autograph collecting: preservation, framing and storage, specialty collections, documents and letters, collectors and dealers. Queries preferred. Pays 5¢ a word, on publication.

BIRD WATCHER'S DIGEST—P.O. Box 110, Marietta, OH 45740. Mary B. Bowers, Ed. Articles, 600 to 3,000 words, on bird-watching experiences and expeditions; information about rare sightings; updates on endangered species. Pays to $50, on publication.

THE BLADE MAGAZINE—P.O. Box 22007, Chattanooga, TN 37422. J. Bruce Voyles, Ed. Articles, 500 to 3,000 words: Historical pieces on knives and old knife factories, etc.; interviews with knifemakers; how-to pieces. Pays from 5¢ a word, on publication.

CHESS LIFE—186 Route 9W, New Windsor, NY 12550. Larry Parr, Ed. Articles, 500 to 3,000 words, for members of the U.S. Chess Federation, on news, profiles, technical aspects of chess. Features on all aspects of chess—

history, humor, puzzles, etc. Fiction, 500 to 2,000 words, related to chess. Photos. Pays varying rates, on acceptance. Query; limited freelance market.

CLASSIC AMERICA—P.O. Box 2516, Westfield, NJ 07090. Articles, 500 to 1,600 words, related to America from 1800 to 1930: historical events, restorations, antiques, collectibles, and life styles. Pays 8¢ to 20¢ a word, on acceptance. "Articles with a 'how it can still be enjoyed today' slant are of particular interest."

COLLECTOR EDITIONS QUARTERLY—170 Fifth Ave., New York, NY 10010. Articles, 750 to 1,500 words, on collectibles: glass, porcelain, *objets d'art,* modern Americana, etc. Pays $150 to $350, within 30 days of acceptance. Query.

COUNTRY NEEDLECRAFT—See *Women's Circle Country Needlecraft.*

CRAFTS 'N THINGS—14 Main St., Dept. W, Park Ridge, IL 60068. Nancy Tosh, Ed. How-to articles on all kinds of crafts projects, with instructions. Pays $35 to $200, on publication. Send manuscript with instructions and photograph of the finished item.

DOLLS, THE COLLECTOR'S MAGAZINE—170 Fifth Ave., New York, NY 10010. Krystyna Poray Goddu, Ed. Articles, 500 to 2,500 words, for knowledgeable doll collectors: sharply focused with a strong collecting angle, and concrete information: value, identification, dollmaking, restoration, etc. Pays $100 to $350, after acceptance. Query.

FINESCALE MODELER—1027 N. Seventh St., Milwaukee, WI 53233. How-to articles for people who make nonoperating scale models of aircraft, automobiles, boats, figures. Photos and drawings should accompany articles. One-page model-bulding hints and tips. Pays from $30 per published page, on acceptance. Query preferred.

GAMBLING TIMES—1018 N. Cole Ave., Hollywood, CA 90038. Len Miller, Ed. Gambling-related articles, 1,000 to 6,000 words. Pays $100 to $150, on publication.

GAMES—810 Seventh Ave., New York, NY 10019. Articles on games and puzzles. Quizzes, tests, brainteasers, etc. Photos. Pays varying rates, on acceptance.

HANDS-ON ELECTRONICS—500-B Bi County Blvd., Farmingdale, NY 11735. Julian S. Martin, Ed. Features, 1,500 to 2,500 words, for the electronics activist. Pays from $250, on acceptance. Query.

THE HOME SHOP MACHINIST—2779 Aero Park Dr., Box 1810, Traverse City, MI 49685. Joe D. Rice, Ed. How-to articles, on precision metalworking and foundry work. Accuracy and attention to detail a must. Pays $40 per published page, extra for photos and illustrations, on publication. Send SASE for writer's guidelines.

THE LEATHER CRAFTSMAN—Box 1386, Fort Worth, TX 76101. Nancy Sawyer, Ed. Articles on leather crafters, helpful hints and projects of varying difficulty. Pays $50 to $200, on publication.

LOST TREASURE—P.O. Box 937, Bixby, OK 74008. Kathy Dyer, Man. Ed. Factual articles 1,000 to 3,000 words, on treasure hunting, metal detecting, prospecting techniques, and legendary lost treasure. Profiles. Photos. Pays 3¢ a word, extra for photos, on publication.

MINIATURE COLLECTOR—170 Fifth Ave., New York, NY 10010. Articles, 800 to 1,200 words, with photos, on outstanding miniatures and the people who make and collect them. Original, illustrated how-to projects for making miniatures. Pays varying rates, after acceptance. Query with photos.

MODEL RAILROADER—1027 N. Seventh St., Milwaukee, WI 53233. Russ Larson, Ed. Articles, with photos of layout and equipment, on model railroads. Pays $66 per printed page, on acceptance. Query.

NATIONAL DOLL WORLD—306 E. Parr Rd., Berne, IN 46711. Rebekah Montgomery, Ed. Informational articles about doll collecting.

THE NEW YORK ANTIQUE ALMANAC—Box 335, Lawrence, NY 11559. Carol Nadel, Ed. Articles on antiques, shows, shops, museums, art, investments, collectibles, collecting suggestions; related humor. Photos. Pays $5 to $75, extra for photos, on publication.

NOSTALGIA WORLD—Box 231, North Haven, CT 06473. Bonnie Roth, Ed. Articles, 500 to 3,000 words, on all kinds of collectibles: records, comics, gum cards, toys, sheet music, magazines, dolls, movie posters, etc. Pays $10 to $50, on publication.

NUTSHELL NEWS—633 W. Wisconsin Ave., Suite 304, Milwaukee, WI 53203. Colleen Kearney, Assoc. Ed. Articles, 1,200 to 1,500 words, for miniatures enthusiasts, collectors, craftspeople and hobbyists. Pays 10¢ a word, on publication. Query first.

PETERSEN'S PHOTOGRAPHIC—8490 Sunset Blvd., Los Angeles, CA 90069. Bill Hurter, Ed. How-to articles on all phases of still photography of interest to the amateur and advanced photographer. Pays $60 per printed page for article accompanied by photos, on publication.

PLATE WORLD—9200 N. Maryland Ave., Niles, IL 60648. Alyson Sulaski Wyckoff, Ed. Articles on artists, collectors, manufacturers, retailers of limited-edition collector's plates. Internationally oriented. Pays varying rates, on acceptance. Query first.

POPULAR MECHANICS—224 W. 57th St., New York, NY 10019. Bill Hartford, Man. Ed. Articles, 300 to 2,000 words, on latest developments in mechanics, industry, science; features on hobbies with a mechanical slant; how-to's on home, shop, and crafts projects. Photos and sketches. Pays to $1,000, $25 to $100 for short pieces, on acceptance. Buys all rights.

THE PROFESSIONAL QUILTER—Oliver Press, Box 4096, St. Paul, MN 55104. Jeannine M. Spears, Ed. Articles, 500 to 1,500 words, for women in small businesses related to the quilting field: business and marketing skills, personality profiles. Graphics, if applicable; no "how-to" quilt articles. Pays $25 to $75, on publication.

RAILROAD MODEL CRAFTSMAN—P.O. Box 700, Newton, NJ 07860. William C. Schaumburg, Ed. How-to articles on scale model railroading; cars, operation, scenery, etc. Pays on publication.

R/C MODELER MAGAZINE—P.O. Box 487, Sierra Madre, CA 91024. Patricia E. Crews, Ed. Technical and semi-technical how-to articles on radio-controlled model aircraft, boats and cars. Query.

THE ROBB REPORT—1 Acton Pl., Acton, MA 01720. Feature articles on investment opportunities, classic and collectible autos, art and antiques, home interiors, boats, travel, etc. Pays on publication. Query with SASE and published clips. Attn: Jane Doerfer.

SEVEN—Caesars World, Inc., 1801 Century Park E., Suite 2600, Los Angeles, CA 90067. Stewart Weiner, Ed. Resort-oriented, gaming articles, to 2,500 words. Pays $1,000 to $2,000, on acceptance. Query required.

73 AMATEUR RADIO—WGE Center, Peterborough, NH 03458. Perry Donham, Ed. Articles, 1,500 to 3,000 words, for electronics hobbyists and amateur radio operators. Pays $60 per printed page, on acceptance.

SEW NEWS—P.O. Box 1790, News Plaza, Peoria, IL 61656. Linda Turner Jones, Ed. Articles, to 3,000 words, "that teach a specific technique, inspire a reader to try new sewing projects, or inform a reader about an interesting person, company, or project related to sewing, textiles, or fashion." Emphasis is on fashion sewing. Pays $25 to $400, on acceptance. Queries required.

TEDDY BEAR REVIEW—Collector Communications Corp., 170 Fifth Ave., New York, NY 10010. Krystyna Poray Goddu, Ed. Dir. Articles on teddy bears for makers, collectors, and enthusiasts. Pays varying rates, after acceptance.

TREASURE—6745 Adobe Rd., Twenty-Nine Palms, CA 92277. Jim Willliams, Ed. Articles (to 2,500 words) and fillers (300 words) of interest to treasure hunters: How-to (building projects and hunting techniques); Search (where to look for treasure); and Found (stories of discovered treasure). Photos and illustrations welcome. Pays from $30 for fillers, to $125 for features, on publication. Same address and requirements for *Treasure Search* and *Treasure Found*.

TROPICAL FISH HOBBYIST—211 W. Sylvania Ave., Neptune City, NJ 07753. Ray Hunziker, Ed. Articles, 500 to 3,000 words, for beginning and experienced tropical and marine fish enthusiasts. Photos. Pays $35 to $250, on acceptance. Query.

WESTART—Box 6868, Auburn, CA 95604. Martha Garcia, Ed. Features, 350 to 700 words, on fine arts and crafts. No hobbies. Photos. Pays 50¢ per column inch, on publication. SASE required.

WESTERN & EASTERN TREASURES—P.O. Box 1095, Arcata, CA 95521. Rosemary Anderson, Man. Ed. Illustrated articles, to 1,500 words, on metal detecting, treasure-hunting, rocks, and gems. Pays 2¢ a word, extra for photos, on publication.

THE WINE SPECTATOR—Opera Plaza Suite 2040, 601 Van Ness Ave., San Francisco, CA 94102. Harvey Steiman, Exec. Ed. Features, 600 to 1,000 words, preferably with photos, on news and people in the wine world. Pays from $100, extra for photos, on publication. Query required.

WOMEN'S CIRCLE COUNTED CROSS-STITCH—306 E. Parr Rd., Berne, IN 46711. Denise Lohr, Ed. How-to and instructional counted cross-stitch. Interviews and photos of top designers, book reviews, tips, humor. Pays varying rates, on publication.

WOMEN'S CIRCLE COUNTRY NEEDLECRAFT—306 E. Parr Rd., Berne, IN 46711. Denise Lohr, Ed. How-to and instructional needlecrafts; related interviews, humor, book reviews, tips, and short fiction. Photos. Pays varying rates, on publication.

WOODENBOAT—P.O. Box 78, Brooklin, ME 04616. Jonathan Wilson, Ed. How-to and technical articles, 4,000 words, on construction, repair and maintenance of wooden boats; design, history and use of wooden boats; and profiles of outstanding wooden boat builders and designers. Pays $6 per column inch. Query preferred.

THE WOODWORKER'S JOURNAL—P.O. Box 1629, 517 Litchfield Rd., New Milford, CT 06776. Thomas G. Begnal, Man. Ed. Original plans for woodworking projects, with detailed written instructions and at least one B/W photo of finished product. Pays $80 to $120 per published page, on acceptance.

WORKBENCH—4251 Pennsylvania Ave., Kansas City, MO 64111. Robert N. Hoffman, Ed. Articles on do-it-yourself home improvement and maintenance projects and general woodworking articles for beginning and expert craftsmen. Complete working drawings with accurate dimensions, step-by-step instructions, lists of materials, and photos of the finished product must accompany submission. Features on how to reduce energy consumption. Pays from $125 per published page, on acceptance.

YESTERYEAR—P.O. Box 2, Princeton, WI 54968. Michael Jacobi, Ed. Articles on antiques and collectibles, for readers in Wisconsin, Illinois, Iowa, Minnesota and surrounding states. Photos. Will consider regular columns on collecting or antiques. Pays from $10, on publication.

ZYMURGY—Box 287, Boulder, CO 80306. Charles N. Papazian, Ed. Articles appealing to beer lovers and homebrewers. Pays $25 to $75, for pieces 750 to 2,000 words, on publication. Query.

POPULAR & TECHNICAL SCIENCE; COMPUTERS

AIR & SPACE—National Air & Space Museum, Washington, DC 20560. George Larson, Ed. General-interest articles, 1,000 to 3,500 words, on aerospace experience, past, present, and future. Pays varying rates on acceptance. Query first.

ANTIC, THE ATARI RESOURCE—544 Second St., San Francisco, CA 94107. Nat Friedland, Ed. Programs and information for the Atari computer user/owner. Reviews of hardware and software, original programs, etc., 500 words. Game reviews, 400 words. Pays $50 per review, $60 per published page, on publication. Query.

ASTRONOMY—1027 N. Seventh St., Milwaukee, WI 53233. Richard Berry, Ed.-in-Chief. Articles on astronomy, astrophysics, space programs, research. Hobby pieces on equipment; short news items. Pays varying rates, on acceptance.

BIOSCIENCE—American Institute of Biological Science, 730 11th St., NW, Washington, DC 20001. Laura Tangley, Features Ed. Articles, 2 to 4 journal pages, on new developments in biology or science, for professional biologists. Pays $200 per journal page, on publication. Query required.

BYTE MAGAZINE—P.O. Box 372, Hancock, NH 03449. Philip Lemmons, Ed. Features on new technology, how-to articles, and reviews of computers and software, varying lengths, for sophisticated users of personal computers. Payment is competitive. Query.

COMMODORE MAGAZINE—1200 Wilson Dr., West Chester, PA 19380. Jim Gracely, Interim Ed. Software reviews, programs, do-it-yourself projects, buyers guides, etc., for Commodore computer users. Pays varying rates on publication. Query.

COMPUTE!—P.O. Box 5406, Greensboro, NC 27403. Lance Elko, Ed. Timely articles and program listings on applications, tutorials, games and programs that address the needs of the consumer computer user. Length: 500 to 6,000 words. Pays on acceptance.

COMPUTE!'S ATARI ST DISK & MAGAZINE—324 W. Wendover Ave., Ste. 200, Greensboro, NC 27403. Tom R. Halfhill, Ed. Programs and articles, 200 to 3,500 words, for users of Atari ST computers. Pays $100 to $600, on acceptance. Guidelines.

COMPUTE!'S PC MAGAZINE—324 W. Wendover Ave., Ste. 200, Greensboro, NC 27403. Tom R. Halfhill, Ed. Programs and articles, 200 to 3,500 words, for users of IBM PC and compatible computers. Pays $200 to $2,000, on acceptance. Guidelines.

COMPUTER AND SOFTWARE NEWS—425 Park Ave., New York, NY 10022. Charles J. Humphrey, Ed. Newsweekly for hardware and software retailers, distributors and suppliers. News items. Pays 30¢ per published word, on publication.

COMPUTER LANGUAGE—Miller Freeman Publications, 500 Howard St., San Francisco, CA 94105. Regina Starr Ridley, Ed. Articles on programming language issues and trends of importance to programmers and software developers, 2,500 to 4,000 words; include relevant code and diagrams. Pays $60 per published page, on publication.

COMPUTER PRODUCT SELLING—425 Park Ave., New York, NY 10022. Betty J. Taylor, Ed. News and features for computer sales professionals. Pays 30¢ a word, on publication.

DESIGN GRAPHICS WORLD—Communications Channels, 6255 Barfield Rd., Atlanta, GA 30328. James J. Maivald, Ed. Articles 1,500 to 2,000 words, on trends and current methods of engineering, architecture, computer graphics, micrographics, and related design fields. Query required. Pays on publication.

DIGITAL NEWS—33 West St., Boston, MA 02111. Newspaper articles of varying lengths, covering products, applications, and events related to Digital's VAX line of computers. Pay varies, on acceptance. Query required.

DIGITAL REVIEW—800 Boylston St., Ste. 1390, Boston, MA 02199. Jonathan Cohler, Ed.-in-Chief. Tutorials, news analysis, case studies, product profiles, and reviews for users of Digital Equipment Corp.'s computers, to 3,500 words. Pays on acceptance. Guidelines.

DISCOVER MAGAZINE—Family Media, Inc., 3 Park Ave., New York, NY 10016. Uses mostly staff-written material. Query.

80 MICRO—Computer World Communications, 80 Pine St., Peterborough, NH 03458. Address Submissions Ed. Technical articles, programs and tutorials for Tandy microcomputer; no general-interest articles. Pays $50 to $75 per printed page, on acceptance. Query.

ENVIRONMENT—4000 Albemarle St. N.W., Washington, DC 20016. Jane Scully, Ed. Factual articles, 2,500 to 5,000 words, on scientific, technological and environmental policy and decision-making issues. Pays $100 to $300. Query.

FOCUS—The Magazine of the North American Data General Users Group. Turnkey Publishing, 5332 Thunder Creek Rd., Ste. 105, Austin, TX 78759. Greg Farman, Ed. Articles, 700 to 4,000 words, on Data General computers. Photos a plus. Pays to $100, on publication. Query required.

THE FUTURIST—World Future Society, 4916 Elmo Ave., Bethesda, MD 20814. Timothy Willard, Man. Ed. Features 1,000 to 5,000 words, on subjects pertaining to the future: environment, education, science, technology, etc. Pays in copies.

GENETIC ENGINEERING NEWS—1651 Third Ave., New York, NY 10128. John Sterling, Man. Ed. Articles on all aspects of biotechnology; feature articles and news articles. Pays varying rates, on acceptance. Query.

GEOBYTE—P.O. Box 797, Tulsa, OK 74101. Ken Milam, Managing Editor. Quarterly publication of the American Association of Petroleum Geologists. Articles, to 20 typed pages, on computer applications in exploration and production of oil, gas, and energy minerals. Pays varying rates, on acceptance. Queries are required.

HAM RADIO—Greenville, NH 03048. Rich Rosen, Ed. Articles, to 2,500 words, on amateur radio theory and construction. Pays to $40 per printed page, on publication. Query. Guidelines.

HARDCOPY—Box 759, Brea, CA 92621. Dan Reese, Ed. Articles, 2,000 to 3,500 words, for manufacturers, users, and distributors of Digital Equipment Corp. (DEC): how-to pieces on product and system applications. Must have DEC tie-in. Pays $200 to $600, thirty days after acceptance. Query first.

INCIDER—Elm St., Peterborough, NH 03458. Articles for Apple II computer users: applications-oriented, state-of-the-art ready to type in program listings, and how-to pieces. Software and hardware reviews. Pays on acceptance. Query preferred.

LINK-UP—143 Old Marlton Pike, Medford, NJ 08055. Bev Smith, Ed. Dir. How-to pieces, and reviews for small-computer communications enthusiasts, 600 to 2,500 words. Photos are a plus. Pay runs from $80 to $200, on publication.

LOTUS—P.O. Box 9123, Cambridge, MA 02139. Chris Brown, Ed. Articles, 1,500 to 2,000 words, on business and professional applications of Lotus software. Query with outline required. Pays varying rates, on acceptance.

MACWORLD—Editorial Proposals, 501 Second St., Suite 600, San Francisco, CA 94107. How-to articles relating to Macintosh personal computers; varying lengths. Query or send outline with screenshots, if applicable. Pays from $300, on acceptance. Send SASE for writer's guidelines.

MICROAGE QUARTERLY—2308 S. 55th St., Tempe, AZ 85282. Linnea Maxwell, Ed. Distributed through MicroAge stores. Articles on business uses of micro-computers. Query first. Pays varying rates, on publication.

MINI-MICRO SYSTEMS—275 Washington St., Newton, MA 02158. George Kotelly, Ed. Technical monthly for computer system users, manufacturers, and integrators. How-to pieces, profiles, news items, etc. Pays $35 to $100 per printed page, on publication. Query.

MODERN ELECTRONICS—76 N. Broadway, Hicksville, NY 10081. Art Salsberg, Ed.-in-Chief. How-to features, technical tutorials, and construction projects related to latest consumer electronics circuits, products, and personal computer equipment. Lengths vary. Query with outline required. Pays $80 to $150, on acceptance.

NETWORK WORLD—Box 9171, Framingham, MA 01701. Bruce Hoard, Ed. Articles, to 2,500 words, about applications of communications technology for management-level users of data, voice, and video communications systems. Pays varying rates, on acceptance. Query.

NIBBLE—52 Domino Dr., Concord, MA 01742. David P. Szetela, Ed. Programs and programming methods, as well as short articles, reviews and general-interest pieces for Apple Computer users. Send short cover letter and sample program runs with manuscript. Pays $40 to $500 for articles, $20 to $250 for shorter pieces. Send SASE for writers' guidelines.

NIBBLE MAC—52 Domino Dr., Concord, MA 01742. David Szetela, Ed. Articles using popular Macintosh programs; product reviews, tutorials, and general-interest articles for Macintosh users. Pays $50 to $500, after acceptance. Programs must be submitted on disk. Send for guidelines.

OMNI—1965 Broadway, New York, NY 10023. Patrice Adcroft, Ed. Articles 1,000 to 3,500 words, on scientific aspects of the future: space colonies, cloning, machine intelligence, ESP, origin of life, future arts, lifestyles, etc. Pays $800 to $3,000, $150 for short items, on acceptance. Query.

PC TECH JOURNAL—10480 Little Patuxent Pkwy., Ste. 800, Parkview, Columbia, MD 21044. Julie Anderson, Ed. How-to pieces and reviews, for technically sophisticated computer professionals. Pays $100 to $1,000, on acceptance. Query required.

PCM MAGAZINE—Falsoft, Inc. 9509 US Hwy 42, P.O. Box 385, Prospect, KY 40059. Kevin Nichols, Editor. Articles and computer programs for Tandy portable and MS–DOS computers. Pays varying rates, on publication.

POPULAR SCIENCE—380 Madison Ave., New York, NY 10017. C. P. Gilmore, Ed. Articles with photos, on developments in applied science and technology. Short illustrated articles on new inventions and products; photo essays, to 4 pages. Pays from $150 per printed page, on acceptance.

PROFILES—Kaypro Corp., 533 Stevens Ave., Solana Beach, CA 92075. Diane Ingalls, Ed. Tutorials, 2,500 to 3,000 words, geared to beginner and intermediate users of CP/M and MS–DOS computers. Pays $350, on acceptance. Queries required.

THE RAINBOW—Falsoft, Inc., 9509 US Highway 42, P.O. Box 385, Prospect, KY 40059. Jutta Kaphammer, Submissions Ed. Articles and computer programs for Tandy portable and MS–DOS computers. Pays varying rates, on publication.

RUN—CW Communications, Elm St., Peterborough, NH 03458. Dennis Brisson, Ed.-in-Chief. Computer applications, program listings, hints and tips to help readers get the most out of their Commodore home computers, 6 to 10 typed pages. Pays about $100 per published page, after acceptance. Query.

SEA FRONTIERS/SEA SECRETS—3979 Rickenbacker Causeway, Virginia Key, Miami, FL 33149. Jean Bradfisch, Exec. Ed. Illustrated articles, 500 to 3,000 words, on scientific advances related to the sea, biological, physical, chemical, or geological phenomena, ecology, conservation, etc., written in a popular style for lay readers. Send SASE for guidelines. Pays $50 to $300, on acceptance. Query.

SOFT SECTOR MAGAZINE—Falsoft, Inc., 9509 US Hwy 42, P.O. Box 385, Prospect, KY 40059. Belinda Kirby, Editor. Articles and computer programs for PC compatible computers. Pays varying rates, on publication.

SPACE WORLD—National Space Society, 922 Pennsylvania Ave., S.E., Washington, DC 20003. Lively, non-technical features on all aspects of the international space program. Pays $150 per article, on publication. Query; guidelines available.

START/THE ST QUARTERLY—Antic Publishing, 544 Second St., San Francisco, CA 94107. Jon A. Bell, Ed. Articles, 1,500 to 2,500 words, related to the Atari ST computer; programs, to 4,000 words. Submit hard copy and disk copy of manuscript. Pays varying rates, on publication. Guidelines.

TECHNOLOGY REVIEW—Rm. 10–140, Massachusetts Institute of Technology, Cambridge, MA 02139. John Mattill, Ed. General-interest articles, and more technical features, 1,500 to 5,000 words, on technology, the environment and society. Payment varies, on publication. Query.

ANIMALS

CAT FANCY—P.O. Box 6050, Mission Viejo, CA 92690. Linda Lewis, Ed. Articles, from 1,500 to 3,000 words, on cat care, health, grooming, etc. Pays 5¢ a word, on publication.

CATS—P.O. Box 290037, Port Orange, FL 32029. Articles, 1,000 to 2,000 words, with illustrations or photos, on cats: unusual anecdotes, medical pieces, cats in literature, art, or science. Pays 5¢ a word, extra for illustrations, on publication.

DOG FANCY—P.O. Box 6050, Mission Viejo, CA 92690. Linda Lewis, Ed. Articles 1,500 to 3,000 words, on dog care, health, grooming, breeds, activities, events, etc. Photos. Pays 5¢ a word, on publication.

HORSE ILLUSTRATED—P.O. Box 6050, Mission Viejo, CA 92690. Jill-Marie Jones, Ed. Articles 1,500 to 2,500 words, on all aspects of owning and caring for horses. Photos. Pays 3¢ to 5¢ a word, on publication.

HORSEMEN'S YANKEE PEDLAR—785 Southbridge St., Auburn, MA 01501. Nancy L. Khoury, Pub. News and feature-length articles, about horses and horsemen in the Northeast. Photos. Pays $2 per published inch, on publication. Query.

LLAMAS—Box 100, Herald, CA 95638. Articles, fiction, and poetry, related to llamas. Pays on acceptance. Query first to Susan Jones-Ley, Contributing Editor, P.O. Box 1038, Dublin, OH 43017.

PARENTING, CHILD CARE, AND DEVELOPMENT

AMERICAN BABY—249 W. 17th St., New York, NY 10011. Judith Nolte, Ed. Articles, about 2,000 words, for new or expectant parents; pieces on pregnancy and child care. No poetry. Pays on acceptance.

BABY!—230 Park Ave., New York, NY 10169. Andrea Burtman, Man. Ed. Articles, 700 to 1,800 words, on child care, health, and child psychology, for mothers who have just given birth. Pays $500 to $1,200, on acceptance.

BABY TALK—185 Madison Ave., New York, NY 10016. Patricia Irons, Ed. Articles, 1,500 to 3,000 words, by parents or professionals, on babies, baby care, etc. Pays varying rates, on acceptance. SASE required.

CHILD MAGAZINE—477 Madison Ave., 22nd Floor, New York, NY 10022. Jackie Leo, Ed., Nancy Clark, Exec. Ed. Articles 1,500 to 2,500 words, for parents who want the best for their children: schools, health, books, travel, and childcare. Pays $500 to $1,000, on acceptance. Query preferred.

THE EXCEPTIONAL PARENT—605 Commonwealth Ave., Boston, MA 02215. Maxwell J. Schleifer, Ed. Articles, 600 to 3,000 words, with practical information for parents of disabled children. Pays on publication.

EXPECTING—685 Third Ave., New York, NY 10017. Evelyn A. Podsiadlo, Ed. Articles, 700 to 1,800 words, for expectant mothers. Pays $150 to $350, on acceptance.

GROWING CHILD/GROWING PARENT—22 N. Second St., Lafayette, IN 47902. Nancy Kleckner, Ed. Articles, to 1,500 words, on subjects of interest to parents of children under 6, with emphasis on the issues, problems and choices of being a parent. No personal-experience pieces or poetry. Pays 8¢ to 15¢ a word, on acceptance. Query.

GROWING UP—5127 Summit Ave., Greensboro, NC 27405. Joe Benson, Man. Ed. Articles, 2,500 to 4,000 words, for parents of adolescents. Some fiction and poetry. Pays $25 to $50. Query required.

LIVING WITH CHILDREN—127 Ninth Ave. N., Nashville, TN 37234. SuAnne Bottoms, Ed. Articles, 800, 1,450 to 2,000 words, on parent–child relationships, told from a Christian perspective. Pays 5¢ a word, after acceptance.

LIVING WITH PRESCHOOLERS—127 Ninth Ave., N., Nashville, TN 37234. SuAnne Bottoms, Ed. Articles, 800, 1,450 or 2,000 words, and fillers, to 300 words, for Christian families. Pays 5¢ a word, on acceptance.

LIVING WITH TEENAGERS—127 Ninth Ave., N., Nashville, TN 37234. Articles, told from a Christian perspective for parents of teenagers; first-person approach preferred. Poetry, 4 to 16 lines. Photos. Pays 5¢ a word, on acceptance.

MARRIAGE & FAMILY LIVING—St. Meinrad, IN 47577. Kass Dotterweich, Man. Ed. Articles, to 2,000 words, on husband–wife and parent–child relationships. Pays 7¢ a word, on acceptance. Query.

NEW YORK FAMILY—420 E. 79th St., New York, NY 10021. Susan Ross, Ed. Articles on parenting in New York City. Pays $50 to $100, on publication.

PARENTS—685 Third Ave., New York, NY 10017. Elizabeth Crow, Ed.-in-Chief. Articles 2,000 to 3,000 words, on growth and development of infants, children, teens; family; women's issues; community; current research. Informal style with quotes from experts. Pays from $750, on acceptance. Query.

RODALE'S CHILDREN—33 E. Minor St., Emmaus, PA 18098. Eileen Nechas, Ed. Authoritative, informative articles, 1,500 to 3,500 words, that will be of interest to parents of youngsters to age 15. "We look for a friendly writing style with personal and anecdotal accounts." Pays 30¢ a word, on acceptance. Query.

WORKING MOTHER—230 Park Ave., New York, NY 10169. Olivia Buehl, Ed. In-depth articles, 800 to 1,500 words, for working mothers, on child care, home management, the work world, single mothers, etc. Pays varying rates, on acceptance. Query first with detailed outline.

WORKING PARENTS—18 E. 41st St., New York, NY 10017. Janet Spencer King, Ed. Articles, to 1,800 words, of interest to parents with children six years old or younger. Poetry, any length. Pays varying rates, on publication. Query preferred.

MILITARY

THE AMERICAN LEGION MAGAZINE—Box 1055, Indianapolis, IN 46206. Michael D. LaBonne, Ed. Articles, 750 to 1,800 words, on current world affairs, public policy, and subjects of contemporary interest. Pays $100 to $1,000, on acceptance. Query.

ARMY MAGAZINE—2425 Wilson Blvd., Arlington, VA 22201. L. James Binder, Ed.-in-Chief. Features, to 5,000 words, on military subjects. Essays, history, news reports. Pays 10¢ to 17¢ a word, on publication.

INFANTRY—P.O. Box 2005, Fort Benning, GA 31905–0605. Articles, 2,000 to 5,000 words, on military organization, equipment, tactics, foreign armies, etc. for U.S. infantry personnel. Pays varying rates, on publication; no payment made to U.S. Government employees. Query.

LEATHERNECK—Box 1775, Quantico, VA 22134. William V. H. White, Ed. Articles, to 3,000 words, with photos, on U.S. Marines. Pays $50 per printed page, on acceptance. Query.

LIFE IN THE TIMES—The Times Journal Co., Springfield, VA 22159–0200. Barry Robinson, Ed. Articles, to 2,000 words, on current military family life. Pays $100 to $350, on acceptance.

MILITARY LIFESTYLE MAGAZINE—1732 Wisconsin Ave., N.W., Washington, DC 20007. Hope Daniels, Ed. Articles, 800 to 2,000 words, for military families in the U.S. and overseas, on lifestyles, travel, fashion, nutrition, and health. Pays $100 to $600, on publication. Query first.

MILITARY REVIEW—U.S. Army Command and General Staff College, Fort Leavenworth, KS 66027–6910. Phillip W. Childress, Ed.-in-Chief. Articles, 2,000 to 3,000 words, on tactics, national defense, military history and any military subject of current interest and importance. Pays $50 to $300, on publication.

NATIONAL GUARD—One Mass. Ave. N.W., Washington, DC 20001. Reid K. Beveridge, Ed. Articles, 2,000 to 4,000 words, with photos, of interest to National Guard members. Pays on publication.

OFF DUTY—3303 Harbor Blvd., Suite C-2, Costa Mesa, CA 92626. Informative, entertaining and useful articles, 900 to 1,800 words, for military service personnel and their dependents, on making the most of off duty time and getting the most out of service life: military living, travel, personal finance, sports, military people, American trends, etc. Military angle essential. Pays 13¢ to 16¢ a word, on publication. European and Pacific editions also. Guidelines available. Query required.

PROCEEDINGS—U.S. Naval Institute, Annapolis, MD 21402. Fred H. Rainbow, Ed. Articles, to 3,500 words, on naval and maritime subjects; article should come to grips with a problem and offer a solution. Opinion pieces, to 1,000 words. Pays $60 to $150, per published page. Query.

THE RETIRED OFFICER MAGAZINE—201 N. Washington St., Alexandria, VA 22314. Articles, 750 to 2,000 words, of interest to military retirees and their families. Current military/political affairs; recent military history (especially Vietnam and Korea), humor, travel, hobbies, military famliy life styles, and second-career job opportunities. Photos a plus. Pays to $500, extra for photos, on acceptance. Queries preferred; address Manuscript Ed. Guidelines.

VFW MAGAZINE—Broadway at 34th, Kansas City, MO 64111. Magazine for Veterans of Foreign Wars and their families. James K. Anderson, Ed. Articles, 1,000 words, on current issues, solutions to everyday problems, personalities, sports, etc. How-to and historical pieces. Photos. Pays 5¢ to 10¢ a word, extra for photos, on acceptance.

WESTERN

AMERICAN WEST—3033 N. Campbell Ave., Tucson, AZ 85719. Mae Reid-Bills, Man. Ed. Well-researched, illustrated articles, 1,000 to 3,000 words, on western America, past and present, in a lively style appealing to the intelligent general reader. Query required. Pays from $200, on acceptance.

OLD WEST—See *True West*.

PERSIMMON HILL—1700 NE 63rd St., Oklahoma City, OK 73111. Marcia Preston, Ed. Published by the National Cowboy Hall of Fame. Articles, 1,500 to 3,000 words, on Western history and art, cowboys, ranching, and nature. Pays from $100, on publication.

REAL WEST—Charlton Publications, Inc., Division St., Derby, CT 06418. Ed Doherty, Ed. True stories of the Old West, 1,000 to 4,000 words. Photos. Pays from 4¢ a word, on acceptance.

TRUE WEST—P.O. Box 2107, Stillwater, OK 74076. John Joerschke, Ed. True stories, 500 to 4,500 words, with photos, about the Old West to 1930. Some contemporary stories with historical slant. Source list required. Pays 3¢ to 5¢ a word, extra for B&W photos, after acceptance. Same address and requirements for *Old West*.

HISTORICAL

AMERICAN HERITAGE—60 Fifth Ave., New York, NY 10011. Byron Dobell, Ed. Articles, 750 to 5,000 words, on U.S. history and background of American life and culture. No fiction. Pays from $300 to $1,500, on acceptance. Query.

AMERICAN HERITAGE OF INVENTION & TECHNOLOGY—60 Fifth Ave., New York, NY 10011. Frederick Allen, Ed. Articles, 2,000 to 3,500 words, on the history of technology in America, for the sophisticated general reader. Query. Pays on acceptance.

AMERICAN HISTORY ILLUSTRATED—2245 Kohn Rd., P.O. Box 8200, Harrisburg, PA 17105. Articles, 2,000 to 3,500 words, soundly researched. Style should be popular, not scholarly. Pays $300 to $500, on acceptance. Query required.

AMERICANA—29 W. 38th St., New York, NY 10018. Sandra J. Wilmot, Ed. Articles, 1,000 to 2,500 words, with historical slant; restoration, crafts, food, collecting, travel, etc. Pays $400 to $750, on acceptance. Query.

CHICAGO HISTORY—Clark St. at North Ave., Chicago, IL 60614. Russell Lewis, Ed. Articles, to 4,500 words, on urban political, social and cultural history. Pays to $250, on publication. Query.

CLASSIC AMERICA—P.O. Box 2516, Westfield, NJ 07090. Richard O. Aichele, Ed. Articles, 600 to 2,000 words, related to American from 1800 to 1930: historical events, travel, antiques, collectibles, and lifestyle; articles with a "how it can still be enjoyed today" slant are of special interest. Pays 8¢ to 20¢ a word, on acceptance.

EARLY AMERICAN LIFE—Box 8200, Harrisburg, PA 17105. Frances Carnahan, Ed. Illustrated articles 1,000 to 3,000 words, on early American life:

arts, crafts, furnishings, architecture; travel features about historic sites and country inns. Pays $50 to $500, on acceptance. Query.

HEARTLAND JOURNAL—4114 N. Sunset Ct., Madison, WI 53705. Jeri McCormick and Lenore Coberly, Eds. Articles, 100 to 4,000 words, on "times and places that are gone." Pays in copies.

HISTORIC PRESERVATION—1785 Massachusetts Ave., N.W., Washington, DC 20036. Thomas J. Colin, Ed. Articles from published writers, 1,500 to 4,000 words, on historic preservation, maritime preservation and people involved in preservation. High-quality photos. Pays $300 to $850, extra for photos, on acceptance. Query required.

COLLEGE, CAREERS

AMPERSAND—303 N. Glenoaks Blvd., Suite 600, Burbank, CA 91502. Charlotte Wolter, Ed. Articles, 1,000 to 2,000 words, of interest to college students. Focus on films and popular entertainment. Pays 15¢ to 20¢ a word, half on acceptance, half on publication. Query required.

THE BLACK COLLEGIAN—1240 S. Broad St., New Orleans, LA 70125. K. Kazi-Ferrouillet, Man. Ed. Articles, to 2,000 words, on experiences of black students, careers, and how-to subjects. Pays on publication. Query.

CAMPUS LIFE—465 Gundersen Dr., Carol Stream, IL 60188. Gregg Lewis, Sr. Ed. Articles reflecting Christian values and world view, for high school and college students. Pays from $150, on acceptance. Limited free-lance market.

CAMPUS USA—Montrose Office Center, Suite 808, 6001 Montrose Rd., Rockville, MD 20852. Gerald S. Snyder, Ed. Articles, 1,500 to 2,000 words, on careers, travel, movies, fashion, autos, and sports for college students. Pays to $750, on publication. Query first.

CAMPUS VOICE—505 Market St., Knoxville, TN 37902. Lively, in-depth articles, 2,000 to 3,500 words, of interest to college students. Department pieces, 1,000 to 2,000 words. Pays $300 to $2,000, on acceptance. Query required. Send SASE for guidelines.

COLLEGE WOMAN—303 N. Glenoaks Blvd., Suite 600, Burbank, CA 91502. Charlotte Wolter, Ed. Articles, 2,500 words, of interest to college women, on topics from controversial, on-campus issues to fashion and sports. Pays 15¢ to 40¢ a word, on acceptance. Query required.

HIS—See *U*.

JOURNAL OF CAREER PLANNING & EMPLOYMENT—62 Highland Ave., Bethlehem, PA 18017. Patricia A. Sinnott, Man. Ed. Articles, 3,000 to 4,000 words, on topics related to career planning, placement, and recruitment. Pays $200 to $400, on acceptance. Query with clips.

MOVING UP—303 N. Glenoaks Blvd., Suite 600, Burbank, CA 91502. Charlotte Wolter, Ed. Articles, 500 to 2,500 words, of interest to college men, concerning careers, relationships, fitness, personal style, and self-awareness; profiles; opinion pieces. Pays half on acceptance, half on publication. Query required.

PANACHE—4550 38th St., Long Island City, NY 11101. Michael Weiss, Ed. Personality profiles; articles on events and landmarks relating to college life, 500 to 2,000 words. East Coast: address Robin Clark; West Coast: address Catie Lott. Pays $30 to $100, on publication. Query required.

U MAGAZINE (formerly *His*)—5206 Main St., Downers Grove, IL 60515. Verne Becker, Ed. Articles, to 2,000 words, reflecting a Christian world view, for Christian college and university students. Pays on acceptance.

WHAT'S NEW MAGAZINE—Multicom Inc., 11 Allen Rd., Boston, MA 02135. Bob Leja, Ed. General-interest articles, 150 to 300 words, on music, movies, books, cars, travel, sports, food, wine, consumer electronics, computers, arts and entertainment. Pays $25 to $250, on publication. Query required.

ALTERNATIVE MAGAZINES

EAST WEST; THE JOURNAL OF NATURAL HEALTH & LIVING—17 Station St., Box 1200, Brookline, MA 02147. Features, 1,500 to 2,500 words, on holistic health, natural foods, the environment, etc. Material for "Body," "Healing," "In the Kitchen," and "Beauty and Fitness." Interviews. Photos. Pays 7¢ to 12¢ a word, extra for photos, on publication.

FATE—Clark Publishing Co., 500 Hyacinth Pl., Highland Park, IL 60035. Mary M. Fuller, Ed. Documented articles, to 3,000 words, on strange happenings. Pays from 5¢ a word for articles, on publication.

NEW AGE—342 Western Ave., Brighton, MA 02135. Gail Whitney, Ed. Coordinator. Articles for readers who take an active interest in social change and personal growth, health and contemporary issues. Features, 2,000 to 4,000 words; columns, 750 to 1,500 words; and first-person narratives, 750 to 1,500 words. Pays varying rates. Query.

NEW REALITIES—4000 Albemarle St. NW, Washington, DC 20016. Neal Vahle, Ed. Articles on holistic health, personal growth, parapsychology, alternative lifestyles, new spirituality. Query required.

YOGA JOURNAL—2054 University Ave., Berkeley, CA 94704. Stephan Bodian, Ed. Articles, 1,200 to 3,000 words, on holistic health, spirituality, yoga, and transpersonal psychology; "new age" profiles; interviews. Pays $50 to $150, on publication.

OP-ED MARKETS

Op-ed pages in newspapers—those pages that run opposite the editorials—offer writers an excellent opportunity to air their opinions, views, ideas, and insights on a wide spectrum of subjects and in styles from the highly personal and informal essay to the more serious commentary on politics, foreign affairs, and news events. Humor and nostalgia often find a place here.

THE ANCHORAGE DAILY NEWS—Pouch 6616, Anchorage, AK 99502. Seeks articles, 800 to 900 words, that "balance the national and international orientation of the editorial page," on natural resources, local issues, humor, seasonal topics, oil, etc. Preference for local writers. Pays $50, on publication. Submit manuscript with SASE postcard.

THE ATLANTA CONSTITUTION—P.O. Box 4689, Atlanta, GA 30302. Patricia Carr, Op-Ed Ed. Articles related to the Southeast, Georgia or the Atlanta metropolitan area, 200 to 800 words, on a variety of topics: law, economics, politics, science, environment, performing and manipulative arts, humor, education; religious and seasonal topics. Pays $50 to $150, on publication. Submit complete manuscript.

THE BALTIMORE SUN—501 N. Calvert St., Baltimore, MD 21278. Harold Piper, Op-Ed Editor. Articles, 750 to 1,000 words, for Opinion Commentary page, on a wide range of topics: politics, education, foreign affairs, life styles, science, etc. Humor. Pays $75 to $125, on publication.

BOSTON HERALD—One Herald Sq., Boston, MA 02106. Shelly Cohen, Editorial Page Ed. Pieces, 600 to 800 words, on human-interest, political, regional, life style, and seasonal topics. Pays $50 to $75, on publication. Prefer submissions from regional writers.

THE CHICAGO TRIBUNE—435 N. Michigan Ave., Chicago, IL 60611. Richard Liefer, Op-Ed Ed. Pieces, 500 to 800 words, on politics, economics, education, environment, foreign and domestic affairs. Writers *must* have experience in their fields. Pays $50 to $250 on publication.

THE CHRISTIAN SCIENCE MONITOR—One Norway St., Boston, MA 02115. Cynthia Hanson, Opinion Page Coordinator. Pieces, 600 to 700 words, for "Opinion and Commentary" page, on politics, domestic and foreign affairs. Humor. Payment varies. Query preferred.

THE CHRONICLE—901 Mission St., San Francisco, CA 94103. Ms. Lyle York, "This World" Ed. Articles, 1,500 to 2,500 words, on a wide range of subjects. Pays $50 to $100, on publication.

THE CLEVELAND PLAIN DEALER—1801 Superior Ave., Cleveland, OH 44114. William Henson, Deputy Ed. Dir. Pieces, 800 to 1,000 words, on politics, economics, foreign affairs, and regional issues. Pays $50 to $100, on publication.

DAILY NEWS—14539 Sylvan St., Van Nuys, CA 91411. Pieces, 800 words, with special interest in regional focus: politics, environment, law, and economics. Pays $50, on publication. Query first.

DALLAS MORNING NEWS—Communications Center, Dallas, TX 75265. Carolyn Berta, "Viewpoints" Ed. Pieces 750 words (1,000 words for Sunday issue), on politics, education, foreign and domestic affairs, seasonal and regional issues. Pays $75 to $100, on publication. SASE required.

DENVER POST—P.O. Box 1709, Denver, CO 80201. Fred Brown, Asst. Editorial Page Ed. Pieces, 500 to 700 words, on economics, environment, education, law, politics, and science; seasonal and regional issues. Humor. Pays $35 to $50, on publication.

DES MOINES REGISTER—Box 957, Des Moines, IA 50304. James Flansburg, "Opinion" Page Ed. Articles, 600 to 800 words, on all topics. Humor. Pays $25 to $250, on publication.

THE DETROIT FREE PRESS—321 W. Lafayette St., Detroit, MI 48231. Patricia C. Foley, Op-Ed Ed. Articles, 750 to 800 words, on topics of local interest, and opinion pieces. Pays varying rates, on publication.

THE DETROIT NEWS—615 Lafayette Blvd., Detroit, MI 48231. Richard Burr, Ed. Pieces, 500 to 900 words, on science, economics, foreign and domestic affairs, education, environment, regional topics, nostalgia, religion and politics. Humor. Pays varying rates, on publication.

THE HARTFORD COURANT—285 Broad St., Hartford, CT 06115. Elissa Papirno, Deputy Ed. Page Ed. Opinionated articles, 750 words (1,000 for

Sunday "Commentary" section), on science, environment, politics, economics, law, and domestic and foreign affairs; pieces of regional and seasonal interest. Pays from $40, on publication.

THE LOS ANGELES HERALD EXAMINER—Box 2416, Terminal Annex, Los Angeles, CA 90051–0416. Jim Kinsella, Editor, Editorial Page. Articles, to 800 words, on local topics not covered by syndicated columnists. Humor. Pays $75, on publication.

LOS ANGELES TIMES—Times Mirror Sq., Los Angeles, CA 90053. Commentary pieces, to 800 words, on many subjects. Pays $150 to $250, on publication.

LOUISVILLE COURIER-JOURNAL—525 W. Broadway, Louisville, KY 40202. Keith L. Runyon, Op-Ed Ed. Pieces, 400 to 800 words, on politics, economics, regional topics, life styles, law, education, environment, humor, nostalgia, foreign and domestic affairs, and seasonal topics. Pays varying rates, on publication.

THE MIAMI HERALD—One Herald Plaza, Miami, FL 33132–1693. Joanna Wragg, Op-Ed Ed. Informed opinion pieces, to 800 words, on all subjects. Pays $35 to $50, on publication.

MILWAUKEE JOURNAL—Box 661, Milwaukee, WI 53201. James P. Cattey, Op-Ed Ed. Occasional pieces, 600 words, on various subjects. Pays $30 to $35, on publication.

THE NEW YORK TIMES—229 W. 43rd St., New York, NY 10036. Robert Semple, Jr., Op-Ed Ed. Pieces, 750 words, on topics not covered by syndicated columnists. Pays $150, on publication.

NEWSDAY—Long Island, NY 11747. Ilene Barth, "Viewpoints" Ed. Pieces, 600 to 1,500 words, on foreign and domestic affairs, politics, economics, life styles, law, education, and the environment. Seasonal pieces. Prefer policy experts and local writers. Pays $75 to $300, on publication.

THE OAKLAND TRIBUNE—Box 24424, Oakland, CA 94623. Jonathan Marshall, Editorial Page Ed. Articles, 800 words, on a wide range of topics; no humor or life style materials. Pays $20 to $35, on publication.

THE ORANGE COUNTY REGISTER—625 N. Grand Ave., Santa Ana, CA 92711. K. E. Grubbs, Jr. Ed. Articles on a wide range of local and national issues and topics. Pays $40 to $100, on publication.

PITTSBURGH POST GAZETTE—50 Blvd. of the Allies, Pittsburgh, PA 15222. Mike McGough, Editorial Page Ed. Articles, to 800 words, on politics, law, economics, life style, religion, foreign and domestic affairs. Pays varying rates, on publication. SASE required.

THE REGISTER GUARD—P. O. Box 10188, Eugene, OR 97440. Don Robinson, Editorial Page Ed. All subjects; regional angle preferred. Pays $10 to $25, on publication. Limited free-lance market.

THE SACRAMENTO BEE—21st and Q, P.O. Box 15779, Sacramento, CA 95852. Peter Schrag, Editorial Page Editor. Op-ed pieces, to 750 words; topics of regional interest preferred. Pays $100 to $200, on publication. Query.

ST. LOUIS POST DISPATCH—900 N. Tucker Blvd., St. Louis, MO 63101. Articles on economics, education, science, politics, foreign and domestic affairs, and the environment. Pays $50, on publication.

ST. PAUL PIONEER PRESS DISPATCH—345 Cedar St., St. Paul, MN 55101. Robert J. R. Johnson, Ed. Uses occasional pieces, to 750 words, on topics related to Minnesota and western Wisconsin. Pays $50, on publication. Query first.

ST. PETERSBURG TIMES—Box 1121, 490 First Ave., S., St. Petersburg, FL 33731. Daryl Frazell, "Perspective" Section Ed. Authoritative articles, to 2,000 words, on current political, economic, and social issues, for "Perspective" section. Payment varies, on publication. Query first.

SEATTLE POST-INTELLIGENCER—101 Elliott Ave., W., Seattle, WA 98119. Charles J. Dunsire, Editorial Page Ed. Current events articles, 800 to 1,000 words, with Pacific Northwest themes. Pays $75 to $100, on publication.

THE WALL STREET JOURNAL—World Financial Center, 200 Liberty St., New York, NY 10281. Tim Ferguson, Editorial Features Ed. Articles, 850 to 1,100 words, on politics, economics, life styles, law, education, environment, humor, nostalgia, science, foreign and domestic affairs, religion, human-interest, and seasonal topics. Submit manuscript with SASE.

ADULT MAGAZINES

CAVALIER—2355 Salzedo St., Coral Gables, FL 33134. Nye Willden, Man. Ed. Articles with photos, and fiction, 1,500 to 3,000 words, for sophisticated young men. Pays to $400 for articles, to $250 for fiction, on publication. Query for articles.

CHIC—2029 Century Park E., Suite 3800, Los Angeles, CA 90067. Lonn M. Friend, Exec. Ed. Articles, profiles, erotic film and video coverage, 2,500 to 4,500 words. Pays $750 for articles, on acceptance.

FORUM, THE INTERNATIONAL JOURNAL ON HUMAN RELATIONS—1965 Broadway, New York, NY 10023–5965. True, first-person erotic adventures. Pays $800 to $1,000, on acceptance. Send manuscript or proposal.

GALLERY—800 Second Ave., New York, NY 10017. Marc Lichter, Ed.-in-Chief. Articles, investigative pieces, and men and women relationship pieces, to 3,000 words, for sophisticated men. Short humor, satire, service pieces. Photos. Pays varying rates, half on acceptance, half on publication. Query.

GEM—G&S Publications, 1472 Broadway, New York, NY 10036. Will Martin, Ed. Sex-related (not pornographic) articles and fiction, 500 to 2,500 words. Humor, satire, and spoofs of sexual subjects. Pays $50 to $100, after acceptance. All submissions must be accompanied by SASE.

GENESIS—770 Lexington Ave., New York, NY 10021. J. J. Kelleher, Ed.-in-Chief. Articles, 2,500 to 3,500 words; celebrity interviews, 2,500 words. Sexually-explicit features, 3,000 words. Photo essays. Pays 30 days after acceptance. Query.

HARVEY FOR LOVING PEOPLE—Suite 2305, 450 Seventh Ave., New York, NY 10001. Harvey Shapiro, Ed./Pub. Sexually-oriented articles and fiction, to 2,500 words. Pays to $200, on publication. Query for articles.

HUSTLER—2029 Century Park E., Suite 3800, Los Angeles, CA 90067. Tim Conaway, Exec. Ed. Investigative articles and profiles, 4,500 words. Pays from $1,500, on acceptance. Query.

PENTHOUSE—1965 Broadway, New York, NY 10023. Peter Bloch, Exec.

Ed. General-interest or investigative articles, to 5,000 words. Interviews, 5,000 words, with introductions. Pays to 50¢ a word, on acceptance.

PLAYBOY—919 N. Michigan Ave., Chicago, IL 60611. John Rezek, Articles Ed. Alice K. Turner, Fiction Ed. Articles, 3,500 to 6,000 words, and sophisticated fiction, 1,000 to 8,000 words (6,000 preferred), for urban men. Humor; satire. Science fiction. Pays to $5,000 for articles, to $2,000 for fiction ($1,000 for short-shorts), on acceptance.

PLAYERS—8060 Melrose Ave., Los Angeles, CA 90046. H. L. Sorrell, Ed. Articles, 1,000 to 3,000 words, for black men: travel, fashion, grooming, entertainment, sports, interviews, fiction, humor, satire, health and sex. Photos a plus. Pays on publication.

FICTION MARKETS

This list gives the fiction requirements of the general- and special-interest magazines, including those that publish detective and mystery, romance and confession, and science fiction and fantasy stories. Other good markets for short fiction are the little, literary, and college journals (listed on page 671). Though payment is modest—usually in copies only—publication here can help a beginning writer achieve recognition by editors at the larger magazines. Juvenile fiction markets are listed under *Juvenile, Teenage, and Young Adult Magazines*. Publishers of book-length fiction manuscripts are listed under *Book Publishers*.

All manuscripts must be typed double-space and submitted with self-addressed envelopes bearing postage sufficient for the return of the material. Use good white paper; onion skin or erasable bond is not acceptable. Always keep a copy of the manuscript, since occasionally a manuscript is lost in the mails. Magazines may take several weeks—often longer—to read and report on submissions. If an editor has not reported on a manuscript after a reasonable amount of time, write a brief, courteous letter of inquiry.

AIM MAGAZINE—P.O. Box 20554, Chicago, IL 60620. Ruth Apilado, Ed. Short stories, 800 to 1,000 words, geared to promoting racial harmony and peace. Pays from $15 to $25, on publication. Annual contest.

ALFRED HITCHCOCK'S MYSTERY MAGAZINE—380 Lexington Ave., New York, NY 10017. Cathleen Jordan, Ed. Well-plotted, plausible mystery, suspense, detection and crime stories, 1,000 to 14,000 words. Pays 3¢ to 8¢ a word, on acceptance.

ALOHA, THE MAGAZINE OF HAWAII—828 Fort Street Mall, Honolulu, HI 96813. Cheryl Tsutsumi, Ed. Fiction to 4,000 words, on Hawaii and its ethnic groups. Pays 10¢ a word, on publication. Query.

AMAZING STORIES—Box 110, Lake Geneva, WI 53147. Patrick L. Price, Ed. Science fiction and fantasy, to 25,000 words. Pays 6¢ to 8¢ a word, on acceptance.

AMERICAN TRUCKER MAGAZINE—P.O. Box 9159, Brea, CA 92622.

Carl Calvert, Ed. Fiction, 1,200 to 2,500 words, for truck drivers and trucking industry personnel. Pays on publication.

ANALOG: SCIENCE FICTION/SCIENCE FACT—380 Lexington Ave., New York, NY 10017. Stanley Schmidt, Ed. Science fiction, with strong characters in believable future or alien setting: short stories, 2,000 to 7,500 words; novelettes, 10,000 to 20,000 words; serials, to 70,000 words. Pays 5¢ to 8¢ a word, on acceptance. Query for novels.

ARKANSAS TIMES—Box 34010, Little Rock, AR 72203. Mel White, Ed. Fiction, to 6,000 words: must have an Arkansas slant. Pays from $100, on acceptance.

ARRIVAL—48 Shattuck Sq., Suite 194, Berkeley, CA 94704. William Katovsky, Ed. Fiction, 2,000 to 5,000 words, that "takes a sharp, new approach to the people, places, and events that are making and remaking the American landscape today." Pays varying rates, on publication.

THE ATLANTIC ADVOCATE—P.O. Box 3370, Fredericton, N.B., Canada E3B 5A2. H.P. Wood, Ed. Fiction, 1,000 to 1,500 words, with regional angle. Pays to 10¢ a word, on publication.

THE ATLANTIC MONTHLY—8 Arlington St., Boston, MA 02116. William Whitworth, Ed. Short stories, 2,000 to 6,000 (occasionally, to 14,000) words, of highest literary quality. Pays $2,500, on acceptance.

THE ATLANTIC SALMON JOURNAL—1435 St. Alexandre, Suite 1030, Montreal, Quebec, Canada, H3A 2G4. Joanne Eidinger, Ed. Fiction, 1,500 to 2,500 words, related to the conservation of Atlantic salmon. Pays $100 to $400, on publication.

AUGUSTA SPECTATOR—P.O. Box 3168, Augusta, GA 30904. Faith Bertsche, Pub. Fiction, to 2,000 words. Pays $25, on publication.

BANE K. WILKER'S TALES OF THE OLD WEST—PPG Publishing, Box 22866, Denver, CO 80222. Keith Olsen, Ed. Short stories, 500 to 5,000 words, related to the Old West. Pays in copies. SASE required. Annual contest.

BLACK ELEGANCE—475 Park Ave. South, New York, NY 10016. Sharyn J. Skeeter, Ed. Fiction, 1,500 words, with a strong emphasis on relationships, of interest to sophisticated black women aged 25 to 45. Pays on publication.

THE BOSTON GLOBE MAGAZINE—*The Boston Globe,* Boston, MA 02107. Ande Zellman, Ed. Short stories, to 2,500 words. Include SASE. Pays on publication.

BOY'S LIFE—1325 Walnut Hill Lane, Irving, TX 75038–3096. W. E. Butterworth IV, Fiction Ed. Publication of the Boy Scouts of America. Fiction, 1,000 to 2,000 words, for 8- to 18-year-old boys. Pays from $500, on acceptance.

BUFFALO SPREE MAGAZINE—Box 38, Buffalo, NY 14226. Johanna V. Shotell, Ed. Fiction and humor, to 1,800 words, for readers in the western New York region. Pays $75 to $100, on publication.

BURLINGTON MAGAZINE—333 S. Union St., Burlington, VT 05401. Tim Etchells, Ed. Fiction with Burlington area tie-in. Pays varying rates, on acceptance.

CAMPUS LIFE—465 Gundersen Dr., Carol Stream, IL 60188. James Long, Sr. Ed. Fiction and humor, reflecting Christian values (no overtly religious material), 1,000 to 4,000 words, for high school and college students. Pays from $150 to $400, on acceptance. Limited free-lance market.

CAPPER'S—616 Jefferson Ave., Topeka, KS 66607. Nancy Peavler, Ed. Novel-length mystery and romance stories: no short stories. Pays $150 to $200. Query.

CAT FANCY—P.O. Box 6050, Mission Viejo, CA 92690. Linda W. Lewis, Ed. Fiction, to 3,000 words, about cats. Pays 5¢ a word, on publication.

CATHOLIC FORESTER—425 W. Shuman Blvd., Naperville, IL 60566. Barbara A. Cunningham, Ed. Official publication of the Catholic Order of Foresters. Fiction, to 3,000 words (prefer shorter). No sex or violence or "preachy" stories; religious angle not essential. Pays from 5¢ a word, on acceptance.

CAVALIER—2355 Salzedo St., Coral Gables, FL 33134. Maurice DeWalt, Fiction Ed. Sexually-oriented fiction, to 3,000 words, for sophisticated young men. Pays to $300, on publication.

CHESAPEAKE BAY MAGAZINE—1819 Bay Ridge Ave., Annapolis, MD 21403. Betty Rigoli, Ed. Short stories, to 15 pages; must be related to Chesapeake Bay area. Pays $85 to $100, on publication.

CLINTON STREET QUARTERLY—P.O. Box 3588, Portland, OR 97208. David Milholland, Ed. Short stories, 2 to 20 pages: "First-person accounts, thought-provoking, non-rhetorical essays and idea pieces." Pays varying rates, on publication.

CLUBHOUSE—Berrien Springs, MI 49103. Elaine Meseraull, Ed. Action-oriented Christian stories: features, 1,000 to 1,200 words. Children in stories should be wise, brave, funny, kind, etc. Pays $30 to $35, on acceptance. Submit in April.

COBBLESTONE—20 Grove St., Peterborough, NH 03458. Carolyn P. Yoder, Ed. Fiction, related to monthly theme, 500 to 1,200 words, for children aged 8 to 14 years. Pays 10¢ to 15¢ a word, on publication. Send SASE for editorial guidelines.

COMMENTARY—165 E. 56th St., New York, NY 10022. Marion Magid, Ed. Fiction, of high literary quality, on contemporary social or Jewish issues. Pays on publication.

THE COMPASS—Mobil International Aviation and Marine Sales, Inc., 150 E. 42nd St., New York, NY 10017. R. G. MacKenzie, Ed. Short stories, to 3,500 words, on the sea and sea trades. Pays to $250, on acceptance. Query.

CORVETTE FEVER—Box 44620, Ft. Washington, MD 20744. Pat Stivers, Ed. Corvette-related fiction, about 300 lines. Pays 10¢ a word, on publication.

COSMOPOLITAN—224 W. 57th St., New York, NY 10019. Betty Kelly, Fiction and Books Ed. Short-shorts, 1,500 to 3,000 words, and short stories, 4,000 to 6,000 words, focusing on contemporary man-woman relationships. Solid, upbeat plots, sharp characterization; female protagonists preferred. Pays $300 to $600 for short-shorts, from $1,000 for short stories. Payment negotiable.

COUNTRY WOMAN (formerly *Farm Woman*)—P.O. Box 643, Milwaukee, WI 53201. Eleanor Jacobs, Man. Ed. Fiction, to 1,000 words, of interest to rural women. Pays $30 to $250, on publication.

CRICKET—Box 300, Peru, IL 61354. Marianne Carus, Ed.-in-Chief. Fiction, 200 to 1,500 words, for 6- to 12-year-olds. Pays to 25¢ a word, on publication.

DISCOVERIES—6401 The Paseo, Kansas City, MO 64131. Cheryl Turner, Ed. Fiction, 600 to 800 words, for children grades 3 to 6, defining Christian experiences and values. Pays 3½¢ a word, on acceptance.

DIVER MAGAZINE—#295, 10991 Shellbridge Way, Richmond, B.C. Canada V6X 3C6. Neil McDaniel, Ed. Fiction, related to diving. Humor. Pays $2.50 per column inch, on publication. Query.

DOG FANCY—P.O. Box 6050, Mission Viejo, CA 92690. Linda W. Lewis, Ed. Fiction, to 2,500 words: dog must be central element of the story; no "talking dog" stories. Pays 5¢ a word, on publication.

EASYRIDERS MAGAZINE—Box 52, Malibu, CA 90265. Lou Kimzey, Ed. Fiction, 3,000 to 5,000 words. Pays from 10¢ a word, on acceptance.

ELLERY QUEEN'S MYSTERY MAGAZINE—380 Lexington Ave., New York, NY 10017. Eleanor Sullivan, Ed. High-quality detective, crime, and mystery stories, 4,000 to 6,000 words. "First Stories" by unpublished writers. Pays 3¢ to 8¢ a word, on acceptance.

ENTERTAINER MAGAZINE—One Lytle Place, Suite 802, 621 Mehring Way, Cincinnati, OH 45202. Brian Baker, Ed. General comedy, 750 words, related to Cincinnati. Pays $15 and copies, on publication.

ESPIONAGE—Leo 11 Publications, P.O. Box 1184, Teaneck, NJ 07666. Jackie Lewis, Ed. Spy stories, 1,000 to 6,000 words: no horror, extreme violence, or explicit sex. Pays 3¢ to 8¢ a word, on publication.

ESQUIRE—1790 Broadway, New York, NY 10019. Lee Eisenberg, Ed.-in-Chief. No unsolicited manuscripts.

ESSENCE—1500 Broadway, New York, NY 10036. Susan L. Taylor, Ed.-in-Chief. Fiction, 800 to 3,000 words, for largely black, female readership. Pays $500 to $1,300, on acceptance.

FAMILY CIRCLE—110 Fifth Ave., New York, NY 10011. Nicole Gregory, Sr. Ed. No unsolicited manuscripts.

FAMILY MAGAZINE—P.O. Box 4993, Walnut Creek, CA 94596. Address Editors. Short stories, to 2,000 words, of interest to high school-educated military wives between 20 and 35. Pays from $100 to $300, on publication.

FARM WOMAN—See *Country Woman.*

FICTION INTERNATIONAL—English Dept., San Diego State Univ., San Diego, CA 92182. Harold Jaffe and Larry McCaffery, Eds. Post-modernist and politically committed fiction and theory. Submit between Sept. and Jan.

GALLERY—800 Second Ave., New York, NY 10017. Marc Lichter, Ed.-in-Chief. Fiction, to 4,000 words, for sophisticated men. Pays varying rates, half on acceptance, half on publication.

GENTLEMEN'S QUARTERLY (GQ)—350 Madison Ave., New York, NY 10017. Tom Jenks, Sr. Ed. Fiction, to 3,000 words. Pays on acceptance. No unsolicited manuscripts.

GOLF DIGEST—5520 Park Ave., Trumbull, CT 06611. Jerry Tarde, Ed. Unusual or humorous stories, to 2,000 words, about golf; golf "fables," to 1,000 words. Pays 50¢ a word, on acceptance.

GOOD HOUSEKEEPING—959 Eighth Ave., New York, NY 10019. Naome Lewis, Fiction Ed. Short stories, 1,000 to 3,000 words, with strong identification figures for women, by published writers and "beginners with demonstrable talent." Novel condensations or excerpts. Pays top rates, on acceptance.

GUN DOG—P.O. Box 35098, Des Moines, IA 50315. Bob Wilbanks, Man. Ed. Occasional fiction, humor related to gun dogs and bird hunting. Pays $100 to $350, on acceptance.

HICALL—1445 Boonville Ave., Springfield, MO 65802. Rick Knoth, Ed. Fiction, to 1,800 words, for 12- to 19-year olds. Strong evangelical emphasis a must: believable characters working out their problems according to biblical principles. Pays 3¢ a word for first rights, on acceptance.

HIGHLIGHTS FOR CHILDREN—803 Church St., Honesdale, PA 18431. Kent L. Brown, Jr., Ed. Fiction on sports, humor, adventure, mystery, etc., 900 words, for 9- to 12-year olds. Easy rebus form, 200 to 250 words, and easy-to-read stories, to 600 words, for beginning readers. Pays on acceptance. Buys all rights.

HIS—See *U*.

INSIDE CHICAGO—2501 W. Peterson Ave., Chicago, IL 60659. Deborah Loeser, Ed. Fiction related to life in Chicago. Pays to $250, on acceptance.

INSIDE RUNNING & FITNESS—9514 Bristlebrook Dr., Houston, TX 77083. Joanne Schmidt, Ed. Fiction, related to running. Pays $35 to $100, on acceptance.

ISAAC ASIMOV'S SCIENCE FICTION MAGAZINE—380 Lexington Ave., New York, NY 10017. Gardner Dozois, Ed. Short science fiction and fantasies, to 15,000 words. Pays 6¢ to 8¢ a word, on acceptance.

JACK AND JILL—Box 567, Indianapolis, IN 46206. Steve Charles, Ed. Fiction, to 1,200 words, for early-elementary-age readers. Pays about 6¢ a word, on publication.

LADIES' HOME JOURNAL—100 Park Ave., New York, NY 10017. Fiction with strong identification for women. Short stories and full-length manuscripts *accepted through agents only*.

LIVE—1445 Boonville Ave., Springfield, MO 65802. John T. Maempa, Adult Ed. Fiction, 1,500 to 2,000 words, on applying Bible principles to everyday living. Send SASE for writers' guidelines (required). Pays 2¢ to 3¢ a word, on acceptance.

LOLLIPOPS—Good Apple Inc., P.O. Box 299, Carthage, IL 62321–0299. Jerry Aten, Ed. Short stories, to 1,200 words; teaching ideas and activities covering all areas of the curriculum for young children. Rates vary.

THE LOOKOUT—8121 Hamilton Ave., Cincinnati, OH 45231. Fiction Ed: Mark Taylor. Inspirational short-shorts, 1,000 to 1,800 words. Pays to 5¢ a word, on acceptance.

MCCALL'S—230 Park Ave., New York, NY 10169. Helen DelMonte, Fiction Ed. Short stories, to 3,000 words; short-shorts, 1,000 words: contemporary themes with strong identification for intelligent women. Family stories, love stories, humor, suspense. Pays from $2,000 for stories, $1,500 for short-shorts, on acceptance.

MADEMOISELLE—350 Madison Ave., New York, NY 10017. Eileen Schnurr, Fiction Ed. Short stories, 1,500 to 5,000 words, of interest to young single women. Looking for good writing, strong voices, fresh insights, generally classic form—no genre fiction. Male point-of-view about personal relationships welcome. Pays $1,000 for short-shorts, to $2,000 for stories, on acceptance.

THE MAGAZINE OF FANTASY AND SCIENCE FICTION—Box 56, Cornwall, CT 06753. Edward Ferman, Ed. Fantasy and science fiction stories, to 10,000 words. Pays 5¢ to 7¢ a word, on acceptance.

A MATTER OF CRIME (formerly *The New Black Mask Quarterly*)—2006 Sumter St., Columbia, SC 29201. Matthew J. Bruccoli, Richard Layman, Eds. Mystery fiction, 3,000 to 6,000 words. Pays to 10¢ a word, on publication.

MATURE LIVING—127 Ninth Ave., N., Nashville, TN 37234. Jack Gulledge, Ed. Zada Malugen, Ass't Ed. Fiction, 900 to 1,475 words, for senior adults. Must be consistent with Christian principles. Pays 5¢ a word, on acceptance.

MICHIGAN, THE MAGAZINE OF THE DETROIT NEWS—615 W. Lafayette Blvd., Detroit, MI 48231. Cynthia Boal-Janssens, Ed. Fiction, with *Michigan* slant, to 3,000 words. Pays $200 to $500, on publication.

MID-ATLANTIC COUNTRY—P.O. Box 246, Alexandria, VA 22313. Jim Scott, Ed. Fiction, related to the mid-Atlantic region, varying lengths. Include SASE.

MID-SOUTH MAGAZINE—*The Commercial Appeal,* 495 Union, Box 334, Memphis, TN 38101. Scott Hill, Ed. Fiction, to 1,500 words, with a regional focus. Pays on publication.

MIDSTREAM—515 Park Ave., New York, NY 10022. Fiction on Jewish themes, to 3,000 words. Pays 5¢ a word, after publication.

MILITARY LIFESTYLE—1732 Wisconsin Ave. NW, Washington, DC 20007. Hope Daniels, Ed. Fiction, to 2,000 words, for military families in the U.S. and overseas. Pays to $200, on publication.

MILWAUKEE—312 E. Buffalo, Milwaukee, WI 53202. Charles Sykes, Ed. Regional fiction. Pays on publication.

MS.—One Times Sq., New York, NY 10036. Address Ed. Dept., Fiction. Short stories, to 3,000 words, on women's changing self-image and status. SASE required. Limited market.

NA'AMAT WOMAN—200 Madison Ave., 18th fl., New York, NY 10016. Judith A. Sokoloff, Ed. Short stories, 2,500 words, with Jewish theme. Pays 8¢ a word, on publication.

NATIONAL RACQUETBALL—P.O. Drawer 6126, Clearwater, FL 33528. Sigmund Brouwer, Ed. Fiction, related to racquetball. Pays $25 to $150, on publication.

THE NEW BLACK MASK QUARTERLY—See *A Matter of Crime.*

THE NEW YORKER—25 W. 43rd St., New York, NY 10036. Short stories, humor, and satire. Pays varying rates, on acceptance. Include SASE.

NORTHEAST MAGAZINE—*The Hartford Courant,* 285 Broad St., Hartford, CT 06115. Lary Bloom, Ed. Short stories, to 4,000 words; must have

Connecticut tie-in, or be universal in theme and have non-specific setting. Pays $300 to $600, on acceptance. SASE required.

NORTHERN LIGHTS—Box 8084, Missoula, MT 59807–9962. Dan Whipple, Ed. Occasional fiction about the West (especially the Rocky Mountains). Pays on publication.

OMNI—1965 Broadway, New York, NY 10023–5965. Ellen Datlow, Fiction Ed. Strong, realistic science fiction, to 9,000 words. Some contemporary hard-edge fantasy. Pays to $2,000, on acceptance.

OUR FAMILY—Box 249, Battleford, Sask., Canada S0M 0E0. N. Gregoire, O.M.I., Ed. Fiction, 1,000 to 3,000 words, on the struggle to live the Christian life in the face of modern-day problems. Pays 7¢ to 10¢ a word, on acceptance. Write for guidelines. Enclose *international postal reply coupons* with SAE.

PENTHOUSE—1965 Broadway, New York, NY 10023. No unsolicited fiction.

PLAYBOY—919 N. Michigan Ave., Chicago, IL 60611. Alice K. Turner, Fiction Ed. Quality fiction, 1,000 to 10,000 words (average 6,000): suspense, mystery, adventure and sports short stories; stories about contemporary relationships; science fiction. Active plots and strong characterization. Pays from $1,000 to $3,000, on acceptance.

PLAYGIRL—801 Second Ave., New York, NY 10017. Mary Ellen Strote, Fiction Ed. Contemporary, romantic fiction, 1,000 to 4,000 words. Pays from $300, after acceptance.

POCKETS—1908 Grand Ave., Box 189, Nashville, TN 37202. Shirley Paris, Assistant Ed. Contemporary fiction and scripture stories, 600 to 1,500 words, for children aged 6 to 12: a Christian focus is required. Pays 7¢ a word, on acceptance. Guidelines.

PRIME TIMES—Suite 210, 2802 International Ln., Madison, WI 53704. Journal for the National Assn. for Retired Credit Union People. Joan Donovan, Exec. Ed. Fiction, 2,500 to 4,000 words; dynamic, upbeat, young themes. Pays varying rates, on publication. Query.

PULPSMITH—5 Beekman St., New York, NY 10038. Harry Smith, General Ed. Literary genre fiction; mainstream, mystery, SF, westerns. Pays $35 to $100 for fiction, on acceptance.

PURPOSE—616 Walnut Ave., Scottdale, PA 15683–1999. James E. Horsch, Ed. Fiction 1,200 words, on problem solving from a Christian point of view. Poetry, 3 to 12 lines. Pays up to 5¢ a word, to $1 per line for poetry, extra for photos, on acceptance.

RANGER RICK MAGAZINE—8925 Leesburg Pike, Vienna, VA 22184–0001. Betty Athey, Fiction Ed. Nature- and conservation-related fiction, for 7- to 12-year olds. Maximum: 900 words. Pays to $350, on acceptance. Buys all rights.

REDBOOK—224 W. 57th St., New York, NY 10019. Deborah Purcell, Fiction Ed. Fresh, distinctive short stories, of interest to women, about love and relationships, friendship, careers, parenting, family dilemmas, confronting basic problems of contemporary life and women's issues. Pays $850 for short-shorts (about 9 manuscript pages), from $1,000 for short stories (to 20 pages). Allow 8 to 10 weeks for reply. Manuscripts without SASEs will not be returned. No unsolicited novellas or novels accepted.

657

ROAD KING—P.O. Box 250, Park Forest, IL 60466. George Friend, Ed. Short stories, 1,200 to 1,500 words, for and/or about truck drivers. Pays to $400, on acceptance.

ROD SERLING'S THE TWILIGHT ZONE MAGAZINE—800 Second Ave., New York, NY 10017. Tappan King, Ed.-in-Chief. Fiction, to 7,500 words: human-centered fantasies, horror, and science fiction, involving "ordinary people in extraordinary events." Avoid genre cliches. Pays 6¢ to 10¢ a word, half on acceptance, half on publication.

RURAL LIVING—P.O. Box 15248, Richmond, VA 23227–0648. Richard G. Johnstone, Jr., Ed. Family-oriented fiction, 1,000 to 1,500 words. Pays on acceptance.

ST. ANTHONY MESSENGER—1615 Republic St., Cincinnati, OH 45210. Norman Perry, Ed. Fiction that makes readers think about issues, lifestyles and values. Pays 12¢ a word, on acceptance. Query first.

SAN FRANCISCO FOCUS—680 Eighth St., San Francisco, CA 94103. Mark Powelson, Ed. Short stories, 1,500 to 5,000 words. Pays from $250, on publication.

THE SATURDAY EVENING POST—1100 Waterway Blvd., Indianapolis, IN 46202. Dan Anger, Fiction Ed. Upbeat short stories, 500 to 4,000 words, that lend themselves to illustration. Humor. Pays varying rates, on publication.

SCHOLASTIC SCOPE—Scholastic, Inc., 730 Broadway, New York, NY 10003. Fran Claro, Ed. Fiction for 15- to 18-year olds, with 4th to 6th grade reading ability. Short stories, 500 to 1,000 words, on teen-age interests and relationships; family, job and school situations. Pays good rates, on acceptance.

SEA KAYAKER—1670 Duranleau St., Vancouver, BC, V6H 3S4 Canada. John Dowd, Ed. Short stories related to ocean kayaking, 1,500 words. Pays on publication. Enclose international reply coupons for return of material.

SEVENTEEN—850 Third Ave., New York, NY 10022. Sara London, Fiction Ed. High-quality literary fiction for young adults. Pays on acceptance.

SOUTHERN—P.O. Box 3418, 201 E. Markham, Suite 200, Little Rock, AR 72203. Linton Weeks, Ed. Short stories by Southern writers. Pays on acceptance.

SPORTS AFIELD—250 W. 55th St., New York, NY 10019. Tom Paugh, Ed. Fiction, on hunting, fishing, and related topics. Outdoor adventure stories. Humor. Pays top rates, on acceptance.

STORY CARDS—P.O. Box 11575, Washington, DC 20008–0775. Bill Adler, Pub. Short stories, to 2,000 words, for greeting card-sized literary publication. SASE required. Pays $100 to $900. Guidelines.

STRAIGHT—8121 Hamilton Ave., Cincinnati, OH 45231. Dawn Korth, Ed. Well-constructed fiction, 1,000 to 1,500 words, showing Christian teens using Bible principles in everyday life. Contemporary, realistic teen characters a must. Most interested in school, church, dating, and family life stories. Pays about 3¢ a word, on acceptance. Send SASE for guidelines.

SUNDAY DIGEST—850 N. Grove Ave., Elgin, IL 60120. Janette L. Pearson, Ed. Short, reflective anecdotes (500 words) and personal experience short stories (1,000 to 1,500 words), with evangelical religious slant. Pays 10¢ a word, on acceptance.

SUNDAY MAGAZINE—*The Minneapolis Star & Tribune,* 425 Portland Ave., Minneapolis, MN 55488. Fiction, to 3,000 words, with a regional slant. Query first. Pays on publication.

SUNDAY MAGAZINE—*Providence Sunday Journal,* 75 Fountain St., Providence, RI 02902. Alan Rosenberg, Ed. Fiction, 1,000 to 1,500 words. Pays from $75, on publication.

SUNSHINE MAGAZINE—Litchfield, IL 62056. Peggy Kuethe, Ed. Wholesome fiction, 900 to 1,200 words; short stories for youths, 400 to 700 words. Pays to $100, on acceptance. Guidelines.

SWANK—888 Seventh Ave., New York, NY 10106. Bob Rosen, Fiction Ed. Graphic erotic short stories, to 2,500 words. Pays on publication. Limited market.

'TEEN—8490 Sunset Blvd., Los Angeles, CA 90069. Address Fiction Dept. Short stories 2,500 to 4,000 words: mystery, travel, adventure, romance, humor for teens. Pays from $100, on acceptance.

TQ/TEEN QUEST—Box 82808, Lincoln, NE 68501. Nancy Bayne, Man. Ed. Fiction, to 2,000 words, for Christian teens. Pays 4¢ to 10¢ a word, on acceptance.

TEENS TODAY—Nazarene Publishing House, 6401 The Paseo, Kansas City, MO 64131. Karen De Sollar, Ed. Short stories 1,200 to 1,500 words, that deal with teens demonstrating Christian principles in real-life situations; adventure stories. Pays 3½¢ a word, on acceptance.

THIRD COAST—P.O. Box 592, Austin, TX 78767. Kate Berger, Man. Ed. Some fiction, with an Austin slant. Pays from 10¢ a word, after publication.

TOLEDO MAGAZINE—*The Sunday Blade,* 541 Superior St., Toledo, OH 43660. Sue Stankey, Ed. Fiction, with a Toledo/Ohio slant. Pays on publication. Query.

TRIFLE MAGAZINE—P.O. Box 182, Dover, NH 03820. Mary Pat Kingsbury, Ed./Pub. Fiction, to 2,000 words, in news article format: "Humorous fictional news presented in standard news magazine format." Send complete manuscript and SASE. Pays to $150, on publication. Guidelines.

TRISTATE MAGAZINE—*The Cincinnati Enquirer,* 617 Vine St., Cincinnati, OH 45201. Alice Hornbaker, Ed. Short stories, related to Ohio, Northern Kentucky and Indiana. Pays on publication. Query first.

TRUCKS—20 Waterside Plaza, New York, NY 10010–2615. John Stevens, Ed. Fiction, to 1,500 words, of interest to long-haul truck drivers. Pays $50 to $100 per published page.

U (formerly *His*)—P.O. Box 1450, Downers Grove, IL 60515. Verne Becker, Ed. Fiction about college students who experience emotional and/or spiritual growth, to 2,000 words. No fantasy, parables or Bible retellings. Pays 2¢ to 5¢ a word, on acceptance.

VANITY FAIR—350 Madison Ave., New York, NY 10017. Joyce Johnson, Fiction Ed. Fiction of high literary quality. Pays varying rates.

VIRTUE—Box 850, Sisters, OR 97759. Becky Durost Fish, Ed. Fiction with a Christian slant. Pays 10¢ a word, on publication.

WE ALASKANS—*Anchorage Daily News,* Box 6616, Anchorage, AK

99502. Kathleen McCoy, Ed. Short stories on Alaskan topics. Pays on publication.

WESTERN PEOPLE—Box 2500, Saskatoon, Sask., Canada S7K 2C4. Short stories, 1,000 to 2,500 words, on subjects or themes of interest to rural readers in Western Canada. Pays $40 to $150, on acceptance. Enclose international postal reply coupons and SASE.

WILDFOWL—1901 Bell Ave., Suite #4, Des Moines, IA 50315. B. Wilbanks, Man. Ed. Occasional fiction, humor, related to duck hunters and wildfowl. Pays $200 to $300, on acceptance.

WISCONSIN TRAILS—P.O. Box 5650, Madison, WI 53705. Geri Nixon, Man. Ed. Fiction, with regional slant. Pays $100 to $300, on acceptance and on publication.

WOMAN'S DAY—1515 Broadway, New York, NY 10036. Eileen Herbert Jordan, Fiction Ed. Short fiction, humorous or serious. Pays top rates, on acceptance.

WOMAN'S WORLD—P.O. Box 6700, Englewood, NJ 07631. Elinor Nauen, Fiction Ed. Fast-moving short stories, about 4,500 words, with light romantic theme. Mini-mysteries, 1,600 to 1,700 words, with "whodunit" or "howdunit" theme. No science fiction, fantasy or historical romance. Pays $1,000 for short stories, $500 for mini-mysteries, on acceptance. Submit manuscript with SASE.

WOODMEN OF THE WORLD MAGAZINE—1700 Farnam St., Omaha, NE 68102. Leland A. Larson, Ed. Family-oriented fiction. Pays 5¢ a word, on acceptance.

WORKING MOTHER—230 Park Ave., New York, NY 10169. Maria Buhl, Assoc. Ed. Realistic short stories, 750 to 2,500 words, for working mothers. Pays $400 to $800, on acceptance.

YANKEE—Dublin, NH 03444. Judson Hale, Ed. Edie Clark, Fiction Ed. High-quality, literary short fiction, to 4,000 words, with setting in or compatible with New England. Pays $1,000, on acceptance.

DETECTIVE AND MYSTERY

ALFRED HITCHCOCK'S MYSTERY MAGAZINE—380 Lexington Ave., New York, NY 10017. Cathleen Jordan, Ed. Well-plotted mystery, detective, suspense and crime fiction, 1,000 to 14,000 words. Submissions by new writers strongly encouraged. Pays 5¢ a word, on acceptance.

ARMCHAIR DETECTIVE—129 W. 56th St., New York, NY 10019. Michael Seidman, Ed. Articles on mystery and detective fiction; biographical sketches, reviews, etc. Pays in copies.

DETECTIVE DRAGNET—1440 St. Catherine W., Suite 625, Montreal, Quebec, Canada H3G 1S2. Dominick A. Merle, Ed. Well-researched true crime stories, 3,500 to 6,000 words, with photos, involving mystery, suspense and lots of human interest. No fiction. Include clippings describing the case, with date, location and names of victims and suspects. Pays $200 to $300, on acceptance. Same address and requirements for *Detective Cases, Detective Files, Headquarters Detective, Startling Detective,* and *True Police Cases.*

ELLERY QUEEN'S MYSTERY MAGAZINE—380 Lexington Ave., New

York, NY 10017. Eleanor Sullivan, Ed. Detective, crime, mystery and spy fiction, 4,000 to 6,000 words. Suspense or straight detective stories. No sex, sadism or sensationalism. Particularly interested in new writers and "first stories." Pays 3¢ to 8¢ a word, on acceptance.

FRONT PAGE DETECTIVE—See *Inside Detective*.

HEADQUARTERS DETECTIVE—See *Detective Dragnet*.

INSIDE DETECTIVE—Reese Communications, Inc., 460 W. 34th St., New York, NY 10001. Rose Mandelsberg, Ed. Timely, true detective stories, 5,000 to 6,000 words. No fiction. Pays $250, extra for photos, on acceptance. Query. Same address and requirements for *Front Page Detective*.

MASTER DETECTIVE—460 W. 34th St., New York, NY 10001. Art Crockett, Ed. Detailed articles, 5,000 to 6,000 words, with photos, on current cases, emphasizing human motivation and detective work. Pays to $250, on acceptance. Query.

A MATTER OF CRIME (formerly *The New Black Mask Quarterly*)—2006 Sumter St., Columbia, SC 29201. Matthew J. Bruccoli, Richard Layman, Eds. Mystery fiction, 3,000 to 6,000 words. Pays to 10¢ a word, on publication.

OFFICIAL DETECTIVE STORIES—460 W. 34th St., New York, NY 10001. Art Crockett, Ed. True detective stories, 5,000 to 6,000 words, on current investigations, strictly from the investigator's point of view. No fiction. Photos. Pays $250, extra for photos, on acceptance. Query.

STARTLING DETECTIVE—See *Detective Dragnet*.

TRUE DETECTIVE—460 W. 34th St., New York, NY 10001. Art Crockett, Ed. Articles, from 5,000 words, with photos, on current police cases, emphasizing detective work and human motivation. No fiction. Pays $250, extra for photos, on acceptance. Query.

TRUE POLICE CASES—See *Detective Dragnet*.

SCIENCE FICTION AND FANTASY

ABORIGINAL SF—P.O. Box 2449, Woburn, MA 01888–0849. Charles C. Ryan, Ed. Short stories, 2,500 to 4,500 words, and poetry, 1 to 2 typed pages, with strong science content, lively, unique characters, and well-designed plots. No sword and sorcery or fantasy. Pays $200 for fiction, $20 to $25 for poetry, $5 for SF jokes, and $15 for cartoons, on publication.

AMAZING STORIES—Box 110, Lake Geneva, WI 53147. Patrick L. Price, Ed. Science fiction and fantasy, to 15,000 words. Also general-interest science articles; query first or nonfiction. Pays 5¢ to 8¢ a word, on acceptance.

ANALOG SCIENCE FICTION/SCIENCE FACT—380 Lexington Ave., New York, NY 10017. Stanley Schmidt, Ed. Science fiction, with strong characters in believable future or alien setting: short stories, 2,000 to 7,500 words; novelettes, 10,000 to 20,000 words; serials, to 80,000 words. Also uses future-related articles. Pays to 7¢ a word, on acceptance. Query on serials and articles.

THE ASYMPTOTICAL WORLD—P.O. Box 1372, Williamsport, PA 17703. Michael H. Gerardi, Ed. Psychodramas, fantasy, experimental fiction, 1,500 to 2,500 words. Illustrations, photographs. Pays 2¢ a word, on acceptance.

DIFFERENT WORLDS—2814–19th St., San Francisco, CA 94110. Tadashi

Ehara, Ed. Articles, to 5,000 words, on role-playing games: reviews, variants, source materials, etc. Pays 1¢ a word, on publication. Query preferred.

DRAGON MAGAZINE—P.O. Box 110, Lake Geneva, WI 53147. Roger E. Moore, Editor-In-Chief. Patrick L. Price, Fiction Ed. Articles 1,500 to 10,000 words, on fantasy and SF role-playing games. Fiction, 1,500 to 8,000 words. Pays 5¢ to 8¢ a word for fiction, slightly lower for articles, on publication. Query.

EMPIRE/WAYSTATION FOR THE SF WRITER—1025 55th St., Oakland, CA 94608. Millea Kenin, Ed. Articles, 2,000 words preferred, on the craft of writing science fiction and fantasy. Cartoons, illustrations, poetry. Pays negotiable rates, on publication. Query. Send SASE for guidelines.

FANTASY MACABRE—P.O. Box 20610, Seattle, WA 98120. Jessica Salmonson, Ed. Fiction, to 3,000 words, and poetry of any length. "We look for a tale that is strong in atmosphere, with menace that is suggested and threatening rather than the result of dripping blood and gore." Pays 1¢ a word, to $30 per story, on publication.

FANTASY REVIEW—College of Humanities, Florida Atlantic University, Boca Raton, FL 33431. Robert A. Collins, Ed. Articles and interviews, to 5,000 words, on SF, fantasy, horror. No fiction. Occasional poetry. Cartoons, photos, artwork. Pays varying rates.

FOOTSTEPS—Box 75, Round Top, NY 12473. Bill Munster, Ed. Material related to horror, supernatural, or the weird tale: essays, reviews, profiles, fiction, to 3,500 words. Poetry to 40 lines. Pays 1¢ a word.

GRUE MAGAZINE—Box 370, Times Square Sta., New York, NY 10108. Peggy Nadramia, Ed. Fiction, 3,500 words, and macabre/surreal poetry of any length. "We're looking for stories about people; characterization and motivation are important to us." Pays ½¢ per word for fiction, $5 per poem, on publication.

THE HORROR SHOW—Phantasm Press, 14848 Misty Springs Lane, Oak Run, CA 96069. David B. Silva, Ed. Contemporary horror fiction, to 4,000 words, with a style that keeps the reader's hand trembling as he turns the pages. Pays ½¢ to 1¢ a word, on acceptance. Send SASE for guidelines.

ISAAC ASIMOV'S SCIENCE FICTION MAGAZINE—380 Lexington Ave., New York, NY 10017. Gardner Dozois, Ed. Short, character-oriented science fiction and fantasy, to 15,000 words. Pays 4¢ to 7¢ a word, on acceptance. Send SASE for requirements.

THE MAGAZINE OF FANTASY AND SCIENCE FICTION—Box 56, Cornwall, CT 06753. Edward Ferman, Ed. Fantasy and science fiction stories, to 10,000 words. Pays 5¢ to 7¢ a word, on acceptance.

THE MAGE—The Colgate Science Fiction & Fantasy Assn., CUSA, Colgate Univ., Hamilton, NY 13346. Jeffrey V. Yule, Ed. Science fiction and fantasy stories, varying lengths. Articles, reviews. poetry. Pays in copies. Include SASE.

MAGICAL BLEND—Box 11303, San Francisco, CA 94101. Steven Spears, Literary Ed. Positive, uplifting articles on spiritual exploration, lifestyles, occult, white magic and fantasy. Fiction and features to 5,000 words, Poetry, 4 to 40 lines. Pays in copies.

MYTHOS—Crown Creations Associates, Box 11626, St. Paul, MN 55111–

0626. Steven Mark Deyo, Ed. "A journal of mythopoeic art, studies, and humor, treating any aspect of myth or the 'secondary worlds' of fantasy/SF authors in the vein of mythopoeia." Poetry, fiction, and literary studies. Pays in copies, on publication.

NIGHT CRY—800 Second Ave., New York, NY 10017. Alan Rodgers, Ed. Horror fiction and poetry. Some fantasy, mystery, and science fiction. Pays 5¢ to 7¢ a word, half on acceptance, half on publication.

OMNI—1965 Broadway, New York, NY 10023–1965. Ellen Datlow, Ed. Strong, realistic science fiction, 2,000 to 9,000 words, with real people as characters. Some fantasy. No horror, ghost or sword and sorcery tales. Pays $1,250–$2,000, on acceptance.

OWLFLIGHT—1025 55th St., Oakland, CA 94608. Millea Kenin, Ed. Science fiction and fantasy, 3,000 to 10,000 words. Since fiction/fantasy poetry, 8 to 100 lines. Photographs, illustrations. Pays 1¢ a word, extra for illustrations, on publication. Send SASE for guidelines.

ROD SERLING'S TWILIGHT ZONE MAGAZINE—800 Second Ave., New York, NY 10017. Tappan King, Ed.-in-Chief. Fiction, to 7,500 words: human-centered fantasies of horror, suspense and the supernatural involving "ordinary people in extraordinary events." Pays about 6¢ to 10¢ a word, half on acceptance, half on publication.

SCIENCE FICTION CHRONICLE—P.O. Box 4175, New York, NY 10163. Andrew Porter, Ed. News items, 100 to 1,000 words, for SF and fantasy readers, professionals, and collectors. Photos and short articles on authors' signings, events, conventions. Pays 3¢ to 5¢ a word, on publication.

SPACE AND TIME—138 W. 70th St., #4B, New York, NY 10023. Fantasy fiction, to 15,000 words; science fiction, supernatural, sword and sorcery. Pays ¼¢ a word for fiction, on acceptance.

THRESHOLD OF FANTASY—P.O. Box 70868, Sunnyvale, CA 94086. Randall D. Larson, Ed. Fiction (fantasy, horror, sci-fi), to 5,000 words; book reviews; interviews to 1,000 words. Pays ½¢ a word for fiction, $20 for interviews, copies for reviews and poetry, on acceptance and on publication. Guidelines.

THRUST: SCIENCE FICTION & FANTASY REVIEW—8217 Langport Terrace, Gaithersburg, MD 20877. D. Douglas Fratz, Ed. Articles, interviews, 2,000 to 6,000 words, for readers familiar with SF and related literary and scientific topics. Book reviews, 100 to 800 words. Pays 1¢ to 2¢ a word on publication. Query preferred.

CONFESSION AND ROMANCE

INTIMACY—355 Lexington Ave., New York, NY 10017. Natasha Brooks, Ed. Fiction 2,000 to 3,000 words, for women age 18 to 45; must have contemporary, glamorous plot and contain two explicit love scenes. Pays $75 to $100, on publication. Same address for *Jive,* geared toward younger women seeking adventure, glamour and romance.

JIVE—See *Intimacy.*

MODERN ROMANCES—215 Lexington Ave., New York, NY 10016. Jean Sharbel, Ed. Confession stories with reader-identification and strong emotional tone, 1,500 to 7,500 words. Articles for blue-collar, family-oriented women, 300 to 1,000 words. Pays 5¢ a word, after publication. Buys all rights.

SECRETS—215 Lexington Ave., New York, NY 10016. Jean Press Silberg, Ed. Realistic, emotional confession stories, 1,500 to 10,000 words, emphasizing family, home, and love relationships. Articles on subjects of interest to blue-collar, family-oriented women. Pays 3¢ a word, on publication. Buys all rights.

TRUE CONFESSIONS—215 Lexington Ave., New York, NY 10016. Barbara J. Brett, Ed. Timely, emotional, first-person stories, 2,000 to 10,000 words, on romance, family life, and problems of today's young blue-collar women. Articles, 300 to 700 words, for young wives and mothers. Pays 5¢ a word, after publication.

TRUE EXPERIENCE—215 Lexington Ave., New York, NY 10016. Paula Sciarrino, Ed. Realistic first-person stories, 4,000 to 8,000 words (short-shorts, to 2,000 words), on family life, love, courtship, health, religion, etc. Pays 3¢ a word, after publication.

TRUE LOVE—215 Lexington Ave., New York, NY 10016. Colleen Brennan, Ed. Fresh, true first-person stories, on young love, marital problems, and topics of current interest. Pays 3¢ a word, a month after publication.

TRUE ROMANCE—215 Lexington Ave., New York, NY 10016. Susan Weiner, Ed. True, romantic first-person stories, 2,000 to 12,000 words. Love poems. Articles, 300 to 700 words, for young wives and singles. Pays 3¢ a word, a month after publication.

POETRY MARKETS

Markets for both serious and light verse are included in the following list of magazines.

Although major magazines pay good rates for poetry, the competition to break into print is very stiff, since editors use only a limited number of poems in each issue. On the other hand, college, little, and literary magazines use a great deal of poetry, and though payment is modest—usually in copies—publication in these journals can establish a beginning poet's reputation, and lead to publication in the major magazines. (The listing of college, literary, and little magazines, which begins on page 671, includes requirements for poetry, fiction, and essays). Poets will find a number of competitions offering cash awards for unpublished poems in the *Literary Prize Offers* list, beginning on page 754.

Poets should also consider local newspapers as possible verse markets. Although they may not specifically seek poetry from free lancers, newspaper editors often print verse submitted to them, especially on holidays and for special occasions.

The market for book-length collections of poetry is extremely limited. Commercial publishers bring out few volumes of poetry. There are a number of university presses that publish poetry collections, however (see page 749), and many of them sponsor annual competitions. Consult the *Literary Prize Offers* list for more information about these contests.

ALCOHOLISM & ADDICTION MAGAZINE—P.O. Box 31329, Seattle,

WA 98103. Neil Scott, Ed. Poetry, 4 to 15 lines, on recovery from chemical or other dependencies; humor. Guidelines available.

ALOHA—828 Fort St. Mall, Suite 640, Honolulu, HI 96813. Rita Ariyoshi, Ed. Poetry relating to Hawaii. Pays $25 per poem, on publication.

AMAZING STORIES—Box 110, Lake Geneva, WI 53147. Patrick Lucien Price, Ed. Serious and light verse, with SF/fantasy tie-in. Pays $1.00 per line for short poems, somewhat less for longer ones, on acceptance.

AMERICA—106 W. 56th St., New York, NY 10019. John Moffitt, Poetry Ed. Serious poetry of high quality, preferably in contemporary prose idiom, 10 to 30 lines. Half-rhyme and occasional light verse. Submit 2 or 3 poems only. Pays $1.40 per line, on publication. Guidelines.

THE AMERICAN SCHOLAR—1811 Q St., N.W., Washington, DC 20009. Joseph Epstein, Ed. Highly original poetry, 10 to 32 lines, for college-educated, intellectual readers. Pays $50, on acceptance.

THE AMICUS JOURNAL—Natural Resources Defense Council, 122 E. 42nd St., Rm. 4500, New York, NY 10168. Peter Borrelli, Ed. Poetry, varying lengths, related to national and international environmental policy. Pays on acceptance.

THE ATLANTIC—8 Arlington St., Boston, MA 02116. Peter Davison, Poetry Ed. Poetry of highest quality. Limited market; only 3 to 4 poems an issue. Interest in young poets. Occasionally uses light verse. Pays excellent rates, on acceptance.

THE ATLANTIC ADVOCATE—P.O. Box 3370, Fredericton, N.B., Canada E3B 5A2. Poetry related to Canada's Atlantic provinces. Pays to $5 per column inch, on publication.

BLACK ELEGANCE—475 Park Ave. South, New York, NY 10016. Sharyn J. Skeeter, Ed. Poetry, to 25 lines, of interest to sophisticated black women ages 25 to 45. Pays on publication.

BURLINGTON MAGAZINE—333 S. Union St., Burlington, VT 05401. Tim Etchells, Ed. Poetry with Burlington area tie-in. Pays varying rates, on acceptance.

CAPE COD LIFE—P.O. Box 222, Osterville, MA 02655. Mary Shortsleeve, Ed. Poetry, all kinds, with special interest in nature or coastal themes. Pays on publication.

CAPPER'S—616 Jefferson St., Topeka, KS 66607. Dorothy Harvey, Ed. Traditional poetry and free verse, 4 to 16 lines. Submit up to 6 poems at a time, with SASE. Pays $3 to $5, on acceptance.

CHILDREN'S PLAYMATE—P.O. Box 567, Indianapolis, IN 46206. Elizabeth A. Rinck, Ed. Poetry for children, 5 to 7 years old, on good health, nutrition, exercise, safety, seasonal and humorous subjects. Pays from $10, on publication. Buys all rights.

THE CHRISTIAN SCIENCE MONITOR—One Norway St., Boston, MA 02115. Maggie Lewis, Ed., The Home Forum. Fresh, vigorous nonreligious poems of high quality, on various subjects. Short poems preferred. Pays varying rates, on acceptance. Submit no more than 5 poems at a time.

CLASS—27 Union Sq., West, New York, NY 10003. Velma R. Dortch, Ed. Poetry, 8 to 10 lines, related to the Third World population in the U.S. Payment varies, after publication.

COBBLESTONE—20 Grove St., Peterborough, NH 03458. Carolyn P. Yoder, Ed. Poetry, to 100 lines, on monthly themes, for 8- to 14-year olds. Pays varying rates, on publication. Send SASE for guidelines and themes.

COMMONWEAL—15 Dutch St., New York, NY 10038. Rosemary Deen, Ed. Catholic. Serious, witty poetry. Pays 50¢ a line, on publication.

COMPLETE WOMAN—1165 N. Clark St., Chicago, IL 60610. Address Mary James, Assoc. Ed. Poetry. Pays $10, on publication. SASE necessary for return of material.

COSMOPOLITAN—224 W. 57th St., New York, NY 10019. Karen Burke, Poetry Ed. Poetry about relationships, for young, active career women. Pays from $25, on acceptance.

COUNTRY WOMAN (formerly *Farm Woman*)—P.O. Box 643, Milwaukee, WI 53201. Eleanor Jacobs, Man. Ed. Traditional rural poetry and light verse, 20 to 25 lines, on rural experiences, for farm and ranch women. Pays $40 to $60, on acceptance.

DECISION—Billy Graham Evangelistic Assn., 1300 Harmon Pl., Minneapolis, MN 55403. Roger C. Palms, Ed. Poems, 5 to 20 lines, on devotional and other subjects; preference for free verse. Pays on publication.

THE DISCIPLE—Box 179, St. Louis, MO 63166. James L. Merrell, Ed. Londia R. Darden, Poetry Ed. Journal of Disciples of Christ. Poetry, on religious, seasonal, and historical subjects. Pays $5 to $15, on publication.

ESSENCE—1500 Broadway, New York, NY 10036. Susan L. Taylor, Ed.-in-Chief. Poetry, to 29 lines, for black women. Pays $25.

THE EVANGEL—Dept. of Christian Education, Free Methodist Headquarters, 901 College Ave., Winona Lake, IN 46590. Vera Bethel, Ed. Free Methodist. Devotional or nature poetry, 8 to 16 lines. Pays $5, on publication.

EVANGELICAL BEACON—1515 E. 66th St., Minneapolis, MN 55423. George Keck, Ed. Denominational publication of Evangelical Free Church of America. Some poetry related to Christian faith. Pays 4¢ a word. $2.50 minimum, on publication.

FAMILY CIRCLE—110 Fifth Ave., New York, NY 10011. No unsolicited poetry.

FARM AND RANCH LIVING—5400 S. 60th St., Greendale, WI 53129. Bob Ottum, Ed. Poetry, to 20 lines, on rural people and situations. Photos. Pays $35 to $75, extra for photos, on acceptance and on publication. Query.

FARM WOMAN—See *Country Woman*.

GEORGIA JOURNAL—Agee Publishers, P.O. Box 526, Athens, GA 30603. Janice Moore, Ed. Poetry, to 20 lines, related to Georgia. Pays on acceptance.

GOLF DIGEST MAGAZINE—5520 Park Ave., Trumbull, CT 06611–0395. Lois Hains, Ass't. Ed. Humorous golf-related verse, 4 to 8 lines. Pays $20 to $25, on acceptance. Send SASE.

GOOD HOUSEKEEPING—959 8th Ave., New York, NY 10019. Rosemary Leonard, Ed. Light, humorous verses, quips, and poems. Pays $25 for four lines, $50 for eight lines, on acceptance.

GRIT—208 W. Third St., Williamsport, PA 17701. Joanne Decker, Assignment Ed. Traditional poetry and light verse, 4 to 16 lines, for readers in small-town and rural America. Pays $6 for poems up to 4 lines, 50¢ a line for each additional line, on acceptance.

HOME LIFE—127 Ninth Ave., N., Nashville, TN 37234. Reuben Herring, Ed. Southern Baptist. Short lyrical verse, humorous, marriage and family, seasonal, and inspirational. Pays to $24, on acceptance.

LADIES' HOME JOURNAL—100 Park Ave., New York, NY 10017. No unsolicited poetry; submit through an agent only.

LEATHERNECK—Box 1775, Quantico, VA 22134. W.V.H. White, Ed. Publication related to the U.S. Marine Corps. Marine-related poetry. Pays from $10, on acceptance. SASE required.

MCCALL'S MAGAZINE—230 Park Ave., New York, NY 10169. Over-stocked.

MARRIAGE AND FAMILY LIVING—Abbey Press Publishing Div., St. Meinrad, IN 47577. Kass Dotterweich, Man. Ed. Verse, on marriage and family. Pays $15, on publication.

MATURE YEARS—201 Eighth Ave. S., Nashville, TN 37202. John P. Gilbert, Ed. United Methodist. Poetry, to 14 lines, on pre-retirement, retirement, seasonal subjects, aging. No saccharine poetry. Pays 50¢ to $1.00 per line.

MIDSTREAM—515 Park Ave., New York, NY 10022. Joel Carmichael, Ed. Poetry, of Jewish interest. Pays $25, on publication.

THE MIRACULOUS MEDAL—475 E. Chelten Ave., Philadelphia, PA 19144. Robert P. Cawley, C.M., Ed. Catholic. Religious verse, to 20 lines. Pays 50¢ a line, on acceptance.

MODERN BRIDE—One Park Ave., New York, NY 10016. Mary Ann Cavlin, Man. Ed. Short verse of interest to bride and groom. Pays $25 to $35, on acceptance.

MODERN MATURITY—3200 E. Carson St., Lakewood, CA 90712. Ian Ledgerwood, Ed. Short verse to 40 lines. Pays from $50, on acceptance.

MS.—One Times Sq., New York, NY 10036. Address Poetry Ed. Poetry of high quality, on feminist subjects. Pays $75, on acceptance.

THE NATION—72 Fifth Ave., New York, NY 10011. Grace Schulman, Poetry Ed. Poetry of high quality. Pays after publication.

NATIONAL ENQUIRER—Lantana, FL 33464. Jim Allan, Asst. Ed. Short poems of a philosophical or amusing nature. Pays $20, on publication. Include SASE.

NEW ENGLAND ENTERTAINMENT—P.O. Box 735, Marshfield, MA 02050. Paul J. Reale, Ed. Light verse, of any length, related to the entertainment field. Pays $1 to $2, on publication.

THE NEW REPUBLIC—1220 19th St., N.W., Washington, DC 20036. Richard Howard, Poetry Ed. Poetry, of interest to liberal, intellectual readers. Pays $75, after publication.

THE NEW YORKER—25 W. 43rd St., New York, NY 10036. First-rate poetry and light verse. Pays top rates, on acceptance. Include SASE.

NORTHWEST MAGAZINE—*The Oregonian,* 1320 SW Broadway, Portland, OR 97201. Address Poetry Ed. Traditional and experimental poetry, by Northwest poets only. Pays $10 on acceptance.

OUR FAMILY—Box 249, Dept. E., Battleford, Sask., Canada, S0M 0E0. Rev. Albert LaLonde, O.M.I. Catholic. Verse, for family men and women. Pays 75¢ to $1.00 a line, on acceptance. Send SAE with *international reply coupons* for guidelines.

PENTECOSTAL EVANGEL—1445 Boonville, Springfield, MO 65802. Richard G. Champion, Ed. Journal of Assemblies of God. Religious and inspirational verse, 12 to 30 lines. Pays to 40¢ a line, on publication.

POCKETS—1908 Grand Ave., Box 189, Nashville, TN 37202. Shirley Paris, Assistant Ed. Short poems, for children aged 6 to 12, that illuminate a Christian life style. Pays $25 to $50, on acceptance. Guidelines.

PURPOSE—616 Walnut Ave., Scottdale, PA 15683–1999. James E. Horsch, Poetry Ed. Poetry, to 12 lines, with challenging Christian discipleship angle. Pays 50¢ to $1 a line, on acceptance.

ST. JOSEPH'S MESSENGER—P.O. Box 288, Jersey City, NJ 07303. Sister Ursula Marie Maphet, Ed. Light verse and traditional poetry, 4 to 40 lines. Pays $5 to $15, on publication.

THE SATURDAY EVENING POST—1100 Waterway Blvd., Indianapolis, IN 46202. Address Post Scripts Ed. Light verse and humor. Pays $15, on publication.

SCORE, CANADA'S GOLF MAGAZINE—287 MacPherson Ave., Toronto, Ont., Canada M4V 1A4. Poetry, to 50 words, on the Canadian and U.S. golf scene. Pays to $20, on publication.

SEVENTEEN—850 Third Ave., New York, NY 10022. Poetry, to 40 lines, by teens. Submit up to 5 poems. Pays $15, after acceptance.

UNITED METHODIST REPORTER—P.O. Box 660275, Dallas, TX 75266–0275. Spurgeon M. Dunnam III, Editor. Religious verse, 4 to 16 lines. Pays $2, on acceptance.

WESTERN PEOPLE—P.O. Box 2500, Saskatoon, Sask., Canada S7K 2C4. Mary Gilchrist, Man. Ed. Short poetry, with Western Canadian themes. Pays on acceptance. Send SAE with *international reply coupons*.

YANKEE—Dublin, NH 03444. Jean Burden, Poetry Ed. Serious poetry of high quality, to 30 lines. Pays $35 per poem for all rights, $25 for first rights, on publication.

POETRY SERIES

The following university presses publish book-length collections of poetry by writers who have never had a book of poems published. Each has specific rules for submission, so before submitting any material, be sure to write well ahead of the deadline dates for further information. Some organizations sponsor competitions in which prizes are offered for book-length collections of poetry; see *Literary Prize Offers* list on page 754.

THE ALABAMA PRESS POETRY SERIES—Dept. of English, Drawer A1, Univ. of Alabama, University, AL 35486. Address Thomas Rabbitt or Dara Wier. Considers unpublished book-length collections of poetry for publication as part of the Alabama Press Poetry Series. Submissions accepted during the months of September, October, and November only.

UNIVERSITY OF GEORGIA PRESS POETRY SERIES—Athens, GA 30602. Poets who have never had a book of poems published may submit book-length poetry manuscripts for possible publication. Open during the month of September each year. Manuscripts from poets who have published at least one volume of poetry (chapbooks excluded) are considered during the month of January.

WESLEYAN UNIVERSITY PRESS—110 Mt. Vernon St., Middletown, CT 06457. Considers unpublished book-length poetry manuscripts, by poets who have never had a book published, for publication in the Wesleyan New Poets Series. There is no deadline. Submit manuscript and $15.00 reading fee.

GREETING CARD MARKETS

Greeting card companies often have their own specific requirements for submitting ideas, verse, and artwork. The National Association of Greeting Card Publishers, however, gives the following general guidelines for submitting material: Verses and messages should be typed, double-spaced, each one on 3 × 5 or 4 × 6 card. Use only one side of the card, and be sure to put your name and address in the upper left-hand corner. Keep a copy of every verse or idea you send. (It's also advisable to keep a record of what you've submitted to each publisher.) Always enclose a stamped, self-addressed envelope, and do not send out more than ten verses or ideas in a group to any one publisher.

The Greeting Card Association brings out a booklet for free lancers, *Artists and Writers Market List,* with the names, addresses, and editorial guidelines of greeting card companies. This may be obtained by sending a self-addressed stamped envelope and $5.00 to The Greeting Card Association at 1350 New York Ave., NW, Suite 615, Washington, DC 20005.

AMBERLEY GREETING CARD COMPANY—11510 Goldcoast Dr., Cincinnati, OH 45249–1695. Ned Stern, Ed. Humorous ideas for birthday, illness, friendship, congratulations, "miss you," etc. Risqué and non-risqué humor. No seasonal cards. Pays $40. Buys all rights.

AMERICAN GREETING CORPORATION—10500 American Rd., Cleveland, OH 44144. Kathleen McKay, Ed. Recruitment. Studio and humor. Study current offerings and query before submitting.

BLUE MOUNTAIN ARTS, INC.—P.O. Box 1007, Boulder, CO 80306. Attn: Editorial Staff, Dept. TW. Poetry and prose about love, friendship, family, philosophies, etc. Also material for special occasions and holidays, birthdays, get well, Christmas, Valentine's Day, etc. No artwork or rhymed verse. Pays from $25.

BRETT-FORER GREETINGS, INC.—790 Madison Ave., New York, NY 10021. Ideas and designs for whimsical everyday and Christmas lines. Pays on acceptance.

CELEBRATION GREETINGS—Box 9500-WR, Boulder, CO 80301. Attn.: Edit. Ass't. Verse with a Christian theme, on strength, relationships, love.

Sincerity a must. Pays $35 a verse, on publication. Query with SASE for guidelines first.

FRAVESSI-LAMONT, INC.—11 Edison Pl., Springfield, NJ 07081. Address Editor. Short verse, mostly humorous or sentimental; cards with witty prose. No Christmas material. Pays varying rates, on acceptance.

FREEDOM GREETING CARD COMPANY—P.O. Box 715, Bristol, PA 19007. Submit to Jay Levitt. Verse, traditional, humorous, and love message. Inspirational poetry for all occasions. Pays $1 a line, on acceptance. Query with SASE.

GALLANT GREETINGS CORPORATION—2654 West Medill, Chicago, IL 60647. Ideas for humorous and serious greeting cards. Pays $35 per idea, in 45 days.

HALLMARK CARDS, INC.—Public Affairs & Communications #276, 2501 McGee, Box 419580, Kansas City, MO 64141–6580. No unsolicited material.

LEANIN' TREE PUBLISHING CO.—Box 9500, Boulder, CO 80301. Address Editorial Assistant. Verse with a western flavor or theme, friendship and inspirational verse, Christian verse for holiday and friendship cards, and short love poems of upbeat, contemporary nature. Pays $35, on publication. Send SASE for guidelines first (required).

THE MAINE LINE COMPANY—P.O. Box 418, Rockport, ME 04856. Attn. Perri Ardman. Untraditional humorous cards. Send SASE with three first class stamps for guidelines. Pays $50 per card.

MARK I—1733 W. Irving Park Rd., Chicago, IL 60613. Overstocked.

OATMEAL STUDIOS—Box 138 TW, Rochester, VT 05767. Dawn Abraham, Ed. Humorous, clever, and funny ideas needed for birthday, anniversary, get well, etc., also Valentine's Day, Christmas, Mother's Day, Father's Day, etc. Note pads. Query with SASE.

OUTREACH PUBLICATIONS—P.O. Box 1010, Siloam Springs, AR 72761. Christian greeting cards for most occasions. Pays varying rates, on acceptance. Address Creative Editor.

RED FARM STUDIOS—P.O. Box 347, 334 Pleasant St., Pawtucket, RI 02862. Traditional cards, for graduations, weddings, birthdays, get-wells, anniversaries, friendship, new baby, Christmas, and sympathy. No studio humor. Pays varying rates. SASE required.

ROUSANA CARDS—28 Sager Pl., Hillside, NJ 07205. Attn: Ed Briscoe, Ed. Verse, prose, cutes, and humor for Everyday and all Seasonal lines.

VAGABOND CREATIONS, INC.—2560 Lance Dr., Dayton, OH 45409. George F. Stanley, Jr., Ed. Greeting cards with graphics only on cover (no copy) and short tie-in copy punch line on inside page: birthday, everyday, Valentine, Christmas, and graduation. Mildly risqué humor with *double entendre* acceptable. Ideas for humorous buttons and illustrated theme stationery. Pays $15, on acceptance.

WARNER PRESS PUBLISHERS—1200 E. Fifth St., Anderson, IN 46012. Cindy M. Grant, Product Editor. Sensitive prose and inspirational verse card ideas; religious themes. Submit everyday ideas in March and April; Christmas material in July and Aug. Pays $10 to $30 on acceptance. Guidelines.

COLLEGE, LITERARY AND LITTLE MAGAZINES

FICTION, NONFICTION, POETRY

The thousands of literary journals, little magazines, and college quarterlies being published today welcome work from novices and pros alike; editors are always interested in seeing traditional and experimental fiction, poetry, essays, reviews, short articles, criticism, and satire, and as long as the material is well-written, the fact that a writer is a beginner doesn't adversely affect his chances for acceptance.

Most of these smaller publications have small budgets and staffs, so they may be slow in their reporting time—several months is not unusual. In addition, they usually pay only in copies of the issue in which published work appears and some—particularly college magazines—do not read manuscripts during the summer.

Publication in the literary journals can, however, lead to recognition by editors of large-circulation magazines, who read the little magazines in their search for new talent. There is also the possibility of having one's work chosen for reprinting in one of the prestigious annual collections of work from the little magazines.

Because the requirements of these journals differ widely, it is always important to study recent issues before submitting work to one of them. Copies of magazines may be in large libraries, or a writer may send a postcard to the editor, and ask the price of a sample copy. When submitting a manuscript, always enclose a self-addressed envelope, with sufficient postage for its return.

For a complete list of literary and college publications and little magazines, writers may consult such reference works as *The International Directory of Little Magazines and Small Presses,* published annually by Dustbooks (P.O. Box 100, Paradise, CA 95969).

THE AGNI REVIEW—P.O. Box 660, Amherst, MA 01004. Sharon Dunn, Ed. Short stories and poetry. Pays in copies.

ALASKA QUARTERLY REVIEW—Dept. of English, Univ. of Alaska, 3211 Providence Dr., Anchorage, AK 99508. Address Eds. Short stories, novel excerpts, poetry (traditional and unconventional forms). Submit manuscripts between August 15 and May 15. Pays in copies.

ALTERNATIVE FICTION & POETRY—7783 Kensington Ln., Hanover Park, IL 60107. Philip Athans, Ed. Politically/socially/ethically challenging fiction and poetry, any length. Pays in copies, on publication.

AMELIA—329 E St., Bakersfield, CA 93304. Poetry, to 100 lines; critical essays, to 2,000 words; reviews, to 500 words; belles lettres, to 1,000 words; fiction, to 3,500 words; fine pen and ink sketches; photos. Pays $35 for fiction and criticism, $10 to $25 for other nonfiction and artwork, $2 to $25 for poetry. Annual contest.

THE AMERICAN BOOK REVIEW—P.O. Box 188, Cooper Sta., New York, NY 10003. Rochelle Ratner, John Tytell, Ronald Sukenick, Eds. Book reviews, 700 to 1,200 words. Pays $25 honorarium and copies. Query first.

THE AMERICAN POETRY REVIEW—1616 Walnut St., Rm. 405, Philadelphia, PA 19103. Address Eds. Highest-quality contemporary poetry. Responds in 8 weeks. SASE a must.

AMERICAN QUARTERLY—307 College Hall, Univ. of Pennsylvania,

Philadelphia, PA 19104–6303. Janice Radway, Ed. Scholarly essays, 5,000 to 10,000 words, on any aspect of U.S. culture. Pays in copies.

THE AMERICAN SCHOLAR—1811 Q St. N.W., Washington, DC 20009. Joseph Epstein, Ed. Articles, 3,500 to 4,000 words, on science, politics, literature, the arts, etc. Book reviews. Pays $450 for articles, $100 for reviews, on publication.

ANOTHER CHICAGO MAGAZINE—Box 11223, Chicago, IL 60611. Fiction, essays on literature, and poetry. Pays $5 to $25, on acceptance.

ANTAEUS—18 W. 30th St., New York, NY 10001. Daniel Halpern, Ed. Short stories, essays, documents, parts-of-novels, poems. Pays on publication.

ANTIETAM REVIEW—Room 215, 33 W. Washington St., Hagerstown, MD 21740. Ann Knox, Ed.-in-Chief. Fiction, to 5,000 words; poetry. Submissions from regional artists only (MD, PA, WV, VA, DC), from Oct. through Feb. Pays from $25 to $100. Annual Literary Award for fiction.

THE ANTIGONISH REVIEW—St. Francis Xavier Univ., Antigonish, N.S., B2G1CO, Canada. George Sanderson, Ed. Poetry; short stories, essays, book reviews, 1,800 to 2,500 words. Pays in copies.

ANTIOCH REVIEW—P.O. Box 148, Yellow Springs, OH 45387. Robert S. Fogarty, Ed. Timely articles, 2,000 to 8,000 words, on social sciences, literature, and humanities. Quality fiction. Poetry. No inspirational poetry. Pays $10 per printed page, on publication.

APALACHEE QUARTERLY—Apalachee Press, P.O. Box 20106, Tallahassee, FL 32316. Barbara Hamby and Elizabeth Woodsmall, Eds. Fiction, to 30 manuscript pages; poems (3 to 5). Pays in copies.

APOCALYPSO—673 Ninth Ave., New York, NY 10036. Articles and fiction, to 3,000 words. Poetry, any length. Archival material and graphics. Pays in copies.

ARIZONA QUARTERLY—Univ. of Arizona, Tucson, AZ 85721. Albert F. Gegenheimer, Ed. Literary essays; regional material; general-interest articles. Fiction, to 3,500 words. Poetry (up to 30 lines)—any form or subject matter. Pays in copies.

THE ATAVIST—P.O. Box 5643, Berkeley, CA 94705. Robert Dorsett, Loretta Ko, Eds. Poetry, poetry criticism, translations, varying lengths. Pays in copies.

AURA LITERARY/ARTS REVIEW—P.O. Box 76, Univ. Center, UAB, Birmingham, AL 35294. Randy Blythe, Ed. Fiction and essays on literature, to 6,000 words; poetry; photos and drawings. Pays in copies.

BACKBONE—P.O. Box 95315, Seattle, WA 98145. Journal of Women's Literature. Mildred Jesse, Ed. Essays, fiction, and poetry that "inspire poetic, feminist, and political dialogue." Pays in copies.

BALL STATE UNIVERSITY FORUM—Ball State Univ., Muncie, IN 47306. Bruce W. Hozeski and Frances Mayhew Rippy, Eds. Short stories and general-interest articles, 500 to 4,000 words. One-act plays. Poetry. Pays in copies.

BANE K. WILKER'S TALES OF THE OLD WEST—PPG Publishing, Box 22866, Denver, CO 80222. Keith Olsen, Ed. Poetry, 3 to 100 lines, related to the Old West. Pays in copies.

BELLES LETTRES—Box 987, Arlington, VA 22216. Janet Mullaney, Ed. Reviews and essays, 250 to 2,000 words, on literature by women. Literary puzzles. Query required. Pays in copies.

THE BELLINGHAM REVIEW—932 Monitor Ave., Wenatchee, WA 98801. Randy Jay Landon, Ed. Fiction, to 5,000 words; poetry; short dramas. Submit manuscripts between Sept. 15 and May 1. Pays in copies. Annual contest.

THE BELOIT FICTION JOURNAL—Box 11, Beloit College, Beloit, WI 53511. Clint McCown, Ed. Short fiction, 15 to 20 pages, of all themes (no pornography, political propaganda, religious dogma). Manuscripts read from Sept. through Apr. Pays in copies.

BELOIT POETRY JOURNAL—RFD 2, Box 154, Ellsworth, ME 04605. First-rate contemporary poetry, of any length or mode. Pays in copies. Send SASE for guidelines.

BERKELEY POETS COOPERATIVE—P.O. Box 459, Berkeley, CA 94701. Charles Entrekin, Ed. Poetry, all forms; no restrictions. Submissions accepted from April 1 to August 1 and from October 1 to February 1. Pays in copies.

BITTERROOT—P.O. Box 489, Spring Glen, NY 12483. Menke Katz, Ed.-in-Chief. Poetry, to 50 lines; B&W camera ready drawings. Pays in copies. Annual contests. Send SASE for information.

BLACK MARIA—P.O. Box 25187, Chicago, IL 60625. Feminist. Short stories and experimental fiction, to 3,500 words. Poetry of any form. Articles; essays; B & W photos, graphics. Pays in copies.

BLACK MULLET REVIEW—P.O. Box 22814, Tampa, FL 33622. Gina Bergamino-Frey, Ed. High-quality short fiction, poetry, to 3 pages, and art. Pays in copies.

BLACK RIVER REVIEW—855 Mildred Ave., Lorain, OH 44052. Kaye Coller, Assoc. Ed. Poetry; short book reviews; essays; B&W artwork. Payment in copies. Contests.

THE BLACK WARRIOR REVIEW—P.O. Box 2936, Tuscaloosa, AL 35487. Janet McAdams, Ed. Fiction; poetry with intention; reviews and essays. Pays per printed page. Annual awards.

THE BLOOMSBURY REVIEW—P.O. Box 8928, Denver, CO 80201. Tom Auer, Ed.; Carol Arenberg, Senior Ed.; Ray Gonzalez, Poetry Ed. Book reviews, publishing features, interviews, essays, poetry, up to 800 words. Pays $5 to $25, on publication.

BLUELINE—Blue Mountain Lake, NY 12812. Alice Gilborn, Ed. Essays, fiction, to 2,500 words, on Adirondack region or similar areas. Poetry, to 44 lines. No more than 5 poems per submission. Pays in copies.

BOOK FORUM—38 E. 76th St., New York, NY 10021. Essays, 800 to 1,600 words, on books, writers, art, politics, etc. Interviews. Book reviews assigned. Pays $25 to $50, on acceptance. Query.

BOSTON REVIEW—33 Harrison Ave., Boston, MA 02111. Margaret Ann Roth, Ed.-in-Chief. Reviews and essays, 800 to 3,000 words, on literature, art, music, film, photography. Original fiction, to 5,000 words. Poetry. Pays $40 to $150.

BOTTOMFISH—De Anza College, 21250 Stevens Creek Blvd., Cupertino,

CA 95014. Robert E. Brock, Ed. Short, contemporary fiction, to 3,500 words; poetry, prefer tight lyric. Pays in copies.

BUCKNELL REVIEW—Bucknell Univ., Lewisburg, PA 17837. Interdisciplinary journal in book form. Scholarly articles on arts, science, and letters. Pays in copies.

CAESURA—English Dept., Auburn Univ., Auburn, AL 36849. R. T. Smith, Man. Ed. Short stories, to 3,000 words; narrative and lyric poetry, to 150 lines. Pays in copies.

CALLIOPE—Creative Writing Program, Roger Williams College, Bristol, RI 02809. Martha Christina, Ed. Short stories, to 2,500 words; poetry (query first for themes). Pays in copies. No submissions Apr. through July.

CALYX, A JOURNAL OF ART & LITERATURE BY WOMEN—P.O. Box B, Corvallis, OR 97339. M. Donnelly, Man. Ed. Fiction, 5,000 words, reviews, 250 to 1,000 words; poetry, to 6 poems; poetry book reviews, to 1,000 words. Query first. Pays in copies. Include short bio and SASE. Send for guidelines.

CANADIAN FICTION MAGAZINE—Box 946, Sta. F., Toronto, Ontario, Canada M4Y 2N9. High-quality short stories, novel excerpts, and experimental fiction, to 5,000 words, by Canadians. Interviews with Canadian authors; translations. Pays $10 per page, on publication. Annual prize.

THE CAPILANO REVIEW—Capilano College, 2055 Purcell Way, North Vancouver, B.C., Canada V7J 3H5. Dorothy Jantzen, Ed. Fiction; poetry; drama; visual arts. Pays $10 to $40.

CAROLINA QUARTERLY—Greenlaw Hall 066A, Univ. of North Carolina, Chapel Hill, NC 27514. Emily Stockard, Ed. Fiction, to 7,000 words, by new or established writers. Poetry (no restrictions on length, though limited space makes inclusion of works of more than 300 lines impractical). Pays $3 per printed page for fiction, $5 per poem, on acceptance.

THE CENTENNIAL REVIEW—110 Morrill Hall, Michigan State Univ., East Lansing, MI 48824–1036. Linda Wagner, Ed. Articles 3,000 to 5,000 words, on sciences, humanities, and interdisciplinary topics. Poetry; reviews. Pays in copies.

THE CHARITON REVIEW—Northeast Missouri State Univ., Kirksville, MO 63501. Jim Barnes, Ed. Highest quality poetry and fiction, to 6,000 words. Modern and contemporary translations. Book reviews. Pays $5 per printed page for fiction and translations.

THE CHICAGO REVIEW—Univ. of Chicago, Faculty Exchange Box C, Chicago, IL 60637. Robert Sitko Ed. Essays; interviews; reviews; fiction; translations; poetry. Pays in copies.

CIMARRON REVIEW—Oklahoma State Univ., Stillwater, OK 74078. Jeanne Adams Wray, Man. Ed. Articles, 1,500 to 2,500 words, on history, philosophy, political science, etc. Serious contemporary fiction. Pays in copies.

CINCINNATI POETRY REVIEW—Dept. of English, 069, Univ. of Cincinnati, Cincinnati, OH 45221. Dallas Wiebe, Ed. Poetry. Pays in copies.

CLINTON STREET QUARTERLY—P.O. Box 3588, Portland, OR 97208. David Milholland, Ed. Compelling first-person accounts, essays and idea pieces (3 to 15 pages) and short stories (2 to 20 pages). Pays $60 to $100, on publication.

COLORADO REVIEW—English Dept., 322 Eddy, Colorado State Univ.,

Fort Collins, CO 80523. Fiction submissions accepted from August 1 to December 31; poetry from January 1 to April 30 every year. Poetry, fiction, translations, interviews, reviews, articles.

COLUMBIA, A MAGAZINE OF POETRY & PROSE—404 Dodge, Columbia Univ., New York, NY 10027. Address appropriate Ed. Articles and fiction, to 25 typed pages. Poetry. Pays in copies. Annual award. SASE *required*.

CONFRONTATION—Dept. of English, C.W. Post of L.I.U., Greenvale, NY 11548. Martin Tucker, Ed. Serious fiction, 750 to 6,000 words. Crafted poetry, 20 to 200 lines. Pays $5 to $40, on publication.

THE CONNECTICUT POETRY REVIEW—P.O. Box 3783, New Haven, CT 06525. J. Claire White and James Chichetto, Eds. Poetry, 5 to 20 lines, and reviews, 700 words. Pays $5 per poem, $10 for a review, on acceptance.

CONNECTICUT RIVER REVIEW—30 Burr Farms Rd., Westport, CT 06880. Peggy Heinrich, Ed. Poetry, to 40 lines. Pays in copies.

COTTON BOLL/ATLANTA REVIEW—Sandy Springs P.O. Box 76757, Atlanta, GA 30358. Mary Hollingsworth, Ed. Literary short stories, to 3,500 words; poetry, to 2 pages; literary fillers; humor. Payment varies. Send SASE for guidelines. Contests.

COW IN THE ROAD—P.O. Box 90236, San Jose, CA 95109-3236. Timothy Barnes, Ed. Fiction (to 10,000 words), essays, and poetry for readers interested in contemporary literature and arts. Pays in copies.

CRITICAL INQUIRY—Univ. of Chicago Press, Wieboldt Hall, 1050 E. 59th St., Chicago, IL 60637. W. J. T. Mitchell, Ed. Critical essays that offer a theoretical perspective on literature, music, visual arts, popular culture, etc. Pays in copies.

CROTON REVIEW—P.O. Box 277, Croton-on-Hudson, NY 10520. Quality short-short fiction (to 14 pages), poetry (to 75 lines), and literary essays. Submissions accepted from September to February only. Pays with copy and honorarium. Send SASE for guidelines.

CUMBERLAND POETRY REVIEW—P.O. Box 120128, Acklen Sta., Nashville, TN 37212. Address Eds. High-quality poetry and criticism; translations. No restrictions on form, style or subject matter. Pays in copies.

DENVER QUARTERLY—Univ. of Denver, Denver, CO 80208. David Milofsky, Ed. Literary, cultural essays, and articles; poetry; book reviews; fiction. Pays $5 per printed page for fiction; $10 per page for poetry, after publication.

DESCANT—Texas Christian Univ., T.C.U. Sta., Fort Worth, TX 76129. Betsy Colquitt, Ed. Fiction, to 6,000 words. Poetry, to 40 lines. No restriction on form or subject. Pays in copies. Submit Sept.–May only.

THE DEVIL'S MILLHOPPER—The Devil's Millhopper Press, Persimmon Fork Rd., Blythewood, SC 29016. Jim Peterson, Ed. Poetry. Pays in copies. Writes for guidelines.

ELECTRUM MAGAZINE—222 Silk Tree Dr., Tustin, CA 92680. Roger Suva, Ed. Poetry, from traditional to avant-garde and free verse; limit to 80 lines. Limit 5 poems. Pays in copies.

EMBERS—Box 404, Guilford, CT 06437. Katrina Van Tassel, Ed. Poetry, varying lengths. Pays in copies. Annual contest.

EPOCH—245 Goldwin Smith Hall, Cornell Univ., Ithaca, NY 14853. Serious fiction and poetry. Pays $10 a page for prose; $1 a line for poetry. No submissions between May and Aug. Send for guidelines.

EVENT—Douglas College, Box 2503, New Westminister, BC, Canada, V3L 5B2. Dale Zieroth, Ed. Short fiction; short plays; poetry. Pays modest rates, on publication.

EXPRESSIONS: FIRST STATE JOURNAL—P.O. Box 4064, Greenville, DE 19807. Joanne Petrizzi, Ed. Poetry: contemporary, historical, literary, regional, juvenile, and experimental. Submit up to 8 poems. Pays in copies.

FARMER'S MARKET—P.O. Box 1272, Galesburg, IL 61402. Short stories and novel excerpts, to 20 pages, and poetry, related to the Midwest. Pays in copies.

FAT TUESDAY—419 N. Larchmont, Ste. 104, Los Angeles, CA 90004. F. M. Cotolo, Ed. Annual. Short fiction, poetry, parts-of-novels, paragraphs, crystal thoughts of any dimension—up to 5 pages. Pays in copies.

FICTION INTERNATIONAL—English Dept., San Diego State Univ., San Diego, CA 92182. Harold Jaffe and Larry McCaffery, Eds. Post-modernist and politically committed fiction and theory. Payment varies.

THE FIDDLEHEAD—Dept. of English, Univ. of New Brunswick, Fredericton, N.B., Canada E3B 5A3. Serious fiction, 2,500 words, preferably by Canadians. Pays about $10 per printed page, on publication.

FIELD—Rice Hall, Oberlin College, Oberlin, OH 44074. Stuart Friebert, David Young, Eds. Serious poetry, any length, by established and unknown poets; essays on poetics by poets. Translations by qualified translators. Pays $20 to $30 per page, on publication.

FINE MADNESS—P.O. Box 15176, Seattle, WA 98115. Address Eds. Poetry, any length; occasional reviews. Pays in copies.

FM FIVE—See *The Short Story Review.*

FOOTWORK—Cultural Affairs Office, Passaic County Comm. College, College Blvd., Patterson, NJ 07509. Maria Gillan, Ed. High quality fiction, to 4 pages, and poetry, to 3 pages, any style. Pays in copies.

THE GAMUT—1216 Rhodes Tower, Cleveland State Univ., Cleveland, OH 44115. Lively articles on general-interest topics preferably concerned with the region, 2,000 to 6,000 words. Quality fiction and poetry. Photos. Pays $25 to $250, on publication. Send SASE for guidelines.

GARGOYLE—P.O. Box 30906, Bethesda, MD 20814. Richard Peabody, Ed. Fiction, 3 to 30 typed pages; poetry, 5 to 25 lines. Photos. Pays in copies.

THE GEORGIA REVIEW—Univ. of Georgia, Athens, GA 30602. Stanley W. Lindberg, Ed.; Stephen Corey, Asst. Ed. Short fiction; interdisciplinary essays on arts and the humanities; book reviews; poetry. No submissions in June, July, and August.

GRAIN—Box 1154, Regina, Sask., Canada, S4P 3B4. Brenda Riches, Ed. Short stories, to 30 typed pages. Songs, essays, and drama. Poems (send no more than 6). Pays $30 to $100 for prose; $20 per poem, on publication.

GREAT RIVER REVIEW—211 W. 7th St., Winona, MN 55987. Fiction and creative prose, 2,000 to 10,000 words. Quality contemporary poetry; send 4 to 8 poems. Special interest in Midwestern writers and themes.

THE GREENFIELD REVIEW—R.D. 1, Box 80, Greenfield Center, NY 12833. Contemporary poetry by established and new poets and Third World writers. Pays in copies.

GREEN'S MAGAZINE—P.O. Box 3236, Regina, Sask., Canada S4P 3H1. David Green, Ed. Fiction for family reading, 1,500 to 4,000 words. Poetry, to 40 lines. Pays in copies.

THE GREENSBORO REVIEW—Univ. of North Carolina, Greensboro, NC 27412. Jim Clark, Ed. Semi-annual. Poetry and fiction. Submission deadlines: Sept. 15 and Feb. 15. Pays in copies.

HARVARD REVIEW—Byerly Hall 200, 8 Garden St., Cambridge, MA 02138. Nancy Bauer, Man. Ed. Articles, academic papers, and essays on all topics in the arts and sciences (5,000 to 15,000 words), by graduate students only. Pays in copies.

HAUNTS—Nightshade Publications, Box 3342, Providence, RI 02906. Joseph K. Cherkes, Ed. Short stories, 1,500 to 10,000 words: horror, science-fantasy, and supernatural tales with strong characters. Pays ¼¢ to ⅓¢ a word, on publication.

THE HAVEN, NEW POETRY—5969 Avenida la Barranca NW, Albuquerque, NM 87114. Poetry, to 20 lines. Pays $5 to $15, on acceptance.

HAWAII REVIEW—Dept. of English, Univ. of Hawaii, 1733 Donaghho Rd., Honolulu, HI 96882. Quality fiction, poetry, interviews, and literary criticism reflecting both regional and universal concerns.

HELICON NINE, THE JOURNAL OF WOMEN'S ARTS AND LETTERS—P.O. Box 22412, Kansas City, MO 64113. Poetry and fiction about women. Include SASE.

HERESIES—Box 1306, Canal St. Sta., New York, NY 10013. Feminist art/political slant/ thematic issues. Fiction, to 12 typed pages; nonfiction; poetry.

HIGH COUNTRY NEWS—Box 1090, Paonia, CO 81428. C. L. Rawlins, Poetry Ed. Poetry, solidly grounded in Western U.S. life and issues.

HIGH PLAINS LITERARY REVIEW—180 Adams St., Ste. 250, Denver, CO 80206. Robert O. Greer, Ed. Fiction (3,000 to 6,000 words), essays, and poetry (to 5 pages). Pays $5 a page for prose, $10 a page for poetry, on publication.

HUBBUB MAGAZINE—5344 S.E. 38th, Portland, OR 97202. Lisa Steinman, Carlos Reyes, Eds. Poetry. Pays in copies. Rarely accepts unsolicited manuscripts.

HURRICANE ALICE: A FEMINIST REVIEW—207 Lind Hall, 207 Church St., SE, Minneapolis, MN 55455. Articles, essays, fiction, interviews, and reviews (500 to 3,000 words), with a feminist perspective. Pays in copies.

INDIANA REVIEW—316 N. Jordan Ave., Bloomington, IN 47405. Elizabeth Dodd, Jim Brock, Eds. Fiction with an emphasis on style. Poems that are well executed and ambitious. Pays $5 a page for poetry; $25 per story.

INLET—Dept. of English, Virginia Wesleyan College, Norfolk, VA 23502. Joseph Harkey, Ed. Short fiction, 500 to 3,000 words (short lengths preferred). Poems of 4 to 40 lines; all forms and themes. Submit between September and March 1st, each year. Pays in copies.

INTERNATIONAL POETRY REVIEW—Box 2047, Greensboro, NC

27402. Evalyn P. Gill, Ed. Contemporary poetry and translations (with original). Pays in copies.

INVISIBLE CITY—P.O. Box 2853, San Francisco, CA 94126. John McBride, Ed. Reviews, translations, especially contemporary European literature.

THE IOWA REVIEW—EPB 308, Univ. of Iowa, Iowa City, IA 52242. David Hamilton, Ed. Essays, poems, stories, reviews. Pays $10 a page for fiction and nonfiction, $1 a line for poetry, on publication.

JAM TO-DAY—372 Dunstable Rd., Tyngsboro, MA 01879. Don Stanford and Judith Stanford, Eds. Fiction, to 7,000 words. Concrete/shaped poetry. Especially interested in traditional forms. Pays $5 per printed page for fiction, $5 per poem, plus copies, on publication.

JAPANOPHILE—Box 223, Okemos, MI 48864. Earl R. Snodgrass, Ed. Fiction, to 10,000 words, with a Japanese setting. Each story should have at least one Japanese character and at least one non-Japanese. Pays to $20, on publication. Annual contest.

JOURNAL OF POPULAR LITERATURE—Center for the Study of Popular Culture, Bowling Green State Univ., Bowling Green, OH 43403. Ray B. Browne, Ed. Articles. Pays in copies.

KANSAS QUARTERLY—Dept. of English, Denison Hall 122, Kansas State Univ., Manhattan, KS 66506. Literary criticism, art and history. Fiction and poetry. Pays in copies. Annual awards. Query for articles and special topics.

KARAMU—Dept. of English, Eastern Illinois Univ., Charleston, IL 61920. John Guzlowski, Ed. Contemporary or experimental fiction. Poetry. Pays in copies.

LIGHT YEAR—Bits Press, Dept. of English, Case Western Reserve Univ., Cleveland, OH 44106. Robert Wallace, Ed. Annual. "The best funny, witty, or merely levitating verse being written." No restrictions on style or length. Pays $4 per poem plus 10¢ per line, on publication. Material will not be returned unless accompanied by SASE.

LILITH—250 W. 57th St., New York, NY 10017. Susan Weidman Schneider, Ed. Fiction, 1,500 to 2,000 words, on issues of interest to Jewish women. Pays in copies.

THE LION AND THE UNICORN—English Dept., Brooklyn College, NY 11210. Geraldine DeLuca, Roni Natov, Eds. Articles, from 2,000 words, offering criticism of children's and young adult books, for teachers, scholars, artists, and parents. Query preferred. Pays in copies.

LITERARY MAGAZINE REVIEW—English Dept., Kansas State Univ., Manhattan, KS 66506. Reviews and articles concerning literary magazines, 1,000 to 1,500 words, for writers and readers of contemporary literature. Pays modest fees and copies. Query.

THE LITERARY REVIEW—Fairleigh Dickinson Univ., 285 Madison Ave., Madison, NJ 07940. Walter Cummins, Martin Green, Harry Keyishian, William Zander, Eds. Serious fiction; poetry; translations; reviews; essays on literature. Pays in copies.

THE LONG STORY—11 Kingston St., N. Andover, MA 01845. Stories, 8,000 to 20,000 words; prefer committed fiction. Pays $1 a page, on publication. Poetry.

THE MALAHAT REVIEW—Univ. of Victoria, P.O. Box 1700, Victoria, B.C., Canada V8W 2Y2. Constance Rooke, Ed. Fiction and poetry, including translations, and occasional articles. Pays from $10 to $15 per page, on acceptance.

THE MANHATTAN REVIEW—304 Third Ave., New York, NY 10010. Highest quality poetry. Pays in copies.

MASSACHUSETTS REVIEW—Memorial Hall, Univ. of Massachusetts, Amherst, MA 01003. Literary criticism; articles on public affairs, scholarly disciplines. Short fiction. Poetry. No submissions between June and October. Pays modest rates, on publication. SASE required.

MEMPHIS STATE REVIEW—Dept. of English, Memphis State Univ., Memphis, TN 38152. Short stories, novel excerpts, to 4,500 words; poetry, to one page. Pays in copies. Annual award.

METROSPHERE—Metropolitan State College, 1006 11th St., Office of Publications, Box 57, Denver, CO 80204. Interviews and profiles of writers and artists, 1,200 words; fiction, to 2,000 words; and poetry, to 50 lines. Pays in copies.

MICHIGAN HISTORICAL REVIEW—Clark Historical Lib., Central Michigan Univ., Mt. Pleasant, MI 48859. Address Ed. Articles related to Michigan's political, social, economic, and cultural history. SASE.

MICHIGAN QUARTERLY REVIEW—3032 Rackham Bldg., Univ. of Michigan, Ann Arbor, MI 48109. Laurence Goldstein, Ed. Scholarly essays on all subjects; fiction; poetry. Pays $8 a page, on publication. Annual contest.

MID-AMERICAN REVIEW—Dept. of English, Bowling Green State Univ., Bowling Green, OH 43403. Robert Early, Ed. High-quality fiction, poetry, articles and reviews of contemporary writing. Fiction to 20,000 words. Reviews, articles, 500 to 2,500 words. Pays to $75, on publication.

MIDCOASTER—P.O. Box 12590, Milwaukee, WI 53212. Peter Hickey, Ed. High quality fiction, nonfiction (to 20 pages) and poetry. Pays in copies.

MIDWEST QUARTERLY—Pittsburg State Univ., Pittsburg, KS 66762. James B. Schick, Ed. Scholarly articles, 2,500 to 5,000 words, on contemporary issues. Pays in copies.

MILKWEED CHRONICLE—Box 24303, Minneapolis, MN 55424. Emilie Buchwald, Ed. Poems that reflect a unique voice. No overly religious or political material. Pays $15 per poem, $50 to $100 for essays (1,200 to 3,000 words), on publication.

MIND IN MOTION—P.O. Box 1118, Apple Valley, CA 92307. Celeste Goyer, Ed. Fiction, 500 to 2,500 words: allegory, fable, surrealism, parody; poetry, to 45 lines: emphasis on universal concerns artfully directed toward everyday and esoteric. Pays in copies.

THE MINNESOTA REVIEW—Dept. of English, SUNY, Stony Brook, NY 11794. Michael Sprinker, Helen Cooper, Susan Squier, Eds. Poetry, fiction, essays, reviews. Pays in copies.

MISSISSIPPI REVIEW—Center for Writers, Univ. of Southern Mississippi, Southern Sta., Box 5144, Hattiesburg, MS 39406–5144. Frederick Barthelme, Ed. Serious fiction, poetry, criticism, interviews. Payment in copies and small honorarium, on publication.

THE MISSISSIPPI VALLEY REVIEW—Dept. of English, Western Illinois

Univ., Macomb, IL 61455. Forrest Robinson, Ed. Short fiction, to 20 typed pages. Poetry; send 3 to 5 poems. Pays in copies.

THE MISSOURI REVIEW—Dept. of English, 231 Arts & Science, Univ. of Missouri-Columbia, Columbia, MO 65211. Greg Michalson, Man. Ed. Poems, of any length. Fiction and essays. Pays $5 to $10 per printed page, on publication.

MODERN HAIKU—P.O. Box 1752, Madison, WI 53701. Robert Spiess, Ed. Haiku and articles about haiku. Pays $1 a haiku, $5 a page for articles.

MONTHLY REVIEW—155 W. 23rd St., New York, NY 10011. Paul M. Sweezy, Harry Magdoff, Eds. Analytic articles, 5,000 words, on politics and economics, from independent socialist viewpoint. Pays $50, on publication.

THE MOVEMENT—P.O. Box 19458, Los Angeles, CA 90019. Roberts C. Taylor, Ed. Articles dedicated to spiritual/transformational interests, 1,000 words. Pays in copies. Must include SASE.

MUNDUS ARTIUM—Univ. of Texas at Dallas, Box 688, Richardson, TX 75080. Rainer Schulte, Ed. Short fiction, poetry, translations, interdisciplinary essays on the humanities. Pays in copies.

NATIONAL POETRY JOURNAL—177 S. Front St., Souderton, PA 18964. W. Bruce Fenstermacher, Ed. Poetry, any length. Quarterly.

NEBO—Dept. of English, Arkansas Tech. Univ., Russellville, AR 72801. Poetry; mainstream fiction, to 20 pages; critical essays, to 10 pages. Pays in copies.

NEGATIVE CAPABILITY—6116 Timberly Rd. N., Mobile, AL 36609. Sue Walker, Ed. Poetry, any length; fiction, essays, art. Pays in copies. Annual Eve of St. Agnes poetry competition and annual essay contest.

THE NEW CRITERION—850 Seventh Ave., New York, NY 10019. Robert Richman, Poetry Ed. Poems of varying lengths. Pays in copies.

NEW LETTERS—5216 Rockhill Rd., Kansas City, MO 64110. James McKinley, Ed. Fiction, 10 to 25 pages; nonfiction, 20 to 30 pages. Poetry; submit 3 to 6 at a time.

NEW MEXICO HUMANITIES REVIEW—Box A, New Mexico Tech., Socorro, NM 87801. Poetry, any length, any themes; essays dealing with southwestern and native American themes. Pays with subscription.

NEW ORLEANS REVIEW—Loyola Univ., New Orleans, LA 70118. John Mosier, Ed. Literary or film criticism, to 6,000 words. Serious fiction and poetry.

THE NEW SOUTHERN LITERARY MESSENGER—400 S. Laurel St., Richmond, VA 23220. Charles Lohmann, Ed. Ingraham Kirkland, Fiction Ed. Quarterly. Short stories, satire, science fiction, contemporary history, 1,000 to 5,000 words. One-act plays and short film scripts. Pays $5 for one-time reprint rights, plus one copy, on publication. Send SASE for guidelines.

NEXUS—Wright State Univ., 006 Univ. Center, Dayton, OH 45435. Vance Wissinger, Jr., Ed. Quality short fiction, to 2,500 words; poetry; B&W photos.

NIMROD—2210 S. Main St., Tulsa, OK 74114. Quality poetry and fiction, experimental and traditional. Pays in copies. Annual awards for poetry and fiction. Send SASE for guidelines.

THE NORTH AMERICAN REVIEW—University of Northern Iowa, Cedar Falls, IA 50614. Peter Cooley, Poetry Ed. Poetry of high quality. Fiction, of highest quality (address Fiction Ed. Submissions accepted Jan.–March only). Pays 50¢ a line for poetry, $10 per published page for fiction, on acceptance.

THE NORTH DAKOTA QUARTERLY—Box 8237, Univ.of North Dakota, Grand Forks, ND 58202. Nonfiction essays in the humanities; fiction, reviews, graphics, and poetry. Limited market. Pays in copies.

THE NORTHERN REVIEW—U-Wisc./Stevens Point, Stevens Point, WI 54481. Essays and articles (1,200 to 4,000 words) related to the north. Pays in copies.

NORTHWEST REVIEW—369 PLC, Univ. of Oregon, Eugene, OR 97403. John Witte, Ed. Serious fiction, commentary, and poetry. Reviews. Pays in copies. Send SASE for guidelines.

NYCTICORAX—P.O. Box 8444, Asheville, NC 28814. John A. Youril, Ed. Short-short fiction and poetry (submit 4 to 8 poems at a time). Query about essays on literary criticism. Pays in copies.

OAK SQUARE—Box 1238, Allston, MA 02134. Philip Borenstein, Ed. Experimental and traditional stories, about 2,500 words; some poetry; non-political essays and interviews. Pays in copies.

OBSIDIAN II—Dept. of English, Box 8105, North Carolina State Univ., Raleigh, NC 27695–8105. Gerald Barrax, Ed. Fiction, poetry and short plays by blacks; reviews, interviews and scholarly articles on black authors and their works. Pays in copies.

THE OHIO JOURNAL—164 W. 17th Ave., Columbus, OH 43210. David Citino, Ed. Short stories, personal essays, poetry, book reviews. No submissions during this summer. Pays in copies. Annual poetry award.

OHIO RENAISSANCE REVIEW—P.O. Box 804, Ironton, OH 45638. James R. Pack, Ed. Ron Houchin, Poetry Ed. Science fiction, fantasy, and mystery stories, 400 to 3,000 words. Contemporary, avant-garde poetry, any length. Pays $2.50 per column for fiction, 25¢ a line for poetry, on publication. Include bio and SASE.

THE OHIO REVIEW—Ellis Hall, Ohio Univ., Athens, OH 45701–2979. Short stories, poetry, essays, reviews. Pays from $5 per page, plus copies, on publication.

THE ONTARIO REVIEW—9 Honey Brook Dr., Princeton, NJ 08540. Raymond J. Smith, Ed. Poetry and fiction. No unsolicited manuscripts.

OREGON EAST—Hoke College Center, Eastern Oregon State College, La Grande, OR 97850. Short fiction, nonfiction (to 3,000 words), and poetry (to 60 lines). Regional angle preferred. Pays in copies.

ORPHIC LUTE—1675A 16th St., Los Alamos, NM 87544. Patricia Doherty Hinnebusch, Ed. Lyric poetry, traditional and contemporary (submit up to 4 poems at a time). Pays in copies.

OTHER VOICES—820 Ridge Rd., Highland Park, IL 60035. Dolores Weinberg, Ed. Semiannual. Fresh, accessible short stories and novel excerpts, to 5,000 words. Pays in copies and modest honorarium.

OUROBOROS—P.O. Box 141, Mansfield Depot, CT 06251. Erskine Carter, Ed. Short stories (to 3,500 words) and poetry (limit 10 poems). Pays in copies.

PAINTED BRIDE QUARTERLY—230 Vine St., Philadelphia, PA 19106. Louis McKee, Ed. Fiction, nonfiction, and poetry, varying lengths. Pays in copies.

PANDORA—Empire Books, P.O. Box 625, Murray, KY 42071. Science fiction and speculative fantasy stories, to 5,000 words. Pays 1¢ a word, on acceptance. SASE for guidelines.

PARIS REVIEW—541 E. 72nd St., New York, NY 10021. Address Fiction and Poetry Eds. Fiction and poetry of high literary quality. Pays on publication.

PARNASSUS—205 W. 89th St., New York, NY 10024. Herbert Leibowitz, Ed. Critical essays and reviews on contemporary poetry. International in scope. Pays in cash and copies.

PARTISAN REVIEW—Boston Univ., 141 Bay State Rd., Boston, MA 02215. William Phillips, Ed. Serious fiction, poetry and essays. Payment varies.

PASSAGES NORTH—William Bonifas Fine Arts Center, Escanaba, MI 49829. Elinor Benedict, Ed. Quality short fiction and contemporary poetry. Pays in copies, frequent prizes and honoraria.

THE PENNSYLVANIA REVIEW—Dept. of English, 526 Cathedral of Learning, Univ. of Pittsburgh, Pittsburgh, PA 15260. Articles and fiction, to 5,000 words, and poetry (send as many as six at one time). Pays $5 a page for prose, $5 for poetry.

PERMAFROST—English Dept., Univ. of Alaska, Fairbanks, AK 99775. Poetry, short fiction, essays, translations, and B&W photos and graphics. No manuscripts accepted between Mar. 1 and Aug. 1. Pays in copies.

PIEDMONT LITERARY REVIEW—P.O. Box 3656, Danville, VA 24543. Fiction, to 4,000 words. Poems, of any length and style. Special interest in young poets. Pays in copies. Submit up to 5 poems.

PIG IRON—P.O. Box 237, Youngstown, OH 44501. Rose Sayre, Jim Villani, Eds. Fiction and nonfiction, to 8,000 words. Poetry, to 100 lines. Humor. Pays $2 per published page, on publication.

PINCHPENNY—4851 Q St., Sacramento, CA 95819. Tom Miner, Elisabeth Goossens, Ed. Prose poems, tiny poems short-short stories, B&W art. New writers welcome. Pays in copies.

PLAINS POETRY JOURNAL—Box 2337, Bismarck, ND 58502. Jane Greer, Ed. Poetry using traditional conventions in vigorous, compelling ways; no "greeting card"-type verse. No subject is taboo. Pays in copies.

PLOUGHSHARES—Box 529, Dept. M, Cambridge, MA 02139. Address Fiction or Poetry Ed. Serious fiction, to 7,000 words. Poetry. Pays $10 to $50, on publication. Query.

POEM—c/o English Dept., U.A.H., Huntsville, AL 35899. Nancy Frey Dillard, Ed. Serious poetry, any length. Pays in copies.

POET AND CRITIC—203 Ross Hall, Iowa State Univ., Ames, IA 50011. Michael Martone, Ed. Poetry, fiction, essays on contemporary poetry. Pays in copies.

POETIC JUSTICE—8220 Rayford Dr., Los Angeles, CA 90045. Alan Engebretsen, Ed. Quarterly. Poetry, 4 to 70 lines. Pays in copies.

POET LORE—The Writer's Center, 7815 Old Georgetown Rd., Bethesda,

MD 20814-2415. Ed Taylor, Man. Ed. Original poetry, all kinds. Translations, reviews. Pays in copies. Annual narrative contest.

POETRY—P.O. Box 4348, 601 S. Morgan St., Chicago, IL 60680. Joseph Parisi, Ed. Poetry of highest quality. Pays $1 a line, on publication.

POETS ON:—Box 255, Chaplin, CT 06235. Ruth Diagon, Ed. Thematic issues, query about current editorial needs. Payment is in copies.

THE PORTABLE LOWER EAST SIDE—463 West St., #344, New York, NY 10014. Kurt Hollander, Ed. Quality fiction, to 15 pages; poetry, to 3 pages. Articles related to the Lower East Side of New York City. Pays in copies.

PRAIRIE SCHOONER—201 Andrew Hall, Univ. of Nebraska, Lincoln, NE 68588. Hugh Luke and Hilda Raz, Eds. Short stories, poetry and essays, to 6,000 words. Pays in copies. Annual contests.

PRIMAVERA—1212 E. 59th St., Chicago, IL 60637. Stories, poems, and personal essays (to 30 typed pages) by or about women. Pays in copies.

PRISM INTERNATIONAL—E459-1866 Main Mall, Dept. of Creative Writing, Univ. of British Columbia, Vancouver, BC, Canada, V6T 1W5. High quality fiction, poetry, drama, translations. Pays in copies. Include *international reply coupons.*

PORTENTS—12 Fir Pl., Hazlet, NJ 07730. Deborah Rassmussen, Ed. Contemporary horror, dark fantasy, exceptional gothic, and supernatural horror short stories, to 3,000 words. No werewolves, vampires, ghouls, religion or sex. Pays in copies.

PROOF ROCK—P.O. Box 607, Halifax, VA 24558. Don Conner, Ed. Fiction, to 2,500 words. Poetry, to 32 lines. Reviews. Pays in copies. Sample copies available.

PUDDING—2384 Hardesty Dr. South, Columbus, OH 43204. Jennifer Welch Bosveld, Ed. Poems—especially free verse and experimental—with fresh language, concrete images, and specific detail. Short articles about poetry in human services.

PUERTO DEL SOL—New Mexico State Univ., Box 3E, Las Cruces, NM 88003. Kevin McIlvoy, Ed. Short stories, to 30 pages; novel excerpts, to 65 pages; articles, to 45 pages, related to the Southwest; and reviews, to 15 pages. Poetry, photos. Pays in copies.

PULPSMITH—5 Beekman St., New York, NY 10038. Harry Smith, General Ed. Literary genre fiction; mainstream, mystery, SF, westerns. Short lyric poems, sonnets, ballads. Essays and articles: Pays $35 to $100 for fiction, $15 to $35 for poetry, on acceptance.

QUEEN'S QUARTERLY—Queens Univ., Kingston, Ont., Canada K7L 3N6. Articles, to 6,000 words, on a wide range of topics, and fiction, to 5,000 words. Poetry; send no more than 6 poems. B&W art. Pays to $150, on publication.

RACCOON—Raccoon Books, Inc., 3387 Poplar Ave., #205, Memphis, TN 38111. David Spicer, Ed. Poetry and poetic criticism, varying lengths. Pays in copies.

RAMBUNCTIOUS REVIEW—1221 W. Pratt Blvd., Chicago, IL 60626, Mary Dellutri, Richard Goldman, Eds. Fiction, poetry, short drama. Pays in copies. Submit material Sept.–May.

RHINO—325 Maple Ave., Wilmette, IL 60091. Sara Esgate, Ed. Fiction, to 3 typed pages; poetry, any length. "Seeking authentic emotion in well-crafted forms using fresh images." Pays in copies.

RIVERSIDE QUARTERLY—P.O. Box 833-044, Richardson, TX 75083. Science fiction and fantasy (to 3,500 words); criticism, reviews. Send fiction to Redd Boggs, Box 1111, Berkeley, CA 94701; poetry to Sheryl Smith at above address. Pays in copies.

ROANOKE REVIEW—Roanoke College, Salem, VA 24153. Robert R. Walter, Ed. Quality short fiction, to 10,000 words, and poetry, to 100 lines. Pays in copies.

SAN FERNANDO POETRY JOURNAL—18301 Halstead St., Northridge, CA 91325. Richard Cloke, Ed. Quality poetry, 20 to 100 lines, with social content; scientific, philosophic and historical themes. Pays in copies.

SAN JOSE STUDIES—San Jose State Univ., San Jose, CA 95192. Fauneil J. Rinn, Ed. Poetry, fiction, and essays on interdisciplinary topics. Pays in copies. Annual awards.

SANDS—P.O. Box 638, Addison, TX 75001. Susan C. Baugh, Ed. Quality fiction, poetry. Pays in copies.

SCANDINAVIAN REVIEW—127 E. 73rd St., New York, NY 10021. Essays on contemporary Scandinavia. Fiction and poetry, translated from Scandinavian. Pays to $100, on publication.

SCRIVENER—McGill Univ., 853 Sherbrooke St. W., Montreal, Quebec, Canada H3A 2T6. Andrew Burgess, Ed. Poetry, 5 to 25 poems; prose, to 25 pages; reviews, to 3 pages; essays, to 8 pages. Photography and graphics. Pays in copies.

THE SEATTLE REVIEW—Padelford Hall, GN–30, Univ. of Washington, Seattle, WA 98195. Donna Gerstenberger, Ed. Short stories and poetry, to 2 pages. Payment is in copies.

SENECA REVIEW—Hobart & William Smith Colleges, Geneva, NY 14456. Poetry. Pays in copies.

SEVEN—3630 N.W. 22, Oklahoma City, OK 73107–2893. James Neill Northe, Ed. Serious poetry, in any form. Pays $5, on acceptance. Query. Guidelines available.

SEWANEE REVIEW—Sewanee, TN 37375. George Core, Ed. Fiction, to 7,500 words. Serious poetry, to 40 lines, of highest quality. Pays about $12 per printed page for fiction, 60¢ per line for poetry, on publication. Send cover letter and SASE.

SHENANDOAH—Washington and Lee Univ., P.O. Box 722, Lexington, VA 24450. James Boatwright, Ed. Richard Howard, Poetry Ed. Highest quality fiction, poetry, criticism, essays and interviews. Annual contest.

THE SHORT STORY REVIEW (formerly *FM Five*)—P.O. Box 882108, San Francisco, CA 94188. Dwight Gabbard, Ed. Short stories, to 3,500 words; interviews; book reviews, to 600 words. Query required for interviews and reviews. Send SASE for guidelines. Pays in copies for stories, $180 for interviews.

SIDEWINDER—Division of Arts and Humanities, College of the Mainland, Texas City, TX 77591. Brett Jarrett, Ed. Fiction and poetry of any length:

"Our main concern is with the originality and skill in presentation, so we are not interested in genre or formula stories." Manuscripts only. Pays $50 to $100.

SING HEAVENLY MUSE! WOMEN'S POETRY & PROSE—P.O. Box 13299, Minneapolis, MN 55414. Short stories and essays, to 5,000 words. Poetry. Pays $25, plus copies, on publication.

SINISTER WISDOM—P.O. Box 1308, Montpelier, VT 05602. Melanie Kaye/Kantrowitz, Ed. Articles, fiction, poetry, reviews, and plays, from feminist and lesbian perspective, varying lengths. Pays in copies.

SLIPSTREAM—Box 2071, New Market Sta., Niagara Falls, NY 14301. Fiction, 2 to 25 pages, and contemporary poetry, any length. Pays in copies. Query for themes.

SMALL PRESS REVIEW—Box 100, Paradise, CA 95969. Len Fulton, Ed. News pieces and reviews, to 250 words, about small presses and little magazines. Pays in copies.

SNAPDRAGON—English Dept., Univ. of Idaho, Moscow, ID 83843. Ron McFarland, Tina Foriyes, Eds. Fiction and articles, 2,000 to 4,000 words, and poetry. Pays in copies.

SNOWY EGRET—205 S. Ninth St., Williamsburg, KY 40769. Humphrey A. Olsen, Alan Seaburg, Eds. Poetry to 10,000 words, related to natural history. Fiction and nonfiction, about 3,000 words, related to natural history. Pays $2 per page for prose, $2 to $4 for poetry, on publication. Send fiction and poetry to Alan Seaburg, Ed., 67 Century St., W. Medford, MA 02155.

SONORA REVIEW—Dept. of English, Univ. of Arizona, Tucson, AZ 85721. Scott Wigton and Alison Hicks, Eds. Fiction, poetry, reviews. Pays in copies. Annual prizes for fiction and poetry.

SOUTH CAROLINA REVIEW—c/o Dept. of English, Clemson Univ., Clemson, SC 29631. Martin Jacobi, Man. Ed. Short stories, 3,000 to 5,000 words. Poetry. Criticism. Pays in copies.

SOUTH DAKOTA REVIEW—Box 111, Univ. Exchange, Vermillion, SD 57069. John R. Milton, Ed. Exceptional fiction, 3,000 to 5,000 words, and poetry, 10 to 25 lines. Critical articles, especially on American literature, Western American literture, theory and esthetics, 3,000 to 5,000 words. Pays in copies.

SOUTHERN HUMANITIES REVIEW—9088 Haley Center, Auburn Univ., AL 36849. Thomas L. Wright and Dan R. Latimer, Eds. Short stories, essays, and criticism, 3,500 to 5,000 words; poetry, to 2 pages.

SOUTHERN POETRY REVIEW—Dept. of English, Univ. of North Carolina, Charlotte, NC 28223. Robert W. Grey, Ed. Poems. No restrictions on style length or content.

SOUTHERN REVIEW—43 Allen Hall, Louisiana State Univ., Baton Rouge, LA 70803. Lewis P. Simpson, James Olney, Eds. Fiction, and essays, 4,000 to 8,000 words. Serious poetry of highest quality. Pays $12 a page for prose, $20 a page for poetry, on publication.

SOUTHWEST REVIEW—Southern Methodist Univ., Dallas, TX 72575. Willard Spiegelman, Ed. Fiction and essays, 3,000 to 7,500 words; book reviews. Poetry. Pays in copies.

SOU'WESTER—Dept. of English, Southern Illinois Univ. at Edwardsville,

Edwardsville, IL 62026–1438. Dickie Spurgeon, Ed. Fiction to 10,000 words. Poetry, especially poems over 100 lines. Pays in copies.

THE SPIRIT THAT MOVES US—P.O. Box 1585 TW, Iowa City, IA 52244. Morty Sklar, Ed. Biannual. Fiction, poetry, that is expressive rather than formal or sensational. Each issue focuses on a specific theme—query. Pays in copies.

STONE COUNTRY—P.O. Box 132, Menemsha, MA 02552. Judith Neeld, Ed. High-quality contemporary poetry in all genres. Pays in copies. Semiannual award. SASE required. Guidelines.

STONY HILLS; NEWS & REVIEWS OF THE SMALL PRESS—Weeks Mills, New Sharon, ME 04955. Diane Kruchkow, Ed. Reviews of small press books and magazines nationwide, to 500 words. Some short poetry. Pays in copies. Query on nonfiction preferred.

STORY QUARTERLY—P.O. Box 1416, Northbrook, IL 60065. Anne Brashler, Diane Williams, Eds. Short stories and interviews. Pays in copies.

STUDIES IN AMERICAN FICTION—English Dept., Northeastern Univ., Boston, MA 02115. James Nagel, Ed. Reviews, 750 words; scholarly essays, 2,500 to 6,500 words, on American fiction. Pays in copies.

SUNRUST—P.O. Box 58, New Wilmington, PA 16142. James Ashbrook Perkins, Nancy Esther James, Eds. Nonfiction, to 2,000 words, and poetry, to 75 lines, about rural life, nature, memories of the past, and small communities. Pays in copies.

TAR RIVER POETRY—Dept. of English, East Carolina Univ., Greenville, NC 27834. Peter Makuck, Ed. Poems, all styles. Submit between September and May. Pays in copies.

TERRA POETICA—Dept. of Modern Languages and Literatures, SUNY at Buffalo, Buffalo, NY 14260. Jorge Guitart, Ed. Poetry: originals in all languages, and English translations. Pays in copies. Query preferred.

TESTIMONY—P.O. Box 495, Montclair, NJ 07042. Sandra West, Ed. "Creative, soul-stirring poetry, sonnets and haiku, political poems, and verse about the black religious experience." Pays in copies.

THE TEXAS REVIEW—English Dept., Sam Houston State Univ., Huntsville, TX 77341. Paul Ruffin, Ed. Fiction, poetry, articles, to 20 typed pages. Reviews. Pays in copies.

THE THREEPENNY REVIEW—P.O. Box 9131, Berkeley, CA 94709. Wendy Lesser, Ed. Fiction, to 5,000 words. Poetry, to 40 lines. Essays, on books, theater, film, dance, music, art, television, and politics, 1,500 to 3,000 words. Pays $25 to $50, on acceptance. Limited market. Query first with SASE.

TOUCHSTONE—P.O. Box 42331, Houston, TX 77042. Bill Laufer, Pub. Quarterly. Fiction, 750 to 2,000 words: mainstream, experimental. Interviews, essays, reviews. Poetry, to 40 lines. Pays in copies.

TRANSLATION—The Translation Center, 307A Mathematics Bldg., Columbia Univ., New York, NY 10027. Frank MacShane, Dir. Diane G. H. Cook, Man. Ed. Semiannual. New translations of contemporary foreign poetry and prose.

TRIQUARTERLY—1735 Benson Ave., Northwestern Univ., Evanston, IL 60201. Serious, aesthetically informed and inventive poetry and prose, for an international and literate audience. Pays $10 per page.

TWISTED—6331 N. Lakewood Ave., Chicago, IL 60660. Christine Hoard, Ed. Articles and poetry related to horror and dark fantasy. Overstocked with fiction. Pays in copies.

2AM—P.O. Box 50444, Chicago, IL 60650–0444. Gretta Anderson, Ed. Articles, reviews and personality profiles (500 to 2,000 words); fantasy, horror and some science fiction/sword and sorcery short stories (500 to 5,000 words). Pays ½¢ a word, on acceptance.

THE UNIVERSITY OF PORTLAND REVIEW—Univ. of Portland, Portland, OR 97203. Thompson H. Faller, Ed. Scholarly articles and contemporary fiction, 500 to 2,500 words. Poetry. Book reviews. Pays in copies.

UNIVERSITY OF WINDSOR REVIEW—Dept. of English, Univ. of Windsor, Windsor, Ont., Canada N9B 3P4. Eugene McNamara, Ed. Short stories, poetry, criticism, reviews. Pays $10 to $25, on publication.

THE VILLAGER—135 Midland Ave., Bronxville, NY 10708. Amy Murphy, Ed. Fiction, 900 to 1,500 words: mystery, adventure, humor, romance. Short, preferably seasonal poetry. Pays in copies.

VIRGINIA QUARTERLY REVIEW—One W. Range, Charlottesville, VA 22903. Quality fiction and poetry. Serious essays and articles, 3,000 to 6,000 words, on literature, science, politics, economics, etc. Pays $10 per page for prose, $1 per line for poetry, on publication.

WASCANA REVIEW—c/o Dept. of English, Univ. of Regina, Regina, Sask., Canada S4S 0A2. Joan Givner, Ed. Short stories, 2,000 to 6,000 words; critical articles; poetry. Pays $3 per page, after publication.

WASHINGTON REVIEW—P.O. Box 50132, Washington, DC 20004. Clarissa Wittenberg, Ed. Poetry; articles on literary, performing and fine arts in the Washington, D.C. area, 1,000 to 2,500 words. Fiction, to 1,000 words. Area writers preferred. Pays in copies.

WAVES: FINE CANADIAN WRITING—79 Denham Dr., Richmond Hill, Ont., L4C 6H9, Canada. Excerpts and short stories, 500 to 5,000 words. Haiku; poetry to 500 lines. Reviews of and interviews with Canadian writers. Pays $10 per printed page, on publication. Include *international reply coupons.*

WEBSTER REVIEW—Webster Univ., 470 E. Lockwood, Webster Groves, MO 63119. Nancy Schapiro, Ed. Fiction; poetry; interviews; essays; translations. Pays in copies.

WEST BRANCH—English Dept., Bucknell Univ., Lewisburg, PA 17837. Karl Patten, Robert Taylor, Eds. Poetry and fiction. Pays in copies and subscriptions.

THE WINDLESS ORCHARD—Dept. of English, Indiana-Purdue Univ., Ft. Wayne, IN 46805. Robert Novak, Ed. Contemporary poetry. Pays in copies.

WITHOUT HALOS—Ocean County Poets Collective, P.O. Box 1342, Point Pleasant Beach, NJ 08742. Frank Finale, Ed. Poetry accepted between Jan. 1 and June 30. Pays in copies.

WOMAN OF POWER—Box 827, Cambridge, MA 02238–0827. Char McKee, Linda Roach, Eds. Fiction, to 3,500 words; nonfiction, to 3,500 words. Poetry, submit up to 5 poems at a time. Pays in copies.

WRITERS FORUM—Univ. of Colorado, Colorado Springs, CO 80933–7150. Alex Blackburn, Ed. Annual. Mainstream and experimental fiction, 1,000 to 10,000 words. Poetry (1 to 5 poems per submission). Emphasis on Western themes and writers. Send material October through May. Pays in copies.

WYOMING, THE HUB OF THE WHEEL—The Willow Bee Publishing, Box 9, Saratoga, WY 82331. Lenore A. Senior, Man. Ed. Fiction, to 2,500 words; nonfiction, to 2,500 words; poetry, to 80 lines. "An international literary/arts magazine devoted to peace, the human race, positive relationships, and the human spirit and possibilities." Pays in copies.

XANADU—Long Island Poetry Collective, Box 773, Huntington, NY 11743. Pat Nesbitt, Mildred Jeffrey, Barbara Lucas, Eds. Short poetry on a variety of topics. Pays in copies.

YALE REVIEW—1902A Yale Sta., New Haven, CT 06520. Kai Erikson, Ed. Serious poetry, to 200 lines and fiction, 3,000 to 5,000 words. Pays nominal sum.

HUMOR, FILLERS, AND SHORT ITEMS

Magazines noted for their excellent filler departments, plus a cross-section of publications using humor, short items, jokes, quizzes, and cartoons, follow. However, almost all magazines use some type of filler material, and writers can find dozens of markets by studying copies of magazines at a library or newsstand.

Many magazines do not acknowledge or return filler material, and in such cases, writers may assume that after 90 days have passed from the time of submission, a filler may be submitted to another market.

ALCOHOLISM & ADDICTION MAGAZINE—P.O. Box 31329, Seattle, WA 98103. "Coffee Break Page": short, true-experience pieces, jokes and anecdotes relating to alcoholism and chemical dependency for professionals in the treatment field and recovering persons.

AMERICAN CLAY EXCHANGE—P.O. Box 2674, La Mesa, CA 92041. Short items on American-made pottery. Pays $5, on acceptance.

THE AMERICAN FIELD—222 W. Adams St., Chicago, IL 60606. W. F. Brown, Ed. Short fact items and anecdotes on hunting dogs, and field trials for bird dogs. Pays varying rates, on acceptance.

THE AMERICAN LEGION MAGAZINE—Box 1055, Indianapolis, IN 46206. Parting Shots Page: short humorous anecdotes, appealing to military veterans and their families. General humor: no sex, religion, ethnic humor or political satire. Pays $15 for definitions, anecdotes and gags, on acceptance. No fillers or poetry.

THE AMERICAN NEWSPAPER CARRIER—P.O. Box 15300, Winston-Salem, NC 27103. Short, humorous pieces, to 1,000 words, for pre-teen and teen-age newspaper carriers. Pays to $25, on publication.

AMERICAN WAY—P.O. Box 619616, MD 2G23, DFW Airport, TX 75261–9616. Charles Marsh, Ed. American Airlines' inflight magazine. Short pieces, 700 words, for "American Observer." Pays $100, on acceptance.

ARMY MAGAZINE—2425 Wilson Blvd., Arlington, VA 22201. L. James Binder, Ed.-in-Chief. True anecdotes on military subjects. Pays $10 to $35, on publication.

ART & ANTIQUES—89 Fifth Ave., New York, NY 10003. Judith Cressy, Man. Ed. News items, 300 to 500 words, related to arts or antiques. Pays on publication.

THE ATLANTIC—8 Arlington St., Boston, MA 02116. Sophisticated humorous or satirical pieces, 1,000 to 3,000 words. Some light poetry. Pays from $750 for prose, on acceptance.

BASSMASTER MAGAZINE—B.A.S.S. Publications, Box 17900, Montgomery, AL 36141. Dave Precht, Ed. Anecdotes, short humor and news breaks related to bass fishing, 250 to 500 words. Pays $50 to $100, on acceptance. No clips.

BICYCLING—33 E. Minor Rd., Emmaus, PA 18098. Anecdotes, new trends, and other items for "Paceline" section, 150 to 250 words. Pays $50, on publication.

BIKEREPORT—Bikecentennial, P.O. Box 8308, Missoula, MT 59807. Daniel D'Ambrosio, Ed. News shorts from the bicycling world for "In Bicycle Circles." Pays $5 to $10, on publication.

BIRD WATCHER'S DIGEST—P.O. Box 110, Marietta, OH 45750. Mary Bowers, Ed. Cartoons. Pays $10, on publication.

BLACK FAMILY—1180 Sunrise Valley Dr., Suite 320, Reston, VA 22091. Evelyn Ivery, Ed. Fillers and poetry. Pays $25, after publication.

BUSINESS VIEW—P.O. Box 9859, Naples, FL 33941. Business- or economic-related shorts, 100 to 300 words. Pays $10 to $25, on publication.

CAPPER'S—616 Jefferson St., Topeka, KS 66607. Nancy Peavler, Ed. Household hints, recipes, jokes. Pays varying rates, on publication.

CASCADES EAST—716 N.E. 4th St., P.O. Box 5784, Bend, OR 97708. Geoff Hill, Ed. Fillers, related to travel, history, and recreation in Central Oregon. Pays 3¢ to 10¢ a word, on publication.

CASHFLOW—6255 Barfield Rd., Atlanta, GA 30328. Dick Gamble, Ed. Short pieces, to 1,000 words, on varied aspects of treasury financial management, for treasury managers in public and private institutions. Pays on publication. Query.

CATHOLIC DIGEST—P.O. Box 64090, St. Paul, MN 55164. Fillers, to 300 words, on instances of kindness rewarded, for "Hearts Are Trumps." Stories about conversions, for "Open Door." Reports of tactful remarks or actions, for "The Perfect Assist." Accounts of good deeds, for "People Are Like That." Humorous pieces on parish life, for "In Our Parish." Amusing signs, for "Signs of the Times." Jokes; fillers. Pays $4 to $50, on publication.

CHEVRON USA ODYSSEY—Rm. 3188, 575 Market St., San Francisco, CA 94105. Mark Williams, Ed. Quarterly. True, previously unpublished, humorous anecdotes with a travel tie-in, 200 words. Pays $25, on publication.

CHIC—2029 Century Park E., Suite 3800, Los Angeles, CA 90067. Visual fillers, short humor with visuals, 100 to 200 words, for "Odds and Ends" section. Pays on acceptance.

CHICKADEE—56 The Esplanade, Suite 306, Toronto, Ont., Canada M5E

1A7. Humorous poetry about animals and nature, for children, 10 to 15 lines. Pays on publication.

CHILD LIFE—P.O. Box 567, Indianapolis, IN 46206. Karla Stouse, Ed. Puzzles, games, mazes, and rebuses, on health or safety-related subjects, simple craft ideas, for children 7 to 9 years. Pays $10 to $15, on publication.

CHILDREN'S PLAYMATE—1100 Waterway Blvd., P.O. Box 567, Indianapolis, IN 46206. Elizabeth Rinck, Ed. Puzzles, games, mazes for 5- to 7-year-olds, emphasizing health, safety, nutrition. Pays about 6¢ a word (varies on puzzles), on publication.

CHRISTIAN HERALD—40 Overlook Dr., Chappaqua, NY 10514. Dean Merrill, Ed. Poetry and true anecdotes, humorous or instructive, on Christian marriage and child-rearing. Pays $20, on acceptance.

THE CHURCH MUSICIAN—127 Ninth Ave. N., Nashville, TN 37234. W. M. Anderson, Ed. For Southern Baptist music leaders. Humorous fillers with a music slant. No clippings. Pays around 5¢ a word, on acceptance. Same address and requirements for *Glory Songs* (for adults), and *Opus One* and *Opus Two* (for teen-agers).

CLAVIER MAGAZINE—200 Northfield Rd., Northfield, IL 60093. Barbara Kreader, Ed. Fillers, humor, and jokes of interest to keyboard performers and teachers. Pay varies, on publication.

COLUMBIA—Box 1670, New Haven, CT 06507. Elmer Von Feldt, Ed. Journal of the Knights of Columbus. Catholic family magazine. Humor and satire, to 1,000 words; captionless cartoons. Pays $200, $50 for cartoons, on acceptance.

COLUMBIA JOURNALISM REVIEW—700 Journalism Bldg., Columbia Univ., New York, NY 10027. Gloria Cooper, Man. Ed. Amusing mistakes in news stories, headlines, photos, etc. (original clippings required), for "Lower Case." Pays $10, on publication.

CONNECTICUT—Communications International, P. O. Box 6480, Bridgeport, CT 06606. Dale P. Salm, Man. Ed. Short "About and Around" pieces on subjects related to life in Connecticut. Pays $50, on publication.

COUNTRY—5400 S. 60th, Greendale, WI 53129. Dan Johnson, Associate Ed. Fillers, 50 to 200 words, for a rural audience. Taboos: tobacco, liquor, and sex. Pays on acceptance.

COUNTRY WOMAN (formerly *Farm Woman*)—P.O. Box 643, Milwaukee, WI 53201. Eleanor Jacobs, Man. Ed. Short verse, 4 to 20 lines, and fillers, to 250 words, on the rural experience. Pays from $40, on acceptance.

CYCLE WORLD—1499 Monrovia Ave., P.O. Box 1757, Newport Beach, CA 92663. Paul Dean, Ed. News items on motorcycle industry, legislation, trends. Pays on acceptance.

DANCE TEACHER NOW—803 Russell Blvd., Ste. 2, Davis, CA 95616. Short pieces, 100 to 750 words, on dance history or dance teaching theme. Cartoons. Pays on publication.

DOWN EAST—Camden, ME 04843. Anecdotes about Maine, to 1,000 words, for "I Remember." Humorous anecdotes, to 300 words, for "It Happened Down East." Pays $10 to $50, on acceptance.

EBONY—820 S. Michigan Ave., Chicago, IL 60605. Charles L. Sanders,

Man. Ed. "Speaking of People," short features, to 200 words, on blacks in traditionally non-black jobs. Cartoons. Pays $75 for cartoons, on publication.

ELECTRONIC EDUCATION—Electronic Communications, 1311 Executive Center Dr., Suite 220, Tallahassee, FL 32301. Don Wood, Ed. Fillers of interest to educators who use computers.

THE ELKS MAGAZINE—425 W. Diversey Pkwy., Chicago, IL 60614. Judith Keogh, Assoc. Ed. Humor, 1,500 to 3,000 words, for a family audience. No fillers. Query only; send SASE for guidelines. Pays from $150, on acceptance.

EQUINOX—7 Queen Victoria Rd., Camden East, Ont., Canada K0K 1J0. Jody Morgan, Assistant Ed. Department pieces, 300 to 500 words, for "Nexus" (science and medicine) and "Habitat" (man-made and natural environment). Pays $100 to $300, on acceptance.

ESSENCE—1500 Broadway, New York, NY 10036. Susan L. Taylor, Ed. Short items, 300 to 750 words, on the arts, mothering, work, and health, for black women. Pays on acceptance.

THE EVENER—See *Rural Heritage*.

EXPECTING—685 Third Ave., New York, NY 10017. E. Podsiadlo, Ed. Anecdotes about pregnancy, for "Happenings." Pays $15, on publication.

FACES—20 Grove St., Petersborough, NH 03458. Carolyn Yoder, Ed. Puzzles, mazes, crosswords, and picture puzzles, related to monthly themes, for children. Send SASE for list of themes before submitting.

FAMILY CIRCLE—Box 2822, Grand Central Sta., New York, NY 10017. Ideas or suggestions on homemaking and community betterment, for "Readers' Idea Exchange." Pays $50. Unpublished entries cannot be returned or acknowledged. Query.

FARM AND RANCH LIVING—5400 S. 60th St. Greendale, WI 53129. Bob Ottum, Man. Ed. Fillers on rural people and living, 200 words. Pays from $15, on acceptance and on publication.

FARM WOMAN—See *Country Woman*.

FATE—500 Hyacinth Pl., Highland Park, IL 60035. Mary Margaret Fuller, Ed. Factual fillers, to 300 words, on strange or psychic happenings. True stories, to 300 words, on psychic or mystic personal experiences. Pays $2 to $15.

FIELD & STREAM—1515 Broadway, New York, NY 10036. Duncan Barnes, Ed. Fillers on hunting, camping, fishing, etc., to 750 words, for "How It's Done." Cartoons. Pays $250 to $750 for fillers, $100 for cartoons, on acceptance.

FLARE—777 Bay St., Toronto, Ont., Canada M5W 1A7. Sharon Bird, Man. Ed. Career-related items, profiles, 100 to 150 words, for young Canadian working women aged 18 to 34. Pays on acceptance. Query.

FLORIDA KEYS MAGAZINE—Box 818, 2111 O/S Hwy., Marathon, FL 33050. Address David Ethridge. Fillers, humor, with regional tie-in. Pays on publication.

FLY FISHERMAN—Box 8200, Harrisburg, PA 17105. Jack Russell, Assoc. Ed. Fillers, 100 words, on equipment, tackle tips, knots, and fly-tying tips. Pays from $35, on acceptance.

FORD TIMES—One Illinois Ctr., 111 E. Wacker Dr., Suite 1700, Chicago, IL 60601. Lauren Reskin, Man. Ed. Short, 150 words, vacation/travel/dining anecdotes for "Road Show." Pays $50, on acceptance.

GALLERY—800 Second Ave., New York, NY 10017. Marc Lichter, Ed.-in-Chief; Barry Janoff, Man. Ed. Short humor, satire, and short service features for men. Pays varying rates, on acceptance and on publication. Query.

GLAMOUR—350 Madison Ave., New York, NY 10017. Articles, 1,000 words, for "Viewpoint" section: opinion pieces for women. Pays $500, on acceptance. Send SASE.

GLORY SONGS—See *The Church Musician.*

GOLF DIGEST—5520 Park Ave., Trumbull, CT 06611. Lois Hains, Asst. Ed. Short fact items, anecdotes, quips, jokes, light verse related to golf. True humorous or odd incidents, to 200 words. Pays from $25, on acceptance.

GOLF ILLUSTRATED—3 Park Ave., New York, NY 10016. David Earl, Ed. Golf-related fillers; one- to two-paragraph news or personal-experience snippets, preferably of humorous or offbeat nature. Pays $25 to $100, on acceptance.

GOLF MAGAZINE—380 Madison Ave., New York, NY 10017. Robin McMillan, Sr. Ed. Fillers to 750 words, on golf. Pays from $75, on acceptance.

GOOD HOUSEKEEPING—959 Eighth Ave., New York, NY 10019. Rosemary Leonard, Ed. Light verse and very short humorous prose. Pays from $10, on acceptance.

GRIT—208 W. Third St., Williamsport, PA 17701. Joanne Decker, Assignment Ed. Brief anecdotal features, from 30 words, on interesting, amusing, heart-warming, and inspiring subjects. Humorous verse. Pays 12¢ a word for prose, $6 for four lines of verse.

GUIDEPOSTS—747 Third Ave., New York, NY 10017. Jack Haring, Man. Ed. Inspirational anecdotes, to 250 words. Pays $10 to $50, on acceptance.

HARROWSMITH/USA—The Creamery, Ferry Rd., Charlotte, VT 05445. Tom Rawls, Man. Ed. Short pieces for "Screed" (opinions) and "Gazette" (news briefs). Pays from $50, on acceptance.

HOME LIFE—127 Ninth Ave. N., Nashville, TN 37234. Reuben Herring, Ed., Southern Baptist. Personal-experience pieces, 100 to 500 words, on Christian marriage, and family relationships, Pays to 5¢ a word, on acceptance.

HOME MECHANIX—1515 Broadway, New York, NY 10036. Joseph R. Provey, Ed. Single photos with captions and tips for shortcuts in shop, garage or home. Pays $50 to $75, on acceptance.

HOMEOWNERS—The Personal Marketing Co., 8520 Sweetwater, Ste. F57, Houston, TX 77037. Theresa Seegers, Man. Ed. Short articles, 200 to 500 words, on buying and selling real estate, mortgages, investment, home improvements, interior design, etc. Pays 10¢ to 20¢ a word, on acceptance. Query. Newsletter.

THE INTERNATIONAL ASSIGNMENT (formerly *The International American*)—201 E. 36th St., New York, NY 10016. Alison R. Lanier, Ed. Short pieces, 200 to 300 words, by writers who have lived abroad, with advice, suggestions, warnings and information for Americans who are now living overseas. No travel tips, or stories of personal interest. Pays $35, on acceptance.

JACK & JILL—1100 Waterway Blvd., P. O. Box 567, Indianapolis, IN 46206. Christine French Clark, Ed. Poems, puzzles, games, science and craft projects, for 6- to 8-year-olds, with health or holiday themes. Instructions for activities should be clearly written, accompanied by diagrams and a list of needed materials. Pays varying rates, on publication.

KEY TO CHRISTIAN EDUCATION—8121 Hamilton Ave., Cincinnati, OH 45231. Virginia Beddow, Ed. Short pieces, 50 to 250 words, for "This Is How We Did It" (personal experience) column. Pays $5 to $10, on acceptance.

LADIES' HOME JOURNAL—"Last Laughs," 100 Park Ave., New York, NY 10017. Brief anecdotes and poems about the funny business of being a woman today. Pays $25. Submissions cannot be acknowledged or returned.

LIFE IN THE TIMES—Times Publishing Co., Springfield, VA 22159. Barry Robinson, Ed. Short personal-experience pieces, 750 words, for "On the Homefront." Pays from $25.

MAD MAGAZINE—485 Madison Ave., New York, NY 10022. Humorous pieces on a wide variety of topics. No straight text pieces, no poetry. Query with proposal and SASE. Pays top rates, on acceptance.

MAGAZINE DESIGN & PRODUCTION—P. O. Box 7926, Overland Park, KS 66207. Ideas on improving magazine design or being more cost-effective in production management, to 500 words, for "Tip Sheet." Pays $50, on publication.

MATURE LIVING—127 Ninth Ave. N., MSN 140, Nashville, TN 37234. Nostalgia, 900 words, for "I Remember When . . ." Brief, humorous, original items. Profiles of senior adults, 25 lines with photos. Pays after acceptance. Send SASE for guidelines.

MATURE YEARS—201 Eighth Ave. S., Nashville, TN 37202. Jack Gilbert, Ed. Poems, cartoons, puzzles, jokes, anecdotes, to 300 words, for older adults. Pays 4¢ a word, on acceptance.

MIAMI/SOUTH FLORIDA MAGAZINE—P. O. Box 140008, Coral Gables, FL 33114. Rick Eyerdam, Man. Ed. Short, localized, "bright" items, 200 to 400 words, for the "Big Orange" section. Pays 15 days before publication.

THE MICHIGAN WOMAN—P. O. Box 1171, Birmingham, MI 48012. Betsy Hull, Ed. Fillers, to 700 words. Pays on publication.

MIDWAY—Skies Publishing Co., Plaza West, Suite 310, 9600 SW Oak St., Portland, OR 97223. Robert Patterson, Ed. Columns, 500 to 700 words, of interest to business travelers. Pays $50 to $100, on publication.

MID-WEST OUTDOORS—111 Shore Dr., Hinsdale, IL 60521. Gene Laulunen, Ed. Where to and how to fish in the Midwest, 400 to 1,500 words, with 2 photos. Pays $15 to $35, on publication.

MODERN BRIDE—One Park Ave., New York, NY 10016. Mary Ann Cavlin, Man. Ed. Humorous pieces, 500 to 1,500 words, for brides. Pays on acceptance.

MODERN MATURITY—3200 E. Carson St., Lakewood, CA 90712. Ian Ledgerwood, Ed. Money-saving tips; jokes; cartoons; narrative math problems, etc. Submit seasonal material 6 months in advance. Pays from $50, on acceptance. Query.

MODERN PHOTOGRAPHY—825 Seventh Ave., New York, NY 10019. Jason Schneider, Ed. How-to pieces, 200 to 300 words, with photos, on photography. Pays $25 to $500, on acceptance.

MUTUAL FUND PERFORMANCE JOURNAL—824 E. Baltimore St., Baltimore, MD 21202. Robert W. Czeschin, Ed. Tabloid. Short features on all aspects of mutual funds and mutual fund investing: IRA's, switching strategies, non-US funds, taxes, etc. to 1,000 words. Pays to $100, on acceptance.

NATIONAL BEAUTY SCHOOL JOURNAL—3839 White Plains Rd., Bronx, NY 10467. Mary Jane Tenerelli, Ed. Crossword puzzles and cartoons with a cosmetology slant. Pays $25 for puzzles, $50 for cartoons, on publication.

NATIONAL ENQUIRER—Lantana, FL 33464. Jim Allan, Asst. Ed. Short, humorous fillers, witticisms, anecdotes, tart comments. Original items preferred, but others considered if source and date given. Short poems of a philosophical or amusing nature. Pays $20, on publication. Self-addressed, stamped envelope required.

NATIONAL REVIEW—150 E. 35th St., New York, NY 10016. William F. Buckley, Ed. Satire, to 900 words. Short, satirical poems. Pays $35 to $100, on publication.

NEW ENGLAND MONTHLY—P. O. 446, Haydenville, MA 01039. Paul Keegan, Associate Ed. Short items, 600 to 800 words, on politics, arts, business, education, crime, in New England area. Pays $150 to $200, on acceptance.

NEW JERSEY MONTHLY—7 Dumont Pl., Morristown, NJ 07960. Patrick Sarver, Man. Ed. Short pieces related to life in New Jersey. Pays $35 to $75, on acceptance.

NEW YORK—755 Second Ave., New York, NY 10017. Eric Pooley, Assoc. Ed. Short, lively pieces, to 400 words, highlighting events and trends in New York City for "Fast Track." Profiles to 300 words for "Brief Lives." Pays $25 to $150, on publication. Include SASE.

NEW YORK ALIVE—152 Washington Ave., Albany, NY 12210. Mary Grates Stoll, Ed. Department pieces, including "Great Escapes" (travel ideas) and "Expressly New York" (unusual places, products or events in New York). Pays $50 to $150.

THE NEW YORKER—25 W. 43rd St., New York, NY 10036. Amusing mistakes in newspapers, books, magazines, etc. Pays from $10, extra for headings and tag lines, on acceptance. Address Newsbreaks Dept.

NORTHWEST LIVING—130 Second Ave. S., Edmonds, WA 98020. Terry Sheely, Ed. Shorts, 100 to 400 words, related to the natural resources of the Northwest. Query first with SASE. Pays on acceptance.

OHIO MAGAZINE—40 S. Third St., Columbus, OH 43215. Ellen Stein Burbach, Man. Ed. Short pieces (from 50 words) on regional topics, for departments. Pays on publication.

OMNI—1965 Broadway, New York, NY 10023. Douglas Colligan, Senior Ed. Humorous and satirical pieces, to 800 words, on aspects of the future: science and technology, the arts, lifestyles. Pays from $750, on acceptance.

OPUS ONE and **OPUS TWO**—See *The Church Musician.*

ORBEN'S CURRENT COMEDY—1200 N. Nash St., #1122, Arlington, VA 22209. Robert Orben, Ed. Original, funny, performable one-liners and brief jokes on news, fads, topical subjects, etc. Openings, jokes, roast material, etc., for speakers. Pays $8, after publication. Stamped, self-addressed envelope required.

THE ORIGINAL NEW ENGLAND GUIDE—Historical Times, Inc., 2245 Kohn Rd., Box 8200, Harrisburg, PA 17105. Howard Crise, Ed. Annual. Short pieces, 500 words, focusing on a particular New England attraction or theme. Pays on acceptance.

OUTDOOR LIFE—380 Madison Ave., New York, NY 10017. Clare Conley, Ed. Short instructive items and 1-pagers on hunting, fishing, camping gear, boats, outdoor equipment. Photos. Pays on acceptance.

PARENTS MAGAZINE—685 Third Ave., New York, NY 10017. Short items on solutions of child care-related problems for "Parents Exchange." Pays $20, on publication.

PARISH FAMILY DIGEST—200 Noll Plaza, Huntington, IN 46750. Louis F. Jacquet, Ed. Family- or Catholic parish-oriented humor. Anecdotes, 250 words, of unusual parish experiences. Pays $5 to $12.50, on acceptance.

PENNYWHISTLE PRESS—Box 500-P, Washington, DC 20044. Anita Sama, Ed. Short fillers, puzzlers, word games, humorous stories, for 6- to 12-year-olds. Pays varying rates, on acceptance.

PEOPLE IN ACTION—P. O. Box 10010, Ogden, UT 84409. Profiles, 500 to 700 words, on accomplished cooks, for "Cuisine." Must be accompanied by recipe and color transparency. Query. Pays 15¢ a word, extra for photos, on acceptance.

PGA MAGAZINE—100 Ave. of the Champions, Palm Beach Gardens, FL 33410. Humorous pieces related to golf, to 1,500 words. Pays to $300, on acceptance.

PLAYBOY—919 N. Michigan Ave., Chicago, IL 60611. Address Party Jokes Editor or After Hours Editor. Jokes; short original material on new trends, lifestyles, personalities; humorous news items. Pays $50 for jokes, on acceptance; $50 to $350 for "After Hours" items, on publication.

PLAYGIRL—801 Second Ave., New York, NY 10017. Humorous looks at daily life and relationships from male or female perspective, to 1,000 words, for "The Men's Room" and "The Women's Room." Query Nonfiction Ed. Cartoons dealing with women and women's issues. Kevin G. Loud, Cartoon Ed. Pays varying rates.

POLITICAL WOMAN—4521 Campus Dr., Ste. 388, Irvine, CA 92715. Sally Corngold, Ed. Fillers, jokes, and humor, one to three paragraphs, on current events. Pays on publication.

POPULAR MECHANICS—224 W. 57th St., New York, NY 10019. Bill Hartford, Man. Ed. How-to pieces, from 300 words, with photos and sketches, on home improvement and shop and craft projects. Pays $25 to $200, on acceptance. Buys all rights.

POPULAR SCIENCE—380 Madison Ave., New York, NY 10017. A. W. Lees, Home & Shop Ed. One-column fillers, 350 words, with photo or sketch if demo necessary: general workshop ideas, maintenance tips for home and car. Pays from $100, on acceptance.

PROCEEDINGS—U.S. Naval Institute, Annapolis, MD 21402. Kristine S. Wilcox, Ed. Asst. Short humorous anecdotes of interest to Navy, Marine Corps, and Coast Guard professionals. Pays $25, on acceptance.

READER'S DIGEST—Pleasantville, NY 10570. Anecdotes for "Life in These United States," "Humor in Uniform," "Campus Comedy" and "All in a Day's Work." Pays $300, on publication. Short items for "Toward More Picturesque Speech." Pays $50. Anecdotes, fillers, for "Laughter, the Best Medicine," "Personal Glimpses," etc. Pays $20 per two-column line. No submissions acknowledged or returned. Consult anecdotes page in each issue for additional guidelines.

RECOVERY—P. O. Box 31329, Seattle, WA 98103. Poetry and fillers of interest to those recovering from alcohol and drug dependencies. Guidelines.

ROAD KING—P. O. Box 250, Park Forest, IL 60466. Address Features Ed. Trucking-related cartoons for "Loads of Laughs"; anecdotes to 200 words, for "Trucker's Life." Pays $25 for anecdotes, on publication. SASE required.

RODALE'S PRACTICAL HOMEOWNER—33 E. Minor St., Emmaus, PA 18098. Short pieces, 300 to 400 words, on solo and community efforts, restoration and architectural interests, energy saving ideas, inventions, etc. Pays on acceptance.

ROLL CALL—317 Mass. Ave. N.E., Washington, DC 20002. Sidney Yudain, Ed. Humorous items on Congress; anecdotes, quips. Pays on acceptance.

RURAL HERITAGE (formerly *The Evener*)—P. O. Box 7, Cedar Falls, IA 50613. Anecdotes and newsbreaks, 100 to 750 words, related to draft horses, rural history, antiques, or old-time crafts. Pays 3¢ to 10¢ a word, on acceptance.

RURAL LIVING—P. O. Box 15248, Richmond, VA 23227-0648. Richard G. Johnstone, Jr., Ed. Family humor, 100 to 250 words. Pays on publication.

SACRAMENTO—P. O. Box 2424, Sacramento, CA 95811. "City Lights," interesting and unusual people, places, and behind-the-scenes news items, 75 to 250 words. All material must have Sacramento tie-in. Pays on acceptance.

THE SATURDAY EVENING POST—1100 Waterway Blvd., Indianapolis, IN 46202. Jack Gramling, Post Scripts Ed. Humor and satire, to 300 words; light verse, jokes, for "Post Scripts." Pays $15, on publication.

SCHOOL SHOP—Prakken Publishing, Box 8623, 416 Longshore Dr., Ann Arbor, MI 48107. Alan H. Jones, Exec. Ed. Puzzles and cartoons of interest to technology and industrial education teachers and administrators. Pay varies, on publication.

SCORE, CANADA'S GOLF MAGAZINE—287 MacPherson Ave., Toronto, Ont., Canada M4V 1A4. John Gordon, Man. Ed. Fillers, 50 to 100 words, related to Canadian golf scene. Pays $10 to $25, on publication. Include *international reply coupons.*

SHEET MUSIC MAGAZINE—223 Katonah Ave., Katonah, NY 10536. How-to's and book reviews, for amateur and professional pianists and organists, to 500 words. Pays on publication.

SKI MAGAZINE—380 Madison Ave., New York, NY 10017. Dick Needham, Ed. Short, 100 to 300 word items on events and people in skiing, for "Ski Life" department. Humor, to 2,000 words, related to skiing. Pays on acceptance.

SKIING—One Park Ave., New York, NY 10016. Bill Grout, Ed.-in-Chief.

Articles, to 600 words, on skiing; humorous vignettes, fillers on skiing oddities. Pays from 15¢ a word, on acceptance.

SNOWMOBILE—319 Barry Ave. S., Ste. 101, Wayzata, MN 55391. Dick Hendricks, Ed. Short humor and cartoons on snowmobiling and winter "Personality Plates" sighted. Pays varying rates, on publication.

SOUTHERN—P. O. Box 3418, 201 E. Markham, Suite 200, Little Rock, AR 72203. Linton Weeks, Ed. "We have several monthly departments open to free lancers: politics, sports, business, 'Southern Front' (short, quirky tidbits from around the South, 50 to 600 words), 'Weekends' (nuts and bolts travel pieces), food and drink, and 'Southern Lights' (Southern 'up-and-comers,' success stories—300 to 500 words)." Pays from $50, on acceptance.

SOUTHERN EXPOSURE—P. O. Box 531, Durham, NC 27702. Bob Hall, Ed. Fillers on civil rights, politics, nuclear power, utility reform, land use, southern people, etc. Pays from $50, on publication.

SOUTHERN OUTDOORS—1 Bell Rd., Montgomery, AL 36117. Larry Teague, Ed. Humor, 250 to 800 words, related to the outdoors. Pays 15¢ to 20¢ a word, on acceptance.

SPORTS AFIELD—250 W. 55th St., New York, NY 10019. Unusual, useful tips, 100 to 500 words, for "Almanac" section: hunting, fishing, camping, boating, etc. Photos. Pays $10 per column inch, on publication.

THE STATE: DOWN HOME IN NORTH CAROLINA—P. O. Box 2169, Raleigh, NC 27602. W. B. Wright, Ed. Short fillers. Pays on acceptance.

TOUCH—Box 7259, Grand Rapids, MI 49510. Carol Smith, Man. Ed. Fillers, Bible puzzles from NIV version, for Christian girls aged 8 to 14. Pays 2¢ a word, on acceptance.

TRAILER BOATS—20700 Belshaw Ave., P.O. Box 5427, Carson, CA 90249. Jim Youngs, Ed. Fillers and humor, preferably with illustrations, on boating and related activities. Pays $5 per column inch, extra for photos, on publication.

TRAVEL SMART—Dobbs Ferry, New York 10522. Interesting, unusual or helpful travel-related tips, vacation or business-travel information, to 1,000 words. Pays $5 to $100, on publication. Query.

TRIFLE—Box 182, Dover, NH 03820. Mary Pat Kingsbury, Ed. Humorous non-fiction, 150 to 750 words, for "Spouting Off"; brief fictional news items, 100 to 200 words, accompanied by photos or illustrations, for "Newsnotes." Pays $15 to $75, on publication.

TRUE CONFESSIONS—215 Lexington Ave., New York, NY 10016. Barbara J. Brett, Ed. Warm, inspirational first-person fillers, 300 to 700 words, about love, marriage and family life for "The Feminine Side of Things." Pays after publication. Buys all rights.

THE VIRGINIAN—P. O. Box 8, New Hope, VA 24469. Hunter S. Pierce, IV, Ed. Dir. Fillers, relating to Virginia and adjacent region of the South. Anecdotes and nostalgia preferred. Pays on publication.

VISTA/USA—Box 161, Convent Station, NJ 07961. Kathleen M. Caccavale, Ed. Shorts, 500 to 1,000 words, on mini-trips, American vignettes. Pays from $150, on acceptance.

VOLKSWAGEN'S WORLD—P. O. Box 3951, 888 W. Big Beaver, Troy, MI 48007-3951. Marlene Goldsmith, Ed. Anecdotes, to 100 words, about Volkswagen owners' experiences; humorous photos of Volkswagens. Pays from $15 to $40, on acceptance.

WASHINGTON'S ALMANAC—901 Lenora, Seattle, WA 98121. David Fuller, Man. Ed. Fillers and short items related to WA. Pays varying rates, on publication.

WE ALASKANS—*Anchorage Daily News,* Box 6616, Anchorage, AK 99502. Kathleen McCoy, Ed. Humor on Alaskan topics. Pays on publication.

WESTERN SPORTSMAN—P. O. Box 737, Regina, Sask., Canada S4P 3A8. Rick Bates, Ed. How-to's, humor, cartoons on outdoor experiences in Alberta and Saskatchewan. Pays from $40, on publication.

WISCONSIN TRAILS—P. O. Box 5650, Madison, WI 53705. Geri Nixon, Man. Ed. Short fillers on regional topics. Pays from $100, on acceptance and on publication.

WOMAN—1115 Broadway, New York, NY 10010. Sherry Amatenstein, Ed. Short newsbreaks on medical and legal advances for women for "Let's Put Our Heads Together." Pays on acceptance. Query.

WOMAN'S DAY—1515 Broadway, New York, NY 10036. Heart-warming anecdotes about a "good neighbor"; creative solutions to community or family problems; reader versions of a *Woman's Day*- inspired craft (including photo). For "Tips to Share": short pieces on personal instructive family experiences, practical suggestions for homemakers. Pays $50, on publication.

WOODENBOAT MAGAZINE—Box 78, Brooklin, ME 04616. Jon Wilson, Ed. Wooden boat-related activities and projects. Pays $5 to $50, on publication.

JUVENILE, TEENAGE, AND YOUNG ADULT MAGAZINES

JUVENILE MAGAZINES

ACTION—Dept. of Christian Education, Free Methodist Headquarters, 901 College Ave., Winona Lake, IN 46590. Vera Bethel, Ed. Stories, 1,000 words, for 9- to 11-year-olds. How-to features, 200 to 500 words. Verse. Seasonal material. Pays $25 for stories, $15 for features with photos or sketch, $5 for poetry, on publication.

CHICKADEE—The Young Naturalist Foundation, 56 The Esplanade, Suite 306, Toronto, Ont., Canada M5E 1A7. Janis Nosbakken, Ed. Animal and adventure stories, 200 to 800 words, for children aged 3 to 8. Also, puzzles, activities and observation games, 50 to 300 words. Pays varying rates, on publication. Send complete manuscript and International postal coupons. No outlines.

CHILD LIFE—1100 Waterway Blvd., P. O. Box 567, Indianapolis, IN 46206. Karla Stouse, Ed. Articles, 500 to 1,200 words, for 7- to 9-year olds.

Fiction and humor stories, to 1,600 words. Puzzles. Photos. Pays about 6¢ a word, extra for photos, on publication. Buys all rights.

CHILDREN'S DIGEST—1100 Waterway Blvd., P. O. Box 567, Indianapolis, IN 46202. Elizabeth Rinck, Ed. Health publication for children aged 8 to 10. Informative articles, 500 to 1,200 words, and fiction (especially realistic, adventure, mystery, and humorous), 500 to 1,800 words, with health, safety, exercise, nutrition, or hygiene as theme. Historical and biographical articles. Poetry. Pays 6¢ a word, from $10 for poems, on publication. Buys all rights.

CHILDREN'S MAGIC WINDOW—2416 London Rd., Ste. 721, Duluth, MN 55812. Mary Morse, Ed.-in-Chief. Articles, 500 to 800 words, on topics from science and sports to health and family. Short stories, 350 to 800 words, poetry, columns, games, puzzles, and riddles. Query first for articles and columns. Pays $35 to $200, on publication.

CHILDREN'S PLAYMATE—Editorial Office, 1100 Waterway Blvd., P. O. Box 567, Indianapolis, IN 46206. Elizabeth Rinck, Ed. Humorous and health-related short stories, 500 to 800 words, for 5- to 7-year-olds. Simple science articles and how-to crafts pieces with brief instructions. "All About" features, about 500 words, on health, nutrition, safety, and exercise. Poems. Pays about 6¢ a word, $10 minimum for poetry, on publication.

CLUBHOUSE—Berrien Springs, MI 49103. Elaine Meseraull, Ed. Action-oriented Christian stories: features, 1,000 to 1,200 words; "Story Cubes" and "Thinker Tales" (parables), about 800 words. Children in stories should be wise, brave, funny, kind, etc. Pays to $35 for lead stories, $30 for parables and other stories.

COBBLESTONE—20 Grove St., Peterborough, NH 03458. Carolyn Yoder, Ed. Theme-related biographies, and short accounts of historical events, to 1,200 words, for children aged 8 to 14 years. Fiction, 500 to 1,200 words. Poetry, to 100 lines. Photos. Pays 10¢ to 15¢ a word for prose, varying rates for poetry, on publication. Send SASE for editorial guidelines with monthly themes.

CRICKET—Box 300, Peru, IL 61354. Marianne Carus, Ed.-in-Chief. Articles and fiction, 200 to 1,500 words, for 6- to 12-year-olds. Poetry, to 30 lines. Pays to 25¢ a word, to $3 a line for poetry, on publication. Send SASE for guidelines. Overstocked.

DISCOVERIES—6401 The Paseo, Kansas City, MO 64131. Cheryl Turner, Ed. Stories, 800 to 1,000 words, for 3rd to 6th graders, with Christian emphasis. Poetry, 4 to 20 lines. Cartoons. Pays 3½¢ a word (2¢ a word for reprints), 25¢ a line for poetry (minimum of $2), on acceptance.

THE DOLPHIN LOG—The Cousteau Society, 8440 Santa Monica Blvd., Los Angeles, CA 90069. Pam Stacey, Ed. Articles, 500 to 1,200 words, on a variety of topics related to our global water system: marine biology, ecology, natural history, and water-related stories, for children ages 7 to 15. Pays $25 to $150, on publication. Query.

ELECTRIC COMPANY MAGAZINE—See *3-2-1 Contact*.

THE FRIEND—50 E. North Temple, 23rd Fl., Salt Lake City, UT 84150. Vivian Paulsen, Man. Ed. Stories and articles, 1,000 to 1,200 words. "Tiny tot" stories, to 250 words. Pays from 8¢ a word, from $15 per poem, on acceptance.

HIGHLIGHTS FOR CHILDREN—803 Church St., Honesdale, PA 18431. Kent L. Brown, Ed. Fiction and articles, to 900 words, for 2- to 12-year-olds.

Fiction should have strong plot, believable characters, story that holds reader's interest from beginning to end. No crime or violence. For articles, cite references used and qualifications. Easy rebus-form stories. Easy-to-read stories, 400 to 600 words, with strong plots. Pays from 6¢ a word, on acceptance.

HUMPTY DUMPTY'S MAGAZINE—1100 Waterway Blvd., P. O. Box 567, Indianapolis, IN 46202. Christine French Clark, Ed. Health publication for children ages 4 to 6. Easy-to-read fiction, to 600 words, some with health and nutrition, safety, exercise, or hygiene as theme; humor and light approach preferred. Crafts with clear, brief instructions. Short poems. Stories-in-rhyme. Pays about 6¢ a word, from $7 for poems, on publication. Buys all rights.

JACK AND JILL—Box 567, Indianapolis, IN 46206. Christine French Clark, Ed. Articles, 500 to 1,000 words, for 6- to 8-year-olds, on sports, nature, science, health, safety, exercise. Features, 1,000 to 1,200 words, on history, biography, life in other countries, etc. Fiction, to 1,200 words. Short poems, games, puzzles, projects. Photos. Pays about 6¢ a word, extra for photos, varying rates for fillers, on publication.

JUNIOR TRAILS—1445 Boonville Ave., Springfield, MO 65802. Cathy Ketcher, Ed. Short stories, 1,000 to 1,800 words, with believable characters and moral emphasis; occasional articles, 500 to 1,000 words, on science, nature, and biography. Pays 2¢ or 3¢ a word, on acceptance.

LOLLIPOPS MAGAZINE—Good Apple, Inc., P. O. Box 299, Carthage, IL 62321-0299. Learning games and activities covering all areas of the curriculum; arts and crafts ideas; stories, for ages 4 to 7. Pays varying rates, on publication. Query first.

MERLYN'S PEN—P. O. Box 1058, E. Greenwich, RI 02818. R. James Stahl, Ed. Short stories, plays and poetry, to 2,500 words, by students in grades 7 through 10 only.

MY OWN MAGAZINE—3500 Western Ave., Highland Park, IL 60035. Carolyn Good Quattrocki, Ed. Fiction, 200 or 400 words; poetry, 50 to 100 words, for children ages three to six. Stories and activities should teach concepts in safety, language, science, math, social studies, and health. Pays $150 to $200 for fiction, $100 for poetry, on acceptance. Guidelines available.

ODYSSEY—1027 N. 7th St., Milwaukee, WI 53233. Nancy Mack, Ed. Features, 600 to 1,500 words, on astronomy and space science for 8- to 12-year-olds. Short experiments, projects, and games. Pays $100 to $350, on publication. Query.

ON THE LINE—616 Walnut, Scottdale, PA 15683-1999. Virginia A. Hostetler, Ed. Nature and how-to articles, 500 to 750 words, for 10- to 14-year-olds. Fiction, 800 to 1,200 words. Poetry, puzzles, cartoons. Pays to 4¢ a word, on acceptance.

OWL—The Young Naturalist Foundation, 56 The Esplanade, Suite 306, Toronto, Ont., Canada M5E 1A7. Sylvia Funston, Ed. Articles, 500 to 1,000 words, for children aged 8 to 12 about animals, science, people, technology, new discoveries, activities. Pays varying rates, on publication. Send for guidelines.

PENNYWHISTLE PRESS—Box 500-P, Washington, DC 20044. Anita Sama, Ed. Short fiction, 850 words, for 8- to 12-year-old children, 400 words for 5- to 8-year-olds. Puzzles and word games. Payment varies, on publication.

PLAYS, THE DRAMA MAGAZINE FOR YOUNG PEOPLE—120 Boylston St., Boston, MA 02116. Elizabeth Preston, Man. Ed. Needs one-act plays, programs, skits, creative dramatic material, suitable for school productions at junior high, middle and lower grade levels. Plays with one set preferred. Uses comedies, dramas, satires, farces, melodramas, dramatized classics, folktales and fairy tales, puppet plays. Pays good rates, on acceptance. Send SASE for manuscript specification sheet. Buys all rights.

POCKETS—1908 Grand Ave., Box 189, Nashville, TN 37202. Shirley Paris, Ed. Ecumenical magazine for children aged 6 through 12. Articles, 400 to 600 words, about the Bible, church history, holidays, etc., that will help children experience a Christian life style. Pays 7¢ a word, on acceptance. Guidelines.

RADAR—8121 Hamilton Ave., Cincinnati, OH 45231. Margaret Williams, Ed. Articles, 400 to 650 words, on nature, hobbies, crafts. Short stories, 900 to 1,100 words: mystery, sports, school, family, with 12-year-old as main character; serials of 2,000 words. Christian emphasis. Poems to 12 lines. Pays to 3¢ a word, to 40¢ a line for poetry, on acceptance.

RANGER RICK—8925 Leesburg Pike, Vienna, VA 22184. Trudy Farrand, Ed. Articles, to 900 words, on wildlife, conservation, natural sciences, and kids in the outdoors, for 6- to 12-year-olds. Nature-related fiction and science fiction welcome. Games, crafts, poems, and puzzles. Pays to $350, on acceptance.

SESAME STREET MAGAZINE—See *3-2-1 Contact.*

SHOFAR—43 Northcote Dr., Melville, NY 11747. Alan A. Kay, Exec. Ed. Short stories, 500 to 750 words; articles, 250 to 750 words; poetry, to 50 lines; short fillers, games, puzzles, and cartoons, for Jewish children, 8 to 13. All material must have a Jewish theme. Pays 10¢ a word, on publication. Submit holiday pieces at least three months in advance.

STONE SOUP, THE MAGAZINE BY CHILDREN—Box 83, Santa Cruz, CA 95063. Gerry Mandel, Ed. Stories, poems, plays, book reviews by children under 14. Pays in copies.

STORY FRIENDS—Mennonite Publishing House, Scottdale, PA 15683. Marjorie Waybill, Ed. Stories, 350 to 800 words, for 4- to 9-year-olds, on Christian faith and values in everyday experiences. Quizzes, riddles. Poetry. Pays to 5¢ a word, to $5 per poem, on acceptance.

SUPER TIMES—5600 North University Ave., Provo, UT 84604. Colleen Hinckley, Man Ed. Thematic issues specializing in activities that teach positive character traits. Stories, 350 to 600 words, that feature the life of a famous person relating to the theme of the issue. Pays $20 to $80, on publication. Query.

3-2-1 CONTACT—Children's Television Workshop, 1 Lincoln Plaza, New York, NY 10023. Jonathan Rosenbloom, Ed. Entertaining and informative articles, 600 to 1,000 words, for 8- to 14-year-olds, on all aspects of science, computers, scientists, and children who are learning about or practicing science. Pays $75 to $400, on acceptance. No fiction. Also publishes *Electric Company Magazine* and *Sesame Street Magazine.* Query.

TOUCH—Box 7259, Grand Rapids, MI 49510. Carol Smith, Man. Ed. Upbeat fiction and features, 1,000 to 1,500 words, for Christian girls age 8 to 14; personal life, nature, crafts. Poetry; fillers, puzzles. Pays 2¢ a word, extra for photos, on acceptance. Query for theme with SASE.

TURTLE MAGAZINE FOR PRESCHOOL KIDS—1100 Waterway Blvd., Box 567, Indianapolis, IN 46206. Beth Wood Thomas, Ed. Stories about safety, exercise, health, and nutrition, for preschoolers. Humorous, entertaining fiction, 600 words. Simple poems. Stories-in-rhyme; easy-to-read stories, to 500 words, for beginning readers. Pays about 6¢ a word, on publication. Buys all rights. Send SASE for guidelines.

WEE WISDOM—Unity Village, MO 64065. Verle Bell, Ed. Character-building stories, to 800 words, for 3- to 12-year-olds. Pays 3¢ to 4¢ per word, on acceptance.

WONDER TIME—6401 The Paseo, Kansas City, MO 64131. Evelyn J. Beals, Ed. Stories, 200 to 600 words, for 6- to 8-year-olds, with Christian emphasis to correlate with Sunday School curriculum. Features, to 300 words, on nature, crafts, etc. Poetry, 4 to 12 lines. Pays 3½¢ a word, from 25¢ a line for verse, $2.50 minimum, on acceptance.

YABA WORLD—5301 S. 76th St., Greendale, WI 53129. Peggy Larson, Ed. Articles, 1,500 words, on Young American Bowling Alliance league or tournament bowling. Profiles; how-to's. Photos. Pays $25 to $50, extra for photos, on acceptance. Query preferred.

YOUNG AMERICAN—P. O. Box 12409, Portland, OR 97212. Kristina T. Linden, Ed. Upbeat, positive, sophisticated material for children ages four to fifteen. Fiction, to 1,000 words; articles, to 350 words, on science, humor, history, and newsworthy young people; poetry. Pays 7¢ a word, $5 for photos, on publication.

YOUNG JUDAEAN—50 W. 58th St., New York, NY 10019. Mordecai Newman, Ed. Articles, 500 to 1,000 words, with photos, for 9- to 12-year-olds, on Israel, Jewish holidays, Jewish-American life, Jewish history. Fiction, 800 to 1,500 words, on Jewish themes. Poetry, from 8 lines. Fillers, humor, reviews. Pays 5¢ per word.

THE YOUNG SALVATIONIST—The Salvation Army, 799 Bloomfield Ave., Verona, NJ 07044. Capt. Dorothy Hitzka, Ed. Articles for teens, 800 to 1,200 words, with Christian perspective; fiction, 1,000 to 1,200 words; short fillers. Young Soldier Section: fiction, 600 to 800 words; games and puzzles for children. Pays 3¢ a word, on acceptance.

TEENAGE AND YOUNG ADULT

ALIVE NOW!—P. O. Box 189, Nashville, TN 37202. Mary Ruth Coffman, Ed. Short essays, 250 to 400 words, with Christian emphasis. Poetry, one page. Photos. Pays $5 to $20, on publication.

AMERICAN NEWSPAPER CARRIER—P. O. Box 15300, Winston-Salem, NC 27103. Marilyn Rollins, Ed. Light fiction, 1,000 words, for teenage newspaper carriers; mystery, adventure, etc. Inspirational articles, editorials. Pays $25, on acceptance.

BOP—3500 W. Olive Ave., Suite 850, Burbank, CA 91505. Julie Laufer, Ed. Interviews and features, 500 to 1,000 words, for teenage girls, on stars popular with teenagers. Photos. Pays varying rates, on acceptance. Query preferred.

BOYS' LIFE—1325 Walnut Hill Ln., Irving, TX 75038-3096. William B. McMorris, Ed. Publication of Boy Scouts of America. Articles and fiction, 1,500 words, for 8- to 18-year-old boys. Photos. Fillers. Pays from $500 for major articles and fiction, on acceptance. Query first.

THE CHRISTIAN ADVENTURER—P. O. Box 850, Joplin, MO 64802.

Rosmarie Foreman, Ed. Fiction, 1,500 to 1,800 words, for 13- to 19-year-olds, on Christian living. Fillers. Pays 1½¢ a word, quarterly.

CHRISTIAN LIVING FOR SENIOR HIGH—850 N. Grove, Elgin, IL 60120. Anne E. Dinnan, Ed. Articles and fiction, 1,000 to 1,500 words, of interest to Christian teens. Don't preach. Pays 10¢ a word, on acceptance.

CURRENT CONSUMER & LIFESTUDIES—3500 Western Ave., Highland Park, IL 60035. Carole Rubenstein, Sr. Assoc. Ed. Practical, well-researched articles, 1,000 to 1,200 words, for high school students, on family living, interpersonal relationships, and consumer topics. Pays $100, on publication. Queries only; no unsolicited manuscripts accepted.

EXPLORING—1325 Walnut Hill Ln., Irving, TX 75038-3096. Scott Daniels, Exec. Ed. Publication of Boy Scouts of America. Articles, 500 to 1,800 words, for 15- to 21-year-olds, on education, careers, Explorer post activities (hiking, canoeing, camping), and program ideas for Explorer post meetings. No controversial subjects. Pays $150 to $400, on acceptance. Query. Send SASE for guidelines.

FREEWAY—Box 632, Glen Ellyn, IL 60138. Billie Sue Thompson, Ed. First-person true stories, personal experience, how-to's, fillers, and humor, to 1,000 words, with photos, for 13- to 22-year-olds. Christian emphasis. Pays to 8¢ a word.

GRIT—Williamsport, PA 17701. Joanne Decker, Assignment Ed. Articles, 300 to 500 words, with photos, on young people involved in unusual hobbies, occupations, athletic pursuits, and personal adventures. Pays 12¢ a word, extra for photos, on acceptance.

HICALL—1445 Boonville Ave., Springfield, MO 65802. Rick Knoth, Ed. Articles, 500 to 1,000 words, and fiction, to 1,800 words, for 12- to 19-year-olds; strong evangelical emphasis. Pays on acceptance.

IN TOUCH—Box 2000, Marion, IN 46952. Articles, 500 to 1,000 words, on contemporary issues, athletes and singers from conservative Christian perspective, for 13- to 19-year-olds. Pays 2¢ to 4¢ a word. Send SASE for guidelines. No queries.

KEYNOTER—3636 Woodview Trace, Indianapolis, IN 46268. Jack Brockley, Exec. Ed. Articles, 1,500 to 2,500 words, for high school leaders: general-interest features; self-help; pieces on contemporary teen-age problems. Photos. Pays $75 to $250, extra for photos, on acceptance. Query preferred.

LIGHTED PATHWAY—922 Montgomery Ave., Cleveland, TN 37311. Marcus V. Hand, Ed. Human-interest and inspirational articles, 800 to 1,000 words, for teen-agers. Short pieces, 600 to 800 words. Fiction, 1,000 to 1,200 words. Pays 2½¢ to 5¢ a word, on acceptance.

LISTEN MAGAZINE—6830 Laurel St. N.W., Washington, DC 20012. Gary B. Swanson, Ed. Articles, 1,000 to 1,500 words, on problems of alcohol and drug abuse, for teenagers; personality profiles. Photos. Pays 5¢ to 7¢ a word, extra for photos, on acceptance. Query. Guidelines available.

THE NATIONAL FUTURE FARMER—Box 15160, Alexandria, VA 22309. Wilson W. Carnes, Ed.-in-Chief. Articles, to 1,000 words, preferably with photos, for agriculture students aged 14 to 21, on activities of Future Farmers of America, new developments in agriculture, and general-interest subjects. Pays from 6¢ a word, on acceptance. Query.

NEW ERA—50 E. North Temple, Salt Lake City, UT 84150. Brian Kelley, Ed. Articles, 150 to 3,000 words, and fiction, to 3,000 words, for young Mormons. Poetry. Photos. Pays 3¢ to 10¢ a word, 25¢ a line for poetry, on acceptance. Query.

PROBE—1548 Poplar Ave., Memphis, TN 38104. Michael S. Day, Ed. Southern Baptist. Articles, to 1,500 words, for 12- and 15-year-old boys, on teen problems, current events. Photo essays on Baptist sports personalities. Pays 4¢ a word, extra for photos, on acceptance.

SCHOLASTIC SCOPE—730 Broadway, New York, NY 10003. Fran Claro, Ed. For 15- to 18-year-olds with 4th to 6th grade reading ability. Realistic fiction, 400 to 1,200 words, and plays, to 6,000 words, on teen problems. Profiles, 400 to 800 words, of interesting teenagers, with black and white photos. Pays $125 for 500- to 600-word articles, from $200 for plays and short stories, from $150 for longer pieces, on acceptance.

SEVENTEEN—850 Third Ave., New York, NY 10022. Sarah Crichton, Sr. Ed. Articles, to 2,500 words, on subjects of interest to teens. Sophisticated, well-written fiction, 1,500 to 3,500 words, for young adults. Poetry, to 40 lines, by teens. Short news and features, to 750 words, for "Mini-Mag." Articles, 1,000 words, by teens, for "Your Words." Pays varying rates, on acceptance.

SPLICE—10 Columbus Circle, Suite 1300, New York, NY 10019. Bob Woods, Ed. Articles and personality profiles, 1,000 words, relating to the teen movie and entertainment scene. Music articles dealing with movies or music videos. Pays varying rates, on publication. Queries preferred.

SPRINT—850 N. Grove Ave., Elgin, IL 60120. Paul Woods, Ed. Feature articles from Christian perspective, 800 to 1,000 words, for junior high Sunday school students, on current teen problems and Christian personalities. Fiction, 1,000 to 1,200 words, with realistic characters and dialogue. Poetry. Pays to $100, on acceptance. Submit seasonal material four months in advance. Buys all rights. Query for nonfiction.

STRAIGHT—8121 Hamilton Ave., Cincinnati, OH 45231. Dawn Korth, Ed. Devotional pieces, features on current situations and issues, humor, for Christian teens. Well-constructed fiction, 1,000 to 1,200 words, showing teens using Christian principles. Poetry, by teen-agers. Photos. Pays about 3¢ a word, on acceptance. Guidelines.

TEEN POWER—Box 632, Glen Ellyn, IL 60138. Pam Campbell, Ed. First person (as told to), true teen experience stories with Christian insights and conclusion, 700 to 1,000 words. Include photos. Pays 4¢ to 7¢ a word, extra for photos, on acceptance.

TQ/TEEN QUEST (formerly *Young Ambassador*)—Box 82808, Lincoln, NE 68501. Nancy Bayne, Ed. Articles, to 1,800 words, and well-crafted fiction, to 2,500 words, for conservative Christian teens. B/W photos and color slides. Pays 4¢ to 10¢ a word, extra for photos, on publication.

TEENAGE—928 Broadway, New York, NY 10010. Jeannie Ralston, Ed.-in-Chief. Articles, profiles, interviews, short news reports, essays, humor, celebrity interviews, 500 to 2,000 words, on topics of vital interest to sophisticated young women, ages 14 to 18: sex, relationships, college, careers, sports and fitness, dating, health, money, computers, drugs and alcohol, examples of achievement and leadership among peers, advice on "making it" in the adult world. Some preference given to high school and college-age writers; fiction accepted only from students. Pays $25 to $500, on publication.

TEENS TODAY—Nazarene Publishing House, 6401 The Paseo, Kansas City, MO 64131. Karen De Sollar, Ed. Short stories, 1,200 to 1,500 words, dealing with teens demonstrating Christian principles in real-life situations. Adventure stories; stories about relationships and ethics. Pays 3½¢ a word, on acceptance.

TIGER BEAT—7086 Teaneck Rd., Teaneck, NJ 07666. Diane Umansky, Ed. Articles, to 4 pages, on young people in show business and music industry. Pays varying rates, on acceptance. Query. Unsolicited manuscripts sent without SASE will not be returned.

TIGER BEAT STAR—7086 Teaneck Rd., Teaneck, NJ 07666. Nancy O'Connell, Ed. Light celebrity fan pieces and interviews (pop/rock, movies and TV); occasional serious articles on topics of interest to teens. For articles, 300 words, payment is $50 per published page. Query.

WRITING!—3500 Western Avenue, Highland Park, IL 60035. Alan Lenhoff, Ed. Interviews, 1,200 words, for "Writers at Work" department, for high school students. Pays $200, on publication. Query.

YM—685 Third Ave., New York, NY 10017. No unsolicited material.

YOUNG AMBASSADOR—See *TQ/Teen Quest*.

YOUNG AND ALIVE—4444 S. 52nd St., Lincoln, NE 68506. Richard Kaiser, Ed. Feature articles, 800 to 1,400 words, for blind and visually impaired young adults, on adventure, biography, camping, health, hobbies, and travel. Photos. Pays 3¢ to 5¢ a word, extra for photos, on acceptance. Write for guidelines.

YOUTH!—P. O. Box 801, Nashville, TN 37202. Sidney Fowler, Ed. Articles and fiction, 700 to 2,000 words, that help teenagers develop a Christian identity and faith in contemporary culture. Photos. Pays 4¢ a word, on acceptance.

THE DRAMA MARKET

REGIONAL AND UNIVERSITY THEATERS

Community, regional and civic theaters and college dramatic groups offer the best opportunities today for playwrights to see their plays produced, whether for staged production or for dramatic readings. Indeed, aspiring playwrights who can get their work produced by any of these have taken an important step toward breaking into the competitive dramatic field—many well-known playwrights received their first recognition in the regional theaters. Payment is generally not large, but regional and university theaters usually buy only the right to produce a play, and all further rights revert to the author. Since most directors like to work closely with the authors on any revisions necessary, theaters will often pay the playwright's expenses while in residence during rehearsals. The thrill of seeing your play come to life on the stage is one of the pleasures of being on hand for rehearsals and performances.

Aspiring playwrights should query college and community theaters in their region to find out which ones are interested in seeing original scripts. Dramatic associations of interest to playwrights include the Dramatists Guild (234 W. 44th St., New York, NY 10036), Theatre Communications Group, Inc. (355 Lexington Ave., New York, NY 10017), which publishes the annual *Dramatists Sourcebook,* and The International Society of Dramatists, publishers of *The Dramatist's Bible* P. O. Box 3470, Fort Pierce, FL 33448). *The Playwright's Companion,* published by Feedback Theatrebooks, P. O. Box 606, Nashville, IN 47448, is an annual directory of theatres and prize contests seeking scripts.

Some of the theaters on the following list require that playwrights submit all or some of the following with scripts—cast list, synopsis, resumé, recommendations, return postcard—and with scripts and queries, self-addressed, stamped envelopes (SASE) must *always* be enclosed. Playwrights may also wish to register their material with the U.S. Copyright Office. For additional information about this, write Register of Copyrights, Library of Congress, Washington, DC 20559.

ACADEMY THEATRE—P. O. Box 77070, Atlanta, GA 30357. John T. Liles, Lit. Man. Full length and some and one-act dramas. "Our First Stage New Play Series is our primary forum for new work. We prefer scripts from Atlanta or regional writers, though all areas are considered. We receive so many scripts that we must ask writers to send synopses *only* (with cast list and SASE)." Pays $250.

ACTORS THEATRE OF LOUISVILLE—316 W. Main St., Louisville, KY 40202. Michael Bigelow Dixon, Lit. Man. One-act comedies and dramas (to 60 pages). Annual contest closes April 15. Pays standard contract. Send for guidelines. Six-month reporting time.

A.D. PLAYERS—2710 W. Alabama, Houston, TX 77098. Jeannette Clift George, Artistic Dir. Carol E. Anderson, Lit. Man. Full-length or one-act comedies, dramas, musicals, children's plays and adaptations with Christian world view. Submit script with SAS postcard, resumé, cast list, and synopsis (Christmas plays should be submitted before Oct.). Reports in 2 months. Readings. Pays negotiable rates.

ALASKA REPERTORY THEATRE—705 W. 6th Ave., Suite 201, Anchorage, AK 99501. Andrew Traister, Artistic Dir. Full-length dramas, comedies, and adaptations. Query with synopsis required.

ALLEY THEATRE—615 Texas Ave., Houston, TX 77002. Robert Strane, Lit. Man. One-act and full length dramas, comedies, musicals, children's, and adaptations. Queries are required: include cast list, synopsis, resume, production history. Standard contract. Reports in 6 months.

ALLIANCE THEATRE COMPANY—1280 Peachtree St. NE, Atlanta, GA 30309. Sandra Deer, Lit. Man. Full-length comedies, dramas, musicals, and adaptations. Query with synopsis and cast list. Pay varies.

AMERICAN JEWISH THEATRE—15 W. 28th St., New York, NY 10016. Stanley Brechner, Art. Dir. Full-length comedies and dramas, reflecting Jewish themes. Submit script with SASE to Susan Nanus. Standard contract.

AMERICAN LIVING HISTORY THEATRE—P. O. Box 2677, Hollywood, CA 90078. Dorene Ludwig, Artistic Dir. One-act, historically accurate dramas. Submit script with SASE. Reports in 1 to 6 months. Pays varying rates.

AMERICAN PLACE THEATRE—111 W. 46th St., New York, NY 10036. Chris Breyer, Lit. Man. Full-length plays. Do not prefer commercial comedies;

706

favor plays innovative in both form and content. Send play with SASE. Allow 3 to 5 months for reply.

AMERICAN RENAISSANCE THEATRE—112 Charlton St., New York, NY 10014. Robert Elston, Artistic Dir. Susan Egent, Lit. Man. Full-length and one-act plays with American theme. Submit synopsis with SASE. Reports in 6 months. Pays $100 and royalty. Offers workshops and readings.

AMERICAN REPERTORY THEATRE—64 Brattle St., Cambridge, MA 02138. Arthur Holmberg, Lit. Man. No unsolicited manuscripts. Submit one-page description of play, 10-page sample, and SASE.

AMERICAN STAGE COMPANY—P. O. Box 1560, St. Petersburg, FL 33731. Victoria Holloway, Artistic Dir. Full-length comedies and dramas. Send synopsis with short description of cast and production requirements with self-addressed postcard. Pays negotiable rates. Submit material September through January.

AMERICAN STANISLAVSKI THEATRE—485 Park Ave., #6A, New York, NY 10022. Sonia Moore, Artistic Dir. Full-length or one-act drama with important message. No offensive language. For cast aged 16 to 45. Submit script with SAS postcard in April and May; reports in Sept. No payment.

ANGEL'S TOUCH PRODUCTIONS—11022 Hesby St., N. Hollywood, CA 91601. Philip Nemy, Artistic Dir. Full-length comedies, dramas, musicals and adaptations. Submit script with resumé and SASE. Reports in 3 to 4 months. Pays negotiable rates.

THE APPLE CORPS.—336 W. 20th St., New York, NY 10011. Bob Del Pazzo, Coordinator. All types of one-act and full-length plays. Send bio, synopsis with SASE. Allow 4 to 6 months for response. Payment varies. No phone calls.

ARENA STAGE—6th and Maine Ave., S.W., Washington, DC 20024. Full-length comedies, dramas, musicals and adaptations. Lloyd Rose, Dir. of Play Development. Submit one-page synopsis, first 10 pages of dialogue, resumé and professional recommendations. No unsolicited manuscripts. Pays varying rates. Workshops and readings offered. Allow 2 to 4 months for reply.

ARKANSAS ARTS CENTER CHILDREN'S THEATRE—Box 2137, Little Rock, AR 72203. Bradley Anderson, Art. Dir. Seeks solid, professional (full-length or one-act) scripts. Original, and, particularly, adapted work from contemporary and classic literature. Pays flat rate.

ARTREACH TOURING THEATRE—2926 Millsbrae Ave., Cincinnati, OH 45209. Kathryn Schultz Miller, Art. Dir. One-act dramas and adaptations for touring children's theatre; cast to 4, simple sets. Submit script with synopsis, cast list, resumé, recommendations and SASE. Payment varies.

ASOLO STATE THEATRE—P. O. Drawer E., Sarasota, FL 33578. John Ulmer, Artistic Dir. Full-length dramas, comedies, musicals, and children's plays. Small stage. Pays royalty or varying rates. Readings and workshops offered. No unsolicited manuscripts. Query with synopsis.

AT THE FOOT OF THE MOUNTAIN—2000 S. Fifth St., Minneapolis, MN 55454. Phyllis Jane Rose, Artistic Dir. Full-length, one-act and musical plays by and about women. Query with synopsis, SAS postcard. Reports in 6 weeks. Pays royalty.

ATTIC THEATRE—P. O. Box 02457, 2990 W. Grand Blvd., Suite 406, Detroit, MI 48202. Ron Martell, Assoc. Artistic Director. Produces 1 to 3 new plays per year; interested in full-length comedies, dramas, musicals, and adaptations. Cast to 15; limited wing and fly space. Query with synopsis, cast list, and resume. Best time to submit: spring–summer. Reports in one year. Pays standard royalty.

BARTER THEATER—P. O. Box 867, Abingdon, VA 24210. Rex Partington, Producing Dir. Full-length dramas, comedies, adaptations, musicals and children's plays. Full workshop and reading productions. Allow 6 to 8 months for report. Payment rates negotiable.

BERKELEY REPERTORY THEATRE—2025 Addison St., Berkeley, CA 94704. Sharon Ott, Artistic Director. No unsolicited manuscripts; agent submissions or professional recommendations only. Reporting time: 3 to 4 months.

BERKSHIRE THEATRE FESTIVAL—Box 797, Stockbridge, MA 02162. Josephine Abady, Art. Dir. Full-length comedies, musicals and dramas; cast to 8. Submit through agent only.

BEVERLY HILLS PLAYHOUSE/SKYLIGHT THEATRE—6525 Sunset Blvd., Garden Suite #2, Los Angeles, CA 90028. Full-length and one-act comedies, dramas, and musicals; simple sets. Submit scripts with synopsis, recommendations, and SASE. Reports in 8 weeks. No payment.

BOARSHEAD: MICHIGAN PUBLIC THEATER—425 S. Grand Ave., Lansing, MI 48933. Jim Burton, Dramaturg. One-act and full-length comedies, dramas, musicals, children's and adaptations; limit cast to 12. Submit script with cast list, resume and SASE. Sponsors annual drama festival and readings.

CENTER STAGE—700 N. Calvert St., Baltimore, MD 21202. Full-length and one-act comedies, dramas, musicals, adaptations. No unsolicited manuscripts. Send synopsis, resumé, cast list, recommendations and production history, with return postcard and SASE. Pays varying rates. Allow 4 to 8 weeks for reply.

CHIMERA THEATRE CO.—30 E. 10th St., St. Paul, MN 55101. Larry Whiteley, Artistic Dir. Full-length comedies, dramas, musicals, children's plays, and adaptations. Submit script with resumé, recommendations, cast list, and synopsis. Reports in year and a half. Pays royalty. Offers workshops and readings.

CIRCLE REPERTORY COMPANY—161 Ave. of the Americas, New York, NY 10013. B. Rodney Marriott, Assoc. Art. Dir. Full length and one-act comedies and dramas. Submit script with SASE and credentials; "personal criticism offered as often as possible." Pays $2,500; reports in 5 months.

CITY THEATRE COMPANY—B39CL, Univ. of Pittsburgh, Pittsburgh, PA 15260. Dennis Kennedy, Lit. Man. Full-length comedies and dramas "by twentieth-century writers only." Limit cast to 12; simple set. Reports in 3 months. Query required; include synopsis, cast list, resume and SASE. Best time to submit: Sept.–May. Standard contract.

CLASSIC STAGE COMPANY—136 East 13th St., New York, NY 10003. Carol Ostrow, Producing Dir. Carey Perloff, Artistic Dir. Full-length adaptations and translations of existing classic literature. Submit synopsis with cast list and SASE, Sept.–May. Offers workshops and readings. Pays on royalty basis.

THE CLEVELAND PLAYHOUSE—8500 Euclid Ave., P. O. Box 1989, Cleveland, OH 44106. Wayne S. Turney, Dramaturg. "The Cleveland Playhouse is the oldest professional theatre in the U.S.," reports Mr. Turney, who will consider full-length scripts for all types of plays (comedies, dramas, musicals, etc.). Queries are required; include sample dialogue, synopsis, cast list, SASE. Sponsors annual New Voices/New Directions series of readings.

CREATIVE THEATRE UNLIMITED—133 Drakes Corner Rd., Princeton, NJ 08540. Laurie Huntsman, Acting Dir. One-act participatory plays and adaptations for children; cast to 5; arena stage. Submit manuscript with synopsis and cast list in the spring. Pays $400.

THE CRICKET THEATRE—9 W. 14th St., Minneapolis, MN 55403. William Partlan, Art. Dir. Send full-length comedies, dramas, and musicals ("prefer contemporary plays") with synopsis, resumé. Cast to 11. Reports in 6 months. Workshops and readings.

CROSSROADS THEATRE CO.—320 Memorial Pkwy., New Brunswick, NJ 08901. Lee Richardson, Art. Dir., Sydné Mahone, Lit. Man. Full-length and one-act dramas, comedies, musicals and adaptations; experimental pieces; one man/one woman shows. Queries only, with synopsis, cast list, resumé and SASE.

DELAWARE THEATRE COMPANY—P. O. Box 516, Wilmington, DE 19899. Cleveland Morris, Art. Dir. Full-length comedies, dramas, musicals, and adaptations, with cast to 10; prefer single set. Send cast list, synopsis, and SASE. Reports in 6 months. Pays royalty.

DENVER CENTER THEATRE COMPANY—1050 13th St., Denver, CO 80204. Coleen Bronston, Lit. Man. Send full-length comedies and dramas (cast to 12); June–Dec. Include cast list, resumé. Pay varies.

DETROIT REPERTORY THEATRE—13103 Woodrow Wilson Ave., Detroit, MI 48238. Barbara Busby, Lit. Man. Full-length comedies and dramas. Enclose SASE. Pays royalty. Annual contest.

DORSET THEATRE FESTIVAL—Box 519, Dorset, VT 05251. Jill Charles, Art. Dir. Full-length comedies, musicals, dramas, and adaptations; cast to 8; simple set preferred. Agent submissions and professional recommendations only. Pays varying rates.

EAST WEST PLAYERS—4424 Santa Monica Blvd., Los Angeles, CA 90029. Full-length comedies, dramas and musicals, dealing with Asian American issues and/or including important roles for Asian actors. Cast up to 15. Send manuscript with synopsis, cast list, resumé and SASE. Pays varying rates. Offers workshops and readings. Allow 3 months for reply.

EMPIRE STATE INSTITUTE FOR THE PERFORMING ARTS—Empire State Plaza, Albany, NY 12223. Patricia B. Snyder, Art. Dir. Full-length comedies, dramas, musicals, children's plays, and adaptations suitable for family audience. "We have a special interest in developing new works, and we offer developmental workshops and readings." Queries are preferred, accompanied by synopsis, cast list, and SASE—best time to submit is between June and August. Pays varying rates.

THE EMPTY SPACE THEATRE—95 S. Jackson St., Seattle, WA 98104. Tom Creamer, Lit. Man. Unsolicited scripts accepted only from WA, OR, WY, MT, and ID. Outside five-state NW region: scripts accepted through agents or established theatre groups only.

ENSEMBLE STUDIO THEATRE—549 W. 52nd St., New York, NY 10019. D. S. Moynihan, Lit. Man. 12 to 16 new full-length or one-act plays—with a cast to 10 players—are produced each season. Send complete manuscript with cast list, resume, SAS postcard, and SASE between Sept. and April. Workshops and readings. Payment varies.

THE FAMILY REPERTORY CO.—9 Second Ave., New York, NY 10003. Marvin F. Camillo, Art. Dir. Contemporary, social works on variety of topics. Full-length dramas and musicals for young people and adults. Submit manuscript with synopsis, resumé, and return postcard. Pays small fee.

FLORIDA STUDIO THEATRE—1241 N. Palm Ave., Sarasota, FL 33577. Jeff Mousseau, New Play Development. Innovative smaller cast plays that are pertinent and contemporary. Query first. Pays varying rates.

WILL GEER THEATRICUM BOTANICUM—Box 1222, Topanga, CA 90290. All types of scripts for outdoor theater, with large playing area. Submit manuscript with SASE. Pays varying rates.

GEVA THEATRE—75 Woodbury Blvd., Rochester, NY 14607. Ann Patrice Carrigan, Lit. Dir. Query with synopsis, cast list, and SAS postcard for full-length comedies and dramas with cast of 7 to 10 players. Readings. Pays on contractual basis.

THE GOODMAN THEATRE—200 S. Columbus Dr., Chicago, IL 60603. Tom Creamer, Dramaturg. Send query with synopsis, cast list, resume, SAS postcard, reviews, and to 10 pages of dialogue for full-length plays. Produces 1 to 2 new plays each season. Offers occasional readings and workshops. Reports in 3 months.

THE GROUP THEATRE—3940 Brooklyn Ave. NE, Seattle, WA 98105. Tim Bond, Lit. Man. Full-length comedies, dramas, adaptations, and translations, cast to 10; simple set. Special interest in plays suitable for multi-ethnic casts; serious plays on social/cultural issues; satires. Query with synopsis, sample dialogue and resumé required. Reporting time: 4 weeks.

THE GUTHRIE THEATER—725 Vineland Pl., Minneapolis, MN 55403. Marc Bly, Lit. Man. Full-length comedies, dramas, and adaptations. Manuscripts accepted only from recognized theatrical agents. Query with detailed synopsis, cast size, resumé, return postcard and recommendations. Pays negotiable rates, and travel/residency expenses. Offers readings. Reports in 1 to 2 months.

HARRISBURG COMMUNITY THEATRE—513 Hurlock St., Harrisburg, PA 17110. Thomas G. Hostetter, Artistic Dir. Full-length comedies, dramas, musicals, and adaptations—cast to 20; prefers simple set. Submit script with cast list, resume, synopsis, and SAS postcard. Best time to submit: June to August. Reporting time: 6 months. Pays negotiable rates.

HARTFORD STAGE COMPANY—50 Church St., Hartford, CT 06103. Constance Congdon, Lit. Man. Full-length plays of all types, for cast up to 12. No unsolicited manuscripts; submit through agent or send synopsis. Pays varying rates.

HARTMAN THEATRE COMPANY—P. O. Box 521, Stamford, CT 06904. Michael Bloom, Assoc. Art. Dir. Produces 1 to 2 new plays each season: "Our vision is to make Hartman a thriving regional repertory theatre, where we celebrate the human spirit through a broad repertoire of plays that challenge the mind and entertain the senses." Queries are required for full-length plays with casts to 10 players and one set. Pays percentage.

HIPPODROME STATE THEATRE—25 S.E. Second Place, Gainesville, FL 32601. Gregory von Hausch, Artistic Director. Full-length plays, with unit sets and casts up to 15. Submit in summer and fall. Enclose return postcard and synopsis.

HOLLYWOOD ACTORS THEATRE—P. O. Box 5618, Santa Rosa, CA 95402. Ron Bastone, Art. Dir. Full-length comedies and dramas, for cast of 6 to 8 actors; single or unit set preferred. Send manuscript with synopsis, cast list, resumé, and SASE. Pays 20% of gross receipts.

HONOLULU THEATRE FOR YOUTH—Box 3257, Honolulu, HI 96801. John Kauffman, Art. Dir. Plays, 60 to 90 minutes playing time, for young people/ family audiences. Adult casts. Contemporary issues, Pacific themes, etc. Unit sets, small cast. Query or send manuscript with synopsis, cast list and SASE. Royalties negotiable.

HORIZON THEATRE COMPANY—P. O. Box 5376, Station E, Atlanta, GA 30307. Jeffrey and Lisa Adler, Co-Artistic Directors. Full-length comedies, dramas, and adaptations with strong female roles. Cast to 10. Submit synopsis with cast list, resumé, and recommendations. Reports in 2 months to 1 year. Pays percentage. Readings offered.

HUNTINGTON THEATRE CO.—264 Huntington Ave., Boston, MA 02115. Gary Mitchell, Asst. to the Prod. Dir. Full-length comedies and dramas. Query with synopsis, cast list, resumé, recommendations, and return postcard.

ILLINOIS THEATRE CENTER—400 Lakewood Blvd., Park Forest, IL 60466. Steve S. Billig, Artistic Dir. Full-length comedies, dramas, musicals and adaptations, with unit/fragmentary sets, and cast to 8. Send manuscript with recommendations and return postcard. Pays negotiable rates. Workshops and readings offered.

INVISIBLE THEATRE—1400 N. First Ave., Tucson, AZ 85719. Susan Claasen, Art. Dir. Reads queries for full-length comedies, dramas, musicals, adaptations, Jan.–May. Cast to 10; simple set. One full production, 5 readings, produced each year. Pays royalty.

JACKSONVILLE UNIVERSITY THEATRE—Dept. of Theatre Arts, College of Fine Arts, Jacksonville University, Jacksonville, FL 32211. Davis Sikes, Art. Dir. Annual playwriting contest seeks "original, previously unproduced scripts of distinctive quality and outstanding theatrical values." Full-length and one-act comedies and dramas accompanied by synopsis, cast list, resume, SAS postcard, and SASE should be submitted between Sept. and Jan. Annual contest. Write for guidelines.

JEWISH REPERTORY THEATRE—344 E. 14th St., New York, NY 10003. Ran Avni, Artistic Dir. Full-length comedies, dramas, musicals, children's plays and adaptations, with cast to 10, relating to the Jewish experience. Pays varying rates. Enclose return postcard.

THE JULIAN THEATRE—953 DeHaro St., San Francisco, CA 94107. Address New Plays. Full-length comedies and dramas with a social statement. Send 5- to 10-page scene, synopsis, cast description, and SASE. Pays on contractual basis. Allow 2 to 9 months for reply. Readings offered.

LAMB'S PLAYERS THEATRE—500 Plaza Blvd., P. O. Box 26, National City, CA 92050. Kerry Cederberg, Lit. Man. Full-length and one-act comedies, dramas, translations, adaptations, musicals, and children's plays. Special interest in works with Christian world view. Query with synopsis required. Pays varying rates.

LITTLE BROADWAY PRODUCTIONS—c/o Jill Shawn, P. O. Box 15068,

711

N. Hollywood, CA 91615. Musicals and other plays for children; 55 minutes, no intermission. Submit manuscript with synopsis, return postcard, resumé, and SASE. Pays negotiable rates.

LONG ISLAND STAGE—Box 190, Hempstead, NY 11550. Clinton J. Atkinson, Art. Dir. Full-length dramas and adaptations. Query with SASE in late spring/early summer. Pays varying rates.

LOOKING GLASS THEATRE—175 Matthewson St., Providence, RI 02903. Diane Postoian, Artistic Dir. One-act, participation style children's plays, with cast to 5. Send manuscript with return postcard and SASE. Pays negotiable rates. Allow 6 weeks for reply.

LOS ANGELES DESIGNERS' THEATRE—P. O. Box 1883, Studio City, CA 91604-0883. Richard Niederberg, Artistic Dir. Full-length comedies, dramas, musicals, or adaptations. Prefers controversial topics and unconventional staging. Submit query with synopsis. Pays negotiable rates.

LOS ANGELES THEATER UNIT—P. O. Box 429, Los Angeles, CA 90078. Marla Fisher, Man. Dir. Lanny Thomas, Lit Dir. Full-length and one-act comedies and dramas. Submit script and SASE. Reports in 2 to 3 months. Pays varying rates.

LOS ANGELES THEATRE CENTER—514 S. Spring St., Los Angeles, CA 90013. Mame Hunt, Lit. Man. Full-length comedies, dramas, musicals, and adaptations. Special interest in scripts with social/political content and by women and ethnic minorities. Query with synopsis. Pays advance against royalty, on production, and travel and residence expenses.

McCADDEN PLACE THEATRE—1157 N. McCadden Pl., Hollywood, CA 90038. Joy Rinaldi, Jay Donohue, Co-Art. Dir. Queries are preferred for full-length and one-act comedies, dramas, and adaptations with cast to 10 and no more than 2 sets; enclose synopsis, cast list, resume, and SASE. Offers readings. Payment varies.

McCARTER THEATRE COMPANY—91 University Pl., Princeton, NJ 08540. Robert Lanchester, Assoc. Art. Dir. Send full-length plays with synopsis, cast list, resume, and SAS postcard; best time to submit: summer. Reports in 2 to 3 months. Offers 6 readings and occasional workshops; 2 to 3 new plays produced each season. Pays $250 to $500 for readings, negotiable rates for productions.

MAGIC THEATRE—Bldg. D., Fort Mason, San Francisco, CA 94123. Christine Krolik, Lit. Coordinator. Submit complete manuscript for full-length comedies and dramas, with simple set and cast to 8, between Sept. and May. Reports in 4 to 6 months. 7 new plays produced each season.

MANHATTAN PUNCH LINE—410 W. 42nd St., New York, NY 10036. Steve Kaplan, Art. Dir. Comedies. Showcase contract. SASE required.

MANHATTAN THEATRE CLUB—453 W. 16th, New York, NY 10011. Address Tom Szentgyorgyi. Full-length and one-act comedies, dramas and musicals. No unsolicited manuscripts. Send synopsis with cast list, resumé, recommendations and return postcard. Pays negotiable rates. Allow 6 months for reply.

MARKET HOUSE THEATRE—141 Kentucky Ave., Paducah, KY 42001. April Cochran, Lit. Man. Full-length comedies, dramas, musicals, adaptations, and one-act children's plays. Submit script with resumé, cast list and synopsis. Best time to submit is fall. Pays $30 to $70.

MEGAW THEATRE, INC.—17601 Saticoy St., Northridge, CA 91325. Full-length comedies and dramas, with cast of 6 to 8, and unit set. Send manuscripts with synopsis, cast list, resumé, recommendations, return postcard and SASE. Pays on contractual basis. Offers readings.

MIDWEST PLAYLABS—c/o The Playwrights' Center, 2301 Franklin Ave. E., Minneapolis, MN 55406. Full-length, previously unproduced scripts (no musicals). Query. Pays stipend, room and board, and travel for 2-week August conference.

MILL MOUNTAIN THEATRE—Center in the Square, One Market Square, Roanoke, VA 24011. Jo Weinstein, Lit. Man. At least 1 full-length and 10 one-act plays are produced each year in addition to staged readings. Submit script with cast list, resume, SAS postcard, and recommendations and allow 6 to 8 months for a report. Pays negotiable rates. Annual contest.

MILWAUKEE REPERTORY—929 N. Water St., Milwaukee, WI 53202. Tanda Dykes, Dramaturg. Full-length comedies and dramas; cast to 12. Submit synopsis, ten pages of script, SASE in the fall. Payment varies.

MISSOURI REPERTORY THEATRE—4949 Cherry St., Kansas City, MO 64110. Felicia Londre, Dramaturg. Full-length comedies and dramas. Query with synopsis, cast list, resumé, and return postcard. Pays standard royalty.

MUSIC THEATRE GROUP/LENOX ARTS CENTER—735 Washington St., New York, NY 10014. John Hart, Lit., Man. Innovative musicals, to 1½ hours; cast to 10. Query only, with synopsis and return post card. Best submission time: Sept.–Dec.

MUSICAL THEATRE WORKS—440 Lafayette St., New York, NY 10003. Mark Herko, Assoc. Artistic Dir. Full-length musicals; cast to 10; simple sets. Submit manuscript with SASE and cassette score. No payment.

THE NEGRO ENSEMBLE COMPANY—165 W. 46th St., Suite 409, New York, NY 10036. Douglas Turner Ward, Art. Dir. Full-length comedies, dramas, musicals and adaptations pertaining to the Black experience. Submit March through May. Pays on royalty basis. Enclose return postcard.

NEW DRAMATISTS—424 W. 44th St., New York, NY 10036. Workshop for member playwrights. Write Liz Wright, Assoc. Lit. Dir., for membership information.

NEW TUNERS/PERFORMANCE COMMUNITY—1225 W. Belmont Ave., Chicago, IL 60657. George H. Gorham, Dramaturg. Full-length musicals only, for cast to 15; no wing/fly space. Send manuscript with cassette tape of score, cast list, resumé and return postcard. Pays on a royalty basis.

NEW YORK SHAKESPEARE FESTIVAL/PUBLIC THEATER—425 Lafayette St., New York, NY 10003. Gail Merrifield, Dir. of Plays and Musicals. Plays and musical works for the theater, translations, and adaptations. Submit manuscript, cassette (with musicals), and SASE.

NORTHLIGHT THEATRE—2300 Green Bay Rd., Evanston, IL 60201. Full-length plays, music theatre, translations, and adaptations for cast to 10; small theatre. Special interest in Chicago subjects. Synopses only. Royalties, fees and compensations negotiable.

ODYSSEY THEATRE ENSEMBLE—12111 Ohio Ave., Los Angeles, CA 90025. Ron Sossi, Artistic Dir. Full-length comedies, dramas, musicals, and adaptations: provocative subject matter, or plays that stretch and explore the form and possibilities of theatre. Query with synopsis and return postcard. Pays variable rates. Allow 2 to 6 months for reply. Workshops and readings offered.

OLD GLOBE THEATRE—Simon Edison Center for the Performing Arts, Box 2171, San Diego, CA 92112. Address Robert Berlinger. Full-length comedies and dramas. No unsolicited manuscripts. Submit query with synopsis.

ONE ACT THEATRE COMPANY OF SAN FRANCISCO—430 Mason St., San Francisco, CA 94102. Michael Duff, Lit. Man. One-act and full-length comedies and dramas. Submit synopsis, 2 to 5 pages of sample dialogue with SASE. Pays negotiable rates.

EUGENE O'NEILL THEATER CENTER—234 W. 44th St., Suite 901, New York, NY 10036. Annual competition to select new stage and television plays for development at organization's Waterford, Ct. location. Submission deadline Dec. 1. Send SASE for guidelines to National Playwright's Conference, c/o above address. Pays stipend, plus travel/living expenses during conference.

PAPER MILL PLAYHOUSE—Brookside Dr., Millburn, NJ 07041. Maryan F. Stephens, Lit. Advisor. Full-length musicals only. Submit synopsis, tape, and resumé; reporting time: 6 to 8 weeks.

PENGUIN REPERTORY THEATRE—Box 91, Stony Point, NY 10980. Joe Brancato, Art. Dir. Full-length comedies and dramas; cast to 8. Submit manuscript, resumé and SASE. Pays varying rates, on production.

PENNSYLVANIA STAGE COMPANY—837 Linden St., Allentown, PA 18101. Wendy Liscow, Lit. Man. Full-length plays with cast to 8; one set. Full-length musicals, with unit set and cast to 15. Send synopsis, cast list and return postage. Pays negotiable rates. Allow 6 months for reply. Offers readings.

PEOPLE'S LIGHT AND THEATRE COMPANY—39 Conestoga Rd., Malvern, PA 19355. Alda Cortese, Lit. Man. One-act or full-length comedies, dramas, adaptations. Query with synopsis, resumé, ten pages of script required. Reports in six months. Payment negotiable.

PHILADELPHIA FESTIVAL FOR NEW PLAYS—3900 Chestnut St., Philadelphia, PA 19104. Hilary Missan, Program Coordinator. Full-length and one-act comedies, dramas; must be unproduced. Submit script with return postcard, resumé, and SASE. Pays varying rates.

PLAYHOUSE ON THE SQUARE—51 S. Cooper in Overton Sq., Memphis, TN 38104. Jackie Nichols, Art. Dir. Queries are preferred for full-length comedies and dramas with cast to 15 and single set. Include synopsis and SAS postcard with submission, and allow 3 months for a report. Payment is $500.

THE PLAYWRIGHTS FUND OF NORTH CAROLINA, INC.—P. O. Box 646, Greenville, NC 27835-0646. Address Literary Director. One-act comedies and dramas, from SE playwrights. Submit manuscript with SASE. Pays small honorarium. Readings, workshops, and annual contest. Deadline for season submissions and competition: Oct. 1.

PLAYWRIGHTS HORIZONS—416 W. 42nd St., New York, NY 10036. Tim Sanford, Head Reader. Full-length comedies, dramas, and musicals accompanied by synopsis, resumé, cover letter, and recommendations (if available) are considered for 5 new productions each season. Reporting time: 1 to 6 months. Workshops and readings are offered. Pays $2,500.

PLAYWRIGHTS' PLATFORM—164 Brayton Rd., Boston, MA 02135.

B. A. Creasey, Pres. Script development workshops and public readings for New England playwrights only. Full-length and one-act plays of all kinds. Send scripts with short synopsis, resumé, return postcard and SASE.

PORTLAND STAGE COMPANY—Box 1458, Portland, ME 04112. Barbara Rosoff, Art. Dir. Full-length comedies, dramas, and musicals, for cast to 8. Send synopsis with return postcard. Pays fee, travel, and board for 4-week residency if play is produced.

THE PUERTO RICAN TRAVELING THEATRE—141 W. 94th St., New York, NY 10025. Miriam Colon Valle, Art. Dir. Full-length and one-act comedies, dramas, and musicals; cast to 8; simple sets. Payment negotiable.

THE REPERTORY THEATRE OF ST. LOUIS—Box 28030, St. Louis, MO 63119. Agent submissions only.

THE ROAD COMPANY—Box 5278 EKS, Johnson City, TX 37603. Robert H. Leonard, Artistic Dir. Full-length and one-act comedies, dramas with social/political relevance to small-town audiences. Send synopsis, cast list, and production history, if any. Pays negotiable rates. Reports in 6 to 12 months.

ROUND HOUSE THEATRE—12210 Bushey Dr., Silver Spring, MD 20902. Diane Ruscher, Production Office Man. Full-length comedies, dramas, and adaptations; cast to 15; prefer simple set. No unsolicited manuscripts.

THE SHAKESPEARE THEATRE AT THE FOLGER—301 E. Capitol St. SE, Washington, DC 20003. Michael Kahn, Artistic Dir. New versions or adaptations of classics. Agent submissions or professional recommendations only. Pays negotiable rates.

RICHMOND SHEPARD THEATRE COMPLEX—6476 Santa Monica Blvd., Hollywood, CA 90038. Armina Shepard, Art. Dir. Full-length comedies and dramas; cast to 8; prefer one set. Submit manuscript or synopsis with SASE. Pays varying rates.

SOCIETY HILL PLAYHOUSE—507 S. 8th St., Philadelphia, PA 19147. Walter Vail, Dramaturg. Full-length dramas and comedies; cast to 10; simple set. Submit synopsis and SASE. Reports in 6 months. Nominal payment.

SOHO REPERTORY THEATRE—80 Varick St., New York, NY 10013. Jerry Engelbach, Artistic Dir. Full-length dramas, musicals, adaptations and mixed media works for thrust stage. No unsolicited manuscripts. Send brief precis, cast list, and resumé. Guidelines. Pays from $400. Readings offered.

SOUTH COAST REPERTORY—P. O. Box 2197, Costa Mesa, CA 92628. Jerry Patch, Dramaturg; John Glore, Lit. Man. Queries accompanied by a synopsis are preferred for full-length comedies, dramas, musicals, and children's plays. 5 to 7 new plays are produced each season, and several readings and workshops are offered. Allow 2 to 4 months for a report. Pays negotiable rates.

STAGE ONE: THE LOUISVILLE CHILDREN'S THEATRE—721 W. Main St., Louisville, KY 40202. Dramatized classics, and plays for children ages 5 to 18. Submit script with resumé. Reports in four months.

STAGES—3201 Allen Parkway, Suite 101, Houston, TX 77019. Brenda Dubay, Prod. Dir. Full-length and one-act comedies, dramas, and children's scripts, especially from Texan playwrights; cast to 12; simple set. Submit script, synopsis and resumé.

STUDIO ARENA—710 Main St., Buffalo, NY 14202. Kathryn Long, Dramaturg. Query for full-length comedies, dramas, and children's plays. Cast limited to 12, to 8 for children's plays. Enclose synopsis, cast list, and SAS postcard, and allow 10 to 14 weeks for a report. Offers readings. Pays variable rates and travel expenses.

TAKOMA THEATRE—6833 4th St., NW, Washington, DC 20012. Milton O. McGinty, Art. Dir. Realistic, full-length dramas, comedies and musicals. Submit manuscript with SASE; report in 3 months. Payment negotiable.

MARK TAPER FORUM—135 N. Grand Ave., Los Angeles, CA 90012. Jessica Teich, Lit. Man. For full-length comedies, dramas, musicals, adaptations, and children's plays, send query with synopsis, resumé, and SAS postcard. Reports in 8 to 10 weeks and pays varying rates. Readings and workshops offered.

THEATRE AMERICANA—Box 245, Altadena, CA 91001. Full-length comedies and dramas, preferably with American theme. Send manuscript with cast list and SASE. No payment. Allow 3 to 6 months for reply.

THEATRE/TEATRO—Bilingual Foundation for the Arts, 421 N. Ave., #19, Los Angeles, CA 90031. Margarita Galban, Art. Dir. Full-length plays about Hispanic experience; small casts. Submit manuscript with return postcard. Pays negotiable rates.

THEATREWORKS/USA—131 W. 86th St., New York, NY 10024. Barbara Pasternack, Lit. Man. Queries—accompanied by synopsis, cast list, resume, and SAS postcard—are preferred for children's plays and musicals "dealing with historical characters or events, important issues, classics." Cast is limited to 5 players and set must be simple. Best time to submit: spring and summer. "We prefer to work with writers who live in the New York area." Allow 6 months for a report. Pays standard royalty.

WISDOM BRIDGE THEATRE—1559 W. Howard St., Chicago, IL 60626. Doug Finlayson, Assoc. Art Dir. Queries are required for full-length plays with cast to 12; submissions must include synopsis, cast list, and SAS postcard. 1 to 2 new plays are produced each season. Reports in 4 to 6 months. Payment is negotiable. Offers readings.

WOOLLY MAMMOTH THEATRE COMPANY—Box 32229, Washington, DC 20007. Neil Steyskal, Lit. Man. Query required for full-length comedies, dramas, adaptations wih cast to 8 and simple set. Pay varies.

GARY YOUNG MIME THEATRE—23724 Park Madrid, Casabasas, CA 91302. Gary Young, Artistic Director. Comedy monologues and two-person vignettes, for children and adults, 1 minute to 90 minutes in length; casts of 1 or 2, and portable set. Pays varying rates. Enclose return postcard, resumé, recommendations, cast list and synopsis.

RADIO THEATERS

CHILDREN'S RADIO THEATRE—1314 14th St., NW, Washington, DC 20005. Joan Bellsey, Art. Dir. Children's radio plays. No unsolicited material. Query with resumé and SASE required.

TIC RADIO THEATRE WORKSHOP—Box 519, Marshfield, MA 02050. Alberta Fahnley, Dir. Creative Develop. Accepts 30-minute radio scripts to be aired on closed circuit for the visually impaired. Pays in copy of master tape. Send SASE for guidelines.

716

PLAY PUBLISHERS

ART CRAFT PLAY COMPANY—Box 1058, Cedar Rapids, IA 52406. Three-act comedies, mysteries, and farces, and one-act comedies or dramas, with one set, for production by junior and senior high schools. Pays on royalty basis or by outright purchase.

WALTER H. BAKER COMPANY—100 Chauncy St., Boston, MA 02111. Scripts for amateur production: one-act plays for competition, children's plays, musicals, religious drama, full-length plays for high school production. Three- to four-month reading period. Include SASE.

CHILD LIFE MAGAZINE—P. O. Box 567, Indianapolis, IN 46206. Plays, 700 and 1,000 words, for classroom or living-room production by children 8 to 11 years. Pays about 6¢ a word, on publication. Buys all rights.

CHILDREN'S PLAYMATE MAGAZINE—1100 Waterway Blvd., P. O. Box 567, Indianapolis, IN 46206. Elizabeth A. Rinck, Ed. Plays, 200 to 600 words, for children aged 5 to 7: special emphasis on health, nutrition, exercise, and safety. Pays about 6¢ a word, on publication.

CONTEMPORARY DRAMA SERVICE—Meriwether Publishing, Ltd., Box 7710, 885 Elkton Dr., Colorado Springs, CO 80933. Arthur Zapel, Ed. Easy-to-stage comedies, skits, one-acts, musicals, puppet scripts, full-length plays for schools and churches. Adaptations of classics, and improvisational material for classroom use. Comedy monologues and duets. Chancel drama for Christmas and Easter Church use. Enclose synopsis. Pays by fee arrangement or on royalty basis.

THE DRAMATIC PUBLISHING COMPANY—311 Washington St., P. O. Box 109, Woodstock, IL 60098. Full-length and one-act plays, musical comedies for amateur, children, and stock groups. Must run at least thirty minutes. Pays on royalty basis. Address Sally Fyfe. Reports within 10 to 14 weeks.

DRAMATICS—3368 Central Pkwy., Cincinnati, OH 45225. Don Corathers, Ed. One-act and full-length plays, for high school production. Pays $50 to $200, on acceptance.

ELDRIDGE PUBLISHING COMPANY—P. O. Box 216, Franklin, OH 45005. Nancy Vorhis, Edit. Dept. One-, two- and three-act plays and operettas for schools, churches, community groups, etc. Special interest in comedies and Christmas plays. Include cassette for operettas. Pays varying rates.

SAMUEL FRENCH, INC.—45 W. 25th St., New York, NY 10010. Lawrence R. Harbison, Ed. Full-length plays for dinner, community, stock, college and high school theatres. One-act plays (30 to 45 minutes). Children's plays, 45 to 60 minutes. Pays on royalty basis.

HEUER PUBLISHING COMPANY—Drawer 248, Cedar Rapids, IA 52406. C. Emmett McMullen, Ed. One-act comedies and dramas for contest work; three-act comedies, mysteries or farces, with one interior setting, for high school production. Pays varying rates.

INSTRUCTOR—HBJ Publications, 7500 Old Oak Blvd., Cleveland, OH 44130. Plays, 700 to 2,000 words, for elementary school children. Holiday and seasonal plays only. Send six months in advance. Pays $50 to $100, on acceptance.

PIONEER DRAMA SERVICE—P. O. Box 22555, Denver, CO 80222. Patrick Dorn, Asst. Ed. Full-length and one-act plays for young audiences: musicals, melodramas, religious scripts. No unproduced plays, plays with largely male casts or multiple sets. Query. Pays royalty or outright purchase.

PLAYS, THE DRAMA MAGAZINE FOR YOUNG PEOPLE—120 Boylston St., Boston, MA 02116. Elizabeth Preston, Man. Ed. One-act plays, with simple settings, for production by young people, 7 to 17; holiday plays, comedies, dramas, skits, dramatized classics, farces, puppet plays, melodramas, dramatized folktales, and creative dramatics. Maximum lengths: lower grades, 10 double-spaced pages; middle grades, 15 pages; junior and senior high, 20 pages. Casts may be mixed, all-male or all-female; plays with one act preferred. Manuscript specification sheet available on request. Queries suggested for adaptations. Pays good rates, on acceptance. Buys all rights.

SCHOLASTIC SCOPE—730 Broadway, New York, NY 10003. Fran Claro, Ed. For ages 15 to 18 with 4th to 6th grade reading ability. Plays, to 6,000 words, on problems of contemporary teenagers, relationships between people in family, job and school situations. Some mysteries, comedies, and science fiction; plays about minorities. Pays good rates, on acceptance.

THE TELEVISION MARKET

The almost round-the-clock television offerings available for viewers on commercial and educational television stations—greatly expanded by the mushrooming cable TV offerings—may understandably lead free-lance writers to believe that opportunities to sell scripts or program ideas are infinite.

But unfortunately the realities of the television marketplace are generally quite different from this fantasy. With few exceptions, direct submissions of scripts, no matter how good they are, are not considered by producers or programmers, and in general free-lance writers can achieve success in this almost-closed field by concentrating on getting their fiction (short and in novel form) and nonfiction published in magazines or books, combed diligently by television producers for possible adaptations. A large percentage of the material offered over all types of networks (in addition to the motion pictures made in Hollywood or especially for TV) is in the form of adaptations of what has appeared in print.

Writers who want to try their hand at writing directly for this very limited market should be prepared to learn the special techniques and acceptable format of script writing. Also, experience in playwriting and a knowledge of dramatic structure gained through working in amateur, community, or professional theatres can be helpful, though TV is a highly specialized and demanding field, with unique requirements and specifications.

This section of the *Handbook* includes the names of TV shows scheduled for broadcast during the 1987–88 season, and names and addresses of the production companies responsible for these shows. The lists should not be considered either complete or permanent. A more complete list of shows and production companies may be found in *Ross Reports Television,* published monthly by Television Index, Inc., 40-29 27th St., Long Island City, NY 11101. The cost is $3.96 ($4.25 for New York residents) prepaid for each issue (including first-class postage).

Because virtually all of the producers of these shows tell us that they will read only scripts (and queries) submitted through recognized agents, we've included a list of agents who had indicated to us that they are willing to read queries from writers about television scripts. The names and addresses of other literary and dramatic agents can be found in *Literary Market Place* (Bowker),

718

available in most libraries. A list of agents can also be obtained by sending a self-addressed, stamped envelope to Society of Authors' Representatives, 39½ Washington Sq. S., New York, NY 10012. Before submitting scripts to producers or to agents, authors should query to learn whether they prefer to see the material in television script form, or as an outline or summary.

Writers may wish to register their story, treatment, series format, or script with the Writers Guild of America. This registration doesn't confer statutory rights, but it does supply evidence of authorship which is effective for five years (and is renewable after that). To register material a writer should send one copy of his work, along with a $10 fee, to the Writers Guild of America Registration Service, 8955 Beverly Blvd., Los Angeles, CA 90048. Writers can also register dramatic material with the U.S. Copyright Office—for further information, write Register of Copyrights, Library of Congress, Washington, DC 20559. The Copyright Office is mainly used for book manuscripts, plays, music or lyrics, which the Writers Guild will not register.

TELEVISION SHOWS

ALF (NBC)—Alien Productions/MGM-UA

ALL MY CHILDREN (ABC)—ABC-TV

AMEN (NBC)—Carson Productions

ANOTHER WORLD (NBC)—D'Arcy Masius Benton & Bowles for Proctor & Gamble

AS THE WORLD TURNS (CBS)—D'Arcy Masius Benton & Bowles for Proctor & Gamble

BEAUTY AND THE BEAST (CBS)—Witt-Thomas Prod. with Republic Pictures

BEVERLY HILLS BUNTZ (NBC)—MTM Enterprises

THE BOLD AND THE BEAUTIFUL (CBS)—Bell-Phillip TV/CBS-TV

BUCK JAMES (ABC)—Entertainment Partners/Tri Star Prod.

CAGNEY & LACEY (CBS)—Barney Rosenzweig Prod./Mace Neufeld Prod./Orion TV

THE CHARMINGS (ABC)—Sternin & Fraser Ink, Inc./Embassy TV

CHEERS (NBC)—Charles-Burrows-Charles Prod./Paramount TV

THE COSBY SHOW (NBC)—Carsey-Werner Prod. with Bill Cosby

CRIME STORY (NBC)—Michael Mann Co., Inc./New World TV/NBC-TV

DALLAS (CBS)—Lorimar-Telepictures Prod.

DAYS OF OUR LIVES (NBC)—Corday Prod./Columbia Pictures TV

DESIGNING WOMEN (CBS)—Bloodworth/Thomason Mozark Prod. with Columbia Pictures TV

A DIFFERENT WORLD (NBC)—Carsey-Werner Prod. with Bill Cosby

THE DOLLY SHOW (ABC)—Sandollar Co./ABC Entertainment

DOUBLE DARE (Synd)—Viacom Enterprises

DYNASTY (ABC)—Richard & Esther Shapiro Prod./Aaron Spelling Prod.

719

THE EQUALIZER (CBS)—Universal TV

EVERYTHING'S RELATIVE (CBS)—Fredde Prod./Columbia Pictures TV

THE FACTS OF LIFE (NBC)—Embassy TV

FALCON CREST (CBS)—Lorimar-Telepictures Prod.

FAMILY TIES (NBC)—UBU Prod./Paramount TV

FRANK'S PLACE (CBS)—Viacom Enterprises

FULL HOUSE (ABC)—Miller-Boyett Prod./Lorimar-Telepictures Prod.

GENERAL HOSPITAL (ABC)—ABC-TV

GOLDEN GIRLS (NBC)—Witt-Thomas-Harris Prod./Touchstone Pictures

GOOD MORNING AMERICA (ABC)—ABC Entertainment

GROWING PAINS (ABC)—Warner Bros. TV

THE GUIDING LIGHT (CBS)—D'Arcy, Masius, Benton & Bowles, Inc. for Proctor & Gamble

HEAD OF THE CLASS (ABC)—Eustis/Elias Prod. with Warner Bros. TV

HIGHWAY TO HEAVEN (NBC)—Michael Landon Prod./MGM-UA

HOOPERMAN (ABC)—Adam Prod./20th Century Fox TV

HOTEL (ABC)—Aaron Spelling Prod.

HOUSTON KNIGHTS (CBS)—Jay Bernstein Prod./Columbia Pictures TV

HUNTER (NBC)—Stephen J. Cannell Prod.

I MARRIED DORA (ABC)—Reeves Entertainment

IT'S A LIVING (Synd.)—Witt-Thomas-Harris Prod.

J. J. STARBUCK (NBC)—Stephen J. Cannell Prod.

JAKE AND THE FATMAN (CBS)—Fred Silverman Co. & Strathmore Prod./Viacom

KATE AND ALLIE (ABC)—Mort Lachman/Reeves Entertainment Group

KNOT'S LANDING (CBS)—Rondelay-MF Prod./Lorimar-Telepictures Prod.

L. A. LAW (NBC)—20th Century Fox TV

LATE NIGHT WITH DAVID LETTERMAN (NBC)—NBC-TV with Carson Prod.

THE LAW AND HARRY MCGRAW (CBS)—Universal TV

LEG WORK (CBS)—Treasure Island Prod./20th Century Fox TV

LOVING (ABC)—Dramatic Creations, Inc.

MACGYVER (ABC)—Winkler/Rich Prod. with Paramount TV

MAGNUM, P.I. (CBS)—Belisarius Prod., Glen A. Larson Prod., and TWS Prod. with Universal TV

MAMA'S BOY (NBC)—Witt-Thomas-Harris Prod.

MATLOCK (NBC)—Fred Silverman Co./Strathmore Prod./Viacom Prod.

720

MIAMI VICE (NBC)—Michael Mann Co. with Universal TV

MR. BELVEDERE (ABC)—ABC-TV

MR. PRESIDENT (Fox Broadcasting)—Carson Prod.

MOONLIGHTING (ABC)—Picturemaker Prod./ABC Circle Films

MURDER, SHE WROTE (CBS)—Universal TV

MY SISTER SAM (CBS)—Warner Bros. TV/Pony Prod.

NEWHART (CBS)—MTM Prod.

NIGHT COURT (NBC)—Starry Night Prod./Warner Bros. TV

O'HARA (ABC)—Imagine Films Entertainment Prod./Warner Bros. TV

THE OLDEST ROOKIE (CBS)—Touchstone TV

ONE LIFE TO LIVE (ABC)—ABC-TV

OUR HOUSE (NBC)—Lorimar-Telepictures Prod.

PERFECT STRANGERS (ABC)—Miller-Boyett Prod./Lorimar-Telepictures Prod.

PRIVATE EYE (NBC)—Universal TV

PURSUIT OF HAPPINESS, THE (ABC)—ABC-TV

RAGS TO RICHES (NBC)—Leonard Hill/New World Television/NBC-TV

RYAN'S HOPE (ABC)—ABC-TV

ST. ELSEWHERE (NBC)—MTM Enterprises

SANTA BARBARA (NBC)—Dobson Prod./New World TV

SATURDAY NIGHT LIVE (NBC)—NBC-TV

THE SLAP MAXWELL STORY (ABC)—Slap Happy Prod.

SLEDGE HAMMER! (ABC)—New World TV/ABC-TV

SPENSER: FOR HIRE (ABC)—Jadda Prod./Warner Bros. TV

THIRTY SOMETHING (ABC)—Bedford Falls Prod./MGM-UA

TODAY (NBC)—NBC-TV

TOUR OF DUTY (CBS)—Zev Braun Prod./New World Prod./CBS-TV

TRUE COLORS (ABC)—New World Prod./ABC-TV

227 (NBC)—Embassy TV

VALERIE (NBC)—Miller-Boyett and TAL Prod. with Lorimar-Telepictures Prod.

WHO'S THE BOSS? (ABC)—Embassy TV

WHO'S DAD? (NBC)—Tri-Star

WISE GUY (CBS)—Stephen J. Cannell Prod.

A YEAR IN THE LIFE (NBC)—Universal TV

THE YOUNG AND THE RESTLESS (CBS)—Bell-Phillip TV Prod./Corday Prod./Columbia Pictures TV

TELEVISION PRODUCERS

ABC CIRCLE FILMS—911 W. Pico Blvd., Los Angeles, CA 90067.

ABC ENTERTAINMENT—4151 Prospect Ave., Los Angeles, CA 90027.

ABC PRODUCTIONS—101 W. 67th St., New York, NY 10023.

ABC-TV—1330 Ave. of the Americas, New York, NY 10019

BENTON & BOWLES, INC.—909 Third Ave., New York, NY 10022.

STEPHEN J. CANNELL PRODUCTIONS—7083 Hollywood Blvd., Los Angeles, CA 90028.

CARSEY-WERNER PRODUCTIONS—NBC Studios, 1268 E. 14th St., Brooklyn, NY 11230.

CARSON PRODUCTIONS—10045 Riverside Dr., Toluca Lake, CA 91602.

CBS ENTERTAINMENT—51 W. 52nd St., New York, NY 10019.

CBS TELEVISION CITY—7800 Beverly Blvd., Los Angeles, CA 90036.

COLUMBIA PICTURES TELEVISION—Columbia Plaza, Burbank, CA 91505.

CORDAY PRODUCTIONS, INC.—Colgems Sq., Burbank, CA 91505.

D'ARCY MASIUS BENTON & BOWLES—909 Third Ave., New York, NY 10022.

DOBSON PRODUCTIONS—NBC Studio 11, 3000 W. Alameda Ave., Burbank, CA 91523.

DRAMATIC CREATIONS—320 W. 66th St., New York, NY 10023.

EMBASSY TELEVISION—956 Seward St., Los Angeles, CA 90038.

FOX TELEVISION CENTER—5746 W. Sunset Blvd., Los Angeles, CA 90028.

DAVID GERBER PRODUCTIONS—10000 W. Washington Blvd., Suite 8008, Culver City, CA 90230.

MORT LACHMAN & ASSOCIATES—3500 W. Olive Blvd., Burbank, CA 91505.

LORIMAR-TELEPICTURES PRODUCTIONS—3970 Overland Ave., Culver City, CA 90230.

MGM-UA TELEVISION—10202 W. Washington Blvd., Culver City, CA 90230.

MTM ENTERPRISES—4024 Radford Ave., Studio City, CA 91604.

NBC PRODUCTIONS—NBC-TV, 3000 W. Alameda Ave., Burbank, CA 91523.

NBC-TV—30 Rockefeller Plaza, New York, NY 10020.

MACE NEUFELD PRODUCTIONS—624 N. Arden Dr., Beverly Hills, CA 90210.

ORION PICTURES CORP.—1999 Century Park East, Los Angeles, CA 90067.

PARAMOUNT TELEVISION—5451 Marathon, Los Angeles, CA 90038.

REEVES ENTERTAINMENT GROUP—3500 W. Olive Ave., Suite 500, Burbank, CA 91505.

SLAP HAPPY PRODUCTIONS—ABC-TV, 1330 Ave. of the Americas, New York, NY 10019.

AARON SPELLING PRODUCTIONS—1041 N. Formosa Ave., Los Angeles, CA 91146.

TOUCHSTONE TELEVISION—Walt Disney Studios, 500 S. Buena Vista, Burbank, CA 90038.

TRI-STAR TELEVISION—NBC-TV, 30 Rockefeller Plaza, New York, NY 10020.

20TH CENTURY FOX TELEVISION—10201 W. Pico Blvd., Los Angeles, CA 90064.

UNIVERSAL TELEVISION—100 Universal City Plaza, Universal City, CA 91608.

VIACOM ENTERPRISES—10 Universal City Plaza, Universal City, CA 91608-1097.

WARNER BROTHERS TELEVISION—4000 Warner Blvd., Burbank, CA 91505.

JOE WILLMORE, PRODUCER—221 W. 26th St., New York, NY 10001.

WITT-THOMAS-HARRIS PRODUCTIONS—846 N. Cahuenga Blvd., Hollywood, CA 90038.

TELEVISION SCRIPT AGENTS

ACT 48 MANAGEMENT—1501 Broadway, Suite 705, New York, New York 10036. Address Literary Dept. Reads synopses of scripts for feature films, TV movies, and stage plays, with SASE.

THE BRODY AGENCY—P. O. Box 291423, Davie, FL 33329. Hank Twerl, Script Consultant. Reads queries and scripts with SASEs.

THE CALDER AGENCY—4150 Riverside Dr., Burbank, CA 91505. Reads queries and synopses for features only; no episode TV material.

BILL COOPER ASSOCIATES—224 W. 49th St., New York, NY 10019. Will look at developed ideas for comedies, dramas, theatre, and motion pictures.

HOLLYWOOD TALENT AGENCY—478 Brownridge Dr., Thornhill, Ont., Canada, L4J 3X9. Reads queries, scripts, treatments, and manuscripts.

SCOTT C. HUDSON TALENT REPRESENTATION—215 E. 76th St., New York, NY 10021. Reads queries and treatments, with SASEs.

WILLIAM KERWIN AGENCY—1605 N. Cahuenga Blvd., #202, Hollywood, CA 90028. Reads queries for originals only. No unsolicited manuscripts.

OTTO R. KOZAK LITERARY AGENCY—P. O. Box 152, Long Beach, NY 11561. Query.

L. HARRY LEE LITERARY AGENCY—Box 203, Rocky Point, NY 11778.

Reads queries accompanied by SASE only. Episodic and sitcom for shows produced in NYC.

LONDON STAR PROMOTIONS—7131 Owensmouth Ave., #C116, Canoga Park, CA 91303. Reads queries and synopses.

WILLIAM MORRIS AGENCY—1350 Ave. of the Americas, New York, NY 10019. Reads queries with SASEs.

SUZANNE SHELTON—CNA Associates, 8721 Sunset Blvd., #202, Los Angeles, CA 90069. Reads queries accompanied by SASEs only. No episodic scripts. New series ideas or MFT only.

JACK TANTLEFF—c/o the Tantleff Office, 360 W. 20th St., New York, NY 10011. Reads queries.

VAMP TALENT AGENCY—713 E. La Loma, #1, Somis, CA 93066. Reads queries, treatments and scripts, accompanied by SASEs.

DAN WRIGHT—c/o Ann Wright Representatives, Inc., 136 E. 57th St., New York, NY 10022. Reads queries. Specializes in motion pictures.

BOOK PUBLISHERS

The following list includes the major publishers of trade books (adult and juvenile fiction and nonfiction) and a representative number of small publishers from across the country. All companies in the list publish both hardcover and paperback books, unless otherwise indicated.

Before sending a complete manuscript to an editor, it is advisable to send a brief query letter describing the proposed book. The letter should also include information about the author's special qualifications for dealing with a particular topic and any previous publication credits. An outline of the book (or a synopsis for fiction) and a sample chapter may also be included.

It is common practice to submit a book manuscript to only one publisher at a time, although it is becoming more and more acceptable for writers, even those without agents, to submit the same *query* or *proposal* to more than one editor at the same time.

Book manuscripts may be wrapped in typing paper boxes (available from a stationer) and sent by first-class mail, or, more common and less expensive, by "Special Fourth Class Rate-Manuscript." For rates, details of insurance, and so forth, inquire at your local post office. With any submission to a publisher, be sure to enclose sufficient postage for the manuscript's return.

Royalty rates for hardcover books usually start at 10% of the retail price of the book, and increase after a certain number of copies have been sold. Paperbacks generally have a somewhat lower rate, about 5% to 8%. It is customary for the publishing company to pay the author a cash advance against royalties when the book contract is signed or when the finished manuscript is received. Some publishers pay on a flat fee basis.

ABBEY PRESS—St. Meinrad, IN 47577. Keith McClellan, O.S.B., Pub.

Religious fiction and value-based children's books. Nonfiction Christian books on marriage and family living. Query with table of contents and writing sample.

ABINGDON PRESS—201 Eighth Ave., S., P. O. Box 801, Nashville, TN 37202. Etta Wilson, Children's Books Ed. Picture books, read-aloud books, and middle-grade fiction that "emphasize Christian values and indicate an awareness of child development. We prefer strong story lines and characterization, a sense of movement and adventure, gentle humor or wit, and the fresh perspectives of childhood. We also want books on issues children face, and good stories with ethnic characters." Royalty.

ACADEMIC PRESS—Harcourt, Brace, Jovanovich, Inc., Orlando, FL 32887. Blake E. Vance, Ed. Scientific books for professionals; college science texts. Royalty. Query.

ACADEMY CHICAGO PUBLISHERS—425 N. Michigan Ave., Chicago, IL 60601. Anita Miller, Ed. General quality fiction; mysteries. History; biographies, travel; books by and about women. Royalty. Query with four sample chapters. SASE required.

ACCENT BOOKS—Box 15337, 12100 W. 6th Ave., Denver, CO 80215. Mary Nelson, Man. Ed. Fiction and nonfiction from evangelical Christian perspective. Query with sample chapters. Royalty. Paperback only.

ACE BOOKS (Imprint of *Berkley Publishing Group*)—200 Madison Ave., New York, NY 10016. Susan Allison, V.P., Ed.-in-Chief. Science fiction and fantasy. Royalty. No unsolicited manuscripts.

ADAMA BOOKS—306 W. 38th St., New York, NY 10018. Esther Cohen, Ed. Adult nonfiction. Juvenile fiction, nonfiction, picture books. Most titles have an international focus. Query with outline and sample chapters. Royalty.

ADDISON-WESLEY PUBLISHING CO.—Rt. 128, Reading, MA 01867. General Publishing Group: Adult nonfiction on current topics: education, health, psychology, computers, human resources, business, biography, child care, etc. Royalty.

ADLER & ADLER—4550 Montgomery Ave., Bethesda, MD 20814. Amy Pastan, Ed. Nonfiction on politics and business, memoirs, biography, autobiography, and issue-oriented topics. "We will also consider self-help books, but they should have more substance than the average 'how-to' book; they should be 'why' books, as well. We are particularly concerned with health issues. We will consider fiction, but publish only a few novels a year."

ALADDIN BOOKS—Macmillan Children's Book Group, 866 Third Ave., New York, NY 10022. Sharyn November, Assoc. Ed. "We are on the lookout for original material for very young children (concept books, novelties, etc.) as well as for middle readers (ages 7 to 10). Query with outline and sample chapters. Royalty and outright purchase. Softcover only.

ALASKA NORTHWEST PUBLISHING CO.—130 2nd Ave. S., Edmonds, WA 98020. Ethel Dassow, Sr. Book Ed. Nonfiction, some fiction, 10,000 to 100,000 words, with an emphasis on natural resources and history of Alaska, Northwestern Canada, and Pacific Northwest: how-to books; biographies; cookbooks; gardening; humor; nature; guidebooks. Send query or sample chapters with outline. Limited market.

THE AMERICAN PSYCHIATRIC PRESS—1400 K St., NW, Washington, DC 20005. Carol C. Nadelson, M.D., Ed.-in-Chief. Books that interpret scientific and medical aspects of psychiatry for a lay audience, and that address specific psychiatric problems. Query required. Royalty.

APPLE BOOKS—See *Scholastic, Inc.*

ARBOR HOUSE PUBLISHING COMPANY—105 Madison Ave., New York, NY 10016. Allan Mayer, Ed. Dir. General fiction and nonfiction. Royalty. Query.

ARCHWAY PAPERBACKS (Imprint of *Pocket Books*)—1230 Ave. of the Americas, New York, NY 10020. Erica Farber, Ed. Fiction (mystery, romance, fantasy, problem and YA novels) and nonfiction (sports, biography, music) for young adults. Humor for ages 6 to 12. Query required; include outline and sample chapter. Royalty. Paperback only.

ARCO PUBLISHING *(Prentice Hall Press*/a Div. of *Simon & Schuster)*— Gulf & Western Bldg., One Gulf & Western Plaza, New York, NY 10023. William Mlawer, Ed.-in-Chief. Nonfiction, originals and reprints, from 50,000 words. Career guides, test preparation. Royalty. Query with outline. Return postage required.

ARCSOFT PUBLISHERS—P. O. Box 132, Woodsboro, MD 21798. Anthony Curtis, Pres. Nonfiction hobby books for beginners, personal computing, space science, journalism, and hobby electronics, for laymen, general and public consumers, beginners and novices. Outright purchase and royalty basis. Query. Paper only.

ATHENEUM PUBLISHERS (Subsidiary of *Macmillan Publishing Co.*)— 115 Fifth Ave., New York, NY 10003. Susan Ginsburg, Ed.-in-Chief. General nonfiction, biography, history, current affairs, fiction, belles-lettres. Books for children, grade 3 through young adult. Query with sample chapters and outline, except for picture books, for which complete manuscripts will be considered.

THE ATLANTIC MONTHLY PRESS—420 Lexington Ave., Suite 2304, New York, NY 10170. Gary Fisketjon, Ed. Dir. Fiction, general nonfiction and travel books. Hardcover and trade paperback. Royalty.

AUGSBURG PUBLISHING HOUSE—Box 1209, 426 S. Fifth St., Minneapolis, MN 55440. Roland Seboldt, Dir. of Book Development. Fiction and nonfiction, for adults, children and teens, on Christian themes. Picture books for ages 3 to 6 also considered. Royalty.

AVERY PUBLISHING GROUP—350 Thorens Ave., Garden City Park, NY 11040. Nonfiction, from 40,000 words, on health, childbirth, child care, healthful cooking. Query first. Royalty.

AVIATION PUBLISHERS—Ultralight Publications, Inc., One Aviation Way, Lock Box 234, Hummelstown, PA 17036. Michael A. Markowski, Ed. Nonfiction, from 30,000 words, on aviation, cars, model cars and planes, boats, trains, health, and self-help. Query with outline and sample chapters. Royalty.

AVON BOOKS—105 Madison Ave., New York, NY 10016. Linda Cunningham, Ed. Dir. Modern fiction, general nonfiction, historical romance, 60,000 to 200,000 words. Science fiction, 75,000 to 100,000 words. Query with synopsis and sample chapters. Ellen Edwards, Historical Romance; John Douglas, Science Fiction. *Camelot Books:* Ellen Krieger, Ed. Fiction and nonfiction for 8- to 12-year-olds, 60 to 100 manuscript pages. Query. *Flare Books:* Ellen Krieger, Ed. Fiction and nonfiction for 12-year-olds and up, to 200 manuscript pages. Query. Royalty. Paperback only.

BACKCOUNTRY PUBLICATIONS, INC.—P. O. Box 175, Woodstock, VT

05091. Carl Taylor, Editor. Regional guidebooks, 150 to 300 manuscript pages, on hiking, walking, canoeing, bicycling, and fishing. Royalty. Query first.

BAEN BOOKS—Baen Enterprises, 260 Fifth Ave., New York, NY 10001. Elizabeth Mitchell, Sr. Ed. Jim Baen, Pres. High-tech science fiction; innovative fantasy for *Sign of the Dragon*. Query with synopsis and sample chapters. Royalty.

BAKER BOOK HOUSE—P. O. Box 6287, Grand Rapids, MI 49506. Dan Van't Kerkhoff, Ed., general trade and professional books. Allan Fisher, Ed., academic and reference books. Religious nonfiction. Royalty.

BALLANTINE BOOKS—201 E. 50th St., New York, NY 10022. Robert Wyatt, Ed.-in-Chief. Joelle Delbourgo, Vice Pres. and Ed.-in-Chief. No unsolicited material.

BALLANTINE/EPIPHANY BOOKS—201 E. 50th St., New York, NY 10022. Toni Simmons, Ed. Books with Christian elements or themes, targeted not only to a Christian audience, but to "non-Christian readers with spiritual concerns. We blend Christian guidelines and standards with topics of interest to everyone: divorce, marriage, loneliness, stress, personal tragedy, decision-making, handicaps. Our more deeply spiritual books explore prayer, worship, healing, friendship, love, etc. We have also published biographies. Though we prefer nonfiction books, we are willing to look at proposals of novels with inspirational qualities." Manuscripts should be 60,000 to 75,000 words. Query with outline and sample chapters. Royalty.

BALSAM PRESS—122 E. 25th St., New York, NY 10010. Barbara Krohn, Exec. Ed. General and illustrated adult nonfiction. Royalty. Query.

BANTAM BOOKS, INC.—666 Fifth Ave., New York, NY 10103. Linda Grey, Pres. & Pub. Lou Aronica, Publishing Dir., Bantam Science Fiction/Fantasy. Judy Gitenstein, Ed. Dir., Young Readers Books. Carolyn Nichols, *Loveswept*. Steve Rubin, Ed. Dir., Adult Fiction and Nonfiction. General and educational fiction and nonfiction, 75,000 to 100,000 words. No unsolicited manuscripts.

BARRON'S EDUCATIONAL SERIES, INC.—113 Crossways Park Dr., Woodbury, NY 11797. Francoise Martin, Man. Ed. Nonfiction topics—science, nature, history, hobbies, and how-to—for juveniles, and picture books for ages 3 to 6. Query. Royalty.

BEACON PRESS—25 Beacon St., Boston, MA 02108. Joanne Wyckoff, Carol Birdsall, Sr. Eds. General nonfiction: world affairs, sociology, psychology, women's studies, political science, art, anthropology, literature, history, philosophy, religion. No fiction or poetry. Royalty. Query. Return postage required.

BEAUFORT BOOKS—9 E. 40th St., New York, NY 10016. Fiction and nonfiction. Query with outline and sample chapters for nonfiction, one sample chapter for fiction; include list of previous publications.

BEECH TREE BOOKS (Imprint of *William Morrow and Co., Inc.*)—105 Madison Ave., New York, NY 10016. James Landis, Pub. and Ed.-in-Chief. Adult fiction and nonfiction. No unsolicited manuscripts.

BERKLEY PUBLISHING GROUP—200 Madison Ave., New York, NY 10016. Roger Cooper, Pub. and Ed. Dir. General interest fiction and nonfiction: science fiction; suspense and espionage novels; romance. Submit through agent only. Publishes both reprints and originals. Paper only.

727

BETHANY HOUSE PUBLISHERS—6820 Auto Club Rd., Minneapolis, MN 55438. Address Ed. Dept. Fiction, nonfiction. Religious. Royalty. Query required.

BETTER HOMES AND GARDENS BOOKS—See *Meredith Corporation.*

BLACK LIZARD BOOKS (Imprint of *Creative Arts Book Company*)—833 Bancroft Way, Berkeley, CA 94710. Peg O'Donnell, Ed. Distinctive crime fiction. Query with outline and sample chapters. Royalty.

JOHN F. BLAIR, PUBLISHER—1406 Plaza Dr., Winston-Salem, NC 27103. Gail Lathey Warner, Ed. Dept. Biography, history, fiction, travel and guidebooks, with North Carolina tie-in. Length: at least 75,000 words. Royalty. Query.

BLUEJAY BOOKS—26 Douglas Rd., Chappaqua, NY 10514. James Frenkel, Pub. Science fiction, fantasy, mystery, and related nonfiction. Royalty. Query with SASE required.

BONUS BOOKS—160 E. Illinois St., Chicago, IL 60611. Ellen Slezak, Ed. Nonfiction, from 150 pages. Query. Royalty.

BOOKS FOR PROFESSIONALS—See *Harcourt Brace Jovanovich.*

THOMAS BOUREGY & CO., INC.—401 Lafayette St., New York, NY 10003. Rita Brenig, Ed. Light, wholesome, well-plotted romances, modern Gothics, westerns, and nurse romances, 50,000 words. Send one-page synopsis. SASE required. Hardcover only.

BRADBURY PRESS (An affiliate of *Macmillan, Inc.*)—866 Third Ave., New York, NY 10022. Barbara Lalicki, Ed. Fiction (general, mystery, and science fiction) for grades 4–12; nonfiction (including biographies, sports, and history); humor/poetry (for readers to grade 6); and picture books (to age 8). Query or submit complete manuscript. Royalty. Hardcover only.

BRANDEN PRESS—17 Station St., Box 843, Brookline Village, MA 02147. Adolph Caso, Ed. Novels and biographies, 250 to 350 pages. Query with SASE required. Royalty.

GEORGE BRAZILLER, INC.—60 Madison Ave., New York, NY 10010. Literature, history, philosophy, science, art, social science; fiction. Royalty. No unsolicited manuscripts. Query with SASE required.

BROADMAN PRESS—127 Ninth Ave. N., Nashville, TN 37234. Harold S. Smith, Manager. Religious and inspirational fiction and nonfiction. Royalty. Query.

CAMELOT BOOKS—See *Avon Books.*

CAROLRHODA BOOKS—241 First Ave. N., Minneapolis, MN 55401. Rebecca Poole, Submissions Ed. Picture books, fiction, nonfiction for elementary children. Of interest are biography, science, nature, history, mystery, humor. Outright purchase. Hardcover only.

CARROLL AND GRAF PUBLISHERS, INC.—260 Fifth Ave., New York, NY 10001. Kent E. Carroll, Exec. Ed. General fiction and nonfiction. Royalty. Query with SASE.

CBI PUBLISHING CO.—See *Van Nostrand Reinhold Co., Inc.*

CELESTIAL ARTS (Subsidiary of *Ten Speed Press*)—P. O. Box 7327, Berkley, CA 94707. Paul Reed, Ed. Nonfiction, 25,000 to 80,000 words, on all subjects. No fiction or poetry. Royalty.

728

CHARTER BOOKS (Imprint of *Berkley Publishing Group*)—200 Madison Ave., New York, NY 10016. Roger Cooper, Pub. Adventure, espionage and suspense fiction, women's contemporary fiction, family sagas, and historical novels. Westerns, male action/adventure, and cartoon books. No unsolicited manuscripts. Royalty or outright purchase. Paperback.

CHATHAM PRESS—P. O. Box A, Old Greenwich, CT 06807. Roger H. Lourie, Man. Dir. Books on the Northeast coast, New England and the ocean. Royalty. Query with outline, sample chapters, illustrations and SASE large enough for return of material.

CHELSEA GREEN PUBLISHING CO.—P. O. Box 283, Chelsea, VT 05038. Ian Baldwin, Jr., Ed. Fiction and nonfiction on natural history, biography, history, politics, and travel. Query with outline and sample chapter. Royalty.

CHICAGO REVIEW PRESS—814 Franklin St., Chicago, IL 60610. Linda Matthews, Mary Munro, Eds. Nonfiction: sports, medicine, anthropology, travel, nature, life styles, cookbooks, regional and humor books. Query with outline and sample chapters. Royalty.

CHILDRENS PRESS—1224 W. Van Buren St., Chicago, IL 60607. Fran Dyra, Ed. Dir. Juvenile nonfiction: science, biography, 10,000 to 25,000 words, for supplementary use in classrooms. Query first. Picture books, 50 to 1,000 words. Royalty or outright purchase.

CHILTON BOOK CO.—201 King of Prussia Rd., Radnor, PA 19089. Alan F. Turner, Edit. Dir. Business, crafts and hobbies, automotive. Royalty. Query with outline, sample chapter, and return postage.

CHRONICLE BOOKS—One Hallidie Plaza, Suite 806, San Francisco, CA 94102. William LeBlond, Sen. Ed., Nion McEvoy, Ed. Topical nonfiction: West Coast regional recreational guides, natural history, food, photography, art and architecture. Royalty.

CITADEL PRESS—See *Lyle Stuart, Inc.*

CLARION BOOKS (Juvenile imprint of *Ticknor & Fields,* a *Houghton Mifflin* company)—52 Vanderbilt Ave., New York, NY 10017. James C. Giblin, Ed. Lively juvenile fiction geared to ages 8–12; 10–14; and short novels (40 to 80 pages) for ages 7–10. Mysteries, American historical fiction, and humor are all of interest; picture books should be geared to children pre-school through grade 3. For nonfiction topics—biography, word plays, nature, social studies, and holiday themes—writers should query Senior Editor Ann Troy. Royalty basis. Query preferred on manuscripts of more than 20 pages. SASE required.

CLIFFHANGER PRESS—P. O. Box 29527, Oakland, CA 94604-9527. Nancy Chirish, Ed. Mystery and suspense only. Submit copy of complete manuscript with return postage. Royalty.

CLOVERDALE PRESS—133 Fifth Ave., New York, NY 10003. *Book packager.* "We're looking for books in the following fiction categories: women's contemporary romances, romantic suspense, generational sagas, historicals, inspirational romances, male action adventure, medical fiction, and young adult fiction. Many, but not all, of Cloverdale's books are presented in a series format, but new series ideas and individual manuscripts are also welcome. Payment is usually on a flat fee basis." Send queries and resumes for young adult material to Marion Vaarn; for adult works to Lisa Howell.

COLLIER BOOKS—See *Macmillan Publishing Co.*

COMPCARE PUBLICATIONS—18551 Von Karman Ave., Irvine, CA 92715. Bonnie Hesse, Man. Ed. Adult nonfiction; young adult nonfiction: Books on recovery from addictive/compulsive behavior; growth in personal, couple, and family relationships. Submit complete manuscript. Royalty.

COMPUTE! PUBLICATIONS, INC.—P. O. Box 5406, Greensboro, NC 27403. How-to computer books; specializes in machine-specific publications. Query preferred. Royalty.

CONCORDIA PUBLISHING HOUSE—3558 S. Jefferson Ave., St. Louis, MO 63118. Practical nonfiction with moral or religious values. Very little fiction. No poetry. Royalty. Query.

CONTEMPORARY BOOKS—180 N. Michigan Ave., Chicago, IL 60601. Nancy Crossman, V. P. General nonfiction: health, fitness, nutrition, sports, real estate, business, popular culture, humor, biographies. Query with outline and sample chapter. Royalty.

DAVID C. COOK PUBLISHING CO.—850 N. Grove Ave., Elgin, IL 60120. David Orris, Book Division Dir.; Catherine Davis, Man. Ed., Children's Books. Paul Mouw, Man. Ed., General Titles. Religious children's books and general titles. Pays on royalty and work-for-hire basis. Query with chapter-by-chapter synopsis and two sample chapters. Unsolicited manuscripts returned unopened. Label envelope "query." SASE required.

COPLEY BOOKS—7776 Ivanhoe Ave., La Jolla, CA 92037. Jean I. Bradford, Ed. Nonfiction, with photos/illustrations, on history of California (and Baja) and the Southwest, geared to the general reader. Query with synopsis and SASE. Royalty. Hardcover.

COWARD, MCCANN (Div. of *Putnam Publishing Group*)—200 Madison Ave., New York, NY 10016. Fiction and nonfiction through agents only.

CRAFTSMAN BOOK COMPANY—6058 Corte del Cedro, P. O. Box 6500, Carlsbad, CA 92009. Laurence D. Jacobs, Ed. How-to construction manuals for builders, 450 pages. Royalty. Query. Softcover only.

CREATIVE ARTS BOOK COMPANY—833 Bancroft Way, Berkeley, CA 94710. Peg O'Donnell, Ed. Adult fiction and nonfiction, 200+ pages. Juvenile fiction and nonfiction for ages 7 to 12. "We are currently not interested in looking at the following: art, photography, and technical books, science fiction, poetry, dramatical works, or romances. Anything else goes." Query with outline and sample chapters. Royalty.

THE CROSSING PRESS—22-D Roache Rd., P. O. Box 207, Freedom, CA 95019. Elaine Gill, John Gill, Pubs. How-to books; feminist; gay; cookbooks. Fiction. Royalty.

CROSSWINDS—300 E. 42nd St., 6th Fl., New York, NY 10017. Nancy Jackson, Senior Ed. "We accept all kinds of mysteries for young adults aged 11 to 16—puzzles, detective stories, romantic and psychological suspense. They must be tightly written, fast-paced, and feature young protagonists to whom kids can relate. We also publish young-adult romances; the tone may be tender, funny, down-to-earth, but not overly sentimental, moralistic, graphically sexual. Positive, though not necessarily happy, endings are preferred. Finally, we're looking for general-interest, mass market fiction for young adults—interesting stories, believable characters, humanistic values." Books are 40,000 words. Query. Send for tip sheet. Paperback.

THOMAS Y. CROWELL—See *Harper Junior Books Group.*

CROWN PUBLISHERS, INC.—225 Park Ave. S., New York, NY 10003. Fiction and general nonfiction. Royalty. Query letters only: Address Ed. Dept.; no unsolicited manuscripts. SASE required. *Crown Books for Children:* David Allender, Ed. Dir. Fiction (including horror and SF), nonfiction (biography, science, sports, nature, music, and history), and picture books (from age 3). Query with outline and sample chapters for all but picture books.

JONATHAN DAVID PUBLISHERS, INC.—68-22 Eliot Ave., Middle Village, NY 11379. Alfred J. Kolatch, Ed.-in-Chief. General nonfiction—how-to, sports, cooking and food, self-help, etc.—and nonfiction on Judaica. Royalty or outright purchase. Query with outline, sample chapter, and resume required.

DAW BOOKS, INC.—1633 Broadway, New York, NY 10019. Elizabeth R. Wollheim, Ed.-in-Chief. Science fiction and fantasy, 60,000 to 120,000 words. Royalty.

DELACORTE PRESS (Div. of *Dell Publishing Co., Inc.*)—245 E. 47th St., New York, NY 10017. Jackie Farber, Ed. Adult fiction and nonfiction. *Books for Young Readers:* George Nicholson, Ed. Contemporary fiction. Manuscripts accepted through agents only.

DEL REY BOOKS (Div. of *Random House, Inc.*)—201 E. 50th St., New York, NY 10022. Shelly Shapiro, Lester del Rey, Eds. "We are always looking for new writers—a large number of our first novels come from the 'slush pile'. We look for books that are entertaining, well-plotted—with a logical resolution that does not involve coincidence or a deus ex machina—and with at least some likable characters (certainly the main character must be). For our fantasy books, we require that magic be so basic to the plot that there would be no story without it. Manuscripts are in the range of 70,000 to 120,000 words.

"We prefer to see *complete manuscripts,* but will review partial submissions consisting of the first three chapters plus a detailed outline of the rest of the book. Since we read everything that comes in and employ no outside readers, reporting time can be slow—six months or more during particularly busy times. Contracts are negotiated on an individual basis; advances and royalties are competitive." Send SF manuscripts to Shelly Shapiro; fantasy manuscripts to Lester del Rey.

DELL PUBLISHING CO., INC.—245 E. 47th St., New York, NY 10017. Carole Baron, Pres. and Pub. *Dell Books:* family sagas, historical romances, war action, occult/horror/psychological suspense, true crime, men's adventure. *Delta:* General-interest nonfiction, psychology, feminism, health, nutrition, child care, science. *Juvenile Books: Yearling* (kindergarten through 6th grade; no unsolicited manuscripts); and *Laurel-Leaf* (grades 7 through 12; no unsolicited manuscripts). Submissions policy for *Dell Books:* Send four-page narrative synopsis for fiction, or an outline for nonfiction. Enclose SASE. Don't send any sample chapters, artwork, or manuscripts. Address submissions to the appropriate Dell division and add Editorial Dept.—Book Proposal.

DELTA BOOKS—See *Dell Publishing Co.*

DEMBNER BOOKS—80 Eighth Ave., New York, NY 10011. S. Arthur Dembner, Pres. Therese Eiben, Associate Ed. Self-help, lifestyle, reference, and other nonfiction; good fiction. "We want to hear from writers who take writing seriously; who write passionately, accurately; who understand that writing isn't a hobby like gardening—it's a skill, a talent, a gift, a profession. Most of all, we want to hear from writers who are honest with themselves." Query with outline, sample chapters, and SASE. Royalty.

DEVIN-ADAIR PUBLISHERS, INC.—6 N. Water St., Greenwich, CT

06830. C. de la Belle Issue, Pub. J. Andrassi, Ed. Books on conservative affairs, Irish topics, Americana, computers, self-help, health, ecology. Royalty. Send outline, sample chapters, and SASE.

DIAL BOOKS FOR YOUNG READERS (Div. of *E. P. Dutton*)—2 Park Ave., New York, NY 10016. Phyllis Fogelman, Ed.-in-Chief. Picture books; Easy-to-Read Books; middle-grade readers; young adult fiction and nonfiction. Submit complete manuscript for fiction; outline and sample chapters for nonfiction. Enclose SASE. Royalty. Hardcover only.

DILLON PRESS—242 Portland Ave. S., Minneapolis, MN 55415. Uva Dillon, Ed.-in-Chief. Kathryn Shupe, Fiction Ed. Tom Schneider, Nonfiction Ed. Juvenile nonfiction: U.S. states and cities, foreign countries (especially Third World), contemporary biographies for elementary and middle grade levels; unusual approaches to science topics for primary grade readers, sports, biographies, and contemporary issues of interest to young people. Royalty and outright purchase. Query with outline and sample chapter. *Gemstone Books:* Fiction for grades K–9: mystery, adventure, fantasy, science fiction, contemporary problems, etc. Royalty and outright purchase.

DODD, MEAD & CO.—71 Fifth Ave., New York, NY 10003. Cynthia Vartan, Margaret Norton, Sr. Eds. Joe Ann Daly, Dir., Children's Books. General fiction and nonfiction: biography, history, belles-lettres, travel, mystery, social issues, current events. Juveniles. *Teale Books:* Mary Kennan, Ed. Books "symbolizing the world of the outdoors and nature publishing at its best." Royalty. Query.

THE DONNING COMPANY—5659 Virginia Beach Blvd., Norfolk, VA 23502. Tony Lillis, Ed. Adult fiction and nonfiction: metaphysical, humor, general interest, regional. Query with outline and sample chapters. Royalty.

DOUBLEDAY AND CO., INC.—245 Park Ave., New York, NY 10167. Nancy Evans, Pres. & Pub. Hardcover: Mystery/suspense fiction, romance, science fiction, 70,000 to 80,000 words. Send query and outline to appropriate editor: Crime Club, Starlight Romance, or Science Fiction. SASE required. Paperback: Loretta Barrett, V.P., Exec. Ed. Adult trade books: fiction, sociology, psychology, philosophy, women's, etc. Herman Gollob, Ed.-in-Chief. Query.

DOWN EAST BOOKS—Box 679, Camden, ME 04843. Books about Maine and New England. Query with sample chapters and outline. Royalty.

THOMAS DUNNE BOOKS (Imprint of *St. Martin's Press*)—175 Fifth Ave., New York, NY 10010. Thomas L. Dunne, Ed. Adult fiction (mysteries, trade, SF, etc.) and nonfiction (history, biographies, how-to, etc.). Query with outline and sample chapters and SASE. Royalty.

E. P. DUTTON (Div. of *N.A.L./Penguin*)—2 Park Ave., New York, NY 10016. Lucia Monfried, Ed.-in-Chief, Children's Books. Picture books, easy-to-read books; fiction and nonfiction for preschoolers to young adults. Submit outline and sample chapters with query for fiction and nonfiction, complete manuscripts for picture books and easy-to-read books. *E. P. Dutton Adult Trade:* Richard Marek, Pub., Joyce Engelson, Ed.-in-Chief. General fiction and nonfiction. "Whether sending a query letter or a manuscript (with SASE), the writer should explain briefly and clearly what the book is about, and whether he or she has been published before. Please allow six to eight weeks for a reply." *E. P. Dutton/Seymour Lawrence.* Literary fiction. Query with partial manuscript and SASE.

EAST WOODS PRESS (Imprint of *The Globe Pequot Press*)—429 East Kingston Ave., Charlotte, NC 28203. Sally McMillan, Consulting Ed. Nonfiction on travel, cooking, natural science, regional history, and home improvement. Length requirements and payment rates vary. Query with sample chapters required.

WM. B. EERDMANS PUBLISHING COMPANY, INC.—255 Jefferson Ave., S.E., Grand Rapids, MI 49503. Jon Pott, Ed.-in-Chief. Protestant theological nonfiction; American history; some fiction. Royalty.

EMC CORP.—300 York Ave., St. Paul, MN 55101. Eileen Slater, Ed. Vocational, career, and consumer education textbooks. Royalty. No unsolicited manuscripts.

ENSLOW PUBLISHERS—Bloy St. & Ramsey Ave., Box 777, Hillside, NJ 07205. R. M. Enslow, Jr., Ed./Pub. Nonfiction for young adults and children on social issues and science topics. Also reference and professional books in science, technology, medicine, and business. Royalty. Query first.

PAUL S. ERIKSSON, PUBLISHER—208 Battell Bldg., Middlebury, VT 05753. General nonfiction; some fiction. Royalty. Query with outline and sample chapters.

M. EVANS & CO., INC.—216 E. 49th St., New York, NY 10017. Books on health, self-help, popular psychology, and cookbooks. Commercial fiction for adults. Query with outline and sample chapter. Royalty.

FACTS ON FILE PUBLICATIONS—460 Park Ave. S., New York, NY 10016. Gerard Helferich, Exec. Ed. Reference and trade books on business, science, consumer affairs, the performing arts, etc. Query with outline and sample chapter. Royalty. Hardcover.

FARRAR, STRAUS & GIROUX—19 Union Sq. W., New York, NY 10003. General fiction, nonfiction, juveniles. Address queries to Editorial Dept.

FAWCETT BOOKS—201 E. 50th St., New York, NY 10022. Leona Nevler, Ed.-in-Chief. Fiction and nonfiction. Query. Softcover only.

FREDERICK FELL PUBLISHERS, INC.—2131 Hollywood Blvd., Hollywood, FL 33020. Susan Snider, Ed. Nonfiction: how-to's, especially business and health. Query with letter or outline and sample chapter and SASE. Royalty.

THE FEMINIST PRESS AT THE CITY UNIVERSITY OF NEW YORK—311 E. 94th St., New York, NY 10128. Florence Howe, Pub. Reprints of significant "lost" fiction, autobiographies or other feminist work from the past; biography; original anthologies for classroom use; handbooks; bibliographies. Royalty.

DONALD I. FINE, INC.—128 E. 36th St., New York, NY 10016. Literary and commercial fiction. General nonfiction. No queries or unsolicited manuscripts. Submit through agent only.

FIREBRAND BOOKS—141 The Commons, Ithaca, NY 14850. Nancy K. Bereano, Ed. Feminist and lesbian fiction and nonfiction. Royalty. Softcover.

FIRESIDE BOOKS (Imprint of *Simon & Schuster*)—1230 Ave. of the Americas, New York, NY 10020. Barbara Gess, Tim McGinnis, Senior Eds. General nonfiction and "small amount of issue-oriented fiction." Royalty basis or outright purchase. Submit outline and one chapter. Softcover only.

FLARE BOOKS—See *Avon Books*.

FLEET PRESS CORPORATION—160 Fifth Ave., New York, NY 10010. P. Scott, Ed. General nonfiction. Royalty. Query; no unsolicited manuscripts.

FORTRESS PRESS—2900 Queen Lane, Philadelphia, PA 19129. Harold W. Rast, Th.D., Dir. Serious, nonfiction works, from 100 pages, on theology and religion, for the academic or lay reader. Royalty. Query preferred.

FOUR WINDS PRESS (An imprint of *Macmillan Publishing Co.*)—866 Third Ave., New York, NY 10022. Judith R. Whipple, Pub. Cindy Kane, Ed.-in-Chief. Juveniles: picture books, fiction for all ages. Nonfiction for young children. Query with SASE required. Hardcover only.

THE FREE PRESS—See *Macmillan Publishing Co.*

GAMUT BOOKS (Imprint of *Dodd, Mead & Co.*)—71 Fifth Ave., New York, NY 10003. Barbara Beckman, Assoc. Ed. Self-help on business and careers; inspiration/motivation guides to success in work and life; popular psychology. Submit a prospectus, table of contents, brief outline of each chapter, and two sample chapters. Paperback only.

GARDEN WAY PUBLISHING COMPANY—Storey Communications, Schoolhouse Rd., Pownal, VT 05261. Deborah Burns, Ed. How-to books on gardening, cooking, building, animals, country living. Royalty or outright purchase. Query with outline and sample chapter.

GEMSTONE BOOKS—See *Dillon Press.*

THE K. S. GINIGER CO., INC.—1133 Broadway, Suite 1301, New York, NY 10010. General nonfiction; reference and religious. Royalty. Query with SASE; no unsolicited manuscripts.

THE GLOBE PEQUOT PRESS—Old Chester Rd., Box Q, Chester, CT 06412. Eric Newman, Man. Ed. Nonfiction about New England and the Northeast; cookbooks with natural focus; journalism and media. Travel guidebooks a specialty. Royalty. Query with a sample chapter, contents, and one-page synopsis. SASE a must.

GOLD EAGLE BOOKS (Imprint of *Worldwide Library*)—224 Duncan Mill Rd., Don Mills, Ont., Canada M3B 3K9. Randall Toye, Ed. Dir. Espionage, thrillers and crime/suspense fiction; action adventure series; mystery fiction. Query. Paperback only.

GOLDEN PRESS—See *Western Publishing Co., Inc.*

THE STEPHEN GREENE PRESS, INC. (Div. of *Viking/Penguin*)—15 Muzzey St., Lexington, MA 02173. Thomas L. Begner, Pub. "We are basically nonfiction, category publishers, with heavy emphasis on sports, health and wellness, nature, cooking, popular psychology and certain regional titles. Writers should send only query letters with synopses and sample chapters. We do not return material unless there is an SASE. As far as length is concerned, there is no upper limit, although we find that a manuscript of less than 60,000 words really does not make a book." Royalty.

GREENWILLOW BOOKS (Imprint of *William Morrow and Co., Inc.*)—105 Madison Ave., New York, NY 10016. Susan Hirschman, Ed.-in-Chief. Children's books for all ages. Picture books.

GROSSET AND DUNLAP, INC. (Div. of *Putnam Publishing Group*)—51 Madison Ave., New York, NY 10010. Material accepted through agents only.

GROVE PRESS—920 Broadway, New York, NY 10010. Fred Jordan, Editor-in-Chief. General fiction and nonfiction. Query first.

HAMMOND INCORPORATED—Maplewood, NY 07040. Dorothy Bacheller, Ed. Nonfiction: reference, travel. Payment varies. Query with outline and sample chapters. SASE required.

HANCOCK HOUSE—1431 Harrison Ave., Blaine, WA 98230. David Hancock, Ed. Nonfiction: cookbooks, gardening, outdoor guides, Western history, American Indians, real estate, and investing. Royalty.

HARCOURT BRACE JOVANOVICH—1250 Sixth Ave., San Diego, CA 92101. Adult trade nonfiction and fiction. *Books for Professionals:* test preparation guides and other student self-help materials. *Miller Accounting Publications, Inc.:* professional books for practitioners in accounting and finance; college accounting texts. Juvenile fiction and nonfiction: for beginning readers through young adults, especially contemporary young adult novels and nonfiction with commercial appeal. Nonfiction paperback originals. Query; unsolicited manuscripts accepted for picture books only.

HARLEQUIN BOOKS/CANADA—225 Duncan Mill Rd., Don Mills, Ont., Canada M3B 3K9. *Harlequin Romance:* Karen Stoecker, Sr. Ed. Contemporary romance novels, 50,000 to 60,000 words, any setting, ranging in plot from the traditional and gentle to the more sophisticated and sensuous. Query first. *Harlequin Presents:* Karen Stoecker, Sr. Ed. Romantic novels, 50,000 to 60,000 words, any setting. Query first. *Harlequin Regency and Gothic:* Maryan Gibson, Sr. Ed. Short, traditional novels set in the 19th century, 50,000 to 60,000 words. *Harlequin Historicals:* Margaret Carney, Sr. Ed. Long historical novels, 120,000 to 140,000 words, strongly sensual with good character development. *Harlequin Superromance:* Marsha Zinberg, Sr. Ed. Contemporary romance, 85,000 words, with North American or foreign setting. New writers: query first. Published writers: send manuscript, synopsis, and copy of published work. *Harlequin Temptation:* Lisa Boyes, Sr. Ed. Sensually charged contemporary romantic fantasies, 60,000 to 65,000 words. Send for tip sheets.

HARLEQUIN BOOKS/U.S.—300 E. 42nd St., 6th Fl., New York, NY 10017. *Harlequin American Romance:* Debra Matteucci, Sr. Ed. Contemporary romances, 70,000 to 75,000 words, with American setting and American characters. *Harlequin Romantic Intrigue:* Reva Kindser, Ed. Contemporary romances, 70,000 to 75,000 words, set against backdrop of suspense and adventure. Query. Send for tip sheets. Paperback.

HARPER & ROW—10 E. 53rd St., New York, NY 10022. Fiction, nonfiction, biography, economics, etc.: address Trade Dept. College texts: address College Dept. Nonfiction paperback originals: address Paperback Dept. Religion, theology, etc.: address Religious Books Dept., Ice House One, 151 Union St., San Francisco, CA 94111. No unsolicited manuscripts; query only. Royalty.

HARPER JUNIOR BOOKS GROUP—10 E. 53rd St., New York, NY 10022. K. Magnisson, Admin. Coord. *West Coast:* P. O. Box 6549, San Pedro, CA 90734. Linda Zuckerman, Exec. Ed. (Query one address only.) Juvenile fiction, nonfiction and picture books imprints include: *Thomas Y. Crowell Co., Publishers:* juveniles, etc.; *J. B. Lippincott Co.:* juveniles, picture books, etc.; *Harper & Row:* juveniles, picture books, etc.; *Trophy Books:* paperback juveniles. All publish from preshool to young adult titles. Query. Royalty.

HARVEST HOUSE PUBLISHERS—1075 Arrowsmith, Eugene, OR 97402. Eileen L. Mason, Ed. Nonfiction—how-to's, educational, health—with evangelical theme. No biographies, history or poetry. Query first. SASE required.

HASTINGS HOUSE, PUBLISHERS—c/o Kampmann & Company, 9 E. 40th St., New York, NY 10016. Nonfiction and juveniles. Query with outline and sample chapters. Royalty.

HEALTH PLUS PUBLISHERS—Box 22001, Phoenix, AZ 85028. Paula E. Clure, Ed. Books on health and fitness. Query with outline and sample chapters. Royalty.

HEARST BOOKS and **HEARST MARINE BOOKS**—See *William Morrow and Co.*

HEARTFIRE ROMANCES (Imprint of *Zebra Books*)—425 Park Ave. S., New York, NY 10016. Leslie Gelbman, Ed. Dir. "These historical romances revolve around an innocent heroine who becomes involved with an older, more experienced hero. The books must be 'filled with passion' though 'crass vulgarity' is out; manuscript length, 125,000 words." Query with sample chapters and outline. Royalty.

D. C. HEATH & COMPANY—125 Spring St., Lexington, MA 02173. Textbooks for schools and colleges. Professional books (*Lexington Books* division). Software and related educational material. Query Bruce Zimmerli, College; Albert Bursma, School; Robert Bovenschulte, Lexington Books; Daniel Caton, Collamore Educational Publishing.

IRMA HELDMAN BOOKS (Imprint of *Lyle Stuart, Inc.*)—275 Central Park West, New York, NY 10024. Irma Heldman, Ed. Mystery and suspense fiction. "In addition, I will be looking for mainstream fiction and some nonfiction. I want to be queried only regarding nonfiction, where subject matter is as important as writing quality. For fiction, I prefer whole manuscripts to outlines and/or sample chapters. Manuscripts should be 65,000 words or more. All submissions should be accompanied by an SASE—no checks to cover postage, please."

HERALD PRESS—616 Walnut Ave., Scottdale, PA 15683. Paul M. Schrock, General Book Editor. Christian books for adults and children (age 9 and up): inspiration, Bible study, self-help, devotionals, current issues, peace studies, church history, missions and evangelism, family life. Send one-page summary and sample chapter. Royalty.

HEROICA BOOKS—4286 Redwood Highway, San Rafael, CA 94903. Judith Bonair, Ed. Adult fiction and nonfiction, 50,000 to 60,000 words. No poetry. Query required. All unsolicited manuscripts will be returned unopened. Royalty.

HOLIDAY HOUSE, INC.—18 E. 53rd St., New York, NY 10022. Margery S. Cuyler, Vice Pres. General juvenile and young-adult fiction and nonfiction. Royalty. Query with outline and sample chapter. Hardcover only.

HENRY HOLT AND CO.—521 Fifth Ave., New York, NY 10175. John Macrae, Ed.-in-Chief. Fiction and nonfiction (mysteries, history, autobiographies, national history, travel, business, art, and how-to) of highest literary quality. *Books for Young Readers:* Julie Amper, Senior Ed. Fiction for readers ages 8 to 12; nonfiction for ages 7 to 10; fantasy and science fiction for all ages. Royalty. Query with SASE required.

HOUGHTON MIFFLIN COMPANY—2 Park St., Boston, MA 02108. Fiction: literary, mainstream, historical, suspense and science fiction. Nonfiction: history, biography. Query Submissions Dept. with SASE. Children's Book Division, address Walter Lorraine: picture books, fiction and nonfiction for all ages. Query. Royalty.

H. P. BOOKS (Division of *Price Stern Sloan, Inc.*)—575 East River Rd., Tucson, AZ 85704. Rick Bailey, Pub. Illustrated how-to's, 50,000 to 80,000 words, on cooking, gardening, photography, health & fitness, etc. Royalty. Query.

HUNTER PUBLISHING, INC.—155 Riverside Dr., New York, NY 10024. Michael Hunter, Ed. Travel guides. Query with outline.

IMPACT BOOKS—2 Park Ave., New York, NY 10016. Jonathan Eisen, Ed. Dir. Books on world affairs, science, consumer issues, how-to topics. Query. Royalty.

JAMESON BOOKS—722 Columbus St., Ottawa, IL 61350. J. G. Campaigne, Pres. American historical fiction for "Frontier Library" series. Some nonfiction. Query with outline and sample chapters. Royalty.

JOHNSON BOOKS, INC.—1880 S. 57th Ct., Boulder, CO 80301. Michael McNierney, Ed. Nonfiction: western history, archaeology, geology, natural history, outdoor guidebooks, fly fishing, regional. Royalty. Query.

JOVE BOOKS—200 Madison Ave., New York, NY 10016. Fiction and nonfiction. No unsolicited manuscripts.

JOY STREET BOOKS (Imprint of *Little, Brown & Co.*)—34 Beacon St., Boston, MA 02108. Melanie Kroupa, Ed.-in-Chief. Juvenile fiction (especially for 8- to 12-year-olds), humor, and nonfiction (biographies, sports, science, nature, and history). Query with outline and sample chapters for nonfiction; send complete manuscript for fiction. Royalty.

KEATS PUBLISHING, INC.—27 Pine St., Box 876, New Canaan, CT 06840. An Keats, Ed. Nonfiction: health, inspiration, how-to. Royalty. Query.

ALFRED A. KNOPF, INC.—201 E. 50th St., New York, NY 10022. Sonny Mehta, Pres./Ed.-in-Chief. Distinguished fiction and general nonfiction. Query. *Books for Young Readers:* Frances Foster, Anne Schwartz, Senior Eds. Fiction and nonfiction for children and teens (to age 14), as well as picture books (ages 2 to 10), and humor/poetry. Query for nonfiction; complete manuscript for fiction. Royalty.

JOHN KNOX PRESS—341 Ponce de Leon Ave., N.E., Atlanta, GA 30365. Walter Sutton, Ed. Dir. Books that inform, interpret, challenge and encourage Christian faith and living. Royalty. Send SASE for "Guidelines for a Book Proposal."

LAUREL-LEAF BOOKS—See *Dell Publishing Co.*

LEISURE BOOKS—Dorchester Publishing Co., 6 E. 39th St., New York, NY 10016. Katherine Carlon, Ed. Historical romance novels, from 100,000 words; contemporary women's fiction, from 90,000 words; sensuous historical romantic suspense novels, from 80,000 words. Horror novels, from 80,000 words. Submit query, synopsis, and sample chapters. Royalty or flat fee.

HAL LEONARD BOOKS—Box 13819, 8112 W. Bluemound Rd., Milwaukee, WI 53213. Glenda Herro, Ed. Adult nonfiction; juvenile nonfiction, picture books, and young adult. Prefer subjects related to music and entertainment. Query first. Royalty or flat fee.

LEXINGTON BOOKS—See *D. C. Heath & Co.*

J. B. LIPPINCOTT COMPANY—See *Harper Junior Books Group.*

LITTLE BROWN AND COMPANY—34 Beacon St., Boston, MA 02106.

Address Ed. Dept., Trade Division. Fiction, general nonfiction, sports books; divisions for law, medical and college texts. Royalty. Submissions only from authors who have previously published in professional or literary journals, newspapers or magazines. Query first. *Children's Books:* John Keller, Pub. Maria Modugno, Ed.-in-Chief. "We'll consider fiction (from fantasy and romance to young adult and mystery), nonfiction (including science, history, and nature), picture books (for ages 3–8), and humor/poetry (for ages 8–10). Specific genre doesn't matter as much as the quality of the writing. We prefer complete manuscripts (with SASEs!) to queries."

LODESTAR BOOKS (Div. of *E. P. Dutton*)—2 Park Ave., New York, NY 10016. Virginia Buckley, Ed. Dir. Rosemary Brosnan, Ed. Young adult and middle-grade fiction and nonfiction. Nonfiction picture books. Submit proposal for nonfiction, complete manuscript for fiction. Royalty.

LOTHROP, LEE & SHEPARD BOOKS (Imprint of *William Morrow & Co., Inc.*)—105 Madison Ave., New York, NY 10016. Dorothy Briley, Ed.-in-Chief. Juvenile, picture books, fiction and nonfiction. Royalty. Query.

LOVESWEPT (Imprint of *Bantam Books*)—666 Fifth Ave., New York, NY 10019. Carolyn Nichols, Assoc. Pub. Highly sensual, adult contemporary romances, approx. 55,000 words. Study field before submitting. Query required. Paperback only.

NICK LYONS BOOKS—31 W. 21st St., New York, NY 10010. Peter Burford, Ed. Nonfiction books on the outdoors, including natural history, sports, fishing, and hunting. Query first with outline and sample chapters. Pays royalty.

MARGARET K. MCELDERRY BOOKS—Macmillan Publishers, 866 Third Ave., New York, NY 10022. Margaret K. McElderry, Ed. "We look for originality and quality of craftsmanship. I'm interested in fiction (including fantasy, science fiction, and YA) and some nonfiction and humor—all geared to ages 8–12; 10–14; and 12 and up. I'll also consider picture books (from ages 3 and up); don't submit artwork, and no rhymed verse, please." Query with SASE. Royalty. Hardcover.

MCGRAW-HILL BOOK CO.—11 W. 19th St., 3rd Floor, New York, NY 10011. Fiction and nonfiction. No unsolicited manuscripts. Queries only.

DAVID MCKAY COMPANY—201 E. 50th St., New York, NY 10022. Richard T. Scott, Pub. Nonfiction. Unsolicited manuscripts neither acknowledged nor returned.

MACMILLAN PUBLISHING CO., INC.—866 Third Ave., New York, NY 10022. General Books Division: Religious, sports, science and reference books. No fiction or general nonfiction. Paperbacks, *Collier Books.* College texts and professional books in social sciences, humanities, address *The Free Press.* Royalty. Submit through agent only.

MADRONA PUBLISHERS, INC.—P. O. Box 22667, Seattle, WA 98122. Sara Levant, Acquisitions Ed. General-interest nonfiction trade books (no poetry, children's books or fiction). Royalty.

MEADOWBROOK, INC.—18318 Minnetonka Blvd., Deephaven, MN 55391. Elizabeth C. Barnet, Ed. "Upbeat, useful" books on pregnancy, childbirth, and parenting. Also publishes travel books, humorous books (in good taste), and some fiction. All are in the 60,000-word range. Query with outline and sample chapters. "Be sure to enclose self-addressed envelope with postage sufficient for return of all material." Pays by outright purchase or on royalty basis.

MENTOR BOOKS—See *New American Library.*

MERCURY HOUSE—P. O. Box 640, Forest Knolls, CA 94933. Mrs. Alev Lytle, Exec. Ed. Adult fiction and nonfiction, 250 to 350 pages. Query with outline and sample chapters. Royalty.

MEREDITH CORP., BOOK GROUP *(Better Homes and Gardens Books)*—1716 Locust St., Des Moines, IA 50336. David A. Kirchner, Man. Ed. Address The Editors. Books on gardening, crafts, health, decorating, etc. Outright purchase. Query with outline and sample chapter.

JULIAN MESSNER (Div. of *Simon & Schuster*)—1230 Ave. of the Americas, New York, NY 10020. Jane Steltenpohl, Exec. Ed. High-interest, curriculum-oriented nonfiction. General nonfiction for junior and senior high, about 30,000 words. Royalty basis.

MILLER ACCOUNTING PUBLICATIONS, INC.—See *Harcourt Brace Jovanovich.*

MINSTREL BOOKS (Imprint of *Simon & Schuster*)—1230 Ave. of the Americas, New York, NY 10020. Fiction for girls and boys ages 7 to 11. Query first with detailed plot outline, sample chapter, and SASE. No unsolicited manuscripts. Royalty.

MOREHOUSE-BARLOW CO., INC.—78 Danbury Rd., Wilton, CT 06897. E. Allen Kelley, Pub. Theology, pastoral care, church administration, spirituality, Anglican studies, history of religion, etc. Royalty or outright purchase. Query with outline, contents, and sample chapter.

WILLIAM MORROW AND CO., INC.—105 Madison Ave., New York, NY 10016. Sherry Arden, Pub. Adult fiction and nonfiction. No unsolicited manuscripts. *Morrow Junior Books:* David Reuther, Ed.-in-Chief. Children's books for all ages. *Hearst Marine Books:* Connie Roosevelt, Ed. *Hearst Books:* Ann Bramson, Ed. General nonfiction. Submit through agent only.

MORROW QUILL PAPERBACKS (Div. of *William Morrow*)—105 Madison Ave., New York, NY 10016. Andrew Ambraziejus, Man. Ed. Trade paperbacks. Adult nonfiction. No unsolicited manuscripts.

THE MOUNTAINEERS BOOKS—306 Second Ave. W., Seattle, WA 98119. Ann Cleeland, Man. Ed. Nonfiction on mountaineering, backpacking, canoeing, kayaking, bicycling, skiing. Field guides, regional histories, biographies of outdoor people; accounts of expeditions. Nature books. Royalty. Submit sample chapters and outline.

MULTNOMAH PRESS—10209 SE Division St., Portland, OR 97266. Rodney L. Morris, Ed. Man. Conservative, evangelical nonfiction. Send outline and sample chapters. Royalty.

THE MYSTERIOUS PRESS—129 W. 56th St., New York, NY 10019. William Malloy, Man. Ed. Mystery/suspense novels. Query with synopsis. SASE.

NAL BOOKS (Div. of *New American Library*)—1633 Broadway, New York, NY 10019. Michaela Hamilton, Ed. Dir. Fiction and nonfiction books. Manuscripts and proposals accepted only from agents or upon personal recommendation.

NATUREGRAPH PUBLISHERS—P. O. Box 1075, Happy Camp, CA 96039. Barbara Brown, Ed. Nonfiction: Native American culture, natural history, outdoor living, land and gardening, holistic learning and health, Indian lore, crafts and how-to. Royalty. Query.

THOMAS NELSON INC.—Nelson Place at Elm Hill Pike, Nashville, TN 37214. Bruce A. Nygren, Ed. Dir. Religious adult nonfiction. Royalty. Query with outline and sample chapters.

NEW AMERICAN LIBRARY—1633 Broadway, New York, NY 10019. Pay Taylor, Ed. *Signet Books:* Commercial fiction: historicals, sagas, thrillers, action/adventure, mysteries, westerns. Nonfiction: self-help, how-to, etc. *Plume Books:* Nonfiction: hobbies, business, health, cooking, child care, psychology, etc. *Mentor Books:* Nonfiction originals for high school and college market. Royalty. No unsolicited manuscripts.

NEW REPUBLIC BOOKS (Imprint of *Basic Books*)—10 E. 53rd St., New York, NY 10022. Steve Wasserman, Ed.-in-Chief. Books on politics, contemporary affairs, history, and biography. Query. Royalty.

NEW YORK GRAPHIC SOCIETY BOOKS/LITTLE, BROWN AND CO.—34 Beacon St., Boston, MA 02108. Books on fine arts and photography. Query with outline or proposal and vita. Royalty.

NEWMARKET PRESS—18 E. 48th St., New York, NY 10017. Theresa Burns, Man. Ed. Books on health, self-help, child care, parenting, sports, biography, and cultural history. Some fiction. Query with outline and sample chapters. Royalty.

W. W. NORTON & COMPANY, INC.—500 Fifth Ave., New York, NY 10110. H. Hinzmann, Ed. Fiction and nonfiction. Royalty. Query with synopsis, 2 to 3 chapters, and resume. SASE required.

OAK TREE PUBLICATIONS—9601 Aero Dr., San Diego, CA 92123. Juvenile books for ages preschool to 8: picture books, pop-ups, unique craft, activity, and adventure books for children. Royalty. Query with synopsis, outline, illustrations and credentials. SASE required.

101 PRODUCTIONS—834 Mission St., San Francisco, CA 94103. Jacqueline Killeen, Ed. Nonfiction: gardening, domestic arts, travel. Royalty. Query; no unsolicited manuscripts. Softcover only.

OPEN COURT PUBLISHING COMPANY—Box 599, Peru, IL 61354. Scholarly books on philosophy, psychology, religion, oriental thought, history, public policy, and related topics. Send complete manuscript with outline and resume. Royalty.

ORCHARD BOOKS (Imprint of *Franklin Watts*)—387 Park Ave., New York, NY 10016. Sandra Jordan, Ed.-in-Chief. Hardcover picture books and fiction for juveniles; fiction for young adults. Submit complete manuscript. Royalty.

OSBORNE/MCGRAW-HILL—2600 Tenth St., Berkeley, CA 94710. Cynthia Hudson, Ed.-in-Chief. Microcomputer books for a general audience. Query. Royalty.

OXFORD UNIVERSITY PRESS—200 Madison Ave., New York, NY 10016. Authoritative books on literature, history, philosophy, etc.; college textbooks, medical, and reference books. Royalty. Query.

OXMOOR HOUSE, INC.—Box 2262, Brimingham, AL 35201. John

Logue, Ed. Nonfiction: art, photography, gardening, decorating, cooking and crafts. Royalty.

PACER BOOKS FOR YOUNG ADULTS (Imprint *Berkley Publishing Group*)—200 Madison Ave., New York, NY 10016. Fiction: adventure, fantasy, and role-playing fantasy gamebooks. No unsolicited manuscripts; queries only. Address Hillary Cige. Softcover only.

PACER BOOKS FOR YOUNG ADULTS (Imprint *Putnam Publishing Group*)—51 Madison Ave., New York, NY 10010. Fiction: adventure, fantasy, humor and non-formula romance. Query: attn. Anne O'Connell. Hardcover only.

PACIFIC SEARCH PRESS—222 Dexter Ave. N., Seattle, WA 98109. Carolyn Threadgill, Dir. of Books. Crafts, natural history, travel, outdoor recreation, cooking. Royalty. Query; no unsolicited manuscripts.

PANTHEON BOOKS (Div. of *Random House*)—201 E. 50th St., New York, NY 10022. Address Helena Franklin. Nonfiction: academic level for general reader on history, political science, sociology, etc.; picture books; folklore. Some fiction. Royalty. Query; no unsolicited manuscripts.

PARENTING PRESS—7744 31st Ave., N.E., Seattle, WA 98115. Shari Steelsmith, Ed. Parenting and child guidance books, 78,000 words, as well as social skills building books, 600 to 1,000 words, for children preschool to age 10. Query. Royalty.

PARKER PUBLISHING COMPANY, INC.—West Nyack, NY 10994. James Bradler, Pres. Self-help and how-to books, 65,000 words: health, money opportunities, business, etc. Royalty.

PEACHTREE PUBLISHERS, LTD.—494 Armour Circle, N.E., Atlanta, GA 30324. Church Perry, Exec. Ed. General fiction and nonfiction. Humor, cooking, gardening, health, how-to, travel, sports and recreation. No religious material, sf/fantasy, romance, supernatural/horror fiction, mystery/detective fiction. No business, scientific, technical books. Query, with sample chapters and an outline for nonfiction, complete manuscript for fiction.

PELICAN PUBLISHING CO., INC.—1101 Monroe St., Gretna, LA 70053. James L. Calhoun, Exec. Ed. General nonfiction: Americana, regional, architecture, how-to, travel, cookbooks, inspirational, motivational, music, parenting, etc. Juvenile fiction. Royalty.

PELION PRESS—See *The Rosen Publishing Group.*

PENGUIN BOOKS (Div. of *Viking/Penguin, Inc.*)—40 W. 23rd St., New York, NY 10010. Christine Pevitt, Ed.-in-Chief. Adult fiction and nonfiction. Royalty. No unsolicited material.

PHILOMEL BOOKS (Div. of *Putnam Publishing Group*)—51 Madison Ave., New York, NY 10010. Victoria Rock, Ed. Juvenile trade, picture books, and young adult fiction and nonfiction. "We seek works that are fresh and original, with compelling characters and a truly childlike spirit." Query. Royalty.

THE PILGRIM PRESS/UNITED CHURCH PRESS—132 W. 31 St., New York, NY 10001. Larry E. Kalp, Pub. Religious and general-interest nonfiction. Royalty. Query with outline and sample chapters.

PINEAPPLE PRESS—P. O. Box 314, Englewood, FL 33533. June Cussen, Ed. Serious fiction and nonfiction, 60,000 to 125,000 words. Query with outline and sample chapters. Royalty.

PLENUM PUBLISHING CORP.—233 Spring St., New York, NY 10013. Linda Greenspan Regan, Ed. Nonfiction, 200 to 300 pages, on scientific and social scientific topics. Royalty. Query required. Hardcover only.

PLUME BOOKS—See *New American Library.*

POCKET BOOKS (Div. of *Simon and Schuster*)—1230 Ave. of the Americas, New York, NY 10020. William R. Grose, Ed. Dir. Some original fiction and nonfiction. Query with outline; no unsolicited manuscripts. Royalty.

POINT BOOKS—See *Scholastic, Inc.*

POSEIDON PRESS (Imprint of *Pocket Books*)—1230 Ave. of the Americas, New York, NY 10020. Ann Patty, V. P. & Pub. General fiction and nonfiction. Royalty. No unsolicited material.

CLARKSON N. POTTER, INC.—225 Park Ave. S., New York, NY 10003. Carol Southern, Ed. Dir. General trade books. Submissions accepted through agents.

PRAEGER PUBLISHERS (Div. of *Greenwood Press*)—521 Fifth Ave., New York, NY 10175. Ron Chambers, Pub. General nonfiction; scholarly and reference books. Royalty. Query with outline.

PRENTICE HALL PRESS (Div. of *Simon and Schuster*)—Gulf & Western Bldg., New York, NY 10023. General nonfiction. Queries only. Address Editorial Dept. Royalty.

PRESIDIO PRESS—31 Pamaron Way, Novato, CA 94947. Nonfiction: contemporary military history, from 50,000 words. Selected fiction with military background. Royalty. Query.

PRICE/STERN/SLOAN PUBLISHERS, INC.—360 N. La Cienega Blvd., Los Angeles, CA 90048. L. Spencer Humphrey, Ed. Humor, self-help, and juvenile books. Royalty or outright purchase. Query only.

PRUETT PUBLISHING COMPANY—2928 Pearl, Boulder, CO 80301. Gerald Keenan, Man. Ed. Nonfiction: railroadiana, Western U.S. travel and adventure. Royalty. Query.

PUFFIN BOOKS—See *Viking/Penguin.*

G. P. PUTNAM'S SONS (Div. of *Putnam Publishing Group*)—200 Madison Ave., New York, NY 10016. General fiction and nonfiction. No unsolicited manuscripts or queries.

QUEST BOOKS (Imprint of *The Theosophical Publishing House*)—306 W. Geneva Rd., P. O. Box 270, Wheaton, IL 60189-0270. Shirley Nicholson, Senior Ed. Nonfiction books on Eastern and Western religion and philosophy, holism, healing, meditation, yoga, astrology. Royalty. Query.

QUINLAN PRESS—131 Beverly St., Boston, MA 02114. Sandra E. Bielawa, Exec. Ed. General nonfiction. Query with SASE required. Royalty.

RAINTREE PUBLISHERS INC.—310 W. Wisconsin Ave., Milwaukee, WI 53203. Address Ed. Dept. Juveniles: information and reference books; nonfiction and fiction picture books. Outright purchase or royalty. Query.

RAND MCNALLY & COMPANY—Publishing Group, Editorial Department, 8255 N. Central Park Ave., Skokie, IL 60076. World and U.S. atlases and maps; travel and reference directories; rated publications. Royalty or outright purchase. Query with SASE required.

RANDOM HOUSE, INC.—201 E. 50th St., New York, NY 10022. Joni Evans, Pub. Jason Epstein, Ed. Dir. Janet Schulman, Ed.-in-Chief, Juvenile Books; Stuart Flexner, Ed.-in-Chief, Reference Books. General fiction and nonfiction; reference and college textbooks; juvenile fiction and nonfiction for *Step Into Reading Books* (beginning readers); fiction for 7- to 9-year-olds for *Stepping Stone Books;* picture books, easy-to-read material. Royalty. Query with three chapters and outline for nonfiction; complete manuscript for fiction.

RAWSON ASSOCIATES (Div. of *The Scribner Book Cos.*)—115 Fifth Ave., New York, NY 10003. Kennett L. Rawson, Pres. General nonfiction. Royalty. Query.

REGNERY GATEWAY—1130 17th St., NW, Suite 620, Washington, DC 20036. Hardcover and trade paperback nonfiction on public policy, politics and international issues. Royalty. Query.

RENAISSANCE HOUSE—541 Oak St., P. O. Box 177, Frederick, CO 80530. Eleanor H. Ayer, Ed. Western Americana, World War II, and Rocky Mountain West; biographies and historical books. Submit outline, two sample chapters, and short bio. Royalty.

FLEMING H. REVELL COMPANY—Old Tappan, NJ 07675. Gary A. Sledge, V. P. and Ed.-in-Chief. Inspirational and devotional religious books. Royalty. Query required.

REWARD BOOKS (Div. of *Prentice-Hall*)—Englewood Cliffs, NJ 07632. Ted Nardin, V. P. Nonfiction, how-to, and reference books on business, self-improvement, education, and technical subjects. Hardcover and paperback. Royalty.

RODALE PRESS, BOOK DIVISION—33 E. Minor St., Emmaus, PA 18098. Thomas Woll, Pub. Nonfiction: health, nutrition, alternative energy, gardening; woodworking, sports, fitness, etc. Royalty or outright purchase. Query.

THE ROSEN PUBLISHING GROUP, INC.—29 E. 21st St., New York, NY 10010. Roger Rosen, Pres. Ruth C. Rosen, Ed. Young adult novels, and nonfiction, to 40,000 words, on vocational guidance, journalism, theater, self-help, etc. *Pelion Press:* music, art, history. Pays varying rates.

RUTLEDGE HILL PRESS—513 Third Ave. S., Nashville, TN 37210. Ronald E. Pitkin, Ed. Fiction and nonfiction of Southern interest. Send outline and sample chapters. Pays royalty.

ST. ANTHONY MESSENGER PRESS—1615 Republic St., Cincinnati, OH 45210. Karen Hurley, Man. Ed. Inspirational nonfiction that "support Christian life styles in our culture. We want to be 'popularizers' in the best sense of the word." Subjects of interest include religious education, practical spirituality, and aids for prayer. Query with 500-word summary. Pays royalty.

ST. MARTIN'S PRESS—175 Fifth Ave., New York, NY 10010. General adult fiction (including science fiction and horror, two new lines) and nonfiction. Royalty. Query first.

SANDLAPPER PUBLISHING, INC.—P. O. Box 1932, Orangeburg, SC 29116-1932. Frank N. Handal, Pub. Books on South Carolina history, culture, and cuisine. Submit query with outline and sample chapters. Royalty.

SCHOCKEN BOOKS (Imprint of *Pantheon Books*)—201 E. 50th St., New

York, NY 10022. General nonfiction: family, health, history, Judaica, women's studies, etc. Royalty. Query.

SCHOLASTIC, INC.—730 Broadway, New York, NY 10003. *Point:* Brenda Bowen, Senior Ed. Young adult fiction for readers age 12 and up. *Apple Books:* Brenda Bowen, Senior Ed. Fiction for readers age 9 to 12. Query with outline and sample chapter. Royalty basis. *Sunfire,* Ann Reit, Ed., American historical romances for girls 12 and up, 55,000 words. Query with outline and three sample chapters. Write for tip sheets.

SCOTT, FORESMAN & COMPANY—1900 E. Lake Ave., Glenview, IL 60025. Richard T. Morgan, Pres. Elementary, secondary, and college textbooks and materials. Royalty.

CHARLES SCRIBNER'S SONS (Subsidiary of *Macmillan Publishing Co.*)—866 Third Ave., New York, NY 10022. Robert Stewart, Ed.-in-Chief. Susanne Kirk, Exec. Ed. "We do about 40 titles a year in serious fiction, biography, history, science, music, psychology, current affairs, and other nonfiction areas. We also publish mysteries." Query first. *Children's Books:* Clare Costello, Ed. Fiction (including fantasy, mystery, young adult, science fiction, and problem novels), picture books (age 5 and up), and nonfiction (science and how-to). Query with outline and sample chapter. Royalty.

SEAVER BOOKS—333 Central Park W., New York, NY 10025. Jeannette W. Seaver, Pub. Trade fiction, nonfiction. Accepts no unsolicited manuscripts. Royalty. Query.

SERENADE/SERENATA and **SERENADE/SAGA ROMANCES** (Imprints of *Zondervan Publishing House*)—1415 Lake Dr. S.E., Grand Rapids, MI 49506. Inspirational romances, 80,000 words, for Christian readers. *Serenade/ Serenata:* Contemporary. *Serenade/Saga, Serenade/SuperSaga:* historical. Royalty. Send sample chapter, outline, synopsis and biographical sketch. Send SASE for tip sheet.

SEVEN SEAS PRESS—International Marine, 21 Elm St., Camden, ME 04843. Jonathan Eaton, Man. Ed. Books on boating (both sailing and power), other marine topics. Query first. Royalty.

SIERRA CLUB BOOKS—730 Polk St., San Francisco, CA 94109. Nonfiction: environment, natural history, the sciences; outdoors and regional guidebooks; juvenile fiction and nonfiction. Royalty. Query with SASE.

SIGN OF THE DRAGON—See *Baen Books.*

SIGNET BOOKS—See *New American Library.*

SIGNET VISTA (Imprint of *New American Library*)—1633 Broadway, New York, NY 10019. Susan Donovan, Ed. Contemporary teen fiction and nonfiction, 45,000 to 50,000 words. No tip sheet. No unsolicited manuscripts. Royalty. Paperback only.

SILHOUETTE BOOKS—300 E. 42nd St., New York, NY 10017. Karen Solem, Ed.-in-Chief. *Silhouette Romances:* Mary Tara Hughes, Sr. Ed. Contemporary romances, 53,000 to 58,000 words. *Special Edition:* Leslie Kazanjian, Sr. Ed. Sophisticated contemporary romances, 70,000 to 80,000 words. *Silhouette Desire:* Isabel Swift, Sr. Ed. Sensuous contemporary romances, 53,000 to 58,000 words. *Intimate Moments:* Leslie Wainger, Sr. Ed. Sensuous, sophisticated contemporary romances, 80,000 to 85,000 words. Query with synopsis and SASE to appropriate editor.

SILVER BURDETT PRESS—250 James St., Morristown, NJ 07960. Walter

744

Kossmann, Product Development Ed. Nonfiction for children pre-school through twelfth grade: mathematics, biography, emotional/behavioral problems, sports, music, nature, and history. Query with outline and sample chapter. Royalty.

SIMON & SCHUSTER—1230 Ave. of the Americas, New York, NY 10020. No unsolicited material.

SLAWSON COMMUNICATIONS—3719 Sixth Ave., San Diego, CA 92103. Leslie S. Smith, Ed. Avant Books: Business; health and fitness. Microtrend: computer topics. Mad Hatter Press: Children's books with emphasis on the preschool market. Query with SASE. Royalty.

GIBBS M. SMITH, INC./PEREGRINE SMITH BOOKS—P. O. Box 667, Layton, UT 84041. Madge Baird, Trade Ed. Adult and juvenile fiction and nonfiction. Query. Royalty.

SOHO PRESS—One Union Sq., New York, NY 10003. Juris Jurjevics, Ed. Adult fiction and nonfiction, from 75,000 words. Send query with outline and sample chapters or complete manuscript. Royalty.

SOS PUBLICATIONS—4223-25 W. Jefferson Blvd., Los Angeles, CA 90016. S. Paul Bradley, Pub./Ed. Novels, mystery, romance, and adventure, from 85,000 words, for "Mini-Bound" series. Royalty.

SPECTRA BOOKS (Imprint of *Bantam Books*)—666 Fifth Ave., New York, NY 10103. Lou Aronica, Pub. & Sr. Ed. Science fiction and fantasy, with emphasis on story-telling and characterization. Query; no unsolicited manuscripts. Royalty.

STANDARD PUBLISHING—8121 Hamilton Ave., Cincinnati, OH 45231. Address Mark Plunkett. Fiction: juveniles based on Bible or with moral tone. Nonfiction: biblical, Christian education. Conservative evangelical. Query preferred.

STEIN AND DAY—Scarborough House, Briarcliff Manor, NY 10510. Address Editorial Dept. Adult general fiction and nonfiction. Royalty basis. Query with outline and sample chapter for nonfiction; descriptive letter, up to two pages, for fiction. No unsolicited manuscripts. SASE required.

STEMMER HOUSE—2627 Caves Rd., Owings Mills, MD 21117. Barbara Holdridge, Ed. Juvenile fiction and adult nonfiction. Royalty. Query.

STEP INTO READING BOOKS—See *Random House*.

STEPPING STONE BOOKS—See *Random House*.

STERLING PUBLISHING CO., INC.—Two Park Ave., New York, NY 10016. Burton Hobson, Pres./Ed. Dir. How-to, self-help, hobby, woodworking, health, craft, and sports books. Royalty and outright purchase. Query with outline, sample chapter, and sample of illustration.

STONE WALL PRESS—1241 30th St., N.W., Washington, DC 20007. Nonfiction on fishing, outdoors, conservation, 200 to 300 pages. Royalty. Query first.

STRAWBERRY HILL PRESS—2594 15th Ave., San Francisco, CA 94127. Carolyn Soto, Ed. Nonfiction: biography, autobiography, history, cooking, health, how-to, philosophy, performance arts, and Third World. Query first with sample chapters, outline, and SASE. Royalty.

LYLE STUART, INC.—120 Enterprise Ave., Secaucus, NJ 07094. Allan J.

Wilson, Ed. General fiction and nonfiction. *Citadel Press* division: biography, film, history, limited fiction. Royalty. Query; no unsolicited manuscripts.

SUMMIT BOOKS—1230 Ave. of the Americas, New York, NY 10020. James H. Silberman, Ed.-in-Chief. General-interest fiction and nonfiction. "We look for quality, which means to me the best of its kind—books that entertain or inform or teach. No subject is out of the question and certain subjects seem to turn up with some frequency: American politics, women's rights, books on Jewish subjects, fiction of some seriousness and very little fiction that could be described as category. A query on both fiction and nonfiction is absolutely essential." Royalty.

SUNFIRE—See *Scholastic, Inc.*

SWALLOW PRESS—P. O. Box 2080, Chicago, IL 60690. Self-help, history, biography. Contemporary novels. Western Americana. No unsolicited poetry or fiction. Royalty.

TAB BOOKS INC.—Blue Ridge Summit, PA 17214. Raymond A. Collins, Vice-Pres., Edit. Dept. Nonfiction: electronics, computer, how-to, aviation, business, solar and energy, science and technology, back to basics, automotive, marine and outdoor life. Fiction: military. Royalty or outright purchase. Query.

TAPLINGER PUBLISHING CO.—132 W. 22nd St., New York, NY 10011. Bobs Pinkerton, Roy Thomas, Eds. Serious literary fiction. General nonfiction: history, art, etc. Royalty.

JEREMY P. TARCHER, INC.—9110 Sunset Blvd., Los Angeles, CA 90069. Jeremy P. Tarcher, Ed.-in-Chief. General nonfiction: psychology, personal development, health and fitness, women's concerns, science for the layperson, etc. Royalty. Query with outline, sample chapter and SASE.

TAYLOR PUBLISHING CO.—1550 W. Mockingbird Ln., Dallas, TX 75235. Nonfiction: fine arts, regional, biography, cooking, gardening, sports and recreation, art/photo, and life style. Query with sample chapters and outline required. Royalty.

TEALE BOOKS—See *Dodd, Mead & Co.*

TEN SPEED PRESS—P. O. Box 7123, Berkeley, CA 94707. Kim Knutson, Ed. Self-help and how-to on careers, recreation, etc.; natural science, history, cookbooks. Query with outline and sample chapters. Royalty. Softcover only.

TEXAS MONTHLY PRESS—Box 1569, Austin, TX 78767. Scott Lubeck, Dir. Fiction, nonfiction, related to Texas or the Southwest: 60,000 words. Royalty.

THUNDER'S MOUTH PRESS—93-99 Greene St., New York, NY 10012. Neil Ortenberg, Ed. Literary fiction and poetry collections; books on historical and political topics. Query first. Length requirements: poetry, 96 pages; fiction, to 200 pages. Royalty.

TICKNOR & FIELDS (Subsidiary of *Houghton Mifflin Company*)—52 Vanderbilt Ave., New York, NY 10017. General nonfiction and fiction. Royalty.

TIMES BOOKS (Div. of *Random House, Inc.*)—201 E. 50th St., New York, NY 10022. Jonathan B. Segal, Ed. Dir. General nonfiction. No unsolicited manuscripts or queries accepted.

TOR BOOKS—49 W. 24th St., New York, NY 10010. Beth Meacham, Ed.-in-Chief: Science fiction and fantasy. Michael Seidman, Exec. Ed.: Thrillers, espionage, and mysteries. Melissa Ann Singer, Ed.: Horror and dark fantasy.

746

Wanda June Alexander, Asst. Ed.: Historicals. Length: from 60,000 words. Query with outline and sample chapters. Royalty.

TROLL ASSOCIATES—100 Corporate Dr., Mahwah, NJ 07430. M. Francis, Ed. Juvenile fiction and nonfiction. Royalty or outright purchase. Query preferred.

TROPHY BOOKS—See *Harper Junior Books Group.*

TROUBADOR PRESS—410 N. Cienega Blvd., Los Angeles, CA 90048. Juvenile illustrated games, activity, paper doll, coloring and cut-out books. Royalty or outright purchase. Query with outline and SASE.

TYNDALE HOUSE—336 Gundersen Dr., Box 80, Wheaton, IL 60189. Wendell Hawley, Ed.-in-Chief. Juvenile and adult fiction and nonfiction on subjects of concern to Christians. Submit complete manuscripts. Royalty.

UNION OF AMERICAN HEBREW CONGREGATIONS—838 Fifth Ave., New York, NY 10021. Bruce Black, Marketing Dir. Fiction and nonfiction from pre-school to adult. No poetry. Material that deals with traditional and controversial themes in Judaism that appeal to Jewish and non-Jewish readers. Query with detailed table of contents, outline, and sample chapter or complete manuscript.

UNIVERSE BOOKS—381 Park Ave. S., New York, NY 10016. Louis Barron, Vice-Pres. and Ed. Dir. Art, ballet, history, music, natural history, biographies, crafts, linguistics, design, social science, etc. Royalty. Query with SASE.

VAN NOSTRAND REINHOLD, INC.—115 Fifth Ave., New York, NY 10003. John Connolly, Pres. Business, professional, scientific, and technical publishers of applied reference works. *CBI Publishing Co.:* Food service and hospitality books. Royalty.

THE VANGUARD PRESS, INC.—424 Madison Ave., New York, NY 10017. Bernice Woll, Ed. Adult and juvenile fiction and nonfiction. Royalty. Query with sample chapters.

VIKING PENGUIN, INC.—40 W. 23rd St., New York, NY 10010-5201. Adult fiction and nonfiction. *Viking Kestral:* Children's hardcovers. *Penguin Books:* Adult fiction and nonfiction paperbacks. *Puffin Books:* Children's fiction and nonfiction paperbacks. *Frederick Warne:* Children's paperbacks. Royalty. No unsolicited material.

WALKER AND COMPANY—720 Fifth Ave., New York, NY 10019. Fiction: mysteries, men's action, westerns, Regency romance and espionage. Nonfiction: Americana, biography, history, science, and natural history, medicine, psychology, parenting, sports, outdoors, reference, popular science, self-help. Juveniles, Amy C. Shields, Ed.-in-Chief: "We are currently expanding our list, particularly in the nonfiction area. Biographies, as well as science, history, music, and nature titles are all of interest, as is fiction, including YA and problem novels." Query required. Royalty.

WALLACE-HOMESTEAD—580 Waters Edge, Lombard, IL 60148. William N. Topaz, General Man. Books on quilting, antiques and collectibles, and cooking. Submit query with outline. Royalty. Send for tip sheet.

WANDERER BOOKS (Div. of *Simon & Schuster, Inc.*)—1230 Ave. of the Americas, New York, NY 10020. Rose Lopez, Manuscript Ed. General-interest juveniles, for 8- to 14-year-olds: nonfiction, series fiction. Flat fee and royalty. Query with outline and sample chapter for nonfiction.

FREDERICK WARNE—See *Viking Penguin, Inc.*

WARNER BOOKS—666 Fifth Avenue, New York, NY 10103. Mel Parker, Ed.-in-Chief. Fiction: historical romance, contemporary women's fiction, unusual big-scale horror and suspense. Nonfiction: business books, health and nutrition, self-help and how-to books. Royalty. Query with sample chapters. Also publishes trade paperbacks and hardcover titles.

FRANKLIN WATTS, INC.—387 Park Ave. S., New York, NY 10016. Jeanne Vestal, Edit. Dir. Juvenile nonfiction. Ed Breslin, Ed.-in-Chief. Adult trade fiction and nonfiction. Royalty. Query. SASE required.

PETER WEED BOOKS—Beaufort Books, 9 E. 40th St., New York, NY 10016. Peter Weed, Ed. Fiction and nonfiction. No unsolicited manuscripts. Query first. Royalty.

WESTERN PUBLISHING CO., INC.—850 Third Ave., New York, NY 10022. Doris Duenewald, Pub., Children's Books; Rosanna Hanson, Ed.-in-Chief, Children's Books. Adult nonfiction: Field guides, cookbooks, etc. Children's books, fiction and nonfiction: picture books, storybooks, concept books, novelty books. Royalty and outright purchase. Query. Same address and requirements for *Golden Press.*

ALBERT WHITMAN—5747 W. Howart St., Niles, IL 60648. Kathleen Tucker, Ed. Picture books; novels, biographies, mysteries, and general nonfiction for middle-grade readers. Submit complete manuscript for picture books, three chapters and outline for longer fiction, query for nonfiction. Royalty.

WILDERNESS PRESS—2440 Bancroft Way, Berkeley, CA 94704. Thomas Winnett, Ed. Nonfiction: sports, recreation, and travel in the western U.S. Royalty.

WILSHIRE BOOK COMPANY—12015 Sherman Rd., North Hollywood, CA 91605. Inspirational fiction and nonfiction. Query with synopsis or outline. Royalty.

WINDSWEPT HOUSE PUBLISHERS—Box 159, Mt. Desert, ME 04660. Jeanne Merkel, Submissions Editor. Adult fiction and how-to books. Juvenile fiction, nonfiction, picture books, and young adult. Royalty.

WINGBOW PRESS—2929 Fifth St., Berkeley, CA 94710. Randy Fingland, Ed. Nonfiction: travel/guidebooks for Northern California, San Francisco Bay area, women's interests, health psychology, how-to. Query or sample chapter and outline preferred. Royalty.

WOODBINE HOUSE—10400 Connecticut Ave., Suite 512, Kensington, MD 20895. Terry Rosenberg, Ed. Nonfiction. Query with outline, sample chapter, and short biography. Royalty or outright purchase.

WORKMAN PUBLISHING CO., INC.—1 W. 39th St., New York, NY 10018. General nonfiction. Normal contractual terms based on agreement.

YANKEE BOOKS—Main St., Dublin, NH 03444. Sandra Taylor, Acquisitions Ed. Books relating to Northeastern U.S., cooking, crafts, photography, maritime subjects, travel, gardening, nature, nostalgia, humor, folklore and popular history. No scholarly history, highly technical work, or off-color humor. Regional New England fiction considered. Royalty. Query or send proposal.

YEARLING BOOKS—See *Dell Publishing Co., Inc.*

ZEBRA BOOKS—475 Park Ave. S., New York, NY 10016. Leslie Gelbman, Fiction Ed. Wendy McCurdy, Nonfiction Ed. Biography, how-to, humor, self-help. Fiction: adventure, regency, mainstream fiction, historical romance, gothic, historical, horror, etc. Query required.

CHARLOTTE ZOLOTOW BOOKS (Imprint of *Harper & Row*)—10 E. 53rd St., New York, NY 10022. Juvenile fiction and nonfiction "with integrity of purpose, beauty of language, and an out-of-ordinary look at ordinary thing*.*" Royalty.

ZONDERVAN PUBLISHING HOUSE—1415 Lake Dr., S.E., Grand Rapids, MI 49506. Lori Walburg, Manuscript Review Ed. Religious. General fiction and nonfiction; academic and professional books. Query with outline, sample chapter, and SASE. Royalty. Guidelines.

UNIVERSITY PRESSES

University presses generally publish books of a scholarly nature or of specialized interest by authorities in a given field. A few publish fiction and poetry. Many publish only a handful of titles a year. Always query first. Do not send any manuscripts until you have been invited to do so by the editor.

BRIGHAM YOUNG UNIVERSITY PRESS—209 University Press Bldg., Provo, UT 84602.

BUCKNELL UNIVERSITY PRESS—Lewisburg, PA 17837.

CAMBRIDGE UNIVERSITY PRESS—32 East 57th St., New York, NY 10022.

THE CATHOLIC UNIVERSITY OF AMERICA PRESS—620 Michigan Ave., N.E., Washington, DC 20064.

COLORADO ASSOCIATED UNIVERSITY PRESS—University of Colorado, 1344 Grandview Ave., Boulder, CO 80309.

COLUMBIA UNIVERSITY PRESS—562 West 113th St., New York, NY 10025.

DUKE UNIVERSITY PRESS—Box 6697, College Station, Durham, NC 27708.

DUQUESNE UNIVERSITY PRESS—600 Forbes Ave., Pittsburgh, PA 15282.

FORDHAM UNIVERSITY PRESS—University Box L, Bronx, NY 10458–5172.

GEORGIA STATE UNIVERSITY, COLLEGE OF BUSINESS ADMINISTRATION, BUSINESS PUBLISHING DIVISION—University Plaza, Atlanta, GA 30303.

HARVARD UNIVERSITY PRESS—79 Garden St., Cambridge, MA 02138.

INDIANA UNIVERSITY PRESS—10th and Morton Sts., Bloomington, IN 47401.

THE JOHNS HOPKINS UNIVERSITY PRESS—701 W. 40th St., Suite 275, Baltimore, MD 21211.

KENT STATE UNIVERSITY PRESS—Kent, OH 44242.

LOUISIANA STATE UNIVERSITY PRESS—Baton Rouge, LA 70893.

LOYOLA UNIVERSITY PRESS—3441 North Ashland Ave., Chicago, IL 60657.

MEMPHIS STATE UNIVERSITY PRESS—Memphis, TN 38152.

MICHIGAN STATE UNIVERSITY PRESS—1405 South Harrison Rd., East Lansing, MI 48823-5202.

THE MIT PRESS—55 Hayward St., Cambridge, MA 02142.

NEW YORK UNIVERSITY PRESS—Washington Sq., New York, NY 10003.

OHIO STATE UNIVERSITY PRESS—175 Mount Hall, 1050 Carmack Rd., Columbus, OH 43210.

OHIO UNIVERSITY PRESS—Scott Quadrangle, Athens, OH 45701.

OREGON STATE UNIVERSITY PRESS—101 Waldo Hall, Corvallis, OR 97331.

THE PENNSYLVANIA STATE UNIVERSITY PRESS—215 Wagner Bldg., University Park, PA 16802.

PRINCETON UNIVERSITY PRESS—Princeton, NJ 08540.

RUTGERS UNIVERSITY PRESS—109 Church St., New Brunswick, NJ 08901.

SOUTHERN ILLINOIS UNIVERSITY PRESS—Box 3697, Carbondale, IL 62901.

SOUTHERN METHODIST UNIVERSITY PRESS—Box 415, Dallas, TX 75275.

STANFORD UNIVERSITY PRESS—Stanford, CA 94305.

STATE UNIVERSITY OF NEW YORK PRESS—State Univ. Plaza, Albany, NY 12246.

SYRACUSE UNIVERSITY PRESS—1600 Jamesville Ave., Syracuse, NY 13244-5160.

TEMPLE UNIVERSITY PRESS—Broad and Oxford Sts., Philadelphia, PA 19122.

UNIVERSITY OF ALABAMA PRESS—Drawer 2877, University, AL 35486.

UNIVERSITY OF ARIZONA PRESS—Box 3398, College Station, Tucson, AZ 85722.

UNIVERSITY OF CALIFORNIA PRESS—2120 Berkeley Way, Berkeley, CA 94720.

UNIVERSITY OF CHICAGO PRESS—5801 Ellis Ave., Chicago, IL 60637.

UNIVERSITY OF GEORGIA PRESS—Athens, GA 30602.

UNIVERSITY OF ILLINOIS PRESS—54 E. Gregory Dr., Champaign, IL 61820.

UNIVERSITY OF MASSACHUSETTS PRESS—Box 429, Amherst, MA 01002.

UNIVERSITY OF MICHIGAN PRESS—Ann Arbor, MI 48106.

UNIVERSITY OF MINNESOTA PRESS—2037 University Ave., S.E., Minneapolis, MN 55455.

UNIVERSITY OF MISSOURI PRESS—200 Lewis Hall, Columbia, MO 65211.

UNIVERSITY OF NEBRASKA PRESS—901 North 17th St., Lincoln, NE 68588.

UNIVERSITY OF NEW MEXICO PRESS—Albuquerque, NM 87131.

UNIVERSITY OF NOTRE DAME PRESS—Notre Dame, IN 46556.

UNIVERSITY OF OKLAHOMA PRESS—1005 Asp Ave., Norman, OK 73019.

UNIVERSITY OF PITTSBURGH PRESS—127 North Bellefield Ave., Pittsburgh, PA 15260.

UNIVERSITY OF SOUTH CAROLINA PRESS—USC Campus, Columbia, SC 29208.

UNIVERSITY OF TENNESSEE PRESS—293 Communications Bldg., Knoxville, TN 37996-0325.

UNIVERSITY OF UTAH PRESS—101 U.S.B., Salt Lake City, UT 84112.

UNIVERSITY OF WASHINGTON PRESS—Seattle, WA 98195.

UNIVERSITY OF WISCONSIN PRESS—114 S. Murray St., Madison, WI 53715-1199.

THE UNIVERSITY PRESS OF FLORIDA—15 N.W. 15th St., Gainesville, FL 32603.

THE UNIVERSITY PRESS OF KENTUCKY—102 Lafferty Hall, Lexington, KY 40506–0024.

UNIVERSITY PRESS OF MISSISSIPPI—3825 Ridgewood Rd., Jackson, MS 39211.

UNIVERSITY PRESS OF NEW ENGLAND—Box 979, Hanover, NH 03755.

THE UNIVERSITY PRESS OF VIRGINIA—Box 3608, University Sta., Charlottesville, VA 22903.

WAYNE STATE UNIVERSITY PRESS—5959 Woodward Ave., Detroit, MI 48202.

WESLEYAN UNIVERSITY PRESS—110 Mt. Vernon St., Middletown, CT 06457.

YALE UNIVERSITY PRESS—92A Yale Station, New Haven, CT 06520.

SYNDICATES

Syndicates are business organizations that publish nothing themselves, but buy material from writers and artists to sell to newspapers all over the country and the world. Authors are paid either a percentage of the gross proceeds or an outright fee.

Of course, features by people well known in their fields have the best chance of being syndicated. In general, syndicates want columns that have been popular in a local newspaper, perhaps, or magazine. Since most syndicated fiction has been published previously in magazines or books, beginning fiction writers should try to sell their stories to magazines before submitting them to syndicates.

Always query syndicates before sending manuscripts—their needs change frequently—and be sure to enclose self-addressed, stamped envelopes with queries and manuscripts.

ARKIN MAGAZINE SYNDICATE—761 NE 180th St., N. Miami Beach, FL 33162. Joseph Arkin, Ed. Dir. Articles, 750 to 2,200 words, for trade and professional magazines. Must be slanted to small businesses, written in layman's language, and offer solutions to business problems. Pays 3¢ to 10¢ a word, on acceptance. Query preferred.

BUSINESS FEATURES SYNDICATE—P. O. Box 9844, Ft. Lauderdale, FL 33310. Dana K. Cassell, Ed. Articles, 1,500 to 2,000 words, for the independent retailer or small service business owner, on marketing, security, personnel, merchandising, general management. Pays 50% of sales.

CANADA WIDE FEATURE SERVICE—Box 345, Station A, Toronto, Ontario, M5W 1C2, Canada. Glenn-Stewart Garnett, Ed. Interviews with well-known celebrities and international political figures, 1,500 to 2,000 words, with photos. Pays 50% of gross, on publication.

CARDEN EDITORIAL SERVICES—2601 W. Carandis Rd., W. Palm Beach, FL 33406. Gwen Carden, Ed. Life style pieces, 800 to 2,000 words, for distribution to national and international news syndicates. Information must be from nationally-recognized sources with good credentials. Pays from $60 to $300.

CONTEMPORARY FEATURES SYNDICATE—P. O. Box 1258, Jackson, TN 38301. Lloyd Russell, Ed. Articles, 1,000 to 10,000 words: how-to, money-savers, travel, business, etc. Self-help pieces, for small businesses. Pays from $25, on acceptance.

FICTION NETWORK—Box 5651, San Francisco, CA 94101. Fiction, to 2,500 words. One submission per author; submit manuscript unfolded. SASE required. Pays royalty basis. Allow 12 weeks for response.

HARRIS & ASSOCIATES FEATURES—5353 La Jolla Blvd., #34, La Jolla, CA 92037. Dick Harris, Ed. Sports and family-oriented features, to 1,200 words; fillers and short humor, 500 to 800 words. Queries preferred. Pays varying rates.

HERITAGE FEATURES SYNDICATE—214 Mass. Ave., NE, Washington, DC 20002. Andy Seamans, Man. Ed. Public policy news features; syndicates weekly by-lined columns and editorial cartoons. Query with SASE a must.

HISPANIC LINK NEWS SERVICE—1420 N St. NW, Washington, DC 20005. Charles A. Ericksen, Ed. Trend articles and general features with

Hispanic focus, 650 to 700 words; editorial cartoons. Pays $25 for op/ed column and cartoons, on acceptance. Send SASE for guidelines.

THE HOLLYWOOD INSIDE SYNDICATE—Box 49957, Los Angeles, CA 90049. John Austin, Director. Feature material, 750 to 1,000 words, on TV and motion picture personalities. Story suggestions for 3-part series. Pieces on unusual medical and scientific breakthroughs. Pays on percentage basis for features, negotiated rates for ideas, on acceptance.

INTERNATIONAL MEDICAL TRIBUNE SYNDICATE—257 Park Ave. S., 19th fl., New York, NY 10010. Health and medical news, features, 250 to 1,000 words; technical accuracy and clarity a must. Pays 15¢ to 20¢ a word.

KING FEATURES SYNDICATE—235 E. 45th St., New York, NY 10017. Dennis R. Allen, VP/Creative Dir. Columns, comics; most contributions on contract for regular columns. Feature articles for newspaper supplement "Sunday Woman Plus": query Merry Clark.

LOS ANGELES TIMES SYNDICATE—Times Mirror Sq., Los Angeles, CA 90053. Commentary, features, columns, editorial cartoons, comics, puzzles & games; news services. Query for articles.

NATIONAL NEWS BUREAU—2019 Chancellor St., Philadelphia, PA 19103. Articles, 500 to 800 words, interviews, consumer news, how-to's, travel pieces, reviews, entertainment pieces, features, etc. Pays on publication.

NEW YORK TIMES SYNDICATION SALES—130 Fifth Ave., New York, NY 10011. Paula Reichler, Sr. V.P./Ed. Dir. Previously published articles only, to 2,000 words. Query with published article or tear sheet. Pays varying rates, on publiction.

NEWSPAPER ENTERPRISE ASSOCIATION, INC.—200 Park Ave., New York, NY 10166. Diana L. Drake, Exec. Ed. Ideas for new concepts in syndicated columns. No single stories or stringers. Payment by contractual arrangement.

NORTH AMERICA SYNDICATE—1703 Kaiser Ave., Irvine, CA 92714. Tom Reinken, Exec. Ed. Columns, comic strips, panel cartoons, serials.

OCEANIC PRESS SERVICE—P. O. Box 6538, Buena Park, CA 90622-6538. Nat Carlton, General Manager. Buys reprint rights for foreign markets, on previously published novels, self-help, and how-to books; interviews with celebrities; illustrated features on celebrities, family health, beauty, personal relations, etc.; cartoons, comic strips. Pays on acceptance. Query.

RELIGIOUS NEWS SERVICE—104 E. 56th St., New York, NY 10019. Judy Weidman, Ed. and Director. Religious news stories and features. Photos on religious subjects. Query first.

SELECT FEATURES OF NORTH AMERICA SYNDICATE/TIMES OF LONDON SYNDICATE—235 E. 45th St., New York, NY 10017. Susan Jarzyk, Acquisitions Ed., Select Features. Articles and series dealing with lifestyle trends, psychology, health, beauty, fashion, finance, jobs; personality profiles. Query.

SINGER COMMUNICATIONS, INC.—3164 W. Tyler Ave., Anaheim, CA 92801. Kurt D. Singer, Ed. U.S. and/or foreign reprint rights to romantic short stories, historical and romantic novels, published during last 25 years. Biography, women's interest material, all lengths. Home repair, real estate, crosswords. Interviews with celebrities. Illustrated columns, humor, cartoons, comic strips. Pays on percentage basis or by outright purchase.

TRANSWORLD FEATURE SYNDICATE, INC.—2 Lexington Ave., Suite 1021, New York, NY 10010. Thelma Brown, Syndication Manager. Feature material for North American and overseas markets. Query required.

TRIBUNE MEDIA SERVICES—64 E. Concord St., Orlando, FL 32801. Michael Argirion, Ed. Continuing columns; comic strips, features, electronic data bases.

UNITED FEATURE SYNDICATE—200 Park Ave., New York, NY 10166. Diana L. Drake, Exec. Ed. Syndicated columns; no one-shots or series. Payment by contractual arrangement.

UNITED PRESS INTERNATIONAL—1400 Eye St. NW, Washington, DC 20005. Barry Sussman, Man. Ed. Seldom accepts free-lance material.

LITERARY PRIZE OFFERS

Each year many important prize contests are open to free-lance writers. The short summaries given below are intended merely as guides. Closing dates, requirements, and rules are tentative. No manuscript should be submitted to any competition unless the writer has first checked with the Contest Editor and received complete information about a particular contest.

Send a stamped, self-addressed envelope with all requests for contest rules and application forms.

ACADEMY OF AMERICAN POETS—177 E. 87th St., New York, NY 10128. Offers Walt Whitman Award: Publication and $1,000 cash prize for a book-length poetry manuscript by a poet who has not yet published a volume of poetry. Closes in November.

ACTORS THEATRE OF LOUISVILLE—316 W. Main St., Louisville, KY 40202. Conducts One-Act Play Contest. Offers $1,000 for previously unproduced one-act script. Closes in April.

THE AMERICAN ACADEMY AND INSTITUTE OF ARTS AND LETTERS—633 W. 155th St., New York, NY 10032. Offers Richard Rodgers Production Award, which consists of subsidized production in New York City by a non-profit theater for a musical, play with music, thematic review, or any comparable work other than opera. Closes in November.

AMERICAN HEALTH MAGAZINE—80 Fifth Ave., New York, NY 10011. Offers prize of $2,000 for short story about an intense physical experience. Closes in April.

ASSOCIATED WRITING PROGRAMS—Old Dominion University, Norfolk, VA 23508. Conducts Annual Award Series in Short Fiction, the Novel, and Nonfiction. In each category the prize is book publication and a $1,000 honorarium. Closes in December. Offers the Edith Shiffert Prize in Poetry: $1,000 cash prize and publication by the University Press of Virginia for an unpublished book-length collection of poetry. Closes in December.

ASSOCIATION OF JEWISH LIBRARIES—15 Goldsmith St. Providence,

RI 02906. Address Lillian Schwartz, Secretary. Conducts Sydney Taylor Manuscript competition for best fiction manuscript for readers age 8 to 12. Prize is $1,000. Closes in December.

BEVERLY HILLS THEATRE GUILD—JULIE HARRIS PLAYWRIGHT AWARD—2815 N. Beachwood Dr., Los Angeles, CA 90068. Address Marcella Meharg. Offers prize of $5,000, plus $2,000 for production in Los Angeles area, for a previously unproduced and unpublished full-length play. Closes in November.

THE CHICAGO TRIBUNE—435 N. Michigan Ave., Chicago, IL 60611. Sponsors Nelson Algren Awards for Short Fiction, with a first prize of $5,000 and three runners-up prizes of $1,000 for outstanding unpublished short stories of 10,000 words or less, by American writers. Closes in February.

COURT THEATRE—The University of Chicago, 5706 S. University Ave., Chicago, IL 60637. Offers Sergel Drama Prize: $1,500 for full-length unpublished and unproduced play. Closes in June of odd-numbered years.

EUGENE V. DEBS FOUNDATION—Dept. of History, Indiana State University, Terre Haute, IN 47809. Offers Bryant Spann Memorial Prize of $750 for published or unpublished article or essay on themes relating to social protest or human equality. Closes in April.

DELACORTE PRESS—Dept. BFYR, 1 Dag Hammarskjold Plaza, New York, NY 10017. Sponsors Delacorte Press Prize for an outstanding first young adult novel. The prize consists of one Delacorte hardcover and Dell paperback contract, an advance of $4,000 on royalties, and a $1,000 cash prize. Closes in December.

FICTION NETWORK—P. O. Box 5651, San Francisco, CA 94101. Sponsors Fiction Competition, with a first prize of up to $1,500, for a short story to 2,500 words (no children's or young adult fiction). Closes in July.

FOREST A. ROBERTS-SHIRAS INSTITUTE—Forest Roberts Theatre, Northern Michigan Univ., Marquette, MI 49855. Dr. James A. Panowski, Dir. Conducts annual Playwriting Competition, with prize of $1,000, plus production, for an original, full-length, previously unproduced and unpublished play. Closes in November.

THE FOUNDATION OF THE DRAMATISTS GUILD—234 W. 44th St., New York, NY 10036. Sponsors Young Playwrights Festival. Playwrights under 19 years of age may submit scripts; winning plays will be given full stage productions or staged readings. Closes in October.

FULCRUM, INC.—350 Indiana St., Ste. 510, Golden, CO 80401. Offers Fulcrum American Writing Award for a book of nonfiction or fiction by an American writer on environmental, resource, and social issues. The prize is $2,500, plus publication. Closes in November.

HIGHLIGHTS FOR CHILDREN—803 Church St., Honesdale, PA 18431. Conducts Contest for Juvenile Fiction, with cash prizes and publication for short stories. Closes in March.

HONOLULU MAGAZINE—36 Merchant St., Honolulu, HI 96813. Sponsors an annual fiction contest, with a cash prize of $500, plus publication in *Honolulu,* for an unpublished short story with a Hawaiian theme, setting, and/or characters. Closes in September.

HOUGHTON MIFFLIN COMPANY—2 Park St., Boston, MA 02108. Offers Literary Fellowship for fiction or nonfiction project of exceptional literary merit written by American author. Work under consideration must be unpublished and in English. Fellowship consists of $10,000, of which $2,500 is an outright grant and $7,500 is an advance on royalties. There is no deadline.

HUMBOLDT STATE UNIVERSITY—English Dept. Arcata, CA 95521. Sponsors the Raymond Carver Short Story Contest, with a prize of $500, plus publication in the literary journal *Toyon,* for an unpublished short story by a writer living in the U.S. Closes in November.

ILLINOIS STATE UNIVERSITY—Dept. of Theatre, Illinois State Univ., Normal, IL 61761. Address John W. Kirk. Sponsors Fine Arts Competition, with prize of $1,000, plus production, for previously unpublished and unproduced full-length play. Closes in October.

INDIANA UNIVERSITY—PURDUE UNIVERSITY AT INDIANAPOLIS—IUPUI Univ. Theatre, 525 N. Blackford St., Indianapolis, IN 46202. Conducts biennial National Children's Theatre Playwriting Competition, with a prize of $2,000 for an original, previously unproduced one-act children's play. Closes in November.

INTERNATIONAL SOCIETY OF DRAMATISTS—Fulfillment Center, Box 3470, Ft. Pierce, FL 33448. Sponsors Adriatic Award: a prize of $10,000 for a full-length play. Closes in November.

JACKSONVILLE UNIVERSITY—Annual Playwriting Contest, Dept. of Theatre Arts, College of Fine Arts, Jacksonville Univ., Jacksonville, FL 32211. Davis Sikes, Dir. Conducts playwriting contest, with prize of $1,000 and production, for original, previously unproduced script (full-length or one-act). Closes in January.

JEWISH COMMUNITY CENTER THEATRE—3505 Mayfield Rd., Cleveland Heights, OH 44118. Dorothy Silver, Dir. of Cultural Arts. Offers cash award of $1,000 and a staged reading for an original, previously unproduced full-length play on some aspect of the Jewish experience. Closes in December.

CHESTER H. JONES FOUNDATION—P. O. Box 43033, Cleveland, OH 44143. Conducts the National Poetry Competition, with more than $1,800 in cash prizes (including a first prize of $1,000) for original, unpublished poems. Closes in March.

LINCOLN COLLEGE—Lincoln, IL 62656. Address Janet Overton. Offers Billee Murray Denny Poetry Award for original poem by poet who has not previously published a volume of poetry. First prize of $1,000, 2nd prize of $450, and 3rd prize of $200 are offered. Closes in May.

MADEMOISELLE MAGAZINE—350 Madison Ave., New York, NY 10017. Sponsors Fiction Writers Contest, with first prize of $1,000, plus publication, and second prize of $500, for short fiction. Closes in March.

MS. MAGAZINE—One Times Sq., New York, NY 10036. Sponsors annual Fiction Contest for short story. Prize is publication and electronic typewriter. Closes in August.

NATIONAL ENDOWMENT FOR THE ARTS—Washington, DC 20506. Address Director, Literature Program. The National Endowment for the Arts offers fellowships to writers of poetry, fiction, scripts, and other creative prose. Deadlines vary; write for guidelines.

NATIONAL PLAY AWARD—P. O. Box 71011, Los Angeles, CA 90071. National Play Award consists of a $7,500 cash prize, plus $5,000 for production, for an original, previously unproduced play. Sponsored by National Repertory Theatre Foundation. Closes in October of odd-numbered years.

NATIONAL POETRY SERIES—26 W. 17th St., New York, NY 10011. Sponsors Annual Open Competition for unpublished, book-length poetry manuscript. The prize is publication. Closes in February.

THE NEW ENGLAND THEATRE CONFERENCE—50 Exchange St., Waltham, MA 02154. First prize of $500 and second prize of $250 are offered for unpublished and unproduced one-act plays in the John Gassner Memorial Playwriting Award Competition. Closes in April.

NEW VOICES—551 Tremont St., Boston, MA 02116. Conducts Clauder Competition for a full-length play by a New England writer. The prize is $3,000 and workshop production. Closes in June of odd numbered years.

NORTHEASTERN UNIVERSITY PRESS—English Dept., 406 Holmes, Northeastern University, Boston, MA 02115. Guy Rotella, Chairman. Offers Samuel French Morse Poetry Prize—publication of full-length poetry manuscript—by a U.S. poet who has published no more than one book of poems. Closes in September.

O'NEILL THEATER CENTER—234 W. 44th St., Suite 901, New York, NY 10036. Offers stipends, staged readings, and room and board at the National Playwrights Conference, for new stage and television plays. Closes in December.

THE PARIS REVIEW—541 E. 72nd St., New York, NY 10021. Sponsors Aga Khan Prize for Fiction: $1,000, plus publication, for previously unpublished short story. Closes in June. Offers Bernard F. Connors Prize: $1,000, plus publication, for previously unpublished poem. Closes in May. Offers John Train Humor Prize: $1,500, plus publication, for unpublished work of humorous fiction, nonfiction, or poetry. Closes in March.

PEN AMERICAN CENTER—568 Broadway, New York, NY 10012. Sponsors PEN/Nelson Algren Award: stipend of $1,000, plus one-month residency at Edward Albee Foundation's summer residence on Long Island, for uncompleted novel or collection of short stories by an American writer who needs assistance to complete the work. Closes in November. Sponsors Renato Poggioli Translation Award: $3,000 grant for a translator working on his or her first book-length translation from Italian into English. Closes in February. Sponsors the PEN/Jerard Fund Award: $3,000 for a beginning woman writer at an early point in her career for a work in progress of general nonfiction. Closes in May.

PLAYBOY MAGAZINE—919 N. Michigan Ave., Chicago, IL 60611. Sponsors college fiction contest, with first prize of $3,000 and publication in *Playboy,* for a short story by a college student. Closes in January.

POETRY SOCIETY IN AMERICA—15 Gramercy Park, New York, NY 10003. Conducts annual contests—The Celia B. Wagner Memorial Award, the John Masefield Memorial Award, and the Elias Lieberman Student Poetry Award—in which cash prizes are offered for unpublished poems. Contests close in December.

RADIO DRAMA AWARDS—3319 W. Beltline Hwy., Madison, WI 53713. Norman Michie, Exec. Producer. Wisconsin Public Radio conducts annual Radio Drama Awards competition for original scripts by writers in Illinois, Iowa, Michigan, Minnesota, and Wisconsin. Prizes for thirty-minute radio scripts are professional production and cash awards of $500 (first prize), $300 (second), and $200 (third). Closes in January.

REDBOOK MAGAZINE—224 W. 57th St., New York, NY 10019. Conducts Short Story Contest for original fiction. First prize is $1,000, plus publication. Second prize of $500 and third prize of $300 are also offered. Closes in May.

SAN JOSE STATE UNIVERSITY—One Washington Square, San Jose, CA 95192. Address Dr. Howard Burman, Theatre Arts Dept. Sponsors Harold C. Crain Playwriting Contest, with a prize of $500, plus production, for a previously unproduced full-length play. Closes in November.

SEVENTEEN—850 Third Ave., New York, NY 10022. Conducts *Seventeen*/Dell Fiction Contest for original unpublished fiction by writers aged 13 to 20. A first prize of $2,000, second prize of $1,200, and third prize of $700 will be awarded. Winning entries will be considered for publication in *Seventeen* and future publications of Dell Publishing. Closes in January.

SIERRA REPERTORY THEATRE—P. O. Box 3030, Sonora, CA 95370. Offers Cummings/Taylor Award of $400, plus production, for original, previously unpublished, unproduced full-length play or musical. Closes in May.

SUNSET CENTER—P. O. Box 5066, Carmel, CA 93921. Richard Tyler, Director. Offers prize of up to $2,000 for an original, unproduced full-length play in its annual Festival of Firsts Playwriting Competition. Closes in August.

SYRACUSE UNIVERSITY PRESS—1600 Jamesville Ave., Syracuse, NY 13244-5160. Address Director. Sponsors John Ben Snow Prize: $1,500, plus publication, for unpublished book-length manuscript about New York State, especially upstate or central New York. Closes in December.

THEATRE MEMPHIS—630 Perkins Extended, Memphis, TN 38117. Conducts New Play Competition for a full-length play or related one-acts. The prize is $3,000 and production. Closes in September. Biennial.

UNICORN THEATRE—3514 Jefferson, Kansas City, MO 64111. Sponsors National Playwright Competition, with a first prize of $1,000, plus travel and residency while in production, for an original, unpublished and unproduced full-length play. Closes in May.

U.S. NAVAL INSTITUTE—Annapolis, MD 21402. Address Membership Department. Conducts Arleigh Burke Essay Contest, with prizes of $2,000, $1,000, and $750, plus publication, for essays on the advancement of professional, literary, and scientific knowledge in the naval and maritime services, and the advancement of the knowledge of sea power. Closes in December.

UNIVERSITY OF ALABAMA AT BIRMINGHAM—Dept. of Theatre and Dance, University Sta., Birmingham, AL 35294. Rick J. Plummer, Director. Conducts Ruby Lloyd Apsey Playwriting Competition, with $500 cash prize, plus production and travel expenses, for previously unproduced full-length play. Closes in January.

UNIVERSITY OF GEORGIA PRESS—Athens, GA 30602. Offers Flannery O'Connor Award for Short Fiction: a prize of $500, plus publication, for a book-length collection of short fiction. Closes in July.

UNIVERSITY OF HAWAII—Kennedy Theatre, Univ. of Hawaii, 1770 East-West Rd., Honolulu, HI 96822. Conducts annual Kumu Kahua Playwriting Contest with cash prizes for original plays dealing with some aspect of Hawaiian experience. Closes in January.

758

UNIVERSITY OF HAWAII PRESS—2840 Kolowalu St., Honolulu, HI 96822. Sponsors Pacific Poetry Series competition, with prize of publication and royalty contract, for unpublished book-length poetry manuscript by a writer who has not previously published a volume of poetry. Closes in March of odd-numbered years.

UNIVERSITY OF IOWA—Iowa School of Letters Award, Dept. of English, English-Philosophy Bldg., Univ. of Iowa, Iowa City, IA 52242. Offers The John Simmons Short Fiction Award and the Iowa School of Letters Award—$1,000, plus publication, for each—for book-length collections of short stories by writer who has not yet had a book published. Closes in September.

UNIVERSITY OF MASSACHUSETTS PRESS—Juniper Prize, Univ. of Massachusetts Press, c/o Mail Office, Amherst, MA 01003. Offers Juniper Prize of $1,000, plus publication, for book-length manuscript of poetry. Closes in October.

UNIVERSITY OF PITTSBURGH PRESS—Pittsburgh, PA 15260. Sponsors Drue Heinz Literature Prize—$5,000, plus publication and royalty contract—for unpublished collection of short stories. Closes in August. Also sponsors Agnes Lynch Starrett Poetry Prize—$1,000, plus publication and royalty contract—for book-length collection of poems by poet who has not yet published a volume of poetry. Closes in April.

UNIVERSITY OF WISCONSIN-PARKSIDE—Fine Arts Division, Univ. of Wisconsin-Parkside, Box 2000, Kenosha, WI 53141. Address Judith Tucker Snider. Offers award of $1,000, plus production, for an unpublished, unproduced, full-length original play or musical. Closes in December.

UNIVERSITY OF WISCONSIN PRESS—Poetry Series, 114 N. Murray St., Madison, WI 53715. Ronald Wallace, Admin. Offers Brittingham Prize in Poetry: $500 plus publication, for unpublished book-length poetry manuscript. Closes in September.

WALT WHITMAN CENTER FOR THE ARTS AND HUMANITIES—2nd and Cooper Sts., Camden, NJ 08102. Sponsors the annual Camden Poetry Award: $1,000, plus publication, for an unpublished book-length collection of poetry. Closes in November.

WORD WORKS—P.O. Box 42164, Washington, DC 20015. Offers the Washington Prize of $1,000 for unpublished poem by American poet. Closes in November.

YALE UNIVERSITY PRESS—Box 92A, Yale Sta., New Haven, CT 06520. Address Editor, Yale Series of Younger Poets. Conducts Yale Series of Younger Poets Competition, in which the prize is publication of a book-length manuscript of poetry, written by a poet under 40 who has not previously published a volume of poems. Closes in February.

WRITERS COLONIES

A writers colony offers isolation and freedom from everyday distractions to writers who want a quiet place to concentrate on their work. Though some colonies are quite small, with space for just three or four writers at a time, others can provide accommodations for as many as thirty or forty. The length of a residency may vary, too—from a couple of weeks to five or six months. These programs have strict admissions policies, and writers must submit a formal application or letter of intent, a resume, writing samples, and letters of recommendation. Write for application information first, enclosing a stamped, self-addressed envelope (SASE).

CENTRUM FOUNDATION—The Centrum Foundation sponsors residencies of two to three months at Fort Worden State Park, a Victorian fort on the Strait of Juan De Fuca in Washington. Nonfiction, fiction, and poetry writers may apply for residency awards, which include stipend of $600 a month. Application deadline is in early December; send letter explaining the project, short biographical note, and sample of published work. For details, send SASE, in fall, to Carol Jane Bangs, Director of Literature Programs, Centrum Foundation, Fort Worden State Park, P. O. Box 1158, Port Townsend, WA 98368.

CUMMINGTON COMMUNITY OF THE ARTS—Residencies of one month or more in the Berkshires. Quarterly deadlines. For more information, send SASE to Cummington Community of the Arts, Cummington, MA 01026.

DORLAND MOUNTAIN COLONY—Novelists, playwrights, and poets may apply for residencies at the Dorland Preserve of the Nature Conservancy in the Palomar Mountains of Southern California. Cottages, firewood, and kerosene are provided. Application deadlines are March 1 and September 1. For further information and application forms, send SASE to Resident Director, Dorland Mountain Colony, P. O. Box 6, Temecula, CA 92390.

DORSET COLONY HOUSE—Writers and playwrights are offered low-cost room with kitchen facilities at the Colony House in Dorset, Vermont. Periods of residency are 3 to 6 weeks, and are available between October 1 and June 1. Application deadlines are September 15, December 15, and February 15 for the periods immediately following the deadlines. For more information, send SASE to John Nassivera, Director, Dorset Colony House, Dorset, VT 05251.

FINE ARTS WORK CENTER IN PROVINCETOWN—Fellowships including living and studio space and monthly stipends at the Fine Arts Work Center on Cape Cod, for writers to work independently. Residencies are for seven months only; apply before the February 1 deadline. For details, send SASE to Susan Slocum, Dir., Fine Arts Work Center, P. O. Box 565, 24 Pearl St., Provincetown, MA 02657.

THE HAMBIDGE CENTER—Two-week to two-month residencies are offered to writers, artists, composers, historians, humanists and scientists at the Hambidge Center for Creative Arts and Sciences located on 600 acres of quiet woods in the north Georgia mountains. Send SASE for application form to Executive Director, The Hambidge Center, P. O. Box 339, Rabun Gap, GA 30568.

THE MACDOWELL COLONY—Studios, room and board at the Mac-Dowell Colony of Peterborough, New Hampshire, for writers to work without interruption in semi-rural woodland setting. Selection is competitive. Apply at least six months in advance of season desired; residencies average 5 to 6 weeks. For details and admission forms, send SASE to Admissions Coordinator, The MacDowell Colony, 100 High St., Peterborough, NH 03458.

THE MILLAY COLONY FOR THE ARTS—At Steepletop in Austerlitz, New York—former home of Edna St. Vincent Millay—studios, living quarters, and meals are provided to writers at no cost. Residencies are for one month. Application deadlines are February 1, May 1, and September 1. To apply, send SASE to the Millay Colony for the Arts, Inc., Steepletop, Austerlitz, NY 12017.

MONTALVO CENTER FOR THE ARTS—Three-month, low-cost residencies at the Villa Montalvo in the foothills of the Santa Cruz Mountains south of San Francisco, for writers working on specific projects. There are a few small fellowships available to writers with demonstrable financial need. Send self-addressed envelope and 73¢ stamp for application forms to Montalvo Residency Program, P. O. Box 158, Saratoga, CA 95070.

UCROSS FOUNDATION—Residencies, two weeks to four months, at the Ucross Foundation in the foothills of the Big Horn Mountains in Wyoming, for writers to concentrate on their work without interruptions. Residencies are available from August through May. The application deadline is October 1; for more information, send SASE to Director, Residency Program, Ucross Foundation, Ucross Route, Box 19, Clearmont, WY 82835.

VIRGINIA CENTER FOR THE CREATIVE ARTS—Residencies of one to three months at the Mt. San Angelo Estate in Sweet Briar, Virginia, for writers to work without distraction. Apply at least three months in advance. A limited amount of financial assistance is available. For more information, send SASE to William Smart, Director, Virginia Center for the Creative Arts, Sweet Briar, VA 24595.

HELENE WURLITZER FOUNDATION OF NEW MEXICO—Rent-free and utility-free studios at the Helene Wurlitzer Foundation in Taos, New Mexico, are offered to creative writers and artists in all media. Length of residency varies from three to six months. The Foundation is closed from October 1 through March 31 annually. For details, send SASE to Henry A. Sauerwein, Jr., Exec. Dir., The Helene Wurlitzer Foundation of New Mexico, Box 545, Taos, NM 87571.

YADDO—Artists, writers, and composers are invited for short-term residencies at the Yaddo estate in Saratoga Springs, New York. Although there is no fixed charge, voluntary contributions are encouraged. Requests for applications should be sent with SASE before January 15 or August 1 to Myra Sklarew, President, Yaddo, Box 395, Saratoga Springs, NY 12866. An application fee of $10.00 is required.

WRITERS CONFERENCES

Each year, hundreds of writers conferences are held across the country. The following list, arranged geographically, represents a sampling of conferences; each listing includes the location of the conference, the month during which it is usually held, and the name of the person from whom specific information can be received. Additional conferences are listed annually in the May issue of *The Writer* Magazine.

ARKANSAS

ARKANSAS WRITERS' CONFERENCE—North Little Rock, AR. June. Write Clovita Rice, 1115 Gillette Dr., Little Rock, AR 72207.

CALIFORNIA

ANNUAL WRITERS CONFERENCE IN CHILDREN'S LITERATURE—Los Angeles, CA. August. Write Lin Oliver, Dir., SCBW, PO Box 296, Mar Vista Station, Los Angeles, CA 90066.

SQUAW VALLEY COMMUNITY OF WRITERS—Olympic Valley, CA. August. Write Carolyn Doty, PO Box 2352, Olympic Valley, CA 95730.

STANFORD PUBLISHING COURSE—Stanford, CA. July. Write Dir., Alumni Assoc., Bowman House, Stanford Univ., Stanford, CA 94305.

CABRILLO SUSPENSE WRITERS CONFERENCE—Mills College, Oakland, CA. July. Write Dr. Timothy Welch, Dir., PO Box 851, Aptos, CA 95001.

COLORADO

ASPEN WRITERS CONFERENCE—Aspen, CO. August. Write Dir., Box 7726D, Aspen, CO 81612.

CONNECTICUT

WESLEYAN WRITERS CONFERENCE—Middletown, CT. July. Write Anne Greene, Wesleyan Writers Conference, Wesleyan Univ., Middletown, CT 06457.

DEAF PLAYWRIGHT CONFERENCE—Chester, CT. June. Write Shanny Mow, Dir., National Theatre of the Deaf, Chester, CT 06412.

FLORIDA

FLORIDA SUNCOAST WRITERS' CONFERENCE—St. Petersburg, FL. January. Write Writers' Conference, Univ. of Southern Florida/St. Petersburg, 830 First St., South, St. Petersburg, FL 33701.

GEORGIA

DIXIE COUNCIL OF AUTHORS AND JOURNALISTS INC.—St. Simonds Island, GA. June. Dr. James C. Bryant, Dir. Write Leara Rhodes, 1041 Latham Rd., Decatur, GA 30033.

ILLINOIS

INTERNATIONAL BLACK WRITERS—Chicago, IL. June. Write Mable J. Terrell, PO Box 1030, Chicago, IL 60617.

ILLINOIS WESLEYAN UNIVERSITY WRITERS' CONFERENCE—Bloomington, IL. July–August. Write Illinois Wesleyan Univ. Writers' Conference, Illinois Wesleyan Univ., PO Box 2900, Bloomington, IL 61702.

MISSISSIPPI VALLEY WRITERS CONFERENCE—Augustana College, Rock Island, IL. June. Write David R. Collins, 3403 45th St., Moline, IL 61265.

ANNUAL CHRISTIAN WRITERS INSTITUTE CONFERENCE AND WORKSHOPS—Wheaton College, Wheaton, IL. June. Write June Eaton, Dir., CWI, 388 E. Gundersen Dr., Wheaton, IL 60188.

Indiana

OHIO RIVER WRITERS' CONFERENCE—Evansville, IN. October. Write Carol D. Gottliebsen, Program Coord., Evansville Arts & Education Council, 16½ SE Second St., Suite 210, Evansville, IN 47708.

INDIANA UNIVERSITY WRITERS' CONFERENCE—Bloomington, IN. June. Write Maura Stanton, Ballantine Hall 464, Indiana Univ., Bloomington, IN 47405.

Iowa

SUMMER IOWA WRITING PROGRAM—The Univ. of Iowa, Iowa City, IA. July. Write Summer Iowa Writing Program, Div. of Continuing Education, The Univ. of IA, C108 Seashore Hall, Iowa City, IA 52242.

Kentucky

ANNUAL APPALACHIAN WRITERS WORKSHOP—Hindman, KY. August. Write Mike Mullins, Box 844, Settlement School, Hindman, KY 41822.

WRITING WORKSHOP FOR PEOPLE OVER 57—Lexington, KY. August. Write Roberta H. James, Council on Aging, Ligon House, Univ. of Kentucky, Lexington, KY 40506-0442.

CREATIVE WRITING CONFERENCE—Richmond, KY. June. Write William Sutton, Dept. of English, Eastern Kentucky Univ., Richmond, KY 40475.

Louisiana

ANNUAL LOUISIANA WRITERS CONFERENCE—Centenary College, Shreveport, LA. June. Write Dr. David Jackson, Co-Dir., PO Box 4633, Shreveport, LA 71134-0633.

DEEP SOUTH WRITERS CONFERENCE—Univ. of Southwestern Louisiana, Lafayette, LA. September. Write Herb Fackler, Deep South Writers Conference, USL Box 44691, Univ. of Southwestern Louisiana, Lafayette, LA 70504-4691.

Maine

STONECOAST WRITERS' CONFERENCE—Univ. of Southern Maine, Gorham, ME. July. Write Kenneth Rosen, English Dept., USM, Portland, ME 04038.

MAINE WRITERS WORKSHOP—Oceanville, ME. July and August. Write George F. Bush, Dir., PO Box 905W, Stonington, ME 04681.

STATE OF MAINE WRITERS CONFERENCE—Ocean Park (Old Orchard Beach), ME. August. Write Richard F. Burns, Box 296, Ocean Park, ME 04063.

MARYLAND

THE JOHNS HOPKINS UNIVERSITY SUMMER WRITERS' CON-FERENCE—Baltimore, MD. June. Write Summer Writers' Conference, The Johns Hopkins Univ., School of Continuing Studies, 102 Macaulay Hall, Baltimore, MD 21218.

MASSACHUSETTS

HARVARD SUMMER WRITING PROGRAM—Cambridge, MA. June–August. Write Harvard Summer School, 20 Garden Street, Dept. 274, Cambridge, MA 02138.

EASTERN WRITERS' CONFERENCE—Salem, MA. June. Write Claire Keyes, English Dept., Salem State College, Salem, MA 01970.

CAPE COD WRITERS' CONFERENCE—Craigville, MA. August. Write Marion Vuilleumier, Box 111, West Hyannisport, MA 02672.

NEW ENGLAND WRITERS' WORKSHOP AT SIMMONS COLLEGE—Boston, MA. July. Write Theodore Vrettos, Dir., Simmons College, 300 The Fenway, Boston, MA 02115.

MICHIGAN

CLARION SCIENCE FICTION AND FANTASY WRITERS' WORK-SHOP—East Lansing, MI. June–August. Write Mary Sheridan, E-35 Holmes Hall, Lyman Briggs School, MSU, E. Lansing, MI 48854.

ANNUAL BAY DE NOC WRITERS' CONFERENCE—Escanaba, MI. June. Write Larry Leffel, Bay de Noc Community College, Escanaba, MI 49829.

MINNESOTA

MISSISSIPPI RIVER CREATIVE WRITING WORKSHOP IN POETRY AND FICTION—St. Cloud, MN. June. Write Bill Meissner, St. Cloud State Univ., Dept. of English, St. Cloud, MN 56301.

DECISION MAGAZINE'S SCHOOL OF CHRISTIAN WRITING—Roseville, MN. August. Write Lori J. P. Sorensen, Dir., Box 779, Minneapolis, MN 55440.

ANNUAL UPPER MIDWEST WRITERS' CONFERENCE—Bemidji, MN. July. Write Dr. William D. Elliott, Box 48, Hagg-Sauer Hall, Bemidji State Univ., Bemidji, MN 56601.

MISSOURI

AVILA COLLEGE WRITERS CONFERENCE—Kansas City, MO. August. Write Marcy Caldwell, Dept. of Cont. Ed., Avila College, 11901 Wornall Rd., Kansas City, MO 64145.

MONTANA

ANNUAL OUTDOOR WRITERS ASSOCIATION OF AMERICA CON-FERENCE—Kalispell, MT. June. Write Sylvia G. Bashline, 2017 Cato Ave., Suite 101, State College, PA 16801.

New Hampshire

ANNUAL SEACOAST WRITERS CONFERENCE—Portsmouth, NH. September. Write Alice Currie, Box 704, Kennebunkport, ME 04046.

MILDRED I. REID WRITERS CONFERENCE—Contoocook, NH. July–August. Write Mildred I. Reid, Writers Colony, Penacook Rd., Contoocook, NH 03229.

New Mexico

ANNUAL SOUTHWEST WRITERS WORKSHOP CONFERENCE—Albuquerque, NM. September. Write Barbara Fitzgerald, 14225 Copper NE, E-503, Albuquerque, NM 87123.

New York

WRITERS WORKSHOP—Univ. of Rochester, NY. July. Write Anne Ludlow, Writers Workshop, 127 Lattimore Hall, Univ. of Rochester, Rochester, NY 14627.

SOUTHAMPTON WRITERS' CONFERENCE—Southampton, NY. July. Write William Roberson, Library, Southampton Campus/LIU, Southampton, NY 11968.

THE TECHNICAL WRITERS INSTITUTE—Troy, NY. June. Write Dr. Philip Rubens, Sage Bldg., Office of Cont. Studies, RPI, Troy, NY 12180-3590.

CORNELL UNIVERSITY WRITERS PROGRAM—Ithaca, NY. June–August. Write Dean Charles W. Jermy, Jr., Dir., B12L Ives Hall, Cornell Univ., Ithaca, NY 14853.

HOFSTRA UNIVERSITY'S ANNUAL WRITERS' CONFERENCE—Hempstead, NY. July. Write Dr. James J. Kolb, Dir., 017 Weller Hall, Hofstra Univ., Hempstead, NY 11550.

VASSAR INSTITUTE OF PUBLISHING AND WRITING: CHILDREN'S BOOKS IN THE MARKETPLACE—Poughkeepsie, NY. June. Write Publishing Institute, Box 300, Vassar College, Poughkeepsie, NY 12601.

IWWG WOMEN'S WRITING CONFERENCE—Skidmore Coll., Saratoga Springs, NY. July. Write Hannelore Hahn, Exec. Dir., International Women's Writing Guild, PO Box 810, Gracie Station, New York, NY 10028.

NYU SUMMER WRITERS' CONFERENCE—New York University. July. Write Walter James Miller, NYU School of Continuing Education, 332 Shimkin Hall, New York, NY 10003.

North Carolina

DUKE UNIVERSITY WRITERS' CONFERENCE—Durham, NC. June. Write Deborah Pope, Office of Cont. Ed., The Bishop's House, Duke University, Durham, NC 27708.

BLUE RIDGE CHRISTIAN WRITERS CONFERENCE—Black Mountain, NC. July. Write Yvonne Lehman, PO Box 188, Black Mountain, NC 28711.

Ohio

ANNUAL QUEEN CITY WRITERS' SEMINAR—Cincinnati, OH. May.

Write Juanita K. Pence, Pres., Queen City Writers, 8413 Flamingo Ln., Cincinnati, OH 45239.

ANTIOCH WRITERS WORKSHOP—Yellow Springs, OH. July. Write Antioch Writers Workshop, Antioch Univ., Yellow Springs, OH 45387.

Oklahoma

ANNUAL WRITERS OF CHILDREN'S LITERATURE CONFERENCE— Lawton, OK. June 7. Write Dr. George E. Stanley, PO Box 16355, Cameron Univ. Station, Lawton, OK 73505.

Oregon

HAYSTACK PROGRAM IN THE ARTS—Cannon Beach, OR. June–August. Write Steve Reischman, PO Box 1491, Portland State Univ., Portland, OR 97207.

Pennsylvania

ST. DAVIDS CHRISTIAN WRITERS—St. Davids, PA. June. Write Shirley Eaby, Registrar, 1775 Eden Rd., Box W, Lancaster, PA 17601.

ANNUAL OUTDOOR WRITERS ASSOCIATION OF AMERICA CONFERENCE—Harrisburg, PA. June. Write Sylvia G. Bashline, 2017 Cato Ave., Suite 101, State College, PA 16801. For members only.

ANNUAL PHILADELPHIA WRITERS' CONFERENCE—Philadelphia, PA. June. Send SASE to H. Patricia Brown, Registrar-W, PO Box 392, Drexel Hill, PA 19026.

UNIVERSITY OF PENNSYLVANIA PUBLISHING INSTITUTE—Philadelphia, PA. Fall. Spring. Write the Publishing Institute, UPenn, 3808 Walnut St., Philadelphia, PA 19104-6136.

Tennessee

CHRISTIAN WRITERS' GRAND OLE WORKSHOP—Nashville, TN. June. Write Dr. John Warren Steen, 6511 Currywood Dr., Nashville, TN 37205.

Texas

SOUTHWEST WRITER'S CONFERENCE—Houston, TX. July. Write Patricia Robinson, Coordinator, Univ. of Houston, Cont. Ed., 4800 Calhoun Rd., Houston, TX 77004.

Vermont

BENNINGTON WRITING WORKSHOPS—Bennington, VT. June–July. Write Dir., Box H, Bennington College, Bennington, VT 05201.

BREAD LOAF WRITERS' CONFERENCE—Middlebury, VT. August. Write Mrs. Carol Knauss, Bread Loaf Writers' Conference, Middlebury College-TW, Middlebury, VT 05753.

Virginia

ANNUAL HIGHLAND SUMMER CONFERENCE—Radford, VA. June. Write Dr. Grace Toney Edwards, Box 5917, Radford Univ., Radford, VA 24142.

WASHINGTON

PACIFIC NORTHWEST WRITERS' CONFERENCE—Tacoma, WA. July. Write Gladys Johnson, Exec. Secretary, PNWC, 1811 NE 199th, Seattle, WA 98155.

PORT TOWNSEND WRITERS' CONFERENCE—Port Townsend, WA. July. Write Carol Jane Bangs, CENTRUM, PO Box 1158, Port Townsend, WA 98368.

SEATTLE PACIFIC CHRISTIAN WRITERS' CONFERENCE—Seattle, WA. June. Write Rose Reynoldson, Humanities Dept., Seattle Pacific Univ., Seattle, WA 98119.

WISCONSIN

SCHOOL OF ARTS AT RHINELANDER—Rhinelander, WI. July. Write Genevieve Lewis, Admin. Coord., School of Arts at Rhinelander, 610 Langdon Street, Rm. 722, Madison, WI 53703.

MIDWEST WRITERS' CONFERENCE—River Falls, WI. June. Write Michael Norman, Dir., Midwest Writers' Conference, Univ. of Wisconsin-River Falls, River Falls, WI 54022.

WYOMING

WYOMING WRITERS' ANNUAL CONFERENCE—Douglas, WY. June. Write Susan Granquist, Conference Chairman, P. O. Box 802, Green River, WY 82935.

CANADA

MARITIME WRITERS' WORKSHOP—Fredericton, NB. July. Write Steven Peacock, c/o Dept. of Extension and Summer Session, University of New Brunswick, Box 4400, Fredericton, NB E3B 5A3.

SASKATCHEWAN SCHOOL OF THE ARTS—Ft. Sam, Sask. June–August. Write Ann Hewat, Dir., 2550 Broad St., Regina, Sask. S4P 3V7.

INTERNATIONAL

SUMMER WRITING WORKSHOP—Dublin, Ireland. July. Write James McAuley, English Dept., Mail Stop 25, Eastern Washington Univ., Cheney, WA 99004.

WRITERS WORKSHOP IN LONDON—London, England. July. Write Suzanne Robblee, College of Arts and Sciences, Northeastern Univ., Boston, MA 02115.

SCREENPLAY WRITING IN LONDON—London, England. July. Write Lynne Kaufman, Public Information Office, UC Extension, 2223 Fulton St., Berkeley, CA 94720.

ANNUAL WRITERS' SUMMER SCHOOL—Derbyshire, England. August. Write Philippa Boland, The Red House, Mardens Hill, Crowborough, Sussex, TN6 1XN, England.

STATE ARTS COUNCILS

State Arts Councils sponsor grants, fellowships, and other programs for writers. To be eligible for funding, a writer *must* be a resident of the state in which he is applying. For more information, write to the addresses below.

ALABAMA STATE COUNCIL ON THE ARTS AND HUMANITIES
Albert B. Head, Exec. Director
One Dexter Ave.
Montgomery, AL 36130

ALASKA STATE COUNCIL ON THE ARTS
Christine D'Arcy, Director
619 Warehouse Ave., Suite 220
Anchorage, AK 99501-1682

ARIZONA COMMISSION ON THE ARTS
Shelley Cohn, Executive Director
417 W. Roosevelt
Phoenix, AZ 85003

OFFICE OF ARKANSAS STATE ARTS AND HUMANITIES
Bev Lindsey, Executive Director
The Heritage Center, Suite 200
225 E. Markham
Little Rock, AR 72201

CALIFORNIA ARTS COUNCIL
JoAnn Anglin, Public Information Officer
1901 Broadway, Suite A
Sacramento, CA 95818-2492

COLORADO COUNCIL ON THE ARTS AND HUMANITIES
Barbara Neal, Executive Director
770 Pennsylvania St.
Denver, CO 80203

CONNECTICUT COMMISSION ON THE ARTS
John Ostrout, Deputy Director
190 Trumbull St.
Hartford, CT 06103

DELAWARE STATE ARTS COUNCIL
Cecelia Fitzgibbon, Exec. Administrator
Carvel State Building
820 N. French St.
Wilmington, DE 19801

FLORIDA ARTS COUNCIL
Chris Doolin
Dept. of State
Div. of Cultural Affairs
The Capitol
Tallahassee, FL 32399-0250

GEORGIA COUNCIL FOR THE ARTS
2082 E. Exchange Place, Suite 100
Tucker, GA 30084

HAWAII STATE FOUNDATION ON CULTURE AND THE ARTS
Sarah M. Richards, Executive Director
335 Merchant St., Rm. 202
Honolulu, HI 96813

IDAHO COMMISSION ON THE ARTS
304 W. State St.
Boise, ID 83720

ILLINOIS ARTS COUNCIL
Bill Seeback, Director, Performing & Communication Arts Programs
State of Illinois Center
100 W. Randolph, Suite 10-500
Chicago, IL 60601

INDIANA ARTS COMMISSION
32 E. Washington St., 6th Fl.
Indianapolis, IN 46204

IOWA STATE ARTS COUNCIL
Julie Baily, Grants Officer
State Capitol Complex
Des Moines, IA 50319

KANSAS ARTS COMMISSION
700 Jackson, Suite 1004
Topeka, KS 66603-3714

KENTUCKY ARTS COUNCIL
Roger L. Paige, Director
Berry Hill, Louisville Rd.
Frankfort, KY 40601

LOUISIANA COUNCIL FOR MUSIC AND PERFORMING ARTS, INC.
Literature Program Associate
7524 St. Charles Ave.
New Orleans, LA 70118

MAINE ARTS COMMISSION
Stuart Kestenbaum
State House, Station 25
Augusta, ME 04333

MARYLAND STATE ARTS COUNCIL
Linda Vlasak, Program Director
Artists-in-Education and Poets-in-the-Schools
15 W. Mulberry St.
Baltimore, MD 21201

MASSACHUSETTS COUNCIL ON THE ARTS AND HUMANITIES
Pat Dixon, Literature Program Director
80 Boylston St., 10th Fl.
Boston, MA 02116

MICHIGAN COUNCIL FOR THE ARTS
Barbara K. Goldman, Executive Director
1200 Sixth Ave.
Detroit, MI 48226-2461

COMPAS: WRITERS IN THE SCHOOLS
Molly LaBerge, Executive Director
Randy Jennings, Program Director
308 Landmark Center
75 W. 5th St.
St. Paul, MN 55102

MINNESOTA STATE ARTS BOARD
Karen Mueller
Artist Assistance Program Associate
432 Summit Ave.
St. Paul, MN 55102

MISSISSIPPI ARTS COMMISSION
Marian Bordeaux, Program Administrator
301 N. Lamar St., Suite 400
Jackson, MS 39201

MISSOURI ARTS COUNCIL
Teresa Goettsch, Program Administrator for Literature
Wainwright Office Complex
111 N. 7th St., Suite 105
St. Louis, MO 63101-2188

MONTANA ARTS COUNCIL
Julia A. Cook, Director, Artist Services
35 S. Last Chance Gulch
Helena, MT 59620

NEBRASKA ARTS COUNCIL
Douglas D. Elliott, Associate Director/Programs
1313 Farnam On-the-Mall
Omaha, NE 68102-1873

NEVADA STATE COUNCIL ON THE ARTS
William L. Fox, Executive Director
329 Flint St.
Reno, NV 89501

NEW HAMPSHIRE STATE COUNCIL ON THE ARTS
Phenix Hall, 40 N. Main St.
Concord, NH 03301

NEW JERSEY STATE COUNCIL ON THE ARTS
Ronnie B. Weyl, Publications Coordinator
109 W. State St.
Trenton, NJ 08625

NEW MEXICO ARTS DIVISION
Santa Fe Poets-in-the-Schools Program
224 E. Palace Ave.
Santa Fe, NM 87501

NEW YORK STATE COUNCIL ON THE ARTS
Gregory Kolovakos, Director, Literature Program
915 Broadway
New York, NY 10010

NORTH CAROLINA ARTS COUNCIL
Jean W. McLaughlin, Literature Program
Dept. of Cultural Resources
Raleigh, NC 27611

NORTH DAKOTA COUNCIL ON THE ARTS
Donna Evenson, Exec. Director
Black Building, Suite 606
Fargo, ND 58102

OHIO ARTS COUNCIL
727 E. Main St.
Columbus, OH 43205-1796

STATE ARTS COUNCIL OF OKLAHOMA
Ellen Jonsson, Assistant Director
Jim Thorpe Bldg., Rm. 640
Oklahoma City, OK 73105

OREGON ARTS COMMISSION
835 Summer St., NE
Salem, OR 97301

PENNSYLVANIA COUNCIL ON THE ARTS
Peter Carnahan, Literature and Theatre Programs
Kimberly Camp, Artists-in-Education Program
Room 216, Finance Bldg.
Harrisburg, PA 17120

RHODE ISLAND STATE COUNCIL ON THE ARTS
Iona B. Dobbins, Executive Director
312 Wickenden St.
Providence, RI 02903

SOUTH CAROLINA ARTS COMMISSION
Steve Lewis, Director, Literary Arts Program
1800 Gervais St.
Columbia, SC 29201

SOUTH DAKOTA ARTS COUNCIL
108 W. 11th St.
Sioux Falls, SD 57102

TENNESSEE ARTS COMMISSION
320 Sixth Ave., N., Suite 100
Nashville, TN 37219

TEXAS COMMISSION ON THE ARTS
P. O. Box 13406, Capitol Station
Austin, TX 78711

UTAH ARTS COUNCIL
G. Barnes, Literary Arts Coordinator
617 East South Temple
Salt Lake City, UT 84102

VERMONT COUNCIL ON THE ARTS
Janet Ressler, Grants Coordinator
136 State St.
Montpelier, VT 05602

VIRGINIA COMMISSION FOR THE ARTS
Peggy J. Baggett, Executive Director
James Monroe Bldg., 17th Floor
101 N. 14th St.
Richmond, VA 23219

WASHINGTON STATE ARTS COMMISSION
110 9th and Columbia Bldg., MS GH-11
Olympia, WA 98504

WEST VIRGINIA DEPT. OF CULTURE AND HISTORY
Arts and Humanities Division
The Cultural Center, Capitol Complex
Charleston, WV 25305

WISCONSIN ARTS BOARD
131 W. Wilson
Madison, WI 53702

WYOMING COUNCIL ON THE ARTS
Joy Thompson, Executive Director
2320 Capitol Ave.
Cheyenne, WY 82002

ORGANIZATIONS FOR WRITERS

THE ACADEMY OF AMERICAN POETS
117 E. 87th St.
New York, NY 10128
Mrs. Edward Chase, *President*
    Founded in 1934 to "encourage, stimulate and foster the art of poetry," the AAP sponsors a series of poetry readings in New York City and numerous annual awards. Membership is open to all: $35 annual fee includes subscription to the monthly newsletter, admission to sponsored readings, and free copies of prize book selection.

AMERICAN MEDICAL WRITERS ASSOCIATION
5272 River Rd., Suite 410
Bethesda, MD 20816
Lillian Sablack, *Executive Director*
    Members of this association are engaged in communication about medicine and its allied professions. Any person actively interested in or professionally associated with any medium of medical communication is eligible for membership. The annual dues are $55.

AMERICAN SOCIETY OF JOURNALISTS AND AUTHORS, INC.
1501 Broadway, Suite 1907
New York, NY 10036
Alexandra Cantor, *Executive Secretary*
    A nationwide organization dedicated to promoting high standards of non-

fiction writing through monthly meetings, annual writers' conferences, etc., ASJA offers extensive benefits and services including referral service, numerous discount services, and the opportunity to explore professional issues and concerns with other writers. Members also receive a monthly newsletter. Membership is open to qualified free-lance writers of nonfiction; qualifications are judged by Membership Committee. Initiation fee: $50; annual dues: $120.

THE AUTHORS LEAGUE OF AMERICA, INC.
(The Authors Guild and The Dramatists Guild)
234 W. 44th St., New York, NY 10036

The Authors League of America is a national organization of over 14,000 authors and dramatists, representing them on matters of joint concern, such as copyright, taxes, and freedom of expression. Membership in the league is restricted to authors and dramatists who are members of The Authors Guild and The Dramatists Guild. Matters such as contract terms and subsidiary rights are in the province of the two guilds.

A writer who has published a book in the last seven years with an established publisher, or one who has published several magazine pieces with periodicals of general circulation within the last eighteen months, may be eligible for active voting membership in The Authors Guild. A new writer may be eligible for associate membership on application to the Membership Committee. Dues: $60 a year.

The Dramatists Guild is a professional association of playwrights, composers, and lyricists, established to protect dramatists' rights and to improve working conditions. Services include use of the Guild's contracts, business counseling, publications, and symposia in major cities. All theater writers (produced or not) are eligible for membership.

THE INTERNATIONAL SOCIETY OF DRAMATISTS
Box 1310
Miami, FL 33153

Open to playwrights, agents, producers, screenwriters, and others involved in the theater. Publishes *Dramatist's Bible,* a directory of script opportunities, and *The Globe,* a newsletter, with information and news of theaters across the country. Also provides free referral service for playwrights.

MYSTERY WRITERS OF AMERICA, INC.
236 W. 27th St.
New York, NY 10001
Priscilla Ridgway, *Executive Secretary*

The MWA exists for the purpose of raising the prestige of mystery and detective writing, and of defending the rights and increasing the income of all writers in the field of mystery, detection, and fact crime writing. Each year, the MWA presents the Edgar Allan Poe Awards for the best mystery writing in a variety of fields. The four classifications of membership are: *active* (open to any writer who has made a sale in the field of mystery, suspense, or crime writing); *associate* (for nonwriters allied to the mystery field); *corresponding* (writers living outside the U.S.); *affiliate* (for unpublished writers and mystery enthusiasts). Annual dues: $50; $25 for corresponding members.

NATIONAL ASSOCIATION OF SCIENCE WRITERS, INC.
P. O. Box 294
Greenlawn, NY 11740

The NASW promotes the dissemination of accurate information regarding science through all media, and conducts a varied program to increase the flow of news from scientists, to improve the quality of its presentation, and to communicate its meaning to the reading public.

Anyone who has been actively engaged in the dissemination of science information is eligible to apply for membership. Active members must be principally involved in reporting on science through newspapers, magazines, TV, or other media that reach the public directly. Associate members report on science through limited-circulation publications and other media. Annual dues: $45.

THE NATIONAL WRITERS CLUB
1450 S. Havana, Suite 620
Aurora, CO 80012
James Lee Young, *Exec. Dir.*
New and established writers, poets, and playwrights throughout the U.S. and Canada may become members of The National Writers Club, a nonprofit representative organization. Membership includes bimonthly newsletter, *Authorship.* Dues: $50 annually ($40 Associates), plus a $15 initiation fee.

NATIONAL WRITERS UNION
13 Astor Pl., 7th Fl.
New York, NY 10003
Any writer who has published one book, play, short story, or three articles, five poems or the equivalent in unpublished work is eligible to join The National Writers Union. The NWU offers advice on contracts, discounts, insurance, and sponsors events across the country. Annual dues range from $35 to $115.

OUTDOOR WRITERS ASSOCIATION OF AMERICA, INC.
2017 Cato Ave., Suite 101
State College, PA 16801
Sylvia G. Bashline, *Executive Director*
The OWAA is an organization for professional print and broadcast journalists who report on outdoor recreational activities and concerns. Membership (by nomination only) includes a monthly publication, *Outdoors Unlimited;* annual conference; members' directory; and contests. Also provides scholarships.

PEN AMERICAN CENTER
568 Broadway
New York, NY 10012
PEN American Center is one of 80 centers that comprise International PEN, a worldwide association of literary writers, offering conferences, writing programs, financial and educational assistance. Membership is open to writers who have published two books of literary merit, as well as editors, agents, playwrights, and translators who meet specific standards (apply to nomination committee). PEN sponsors annual awards and grants and publishes the quarterly *Pen Newsletter;* and the biennial directory, *Grants and Awards Available to American Writers.*

THE POETRY SOCIETY OF AMERICA
15 Gramercy Park
New York, NY 10003
Judith Baumel, *Administrative Director*
Founded in 1910, The Poetry Society of America seeks through a variety of programs to gain a wider audience for American poetry. The Society offers 17 annual prizes for poetry (with many contests open to non-members as well as members), and sponsors workshops, free public poetry readings, and publications. Maintains the Van Vooris Library of American Poetry. Dues: $30 annually.

POETS AND WRITERS, INC.
201 W. 54th St.
New York, NY 10019
Elliot Figman, *Executive Director*

Poets & Writers, Inc. was founded in 1970 to foster the development of poets and fiction writers and to promote communication throughout the literary community. A non-membership organization, it offers a nationwide information center for writers; *Poets & Writers Magazine* and other publications; as well as sponsored readings and workshops.

PRIVATE EYE WRITERS OF AMERICA
1873 Crowley Circle East
Longwood, FL 32779
Robert J. Randisi, *Executive Director*

Private Eye Writers of America is a national organization that seeks to promote a wider recognition and appreciation of private eye literature. Writers who have published a work of fiction—short story, novel, TV script, or movie screenplay—with a private eye as the central character are eligible to join as active members. Serious devotees of the P.I. story may become associate members. Dues: $20 (active), $10 (associate). Annual Shamus Award for the best in PI fiction.

ROMANCE WRITERS OF AMERICA
5206 FM 1960 West, #208
Houston, TX 77069
Pat Hudgins, Executive Secretary

The RWA is a national organization with over 80 local chapters across the U.S., open to any writer, published or unpublished, interested in the field of romantic fiction. Annual dues of $35; benefits include annual conference, contest, market information, and bimonthly newsmagazine, *Romance Report*.

SCIENCE FICTION WRITERS OF AMERICA
P. O. Box H
Wharton, NJ 07885
Peter D. Pautz, *Executive Secretary*

The purpose of the SFWA, a professional organization of science fiction and fantasy writers, is to foster and further the interests of writers of fantasy and science fiction. SFWA presents the Nebula Award annually for excellence in the field and publishes the *Bulletin* for its members.

Any writer who has sold a work of science fiction or fantasy is eligible for membership. Dues: $50 per year for active members, $35 for affiliates, plus $10 installation fee; send for application and information. *The Bulletin* is available to nonmembers for $10 (four issues).

SOCIETY FOR TECHNICAL COMMUNICATION
815 15th St., NW
Washington, DC 20005
William C. Stolgitis, *Executive Director*

The Society for Technical Communication is a professional organization dedicated to the advancement of the theory and practice of technical communication in all media. The almost 14,000 members in the U.S. and other countries include technical writers and editors, publishers, artists and draftsmen, researchers, educators, and audiovisual specialists.

SOCIETY OF AMERICAN TRAVEL WRITERS
1120 Connecticut Ave., Suite 940

Washington, DC 20036
Ken Fischer, *Administrative Coordinator*
The Society of American Travel Writers represents writers and other professionals who strive to provide travelers with accurate reports on destinations, facilities, and services.

Membership is by invitation. Active membership is limited to salaried travel writers and others employed as free lancers, who have a steady volume of published or distributed work about travel. Initiation fee for active members is $150, for associate members $300. Annual dues: $90 (active); $170 (associate).

SOCIETY OF CHILDREN'S BOOK WRITERS
P. O. Box 296
Mar Vista Station
Los Angeles, CA 90066
Lin Oliver, *Executive Director*
This national organization of authors, editors, publishers, illustrators, librarians, and educators offers a variety of services to people who write for or share an interest in children's literature. Full memberships are open to those who have had at least one children's book or story published. Associate memberships are open to all those with an interest in children's literature. Yearly dues are $35.

WESTERN WRITERS OF AMERICA
1753 Victoria
Sheridan, WY 82801
Barbara Ketcham, *Secretary/Treasurer*
Writers of fiction, nonfiction, and poetry pertaining to the traditions, legends, development, and history of the American West may join the nonprofit Western Writers of America. Its chief purpose is to promote a more widespread distribution, readership, and appreciation of the West and its literature. Dues are $40 a year. Sponsors annual Spur Awards.

WRITERS GUILD OF AMERICA, EAST, INC.
555 W. 57th St.
New York, NY 10019
Mona Mangan, *Executive Director*

WRITERS GUILD OF AMERICA, WEST, INC.
8955 Beverly Blvd.
Los Angeles, CA 90048
Brian Walton, *Executive Director*
The Writers Guild of America (East and West) represents writers in the fields of radio, television and motion pictures.

In order to qualify for membership a writer must fulfill current requirements for employment or sale of material in one of these three fields.

The basic dues are $25 a quarter for the Writers Guild West and $12.50 a quarter in the case of Writers Guild East. In addition, there are quarterly dues based on percentage of the member's earnings in any one of the fields over which the Guild has jurisdiction. The initiation fee is $1,000 for Writers Guild East and $1,500 for Writers Guild West. (Writers living east of the Mississippi join Writers Guild East, and those living west of the Mississippi, Writers Guild West.)

AMERICAN LITERARY AGENTS

Most literary agents do not usually accept new writers as clients. Since the agent's only income is a percentage—10% to 20%—of the amount he receives from the sales he makes for his clients, he must have as clients writers who are selling fairly regularly to good markets. Always query an agent first. Do not send any manuscripts until the agent has asked you to do so. The following list is only a partial selection of representative agents. Addresses which include zip codes in parentheses are located in New York City (the majority of agents in this list are in New York). A list of agents can also be obtained by sending a stamped, self-addressed envelope to Society of Authors' Representatives, 39½ Washington Square South, New York, NY 10012 or Independent Literary Agents Assn., Inc., c/o Sanford J. Greenburger Associates, 55 Fifth Ave., New York, NY 10003.

BRET ADAMS, LTD., 448 W. 44th St. (10036)

JULIAN BACH LITERARY AGENCY, INC., 747 Third Ave. (10017)

LOUIS BERMAN, The Little Theatre Bldg., 240 W. 44th St. (10036)

GEORGES BORCHARDT, INC., 136 E. 57th St. (10022)

BRANDT & BRANDT LITERARY AGENTS, INC., 1501 Broadway (10036)

THE HELEN BRANN AGENCY, INC., 157 W. 57th St. (10019)

CURTIS BROWN, LTD., 10 Astor Place (10003)

KNOX BURGER ASSOCIATES, LTD., 39½ Washington Square South (10012)

COLLIER ASSOCIATES, 875 Sixth Ave., #1003 (10001)

DON CONGDON ASSOCIATES, INC., 111 5th Ave. (10003)

JOAN DAVES, 59 E. 54th St. (10022)

ANITA DIAMANT, 310 Madison Ave., #1508 (10017)

CANDIDA DONADIO & ASSOCIATES, INC., 231 W. 22nd St. (10011)

THE DORSET GROUP, 820 W. Belmont Ave., Chicago, IL 60657

ANN ELMO AGENCY, INC. 60 E. 42nd St. (10165)

JOHN FARQUHARSON, LTD., Suite 1914, 250 W. 57th St. (10107)

ROBERT A. FREEDMAN DRAMATIC AGENCY, INC., 1501 Broadway, #2310 (10036)

SAMUEL FRENCH, INC., 45 W. 25th St. (10010)

GRAHAM AGENCY, 311 W. 43rd St. (10036)

BLANCHE C. GREGORY, INC., Two Tudor City Place (10017)

JOHN W. HAWKINS & ASSOCIATES, INC., 71 W. 23rd St. (10011)

INTERNATIONAL CREATIVE MANAGEMENT, INC., 40 W. 57th St. (10019)

JCA LITERARY AGENCY, INC., 242 W. 27th St., No. 4A (10001)

KIDDE, HOYT & PICARD, 335 E. 51st St. (10022)

PINDER LANE PRODUCTIONS, LTD., 159 W. 53rd St. (10019)

THE LANTZ OFFICE, 888 Seventh Ave. (10106)

LESCHER & LESCHER, LTD., 155 E. 71st St. (10021)

ELLEN LEVINE LITERARY AGENCY, 432 Park Ave. S., #1205 (10016)

LITERISTIC, LTD., 264 Fifth Ave. (10001)

THE STERLING LORD AGENCY, INC., 660 Madison Ave. (10021)

ELISABETH MARTON, 96 Fifth Ave. (10011)

HAROLD MATSON COMPANY, INC., 276 Fifth Ave. (10001)

GERARD MCCAULEY AGENCY, INC., 141 E. 44th St. #208 (10017)

MCINTOSH & OTIS, INC., 310 Madison (10017)

HELEN MERRILL, 435 W. 23rd St., #1A (10011)

WILLIAM MORRIS AGENCY, INC., 1350 Ave. of the Americas (10019)

HAROLD OBER ASSOCIATES, INC., 40 E. 49th St. (10017)

FIFI OSCARD ASSOCIATES, INC., 19 W. 44th St. (10036)

RAINES & RAINES, 71 Park Ave. (10016)

FLORA ROBERTS, INC., Penthouse A, 157 W. 57th St. (10019)

MARIE RODELL-FRANCES COLLIN LITERARY AGENCY, Suite 2004, 110 W. 40th St. (10018)

ROSENSTONE/WENDER, 3 E. 48th St. (10017)

RUSSELL & VOLKENING, INC., 50 W. 29th St. (10001)

JOHN SCHAFFNER ASSOCIATES, INC., 114 E. 28th St. (10016)

JAMES SELIGMANN AGENCY, 175 Fifth Ave., #1101 (10010)

CHARLOTTE SHEEDY LITERARY AGENCY, INC., 145 W. 86th St. (10024)

SUSAN SCHULMAN AGENCY, 454 W. 44th St. (10036)

THE SHUKAT COMPANY, LTD., 340 W. 55th St., #1A (10019)

PHILIP G. SPITZER LITERARY AGENCY, 111-25 76th Ave., Flushing, NY 11375

ROSLYN TARG LITERARY AGENCY, INC., 105 W. 13th St., #15E (10011)

WALLACE & SHIEL AGENCY, INC., 177 E. 70th St. (10021)

THE WENDY WEIL AGENCY, INC., 747 Third Ave. (10017)

MARY YOST ASSOCIATES, INC., 59 E. 54th St., No. 52 (10022)

INDEX TO MARKETS